Ross

Colorblind Injustice

Colorblind Injustice

Minority Voting Rights and the
Undoing of the Second Reconstruction

by J. Morgan Kousser

The University of North Carolina Press ▾ *Chapel Hill & London*

⊗ The paper in this book meets the guidelines for permanence
and durability of the Committee on Production Guidelines for
Book Longevity of the Council on Library Resources.

This book was set in Cycles with Arepo display
by Tseng Information Systems, Inc.

Portions of this book have appeared in substantially different form
in the following publications and are reprinted here with permission
of the publishers: "How to Determine Intent: Lessons from L.A.,"
Journal of Law and Politics 7 (1991): 591–732; "*Shaw v. Reno* and the Real
World of Redistricting and Representation," *Rutgers Law Journal* 26 (1995):
625–710; "The Undermining of the First Reconstruction: Lessons for the
Second," in *Minority Vote Dilution*, edited by Chandler Davidson, 27–46
(Washington, D.C.: Howard University Press, 1984); "The Voting Rights Act
and the Two Reconstructions," in *Controversies in Minority Voting: The Voting
Rights Act in Perspective*, edited by Bernard Grofman and Chandler Davidson,
135–77 (Washington, D.C.: Brookings Institution, 1992); and the author's
testimony as expert witness for the U.S. Department of Justice in the cases
Georgia v. Reno, 881 F. Supp. 7 (D.D.C. 1995); *U.S. v. City of Memphis* (W.D. Tenn.,
Civil Action No. 91-2139); and *Vera v. Richards*, 861 F. Supp. 1304 (S.D. Tex. 1994).

Library of Congress Cataloging-in-Publication Data
Kousser, J. Morgan.
Colorblind injustice : minority voting rights and the undoing
of the second Reconstruction / by J. Morgan Kousser.
       p.   cm.
Includes bibliographical references and index.
ISBN 0-8078-2431-3 (cloth : alk. paper). — ISBN 0-8078-4738-0 (pbk. : alk. paper)
1. Afro-Americans—Suffrage—History.   2. Minorities—Suffrage—United States—
History.   I. Title.
JK1924.K68 1999
328.75'0734—dc21   98-16693
                                                                              CIP

03 02 01 00 99   5 4 3 2 1

For Rachel, Sally, and Thad

And in memory, always, of Alice Morgan Kousser

Contents

Figures and Tables

Colorblind Injustice

Institutions and the Struggle for Equality

*I*nstitutions and institutional rules—not customs, ideas, attitudes, culture, or private behavior—have primarily shaped race relations in America. The most important and longest lasting influence, of course, has been that of the "peculiar institution," slavery—conditioned by law, sustained by law, and, after being devastated by war, finally dispatched and interred by law. More than a generation after slavery's end, segregation and disfranchisement, which maintained white supremacy and largely excluded African-Americans and Latinos from white society and politics, were accomplished or solidified by law (see, e.g., Woodward 1974; Kousser 1974).[1] But other institutions and rules have also had profound impacts on the struggles for and against racial equality: the Constitution, the methods for aggregating votes into legislative seats, the structure and internal organization of political bodies, the regulations issued by the executive branch of government, the actions of political parties, and the pronouncements of the judiciary. The effects of these institutions on minorities have been most favorable when instants of transformation were followed by long periods of gradual change. While liberty may arrive or depart in a moment, equality requires not only eternal vigilance but also consensus and incremental improvement. Institutional stability—with the right kind of institutions— is a prerequisite for minority success. Knowing that their numbers will ultimately preserve them, large groups in a democracy can accept fluctuations in political outcomes and rules. Smaller, more isolated minorities, however, need protective institutions, which cannot be rapidly rebuilt if they are destroyed. Marx was wrong. The poor have much more to lose than their chains. Only the powerful can afford to be radical for long.

This book, which grew out of papers originally produced as part of the struggle to protect minority voting rights, examines distant and recent history in order to determine what institutions and rules are necessary to guarantee equal political opportunities to minority groups in America. It attempts to set voting rights policy straight by getting its history right. Every chapter flows, directly or indirectly, from my work as an expert witness in federal district court cases concerning minority voting rights, in which I testified for the American Civil Liberties Union (ACLU), the U.S. Department of Justice, the Legal Defense Fund of the National Association for the Advancement of Colored People (NAACP-LDF or just LDF), the Mexican-American Legal Defense and Education Fund (MALDEF), and other parties, always on the side identified with minority groups. Because I have a strong point of view on the subjects considered here, I have tried very hard to make my assumptions and arguments clear and to subject every conclusion to the most rigorous criticism that I can manage. Readers will judge where I have failed.

Although the papers began separately, here they have been considerably rewritten and blended into what I hope is a coherent, if complex, argument. At the risk of robbing the reader of the joys of denouement, I will summarize that argument here in order to indicate how the book holds together. The initial chapter considers the analogy between the First and Second Reconstructions, those of the periods after the Civil War and the Second World War, respectively. Since C. Vann Woodward introduced the term "Second Reconstruction" in the 1960s, the parallels between the two have served more as a rhetorical flourish than an invitation to systematic comparison. Focusing on African-American voting rights, I argue that the First Reconstruction failed to preserve those rights because disastrous judicial decisions, stark divisions between the Republican and Democratic parties over black suffrage, and shifting majorities in Congress prevented the necessary elaboration of federal protective laws. The Second Reconstruction has succeeded in fostering political equality for minorities because, until recently, judicial decisions have been much more favorable, partisan divisions over civil rights policy much less pronounced, and congressional lineups much more stable than those of the First Reconstruction. In the past decade, however, radical reinterpretations of the Voting Rights Act proposed by political scientist Abigail Thernstrom and Supreme Court Justice Clarence Thomas and the revolutionary reading of the equal protection clause introduced by the "conservative" Supreme Court majority in *Shaw v. Reno* (1993) and its successors have threatened to reverse the course of minority political success during the Second Reconstruction.

Chapters 2 through 6 present case studies of the adoption of electoral laws and redistrictings in Los Angeles County, California; Memphis, Tennessee; and the states of Georgia, North Carolina, and Texas. I begin in Los Angeles in order to emphasize that southern blacks have not been the only victims of minority vote dilution and to demonstrate that it is possible to discern the intent of redistricters from a pattern of circumstantial evidence alone.[2] From 1959 through 1981, the five Los Angeles County supervisors, who oversaw the government of the most populous local jurisdiction in the country, repeatedly redrew the boundaries of their districts to insure that Latinos could not elect their most preferred candidates. Comprising 28 percent of the county's population by 1980, Latinos had not placed a Latino representative on the Board since 1875. To establish that racial motivation, and not other hypotheses, best accounts for the behavior of the supervisors and their employees, I not only reconstruct maps and demographic statistics but also closely analyze the actions and statements of the large and sophisticated cast of characters involved. The Los Angeles County example represents real racial gerrymandering, redistricting that denied members of a distinct, subordinate group a fair and equal opportunity to elect candidates of their choice.

Chapter 3 moves to Memphis, one of the largest cities in the Deep South. As African-Americans threatened to elect one or more of their group to Memphis's government in the 1950s and 1960s, the city fathers passed laws requiring that candidates run in at-large elections for designated posts, instead of allowing voters to elect the four or more candidates with the highest vote totals, and requiring that they receive a majority vote, rather than a plurality, in what was then a majority-white city. When city leaders completely revised the city charter in 1966, they insured continued white control by requiring that the majority of members of the city council and school board be elected in citywide elections, rather than in separate single-member districts. Numerous indiscreet statements, the history of the city since the 1870s, and the pattern of actions by the voters and by leaders who proposed the changes in electoral laws add up to an overwhelming case that the predominant motive for the passage of these laws was to perpetuate racial discrimination against blacks.

Similar, though not quite so plentiful, evidence establishes the primacy of a racial motive in Georgia's passage of a statewide majority-vote requirement in 1964, discussed in Chapter 4. Even before the passage of the Voting Rights Act (VRA) in 1965, a strong civil rights movement centered in Atlanta fanned out across Georgia to register black voters. Fearing that burgeoning black political organizations would elect African-Americans or their white liberal allies to office, as they had done in the 1950s in Atlanta and Macon, "moderates" eagerly endorsed a hard-line segregationist's proposal to reduce the possibility that a disciplined black minority could rule or even strongly influence elections. Contentions by participants in a lawsuit a generation later that the runoff statute reflected a sudden concern with corruption, long notorious in Georgia elections, or a dedication to individual equality and majority rule—by the leader of the faction most committed to segregation and mal-apportionment!—do not bear scrutiny. Racial purposes clearly predominated in the adoption of the majority vote.

In *Shaw v. Reno* (1993) and other cases, Justice Sandra Day O'Connor has asserted that before 1991, Americans had adhered to such "traditional district-ing principles" as compactness, contiguity, and preserving county or munici-pal boundaries, implying that they have deviated from them only recently, in order to grant special privileges to underrepresented ethnic minorities. Chap-ters 5 and 6, which document the long tradition of antiblack and anti-Latino gerrymandering as well as partisan and incumbent protection in redistricting in North Carolina and Texas before 1991, cast doubt on the justice's unevi-denced assertion. From 1872 through 1900, when blacks were largely disfran-chised in North Carolina, they were "packed" into one overpopulated, heavily black congressional district, the "Black Second." When African-Americans began to register in eastern North Carolina in large numbers after 1965, the boundaries of the congressional district with the largest black concentration, still the Second, were repeatedly manipulated, especially in 1981, in order to insure that blacks could not control its politics. As losers in the redistricting battles freely and frequently charged, districts sprawled all over the state to insure outcomes favorable to particular persons, parties, and ethnic groups. Partisan, personal, and ethnic advantage were the real "traditional districting principles" in North Carolina.

Larger, more urban, and more socially and economically complex than North Carolina, Texas also had a unique brand of rough-and-tumble politics, which spilled over into redistricting. In the Lone Star State, redistricting re-sembled a revenge play more than it did Justice O'Connor's civics textbook exercise. Whether leaders preferred protecting friends to knifing enemies is difficult to say, for the same moves often accomplished both at once. By 1981, the Republican party was strong enough in Texas to control the process, in alliance with conservative Democrats. Conservatives agreed that the redis-tricting should disadvantage minorities and Anglo liberals as much as pos-sible, and only federal court intervention prevented them from doing so. In fact, until 1991, minorities had only very limited influence on the redistricting process, and that influence came primarily as a result of lawsuits. In Texas, as in North Carolina, bitter struggles over redistricting in 1981, centering on minority communities, set the stage for hard-fought rematches in 1991.

The redistricting processes and plans of the 1990s appear very different when placed in the context of previous election laws than when considered as isolated instances, as if the story had begun in 1990 or as though the his-tory of redistricting had been a simple tale of the application of widely shared principles of fairness by unprejudiced, civic-minded nonpartisans.[3] Chapters 2 through 6 reveal a nationwide pattern of electoral laws adopted before 1990 with the intent and effect of discriminating against underrepresented minorities. Whether in cities, counties, or states; for councils, school boards, state legislatures, or Congress; by Democratic or Republican politicians, closely supervised bureaucrats, or independent commissions, the story has been the same, and it is possible, if one digs deeply and evaluates the evidence systematically, to uncover it. There was nothing new about the consideration of race, party, or incumbency in 1991. Every redistricting since the 1960s in any state or locality with a substantial percentage of minorities had concerned itself primarily with such issues. To pretend, as Justice O'Connor did in *Shaw v. Reno*, that the oddly shaped districts adopted in the 1990s uniquely emphasized race, as if race had been invisible in American public policy or electoral law before then, is a considerable distortion. Nor were deal-making or the careful craftsmanship of district lines innovations. After all, the term "gerrymander" originated in 1812. What was different in 1991 was that, for the first time, because of the VRA, minorities enjoyed considerable power during redistricting.

Justice O'Connor's majority opinion in *Shaw v. Reno* stated that for a district to be unconstitutional, it had to be strangely shaped and race had to be the "sole" motive for its boundary, while Justice Anthony Kennedy's majority opinion in *Miller v. Johnson* (1995) held that race need only be the "predominant" motive and that even the most compact district might be illegal. The last sections of Chapters 5 and 6 examine the North Carolina and Texas reapportionments in light of these contradictory standards and determine that racial factors were neither the only nor the most important reasons for the boundaries finally adopted in those states. But how do the Supreme Court's standards in the "minority racial gerrymandering" cases from *Shaw v. Reno* onward compare to its criteria in previous litigation over minority vote dilution and other equal protection cases?

Chapters 7 and 8 turn from the history of redistricting and other electoral laws per se to the history of the development of Supreme Court doctrine. Chapter 7 treats the Court's considerations of the issues of intent and effect in equal protection law, particularly electoral law, from the 1880s through the 1980s. After vacillating for nearly a century on the questions of whether judges could or should be concerned with legislative purpose, of what was the legal relationship between the motives for laws and the impact of those laws, and of whether it was necessary to show one or both to determine that a law was unconstitutional, the Court in the 1970s and 80s settled on an equal protection standard that required proof of both a discriminatory intent and a discriminatory effect. Because this is now settled law, it is important to try to establish a systematic method for organizing the evidence in inquiries into intent. And because intent and effect are essentially empirical rather than legal questions, a historian may have something useful to say on the subject. Focusing on election laws, I propose explicit standards for determining the intent of laws, using Chapters 2 through 6, my experiences in other cases, and the opinions of a number of scholars and judges as guides to general principles.

Chapters 8 and 9 bring the book full circle by considering the undoing of the Second Reconstruction in *Shaw v. Reno* and its progeny and applying the lessons of history to those decisions. Just as no treatment of *Shaw* is complete without a detailed discussion of the history of race and election law in America, no history of race and politics written in the 1990s can be complete without a careful examination of those cases. Defenders of the decisions contend that they are merely the logical outgrowths of the original, "colorblind" goals of the civil rights movement, in particular, of *Brown v. Board of Education* (1954). The "conservative" majority on the Court, they maintain, is the real embodiment of the legacy of Martin Luther King Jr., the true guardian of the equal protection clause of the Fourteenth Amendment, the nonpartisan, idealistic voice of the best intentions of the First Reconstruction. History shows, they believe, that the best governmental policy on racial matters is to ignore racial discrimination, past and present. In any event, they assert, minorities no longer need protection, because white racism is now so insignificant and institutions so fair that the chief hindrances to a world where race no longer matters are quotas and preferences for African-Americans and Latinos. They conclude that the decisions were both inevitable and wholly commendable, because they represent a straightforward and consistent effort to deny special privileges that are sought only by minority politicians and a captured bureaucracy in the Justice Department (Blumstein 1995; Butler 1995, 1996; Thernstrom and Thernstrom 1995; Thernstrom and Thernstrom 1997, 286–312, 462–92; Thernstrom 1995).

By contrast, critics charge that the *Shaw* line of cases represents a counterrevolution, a new "redemption" like the "redemption" of the South from "black Republican rule" after Reconstruction. While critics agree that white racial attitudes have liberalized in many respects, they believe that racial egalitarianism is far from consensual, and that rules that discriminate against minorities are widespread. "Colorblindness," they think, is just a euphemism for a continuation of discrimination, as "separate but equal" was. Far from being descendants of the racially liberating judicial decrees of the 1950s and 60s, or even consistent with each other, *Shaw v. Reno* and the subsequent minority racial gerrymandering decisions are, their opponents declare, heavy-handed, unprincipled interventions into a political process that was finally giving minorities a fair chance. According to *Shaw*'s critics, history demonstrates that minorities need governmental protection from economic, social, and political discrimination against them, and the Reconstruction amendments attempted to guarantee such protection.

The critics, I will argue, have the better case. I go beyond previous dissenters from these decisions by considering their likely practical consequences for the redistricting process following the 2000 census, by showing that the cases are not only riddled with inconsistencies but also with politically and racially biased exceptions and by arguing that *Shaw* fits squarely into a tradition of abstract, formalistic judicial actions, emblemized by the infamous *Dred Scott v. Sandford* (1857) and *Plessy v. Ferguson* (1896) decisions, which did so much to buttress white supremacy. Fortunately, there is another Supreme Court tradition, a practical one that draws on history and other social sciences, instead of on easy slogans; that respects other governmental entities, instead of striking for unfettered judicial supremacy; that protects relatively powerless minorities, instead of ripping apart sheltering institutions—the tradition of *Brown v. Board of Education* and of the key 1973 voting rights case, *White v. Regester*. In order to continue the progress of the Second Reconstruction and to fulfill the egalitarian aims of the First, the Court should return to its pragmatic, realistic precedents. *Shaw* should be reversed.

A SCHEMATIC overview is not meant to convince any reader, and it should not. Persuasion is in the details. There are many of them in the succeeding pages, for three reasons. First, scattered anecdotes are unreliable sources for firm generalizations. To obtain solid answers to such questions as why black voting declined after the First Reconstruction, to the point where blacks could be substantially disfranchised, while it rose and became more potent as the Second Reconstruction wore on, requires a systematic look at election laws, congressional actions, and court decisions in two lengthy periods. To determine whether *Shaw* and its successors are consistent with earlier decisions and with each other necessitates close readings of many judicial opinions. Second, humans are complex, and so is determining their motivation. In the passage of election laws, there are always multiple actors and many potential explanations for their behavior. To choose a hypothesis about the motivation of a particular action as more adequate than the rest, one has to consider arguments and evidence for and against many hypotheses. Third, the easiest way to seem to win an argument is to ignore the best evidence and logic of one's critics. That has often been the practice in debates on voting rights, and one can overcome the possibility of avoiding evidence that doesn't fit only by considering a lot of it. Defenders of *Shaw* sometimes seek to convince their audience by exhibiting a few pictures of irregular boundaries, calling them "political pornography" and demanding that such districts be banned, at least if they contain majorities of minority ethnic populations. This and similar practices avoid all of the difficult and interesting questions.

And there are a lot of interesting questions, events, and personalities in this book—from Ron Smith, the California political consultant and self-described racial egalitarian, whose specialty in campaigns and redistricting plans was pitting one Democratic ethnic group against another; to Russell Sugarmon, the African-American Harvard Law School graduate who seemed to pose such a threat to white supremacy in Memphis in 1959; to Denmark Groover Jr., the legislative wizard and staunch segregationist who framed the Georgia majority-vote law; to L. H. Fountain, the plantation-style congressman whose insistence on an antiblack gerrymander of his congressional seat stalled the North Carolina legislature for six months in 1981; to William Clements, the Texas Republican governor who posed as a friend of Dallas African-Americans in a transparent attempt to win more congressional seats for his party; to Justices Sandra Day O'Connor and Clarence Thomas, one a "moderate" partisan and the other a bitter critic of every achievement of the civil rights movement, especially of *Brown* and the VRA. Such people bring statistics and dry judicial doctrine alive because they insert politics into the analysis and because their struggles show how much the story really matters. Because the cast of characters is large, those mentioned on more than one page (with the exception of authors) are briefly identified in the index entries.

ALTHOUGH *Colorblind Injustice* spans the disciplines of law, political science, and history, it is primarily a history book. And it is not only a work *of* history, but also a work *about* history—about the importance of careful and systematic methods to the understanding of history and, in turn, about the importance of a proper understanding of history to the development of good public policy. Too much public policy is justified on the basis of casual analogies, crude caricatures of facts and trends, and ignorance, willful or otherwise, of even the immediate past. At the same time, too many of today's historians have lost their nerve, doubting not only that one can ever attain truth but also that anyone can determine whether one account of events is superior to another and whether it is ever possible to uncover the causes and motives of action. The postmodern, linguistic turn that dissolves history into a ceaseless, pointless play of "signifiers" (words that stand for actual things, or perhaps only for other words) cedes control over the interpretation of the past to others who are less professional but more self-assured and even more self-interested (Appleby, Hunt, and Jacob 1994, 198–270). It is time that we historians reclaimed our calling. The history of policy is too important to leave to lawyers, judges, and social commentators.

Colorblind Injustice is part of a larger study—a life work, it seems, on race relations in America—and a sketch of the larger themes of that work may alert the reader to otherwise imperceptible overtones in this book. I am neither a pessimist nor an optimist about race relations in this country. Thus, on the one hand, I do not find racism or evil motives everywhere and, on the other, I do not expect any permanent transformation to a new era in which race does not matter. Historians and social scientists, as well as my own research, have taught me better. Although I have learned from many people, my principal working hypotheses are due to two men: my graduate adviser, C. Vann Woodward, who stressed the importance of institutions and institutional rules in shaping race relations (Woodward 1974), and the social psychologist Thomas Pettigrew, who emphasized how variable American race relations have been (Pettigrew 1975, 1979, 1980, 1985, 1989). Racial behavior patterns, I have come to believe, are complex, multidimensional, and variable, subject to change over time and to variation across areas and between people; they are often "thin," that is, not deeply felt or unchangeable; and they are often determined by other, essentially nonracial values or interests, not by racial ideologies or attitudes alone. Institutions and institutional rules bring uniformity to this disorder—sometimes for good, sometimes for ill. Thus, in *The Shaping of Southern Politics* (Kousser 1974), I showed how variable post-Reconstruction politics was from election to election and state to state. African-American and low-status white voters posed a dangerous threat to the dominant Democrats until disfranchisement laws, motivated by a desire to assure that white Democratic supremacy would be unchallengeable, created a new southern order. In my ongoing study of nineteenth-century court cases and legislative actions on racial discrimination in schools (Kousser, 1980a, 1980b, 1986, 1988b, 1991a), I have shown how difficult the struggle for integration often was even in the North but also, in many instances, how easily that policy was accepted once it was authoritatively ordered; how integration policies, as well as segregation policies, could be reversed, casting doubt on the belief that racial change in America is invariably progressive, or as nineteenth-century racial liberals put it, that "revolutions never go backwards"; and how intertwined racial policies were with partisan politics, in courts as well as in legislatures and school boards. Then as now, the best predictor of whether lawyers, judges, or legislators would favor African-Americans or their opponents was each person's political party affiliation. In *Colorblind Injustice*, I investigate changes in electoral structures and rules in a wide array of places, over a considerable portion of time, demonstrating the connection between politicians' self-interest, the structures they wrote into law, and the electoral outcomes that occurred in those jurisdictions. I also show how changing judicial interpretations shaped and continue to shape electoral regulations, which have a crucial impact on racial democracy in America. The history of race relations in America has too often been treated as static, invariant, and isolated from other trends and interests in society. I view it as relatively fluid and heterogeneous, unless regulated by law, and in any event as integrally connected with other facets of society. And that understanding of history, the lessons that I will draw and test in detail in this work, can help to lead us to a more egalitarian society, one where discrimination against members of minority groups is less oppressive than at present.

A WORD about the title: "Colorblind" is the buzzword of opponents of governmental actions to diminish current racial inequality, inequality that results from past and continuing governmental and nongovernmental discrimination against ethnic minorities. As I argue in the body of this book, governmental "neutrality" in this instance is unjust in intent as well as effect. Not only do such policies in fact perpetuate injustice; they are meant to perpetuate injustice. Far from "colorblind," they are deeply color-conscious. To call readers' attention to my skepticism about the "colorblind" slogan, I originally enclosed the word in quotation marks in the title.

I HAVE been at this book for a long time, and I have many friends to thank for inspiration and assistance. The voting rights bar and the community of scholars who work in this field have taught me, provided materials to me, and given me needed criticism, and although I can never adequately repay them, I can at least name them: Jim Blacksher, Neil Bradley, Bruce Cain, Tony Chavez, Dayna Cunningham, Chandler Davidson, Armand Derfner, Richard Fajardo, Luis Fraga, Hugh Davis Graham, Bernie Grofman, Jerry Hebert, Chris Herren, Sam Hirsch, Anita Hodgkiss, Gaye Hume, Bob Kengle, Allan Lichtman, Peyton McCrary, Laughlin McDonald, Rob McDuff, Larry Menefee, the late Frank Parker, Mark Rosenbaum, Steve Rosenbaum, Ed Still, and Rick Valelly. Other friends who have sent materials and/or commented most helpfully include Dale Baum, David Bositis, Canter Brown Jr., Tom Dillard, Ariella Gross, Elsie Hall, Peggy Hargis, Bill Hixson, Sam Hirsch, Greg Keating, Tom Kraemer, David Mayhew, Jack Reynolds, Bryant Simon, and Joe Stewart. I received no grants or fellowships and had no other research assistance for this project. My graduate student Micah Altman and I bounced ideas off of each other on these topics for two years. The comments of Dan Lowenstein and Rick Pildes on earlier versions of Chapters 7–9 were especially extensive and helpful. My friends Vernon Burton and Pam Karlan deserve special attention for encouraging me and giving the entire manuscript close readings. My editor at the University of North Carolina Press, Lewis Bateman, had to wait longer and for a longer manuscript than he wished, but he bore both travails with his usual equanimity. Kathy Malin of the Press pursues the underappreciated profession of copyediting with care, grace, and above all, tact. She saved this book from numerous errors, ambiguities, and infelicities. As always, C. Vann Woodward provided sage advice. His example, as one who has never forgotten that the most important parts of history are the struggles of real people over power and rights, continues to inspire me. It is of more than symbolic importance that the first and last references in this book are to Woodward's work. The book is dedicated to my children Rachel and Thad, who harassed me to finish it, to my wife Sally, who put up with my distraction about it for years, and to the memory of my mother, Alice, who somehow surmounted her small-town southern upbringing to become the most tolerant and thoroughly good person I will ever know.

CHAPTER ONE

The Voting Rights Act
and the Two Reconstructions

*I*t is not only historians who name eras, make analogies, draw lessons from the past. As the Selma March was approaching Montgomery, Alabama, in 1965, and as Congress was pushing House Resolution 6400 toward passage, the *Montgomery Advertiser*, sensing the strong national current, remarked, "It is almost certain that President Johnson's reconstruction bill will be enacted" (*MA*, Mar. 17, 1965, quoted in Lawson 1976, 314). The President Johnson referred to was not Andrew, but Lyndon; the "reconstruction" was not the First, but the Second; and the bill was not the "Force" or "Ku Klux" laws, but the Voting Rights Act. Renewed in 1970, 1975, and 1982, the Voting Rights Act (VRA) has been repeatedly attacked as antisouthern, as an infringement on matters better left to state and local governments, as unconstitutionally color-conscious, and, most important, as unnecessary. It is therefore both desirable and safe, according to VRA opponents, to dismantle this last vestige of the Second Reconstruction.

Such critics endanger the gains of the Second Reconstruction by ignoring or misunderstanding the history of the First. Despite the constitutional guarantees of equal protection of the laws and racially impartial suffrage established by the Fourteenth and Fifteenth Amendments, which were ratified in 1868 and 1870, African-Americans gradually lost political power and the right to vote in the late nineteenth century. Twenty-five years after the passage of the Fifteenth Amendment, for instance, Ben Tillman's faction of the Democratic Party of South Carolina passed a temporary registration law to prevent blacks from voting in a referendum on calling a disfranchising convention, insured that the convention would be held by stuffing the ballot box, struck a deal with the faction's upper-class opponents to disfranchise many poor whites along with nearly all blacks, and proclaimed the new constitution without offering the voters a chance to reject it. The Palmetto State was not alone. By the time the South Carolina convention met in 1895, the Democratic leadership of Mississippi had jammed through a similar constitutional disfranchising scheme without holding any referenda at all; Georgia, Florida, Tennessee, and Arkansas had buttressed white Democratic supremacy with poll tax qualifications; and every other ex-Confederate state except North Carolina had enacted some direct restriction on voting with the predominant intent and effect of disproportionately disadvantaging African-Americans. By the end of the year 1900, thirty years after the enactment of the Fifteenth Amendment, Louisiana and North Carolina had amended their state constitutions to disfranchise the vast majority of blacks, and Alabama and Virginia were in the process of calling or holding disfranchising conventions (Kousser 1974). It would be sixty-five years before African-Americans could vote freely throughout the country, seventy-two before a southern state would elect another black member of Congress.

What a contrast with the situation a generation after the passage of the Voting Rights Act, when notable anniversaries of its passage became the occasions for celebratory conferences! By 1990, when the VRA was the same age as the Fifteenth Amendment had been in 1895, Virginia had become the first state in the nation to elect a black governor, 24 blacks and 10 Latinos sat in Congress, there were 417 black and 124 Latino state legislators and 4,388 black and 1,425 Latino officers of city or county governments, six of the ten largest cities in the country had had black mayors, and nationally, 59 percent of blacks and 64 percent of whites were registered to vote. By 1995, on the VRA's thirtieth birthday, the politics of race were both more and less favorable to minorities, and the joy was mixed with trepidation. On the one hand, the 1990s round of redistricting had fully realized the promise of the 1982 amendments to the Voting Rights Act that minorities should enjoy the same opportunities as whites "to participate [in elections] and to elect candidates of their choice" (U.S. Senate 1982b, 31). In 1993, the number of African-American and Latino elected officials totaled 57 in Congress, 686 in state legislatures, and 6,842 in city or county governments. Voter registration percentages— which stood at 30 percent for Latinos, 58 percent for blacks, and 64 percent for whites in 1994—seemed sure to rise substantially as a result of the 1993 passage of the National Voter Registration Act, or "Motor Voter" Act (U.S. Department of Commerce 1990, 257, 260–61, 264; 1993, 283; 1995, 281, 287). On the other hand, the conservative majority on the U.S. Supreme Court had broadened its assault on guarantees of educational and economic opportunities for minorities to include the electoral arena, attacking "racial gerrymandering" that benefited minorities, a move that threatened ultimately to unseat as many as half of the nation's elected minority officials. The present was bright, but the future was threatening.

Why the contrast between the two Reconstructions? I will argue in this chapter that a detailed comparison of certain aspects of the two Reconstructions will help us to understand both of them more adequately and that such lessons, if absorbed, may allow the nation to avoid the deepest parts of a racist reaction like the one that followed the First Reconstruction, a reaction that currently seems well advanced.[1] On the one hand, by making us more conscious of the problematic nature of outcomes that are too often taken for granted, the comparison provides a new approach to the classic question of why the First Reconstruction failed. On the other hand, the analogy throws a different light on controversies over the intent, development, consequences, and desirability of the Voting Rights Act, its interpretations, amendments, proposed relaxation, and undermining by the courts, and perhaps, in the future, by Congress.

HISTORIANS have spent much more energy in documenting than in explaining the collapse of the First Reconstruction, and there have been almost no serious attempts to explain the reasons for the strange career of the Second Reconstruction. In a 1989 essay, for instance, C. Vann Woodward, the scholar who invented the term "Second Reconstruction" for the period since 1954 and who almost singlehandedly initiated the comparative history of America's First Reconstruction, confessed, in his typically ironic tone, to failure. Not only had the First Reconstruction failed, remarked Woodward, but he personally had failed "to find a satisfactory explanation for the failure of Reconstruction" (1989, 199). In contrast, Eric Foner, no doubt constrained by the textbook format of his masterwork on the First Reconstruction, could not afford Woodward's rather coy reticence. Summarizing much historiography, Foner enumerated six reasons for the demise of Reconstruction, or what he called "America's unfinished revolution": violence, "the weakening of Northern resolve," the inability of southern Republicans to develop a long-term appeal to whites, factionalism and corruption within the GOP, the rejection of land reform, and changing patterns in the national and international economic system (1988, 603). William Gillette added to this list "the resurgence of racism in political campaigning" and judicial restrictions on federal action (1979, xi). Some historians, particularly Marxists, have considered the failure of the First Reconstruction inevitable. Manning Marable, for example, contended that "the failure of the federal government to recognize the necessity for massive land redistribution, along the lines of what blacks themselves called 'forty acres and a mule,' would be the principal reason for the failure of the First Reconstruction" (1991, 6). Applying an only slightly less deterministic approach, the "new institutionalist" perspective in political science, Richard Bensel (1990) saw the failure of the First Reconstruction as predestined because of the underdeveloped condition of national political institutions at the time, particularly their inability to control southern white violence. Less deterministic and more aware of post-1877 events than Bensel, Richard Valelly (1993a, 1993b, 1995) considered the puzzle of disfranchisement to be why the Republican party, once it achieved unified control of the federal government after 1896, did not try very hard to reopen Reconstruction questions, reversing disfranchisement where it had occurred and impeding it where it had not. Why, in other words, did a Second Reconstruction not take place at the turn of the nineteenth century?

Probably because the death rattle of the Second Reconstruction is still sounding and there is no convenient symbol for its demise, as the Compromise of 1877 has usually been taken to have been the endpoint of the First Reconstruction, scholars have been even less inclined to suggest reasons for its combination of successes and failures than for those of its predecessor. Comparisons of the two have rarely gone beyond rhetorical gestures. I will argue that rather different and perhaps more satisfying answers to the general question of why the First Reconstruction failed may be obtained by simultaneously narrowing and lengthening the inquiry. To render the problem tractable, I will concentrate solely on politics. Although a great deal can be learned by comparing race relations in post–Civil War America to those in other post-emancipation societies, keeping the comparative focus within the same country has the advantage of allowing us, in effect, to hold most political institutions constant. And instead of truncating the first period at 1877, when the revolution was not only unfinished, it had perhaps only paused, I will carry my analysis of the First Reconstruction through the end of the nineteenth century. It was only then that white supremacists finally felt relatively safe from the threat of black political power.

BECAUSE the argument of this chapter is novel and because its emphasis on institutions, incrementalism, and intent pervades every chapter of the book, it may help to outline it before considering it in detail. Although highly visible events, such as the passage of the Fifteenth Amendment or the VRA or the upsurge of southern violence in the 1870s, create possibilities for change, progressive or retrogressive, it is smaller, less noticed changes that determine whether those possibilities will be actualized and whether the changes will endure. Thus, incremental changes, legal and extralegal, gradually undermined the constitutional guarantees of equal protection and impartial suffrage in the late nineteenth and early twentieth centuries. Each nineteenth-century tactic became more effective as it allowed others to be employed. Violence and intimidation enabled Democrats to take over the polls, after which they could fabricate election returns. Fraudulently elected officials of state and local governments could then gerrymander election districts, switch from ward-based to at-large elections, or impose other structurally discriminatory devices. Because their numbers were decreased, Republican, Independent, or Populist representatives on governing bodies were thereafter even less able to block the passage of direct legislative and, ultimately, state constitutional restrictions on the suffrage. But federal action by Congress or the judiciary might have short-circuited the process at any point—and repeatedly came close to doing so—not just at the violence stage.

Likewise, a hundred years later, in the Second Reconstruction, political equality for minorities did not come about in a single congressional act. Because no legislation perfectly fulfills all the goals of its proponents, because situations sometimes change in ways that are difficult to predict in advance, and because people sometimes change their goals, laws and administrative practices typically develop incrementally.[2] These truisms are particularly apposite for unpopular minorities, for altering politics, economics, and society to treat them more fairly requires long and especially steady vigilance. The struggle to pass the VRA took a generation, and its development into an effective weapon to guarantee minorities equal opportunities to elect officials of their choice lasted another generation. If persistent pressure is a necessary condition for minority success in a democracy, then the crucial questions become: Which political conditions are most likely to produce a regime of progressive policy incrementalism and, on the other hand, which conditions are more likely to allow or encourage the undermining of hard-won gains?[3] The answer, I suggest, is that too much instability in officeholders and policies threatens minorities. The First Reconstruction failed because the political system was too democratic, too unstable. The Second Reconstruction has succeeded better because, until recently, electoral change and changes in the personnel of the judicial system have come about slowly, allowing minorities and their white allies to learn from and correct the inadequacies of previous policies. Relaxation or reversal of the federal government's tenacious protection of minority rights by the forces of an antigovernment, pro–states' rights counterrevolution risks beginning again a process similar to that which unraveled the First Reconstruction. In a democracy, upheaval is most often the enemy of minority rights.

IN THE minds of both moderate and Radical Republicans, the centerpiece of Reconstruction was the vote. "A man with a ballot in his hand," the abolitionist Wendell Phillips declaimed, "is the master of the situation. He defines all his other rights. What is not already given him, he takes. . . . The Ballot is opportunity, education, fair play, right to office, and elbow-room" (quoted in Gillette 1979, 23). But even as they celebrated passage of the Fifteenth Amendment in 1870, Republicans were not so naïve as to believe that the right to vote was self-executing, as Phillips's and other similar statements might seem to imply.[4] All too aware of the difficulty of struggles over black enfranchisement even in the North, where blacks were largely disfranchised in 1865 and where white voters rejected racially equal suffrage in eight of eleven referenda from 1865 to 1869 (Foner 1988, 223), Radicals fully realized that enfranchisement required practical safeguards against evasion and retrogression. From the first congressional draft of the Fourteenth and Fifteenth Amendments, therefore, proponents of racially impartial suffrage banned abridgement as well as outright denial of the right to vote of any loyal, noncriminal, adult male citizen.[5] Although they never specified in reports or floor debates from 1866 to 1869 exactly what practices "abridgement" prohibited, congressmen probably had in mind the widely known example of New York, where in 1821 Martin Van Buren and his allies in the "Albany Regency" had imposed a $250 property requirement on blacks but not on whites and where attempts to repeal the discriminatory standard had failed, though by ever closer margins, in referenda in 1846, 1860, and 1869 (Field 1982, chaps. 2, 4, 6; Mathews [1909] 1971, 14–15, 25, 34, 38–39).[6]

The meaning of the word "abridge" was by no means the only ambiguity in the deceptively simple Fifteenth Amendment. After Congress enfranchised blacks in ten southern states through the 1867 Military Reconstruction Act, white Democrats in Georgia, reasoning that the right to vote did not imply the right to hold office, expelled all the blacks elected to the subsequent state legislature (Drago 1982, 48–49, 55–56). When in 1869 Congress first explicitly guaranteed the right of African-Americans to hold office, then deleted that provision from the Fifteenth Amendment, did they do so, as historian William Gillette claimed, with the intent of allowing racial restrictions on officeholding? Or, as prominent Radical congressmen and senators asserted at the time, was the connection between voting and officeholding so obviously close as to make formal protection of the latter superfluous, and might mentioning it explicitly be taken to imply that other restrictions were allowed (Gillette 1965, 64–71; Mathews [1909] 1971, 47–8)? Similarly, did Congress's deletion of bans against literacy and property tests, after it had initially included such prohibitions in the Fifteenth Amendment, indicate that such qualifications, which everyone recognized would have a disproportionate impact on blacks, were constitutional (McPherson, [1871] 1972, 399–406; B. Schwartz 1970, 1:184, 371–74, 385–87, 392–95, 408–20)? Or, as the Radicals' position on the controversy over officeholding suggested, did the broad statement of the Fifteenth Amendment, together with the equal protection clause of the Fourteenth, outlaw suffrage restrictions based on literacy, property, and all other similar qualifications?

How wide was congressional power under Section 2 of the Fifteenth Amendment? Did it grant Congress almost unlimited control over local, state, and federal elections, as Democrats and many Radicals agreed during the 1869 debates? In particular, did it authorize Congress to prohibit individuals from interfering with the right to vote of other individuals, and could Congress regulate all elections in an attempt to eliminate fraud? Or was Section 2 essentially meaningless, as Democrats claimed whenever Congress considered bills to implement the Fifteenth Amendment after it had passed (Mathews [1909] 1971, 47-50, 76-77, 90-96)? To what degree did the Fifteenth Amendment, combined with the Fourteenth, constitute a national guarantee of fundamental rights—including the right to be protected by state governments against violence—that might be enforced by courts as well as by Congress?

Acting within two months of the proclamation of the passage of the Fifteenth Amendment,[7] Republicans in Congress sought to protect every male citizen's right to vote against interference through violence, intimidation, or bribery by any persons or groups, official or unofficial. The far-reaching law, which still forms the basis of national protective legislation, undercuts the arguments of those historians who claim that Reconstructionists were constitutional conservatives, seriously constrained by traditional theories of federalism (Benedict 1974, 65-90; Benedict 1978, 39-79). Within a year, Congress had passed two more election acts, one supervising congressional elections from registration through the counting of ballots and the other granting the president extensive powers to suppress the Ku Klux Klan and similar conspiracies (Schwartz 1970, 2:445-53, 548-58, 593-96; Gillette 1979, 25-27; Foner 1988, 454-59). In 1875, the House passed an even stronger "Force Bill," providing more severe penalties, widening the scope of federally criminalized violent offenses, and prohibiting excessive poll taxes (an indication that Republicans believed that the Fifteenth Amendment at least allowed *Congress* to forbid tests that did not explicitly mention race). Democratic defiance and the disillusionment of some Republicans prevented the Senate from acting on the bill (Gillette 1979, 283-84; McPherson 1876, 13-18). In the next Congress in which they composed majorities of both houses, that of 1890, the Republicans came within a single vote of passing the most extensive bill in American history that aimed at corruption in elections (McPherson [1890] 1974, 207-19; Kousser 1974, 29-33).

The Fifteenth Amendment and the Enforcement Acts were more effective than many scholars contend (e.g., Gillette 1979, 292-99). Figure 1.1, which contrasts the numbers of black state and national legislators elected from the eleven ex-Confederate states in each two-year period from 1868 through 1900 with those elected from 1960 through 1992, summarizes better than any other

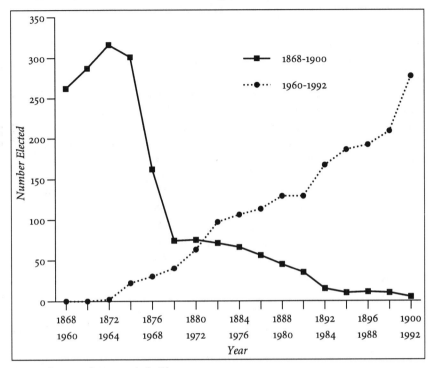

Sources: Congress (1868–1901): Smith 1940.

State legislatures, First Reconstruction (years in parentheses): *Alabama*—Wiggins 1977, 147-51 (1868-78); Taylor 1949 (1880-1900). *Arkansas*—Caldwell 1990. *Florida*—Brown 1995. *Georgia*—Conway 1966, 161 (1868); Foner 1993, passim (1870); Shadgett 1964, 28, 52 (1872-74); Work 1920, 63-119 (1876-78); Bacote 1955, 524-25 (1880-1900). *Louisiana*—Vincent 1976, 228-38 (1868-76); Uzee 1950, 203-4 (1878-1900). *Mississippi*—Harris 1979, 264, 428, 479 (1870-74); Wharton 1947, 202 (1876-92). *North Carolina*—Padgett 1937, 483-84 (1868-88); Work 1920, 63-119 (1890-92, 1900); Edmonds 1951, 116 (1894-98). *South Carolina*—Holt 1977, 97 (1868-76); Tindall 1952, 309-10 (1878-1900). *Tennessee*—Cartwright 1976, 20, 66, 103, 105 (1871-83, 1889-1900); Work 1920, 63-119 (1885-87). *Texas*—Barr 1986, 340-52 (1870); Smallwood 1974, 406-11 (1872-74); Barr 1971, 27 (1876); Rice 1971, 100-111 (1878, 1894-1900); Brewer 1935, 127-28 (1876; 1894-1900). *Virginia*—Blake 1935, 137, 182, 232, 252, (1869-71, 1879, 1891); Buni 1967, 4, 8 (1881); Wynes 1961, 45, 49 (1889); Jackson 1945, 1-43 (1873-77, 1883-87).

Congress and state legislatures: 1964-66—Bass and DeVries 1976, 152; U.S. Commission on Civil Rights 1968, passim. 1968—Southern Regional Council 1968, iii. 1970-92—U.S. Department of Commerce, *Statistical Abstract of the U.S.*, various years.

single document the puzzle of the two Reconstructions. Based on statistics never before collected in one place, the graph suggests a series of questions: Why did the nineteenth-century number start so high,[8] fall so quickly after 1874, continue until 1890 at diminishing levels (but ones that would not be attained again until the 1970s), and then dwindle? Why were the totals in the early 1960s so minuscule, why did they grow gradually, why did they jump in each year after a redistricting (especially in 1992), and what will their future trend be? What were the policy consequences of various levels of black office-holding? Were legislatures more responsive to African-American concerns in the 1880s and 1890s than in the 1860s and 1870s, as implied by the views of those who currently favor trading some black "descriptive representation" for more "substantive representation"—that is, fewer black faces for more sympathetic white ones (Swain 1993)? Since the Fifteenth Amendment and the Voting Rights Act were roughly analogous laws, and since each was followed by a series of enforcing and strengthening acts, the stark divergence in the trends in officeholding demands explanation.

Even after the plunge in black officeholding in the mid-1870s, African-Americans continued to vote in large percentages for another generation. To state that blacks were "politically impotent," as the Thernstroms do, is to ignore a generation of scholarship (Thernstrom and Thernstrom 1997, 29). Although their first preference, then as now, was to be represented by people of their own race, ceteris paribus, most African-Americans were forced after 1877 to settle for whatever influence their votes could buy with overwhelmingly white elected officials. But the notions that disfranchisement was simultaneous with the textbook end of Reconstruction in 1877 and that the South became "solid" immediately after that date are myths. In 1880, three years after Rutherford B. Hayes symbolically confined U.S. troops to their barracks in the South in fulfillment of the Compromise of 1877, an estimated two-thirds of the adult male blacks were recorded as voting, and two-thirds of *those* managed to have their votes recorded for James A. Garfield, whom they had nearly all, no doubt, supported for president. The high black turnout in this election, which was considerably greater than overall national participation a century later, was not atypical, nor did Democrats allow it only because presidential elections were less important to them than those closer to home. An average of six out of ten African-Americans voted in the most heavily contested gubernatorial races in each of the eleven states during the decade of the eighties, despite the fact that none of these elections took place on the same day as voters balloted for president. Of those blacks who voted, at least 60 percent supported the Republican, Greenbacker, or other anti-Democratic candidate.[9] Even in the 1890s, after several states had restricted the suffrage, nearly half of the blacks are estimated to have voted in key gubernatorial contests, although the Populist-Democratic battles were sufficiently severe that Democrats pushed fraud to new levels (Kousser 1974, 15, 28, 42).

It might be imagined that blacks continued to vote in such large numbers for so long in the nineteenth century because paternalistic southern Democrats either wished to keep their pledges to maintain the Constitution or because they needed black votes to combat their lower-class, hill-country white opponents. The first southern white response to threats of Reconstruction had been defiance (Perman 1973). Believing that the Civil War had settled only the questions of secession and slavery and that those who retained power in the states would be allowed to set the status of the freedmen approximately equal to that of the antebellum free people of color, white southerners virulently and often violently opposed all efforts to guarantee blacks equal rights, notably in the 1866 Civil Rights Bill, the Reconstruction Acts, the Fourteenth and Fifteenth Amendments, the various enforcement acts, and the 1875 Civil Rights Act. That the Republican majority, with substantial support from northern public opinion, continued to insist on equal rights, however, convinced white southern Democrats to alter their tactics. While a "white line" faction continued and even, in the mid-1870s, intensified the forcible intimidation of black voters, a more moderate "New Departure" faction of southern Democrats emerged at the same time, assuring the northerners that black rights would be safe if federal protection were withdrawn. The left or moderate hand—the Wade Hampton, L. Q. C. Lamar, and Francis T. Nicholls faction of the party—at least claimed not to know what the right or extreme racist hand—the Martin W. Gary and Ben Tillman faction—was doing. But the combined one-two punch was devastating to black political power in the Deep South.

The moderates' paper pledges were strong, and they persuaded those northerners who, like President Rutherford B. Hayes, were anxious to believe them. The Mississippi state Democratic platform of 1875 affirmed a belief in "the civil and political equality of all men as established by the Constitution of the United States and the amendments thereto." In the words of a modern scholar, however, "the majority of the delegates did not take the document very seriously" (Harris 1979, 654-55). Similarly, another scholar notes that in Louisiana in 1876 "the Democratic Platform also explicitly recognized the binding effect of the 13th, 14th, and 15th amendments to the United States Constitution, and the party pledged itself to protect every citizen, regardless of race, in the exercise of his rights. Every one of these pledges, except possibly the acknowledgement of the 13th Amendment, would be broken within a few years" (Taylor 1974, 483-84).

In Virginia in 1873, the state Democratic party platform "promised to administer equal justice to both races." Nevertheless, the Democrats, including even moderate gubernatorial candidate James L. Kemper, "made much of the color line" during that campaign, and the Virginians took action in the 1874 and 1876 legislative sessions to reduce the black vote (Maddex 1970, 108, 195). In South Carolina, which had the largest percentage of blacks of any state in the union at the time, the 1876 Democratic state platform announced the party's "acceptance, in perfect good faith, of the thirteenth, fourteenth, and fifteenth amendments to the Federal Constitution." The South's best known moderate Redeemer, South Carolina gubernatorial candidate Wade Hampton, promised repeatedly that "not one single right enjoyed by the colored people today shall be taken from them. They shall be equals, under the law, of any man in South Carolina." Blacks would soon convert to the Democratic party, Hampton prophesied, "because they will find that their rights will be better protected by that party" (quoted in Tindall 1952, 12).

Many observers at the time recognized the cynicism that was involved in such pledges and prognostications. As Amos Akerman, who had returned to the South after serving briefly as attorney general under Grant, remarked at the time, "when speaking for effect at the North" the southern Democrats "say much about accepting the results of the war in good faith, and respecting the rights of everybody," but contradicted those statements by their "drastic policy and unguarded utterances" in the South (quoted in Gillette 1979, 313). Even the oft mentioned moderate policy of appointing blacks to some offices was mostly window dressing. As Gov. Francis T. Nicholls of Louisiana, one of the most prominent New Departure Democrats, noted: "[I] appointed a number of [blacks] to small offices sandwiching them on Boards between white men where . . . they were powerless to do harm" (quoted in Hair 1969, 22).

The southern Democrats' promises had been violated even as they were uttered. As U.S. Senate investigations in 1877 and 1878 documented, widespread Ku Klux and Red Shirt violence kept many blacks from the polls, racially discriminatory voting restrictions and facially neutral laws administered in a discriminatory fashion discouraged others, and blatant ballot box stuffing and fraudulent counting negated the votes of many who managed to overcome other obstacles to voting (U.S. Senate 1877, 1878). By 1880, even President Rutherford B. Hayes, whose southern policy was built on the assumption that white moderates would live up to their promises, hold the more openly racist whites in check, and join a Whiggish alliance with Republicans, recognized the southern violations and asked Congress to pass more legislation to protect black rights effectively (Logan 1965, 45).

It was neither conservative honor nor self-interest but the continued struggles of African-Americans and their liberal white allies that preserved partial black suffrage for so long. Indeed, white southern Democrats never ceased scheming to overturn political Reconstruction. Five principal tactics were used in the reversal of Reconstruction, none sufficient by itself, all working together, but, roughly speaking, following a predictable developmental sequence: *violence, fraud, structural discrimination, statutory suffrage restriction,* and *constitutional disfranchisement.* Corresponding to these tactics are four approximate stages in the attack on black voting rights after the First Reconstruction: the *Klan stage,* in which fraud and violence predominated; the *dilution stage,* characterized by structural legal changes; the *disfranchisement stage,* where the last legal underpinnings of the real solid South were put into place; and the *lily-white stage,* the aim of which was to crush any elevation of blacks above the distinctly secondary political status into which the disfranchisement measures had forced them and to reduce, from very slim to none, any chances of blacks being elected or appointed to office or exercising any political muscle whatsoever.

VIOLENCE was important, not only because it killed off or scared off southern Republican leadership, as is often noted, but also because it transfixed northern Republicans. The extent of Reconstruction violence and its political nature have been rightly stressed. Between the gubernatorial election in April and the presidential election in November of 1868, for instance, Louisiana Democrats, according to a congressional investigation, killed 1,081 persons, mostly black. In St. Landry Parish alone in that six-month period, as many as 200 African-Americans fell to the "Knights of the White Camellia"—about four times as many as died in the South as a whole during the civil rights movement of the 1950s and 60s (Trelease 1971, 129–35).[10] Forty-six blacks were massacred in Memphis and 34 in New Orleans in 1866; 25–30 at Meridian, Mississippi, in 1871, and 35 at Vicksburg in 1874; 105 at the tiny hamlet of Colfax, Louisiana, on Easter Sunday, 1873, including 40 or so after they had laid down their arms and surrendered. After 1877, selective assassination of white as well as black Republicans and blunt public threats of fatal violence helped to suppress opposition to the Democrats, especially in the Deep South (Trelease 1971, xliv; Wharton 1947, 189–90; Tunnell 1984, 192; Cresswell 1995). This extensive, systematic political terrorism has no parallel in the modern civil rights movement, and in sheer extent it far surpassed the lynching spree of the last decade of the nineteenth century and the first two decades of the twentieth.[11] Reconstruction violence astonished, mesmerized, and sometimes paralyzed the national Republican leaders, who devoted much—too much—of their legislative attention, as well as a great many "Bloody Shirt" speeches, to the topic.

The attention was excessive because violence was a relatively politically ineffective as well as a dangerous weapon for a conservative, upper-class-dominated group such as the southern Democrats to employ (Cresswell

TABLE 1.1. Republican Share of Vote in Presidential Elections
Following Violent Racial Incidents: Selected Southern Counties, 1866–1876

Town	County	Year of Incident	Black Population of County in 1880 (% of total)	Republican Vote in County[a] (% of total)
Memphis	Shelby, Tenn.	1866	56	64 (1868)
New Orleans	Orleans, La.	1866, 1868	27	38 (1872)
Camilla	Mitchell, Ga.	1868	55	51 (1872)
(None)	St. Landry, La.	1868	49	45 (1872)
Laurens	Laurens, S.C.	1870	60	72 (1872)
Eutaw	Greene, Ala.	1870	82	68 (1872)
Meridian	Lauderdale, Miss.	1872	54	54 (1872)
Colfax	Grant, La.	1873	46	43 (1876)
Coushatta	Red River, La.	1874	71	67 (1876)
Vicksburg	Warren, Miss.	1874	72	23 (1876)
Clinton	Hinds, Miss.	1875	73	25 (1876)
Hamburg	Edgefield, S.C.	1876	65	14 (1880)

Sources: Trelease 1971, xliv, 129; Tunnell 1984, 173–209. Data on black population are from U.S. Bureau of the Census 1883; data on Republican vote from Burnham 1955.
[a] Year of election is shown in parentheses.

1995, 213). If violence had permanently inhibited the political opposition, one would expect presidential returns from counties where there were well-known violent incidents in the 1860s and 70s to show a once-and-for-all destruction of the Republican vote. Table 1.1 demonstrates that this was not the case. In nine of twelve southern counties in which there were well-known "riots" or extensive assassinations, Republicans received approximately the same proportion of the votes as there were blacks in the population in the election after the incidents.[12] Even in the remaining three counties (the last three in the table), the Republicans polled *some* votes.[13] Furthermore, Establishment violence is costly, for those who own and control property and power have much to lose if the labor force leaves or fights back by sabotaging property (Belknap 1987, 23). And outside the region, the southern whites' reputation for violent oppression of blacks fueled campaigns for national intervention (U.S. Senate 1878). As Jonathan Rowell (R-Ill.) stated during the debates on the Lodge Fair Elections Bill in 1890, "It is everywhere in Northern circles believed that the black vote of the Southern States is suppressed. It is everywhere believed that the Fifteenth Amendment to the Constitution of the United States is nullified" (*Cong. Rec.*, 51st Cong., 1st sess., 6555). Thus, the direct political effect of violence, though significant, cannot by itself account for the decline of black voting in the nineteenth century.

Fraud was probably more significant than violence, as composing election returns became a recognized art form and excuses for the loss of official ballots stretched even the southern capacity for hyperbole. Mississippi officials, for instance, reported that horses and mules had developed a taste for ballot boxes (Wharton 1947, 204). Governor Samuel D. McEnery of Louisiana admitted that his state's election law "was intended to make it the duty of the governor to treat the law as a formality and count in the Democrats." He became a zealous enforcer of the legislative will. Virginia elections, according to the author of the state's chief election statute, were "crimes against popular government and treason against liberty." "Any time it was necessary," reported a delegate to the Alabama Constitutional Convention of 1901, whites who controlled the Black Belt "could put in ten, fifteen, twenty or thirty thousand Negro votes." "It is no secret," a leader of the 1890 Mississippi Constitutional Convention admitted, "that there has not been a full vote and a fair count in Mississippi since 1875." But Congress often unseated counted-in candidates, and Republicans twice almost succeeded in strengthening laws against such electoral chicanery (Kousser 1974, 45–47). Like violence, moreover, fraud was a dangerous device for a government of the "best men," one whose propagandistic staple, in the South and especially in the North, was the charge that Reconstructionists had been corrupt. (For the propaganda, see Pike 1874; Herbert 1890.)

SOUTHERN white Democrats in the nineteenth century employed at least eleven legal devices to dilute African-American votes without actually denying them the right to vote explicitly on the basis of race. Many of these devices were neutral on the face of the law and might be upheld by some federal courts in today's climate of judicial opinion. By severely constraining the number of offices that anti-Democratic parties could hope to capture, even in a fair election, such structural changes reduced the amount of overall violence and fraud necessary for the Democrats to carry elections, concentrated the opposition's attention on a few potentially winnable seats, dispirited the Democrats' adversaries, especially in districts where they had no chance to win, and increased the number of legislators willing to support further attacks on ethnic and political minorities. They represented long steps toward disfranchisement then, and might again in the future.

Although they all had the same purpose—the minimization of officeholding by black or black-influenced white officeholders—the specific schemes varied because of differences in the black percentage of the population and its geographic distribution. If blacks were geographically concentrated within the politically relevant area, judicious *gerrymandering* could minimize the number of seats they could hope to win, but single-member districts, always preferred by most whites, could be maintained. If African-Americans were in the minority, *at-large elections* could deny them any representation at all, especially when combined with legalized or informal *white primaries,* which minimized defections by disgruntled white factions in general elections. For temporarily white-controlled cities in black-majority areas, *annexation* or, in suitable circumstances, the strikingly inventive device of *deannexation or retrocession* of territory was available. If the majorities were too large to be overcome, *bonds* for officeholders could be set so high as to deter from running any but the extremely affluent or those with rich and brave friends, or the authorities might arbitrarily *refuse to accept the bonds* as valid, or election officials might *consolidate polling places* to such an extent as to make the trip to the polls or the line at the polls intolerably long, or they might just *fail to open the polls* altogether. In extremes, the legislatures could *impeach or otherwise displace* elected officials or *do away with local elections* altogether and vest the power to choose local officials in the legislature or governor or their appointees.

Gerrymanders were the paradigm of the dilution strategy. Attracting attention from the Supreme Court, editorialists, and other nonhistorians only since the 1993 decision in *Shaw v. Reno,* "racial gerrymandering" in fact appeared in the very first redistricting after the Fifteenth Amendment—that is, the first time that enough African-Americans could vote in the U.S. for anyone to use the gerrymander against them. In North Carolina, the Democrats, who attained a majority in the legislature through extensive violence against and intimidation of black and white Republicans, packed African-Americans into the "Black Second" congressional district (Anderson 1981). The compact southeastern Second District drawn by the Republicans in 1867 had contained a small white majority and a total population that was 8 percent below that of the ideal in the state, and it had only 20 percent more black citizens than could be expected if the state's black population had been divided equally in the nine congressional districts.[14] From the Democratic reapportionment of 1872 until disfranchisement in 1900, the district contained substantial black majorities, from 10 to 18 percent more total population than the average district in the state and, most important, it had approximately twice the number of blacks that an equal division would have dictated. Since the other districts were "stacked" to insure that there was no black majority, the apportionment effectively confined black control in a state that was approximately one-third African-American to a maximum of one district in eight or nine (depending on the state's total population in the decade) and minimized black influence and Republican representation in all the other congressional districts. Republican Governor Tod Caldwell described its shape as " 'extraordinary, inconvenient and most grotesque' " (quoted in Anderson 1981, 3).

It was only after the violently racist "White Supremacy Campaign" of 1898 and the fraudulent passage in 1900 of the disfranchisement amendment—with its literacy test, poll tax, and temporary grandfather clause—that the vast majority of blacks were excluded from politics in North Carolina and that it became safe for the Democrats to reduce the Second District's population, and especially the number of blacks in it, to a more compact size and a population more nearly equal to that of the state's other congressional districts.

The example of South Carolina is even more instructive than that of its northern neighbor. From 1867 to 1875, Republicans spread black (and, therefore, safely Republican) majorities among three of the state's four congressional districts, apparently hoping to hold the Fourth District with a coalition of blacks and upland whites. No county was divided and, nearly a century before *Reynolds v. Sims* (1964), there was little variation in the district populations. In the first reapportionment after the 1870 census, the Republicans proved even craftier, keeping three strongly black-majority districts and adding an at-large seat. (The state as a whole was 59 percent black.) Blacks filled all four black-majority seats. In 1875, the Republicans overreached themselves, drawing two marginal districts with slight preponderances of African-Americans. The two "whitest" districts also contained the most people. Democratic violence and chicanery in the violent "Red Shirt" campaign of 1876 overcame the natural Republican majorities in these two districts.

The first Democratic-run redistricting in South Carolina, which took place in 1881, split so many counties and townships that it is not possible to compute exact racial percentages for all of the districts. The gem of this malapportionment, the 82 percent black Seventh District, contained, according to the *New York Times,* "all the precincts of black voters that could be strung together with the faintest connection of contiguous territory" (see Figure 1.2). Popularly referred to as the "boa constrictor" district, the Seventh stretched between the homes of two incumbent Republican congressmen, a black who resided in coastal Beaufort County and a white who lived at the other end of the district in midlands Sumter County, thus fostering racial and personal Republican fratricide as inconveniently as possible (*NYT,* July 13, 1882, 5).

Mississippi's experience in the Reconstruction and "Redeemer" eras proves that one did not have to slice across county boundaries to construct an effective antiblack racial gerrymander. In 1868, the risk-accepting Republicans created two safe and three competitive districts, splitting the heavily black counties of Bolivar, Sunflower, Coahoma, and Tunica off from their Delta brethren in an attempt to bolster what they hoped would be an appreciable highland white Republican vote. The two most populous districts were also the most heavily black. Apparently to maintain white power within the Republican party, in other words, the Republicans "wasted" many of their votes

FIGURE 1.2. Racial Gerrymandering in South Carolina:
Congressional District Boundaries in 1883 Compared to 1875

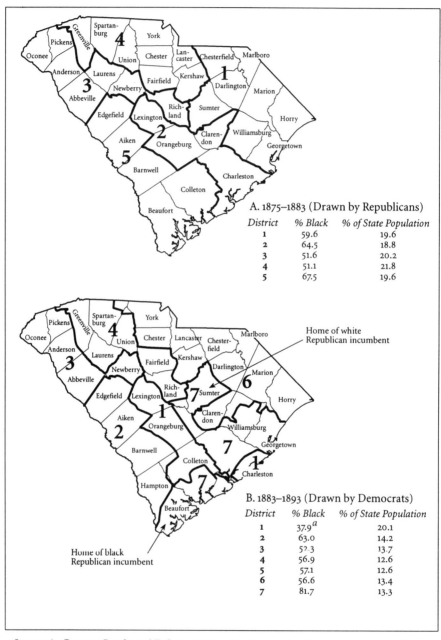

A. 1875–1883 (Drawn by Republicans)

District	% Black	% of State Population
1	59.6	19.6
2	64.5	18.8
3	51.6	20.2
4	51.1	21.8
5	67.5	19.6

B. 1883–1893 (Drawn by Democrats)

District	% Black	% of State Population
1	37.9[a]	20.1
2	63.0	14.2
3	52.3	13.7
4	56.9	12.6
5	57.1	12.6
6	56.6	13.4
7	81.7	13.3

Sources: A—Parsons, Beach, and Dubin 1986, 213; B—Parsons, Beach, and Dubin 1990, 138–43.
[a] 1893–95 figure; 1883–93 figure unavailable.

by concentrating too many people in two districts. After the 1870 census, the Republicans trimmed their majorities but kept fairly safe cushions in five districts, while conceding the First to white Democrats (see Figure 1.3a). The actual results of the electoral process reflected these redistricting changes perfectly, as Republicans carried the five black-majority districts and lost the white-majority First District.

Rather than wait for a new census, the Democrats who had perpetrated the violent "Revolution of 1875" in Mississippi immediately reapportioned the congressional seats, effective with the 1877 elections (see Figure 1.3b). Known throughout the country at the time as the "shoestring district," the new Sixth ran all the way between the northern and southern borders of the state, tracking the Mississippi River and drowning the state's black population in its course. Two of the six districts were safely white (and therefore Democratic), three would require only a limited amount of ballot box stuffing and night riding for the Democrats to carry, and the Sixth was overwhelmingly Republican. Frightened by the assassinations of at least 200 white and black Republicans in the state in 1875, most blacks seem to have given up politics in Mississippi for the next four years (Wharton 1947, 181–98).

In 1881, the Democrats retied the shoestring, which was represented by black congressman John R. Lynch of far-southern Adams County, running it east-west, instead of north-south (see Figure 1.3c). The *New York Times* correspondent reported that "the whole reapportionment scheme, therefore, turned upon the problem of beating Lynch, and an examination of the Sixth District will show that the Bourbons [Democrats] did the best job that it was possible to do. The only trustworthy Republican counties in the whole district are the two that belonged to Mr. Lynch's old district, Adams and Wilkinson." The others were sparsely populated and largely white (*NYT*, July 27, 1882, 5). Lynch lost. In the state as a whole, the Democrats created one overwhelmingly black Delta district, the Third; one substantially black district, the Seventh; and five districts that stacked the African-Americans so skillfully that they ranged only from 49.2 percent to 53.8 percent black. In such districts, including Lynch's home district, it was simple to alter a few tallies, throw out a few thousand votes, or announce solemnly that selected ballot boxes had unaccountably disappeared (Wharton 1947, 204). Fraud worked more easily because gerrymandering had reduced the task to manageable proportions.

In South Carolina and Mississippi, Democratic gerrymanders had transformed a probable 8–3 Republican margin into a 12–1 Democratic one. Since voting was well known at the time to be extremely racially polarized—a conclusion borne out by extensive statistical analyses (see Kousser 1974)—a partisan gerrymander amounted to a racial gerrymander. Similar reapportionments created the "Black Fourth" in Alabama and less notorious con-

FIGURE 1.3. Racial Gerrymandering in Mississippi:
Congressional District Boundaries in 1877 and 1883 Compared to 1873

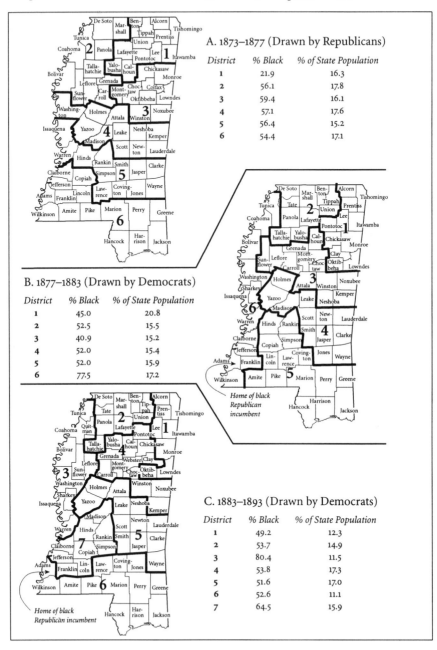

A. 1873–1877 (Drawn by Republicans)

District	% Black	% of State Population
1	21.9	16.3
2	56.1	17.8
3	59.4	16.1
4	57.1	17.6
5	56.4	15.2
6	54.4	17.1

B. 1877–1883 (Drawn by Democrats)

District	% Black	% of State Population
1	45.0	20.8
2	52.5	15.5
3	40.9	15.2
4	52.0	15.4
5	52.0	15.9
6	77.5	17.2

*Home of black
Republican
incumbent*

C. 1883–1893 (Drawn by Democrats)

District	% Black	% of State Population
1	49.2	12.3
2	53.7	14.9
3	80.4	11.5
4	53.8	17.3
5	51.6	17.0
6	52.6	11.1
7	64.5	15.9

*Home of black
Republican incumbent*

Sources: A—Parsons, Beach, and Dubin 1986, 184–87; B—Parsons, Beach, and Dubin 1990, 68–71.

centrations elsewhere (Wiggins 1980, 68–69). In the Texas legislature, the boundaries of all the multicounty "floater" districts in the Black Belt, in the words of the standard work on race relations in that state, "were gerrymandered in order to create a white majority" (Rice 1971, 101, 132). Similar racially tainted gerrymanders "whitened" state legislatures all across the South, as well as in the cities of Richmond, Nashville, Montgomery, Raleigh, Chattanooga, Jackson, Jacksonville (Rabinowitz 1978, 270–73, 323; Cartwright 1976, 158; Akin 1974, 123–45). In the late nineteenth century, "gerrymandering in its various forms was the most effective tactic used by sympathetic legislatures both to redeem the cities [from African-American and Republican control] and to keep them in the hands of white Democrats" (Rabinowitz 1994, 126).

At-large city election schemes, motivated by racial purposes, appeared in the South as early as the first elections in which blacks were allowed to vote. "To guard against the possibility of the election of black city officials," a conservative historian concluded, white Atlanta Democrats in 1868 "secured from the legislature the general ticket system." Two years later, after a temporarily Republican Georgia legislature restored the ward system, two of the ten candidates elected were black. But when the GOP lost control of the legislature in 1871, the Democrats went back to the at-large system, and no more blacks were elected to the Atlanta city government until 1953 (Watts 1974, 273; Rabinowitz 1978, 269). In Mobile, Alabama, the rabidly racist 1874 and 1876 Redeemer legislatures mandated explicit at-large systems for the election of school board and city government officials. In the case of the school board, this replaced a system that had been designed to guarantee "minority representation," and in the instance of the city government, it was a substitute for a vague 1870 law that a local racist faction of white Republicans had interpreted, under Democratic pressure, to require at-large elections. No black was ever elected to either governmental body under these at-large systems, which persisted in Alabama law until overturned by a federal court in 1982 (McCrary 1984; *Bolden v. City of Mobile* [1982]; *Brown v. Board of School Commissioners of Mobile County* [1982]). Chattanooga, Memphis, and Nashville "reformers," too, introduced and at times succeeded in getting the Tennessee legislature to pass at-large election statutes for their cities. "Their efforts stemmed from partisan and racial motives," says the leading authority on the subject, who titles his chapter on the topic: "Urban Reform: The Nemesis of Black Power" (Cartwright 1976, 119–60, quotation on 159).

The Democratic primary was not at first principally a disfranchising device, for the vast majority of blacks wished only to cast Republican, Populist, or independent votes and have them counted as cast; and, in fact, a few blacks were often allowed to vote in such primaries, in return for pledges of allegiance to the Democrats, in order to cut down the Republican totals in the general elections. But the local Democratic primary soon became the real election in many areas, and it was restricted to whites only in certain Texas counties from 1874 on, in Edgefield and Charleston Counties in South Carolina from 1878 on, in Birmingham from 1888 on, and in Atlanta for various periods before 1895 and from that date until at least the *Smith v. Allwright* decision in 1944 (Rice 1971, 113–27; Tindall 1952, 26, 33; Harris 1977, 58; Watts 1978, 24, 30, 31).

To reduce a black majority in 1877, the city of Montgomery deannexed a predominantly black section, even though the area contained enough valuable industrial property that its retrocession noticeably reduced that city's tax base. Whites in Selma convinced the legislature to reduce that city's size, too, as a Dallas County Democratic state senator later recalled, "in order to cut the negroes out of the city" (Rabinowitz 1978, 273, 323; *MA*, Oct. 9, Nov. 24, 1900 [quote]). To discourage black candidates, the town of Huntsville, Texas, raised the required bond for constables during the 1880s to $20,000 (Rice 1971, 88–89). In Vance County, North Carolina, in 1887, a sheriff's bond was fixed at $53,000 and a treasurer's at $18,000. Since few Republicans were wealthy enough to sign such bonds, only those acceptable to rich Democrats could serve. Even if they had affluent friends, successful Republican candidates in North Carolina sometimes had their bonds arbitrarily refused by county commissioners, who were all appointed by the Democrats. In Warren County in 1886, the commissioners turned down a candidate because he "was a colored man." His white opponent, rejected by the voters, was given the office (Anderson 1981, 162–65, quote on 163; for other examples, see Wiggins 1980, 67; Going 1951, 33; Cartwright 1976, 152–53).

Fraud, notorious and ubiquitous in the postbellum South, was supplemented by somewhat less blatant polling place irregularities, which are best illustrated by one scholar's description of the 1876 election in the Alabama "Black Belt":

> "On election day some polls opened and closed at the whim of election officials while other polls moved several times during the day. Some election officials refused to open the polls at all, and others announced that they were not going to remain at the polls all day to permit blacks to make 'radical majorities.' The failure to open polls in Republican strongholds in Hale, Perry, Marengo, Bullock, Barbour, Greene, Pickens, Wilcox, and Sumter counties undermined Republican strength as effectively as the earlier terror of the Ku Klux Klan, and it involved no bloodshed." (Wiggins 1980, 71–72)[15]

If all else failed, officials could be impeached or forced from office, often on trumped-up charges, and local governments could be made appointive. Thus, North Carolina governor William W. Holden was impeached in 1870 for trying to put down the Klan, and Mississippi governor Adelbert Ames, whom no one credibly charged with any illegal act, was pressured out of office during impeachment proceedings, which also led to resignations by other statewide executive and judicial officials, as well as circuit judges, in that state and in South Carolina (Anderson 1981, 3; Harris 1979, 694–98; Tindall 1952, 15–18). In Tennessee in 1869 and in Virginia in 1870, conservative state legislatures summarily ousted the Nashville and Richmond city governments and replaced Republicans with Democrats (Rabinowitz 1978, 267–69). The Alabama legislature abolished the Dallas County Criminal Court because the elected black Republican judge refused to resign and did away with the elective office of county commissioner in at least five Black Belt counties during the 1870s, substituting officers appointed by the governor (Wiggins 1980, 68; *SSA*, Dec. 24, 1875). The purpose of Alabama's action was later openly avowed by state legislator James Jefferson Robinson:

> Montgomery county came before us and asked us to give them protection of life, liberty and property by abolishing the offices that the electors in that county had elected. Dallas asked us to strike down the officials they had elected in that county, one of them a Negro that had the right to try a white man for his life, liberty, and property. Mr. Chairman, that was a grave question to the Democrats who had always believed in the right of the people to select their own officers, but when we saw the life, liberty and property of the Caucasians were at stake, we struck down in Dallas county the Negro and his cohorts. We put men of the Caucasian race there to try them. (*MA*, Apr. 23, 1899)

In North Carolina, the state legislature first divested the voters of the right to elect county commissioners and justices of the peace, then arrogated to itself the power to name justices of the peace, then gave the justices of the peace the responsibility of choosing the commissioners. The complexion of county government in Wake and other Republican counties changed immediately and irredeemably (Rabinowitz 1978 269–70; Anderson 1981, 56–57).

Although violence, fraud, and restructuring could usually keep political dissent in check, they could not eliminate it. Nineteenth-century Democrats rightly feared national antiviolence and anticorruption bills before legal disfranchisement, for there was a core of black political strength to build on if southern Democrats could be forced to allow "a free ballot and a fair count." The final solution to the problems of political dissent and black suffrage was the adoption of statutory and constitutional restrictions on individuals' rights to vote. In most cases, statutory limitations shrank dissent so that constitutional ones could be imposed (Kousser 1974). But some of the statutory restrictions were passed quite early, as soon as Democrats took even temporary control of state legislatures, and since they served exactly the same function as structural changes, it is a mistake to make too strong a distinction between laws affecting whether individuals could vote and those concerning how votes were translated into the control of offices. Moreover, like structural changes, many of the preliminary disfranchisement measures were subtle and formally "colorblind."

Six tactics related to registration greatly assisted nineteenth-century southern Democrats in keeping the black vote under control: lengthening residency requirements; requiring periodic voter registration at centrally located places during working hours and presentation of registration receipts at the polls, which burdened lower-class voters who were not accustomed, in those pre-bureaucratic days, to keeping records; demanding copiously detailed information, which sometimes had to be vouched for by witnesses, before a voter could register; giving registration boards sufficient discretion to allow them to unfairly pad or purge the rolls; not guaranteeing equal party representation on such boards; and permitting widespread challenges to voters at the polls.

Speaking for local Democrats in February 1875, the *Montgomery Daily Advertiser* pleaded, "if the Legislature does not come to the aid of the negro [*sic*] dominated communities then there is no help for this portion of Alabama." The legislature responded with a strict local registration law (*MA*, Feb. 6, 1875, quoted in Rabinowitz 1978, 274). In Mississippi in the same year, "the new registration law provided an excellent means for local Democrats to reduce Negro voters to a manageable proportion—an opportunity many seized upon immediately" (Harris 1979, 701). Texas in 1874 gave city councils the right to delete "ineligibles" from the rolls after the close of registration, a measure "undoubtedly motivated," in the words of Lawrence D. Rice, "by the mobility of certain portions of the population—principally the Negroes" (Rice 1971, 130). In Tennessee, a municipal registration act was beaten in 1885 only when the Republicans in the state senate walked out, breaking the quorum. When it passed in 1889, along with a secret ballot act, which served as a de facto literacy test, since illiterates were not allowed assistance in voting, registration devastated the black vote in the four major Tennessee cities, as it was intended to (Kousser 1973; Cartwright 1976, 134–35, 223–54).

Usually treated by historians as a "good government reform," the secret ballot was employed in eight southern and many northern states with the intent and effect of disfranchising illiterates, who were very disproportionately African-Americans or immigrants. Complicated ballot forms, often with the candidates' party designations deleted, could make it difficult for all but the well-educated and those whom the election officials chose to help to vote at all (Kousser 1974, 51–56).

The South Carolina registration and eight-box law was one of the most clever stratagems, and its provisions illustrate how ingenious southern authors could twist seemingly neutral devices for partisan and racist purposes. As first introduced, the bill took the "neutral principle" of voter registration and turned it into a literacy test by requiring potential registrants to sign their names. Its author, the "patrician" Edward McCrady Jr., estimated that this would disfranchise a majority of the blacks. To those who pointed out that a literacy test would also affect many whites, McCrady proposed as an escape mechanism the first form of the grandfather clause. Massachusetts in 1857 had required literacy of all future voters, but allowed those already on the rolls to stay. McCrady simply adopted the principle of the Massachusetts provision, along with its 1857 date, which, as everyone realized, predated black suffrage. As the bill finally passed, the literacy test was shifted to a new section of the law which provided for separate ballot boxes for each of eight offices, required election officials to shift the boxes around during the voting to make it impossible for a literate friend to put an illiterate's tickets in the correct order before he entered the polling place, and prohibited anyone but the election officers, all but one or two of whom in the entire state seem to have been Democrats, from assisting unlettered voters. In place of the grandfather clause, the registration provision that finally passed allowed the registrar at the close of the registration period to add to the list any voter who had failed to register if the official, to quote the law, "upon such evidence as he may think necessary, in his discretion" judged that the voter should be on the rolls. This open invitation to fraud and discrimination was designed to let registrars enfranchise all whites. Black turnout in South Carolina in the presidential election of 1884 dropped by an estimated 50 percent from its 1880 level (Kousser 1974, 84–92).

The poll tax, according to a member of the 1890 Mississippi Constitutional Convention's Franchise Committee, was "the most effective instrumentality of Negro disfranchisement," According to a prominent North Carolina disfranchiser, it "practically disfranchised the Negroes" in Georgia. Georgia Republicans suspended the tax as a suffrage prerequisite in 1870, but the Democratic Redeemer legislature promptly restored it in 1871, and the 1877 Georgia Constitutional Convention not only fixed it in the fundamental law, but made it cumulative—that is, taxes for all previous years had to be paid before one could vote. Tennessee Democrats in 1870 and Virginia Democrats in 1876 followed Georgia's lead, but anti-Democratic "independent" movements, which were allied with the heavily black Republican parties in each state, made poll tax repeal one of their first orders of business during the 1870s. By 1908, all eleven ex-Confederate states had made the poll tax a suffrage prerequisite, and the African-American was always its chief intended victim (Kousser 1974, 63–72).

Laws and constitutional provisions also disfranchised people for having committed various crimes. While the effect of such provisions is unclear, since many were apparently adopted primarily as insurance should courts strike down more blatantly unconstitutional clauses or mandated fair implementation of those clauses, their intent is obvious. According to the *Petersburg Index and Appeal,* Virginia's petty crimes provision, along with the poll tax, effected "almost . . . a political revolution" in cutting down the black vote (*PIA,* Nov. 8, 1877, quoted in Maddex 1970, 198; Lewinson [1932] 1963, 66). Mississippi's infamous 1875 "pig law" defined the theft of property valued at ten dollars or more, or of any cattle or swine, whatever their value, as grand larceny, thus bringing those convicted of such minor offenses under the previous state constitutional suffrage ban (Woodward 1951, 212–13). During the debate in the 1895 South Carolina Constitutional Convention, a delegate moved to add to the list of disfranchising crimes housebreaking, receiving stolen goods, breach of trust with a fraudulent intention, fornication, sodomy, assault with intent to ravish, miscegenation, incest, and larceny, and to strike out theft and the middle-class crime of embezzlement. The conventioneers agreed, as they did to another member's proposal to include wife beating. Murderers, however, were allowed to vote (South Carolina Constitutional Convention 1895, 298, 487; Tindall 1952, 82). The framer of the crimes provision in the Alabama Constitutional Convention of 1901 thought that its wife-beating provision alone would disqualify two-thirds of the black males in the state (Gross 1969, 244; McMillan 1955, 275).[16] In 1985, the U.S. Supreme Court, relying on evidence of the general intent of the framers of the 1901 Alabama Constitution, invalidated the state's petty crimes provision (*Hunter v. Underwood* [1985]).

USUALLY after special registration laws were passed or extremely complicated ballot forms were mandated and almost always after blatantly fraudulent elections, five southern states held constitutional conventions that were primarily aimed at disfranchising African-Americans. Thereafter in these states, plus two others that adopted suffrage amendments in referenda, voters would have to be literate, own a certain assessed value of real estate, or be able to understand sections of laws or constitutions read to them to the satisfaction of white voting registrars. To win the support of white voters in referenda, there were "grandfather" or "fighting grandfather" clauses that temporarily exempted those who could vote before blacks were enfranchised or who were descendants of those voters or of former soldiers. The key to all of these laws was the administrative flexibility that allowed for discrimination by registrars, not only against African-Americans but also against Latinos in Texas as well as poor whites nearly everywhere and other white members of opposition parties in case they became a threat to Democratic supremacy. Embedded in fundamental laws, these disfranchising provisions were much more difficult to attack through national legislation than violence, fraud, or mere state statute law had been, and the Supreme Court refused initially even to rule squarely on their constitutionality. The disfranchisement of most blacks and potential white supporters of opposition political parties so greatly reduced the chances of beating Democratic nominees that those African-Americans or white oppositionists who might have still qualified to vote often did not bother. By denying the suffrage to most members of these groups, Democrats diluted its value for all individual members. Thus, suffrage restriction exposed the distinction between group and individual rights as unreal. If voting preferences are correlated with race, then the value of an individual's right depends on how her group is treated (Kousser 1974).

EVEN AFTER the institution of registration and secret ballot laws, literacy tests and poll taxes, some southern blacks continued to register and vote, and many others could have done so if one political faction or another had decided to instruct registrars to treat them fairly or if courts had made any effort to enforce the Fourteenth or Fifteenth Amendments (Kousser 1974, 61). It is a mistake to suggest, as some historians have, that such post-disfranchisement "reforms" as city commissions could not have had racially discriminatory purposes because no blacks could vote or influence elections anyway.[17] In close contests, especially in the often desultory municipal elections, geographically concentrated minority votes might hold the balance of power. In Mobile in 1908, for instance, nearly 200 blacks were registered, in an era when the normal turnout was about 3,000 in municipal campaigns. When the legislature temporarily shifted to a scheme in which the members of one part of the bicameral city governing body would be selected on a ward basis, there was a real fear that blacks might influence the selection of a member from one or two wards. The answer to this threat was, first, to ban blacks altogether from the local Democratic primary—some had previously been allowed to vote, and others then apparently desired to—and, second, to return to totally at-large elections, which the legislature ordered in 1911 (McCrary 1984).

Throughout the South, whites in the "Progressive Era" feared that their "solution" to the "Negro problem" might unravel. To counter the possibility that blacks might be able to take advantage of splits within the white community, Democrats sought to impede the growth of any potential opposition party by legalizing the direct primary, creating a simulacrum of two-party competition by requiring a runoff election in many states if no candidate received a majority of the primary vote, and banning defeated primary candidates from running in general elections. All whites, they hoped, would

come to consider the primary the real election, and organized party opposition would fade. The scheme succeeded. Increasingly completely excluded
from what became known at that time as the "white primary," blacks could
thereafter no longer cherish even the slightest hope that they could ally with
a disgruntled white faction or party and thereby regain some political influence, except in nonpartisan municipal elections in such cities as Jacksonville,
Macon, and Memphis (Kousser 1974, 72–82).

White southerners in the early part of the twentieth century insisted upon
absolutely lily-white government, strenuously protesting against appointments of even the best-qualified blacks to the least important federal offices in
the South, appointments that had been conventional since the Civil War and
that had rarely aroused much opposition (Kousser 1984d, 39–40). To suggest
that suffrage laws passed in this lily-white stage of southern politics could not
have had racist purposes is like saying that segregation laws passed during the
same period were "race-neutral," because fear and cultural norms kept most
blacks and whites separate on streetcars and trains, in opera houses and restaurants, and in other public venues before Jim Crow laws were passed. Until
this final stage of post-Reconstruction southern politics, African-American
voters had been a threat or a potential threat. During the last stage, they remained, for southern whites, an obsession.

BEFORE constitutional disfranchisement, then, the federal government could
have intervened to preserve at least some black political rights and perhaps
to reverse the downward spiral of black political power. Why was there no
move to attack the discriminatory southern electoral structures,[18] which were
widely known and condemned in the late nineteenth century,[19] and why were
congressional efforts to punish violence and prevent fraud much less successful than those made in the period since 1957? The most common answer
to this question, a marked liberalization in white racial attitudes, is at best
misleading and at worst flatly wrong. The real answers are congressional partisanship and judicial perfidy.

Tables 1.2 and 1.3 present a remarkably sharp and little-noticed contrast.
Civil rights was an entirely partisan issue in the nineteenth century, but in the
North at least, voting rights has enjoyed nearly unanimous support since 1957.
That partisanship helped consolidate Republican support for civil rights in
the postbellum period has often been noted, and Republicans have repeatedly
been derided for it (Gillette 1965). Many Republicans did not "really" support
black rights, the line goes, but only "expediently" endorsed bills under the
party whip. Whatever the validity of this argument, its converse surely holds
for the Democrats (Woodward 1960, 97). From 1866 to the turn of the century, not a *single* Democrat in the House or Senate *ever* voted in favor of a piece

TABLE 1.2. Partisan Lineups in House and
Senate Votes on Civil Rights Laws, 1866–1890

Year	Law	House Vote		Senate Vote	
		Republican	Democrat	Republican	Democrat
1866	Civil Rights Bill	111–5	0–33	33–2	0–10
1866	Fourteenth Amendment	138–0	0–36	33–4	0–7
1869	Fifteenth Amendment	144–3	0–41	39–2	0–11
1870	Enforcement Act	133–0	0–58	48–1	0–10
1871	Ku Klux Klan Act	93–0	0–74	36–2	0–11
1872	Enforcement Act	102–0	0–79	39–4	0–13
1875	Civil Rights Bill	147–14	0–79	38–7	0–19
1875	Enforcement Act	135–51	0–78	No vote	
1890	Lodge Bill	155–2	0–147	34–8	0–27

Sources: Civil Rights Bill (1866)—*Congressional Globe*, 39 Cong., 1 sess., 606–7; Fourteenth Amendment (1866), Fifteenth Amendment (1869), and Enforcement Act (1870)—McPherson [1871] 1972, 102, 399, 550; Ku Klux Klan Act (1871) and Enforcement Act (1870)—McPherson 1872, 85, 91; Civil Rights Bill (1875) and Enforcement Act (1875)—McPherson 1876, 3, 8, 18; Lodge Bill (1890)—for House vote, McPherson [1890] 1974, 218–19, 1368; for Senate vote to consider, *Congressional Record*, 51 Cong., 2 sess., 1740.

of civil rights legislation! Northern Democrats repeatedly defended southern violence and fraud or denied their obvious existence, and they staunchly supported the endless filibusters—for instance, a month-long one in the Senate in 1890—against civil rights laws (Grossman 1976, 48–49, 143–55).[20] This was true in spite of the fact that a considerable number of Democrats defected from their party's racist tradition from time to time on local issues in the North. As governor of New York, Democrat Grover Cleveland signed a school integration measure that applied to Manhattan in 1883; and Democratic governor George Hoadly of Ohio convinced some Democrats to vote for school integration bills in that state's legislature in 1884. Democrats all over the North either supported or acquiesced in the passage of state laws mandating integrated public accommodations after the Supreme Court's abrogation of the 1875 national civil rights law in 1883 (Grossman 1976, 66–67, 82–106). It was neither constituency pressure nor personal racist belief that kept Democrats from backing voting rights bills in the nineteenth century, for at home some were willing to defect from the party's traditional racism.

Since 1957, support for voting rights has been overwhelming and constant from northern Democrats in both houses of Congress, and from northern Republicans in the Senate.[21] There was a substantial anti-VRA shift among House Republicans during the Nixon administration, but that "southern strategy" quickly faded. The southern pattern is one of a dramatic shift toward civil

TABLE 1.3. Partisan Lineups in House
and Senate Votes on Civil Rights Laws, 1957–1982

Year	Southern States[a]		Nonsouthern States	
	Democrat	Republican	Democrat	Republican
House Votes				
1957	0–99	1–3	118–8	167–16
1960	5–82	2–3	174–12	130–12
1964	8–83	0–11	145–8	136–24
1965	22–59	1–15	199–2	111–9
1970	27–49	3–21	145–7	97–55
1975	49–23	10–17	198–4	84–26
1981–82	62–6	23–13	167–1	137–4
Senate Votes				
1957	5–17	0	26–1	43–0
1960	4–18	0	38–0	29–0
1964	1–20	0–1	45–1	27–5
1965	3–17	0–2	44–0	30–0
1970	3–9	1–1	28–2	32–0
1975	9–5	2–5	40–1	26–1
1981–82	11–0	6–4	31–1	37–3

Source: Congressional Quarterly Almanac, relevant years.
Note: Votes in 1957, 1960, and 1964 were on Civil Rights Acts; those in 1965, 1970, 1975, and 1981–82 on Voting Rights Act and renewals.
[a]Eleven former Confederate states: Alabama, Arkansas, Florida, Georgia, Louisiana, Mississippi, North Carolina, South Carolina, Tennessee, Texas, Virginia.

rights, most strikingly among House Democrats, who opposed the extremely weak 1957 law unanimously but backed the much more stringent 1982 act by a 10:1 ratio. At the height of the Reagan administration's power, six out of ten southern Republicans supported the VRA on final passage.

Why was there such unanimity within and such division between the parties on this issue in the nineteenth century, and why did the two centuries' patterns contrast so starkly? Evidence in the graphs below will show that reapportionments of the post–Civil War era created many more marginal seats than did those of the post–World War II era, that the composition of Congress in the nineteenth century often shifted violently, and that few northern members in that era had secure seats. Instead, and in stark contrast to the safe and relatively autonomous congresspersons of the period from 1954 to 1994, nineteenth-century congressmen were almost wholly dependent on their parties for their brief tenures.[22] At the presidential level, electoral mar-

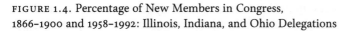

FIGURE 1.4. Percentage of New Members in Congress,
1866–1900 and 1958–1992: Illinois, Indiana, and Ohio Delegations

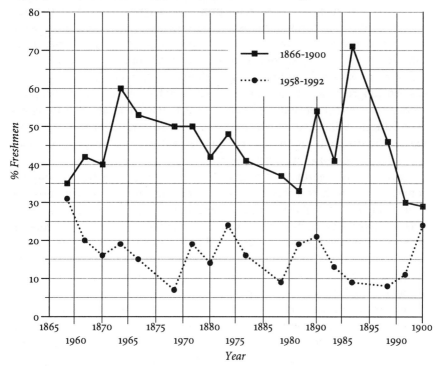

Sources: Author's calculations based on Congressional Quarterly 1975; Scammon and McGillivray, 1976–1991.

gins in the late nineteenth century were sufficiently narrow as to encourage each party to strain for every vote and to compete in every region. If blacks voted freely, Republicans would have been able to carry at least some southern states and, almost certainly, the presidency. It was not differences in racial attitudes between themselves and the Republicans alone, or perhaps even primarily, that drove Democrats to abandon democratic ideals in the nineteenth century and induced Republican allegiance to those ideals; it was the drive for national political power. In the post–World War II period, on the other hand, the South was seldom a swing region in presidential elections, and incumbents were safe enough to vote for democracy.

Figure 1.4, which is based on electoral history in Illinois, Indiana, and Ohio, the homes of four late-nineteenth-century presidents, suggests the volatility of membership in Congress then as compared to now.[23] On average, 45 percent of the congressmen from those three states in the 40th through 57th Congresses had not served in the previous Congress; in the 86th through 103rd, the average of new congresspeople was only 16 percent. In only the 1898 and 1900 elections was the turnover as small as it was in the 1958 election, which had the highest replacement rate in the contemporary period.

Figure 1.5 shows how little congressional experience the average midwestern congressman of the nineteenth century had, in contrast to his post-1956 counterpart. Eighty-five percent of those who held seats in Congress from Illinois, Indiana, and Ohio from 1865 to 1902 served for three or fewer terms, whereas from 1957 to 1993 only 45 percent were as inexperienced (see Figure 1.5a). Viewed another way, the figures show that 65 percent of the time in the nineteenth century, but only 15 percent in the twentieth, the congressional seats from these states were filled by people who sat for three terms or less (see Figure 1.5b). The prospect of repeated interaction in the future gave careerist twentieth-century members of Congress an incentive to develop patterns of cooperation across party and regional boundaries. Congressmen in the nineteenth century, who could not expect to sit long enough to benefit from a "tit-for-tat" strategy, had less reason to compromise and less stake in the incremental development of policy (Axelrod 1984).

The nineteenth-century congressman was more evanescent because elections in each district were closer. Figure 1.6a shows that in the same three midwestern states from 1864 to 1900 there were landslide margins (more than 55 percent for one major party candidate) in an average of only two-fifths of the districts, while from 1956 to 1992 more than four-fifths of the elections were landslides.[24] Even more impressive is the fact that in the earlier period nearly 30 percent of the contests were decided by margins of 52–48 percent or less, compared to less than 8 percent of the elections since 1956 (see Figure 1.6b).

With such small margins, the shift of relatively few votes could produce a dramatic alteration in congressional seats won, as Figure 1.7 shows. From 1864 to 1900, the average Republican percentage of the two-party congressional vote in the same three midwestern states was 52 percent, with a standard deviation of 2.5 percent.[25] In the elections from 1956 to 1992, the average was 50.1 percent, but with a 3.3 percent standard deviation, the votes cast by the electorate were actually more erratic than in the late nineteenth century. However, because the margins for each congressional seat were so much thinner in the nineteenth century than in the twentieth century, the number of seats held by each party fluctuated much more widely in the earlier period, as demonstrated by the contrast between the wildly oscillating line relating to the percentage of seats won in Figure 1.7a and the much more stable one

FIGURE 1.5. Members' Length of Service in Congress,
1865–1903 and 1957–1993: Illinois, Indiana, and Ohio Delegations

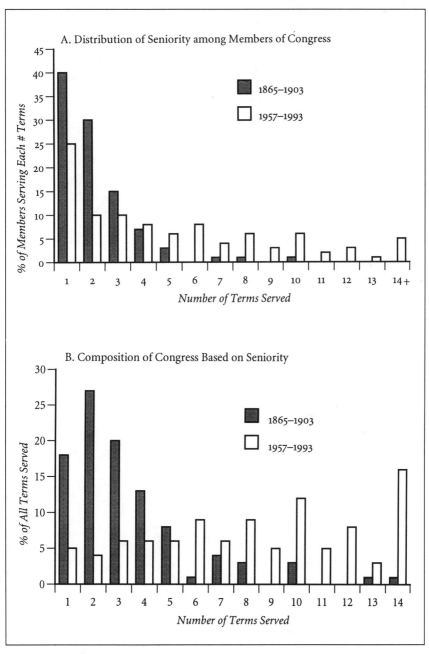

A. Distribution of Seniority among Members of Congress

B. Composition of Congress Based on Seniority

Sources: Same as Figure 1.4.

FIGURE 1.6. Margins of Victory in Congressional Elections,
1864–1900 and 1956–1992: Illinois, Indiana, and Ohio

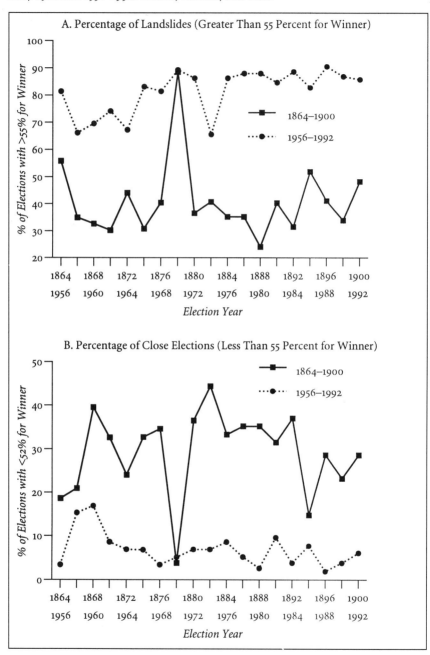

Sources: Same as Figure 1.4.

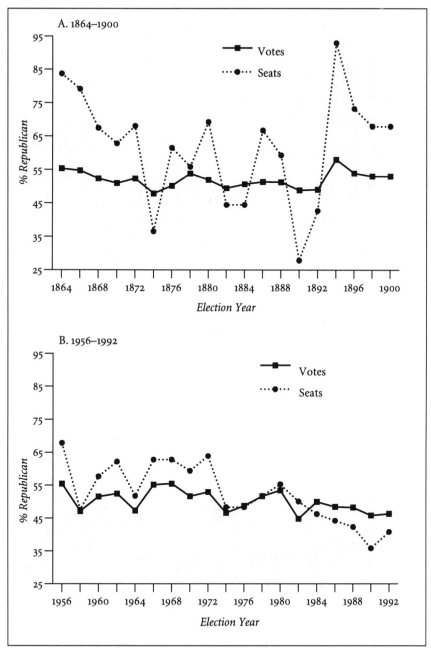

FIGURE 1.7. Volatility in Congressional Elections, 1864–1900 and 1956–1992:
Republican Votes vs. Republican Seats Won in Illinois, Indiana, and Ohio

Sources: Same as Figure 1.4.

FIGURE 1.8. Party Balance in Congress in Election Years, 1864–1900 and 1956–1992

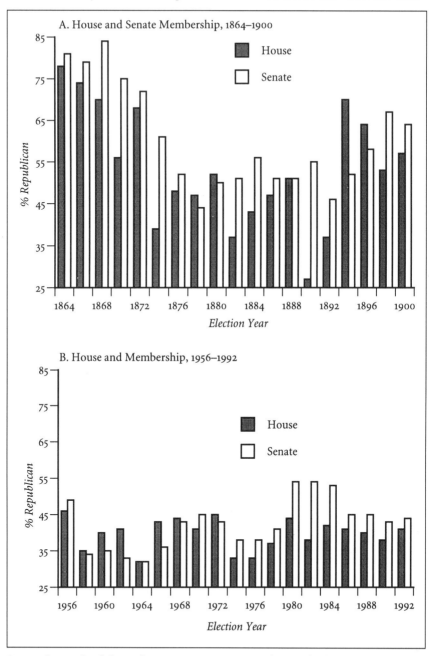

Sources: Congressional Quarterly 1981, 1148–49; *Congressional Quarterly Almanac* 1983–94.

in Figure 1.7b. It was not the way people voted but the way district lines were drawn that accounted for the enormous turnover of congressional seats in the late nineteenth century. Apportionments in the South kept African-Americans from exercising power in proportion to their votes; those in the North kept the federal government from sustaining a policy of protecting southern blacks against discrimination.[26] Redistricting, not racial attitudes, primarily determined congressional policies on race in both the late nineteenth and the late twentieth centuries.

Figure 1.8 reveals the extent of partisan instability in the whole Congress during the two periods. The Midwest was a microcosm, not a deviant case. In the first period, no party majority, no matter how large, was safe for long. The standard deviation of the Republican percentage of House members for the nineteen sessions from 1865 through 1902 was more than four times as high as that for the nineteen sessions from 1957 through 1993; for the Senate, that statistic was nearly twice as high in the first as in the second period. Politicians took note of such facts. James G. Blaine, for instance, remarked in his memoirs that new members composed majorities of nine of the ten sessions of the House from 1861 to 1881 (Blaine 1886, 2:675). When they arrived in Washington in the nineteenth century, congressmen had little identity apart from their political parties, and few remained long enough to develop one. They therefore naturally adopted their party's dominant view. As the Senate leader of the fight for the Fair Elections Bill of 1890 phrased it, a free ballot was the "very definition of Republicanism" (Hoar 1891). The only way to alter the party identity was to experience a series of whipsawing elections, such as those from 1890 through 1894, which first leveled Republican incumbents and then did the same thing to the Democrats, resulting in the retirement of large numbers of core members of each party.

That it was not the fickleness of the nineteenth-century electorate that led to the relatively extreme fluctuations in congressional representation is substantiated by Figure 1.9, which shows that in presidential elections it is the *recent* period that has been unstable, while the earlier one was comparatively immobile. This holds for the nation as a whole, and not just for the Midwest. Nationally, in both the percentage of the popular vote and that of the electoral vote, the standard deviation in the presidential contests from 1956 through 1988 was more than twice that in the nine elections from 1868 through 1900. Presidential elections in the late nineteenth century were so close and candidates before "civil service reform" were so dependent on party activists and so independent of nonpartisan special interest groups, compared to their counterparts today, that they had to enliven the faithful with appeals to traditional issues—the Civil War and its associated racial issues as well as the tariff and monetary policy. Furthermore, since Republicans realis-

FIGURE 1.9. Volatility in Presidential Elections, 1868–1900 and 1956–1988: All States

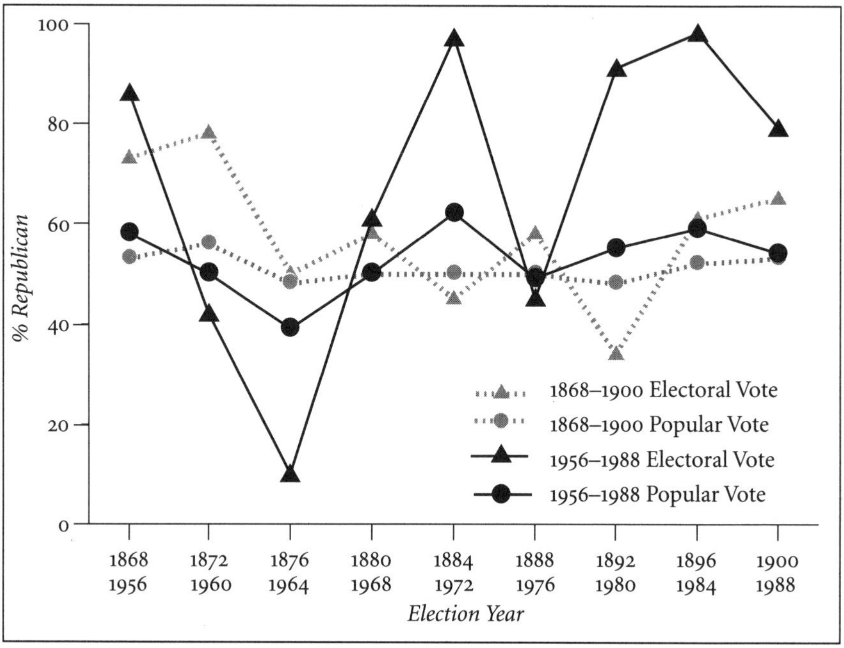

Sources: Congressional Quarterly 1976; Scammon and McGillivray 1976–88.

tically believed that with a fair count, they could carry some southern states during this period, and since Democrats needed every southern electoral vote to win the presidency, control of the southern ballot box was crucial to both parties. By contrast, in recent years only in 1960, 1976, and 1980 have the two parties closely contested the majority of southern electoral votes. Usually the Republicans have been able to count on them, whether blacks voted overwhelmingly for the Democrats or not. Republican presidents therefore have had little incentive to oppose even a strengthened VRA, while Democrats, heavily dependent on their black constituents if they were to have a chance of carrying a national election, have had no choice but to support civil rights enthusiastically.

The consequences of these contrasting trends for the democratization of American politics through the extension and protection of minority voting rights are deeply ironic. In the nineteenth century, the parties were too competitive, too "responsible," too dependably committed to a program, and the voters were too civically conscious to let party elites stray from orthodoxy. Black votes counted for too much nationally. In the post–World War II era, however, it is just those political trends that are so often decried by pundits—presidential landslides, the durability of congressional incumbents, the decline of party loyalty among voters and elites, and the inattention of the public in the last generation—that explain why voting rights for blacks and browns became a consensus issue. The First Reconstruction died from too much democracy, while the Second thrived precisely because, until very recently, competition for congressional seats and for southern electoral votes has been comparatively desultory. It is not only the shift in the Republican center of gravity to the South but also the heightened turnover and competitiveness of congressional seats throughout the country that has put the gains of the Second Reconstruction at risk.

Even if political conditions had favored congressional action on civil rights after 1874, the Supreme Court might have invalidated or undermined any resulting laws. The Supreme Court may not be as effective in bringing about positive social change as liberals thought in the 1960s, but it was demonstrably potent in protecting white supremacy in the late nineteenth century, and it has been just as much a leader in that task in the late twentieth as it was a century earlier. Two opinions of 1876, *U.S. v. Reese* and *U.S. v. Cruikshank,* ruled unconstitutional or largely unenforceable those sections of the 1870–72 Enforcement Acts that attempted to protect all citizens against violence or fraud, state-sponsored or private, in connection with state or local elections. Kentucky officials had refused to accept the ballots of citizens because they were black, while Louisiana had failed both to protect the victims of the Colfax "riot" and to indict the perpetrators of that crime, the largest racial mass murder in American history. Yet, according to Chief Justice Morrison Waite, convictions for these actions in federal courts must be overturned. In each case, the key to the ruling was Waite's insistence that laws and indictments focus on racial intent.

The Enforcement Act at issue in *Reese* had four relevant sections, the first two of which mentioned race, while the last two did not but referred, for instance, to the "wrongful act or omission as aforesaid"—that is, the act by which blacks, on account of their race, were denied the right to become legally qualified to vote.[27] Waite ruled that Sections 3 and 4 were unconstitutional because they did not directly mention race and the only national power to protect citizens' right to vote in state and local elections derived from the Fifteenth Amendment. Likewise, in *Cruikshank,* after a preliminary disquisition on federalism that echoed Democratic rhetoric during the "Force Bill" debates, Waite dismissed the case, not on the ground that the law was unconstitutional, but because the indictment did not aver that the blacks were murdered or denied the right to vote *because* they were black.

The decisions were deeply disturbing for five reasons. First, the Lexington blacks were admittedly denied the right to vote on account of their race; all the victims at Colfax were black; the laws perfectly fit the situations in each instance; indictments were filed, and southern juries convicted the malefactors; yet the Republican Supreme Court let them off. The Reconstruction attempt to use the normal instrumentalities of government to protect the new citizens had failed at the top. Second, the Fourteenth Amendment, which sought, without explicitly mentioning race at all, to protect all citizens against discrimination and deprivation of liberty, was significantly weakened.[28] Waite might have severed Sections 3 and 4 from Sections 1 and 2 and still sustained them as protections of citizens' rights to enjoy the suffrage impartially under the equal protection or privileges or immunities clauses of the Fourteenth Amendment. He might then have ruled that the rights of peaceable assembly and life were guaranteed by the nation under the Fourteenth Amendment and that they were rights that applied to all citizens, rather than depending on race.[29] Third, by insisting on proof of a racist intent, perhaps even of racial hostility, Waite was making it much more difficult to obtain convictions. If over 100 dead black bodies did not prove racial animosity, what would? Fourth, these two decisions severely constrained potential congressional action (Warren 1922, 3:324-30; Benedict 1978, 39-79; Kaczorowski 1985, 199-229; Braeman 1988, 65-66; Simpson 1992).[30] Fifth, the decisions not only inhibited federal action against private interference with the right to vote in local and state elections, but they also encouraged states to pass laws diluting or denying minority political power, which, as we have seen, they avidly did.

Like *Dred Scott* before it and many "conservative" decisions of the Supreme Court more recently, *Cruikshank* was presented as a triumph of liberty. Thus, Robert H. Marr, a leader of a smaller but similar massacre of Republicans in New Orleans and a future judge of the Louisiana Supreme Court, declared that if Cruikshank's conviction for depriving two African-Americans of their civil rights by murdering them were upheld, "The shackles will have fallen in vain from 4 millions of blacks, who were born slaves, if fetters more galling are to be riveted on so many more millions of white people, who were born free." The *New York Times* asserted that the Supreme Court's decision in favor of Cruikshank would "enhance the value of the Supreme Court as a means of securing the rights of citizens" (quoted in Simpson 1992, 46).

But Supreme Court decisions rarely travel in an entirely unambiguous direction for long. In *Ex parte Siebold* (1880), *Ex parte Clarke* (1880), and *Ex parte Yarbrough* (1884), the high court interpreted Congress's plenary power under Article I, Section 4 to regulate the "times, places and manner of holding elections" to Congress broadly enough to allow it to guarantee peaceable assembly and restrict fraud and violence. These decisions later encouraged the sponsors of the 1890 Fair Elections Bill. Moreover, in the 1880 jury exclusion case of *Strauder v. West Virginia* and the 1886 Chinese laundry case of *Yick Wo v. Hopkins,* the Supreme Court struck down racially discriminatory laws not related to voting in such expansive language as to suggest that the justices had not entirely forgotten the original purposes of the Reconstruction Amendments, after all. Despite the Court's narrow construction of the powers of the federal government in *The Civil Rights Cases* (1883), the other, more moderate decisions allowed some scope for national action to protect minority rights if Republicans took firm control of the government again.

Whatever potential the Waite Court left, the Fuller Court destroyed.[31] In *Williams v. Mississippi* in 1898, the Court denied disfranchised blacks a remedy by very strictly construing its earlier decision in *Yick Wo.* Counsel for the Chinese laundrymen had shown that a San Francisco ordinance was adopted with both the intent and effect of discriminating against Chinese. While Henry Williams's lawyer quoted extensively from the Mississippi disfranchising convention of 1890 to demonstrate its racist intent, he apparently took the exclusion of blacks from the Greenville voter rolls, and therefore jury rolls, to be proof enough of the state constitution's discriminatory impact. The Court's crabbed reading of *Yick Wo* cost Williams, convicted of murder by an all-white jury, his life. Yet when a lawyer representing disfranchised Alabama blacks presented extensive evidence of discriminatory effect, as well as intent, the Court, in a decision written by the "liberal" Oliver Wendell Holmes, declared that the Court could do nothing, because suffrage was a "political question." [32]

How DID justices who would make such decisions get appointed to the Supreme Court? Some were Democrats—Stephen J. Field and Nathan Clifford at the time of *Reese* and *Cruikshank*; Melville Westin Fuller, Edward Douglass White, and Rufus W. Peckham at the time of *Williams* and *Giles.* As in Congress, no Democratic member of the U.S. Supreme Court up to 1915 ever voted for black civil rights. But all the other justices in the four most crucial voting rights cases were, nominally at least, Republicans. Partisanship as a motive or as an index of racial attitudes was significant, but it does not by itself explain the decisions. Nor will a second potential reason for the court's undercutting of black voting rights—changes in public attitudes—bear careful scrutiny. As pointed out above, in Congress, few Republicans switched on the issue until after 1890. Almost all nonsouthern state legislatures passed public accommodations integration bills between 1866 and 1890, and at least fourteen mandated school integration. White racial opinion made its major shift only *after* 1890, after the Supreme Court had allowed the white Democratic South to begin to undermine the foundations of black political power.

A third possible explanation is luck or other ambitions. Chief Justice Salmon P. Chase, a brilliant lawyer and stalwart racial egalitarian, died at the age of 65, after only eight and a half years on the bench, the second shortest chief justiceship between 1801 and the present (Epstein, Segal, Spaeth, and Walker 1994, 301). His two immediate predecessors, John Marshall and Roger B. Taney, had served for three decades each, dying in office at the ages of 80 and 88, respectively. Had Chase's tenure been as long as Marshall's, he would have retired in 1899, and it is impossible to imagine him acceding to *Reese, Williams,* or *Plessy v. Ferguson* (1896).[33] Since even on a Court filled with strong-willed judges, Chase was able to prevail on the issues he cared most about, those involving Reconstruction, he probably would have commanded much more than his own vote on civil rights issues had he lived longer. (On Chase, see Friedman 1969; Blue 1987, 40, 49, 53–54, 196, 248–49, 258–59, 300–302, 306–7, 321; Niven 1995, 376, 380–83, 401, 416, 446–47, 450.) Two other strong personalities and staunch advocates of civil rights, Roscoe Conkling and George F. Edmunds, were each twice offered Supreme Court appointments, which they refused out of ambitions for higher office and higher salaries.[34] Waite, whose civil rights views were as unknown before his appointment as he himself was, was Grant's *seventh* choice for chief justice (Abraham 1974, 122). In addition, the civil rights stances of some justices, such as Joseph P. Bradley, changed while they were on the Court, while others, such as William Strong, sometimes seemed loyal advocates of civil rights and sometimes silently concurred in reactionary opinions (Whiteside 1981; Kutler 1969; Strong 1985). Furthermore, many justices, such as David J. Brewer, were chosen by presidents primarily for their views on economic issues or for their specialized knowledge, as was the case with admiralty law expert Henry B. Brown, and they turned out to be relatively conservative on civil rights (Abraham 1974, 136–39; Paul 1969; Goldfarb 1969).[35]

There were, then, a variety of reasons for the shift by the late-nineteenth-century Supreme Court. The relatively small numbers of men involved, the anomalies of the judicial nomination process during the period, with its emphasis on seats for people from particular states, the very low salaries, which kept some of the best candidates off the bench, and the dearth of organized interest groups to vet nominees and to push for and against specific candidates, compared to the experience of more recent times, made members of the nineteenth-century Court less predictable and less easily influenced than elective officeholders were. That popularly elected Republicans stayed loyal to civil rights long after the Supreme Court deserted the cause is evidence of the liberalism, not the conservatism, of northern whites' racial opinions in the nineteenth century.

If, as argued earlier, one line on the tombstone of Reconstruction should read "died of democracy," the next should have chiseled on it "and of an undemocratic institution's failure to protect democracy."[36] The contrast between the actions of the Waite and Fuller Courts and those of the Stone, Warren, and Burger Courts could hardly be stronger. Unfortunately, the Rehnquist Court seems bent on reversing the decisions of its conservative, as well as its liberal, predecessors.

THE SECOND Reconstruction not only reversed the outcome of the first, but protections for minority voting rights were increased by the Supreme Court for nearly fifty years and by Congress for nearly forty. To be sure, there were fits and starts in the Supreme Court in nearly every decade. But most of the justices did agree that the purposes of the Fourteenth and Fifteenth Amendments and the Voting Rights Act were so closely related that analyses under one provision could not and should not be starkly distinguished from those under another, and that racial discrimination in the political process was so harmful to the nation that congressional power to protect voting rights ought to be construed liberally. The Court's willingness to protect the rights of minority citizens or to let Congress do so, along with the stable majority of experienced and sympathetic members of Congress from 1954 to 1994, allowed judges, Congress, bureaucrats, and interest groups to improve federal protections gradually and pragmatically. Radical ideologues, who now threaten large reductions in the representation and influence of minority groups in American national, state, and local governments, have willfully distorted or disregarded the history of these years, as well as of the nineteenth century.

THE SUPREME COURT began the protection of African-American voting rights in 1944 in a case that illustrated the connection between individual and structural discrimination against minorities in politics and the Court's willingness to replace an empty formalism with a practical concern for political reality. The white Democratic primary did not disfranchise anyone. Any black could still vote in the general election. But in *Smith v. Allwright* (1944), the Court recognized that in the dominant-party South, the Democratic nomination was tantamount to election, and that an electoral rule that prohibited blacks from a crucial part of the electoral process abrogated the Fifteenth Amendment.[37]

In the second landmark minority voting rights case of the liberal era, *Gomillion v. Lightfoot* (1960), the Court in effect ran the film of the decisions from *Reese* to *Giles* backwards.[38] Despite craven intransigence and crafty ruses by white officials in the nation's most heavily black county, enough African-

Americans managed to register to vote to threaten white control of the town of Tuskegee. Macon County representative Sam Englehardt therefore pushed through the Alabama legislature a bill redefining the boundaries of Tuskegee to make it an almost wholly white town (Norrell 1985, 79–110). Although no individual had her right to vote taken away—she could still vote in county, state, and federal elections—the blatant racial gerrymander preserved white power in the most important local decisions, those made by the city government.

Justice Felix Frankfurter's opinion in *Gomillion* smashed the "political question" or "justiciability" roadblock. Even Frankfurter, who had held back consideration of rotten borough cases in *Colegrove v. Green* (1946), was shocked by the "strangely irregular 28-sided-figure" drawn to "fence out" blacks from Tuskegee. The decision also reunited the Fourteenth and Fifteenth Amendments, sundered in *Reese* and *Cruikshank*, ruling that a lack of equal protection through a racially discriminatory electoral structure was also a denial of the right to vote guaranteed by the Fifteenth Amendment, with different justices resting its holding on the grounds of each amendment. Finally, the case implicitly ruled that a racially discriminatory intent could be proven solely on the basis of its effect. Robert Carter of the NAACP began his oral argument before the Supreme Court by saying: "Your Honors, our position is simple. This is purely a case of racial discrimination. The *purpose* of this legislation—Alabama Act 140—was discriminatory." When Justice William O. Douglas asked Carter whether purpose was "the central aspect of your case," Carter replied, "Purpose and effect—the effect reveals the purpose" (quoted in Taper 1962, 86, 88–89, italics added). Although the NAACP introduced no direct evidence of intent, no "smoking gun" statements, for instance, the Supreme Court ruled in its favor, declaring that "Acts generally lawful may become unlawful when done to accomplish an unlawful *end*" (*Gomillion*, 130, quoting *U.S. v. Reading Co.* [1913], italics added). The nineteenth-century decisions were tacitly buried.

The *Gomillion* case had been brought by the U.S. Department of Justice under the 1957 Civil Rights Act, an extremely mild measure whose chief significance was that it proved that the Senate filibuster used against the Lodge Fair Elections Bill in 1890 and every other civil rights bill since then could be broken. Three years later, the 1960 Civil Rights Act added a little more authority for the Justice Department to bring suits and for the U.S. Commission on Civil Rights to study discrimination. Hearings and reports by the Commission, which were referred to often in Congress and public debates, as well as the experiences of civil rights workers during frustrating and often brutally suppressed campaigns to register black voters in the Deep South, taught four major lessons for public policy: first, discriminatory administration, especially of registration and literacy tests, was the chief barrier to qualifying more African-American voters; second, bringing individual suits against registration officials before southern federal judges was a painfully slow and ineffective means of adding to the suffrage rolls; third, southern jurisdictions were so adept at adding ingenious subterfuges to replace more obvious means of discrimination that a flexible administrative procedure was needed to stop discriminators from circumventing the effort to give black citizens equal political rights; and fourth, decisive action by the federal government was necessary to convince southern officials to comply with the Fifteenth Amendment and to persuade potential African-American voters that it was safe to take part in politics (U.S. Commission on Civil Rights 1959b, 1961, 1963, 1965a, 1965b; Lawson 1976, 227–35, 289–99). The result, made possible by the Democratic landslide in the 1964 elections and catalyzed by the 1965 Selma March, was the Voting Rights Act.

Section 2 of the Act, which was permanent and applied nationally, prohibited any "voting qualification or prerequisite to voting, or standard, practice, or procedure" that denied or abridged the right to vote on the basis of race or color. Section 4, which was initially imposed for only five years, suspended any "test or device" imposed as a voting prerequisite in jurisdictions, all in the Deep South, that had especially low political participation.[39] Section 5, by implication set to expire in 1970, required that every state or local government subject to Section 4 submit all changes in election laws to the Department of Justice before putting them into effect. If a law was disallowed, the jurisdiction could sue in the federal court in the District of Columbia, not in the often much more racist southern federal courts, to overturn the Justice Department ruling. Section 6 authorized the appointment of federal voting registrars if local registrars continued to discriminate (U.S. Commission on Civil Rights 1968, 202–11).

Within two years after the passage of the VRA, African-American registration in the Deep South surged. Most dramatic were the increases from 19 to 52 percent in Alabama and from 7 to 60 percent in Mississippi. But, as the Civil Rights Commission brought to the attention of Congress and the public, those and other states responded by erecting structural barriers to black power—gerrymandering, changing from single-member-district to at-large elections, prohibiting "single-shot" voting in multimember district contests, and making elective offices appointive (U.S. Commission on Civil Rights 1968, 11–39; Parker 1990, 15–77).[40] Contending that none of these laws denied anyone the right to vote, and that the VRA was not concerned with such structural changes, the covered southern jurisdictions generally did not submit these statutes to the Justice Department for preclearance. Reasoning that it was exactly such circumventions that Section 5 was intended to preclude, black plaintiffs sued in the third crucial minority vote dilution case, *Allen v. Board of Elections* (1969).

In its decision in *Allen*, the Supreme Court continued in the *Gomillion* tradition. Referring extensively to the congressional hearings and debates on the VRA, Chief Justice Earl Warren held that Section 5 applied to election laws in Virginia and Mississippi even if those laws had no direct connection with voter registration or casting a ballot.[41] To have ruled otherwise would have opened a huge loophole for every state. A year later, Congress extended Section 5 for another five years, implicitly endorsing the *Allen* decision, which, along with the Civil Rights Commission study that covered the same grounds, was repeatedly mentioned in the extensive hearings in both houses (U.S. House of Representatives 1969, 3–4, 7, 17, 150; U.S. Senate 1970, 9, 47–48, 52, 96–97, 132, 164, 168–69, 195–96, 252, 427, 516–18). Although the Nixon Administration proposed to repeal Section 5's preclearance requirement and return to litigation as the sole federal remedy for discriminatory voting practices, no one seriously suggested rejecting *Allen*'s interpretation of the intent of the statute, and Congress finally rebuffed the Nixon repeal effort (Lawson 1985, 121–57; Graham 1990, 346–65).

Where Sections 4 and 5 did not apply, minority plaintiffs often relied on the Fourteenth and Fifteenth Amendments, but as the fourth major vote dilution case, *White v. Regester* (1973), shows, legal standards under the Constitution and the VRA intermingled. Because Texas set up multimember legislative districts in Dallas and San Antonio and powerful "slating groups" (unofficial organizations that circulated lists of candidates whom they endorsed) rarely included black or Latino candidates on their lists, few or no minority candidates could hope to be elected from those cities. In a unanimous decision, Justice Byron White ruled that at-large elections violated the equal protection clause of the Fourteenth Amendment when an analysis of "the totality of the circumstances" indicated that jurisdictions that used the device denied minorities an "equal opportunity to participate in the political processes and to elect legislators of their choice." The emphasis on an equal chance to *elect* candidates, and not just to vote, practically wrote *Allen* into the Constitution, and the "totality of the circumstances" test was applied in cases brought under the VRA and served as the basis for the congressional amendments to the VRA in 1981–82.

In 1975 Congress again extended Sections 4 and 5 for another five-year period and, following the recommendations of the Civil Rights Commission and the federal courts' findings in *White v. Regester*, took notice of discrimination against Latinos and explicitly added language minorities to the VRA's coverage. Members of Congress and witnesses at the congressional hearings specifically approved *Allen* (U.S. Senate 1975a, 124; 1975b, 15–19, 24–35; U.S.

House of Representatives 1975a, 629-34, 640-46; 1975b, 8-11; U.S. Commission on Civil Rights 1975, 356). During the mid-1970s, too, the Supreme Court read an intent requirement into the Fourteenth Amendment (*Washington v. Davis* 1976), and it refused to overturn electoral district lines drawn in a race-conscious manner when the lines were adopted to allow ethnic groups that were underrepresented in the political system a chance to elect some candidates of their choice (*United Jewish Organizations v. Carey* 1977). But in *Beer v. U.S.* (1976), the Court construed Section 5's impact on electoral structures narrowly by holding that it only prevented "retrogression." If the New Orleans City Council before redistricting had one black-majority district, then the Justice Department, the Court said, could not reject a plan containing only one such district, even if more generous plans could have been drawn and even if the scheme, in the presence of racial bloc voting, gave whites more than their proportional share of seats. *Beer* encouraged plaintiffs to file suits under Section 2 and under the Fourteenth and Fifteenth Amendments, rather than relying on Justice Department action under Section 5, a trend that might have occurred in any event, because Section 5 applied only to electoral changes enacted from 1965 on.

The first Supreme Court case to apply the new intent emphasis to voting arose in one of the early Section 2 cases. No blacks had been elected to the city commission or school board of Mobile, Alabama, which were chosen by at-large elections, since those forms of election had been mandated, long before the passage of the VRA. African-American plaintiffs convinced a federal district judge that the totality of the circumstances established that the system was discriminatory. But in a confusing split opinion, the Supreme Court reversed the lower court (*City of Mobile v. Bolden* 1980). Three other justices endorsed Justice Potter Stewart's opinion that the Fifteenth Amendment and the VRA applied only to interference with an individual's right to vote and not to structural discrimination, that the Fourteenth and Fifteenth Amendments and Section 2 of the VRA required proof of purpose, and that, piece by piece, the objective evidence presented by the Mobile plaintiffs did not satisfy that standard.

Bolden's troubled life, however, was cut short in less than twenty-seven months. After a surprisingly successful struggle with the Reagan administration, Congress overwhelmingly passed a revised VRA with Section 2 amended specifically to overturn *Bolden* by making it clear that it applied to any law that had the *effect* of discriminating, whether or not judges would accept the contention that the law was passed with a discriminatory *intent*. Congress also extended Sections 4 and 5 for twenty-five more years (U.S. Senate 1982b, 8-43). Moreover, just two days after President Reagan signed the revised law, the Supreme Court handed down *Rogers v. Lodge*, which gingerly sidestepped

Bolden and echoed Congress's actions. In his opinion for a 6–3 majority, Justice White, who had dissented in *Bolden,* merged the effect-based standards of *White v. Regester* with the intent notions of a series of Fourteenth Amendment cases. Thereafter, to prove intent, plaintiffs could use many of the same sorts of evidence that would previously have been considered indicative of effect. Four years later in *Thornburg v. Gingles,* Justice William Brennan focused judicial attention on two of the congressional list of seven circumstances that were particularly important factors for determining a violation of the VRA — a list derived from the constitutional case of *White v. Regester* (U.S. Senate 1982b, 28–29). The crucial inquiries, later considered preconditions for Section 2 cases, became whether voting was racially polarized and whether minority candidates generally lost in contests for those offices. Unfortunately for supporters of minority voting rights in subsequent cases, Brennan added a third factor, not mentioned in *Regester* or the Senate report but suggested as a criterion in at-large cases during 1981 House testimony — whether the minority group was sufficiently large and geographically compact enough to form a majority of a district in the governmental body at issue (U.S. House 1981, 2038). Brennan also rejected an attempt to make it much more difficult to prove that voting was racially polarized. Plaintiffs did not have to demonstrate that racism was the sole or most important *cause* of differences in voting patterns, but only that the electorate *did,* as a matter of fact, split along racial lines. Even though four justices disagreed with parts of the Court's reasoning, all nine agreed that Section 2 did not merely bar discrimination against individuals' exercise of the franchise but also prohibited vote dilution (*Thornburg v. Gingles* 1986, 2786).

THE PRECEDING interpretation of post-1944 voting rights, conventional among most experts in the field, has not gone unchallenged. Like any interpretation of a set of historical events, it cannot be accepted without considering alternative explanations and criticisms. The two principal critics of this line of Supreme Court decisions and congressional actions are Abigail Thernstrom and Justice Clarence Thomas. Pairing the two is hardly coincidental. Thomas's first reference in *Holder v. Hall,* the case in which he made his most extended remarks on the subject, is to Thernstrom's 1987 book *Whose Votes Count?,* and Thernstrom in turn has praised Thomas's opinion in that case as "eloquent . . . a refreshing and candid analysis of the judicial failures in this area" (*Holder v. Hall* [1994], 2592; Thernstrom 1994, 35 n. 4). What is the Thernstrom/Thomas argument and how well does it hold up, particularly in light of the events of the First and Second Reconstructions?

"The aim of the Voting Rights Act — the *single* aim," Thernstrom asserted in 1987, "was black enfranchisement in the South." Four years later, in *Allen,* she argues, the U.S. Supreme Court went well beyond the original intent of the law when it "turned a minor provision of the act—section 5—into a major tool with which to combat white resistance to black power." Nevertheless, presumably because of Mississippi's notorious record of discrimination and because its attempt to counteract increased black registration was so blatant, Thernstrom grudgingly approves of *Allen,* calling it "both correct and inevitable." To her, however, *Allen*'s consequences for other jurisdictions are "troubling." By "implicitly enlarg[ing] the definition of enfranchisement," the Court has made "proportionate ethnic and racial representation . . . an entitlement" that required "gerrymandering to maximize minority officeholding." These "large and unanticipated results" brought the nation to "a point no one envisioned in 1965." "[N]either the aims of that earlier era nor the means of attaining them bear any resemblance to those of today." In her view, because Section 5 was proposed only to meet a temporary "emergency," and because discrimination against southern blacks in the administration of literacy tests has been eliminated, it is now safe to repeal it. Repeal is also desirable, because, as it has been interpreted since *Allen,* it represents an "extraordinary usurpation of traditional local prerogatives by federal authorities," by which "the career attorneys who roam the halls of the Department of Justice, but seldom the streets of a southern town" can "override decisions arrived at democratically" (Thernstrom 1987, 3–9, 30–31, 46, 104, 25, 168, 78, 233, 237, italics in original; similarly, see Thernstrom and Thernstrom 1997, 476).[42]

Thomas's position in *Holder v. Hall* (1994) was even more extreme, not only blasting *Allen* and its successors as "a disastrous misadventure" but also strongly implying that the Fourteenth and Fifteenth Amendments should be held not to prohibit, or to allow Congress to prohibit, discrimination against minorities in the design of electoral structures. Since, according to Justice Thomas, dilution litigation requires judges to choose arbitrarily from among the "infinite number of theories of effective suffrage, representation, and the proper apportionment of political power in a representative democracy," courts should abandon it entirely. The "weight" of a vote or whether or not a vote is "effective," he argues, is irrelevant to the VRA or the Constitution.[43] Nor does it matter whether voting is racially polarized, for the very idea that members of different racial groups have different political interests "should be repugnant to any nation that strives for the ideal of a color-blind Constitution." Construing the terms "standard, practice, or procedure" in the VRA to refer narrowly only to registering, voting, and having one's vote counted, Thomas asserted that the fact that Congress never explicitly amended this language in Sections 2 or 5 after *Allen* was handed down indicated that it never meant the VRA to reach dilutive devices (*Holder v. Hall* 1994, 2592, 2594–96, 2603, 2606).

Stronger on rhetoric than on research, Thernstrom and Thomas have dis-

regarded the events that led up to the passage of the VRA, the broader purposes of that act, and plentiful evidence of congressional intent in 1965 and
thereafter. More important for the general argument of this book, they also
have ignored the lessons of disfranchisement and the incremental nature of
the process of reform by laws and litigation. All these flaws have led them to
misinterpret the intent of the Reconstruction Amendments and the VRA.

The very nature of Section 5 of the VRA militated against clear definition, for it was an administrative remedy designed to prevent southern states
from using new as well as familiar means of inhibiting black voting power.
The few discussions of what the section was meant to cover, therefore, were
necessarily vague. In his opening statement in the House hearings, for instance, Attorney General Nicholas Katzenbach, the Johnson administration's
most important witness, noted that "the tests and devices with which the bill
deals include the usual literacy, understanding, and interpretation tests that
are easily susceptible to manipulation, *as well as a variety of other repressive
schemes,*" and he prominently mentioned *Gomillion.* Inviting an even broader
interpretation, Assistant Attorney General Burke Marshall declared that the
changes in election laws that would be disallowed under Section 5 were not
limited to "tests and devices" but included such measures as poll taxes, while
Katzenbach declined to enumerate the sorts of changes that might be legitimate, "because there are an awful lot of things that could be started for purposes of evading the Fifteenth Amendment if there is the desire to do so" (U.S.
House of Representatives 1965b, 9, 15, 72, 95, italics added). Within the Justice
Department in 1965, the expansive potential of Section 5 was clearly recognized and hotly debated. Reflecting these discussions, Katzenbach noted later
that "when we drafted this legislation, we recognized that increased black
voting strength might encourage a shift in the tactics of discrimination. Once
significant numbers of blacks could vote, communities could still throw up
obstacles to discourage those voters or *make it difficult for a black to win elective office*" (Graham 1990, 169; U.S. Senate 1975a, 123, italics added).[44] Even as
originally introduced, therefore, Section 5 seems easily open-ended enough
to have covered structural changes in voting systems.

But the section was amended in the House in 1965 to prohibit not only
"qualifications or procedures for voting" but in addition any "standard, practice, or procedure with respect to voting," and Section 2 was similarly expanded (U.S. House of Representatives 1965c, 3; 1965b, 864). This final language was arguably as broad as the proposal made by liberal congressman
Don Edwards, which would have prohibited any covered jurisdiction from
enacting "any election law or ordinance different than those in force and
effect on Nov. 1, 1964," a suggestion that Edwards said was offered in an attempt "to preclude other devices which might be used to discriminate, such

as changing the boundaries of voting districts or qualifications for holding office" (U.S. House of Representatives 1965b, 767). Thus, the nature of the remedy established by Section 5, its language, and authoritative comments at the relevant hearings strongly support Chief Justice Warren's opinion in *Allen* and seriously undermine Thernstrom's case about the initial insignificance of Section 5 and the *exclusive* concern of Congress and the Johnson administration with getting blacks registered.[45] Justice Thomas simplified his task by ignoring direct and circumstantial evidence of congressional intent in 1965 altogether.

Suppose, however, that an unruly Justice Department and an ideologically committed Supreme Court had overstepped the clear bounds that Congress had meant to impose in 1965 and that Congress wished to adhere to that original intent, refusing to learn from experience. Why, then, in 1970, with a Nixon administration elected by pursuing a "southern strategy" and George Wallace's segregationist following ripe for Republican picking, was there no strong effort to confine the language of Sections 2 and 5 to pure registration and ballot-casting so unambiguously that *Allen* would be reduced to a curiosity? A decade later, when the Supreme Court, according to civil rights supporters, distorted the original intent of Section 2 in its *Bolden* decision, there was a tremendous outcry and a massive and effective campaign to amend Section 2 to reinstate the pre-*Bolden* understanding of the law. But instead of repudiating *Allen* in 1970, 1975, or 1981, Congress explicitly celebrated it. As one of the principal Republican spokesmen on voting rights, Rep. William McCulloch of Ohio, remarked during the 1970 debate, *Allen* guaranteed that "at long last after 4 years Section 5 will become effective" (Graham 1990, 359). Although the Supreme Court in *United Jewish Organizations of Williamsburgh v. Carey* (1977), 1006, showed through extensive citations to congressional hearings and reports that Congress in its renewal of Section 5 in 1970 and 1975 was well aware of *Allen* and clearly meant to approve it, Thernstrom and Thomas ignore the evidence from both Congress, cited earlier, and the Court, evidence that severely undermines their case.

But Thernstrom and Thomas have gone far beyond glossing over inconvenient evidence.[46] Their abstract, formalistic style of analysis forecloses any appreciation of institutional mechanisms—of the conventions adopted to resolve problems such as determining the intent of a body of several hundred people, of the pragmatic compromises necessary to prevent gridlock, or of the fact that every decision by a complex, ongoing institution is the product of past events and decisions. Often termed "conservatives," they are certainly no followers of Edmund Burke. Instead, they are doctrinaire proponents of a counterrevolution against the "quiet revolution in voting rights" (McDonald 1989), whose radical disregard for institutions finds expression in their bitter scorn of Congress and their willingness to overturn as many judicial decisions as necessary to attain the results they desire.

Thus, to Thernstrom, almost all members of Congress are either blind, gullible, unobservant, incompetent, or Machiavellian. The mention of "effect" in Section 5 of the VRA in 1965 was "unnoticed," she charges. The 1970 amendments "reinforced the act in unintended and unforeseen ways." "[S]lapdash, inattentive" House members cast merely "symbolic votes" in 1981, while the strategy of the leading prospective opponent of the Voting Rights Act, Rep. Henry Hyde, was so inept that it presented "a gift" to the bill's supporters, and the Reagan administration's indecisiveness robbed it of any influence whatsoever in the struggle. Sen. Orrin Hatch, her book's only heroic figure, was a man of considerable "political acumen," who had, she thought, the best of all the arguments, but who commanded almost no votes, betrayed as he was by such ambitious opportunists as Sen. Robert Dole. By contrast, Rep. Don Edwards and the "diehards," a "determined minority hewing to a hard line" within the voting rights lobby, were insidiously crafty, seeking to "deflect scrutiny" of changes in Section 2 that aimed at overruling *Bolden,* harassing potential witnesses for the other side, and, with their "self-proclaimed moral superiority" and deplorable perseverance, overwhelming "moderates" who had "soft hearts and weak stomachs." Even before 1981, members of Congress, as well as lobbyists, had deliberately obfuscated the voting rights issue by conflating disfranchisement and dilution. The black and brown masses, she thinks, were in no danger of losing their votes, but by charging that they were, the civil rights forces could create safe seats for African- and Mexican-American politicians (Thernstrom 1987, 26, 38, 101–2, 84, 114–16, 135–36, 83, 87, 98–99, 41, 45–46, 53, 58, 104, 118–19).

Justice Thomas, whose enmity toward Congress seems to be exceeded only by his resentment of civil rights leaders and liberal judges, disdained any pretense of deference to members of the legislative branch, whom he had once dismissed as "petty despots" (Phelps and Winternitz 1992, 28–30, 66, 79, 104, 109, 121, 173; Mayer and Abramson 1994, 117–18, 360; Roberts 1995, 132). In his view, legislative hearings and remarks on the floor of Congress are irrelevant to determining the intent of laws, legislative histories are shams, and committee reports are merely "a series of partisan statements about purposes and objectives collected by staffers" (*Holder v. Hall,* 2612).[47] Rather than submit to such congressional attempts to fetter the power of judges to interpret a law in any way they please, Thomas argues, judges should merely concern themselves with the text of a statute, which he treats as transparent to "common sense."

Yet in a move inconsistent with his derogation of extratextual evidence, Thomas went on in his *Holder v. Hall* opinion to charge that Justice William

Brennan misinterpreted such evidence of congressional intent in *Thornburg v. Gingles* (1986), which Thomas apparently considered the only Supreme Court case to interpret Section 2 of the VRA as applying to structural discrimination. Brennan had assumed wrongly, Thomas contended, that the words "standard, practice, or procedure" in Section 2 meant what *Allen* had said the same words meant when used in Section 5. The plurality in *Bolden* had ruled, without considering *Allen*, that Section 2 did not reach structural discrimination, and if Congress had wanted to repeal that part of *Bolden*, Thomas asserted, it would have explicitly said so in the text of the law.[48] The justice admitted that Congress shifted from *Bolden*'s discriminatory intent requirement to a discriminatory effect test. But he contended that the mention of effect did not necessarily refer to an effect on the ability to elect candidates of choice, because Congress might have meant to make it possible, for example, to invalidate a registration law that disproportionately disfranchised blacks without plaintiffs having to show that it was adopted with a discriminatory intent. By referring to the legislative history of the law to resolve ambiguities, Thomas declared disdainfully, Brennan had engaged in "statutory construction through divination," employing "a selective reading of legislative history." Instead of such a reading, according to Thomas, Brennan should have ignored the Senate and House committee reports, all the hearings, and almost all of the floor debate and concentrated his attention on a rather vague two-page Senate committee report addendum and one floor statement by Sen. Robert Dole (*Holder v. Hall* 1994, 2602–14).

Thernstrom's 1987 book was hardly less acerbic toward Supreme Court decisions than Thomas was. Thus, she called *White v. Regester*'s judgment "abstruse" and its findings of fact "unexplained assertions of indeterminate weight" that "lacked coherence." Without a complete definition of a fair democratic process, which she apparently thinks the Court had a duty to provide, the list of factors in *Regester* was "arbitrary," and therefore unconstitutional, because "arbitrary federal interference with local and state electoral arrangements is in clear violation of the Constitution." Yet the attempt to codify the decision, she wrote, "simplifies what cannot be simplified; makes orderly a process that is inherently disorderly." *Regester*'s was a "Chinese menu approach," a formula that "never worked," in which factors can be chosen "at random" to prove tautologically the existence of racial discrimination. *Rogers v. Lodge* she condemned as unfaithful to *Mobile v. Bolden*, a decision that she termed "principled, simple, and tight" at one point and condemned as vague at another. Nor did Thernstrom or Thomas like *Gingles*'s rejection of the "multicausal" attack on the statistical methods that are commonly used to determine racially polarized voting. Both the political scientist and the justice agreed that Brennan had "distort[ed] the meaning of electoral opportunity." If blacks are a minority in a jurisdiction, Thernstrom and Thomas insisted, they have no right to any representation at all (Thernstrom 1987, 73–75, 127, 136, 75–76, 133, 206, 227; *Holder v. Hall* 1994, 2596–98).

The radicals' indictment of Congress and the Court is as unfair as it is inattentive to the ways of institutions.[49] Congress usually operates by compromise and cooperation, as well as by conflict and debate. It draws on the expertise and knowledge of bureaucrats, scholars, and spokespersons for the interest groups most affected by a potential action and particularly from the past experiences of members of Congress who specialize in an area of policy. In the instance of voting rights, Congress acted in an exemplary manner, conducting extensive hearings in 1965, 1969–70, 1975, and 1981–82, and listening to large numbers of knowledgeable witnesses on every side of issues of ethnic politics and electoral rules. These are issues that require no technical expertise to grasp and that are necessarily familiar to every politician. Recognizing that statutory language is necessarily general and may be ambiguous, as well as that busy members of Congress do not have time to read voluminous records of hearings, Congress conventionally sets out in committee reports detailed interpretations of the meaning of laws and distills positions on issues raised in the hearings. The reports on the VRA are especially clear and detailed. Although congresspersons may not always have understood every nuance of every amendment, it is difficult to imagine many other subjects on which Congress has acted in a more considered fashion. To take one important instance that contradicts Thernstrom's indictment, civil rights lobbyists in 1981–82 did not attempt to "deflect scrutiny" from *Bolden,* as she charged. Instead, they spotlighted it from the initial hearing in the House, when the very first witness, Vernon Jordan, pointed to the repeal of *Bolden* as one of the chief purposes of the proposed amendments to the VRA. Congress kept its focus on *Bolden* for the next year, climaxing in the Senate Report on the amended act, which devoted at least seventy-three pages to the issue (U.S. House of Representatives 1981, 18–19; U.S. Senate 1982b, 15–43, 127–58, 169–73, 177–87; Boyd and Markman 1983). Thus, the radicals' censure of the national legislature reflects little more than resentment over the defeat of policies that they favored.

Likewise, their criticisms of Supreme Court decisions are inconsistent, illogical, and unreflective. Spinning extremely strained theories about what Congress might conceivably have meant while ignoring the overwhelming evidence in documents that are designed to specify what Congress actually did mean, as Justice Thomas did, is disrespectful of a coequal branch. Denouncing Justice Brennan for using evidence selectively while failing to refrain from quoting selectively—and shockingly misleadingly—oneself is self-contradictory. On the page of the *Congressional Record* (128:14132) before the one that Thomas's opinion quotes, Sen. Dole had said that Section 2 applied "if a voting practice *or structure* operates to exclude members of a minority group from a fair opportunity to participate in the political process." "Citizens of all races," Dole said, "are intended [by Section 2] to have an equal chance *of electing candidates of their choice.*" The standard, he went on—referring to *White v. Regester*'s ruling that at-large elections, in certain circumstances, may unconstitutionally discriminate against minorities—is whether "members of a protected class have the same opportunity as others to participate in the political process *and to elect candidates of their choice*" (italics added). Sen. Dole clearly did not mean, as Justice Thomas's out-of-context quotation suggests, that Section 2 applies only to actions aimed at preventing individuals from registering or voting. Moreover, the "totality of the circumstances" rubric outlined in *White v. Regester* and subsequent court decisions and congressional reports merely reflects an effort to organize inquiries into intent and effect, such as the examinations that Thernstrom and Thomas have made into the intent of Sections 2 and 5 of the VRA and the impacts that they have attributed to rulings that prohibited structural discrimination against minorities. The choice in analyzing empirical evidence about social or political facts is not between looking at the totality of the circumstances and some other approach; it is between looking at a biased selection of the circumstances, as the radicals did, and all of them, as *White v. Regester* advised.

Although both Thomas and Thernstrom have opposed moves by Congress or the courts to protect ethnic minorities against gerrymandering or other structural devices that disadvantage them, they vociferously supported the Court's 5–4 decisions in *Shaw v. Reno* (1993) and *Miller v. Johnson* (1995), which allowed whites to sue under the Fourteenth Amendment if race was assertedly the "predominant factor" in the drawing of election districts. In these cases, Justice Thomas did not, as he did in *Holder v. Hall* (2595–96), raise the specter of courts having to choose from among an "infinite number" of theories of representation, or suggest that the vote might be considered merely a matter of self-expression, no more than a symbol of participation in the polity, or imply that whites ought to be satisfied if they could influence but not control the outcome in a district in which they were not in the majority. When Mississippi in 1967 redrew districts, changed from single-member-district to at-large elections, or, in black-majority areas, switched from electing officials to having white higher-ups appoint them, there was no violation of the law or the Constitution, according to Justice Thomas. When North Carolina in 1991–92 redrew districts to create the most integrated ones in the state, which gave African-Americans the first opportunity of the twentieth century to elect candidates of their choice, Thomas denounced it as unconstitutional "political apartheid." Nor was Thernstrom any less enamored of racial double standards. While in her 1987 book she said she believed that there was too little evidence of voting discrimination against Latinos to justify bringing them under the coverage of the VRA, she showed no such hesitation about *Shaw v. Reno,* when white control of election districts was not maximized (Thernstrom 1987, 55–62; *NYT,* Dec. 7, 1994, A19). Earlier, she had advised civil rights advocates to "trust in the political process left substantially to its own devices," instead of challenging structural discrimination in court (Thernstrom 1987, 240). She gave no such admonitions to white plaintiffs in "racial gerrymandering" cases, nor did she require that they produce a full-blown democratic theory before their plea could be approved, as she had insisted minority plaintiffs in vote dilution cases must do.

Logic aside, the radicals' principal failures lie in their impractical, ahistorical approaches to their topics. The politicians who passed and those who opposed dilutive and disfranchising laws in the nineteenth as well as the twentieth century believed that politics is about who gets and keeps power and what they use it for. They knew that dilution and disfranchisement were not pure concepts, because one may facilitate the other and because both affect the amount of influence that identifiable groups of voters wield over policies. Because the nineteenth-century veterans of the abolitionist movement and the Civil War knew that the political process, left to itself, would not protect African-Americans, they passed the Reconstruction Amendments and pushed, at first quite successfully, for various laws to enforce them. More recent advocates of voting rights for minorities have reshaped the tools provided by the First Reconstruction, learning from their predecessors' failures and the inadequacies of laws in their own time, in a pragmatic effort that has gradually expanded minority political rights until, after the 1991–92 round of redistricting, the rights of minority citizens finally began to approximate those of whites. The congressional and judicial majorities of the period from 1957 to 1993 approached protection of minority electoral rights pragmatically, realizing that the political influence of individual members of minority groups depended on the degree of legal and private discrimination against them *because of their group membership* and approving methods of determining the degree of that discrimination. Since the discrimination was group-based, the remedy had to be group-conscious.[50] Where there was little discrimination, judicial economy dictated that there be little protection by the national intervention. Unlike Thernstrom and Thomas, however, most other officials thought the degree of discrimination a matter of fact, not assumption. But in 1993–94, with the *Shaw* decision and the Republican takeover of Congress, the consensus that had sustained the expansion of minority voting rights was disrupted and the institutions destabilized. While radicals like Thernstrom and Thomas cheered such upheaval, those who knew the history of the First and Second Reconstructions, who recognized the depth of American race-consciousness and the fragility of white support for the rights of minorities, who had painstakingly constructed increasingly effective barriers to discrimination, were much less sanguine about the future. In this instance, it was the "liberal" supporters of voting rights whose historical consciousness, skepticism about human nature, and commitment to reasoned, gradual change fit the classic definitions of "conservative" (Sperber and Trillschuh 1962, 94–95; Plano and Greenberg 1976, 5; Safire 1978, 137).

In *The Civil Rights Cases*, which overturned the 1875 national public accommodations law, Justice Joseph Bradley announced that after slavery and its "concomitants" had been abolished, "there must be some stage in the progress of [the African-American's] elevation when he takes the rank of a mere citizen, and ceases to be the special favorite of the laws, and when his rights as a citizen, or a man, are to be protected in the ordinary modes by which other men's rights are protected" (*Civil Rights Cases* 1883, 31). In an eerie echo of Bradley, Thernstrom asked rhetorically "how much special protection from white competition are black candidates entitled to?" (Thernstrom 1987, 5). Like Bradley, she and Justice Thomas would remove most of the legislative and judicial protections of the most recent Reconstruction. And we know, even if they have forgotten, what happened the first time.

And it could happen again, even though white racism is much less widespread today than it was in the nineteenth century. As the record of the northern Democrats on civil rights roll calls in the nineteenth century shows, it was not simple racism or racial hostility that undermined support for black voting rights, and as a more detailed look at the history of late nineteenth-century and early twentieth-century disfranchisement and Jim Crow would demonstrate, it was not so much that southern whites hated blacks or found contact with them distasteful. Black voting rights and even legalized segregation were more matters of racial *power* than of unthinking racial *animosity*. Consequently, a decline in the overall level of white racism, which has occurred since 1960 (Schuman, Steeh, and Bobo 1985), does not guarantee the fair treatment of racial minorities if, as in the nineteenth century, national legal and judicial safeguards were to be removed or radically reinterpreted. Indeed, the First Reconstruction provides a realistic counterfactual to which the period since 1965 can be usefully compared. Replace *Allen* with *Reese* and *Cruikshank*, emasculating congressional protections of the right to vote in a fair electoral structure; repeal Section 5, as Democrats repealed the Supervisory Law in 1894; fail to overthrow the murky intent-based *Bolden* decision, as 1890 Republicans barely failed to pass the Lodge Fair Elections Bill; or give *Shaw v. Reno* the wide-ranging implications that some of its proponents have found in it, and the Second Reconstruction might well begin to unravel as the First Reconstruction did. Redraw congressional and state legislative districts that after 1992 were occupied by minority representatives in a way that submerges minority voters in hopelessly conservative districts, as was the case in North Carolina congressional districts before 1991; with the most vigorous proponents then unrepresented, repeal or emasculate the National Voter Registration Act (the "motor voter" act) and Sections 2 and 5 of the VRA; rely on term limits to remove the most experienced state legislators and to reduce the incentive of all legislators to compromise, since they would not be interacting with each other long enough to be able to expect that favors will be returned (Schrag 1996); divide and defeat Democrats by emphasizing such racially tinged issues as California's Proposition 187 denying nearly all government services to undocumented immigrants and Proposition 209 banning affirmative action for minorities; use the resulting Republican majorities, now that all racial issues have become partisan, to make voter registration much more difficult, as Republicans have attempted to do nationally (*LAT*, Mar. 16, 1998, A:3); and the country would be solidly mired in a Second Redemption, led, as it was during that first anti-Reconstruction era, by a party that believes, correctly, that it has more to gain by attacking than by appealing to minorities.

If Bradley's pronouncement in *The Civil Rights Cases* helped to usher out the First Reconstruction, Justice Harlan Fiske Stone's famous footnote 4 in *U.S. v. Carolene Products Co.* (1938, 152–53) was both a precursor and a precondition of the Second. The Supreme Court had abandoned its guise as protector of an extremely powerful minority, large corporations, in 1937. Henceforth, Stone indicated, the Court would have to consider, among other roles for itself, "whether prejudice against discrete and insular minorities may be a special condition, which tends seriously to curtail the operation of those political processes ordinarily to be relied upon to protect minorities, and which may call for a correspondingly more searching judicial inquiry." Instead of defending the powerful, who could take care of themselves through the normal political processes, the Court would shield the relatively powerless. Nowhere did the Court more perfectly fulfill this function than in the series of minority vote dilution cases, beginning in 1944 and coming to a sudden halt in 1993, cases that made the efforts of members of Congress, the executive branch, and civil rights groups possible and effective. Justice Thomas has already announced that in matters of economic regulation, he would like to turn the judicial clock back to 1895 (*U.S. v. Lopez* 1995, 1648–49). It was only a year later that the same Court decided *Plessy v. Ferguson*.

CHAPTER TWO

Real Racial Gerrymandering—
Lessons from L.A.

Duration the debate on the renewal of Sections 4 and 5 of the Voting Rights Act in 1969 and 1970, the Nixon administration and many southern Democrats taunted civil rights supporters for ignoring voting rights abuses outside the South. Presenting his proposal to shift the focus from the South by repealing Section 5 of the VRA, require the Justice Department to monitor voting rights problems throughout the country, and leave the Department with only the pre-1965 remedy of bringing individual suits to counter electoral discrimination, Attorney General John Mitchell declared: "Voting rights is not a regional issue. It is a nationwide concern for every American which must be tested on a nationwide basis." In a brilliant, if exaggerated, reply, Rep. William McCulloch, the ranking Republican on the House Judiciary Committee, offered this assessment: "The proposal sweeps broadly into those areas where the need is least, and retreats from those areas where the need is the greatest. The Administration has created a remedy for which there is no wrong and leaves grievous wrongs without adequate remedy." McCulloch's view persists. Dissenting in a 1992 reapportionment case, California Supreme Court Justice Stanley Mosk asserted that the VRA "was obviously aimed at states, mainly in the South, that sought directly or indirectly to disenfranchise minorities or to curtail their potential political influence. It is obvious that such an enactment was unnecessary for California, and in some respects it may be counterproductive" (quotes from Lawson 1985, 136; Ball, Krane, and Lauth 1982, 69–70; *Wilson v. Eu* 1992, 736).

In fact, both sides in the 1970s had good arguments. Nonsoutherners justly pointed out that with very limited resources, the worst problems, those of the Deep South, deserved the earliest attention. Southern strategists correctly emphasized that the problem was nationwide and that it was not confined to relations between whites and African-Americans. Responding to the criticism, Congress in 1970 extended the ban on literacy tests nationwide, which affected fourteen nonsouthern states, and brought counties or election districts with especially low turnout or registration rates in ten nonsouthern states under Section 5 coverage. In 1975, when VRA renewal came up once more, liberals made the nationwide prohibition of literacy tests permanent, brought groups that had many members who did not communicate well in English (termed "language minorities") under the protection of the Act, and subjected counties throughout the country to the preclearance requirements of Section 5 if they had large proportions of language minorities and currently conducted elections using English-only ballots (Davidson 1992; U.S. House of Representatives 1975b, 2–3). Although most legal cases concerning voting rights continued to be filed in the South, there were significant cases that reached the Supreme Court from New York and Indiana, reflecting an understanding that racial bloc voting and discriminatory electoral structures were not confined to the South (*Wells v. Rockefeller* [1969]; *Whitcomb v. Chavis* [1971]).

Until 1988, however, no voting rights case stressing that a system had been adopted and/or maintained with a racially discriminatory intent had been brought outside the South, at least in a state or large metropolitan area. Indeed, even before the *Bolden* case in 1980, voting rights lawyers were justifiably wary of intent cases, since so much seemed to depend on the willingness of a judge to look skeptically, even harshly, at the motives of legislators or local officials, people in most instances very much like himself (most judges were and are upper-class white males) and in some situations, men who were in fact his friends or acquaintances (Parker 1983, 740–46). It was with some trepidation, therefore, that lawyers from the Mexican-American Legal Defense and Education Fund (MALDEF), the American Civil Liberties Union (ACLU), and the U.S. Department of Justice approached adding an intent element as a major focus of their racial gerrymandering case *Garza v. Los Angeles County Board of Supervisors*. The rest of this chapter is a rearranged and somewhat abridged version of the expert witness report that convinced the lawyers and every judge who ruled in the case that discriminatory intent could be demonstrated with circumstantial evidence in a nonsouthern jurisdiction. What motivated those who drew district lines in Los Angeles were not pure feelings of civic virtue or a desire to benefit minorities, as defendants in the case insisted, but the drive to protect Anglo incumbents from challenges by candidates who were the first choice of minority voters.

TWO OF the three members of the first governing body of Los Angeles County after statehood, Augustin Olvera and Luis Roubideau, were Californios, that is, people of Mexican descent who had lived in California before 1849 and continued to reside there after California became part of the United States. County judge Olvera, the head of the Court of Sessions that ruled the county from 1850 until the formation of the Board of Supervisors in 1852, reportedly spoke no English. Although the county was geographically much larger than it is today, the population, according to a state census, was only 7,831, or approximately 1,000 times less than in 1990, and only 377 men voted in the county's first election. In that year, each of its five members represented 1,566 people (Guinn 1902, 132–37).

With the exception of the years from 1882 to 1885, the size of the Los Angeles County Board of Supervisors has been five since 1852.[1] Repeated proposals by Board members and official and citizens' committees to increase the number have failed, the most recent serious ones being defeated in referenda in 1962 and 1976. There is no state policy constraining the number, and San Francisco, with a 1980 population of 679,000, had eleven county supervisors. Los Angeles County Board members are elected for four-year terms by the voters of each district. The terms are staggered, with three members elected in years that are divisible by four, and two members two years later. There is a nonpartisan primary election in the spring or early summer. If no candidate gains a majority, there is a runoff election between the top two vote-getters in November.

In 1990, Los Angeles County had a population of 8,863,164 people—far and away the largest county in the nation—but the number of supervisors had not changed since 1885. Each of the five represented about 1.75 million people. The county's population growth between 1980 and 1990 alone—1,385,926— was 177 times its *total* population when the number of supervisors was first fixed at five. In terms of population, each one of the supervisorial districts was larger than seventeen of the fifty states and larger than three average-size U.S. congressional districts combined. If a candidate had attempted to campaign door to door talking to each constituent for ten minutes, it would have taken over fifty years to complete the task. With officials from eighty-five cities in the county competing for media attention, Los Angeles County supervisors were probably the least well known truly powerful civilian officials in the country, presiding over health, fire, police, park, library, street repair, and many other services. In land area, Los Angeles County is nearly four times as large as the state of Rhode Island and more than twice as large as the state of Delaware (Stern 1989, chap. 11; U.S. Department of Commerce 1994, 46).

The population per elected official in the 1980s was much larger in the Los Angeles County government than in any other county government in the nation, and the county had by far the largest population per district of any county that selected its officials from single-member districts. Cook County,

Illinois, the nation's second largest county, for example, elected fifteen commissioners from single-member districts. Each represented 353,193 persons in 1986, or about a fifth as many as in Los Angeles County. The thirty-five councilpersons from the five boroughs that made up New York City each represented slightly over 200,000 persons. In California, San Diego County's five supervisors each represented 440,260 persons, while Orange County's represented 433,360, and Santa Clara County's 280,320. The county closest to Los Angeles in district size was Harris County, Texas, home to Houston, whose five county commissioners represented an average of 559,660 persons (U.S. Department of Commerce 1994, 42, 55, 120, 354, 497).

Until 1874, one and often two of the five Los Angeles County supervisors had Spanish surnames. From 1875 to 1991, no person with a Spanish surname served on the Board. Before 1992, no black person, white woman, or person of Asian descent had ever been elected to the Board.

IN THE post–World War II era, Los Angeles County supervisorial seats have been very secure. From 1945 to 1990 only eighteen different persons occupied one of the five county seats of power. The average tenure of those eighteen persons (including the time, if any, before 1945) was fourteen years. Most either retired voluntarily or died in office. From 1970 to 1990, only three incumbents were defeated for reelection and, indeed, incumbents were rarely seriously challenged. Their margin over their chief opponents averaged a whopping 36 percent, and they usually gathered a sufficiently large majority (not just a plurality) of the vote to avoid runoff elections. In only four of twenty-four primary contests from 1970 to 1990 did an incumbent fail to obtain a majority. Overall, incumbents averaged a hefty 65 percent of the votes.

Open seat contests, on the other hand, often attracted well-known, well-financed competitors, and margins of victory correspondingly shrank. Assemblyman James Hayes, who had the endorsement of retiring supervisor Burton Chace in 1972, battled Los Angeles city councilman Marvin Braude in the primary.[2] Two years later, three Los Angeles city councilmen—Ed Edelman, John Ferraro, and Ernani Bernardi—struggled for the Third District seat of retiring supervisor Ernest Debs. Despite Debs's endorsement of Ferraro, Edelman won, but his margin was much less than it was in any of his subsequent contests.[3]

There are two major reasons that incumbent supervisors win so overwhelmingly. First, they are able to raise so much money that they frighten away most opponents and heavily outspend those who do run against them. The best funded nonincumbent campaign since 1980, county assessor Alexander Pope's 1984 race against first-term incumbent Deane Dana, was outspent by nearly three to one. Pope lost the primary by a margin of 57 percent to

36 percent. In 1987, three years before they were scheduled to run for reelection, incumbents Peter F. Schabarum and Edmund Edelman between them had on hand campaign funds totaling nearly $1.5 million. The Republican Schabarum's political action committee distributed at least $850,000 to other candidates and campaigns from 1981 to 1987, including $213,000 to Dana in 1984. Although he failed in attempts to interest candidates in running against his longtime enemy, liberal supervisor Kenneth Hahn, Schabarum did arouse Hahn's anger sufficiently to lead Hahn to donate about $100,000 to opponents of supervisors Schabarum, Dana, and Antonovich. Incumbent supervisors collected 91 percent of the campaign contributions given to supervisorial candidates from 1981 to 1986. Seriously challenged in the primary and run-off in 1988, Antonovich spent $2.8 million in winning reelection. When Dana finally retired, after four terms in office, he endorsed his chief deputy, who raised four times as much as his best-financed opponent, much of it from county employees' associations and construction firms that did business with the county. As contributors of less than $100 have become less important, accounting for only 2 percent of the total contributions in the 1980s, favor-seeking businesses, developers, and lobbyists have bought in. The Summa Corporation, which planned to build a marina north of the Los Angeles International Airport, contributed $195,000 to various supervisors from 1980 to 1988 (Stern 1989, chap. 11; *LAT*, Mar. 19, 1996, B:1, 3). For all the ideological struggle on the Board, contributors seem to be markedly nonpartisan. For example, former Edelman aide Jeff Seymour, a longtime Democratic activist who later became a lobbyist for developers and other people with special interests in county actions, contributed to every supervisor and encouraged his clients to do likewise (Seymour dep., 74–78). In sum, most Los Angeles County elections have been characterized by massive incumbent fundraising.

The second means of incumbents' maintaining their positions has been redistricting. One gauge of how much redistricting mattered to a supervisor is the fact that after the very minor line-changing that took place in 1981, the two supervisors whose boundaries were shifted most, Edelman and Hahn, both sent out letters blanketing the areas added to their districts. Hahn, who had received 88 percent of the vote in 1980, enclosed a brochure describing the paramedic program in the City of Los Angeles with his effusive letter offering his new downtown Los Angeles constituents assistance with any county service. An Edelman aide, the day after the supervisors finalized the reapportionment plan, encouraged his boss, who had won reelection in 1978 with 74 percent of the vote, to send a similar letter puffing Edelman's "14 point program" as well as his housing, health, and anti-gang efforts.

The supervisors redrew their district boundaries seven times between 1953 and 1981. Five of those seven instances were not immediately after the decadal census, and, as numerous records from the County Regional Planning group show, the 1953, 1955, 1959, 1963, and 1965 reapportionments were based on county estimates of intercensal population, not on U.S. census data alone. Population growth has been uneven in the county, especially during the 1950s and 60s, but the redistricting often did not respond adequately to imbalances in the populations in the districts and in some crucial cases was obviously not a response to malapportionment at all. For instance, the reapportionment of 1955 *raised* the population of the three most populous districts and *lowered* the population of the two least populous districts (Kousser 1991b, 620). Apart from the mandates of state and national law, the redistrictings have in fact been responses to politics.

SEVERAL facets of state and Los Angeles County law affected the *form* of the county's struggles over redistricting, and one significantly affected the actual *outcomes*. Any board of supervisors in California can reapportion itself at any time within one year after a general election. Since the 1965 case of *Miller v. Board of Supervisors of Santa Clara County* and perhaps since the 1964 U.S. Supreme Court case of *Reynolds v. Sims*, boards have been required to reapportion themselves on a population basis after every decadal census. To assist in reapportioning itself, a board of supervisors may appoint a boundary commission of any size, but the commission proposals are only advisory, not binding. Nor were the guidelines in the State Election Code in 1981 constraining, holding only that in reapportioning itself the Board "*may* give consideration to the following factors: (a) topography; (b) geography; (c) cohesiveness; (d) community of interests of the districts." In 1971, the Los Angeles County Supervisors' Boundary Commission adopted for itself additional guidelines: to "(a) preserve the historical representation of certain areas closely identified with a particular district; (b) insofar as possible not divide cities by supervisorial district boundaries; and (c) insofar as possible not separate cities or communities sharing common interests and problems peculiar to a section of the county." Nonetheless, even before strict population equality in apportionment was mandated, which almost always necessitates dividing cities and communities, cities were always split by redistrictings. In 1962, for example, twelve of the county's cities were divided between different supervisorial districts. One small and poor community, South Gate, was shared by four different districts. Although in theory the county adhered to what *Shaw v. Reno* (1993) referred to as a "traditional districting principle" of not severing municipalities or undefined "communities of interest," in fact it never came close to adhering to that principle.

The most significant provisions of the election code for reapportionment required that four of the five supervisors, rather than a simple majority of the board, concur before any reapportionment was legal, and set a deadline (September 24 in 1981) for the board to act. At least, this has been the usual interpretation of the ambiguous "two-thirds" language in the 1913 county charter, which was evidently copied from an equally ambiguous 1889 state law. (Two-thirds or 67 percent is closer to three-fifths or 60 percent than it is to four-fifths or 80 percent.) Before 1963, the four-vote requirement does not seem to have been questioned. In 1965, it was believed that only three votes were necessary, even though the final plan received four. By 1971, the county counsel's office was unsure whether three or four votes were required, but, again, consensus precluded the testing of this matter in the courts. Finally, in 1981, when it finally really mattered whether a simple or an extraordinary majority was needed to accept a final plan, the county counsel's office casually issued only oral advice on the matter.[4] If no plan were adopted before the deadline, said the counsel, the line-drawing would be taken out of the supervisors' hands and delegated to a three-person committee consisting of the district attorney, the county assessor, and the sheriff, which would have the power to act, before the end of the calendar year, without the approval of the Board. Provisions of the election code and county charter required supervisors to live within the boundaries of their districts and were interpreted as disallowing any boundary change that placed a supervisor's home in a district other than the one from which he was elected (see Kousser 1991b, 613–14 for references).

REDISTRICTING is a game in which territories containing people with certain political proclivities and ethnic identifications are rearranged to benefit one interest or another. As the chief consultant to the California Assembly's Special Committee on Reapportionment in 1981, Professor Bruce E. Cain, put it, "Every plan is going to have a bias. Every plan is going to have a slant. And therefore every plan is going to be a gerrymander in some sense. It is going to have an intention to it. It is going to favor some groups and not others" (Cain 1983, 56). Because of their numbers, settlement patterns, strong identification with the Democratic party, and, until very recently, relative lack of political power, Latinos in Los Angeles have been more often the objects or pawns of redistricting than its shapers or beneficiaries.

By 1960, Spanish-surnamed individuals had become the largest minority ethnic group in Los Angeles County. During the decade of the 1950s, the number of people in the county with Spanish surnames doubled, and by 1960 the census counted 576,716 of them, which amounted to 9.6 percent of the population. In 1970, 15 percent of Los Angeles County's people considered themselves Mexican-Americans, and another 3 percent, non-Mexican Latino. From 1970 to 1980, there was a 68 percent increase in the county's Hispanic population, a 21 percent increase in its African-American population, and a 20.9

FIGURE 2.1. The Third District and the Hispanic Population Grew in Opposite Directions, 1958–1981

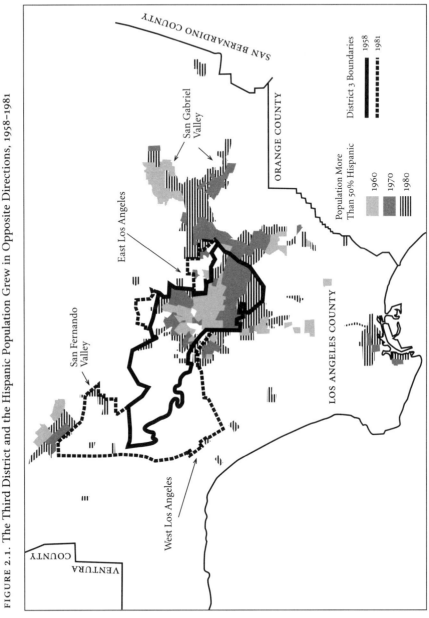

Sources: Based on maps provided to the author by the U.S. Department of Justice in connection with the *Garza* case.

percent *decline* in the county's non-Hispanic white population. By 1980, 27.6 percent of the county's population was Hispanic, and the Health Department and County Regional Planning Group estimated that from 30.4 to 31.7 percent of the population was Hispanic in 1985. In 1990, 37.8 percent of the county's residents reported their ethnicity as Hispanic. By 1995, Hispanics surpassed Anglos as the largest ethnic group in the county, comprising 43.5 percent of the population compared to 35.1 percent for Anglos, 9.9 percent for African-Americans, and 11.4 percent for Asians. As Figure 2.1 shows, the growth in the Hispanic population during the 1960s and 70s took place not only in what demographers referred to as the "Hispanic core" just east and south of down-town Los Angeles, but also south into South Central Los Angeles, east into the San Gabriel Valley, and, largely jumping over Glendale, north around the city of San Fernando (Kousser 1991b, 643–45; U.S. Department of Commerce 1994, 47; *LAT*, March 14, 1996, A4).

Hispanics in California are somewhat less segregated from other ethnic groups than are African-Americans or Anglos, a fact that is widely understood by reapportionment experts. The Los Angeles City Community Development Department identified Anglo, black, "Spanish," "mixed," and "Asian" housing clusters from 1950 through 1980. On average, Anglo clusters were 87.5 per-cent Anglo and black clusters were 81.2 percent black, but "Spanish" clusters were only 61.2 percent Hispanic and Asian clusters were a mere 36 percent Asian. Because of the degree of segregation, it is easiest to draw safe Anglo political districts, but Hispanics are clearly not so mixed within the Southern California community as to make it very difficult to cluster them politically, or, alternatively, to determine where to divide them (Cain 1983, 40; Navarro 1981, 142).

That there is a greater proportion of noncitizens and children among Hispanics than among Anglos or blacks is also a well-recognized factor in reapportionments. The Rose Institute at Claremont McKenna College esti-mated in 1988 that 38 percent of California Hispanics were less than 18 years old, while another 38 percent were not U.S. citizens. The rate of voter regis-tration among California Anglos, they believed, was about 61 percent, while for Hispanics who were U.S. citizens the rate was only 45 percent (Estrada 1983, 15; Rose Institute 1988b). Although none of the Los Angeles County reapportionment experts in 1981 or earlier seems to have used citizenship or Hispanic voter registration estimates explicitly, and although supervisors' offices denied that they gave any less attention to the problems of noncitizens than they did to those of citizens, it is universally understood that the pro-portion of voters to population is lower among Hispanics than among Anglos (Bannister dep., 97–100; Dana dep., 327; Duron dep., 58–59; Edelman dep., 161–62, 165–66; Fitch dep., 69, 172–73, 186–87; Fonda-Bonardi dep., 79; Fukai dep., 78–79, 95; Garcia dep., 29–30; Heslop dep., 310; Hoffenblum dep., 243–44; Murdoch dep., 75; Neri dep., 121; Quevedo dep., 41–42; Shumate dep., 86–87, 341; Smith dep., 186; Turner dep., 79, 241–42, 378; Walters dep., 82).

It is the disproportionately Democratic affiliation of Hispanics in Los Angeles that makes them useful in gerrymanders. According to the Rose Institute, 70.4 percent of the Latino registered voters in Los Angeles County in 1988 were Democrats, 20.4 percent were Republicans, and 9.2 percent declined to state or were affiliated with minor parties (Rose Institute 1988b). Because of this, according to Prof. Richard Santillan, "the Democratic leadership during times of redistricting has deliberately distributed Chicano voters into as many districts as possible to maximize and take advantage of guaranteed Chicano support for non-Chicano Democratic candidates" (Santillan 1981, 4). Conversely, Prof. Alan Heslop, head of the Rose Institute and former executive director of the California State Republican Central Committee, admitted that "Republicans seek to concentrate Latinos excessively by bringing them together in a single district to waste Democratic votes" (Heslop dep., 227). Or as California Assembly minority leader Republican Ross Johnson put it, "If seats are created in the Hispanic areas that increase the opportunity for Hispanic representation, . . . it follows as the night the day that in the suburban areas there will be greater opportunities to elect Republicans" (Johnson 1983, 60).

And it was not only Republicans who charged that Latinos had often been pawns in California redistricting. That most honestly brash of California politicians, the late Democrat Jesse Unruh, who as assembly speaker presided over the epic post-*Reynolds* reapportionment of the 1960s, acknowledged that "reapportionments are designed by incumbents, for incumbents, as a service to incumbents." Continuing this candor, he announced in 1971 hearings of the California State Advisory Committee of the U.S. Commission on Civil Rights that "quite obviously the Mexican American community has been reapportioned more with regard to how it would maximize the Democratic representation tha[n] it has to how it would maximize the Mexican American representation." According to Los Angeles City Councilman Richard Alatorre, who was chairman of the reapportionment committee of the state assembly in 1981, Hispanic areas had been divided in congressional, state legislative, and Los Angeles City Council apportionments in California before 1981 (California State Advisory Committee to the U.S. Commission on Civil Rights 1971, 9, 23; Alatorre dep., 24–27, 45–46, 51–52).

DID THE Los Angeles County supervisors in the recent past use their almost unlimited power over redistricting to strengthen their own seats? And if this strengthening did indeed take place, did it come at the expense of the most rapidly growing demographic group, Latinos? The answer to both questions is unequivocally affirmative. Pro-Anglo, pro-incumbent racial gerrymandering was the dominant theme of redistricting in Los Angeles County from 1959 through 1981.

One of the most instructive instances is the 1959 reapportionment. In 1958, John Anson Ford retired from the Third District seat that he had held since 1934. Four major candidates jumped into the open seat contest: Los Angeles city councilmen Harold A. Henry, Ernest E. Debs, and Edward R. Roybal, and Board of Education member Paul Burke. Despite a *Los Angeles Times* endorsement of the conservative Republican Henry, Democrats Debs and Roybal proved the top vote-getters in the June primary and waged a hot campaign in the November runoff. The more liberal Roybal, a Mexican-American, counterbalanced Debs's endorsements by the *Los Angeles Times* and much of the business and civic Establishment with the backing of Ford and of Saul Alinsky–trained Latino organizers. On election day, many of Roybal's Latino supporters were challenged—unjustly and irregularly, he claimed—at the polls. The election was sufficiently close that four recounts were needed to determine the winner. Those who were active in his campaign still maintained thirty years later that Roybal was counted out (*LAT*, May 14, 1958, I:23; June 1, 1958, II:7; Sept. 16, 1958, III:3; Oct. 26, 1958, IA:3; Nov. 2, 1958, III:2; Nov. 8, 1958, I:4; Nov. 19, 1958, I:29; Montanez-Davis dep., 30–38; *LAT Magazine*, Oct. 22, 1989, 16).

The year after his hairbreadth victory over Roybal, Debs privately negotiated a deal with Fourth District supervisor Burton Chace, whose seat was up for election in 1960. Chace deeded Debs Beverly Hills, West Hollywood, and West Los Angeles, which comprised about a seventh of the people in his district. According to an insider newsletter that circulated widely in county circles and was distributed to Boundary Commission members in 1962 by the county administrative office, Chace wished to avoid a contest with rich and well-connected Los Angeles city councilwoman Rosalind Wyman. Wyman, a Democrat, probably would not oppose Democrat Debs, the newsletter explained, though she had been expected to mount a contest against Republican Chace. As predicted, Wyman did not declare her candidacy against Debs in 1962 or later (*LAN*, Nov. 24, 1962).

It is clear enough why Chace wanted to act at all (to avoid a challenge from Wyman), why he wanted to move then (because he was up for reelection in 1960), and why he could not make a deal with anyone else (only Hahn's and Debs's districts bordered on West Los Angeles, and Hahn preferred to run in a working-class, ethnically mixed constituency, not Beverly Hills). But why was Debs receptive to the deal? Why help a partisan and, presumably, ideological foe, Chace, against a more compatible possible colleague, Wyman, especially since forcing her into Debs's district might have led her to run against Debs? Why the timing? Since there was no effective equal population requirement in California before 1965, there was no legal pressure to act, and, since the 1960 census was but a year off, there were practical reasons for waiting. Why move the district west, instead of east? Debs did not attempt to take in any of Frank Bonelli's First District, the largest of the five in population, even though the largely working-class area to the east of Debs's district might seem natural territory for a Democrat. The obvious problem was that gaining territory from Bonelli would have moved Debs farther into the Latino core area, the stronghold of Ed Roybal, the candidate who had come so close to beating Debs a few months earlier. Roybal had lost neither his city council seat nor his ambition. Before Debs took in Beverly Hills, West Hollywood, and West Los Angeles, 22.7 percent of the population in his Third District had Spanish surnames. By contrast, the western area that he annexed from Chace was but 2.6 percent Spanish-surnamed, bringing the district's total in 1960 below 20 percent. Circumstances suggest, in other words, that Debs moved west to "whiten" his district. Figure 2.2 shows the 1959 addition at the western edge of the Third District.

The enactment of a new law in 1961 that mandated periodic reapportionments and required that a boundary commission be appointed to make recommendations for new lines did not change the basic mode of operation: the supervisors still negotiated changes among themselves. The commissioners were lightning rods to deflect attention and criticism away from the supervisors, as the events of 1962–63 demonstrated clearly. At a meeting on March 1, 1962, each supervisor appointed a boundary commissioner. Under chairman Emmett M. Sullivan, an experienced Long Beach politician appointed by Fourth District supervisor Burton W. Chace, the Boundary Commission delayed action until after a November referendum on expansion of the Board to seven members (*LAT*, May 15, 1963, 1, 3). Before the Board voted to put the expansion measure on the ballot, an insider publication, the *Los Angeles Newsletter*, reported that if the number of seats remained at five, there were plans to move the Third District north into the San Fernando Valley, transfer the city of Compton from Chace's Fourth District to Hahn's Second District, and shift East Los Angeles from Debs to Hahn (*LAN*, Apr. 28, 1962). This is yet another indication of Debs's apparent desire to shed Hispanic East Los Angeles.

After the defeat of the expansion proposal in November, the Boundary Commission reconvened. Again the *Newsletter* stated that Debs wanted to move his district into the San Fernando Valley and that "Debs will have to give up East Los Angeles and surrounding territory to Hahn" (*LAN*, Nov. 24, 1962). Working not only with population data but also with information

FIGURE 2.2. The Third District's Trek West and North, 1958–1971

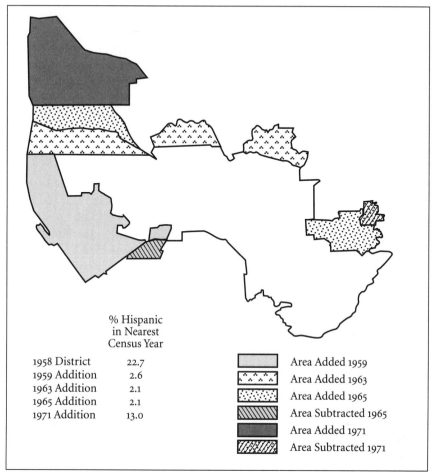

	% Hispanic in Nearest Census Year		
1958 District	22.7		Area Added 1959
1959 Addition	2.6		Area Added 1963
1963 Addition	2.1		Area Added 1965
1965 Addition	2.1		Area Subtracted 1965
1971 Addition	13.0		Area Added 1971
			Area Subtracted 1971

Sources: Based on Kousser 1991b, 619–29.

on voter registration by party, the Boundary Commission members acted as agents for their supervisors. As George Marr, a 36-year veteran in the county regional planning department who carried out staff work for the supervisorial reapportionments during this period, phrased it, each boundary commissioner "had their wish list and 'don't you dare give me that area' or 'don't you dare take this area away from me' and they would sit down and argue— pardon me—discuss the information. And then they would go back and refer to their appointers [the supervisors] to see if they should change their attitude" (Marr dep., 74). And as Boundary Commission coordinator John Leach commented in a memo to commission chairman Sullivan, after the commission had completed its report but before that report was made public: "The [Boundary] Committee approved everything that the supervisors had agreed to. . . . None of the [Boundary] Committee members will be at the Board meeting on Tuesday. I suggested they stay away, so they would not have any questions asked of them. . . . I get the definite feeling that the Board members feel adjustments will be necessary right after the 1964 elections" (Kousser 1991b, 622–23).

While secrecy facilitated horse-trading, it outraged the *Los Angeles Times* and the League of Women Voters. The report was "submitted" to the Board on April 11, 1963, but made public only on May 13, when the supervisors, after a full five minutes of discussion, with no attempt to allow comments from (other) interested parties, voted four to one to adopt it, with Hahn in dissent. The commission had considered switching 154,300 people in Alhambra, San Gabriel, Monterey Park, and South San Gabriel from the First to the Third District, but for unstated reasons left all these greater East Los Angeles areas with First District Supervisor Frank Bonelli. The principal alterations switched 52,500 people in the San Fernando Valley and 41,300 in Eagle Rock from Warren Dorn's Fifth District to Debs's Third, 52,000 in Long Beach from Bonelli's First to Chace's Fourth, and 117,300 people in Torrance, Culver City, and the Mar Vista area from the Fourth to Hahn's Second. The additions further diluted the Hispanic percentage in the Third District's population, which had been 19.8 percent in 1960, by adding territory that was only 2.1 percent Hispanic. Even after the May 13 vote, Bonelli publicly moved to shift Monterey Park and Alhambra from his bloated First District, which contained 25.9 percent of the county's population, to Debs's underpopulated Third, which included only 18.7 percent. Bonelli also proposed to shift much of the east San Gabriel Valley from his district to Dorn's Fifth, but the Board took no further action before the October 6 legal deadline. Again, Debs had shunned the offer of more territory in the Hispanic core, moving instead north over the San Gabriel Mountains and into the then predominantly Anglo San Fernando Valley areas of Sherman Oaks and Studio City and northeast into ethnically similar Eagle Rock (see Figure 2.2 above). Overall, the changes did not equalize the population between districts very much. In fact, Chace's district, which had contained 18.2 percent of the population before the 1963 redistricting, held only 17.2 percent after it (*LAT*, May 14, 1963, 1, 3; May 15, 1963, 1, 3; May 22, 1963, 1, 2).

Because the variation in population between Los Angeles County supervisorial districts was greater than allowed by the California Supreme Court decision of *Miller v. Santa Clara County* (1965), the supervisors had to redistrict again in 1965. A majority of the 1965 boundary commission had served on that of 1962–63. The commission considered a proposal by Russell Quisenberry, the appointee of Supervisor Dorn, to dislodge 90,000 people in Alhambra and San Gabriel, areas close to the Hispanic core, from Bonelli's First District and transfer them to Debs's Third. Dorn himself proposed that the change take place after the 1966 elections, apparently to decrease the threat to Debs, who was up for election then. Instead, the final report pushed Alhambra and San Gabriel into Dorn's Fifth District and moved 87,000 San Fernando Valley residents from Dorn to Debs (see Figure 2.3). Dorn termed this needlessly complicated two-stage shift "ridiculous" (Kousser 1991b, 624–26). Why did Debs insist on it? According to George Marr, the "general feeling" that Debs's staff conveyed as to why their boss desired to move further north instead of east was that the (Anglo) voters in the San Fernando Valley are "our kind of people." As Figure 2.2 shows, the population of the total area shifted to the Third District in 1965 had been only 8.3 percent Hispanic in 1960 (Marr dep., 75–76).

Perhaps seeking to avoid protests against secrecy, which the League of Women Voters had repeated in 1965, the boundary commission that was set up in 1971 (two of whose members were veterans of earlier reapportionments) cosmetically opened their hearings to the public. Appointed on April 20, the 1971 commission met three times from June 21 to July 13, adopting a plan that was subsequently ratified by the supervisors. Whether because they recognized the charade for what it was or not, members of the public did not, in fact, bother the county officers by participating (Schoeni dep., 54–55, 245–46). "Never before," Supervisor Hahn remembered in 1981, "has anyone come in to object or support" a redistricting plan (*LADN*, Sept. 23, 1981). In the words of a newspaper reporter, "redistricting sailed through with no hitches" in 1971 (*PSN*, Aug. 9, 1981). What really happened was that Richard Schoeni of the executive office of the Board met with the chief deputies of each supervisor several times, in order to determine their bosses' desires, and then drafted three comprehensive plans. Schoeni presented these to the Boundary Commission formally on July 1, and twelve days later, presumably after more off-stage negotiation, the commission agreed on a final plan. No member of the commission drew a plan or even part of one (Schoeni dep., 36–43, 54–62, 303–5; Marlow dep., 61–63). As Supervisor Hahn remarked in 1981, speaking of previous reapportionments, "It was all done by the Supervisors" (quoted in Kousser 1991b, 627).

Although neither the Boundary Commission nor the supervisors' offices appear to have been presented with explicit racial or ethnic data regarding proposed changes in each district, the results of the process continued the trends of the redistricting of the 1960s. Population was further equalized by shifting territory from the peripheral First and Fifth Districts to the more central Second, Third, and Fourth, but the switches were accomplished in

FIGURE 2.3. Two Boundary Shifts in 1965 Preserved Anglo Supremacy in the Third District

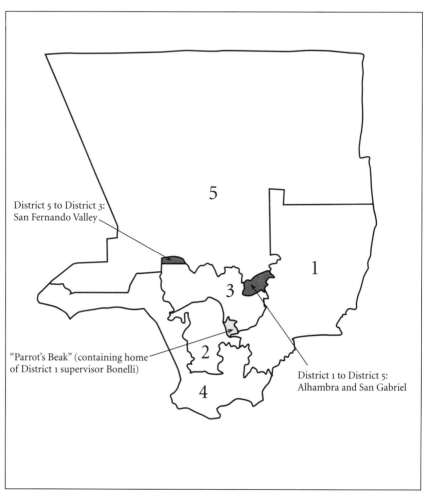

Sources: Based on Kousser 1991b, 625–26.

ways that made key incumbents more secure. Chace's Fourth District, composed predominantly of "beach cities," curled around and moved north and inland to take in conservative areas close to Orange County, such as Lakewood and Cerritos, from Bonelli's vast First District as well as similar areas from the northern part of middle-class Torrance from Hahn's south-central Second. The largest change, involving more than 150,000 people, pushed Debs's Third District farther into the San Fernando Valley, adding the overwhelmingly Anglo Van Nuys and Panorama City sections of the city of Los Angeles (see Figure 2.2 above).

Calculations based on the printed census statistics by tract, which were used in a computerized form by the 1971 redistricters, show that the populations of the districts could have been roughly equalized more simply, without creating divisions in any city except Los Angeles, in a manner that added to, rather than subtracted from the Latino percentage in the Third District. Instead of twisting the Fourth District north at its eastern boundary, it could have been moved directly north at its northern boundary, picking up the demographically similar canyon areas from Brown's Canyon west to the Ventura County line. Since the First District had more than its requisite one-fifth of the population and the Third had less, Bonelli could have deeded Debs two towns on their border, El Monte and Pico Rivera, and could have given up the eastern section of Rosemead, instead of taking in the western section, as actually happened. Such a logical, if hypothetical, shift from the First to the Third District would have given Debs an area that resembled East Los Angeles more and more every day and that in 1970 was 40.8 percent "Spanish language." Just these changes and the shift of the Palms and Rancho Park areas of Los Angeles from the Third to the Second District (which did take place) would have brought all districts within 1 percentage point of the 20.0 percent target.[5] In place of such straightforward changes, however, Debs in fact acquired an area that was not 41 percent but only 13 percent Latino. East Los Angeles formed, in effect, a semipermeable wall, allowing Hispanics, but not the boundary of the Third District, to move east.

In sum, even before 1981, redistricting was employed to strengthen incumbents, and some direct and much indirect evidence indicates that the supervisors kept the Hispanic core area split in order to preserve their offices against potential challengers who might particularly appeal to Latino voters. Specifically, repeated treks of Supervisor Ernest Debs's Third District in western and northern directions, begun almost as soon as Debs barely vanquished the first major Latino politician in modern California history, Edward Roybal, diluted the Hispanic percentage of the population in the Third District markedly. Had the Third District moved east into Alhambra, San Gabriel, and similar communities, as was proposed in 1965 and at other times, instead of west into Beverly Hills and north into Eagle Rock and the San Fernando Valley, the political and ethnic complexion of the district would have been considerably different, and Debs might well faced one or more challengers who were not, as he put it, the choice of "our kind of people."

ALTHOUGH political scientists or law professors may view redistricting as an exercise in normative or empirical theory, politicians typically approach it

FIGURE 2.4. Hypothetical and Actual 1971 Redistricting

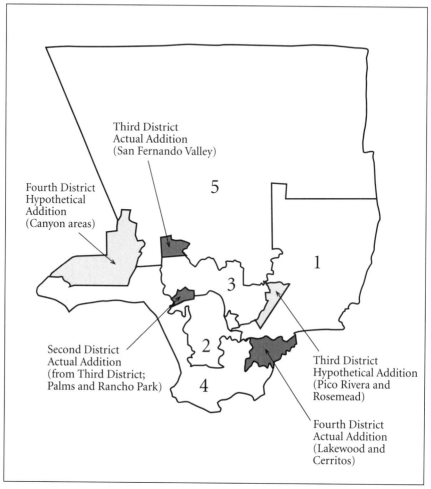

Sources: Based on Kousser 1991b, 627–28.

as a practical matter of survival and advantage. Their expectations about the effects of shifting lines in particular manners are not drawn from theory, but from their own experience. While the experience of the Los Angeles County Board of Supervisors from 1959 through 1971 provided a guide only to what would happen if the Latino percentage in a district were kept too low to be challenging to incumbent Anglos, the actions of the Los Angeles City Council in 1972 showed how to draw a possibly winnable Latino district, under what conditions one was likely to be drawn, and how a crafty and hardworking

Anglo incumbent could beat back challenges in even a majority-Hispanic district. The instance is also pertinent here because it involved then city councilman and later county supervisor Edelman, as well as many of the Latino activists who would subsequently participate in the 1981 county reapportionment. The very visible results of that redistricting, well known to everyone who followed Southern California politics during the period, helped to shape both assumptions and tactics in 1981 (Crow dep., 222).

Before 1971, Los Angeles City Council districts had been apportioned according to the number of registered voters. In that year, however, the California Supreme Court ruled in *Calderon v. City of Los Angeles* that apportionment must be based on population, and that it could take "group interests" into account. As the council's Charter and Administrative Code Committee, headed by Edelman, began to weigh different plans, Chicanos for Fair Representation (CFR), an umbrella group active in the contemporaneous statewide reapportionment, began to interest itself in the council redistricting (Santillan 1983, 122, 127–28). Actually a coalition of Hispanics and liberal Anglos, CFR asked the council to redistrict without regard to incumbency, to order all the elections for 1973 (instead of allowing those elected in 1971 to serve out their four-year terms, as the city charter provided), and to adopt a plan drawn by Clifford Lazar that made District 14 74 percent Hispanic in population and District 4 43.5 percent. The *Los Angeles Times* predicted that CFR's plan would "probably turn three incumbents out of their jobs" (*LAT*, Aug. 14, 1972, II:6).

The ambitious Edelman, who reportedly aspired to run for mayor of the City of Los Angeles if Councilman Tom Bradley lost in 1973 to incumbent Sam Yorty, as he had in 1969, was caught in something of a dilemma: No plan that inconvenienced too many incumbents could hope to secure the necessary ten votes from the Council. On the other hand, Latino activists were pressing him to concentrate enough Latinos in a few districts to make it possible to elect Latino candidates. And to become mayor, Edelman would need to attract votes from the increasingly large Hispanic population. In this case, however, Edelman's dilemma also provided an opportunity, and he took it. Another potential mayoral hopeful, Yorty ally Arthur Snyder, held the district with the second highest proportion of Hispanics, the Fourteenth. By combining three East Los Angeles Hispanic communities that had been split into four districts by previous city council lines—Lincoln Heights, Boyle Heights, and El Sereno—Edelman could make a bid for Latino support while causing trouble and perhaps defeat for an enemy (Edelman dep., 145, 154; Fitch dep., 41–49, 62; Santillan 1983, 133–34).[6]

Edelman's statement when he made his plan public in 1972 echoed ironically during the *Garza v. Los Angeles County Board of Supervisors* trial in 1990, as we shall see. Next to equalizing the population of each district, Edelman announced, the most important goal he had had in the 1972 reapportionment was serving "the interests of ethnic minorities." He had increased the Hispanic proportion in Snyder's district from 38 percent to 68 percent and added two "Hispanic growth districts," one 30 percent Hispanic in the Echo Park area and one 23 percent in the northeast San Fernando Valley. He had also kept stable the three districts then represented by African-Americans Gilbert Lindsay, Billy Mills, and Tom Bradley. His plan, he declared,

> provides an opportunity for Mexican-American representation on the Council. . . . It is my belief that the Los Angeles City Council faces both a legal and a moral duty to provide fair representation for the Mexican-American community. I might point out that above and beyond the legal requirements of the *Calderon* case, there is a more pressing moral obligation for the City Council to affirmatively act to provide an opportunity for just representation for the large and vital Mexican-American community of our city. (Kousser 1991b, 630–31)

Neither CFR nor Snyder liked Edelman's plan, both of these strange bedfellows attacking the scheme publicly on the ground that it did not go far enough toward massing the Hispanic population. MALDEF claimed that the Hispanic population proportion in the proposed Fourteenth District was actually only 57 percent and pointed out that Edelman's map still split such Hispanic areas as Echo Park, while Snyder asserted that 45 percent of the Hispanics in the district were under eighteen years old and another 40 percent were not citizens. Although he did not propose a redistricting setup himself, Snyder castigated Edelman's divisions for making it a "practical impossibility" to elect a Latino candidate in any councilmanic district. Apparently in a move to placate incumbents, MALDEF came up with another plan, this one containing three districts that its authors said were 65 percent, 45 percent, and 30 percent Hispanic, respectively. After listening to forty-three Latino witnesses endorse this MALDEF compromise and disapprove Edelman's efforts, however, the Council voted 13–1 and later 10–2 to accept Edelman's lines (Santillan 1983, 130–31; *LAT*, Sept. 9, 1972, II:1, 10).

Mayor Sam Yorty vetoed the plan on the ground that it was unfair to Latinos, although Edelman charged that Yorty's veto was merely a bid for Latino votes in the next year's mayoral race. In any case, the council quickly overrode the mayor's negative, with Snyder and Yorty ally John S. Gibson dissenting along with Marvin Braude, who charged that Edelman's plan did not go far enough, presumably meaning far enough toward creating winnable Hispanic districts. Braude, a liberal Westside Democrat, was then engaged in a hot runoff campaign for county supervisor with former assemblyman and Republican conservative James Hayes. The fact that the Beverly Hills Bar Association, an Anglo organization, was a conspicuous member of CFR, was probably not lost on Braude (*LAT,* Sept. 16, 1972, II:1, 10; Sept. 20, 1972, I:3, 24).[7]

MALDEF and several other groups sued in state court, charging unconstitutional dilution of potential Latino political power. On the basis of the relatively undeveloped case law at the time and the fact that the reapportionment substantially increased the Hispanic proportion in the Fourteenth and other districts, the state appeals court turned down the mandamus petition.[8] Although severely challenged by Hispanic candidates in repeated recalls and regular elections, Snyder survived politically until a series of scandals led him to retire in 1985 (*Castorena v. City of Los Angeles* [1973]; *LAT,* Mar. 5, 1973, II:1; Jan. 3, 1985, I:1, 3; Oct. 3, 1985, II:1, 4).

Political activists drew two contradictory lessons from Snyder's experience. On the one hand, it underlined the fact that a Hispanic population majority was no guarantee of success for Latino candidates against a "masterful" and hardworking Anglo politician who could raise more campaign funds than any other Los Angeles city councilman from oil and developer interests.[9] On the other hand, it is not so easy to be an Anglo politician in a minority district. Snyder was the first Los Angeles city councilman to be faced with a recall election since 1946. After the 1972 reapportionment, Snyder learned Spanish and hustled grants for bricks-and-mortar projects for his district. His chief opponents were Latinos who charged that he did not represent their community adequately. And his reelection victories were often by very tight margins. In 1984, for instance, he won only in a recount (*LAT,* Jan. 13, 1974, I:3; Mar. 20, 1974, I:1, 3, 19; Feb. 24, 1975, I:3; Apr. 2, 1975, I:3; Nov. 13, 1973, II:1; Oct. 3, 1985, II:1, 4; Montanez-Davis dep., 46–48). As a prelude to the 1981 Board of Supervisors' reapportionment, the case of the Fourteenth District has a third implication. The city council, led by Edelman, knew how to draw seats that would provide Latinos with better chances to elect candidates of their choice, they knew that doing so conflicted with the protection of Anglo incumbents, and when a sufficient majority could agree that one colleague was dispensable, redistricting politics could work in favor of previously excluded ethnic groups.[10]

THE HUGE size of Los Angeles County supervisors' districts has led to numerous efforts to expand the number of supervisors, and as the minority proportions of the county's population mushroomed, expansion moves became as entangled with questions of minority representation as redistricting did. Because minorities usually have less ability to raise the vast amounts of money that are necessary to run in such districts, size itself puts minority candidates at a disadvantage. Expansion has not been just a "good government" issue, with calls for closer representation on one side matched by fears that more county employees would mean more taxes on the other. For at least a half century in Los Angeles, arguments over increasing the number of supervisors have involved the representation of minority groups.

In its 1935 report to the Board of Supervisors, the Committee on Governmental Simplification recommended an expansion of the Board to fifteen members, which was large enough, the committee stated, "to be representative of different groups and sections." As the minority population in the county began to grow, supervisors asked for and received precise estimates of minority proportions. As early as 1953, for example, an internal county report focused on ethnic percentages in each supervisorial district, determining that Hahn's Second District contained 64.6 percent of the county's African-American population. In 1962, two weeks before the Board voted to put an expansion measure on the November ballot, staff from the Regional Planning Commission tabulated the number and percentage of blacks in the Second District and a portion of the Fourth District, apparently in response to a request from Hahn's office.

A Charter Study Committee Report of 1958 recommended expanding the Board to eleven members in order to provide more opportunity for people to have direct contact with their supervisors. Although Warren Dorn and Ernest Debs voted to put a proposal for a seven-person Board on the ballot, they could not obtain a third vote from another supervisor. In 1962, another Charter Study Committee Report—after much controversy over moves for a fifteen-, eleven-, or nine-member Board—finally supported a seven-member body. This time obtaining votes from the necessary three supervisors, the charter amendment providing for expansion failed in a referendum. Debs favored the expansion, a *Los Angeles Times* reporter speculated, because he was "hoping to withdraw from the East Los Angeles area into the remaining downtown, Hollywood, Beverly Hills, and West Los Angeles portions of his district." Among the reasons that supervisors gave for opposing expansion in 1962, the most revealing came in a statement at a Board meeting by Burton Chace, who fought against the change: "I can see it coming, and I can see many, many groups that are in certain areas that are going to request that they have representation on the Board of Supervisors, new Districts here and there which will be carved out of other Districts *for certain minority groups*, et cetera" (*LAN*, Apr. 28, 1962; *LAT*, May 15, 1963, I:1, 3; Chace quoted in Kousser 1991b, 635–36, italics added).

Chace was prophetic. Although the 1958 and 1962 charter study commissions had had but one member with an identifiable Spanish surname, by 1969 Latino leaders were speaking for themselves on the expansion issue. First, they pressured the Los Angeles City Council to increase its membership from fifteen to seventeen in order, in a reporter's summary, "to make

possible the election of a Mexican-American." Led by Esteban Torres, then
president of the Congress of Mexican-American Unity and later a congressman; Michael Tirado, a special assistant to Congressman Edward R. Roybal; and Miguel Garcia, then of the California Chicano Law Students Association and in 1981 state president of Californios for Fair Representation,
Latino witnesses strongly backed Councilman Tom Bradley's plea to give
Latinos a "fighting chance" to elect those "who can best articulate" their
needs. The seventeen-member plan lost by a 7-6 council vote on July 27, after
Councilman Ernani Bernardi voiced his opposition to what he called "legalized mandatory gerrymandering," but the council reversed itself three days
later, 9-6. Voters subsequently defeated the proposal, leading to a further
fifteen-year struggle that finally culminated in the election of the council's
first Latino since Roybal, Richard Alatorre, in 1985 (*LAT*, July 28, 1970, II:1;
July 31, 1970, II:1).

Between the defeat and the victory in the Los Angeles City Council, Torres
appeared before the county Board of Supervisors in a parallel effort to get
them to back a similar expansion measure (*LAT*, July 29, 1970, II:1). Torres
had been one of eleven Latino witnesses who appeared before the Los Angeles County Citizens' Economy and Efficiency Commission during its hearings
in 1969-70, where he charged that the all-Anglo Board did not understand
"the basic needs and aspirations of the Mexican-American community." District lines, Torres and his fellows asserted, had been gerrymandered to dilute
the power of Latino voters. This testimony notwithstanding, the committee
voted 14-5 not to recommend an expansion to seven seats, and the Board
voted 3-2 not to put a seven-member proposal on the ballot. The minority of
five on the Economy and Efficiency Commission favored expansion, and even
opponents recognized that the chief aim of increasing the size of the Board
was "to give representation to the minorities" (Los Angeles County Citizens'
Economy and Efficiency Commission, "Report," 1970).

Again in 1974, the Economy and Efficiency Commission debated but could
not agree on proposals for a seven-member Board and a county chief executive, but this time the deadlock apparently led the County Bar Association to
appoint a new commission, the Public Commission on Los Angeles County
Government. Headed by Seth Hufstedler, a leading downtown Los Angeles
lawyer, and Harold Williams, dean of the UCLA School of Management, the
twelve-member blue-ribbon commission, unlike the Economy and Efficiency
Commission, included female, black, and Latino members. Its 1976 report,
"To Serve Seven Million," pointedly remarked that "the narrow band of citizens from which all Supervisors have been drawn is a proper cause of grave
concern. Every successful candidate in the history of the County [since 1875]
has been a white male, as has every Sheriff, every Assessor and every District

Attorney." From 1958 to 1972, the report emphasized, there was no turnover at all in the membership of the Board of Supervisors, and three of the four who were replaced between 1972 and 1974 had either died or resigned. "Each district is so large and diverse that the cost of a serious challenge to the incumbent can be prohibitive." "The scale of these districts has too often led to under representation, particularly in the case of racial and ethnic minorities." To get this "static" government moving and to give citizens a feeling that they were represented, as well as to give minorities and women better chances to break the Anglo male monopoly of offices, the commission proposed that the Board be increased to include nine members (Los Angeles County Citizens' Economy and Efficiency Commission, "Report," 1974, 4-7; Public Commission on Los Angeles County Government 1976, 22, 23, 69-70).

The ethnic representation issue, along with opponents' charges that expansion would lead to an increase in taxes, was central to the subsequent referendum. The first reason that the *Los Angeles Times* gave for endorsing Proposition B, the nine-member move, was that it raised "the probability that [the Board] would become more representative of ethnic districts—and it could also result in the election of the first woman supervisor in history." The Charter Amendment Task Force noted that Proposition B would "increase the ability of the two principal minorities—the black and the Latin Americans— to elect representatives of their own race." As the November vote approached, the *Los Angeles Times*, advertisements, and ballot arguments for Proposition B downplayed the ethnic representation issue, presumably because proponents recognized the unpopularity of such representation with the Anglos who comprised an overwhelming majority of the electorate. Although many leading Democrats and such groups as the AFL-CIO, the League of Women Voters, and the Chamber of Commerce endorsed Proposition B, the only major Republican to do so was Sheriff Peter Pitchess. Supervisors James A. Hayes, Peter F. Schabarum, and Baxter Ward publicly denounced Proposition B, which subsequently lost by a 65-35 margin (*LAT*, June 23, 1976, II:6; Oct. 31, 1976, VIII:1; Nov. 1, 1976, I:24; Nov. 4, 1976, II:1).

AS THE 1980 elections approached, Democrats held a 4-1 majority on the Board of Supervisors. New Deal liberal Kenneth Hahn, first elected in 1952, had been joined by former newscaster and maverick Democrat Baxter Ward, who had upset Warren M. Dorn in the Fifth District in 1972, and by Westside Los Angeles city councilman Edmund Edelman, who had succeeded Ernest Debs in 1974. When Republican James Hayes unexpectedly resigned in 1979, Governor Edmund G. ("Jerry") Brown Jr. appointed Yvonne B. Burke to be the first black and the first woman member in Board history. Burke had been elected to the state assembly in 1967 and to Congress in 1972, both from nonblack-majority districts. She had gained national attention as vice-chair of the 1972 Democratic National Convention and statewide exposure as the Democratic nominee in an open race for state attorney-general against George Deukmejian in 1978. Up to the point that the Deukmejian campaign began running television commercials with ethnic overtones that attacked Burke's views on busing and the death penalty, Burke's polls, she later remembered, showed her 9 percentage points ahead (Burke dep., 8–16, 19–22). She lost by 3 percent of the vote.

Even though the Fourth District was two-thirds Anglo and less than 10 percent black, 61.9 percent of those who registered with one of the two major parties were Democrats, and Jerry Brown had carried the district in the 1978 governor's race by a 59–41 margin. Intelligent, photogenic, diligent, and very accustomed to interacting with overwhelmingly white groups, Burke began a flurry of activity immediately after her appointment—meeting with local officials who had often felt neglected by the distant Hayes, focusing on non-controversial community projects such as cleaning up the beaches and fighting petty crime, and conciliating developers who feared that she would be ideologically opposed to any growth. Born and raised in South Central Los Angeles, but by 1978 a resident of stylish Brentwood, Burke self-consciously presented herself as an "ethnic crossover" politician, a role that easily attracted plentiful positive media coverage. By January 1980, all of Burke's well-known Republican potential opponents—State Senator Bob Beverly, whose district covered a third of the Fourth District, former state controller Houston Flournoy, Assemblyman Paul Priolo, Assemblywoman Marylyn Ryan, State Senator Ollie Speraw, former county assessor Philip Watson, former congressman Alphonzo Bell, and Long Beach mayor Tom Clark—had decided to pass up the race. Burke's name was known to 90 percent of a sample in the district, those sampled were much more likely to view her favorably than unfavorably, and she led Bell and Flournoy by 16 percentage points in a private poll run by Republican political consultant Allan Hoffenblum and probably paid for by Schabarum. Another consideration that eliminated her strongest undeclared opponent, Beverly, was how to deal with the matter of her race. "There are those who want to beat Yvonne who are racists or close to it," Beverly told the *Los Angeles Times*. "That's one thing that bothers me. What do you do with their support? I don't know how you handle that" (*LAT*, June 15, 1979, I:1, 26; Dec. 1, 1979, I:28; Dec. 9, 1979, II:1; Jan. 28, 1980, I:3, 21; Sept. 22, 1980, II:3; *LAT Magazine*, Oct. 22, 1989, 8–18; Burke dep., 79–80; Smith dep., 307–10).

Deane Dana, a plainspoken, undemonstrative, middle-level telephone company executive, who had never before run for public office, and his campaign manager Ron Smith, a Republican political consultant who boasted of his tough campaign tactics, were not as reticent as Beverly. One of ten comparative unknowns facing Burke—it was just the type of contest pollster Hoffenblum had worried in January that Burke would carry by a majority in the primary—Dana had to adopt aggressive tactics to differentiate himself from the pack of conservative, Republican, white male candidates and to hope to force Burke into a two-person November runoff. The Board's single Republican, Schabarum, backed a former lobbyist for apartment house owners, Mike O'Donnell, whose attempt to tie Burke to white liberals Tom Hayden and Jane Fonda apparently fell flat. O'Donnell's distribution just before the primary of a tabloid that contained critical statements about Burke by local officials also did nothing to help his campaign, for several of the officials quickly disavowed the statements attributed to them. O'Donnell finished with 7.9 percent of the vote. By contrast, Dana capitalized on an endorsement by Deukmejian, whose home was in Long Beach, to edge into the runoff with 21 percent of the vote to Burke's 42 percent (Shumate dep., 378; Burke dep., 56; *LAT*, Jan. 28, 1980, I:3, 21; Apr. 26, 1980, I:16; May 29, 1980, II:1, 5; June 5, 1980, I:3, 25).

Behind by 12 percentage points in August and 10 in September, facing an incumbent who had represented areas of the district for thirteen years and who had raised more than twice as much money as all her opponents combined in the primary, Dana and Smith resorted to the most openly racist campaign in the recent history of the Los Angeles County Board of Supervisors (*LAT*, May 6, 1980, II:1; Sept. 22, 1980, II:1, 3; Oct. 17, 1980, II:1, 7).[11] Initially, Smith later admitted, he had not planned to emphasize busing, which he disingenuously characterized as not "a racial issue at all" (Smith dep., 309–10, 322).[12] It seems that Burke's lead changed Smith's mind. Even though the Board had no influence whatsoever over pupil placement policies in the public schools, Smith/Dana's billboards proclaimed that "Yvonne Burke Lied on Busing," their television and radio advertisements echoed the theme, and a slick *Time Magazine*-like brochure reiterated charges of Burke's alleged endorsement of "forced busing" three times in seven pages. Burke edged away from earlier votes to allow—not require—busing for integration purposes in some circumstances and generally attempted to downplay the issue of race. To counter the "soft on crime" image created by her race and her anti–death penalty stance, which Deukmejian had exploited effectively in the 1978 election for attorney general, Burke trumpeted her endorsement by Republican Los Angeles sheriff Peter Pitchess, who was then embroiled in a bitter personal feud with Schabarum. Burke's last leaked poll showed her ahead by 4 points, with 18 percent undecided, while Dana's called the contest a dead heat (*LAT*, Sept. 13, 1980, III:14; Oct. 22, 1980, II:1, 6; Oct. 27, 1980, II:1, 10; Nov. 2, 1980, II:1, 2; Burke dep., 19–22, 41–43, 47, 49–50, 56; Schabarum dep., 341–42).

Undoubtedly realizing that partisan and ideological control of the Board hung in the balance, conservative Republican leader Schabarum provided Dana with a last-minute infusion of $100,000, a sixth of Dana's total spending, that sent a two-page mailer, designed by Smith, into culturally conservative white areas of the district. For a serious challenger to display a photograph of his opponent prominently in his own campaign literature, especially if he is not glamorous and the incumbent is a former model, would seem a foolish campaign tactic under most circumstances. But below a darkened picture of Burke, the flyer emphasized not only the contrast between Dana's opposition to "forced busing of school children" and Burke's purported support of it but also invoked the classic American racist image, accusing Burke of opposing "mandatory prison for rape." Despite denunciations of such tactics as "racist" by prominent white male politicians, the Smith/Dana tactics succeeded, as the Burke lead faded in the last weekend, and Dana won by 53 percent to 47 percent (*LAT*, Nov. 2, 1980, II:1, 2; Nov. 6, 1980, I:17; Nov. 11, 1980, II:1, 2; Burke dep., 41–43, 61–62; Dana dep., 232; Schabarum dep., 87, 109–11).

The Fifth District contest between incumbent Baxter Ward and challenger Mike Antonovich attracted less media attention than that between Burke and Dana. A fiscal conservative, Ward had sometimes voted with Schabarum and Hayes to keep expenditures down, but when health and welfare benefits for the poor were at issue, he was much more generous than the Board's Republicans were. Blunt and outspoken, Ward refused to take money from developers and was willing to look Schabarum in the eye, detail the campaign contributions that Schabarum had received from someone with a matter currently up for a vote, and ask Schabarum to recuse himself. In the primary, the widely known former television newsman had refused to take any contributions over $50 or to hire a professional campaign manager. Antonovich, a personable, very right-wing assemblyman who had run unsuccessfully for the Republican nomination for lieutenant governor in 1978, raised several hundred thousand dollars, much of it from north county developers, with a small, symbolic contribution directly from Schabarum. After a ferocious campaign in which, Ward felt, Antonovich purposely distorted Ward's record, Antonovich won by a 55–45 margin. Last-minute advertisements and targeted mail overcame a reported 5 percent Ward lead (Stern 1989, chap. 11; *LAT*, Apr. 26, 1980, I:16; May 6, 1980, II:1; May 29, 1980, II:1, 5; June 5, 1980, I:3, 21, 25; Oct. 16, 1980, II:1, 5; Antonovich dep., 11–14, 22–23, 120–21; Schwellenbach dep., 38–46, 57–60, 87–88).

In an invisible campaign in the Second District in 1980, Kenneth Hahn, a seven-term Anglo incumbent in a district that was 42.2 percent African-American, buried the second-place finisher by 88 percent to 9 percent.

But with majorities among the lowest in the Board elections since 1970, the new Schabarum-led majority could not have felt very secure. Schabarum, after all, had avoided a runoff in 1978 by a mere 6 percent against the minor opposition of Covina mayor Elaine Donaldson, an underfinanced conservative Republican, and two nominal candidates. A private poll in 1982 showed that only a third of Schabarum's constituents had heard of him and had a favorable opinion of him. Antonovich had ousted Ward by less than landslide proportions, while Dana and Smith might find it even more difficult to overcome a white male opponent. No doubt, Antonovich and Dana could expect increasing funds to flow into their coffers after 1981, and Schabarum had money to spare, but their districts were hardly "ideal" for them, affording "no way to strengthen the Board Majority" through redistricting, as Smith later averred. Moreover, the Hispanic and Asian populations of Schabarum's district were growing rapidly, amounting to 40.3 percent of the district population in 1980 and projected to rise to 48.6 percent by 1985. Like Edelman, whose district was 41.8 percent Latino and 8.7 percent Asian in 1980, Schabarum could not be too sanguine about his political future if his district's boundaries remained the same (*LAT*, May 30, 1978, II:1, 6; Schabarum dep., 269; Smith dep., 54–57, 139; Kousser 1991b, 644).

THE 1981 redistricting—a complex, convoluted process that produced an extremely simple result—was a melodrama fit for the county whose dominant industry is Hollywood. Intricate plotting; fascinating characters, some colorful, some barely visible; bloviated rhetoric that caricatured even politics; false starts, false denouements, and loose ends—all led only to an anticlimax. The hopes of Republicans and Latinos were raised and dashed; the schemes of Republicans and Democrats were intricately woven, only to unravel; in the end, demographic reality and previously irrelevant formal rules about the process of redistricting shaped the outcome. The necessity of obtaining at least four votes from the five supervisors, the unwillingness of politicians to turn their electoral futures over to people over whom they have no control, and the resolve of the two Democrats, Hahn and Edelman, to stick together no matter what and their stubbornness in the face of the onslaught of their partisan/ideological foes and pressures from their usual allies in the Latino community insured that the status quo, designed to split the Hispanic population concentrations, would be maintained.

Hahn and Edelman's strategy took advantage of the fact that population growth in Los Angeles County during the 1970s was spread remarkably evenly across supervisorial districts. The largest district, the Third, was only 1.1 percent over the 20 percent equality level in 1980, while none of the other districts contained less than 19 percent of the people. To express the same figures in another way, the difference between the percentages in the largest and smallest districts was about 10 percent of the population of a single supervisorial district. As county regional planner George Marr noted in a 1978 memo and a later deposition, "if all you were doing was equalizing the population," there was no need to make "massive changes in the boundaries" (Bush dep., 86–87; Dana dep., 388; Edelman dep., 210, 213, 284, 322–23, 326–27; Garcia dep., 60; Hoffenblum dep., 69–70, 159, 186, 189, 221, 296–97, 369; Huerta dep., 45; Marr dep., 174; Pozorski dep., 120; Quezada dep., 31–32, 88–91; Seymour dep., 627–29, 644; Shumate dep., 226–27; Smith dep., 50, 52, 165–66; *SGVT,* Aug. 13, 1981). In retrospect, an incumbent gerrymander that shifted district lines only to satisfy population equality seems to have been inevitable.

At the beginning of 1981, however, different results seemed possible to two groups. To Pete Schabarum and his protégés who formed the new Board majority, and especially to two brash, aggressive Republican political consultants, Ron Smith and Allan Hoffenblum, it seemed likely that the Republicans could solidify their tenuous hold on the suburban Board seats while creating problems for their partisan enemies and building goodwill with Hispanics. To Latino activists, the rapid but uneven growth of the Hispanic population entitled it to ethnic representation or at least more influence, and they were able and willing to combine both insider and outsider tactics to further Latino political power. Anglo Republicans, counting on a de facto alliance of convenience with Hispanics to help them overcome Democratic majorities in the state legislature and to coerce Hahn and Edelman into acquiescing in changes that doomed them to permanent powerlessness, facilitated the organization of the Latino activists and gave them free but limited access to the computerized redistricting operation at the Rose Institute. In the end, however, the curious combination never really came together, incremental changes in boundary lines preserved the supervisorial fault line in East Los Angeles and did nothing further to shore up shaky Republican control, and both the Latino and Republican activists went away discouraged and angry at each other as well as at the Democrats (Dana dep., 274, 369; Edelman dep., 244–45; Heslop dep., 178, 203; Hoffenblum dep., 57, 67, 70–71, 157, 245, 280–81; Huerta dep., 37–38, 40; Quezada dep., 24–26, 48–50, 75, 114, 118; Santillan dep., 17–20, 31–32; Shumate dep., 158, 214–15, 219, 222–23, 235–37, 272, 358–59; Smith dep., 44–46, 67, 89, 104, 223; Uranga dep., 67–69, 72).

A February 1981 "lettergram" sent to Schabarum and Antonovich under Dana's imprimatur, but probably written by Ron Smith, proposed the establishment of a "non-public reapportionment committee" composed of representatives of the three Republicans. Since, in its words, "the power in reapportionment is information," the memo proposed either using the resources of the Rose Institute, a nonprofit group at Claremont McKenna College headed by Alan Heslop, former executive director of the California State Republican Central Committee and still a very active campaign consultant to Republican candidates, or purchasing Rose data and buying data processing services elsewhere. Rose had proposed to make available to the public boundary commission population, ethnic, and political data for $23,950, but the memo writer believed that even more political data would be necessary. Using Rose would save money, but it would mean that the extensive political data would have to be shared with representatives of Hahn and Edelman, who, the writer smirked, "would try to stop our attempts for a fair reapportionment." If the public boundary commission did not make use of Rose, the Democrats would have to rely strictly on nonpolitical data, which was appropriate because "after all, their [the Boundary Commission's] decisions really should not be made on a political basis." This and the additional secrecy it afforded tilted the writer toward an operation that had no connection with Rose, even though it might cost $47,000. In either case, he proposed hiring as an expert Joseph Shumate, Smith's partner in a political consulting firm, who, he noted, "was instrumental in the Republican [state] reapportionment of 1970, 1971, and 1972" (Dana dep., 164–65, 174–76, 179, 182; Heslop dep., 137, 331–33; Smith dep., 72–73, 77–78, 81, 85–87).[13]

Disregarding the fear that employment of Rose would raise suspicions of Republican partisanship, the Republican supervisors bought Shumate's advice for $18,000 and charged data collection and processing costs to the county. Rose, which had collected extensive census and political data and designed a frilly reapportionment software package called REDIS under an $800,000–$1,000,000 grant from the California Business Roundtable, eventually set a price of $30,000 for the county's use of it. The data they proposed to deliver included statistics on "voter turnout and ethnic participation in the political process," and the contract specified a special allocation of $1,500 for unspecified "ethnic Hispanic data"—an indication of how transfixed by ethnicity everyone involved in the 1981 process was from the beginning. Charging $10,000 as "user fee" for the REDIS system, which had already been paid for by the Roundtable grant and $3,000 for training in the use of REDIS— instruction, that, according to Rose's chief technician, Robert Walters, took only one to two hours—the contract, which was let to Rose over the objections of county staff and with no competitive bidding, was no bargain for the financially strapped local government. In fact, it is doubtful that anyone with an official position in the county reapportionment effort used Rose at all. According to their testimony, no boundary commissioner, supervisor, supervisorial deputy, or county employee drew or evaluated a plan at Rose, although an intern in Schabarum's office, Mike Haines, did apparently use Rose facilities to plot a map that lumped minorities into the Hahn and Edelman districts but drew no precise boundaries between the Democratic seats. Shumate, a private employee of the Republicans who had no independent contract with Rose, did use data from Rose but, as he remembers it, drew only one plan, and that mostly by hand calculations from paper copies of computer printout. All of Rose's bells and whistles, then, allowed one intern to sketch out a rough partisan plan that clustered minorities helter-skelter into the Democratic districts and that never seems to have been considered at all seriously by anyone (Bush dep., 46, 48; Crow dep., 37; Fitch dep., 164, 168, 194; Heslop dep., 133–37, 141, 180, 188, 208–9, 211–12, 298, 362, 371; Hoffenblum dep., 78; Lewis dep., 70, 75, 78, 133; Marr dep., 162; Schoeni dep., 112–17, 130, 133–34; Seymour dep., 122–24; Shumate dep., 53, 55, 160–61, 164–66, 174–76, 225–27; Smith dep., 138, 150–53, 157, 160, 164; Turner dep., 234–35; Walters dep., 36–37, 69, 120–21; *LAT*, Aug. 17, 1981, I:26).

IT IS instructive to conjecture how the Democrats would have handled the 1981 county reapportionment if Ward and Burke, instead of Antonovich and Dana, had been successful in 1980. Hahn and Edelman, recently reelected with 88 percent and 74 percent of the vote, respectively, could easily have afforded changes in their districts. Had Ward been reelected after having been outspent by better than ten to one by a vigorous, seasoned campaigner, he would have seemed quite formidable to other potential challengers. Burke's district being adjacent to Hahn's, she, probably the weakest of the Democrats, could have swapped him some working-class whites near Orange County for some of his South Central blacks.[14] Assuming that Latino pressure on the Board would have been as well organized and vociferous as it was in the actual circumstances in 1981, the Democrats probably would have responded as Edelman and his fellow Democrats on the Los Angeles City Council did in 1972: they would have cut up Schabarum's district, as they had done to abrasive, conservative Republican Art Snyder's in 1972, and given him a substantial Hispanic population majority. After all, Hahn disliked Schabarum intensely, both for his politics and for the fact that Schabarum had thwarted Hahn's ambition to succeed in the normal rotation to the chairmanship of the Board of Supervisors. Burke no doubt would have sought revenge for Schabarum's major role in recruiting and financing her opponents. And Ward detested Schabarum, whom he thought a creature of special interests. Furthermore, by uniting the Hispanic core in one district, the Democrats could have appeared responsive to one of their key constituencies, and they might have kept Republican activists so busy trying to save Schabarum that they would have left the Democrats on the Board alone at election time for awhile (Stern 1989, chap. 11; Crow dep., 98; Schwellenbach dep., 38, 64–65; *LAT*, Nov. 2, 1980, II:1, 2; Sept. 29, 1989, II:2).

Since they instead faced a 3–2 Republican majority, the Democrats adopted a strictly defensive posture and, from the beginning, sought a redistricting as close to the status quo as possible. As Hahn's longtime deputy, Mas Fukai, remarked later, Hahn's preference in 1981 was for "just keeping everything he had and keeping it the same . . . he liked the district as it was." Hahn's boundary commissioner Robert Bush told a reporter after the first meeting of the commission, "I don't think that we will be changing all those boundaries very much" (Fukai dep., 64–65, 67; *LADN*, July 9, 1981; similarly, see Fitch dep., 168, 177–78, 219; Seymour dep., 93–94, 682).

The Democrats were just as "political" and secretive in their efforts to maintain the status quo as the Republicans were in their efforts to change it radically. Each supervisor in 1981 designated one aide as a reapportionment liaison. Schabarum and Antonovich named their chief deputies, Mike Lewis and Kathleen Crow, respectively, and Dana picked his former campaign manager, Ron Smith, who had very temporarily been placed on the county payroll. Hahn selected Fukai, while Edelman chose Jeff Seymour. A member of Edelman's city council staff from 1972 to 1974 and of his supervisorial staff from 1974 on, Seymour was intensely partisan, having been president of Young Democratic clubs in high school and at two colleges and a member of the county and state Democratic central committees. Edelman's former chief deputy, Alma Fitch, who worked with Seymour for nearly a decade, ranked him as one of the most "political" persons in Edelman's office, giving him "an eight or nine" for that trait on a scale of one to ten. As Edelman's chief liaison to the Jewish community, Seymour boasted of close personal connections to the Westside "machine" of Howard and Michael Berman and Henry Waxman (Edelman dep., 260–65; Fitch dep., 202; Seymour dep., 21–26, 43, 85, 163; Smith dep., 11).

On May 11, two and a half months after the "private reapportionment" memo circulated among the Republicans, Seymour sent Edelman a parallel lettergram setting out, at least in part, their aims in reapportionment. "I will be preparing a political analysis of the district to show your strongest areas," Seymour told the supervisor. In particular, Seymour asked Edgar Hayes, director of the county's data processing department, and Leonard Panish, county registrar-recorder, to arrange for county staffers to merge population and electoral data for the Third Supervisorial District in order to determine how the people in each census tract voted in the presidential, congressional, and gubernatorial contests from 1976 to 1980, the Burke-Deukmejian attorney-general's race, the Proposition 13 local taxation limit and the 1980 Gann state tax limitation initiative, the 1973 Bradley-Yorty mayoral election, and a few others, apparently later including Edelman's own 1978 supervisorial race, in which he had two Latino opponents. In addition,

Seymour wanted the voter registration by party in each census tract. After a meeting on June 9, attended by county staff members from the offices of Hayes and Panish as well as the engineering department, computer program-mers Donald Gilbert and Peter Fonda-Bonardi matched electoral and census units and spewed out paper copies, giving Seymour what he asked for. Fonda-Bonardi reported being directed by his superiors not to discuss the work he was doing with voting returns: "There was an atmosphere of 'keep it quiet' . . . My impression was that only one supervisor [Edelman, through Seymour] had asked us for this data, and he didn't want the other supervisors to have these services" (Seymour dep., 155, 173–74, 272–94, 300–301; Bannister dep., 59, 69, 75, 85–86, 89, 91; Edelman dep., 260–72; Gilbert dep., 13–14, 20; Marlow dep., 94–95; Marr dep., 144–48; Fonda-Bonardi dep., 23–24, 29, 50–52, 81).

Since the costs of data collection, programming, and computing time were absorbed into county expenses, Seymour's hush-hush political redistricting effort cost Edelman even less—nothing—than the Republicans' effort cost them. Seymour's operation was also entirely negative and defensive in nature. To draw lines that differed much from the status quo, one would need statis-tics on all the districts, but Seymour asked only for data on the Third. Even to make large changes in the Third, a 335-page printed copy by census tract, not aggregated into cities or recognized communities, was very unwieldy. Be-cause Rose's software allowed someone to redraw lines and quickly reaggre-gate population, ethnic, and political totals, it was tailor-made for aggressive, radical blitzkriegs. By contrast, Seymour's handiwork was a Maginot line.

SUPERVISOR Deane Dana's March 17, 1981 motion for the Board to appoint a boundary commission set out as one of the commission's goals to "ensure that ethnic minorities are equitably represented." A colloquy in that day's Board meeting, however, sliced through the affirmative action rhetoric to get to the incumbent-protecting reality. After Supervisor Edelman mused that "certainly this [the appointment of the Commission] will take some of the heat off the Board of Supervisors in doing the reapportionment," Supervisor Hahn shot back: "No, it won't. How do you say that, Mr. Edelman? The heat will all be here. We'll just appoint our people and we'll tell them what to do. And they'll say, 'Cut this person out and put this city in. . . .' That's the way it works" (Kousser 1991b, 652).

The commission's chairman Blake Sanborn, an insurance broker, former city councilman in and mayor of suburban Whittier, Republican activist, and Supervisor Schabarum's representative, does not appear to have played much of a role on the commission and in 1989 recalled almost nothing about the 1981 redistricting. Hahn's choice, Robert Bush, a former newsman who had been a senior deputy in Hahn's office from 1969 to October 1979, played a canny, almost teasing role in the process. Frank to admit that he was "essentially representing his [Hahn's] interests on the Boundary Commission," Bush repeatedly dangled before the Republicans the hope that they might get his vote if they made a few more concessions, but he always drew back, much to their consternation. Bush's ally on the commission, Alma Fitch, had been active in the liberal California Democratic Council during its heyday in the 1950s and 60s. Joining Edelman's city council staff in 1968, she played an active role in the 1972 city council reapportionment and became Edelman's chief deputy when he joined the Board in 1975, resigning in March 1981 to form her own political consulting firm. Like Bush, she reportedly led the Republicans to think that she might go along with a modified version of their proposed lines, but she never really agreed to anything (Bush dep., 9–14, 68, 73, 81; Fitch dep., 40–49, 78–84; Hoffenblum dep., 69–70, 157, 159, 186, 292, 351; Sanborn dep., 8–10; Smith dep., 50, 52, 177–80, 272–74).

The most "vocal" members of the commission, according to Fitch and others, were Ron Smith and Allan Hoffenblum. Smith began working for the Republican Party in high school, and by the time he graduated from college he was a veteran of both a gubernatorial and a presidential campaign. As an employee of the state Republican apparatus in 1971–72, he assisted in the state Republican redistricting effort. Forming a San Francisco political consulting firm in 1973 with two other Republican activists, Joseph Shumate and Emily Pike, he managed several Northern California campaigns before engineering Dana's controversial last-minute triumph in 1980, an achievement that made Smith a hot commodity on the lecture circuit (Burke dep., 56; Fitch dep., 151; Smith dep., 8–9, 285–89; Turner dep., 123–24).

Smith claimed to have acted in civics-textbook fashion in 1981. When approaching redistricting, one should not have in mind "if X gets elected, then they'll have more health services," he later asserted. "What you should be thinking about is the process of how they elect the people, not the result of that election, of the actions of the kinds of people who are elected. That shouldn't come into consideration." Despite the tight margins of the Republican supervisorial victories in 1980, Smith reported, "we weren't trying to make the three Republicans better districts. That was not a goal because it wasn't necessary." Unlike other commissioners, Smith said, "I did not perceive myself to be on that committee as an agent of Deane Dana. . . . In that role, my goal was to have it be as nonpolitical as possible." Not only did he simply want to draw "a fair redistricting plan," he even attributed the same motive to his Democratic adversaries on the commission: "I had a feeling that the politicos on the Boundary Commission all felt this: this was our one chance to propose something that was, quote, good government." He never "ever" felt, he recalled, that Bush and Fitch torpedoed his plan because they saw it as strengthening the Republican majority on the Board. Republicans, so far as Smith, the state chairman for the 1983 Sebastiani reapportionment plan, knew, had never conducted a redistricting "which disadvantaged minorities." He, Hoffenblum, and Shumate "went into this with hopes of coming up with a district that maximized Hispanic empowerment in the county. . . . We weren't going to get any brownie points for having this Hispanic district. We were doing it because it was the right thing to do." "[A] fair redistricting plan," he asserted, "will help Republicans . . . we really wanted to have a process where there were fair lines drawn" (Smith dep., 41, 54–57, 65, 67, 108, 136, 139, 171, 212–13, 220–21).

After graduating from the University of Southern California in 1962 with a major in radio and television broadcasting and serving in the Air Force, Allan Hoffenblum got his first job with the Republican Party, and has been in politics ever since. From 1968 to 1972, he was an area director of the party in Los Angeles County, and in the latter year he became the county director of the Committee to Reelect the President (CREEP). A member of the Republican State Central Committee for a decade, he generally attended the party's state convention (Hoffenblum dep., 9–11, 384).

The first campaign in which Hoffenblum was the de facto campaign manager is particularly relevant to his activities on the Boundary Commission. A series of retirements during 1970 and 1971 left the East Los Angeles Forty-eighth Assembly District open in November 1971 at the same time that the state legislature was trying to negotiate a redistricting arrangement. A tentative agreement on reapportionment hinged on a victory in the Forty-eighth by Richard Alatorre, who hoped to become the assembly's third Mexican-American representative. Seeking to sabotage the pact, Republican activists from Sacramento flew down to try to help Bill Brophy, an Anglo millionaire who was the only Republican in the contest, try to garner over 50 percent of all the votes in what was expected to be a low-turnout primary. When Brophy was forced into a runoff with Alatorre and two candidates from the minor Peace and Freedom and *La Raza Unida* parties, the activists returned north, assuming an Alatorre victory in the overwhelmingly Democratic district (Alatorre dep., 16; Hoffenblum dep., 12, 405–7; *LAT*, Nov. 17, 1971, I:19).

Only Hoffenblum persevered. "I took the initiative and was able to raise the funds necessary to design some mailers that went into selective precincts," he remembered seventeen years later (Hoffenblum dep., 405–7). One last-minute mailer from a nonexistent "Democratic League of Voters" with a mailing address in a vacant lot, signed by a pseudonymous "Patrick S. Sherman" and sent to Anglo areas of the district, denounced Alatorre as not a true Democrat. Another, which featured a darkened picture of Alatorre, attempted to tie him to violent Hispanic groups. Key to Brophy's eventual 4.5

percent plurality was the 7.9 percent of the votes that Raul Ruiz of *La Raza Unida* garnered. "Brophy didn't win this," Ruiz crowed. "We did." According to Henry Waxman, who was then chairman of the Assembly Elections and Reapportionment Committee, "The reason we lost was a cynical alliance of neo-segregationists in the Chicano community with the Republican party" (*LAT*, Nov. 16, 1971, I:3; Nov. 17, 1971, I:19; Nov. 18, 1971, I:3, 23). Alatorre was blunter, charging that "the Republican Party financed" *La Raza Unida*'s campaign, the high point of the minor party's electoral success in the state (Alatorre dep., 72–73).

Hoffenblum proudly claimed credit for the victory. It was "the only campaign that I was basically responsible for the outcome [in] . . . I called the shots," he remembered (Hoffenblum dep., 12, 405–7). This last phrase echoes with doubtless unconscious irony, in light of the most spectacular incident in the Brophy-Alatorre contest. After a late dinner the night before the election, Brophy and his administrative assistant Bill King had just returned to Brophy's Highland Park home when some undetermined person fired eight to ten rounds from a .22 caliber rifle through Brophy's front window. No one was hurt. Dramatic pictures and extensive television and radio coverage on election day "gave Brophy publicity and momentum we had never hoped to achieve," according to an anonymous Republican strategist quoted in the *Los Angeles Times*. Much to the amusement of his Sacramento colleagues, Republican Paul Priolo announced on the assembly floor the day after the election that "he was acting as a broker for [Republican] caucus Chairman [John] Stull, who had worked in Brophy's campaign. 'Mr. Stull has for sale a slightly used .22 rifle,' Priolo said" (*LAT*, Nov. 17, 1971, I:19; Nov. 18, 1971, I:23). Alatorre found the incidents less humorous. The contest, he charged, "was used as the training grounds for what ended up being the dirty tricks during the Nixon re-election campaign" (Alatorre dep., 72–73).

The man who actually drew the plans for the Republicans was Joseph Shumate, Smith's partner in the San Francisco political consulting firm. A user rather than a designer of computer software systems, Shumate had been a campaign strategist for the Republican State Central Committee from 1969 to 1972. Along with Smith and others, he drew redistricting plans for Congress and the state legislature, taking into account, he said later, age, race, income, education, registration, and past voter history in order to maximize Republican representation. At Smith's suggestion, Shumate was hired by the Republican supervisors to draw plans and to advise them of the effects of various plans on "their re-election efforts." More forthright than his partner, he acknowledged that what Dana wanted out of reapportionment was "a district that he could win" and admitted that he did not flesh out a proposal that would have added Hispanics to Schabarum's district primarily because "it would have done political harm to Supervisor Schabarum . . . eventually he would have faced a viable Hispanic" (Shumate dep., 27, 30, 47–48, 136, 158, 219–20).

In 1983, Smith, Hoffenblum, and Shumate collaborated again on the radical Sebastiani Initiative, Smith as state chairman, Hoffenblum as media coordinator, and Shumate as principal line drawer. This state-level reapportionment plan, drawn at the Rose Institute, was opposed by many leaders of both political parties and virtually all African-American and Latino activists. The Sebastiani (or Shumate) plan cut the number of assembly districts that were 35 percent or more Hispanic in population from seven to four. It switched the residences of Assemblyman Alatorre and then newly elected State Senator Art Torres, as well as that of Assembly Speaker Willie Brown, into new districts with much lower percentages of minorities than in their current districts; Torres's district, for example, became 21 percent Hispanic, instead of 71 percent. In San Diego and San Bernardino Counties, it sliced up existing minority concentrations in the districts of incumbent Latinos Peter Chacon and Reuben Ayala. At the congressional level, the scheme destroyed Edward Roybal's district and threw him into a new, 16 percent Hispanic district against six-term incumbent Anglo Republican Carlos Moorhead, merged the districts of freshmen Marty Martinez and Esteban Torres and created a new, population-majority Hispanic district in southern Los Angeles County that included the heavily conservative city of Downey. Two congressional seats then held by blacks in Los Angeles County were merged with two Westside seats that contained Anglo Democratic incumbents, at the least forcing painful black-Jewish conflicts and at the most causing blacks to lose seats. Throughout the state, blacks were packed into fewer and fewer seats. Both MALDEF and African-American leaders joined a successful suit in the state supreme court to keep the Sebastiani-Smith-Shumate-Hoffenblum Initiative off the ballot (Hoffenblum dep., 423–27; *LAT,* July 7, 1983, I:24; July 10, 1983, I:1; Aug. 27, 1983, I:25; Sept. 13, 1983, II:5).

These, then, were the most aggressive members of the 1981 boundary commission: Ron Smith, fresh from ending the political career of the only member of a racial minority group to sit on the Board of Supervisors in a century, and Allan Hoffenblum, who still vividly remembered the first campaign that he had been "responsible" for, one that employed questionable means to choke off, temporarily at least, an opportunity to elect a second Latino assemblyman from Los Angeles County. Their private technician was a practical line drawer who in the 1970s and again in 1983 designed or helped to design districts throughout the state that used every device to minimize the power of ethnic minorities. Asked why he favored creating a "Latino district" on the Board in 1981, Hoffenblum responded: "I've always believed in civil rights . . . and I truly believe that people should have the right to elect their own and not be gerrymandered out of that right" (Hoffenblum dep., 277).

At the Boundary Commission's first public meeting, Latino activists attacked the body because it contained no members of minority groups. "Our interests are not served without a Hispanic on this committee," announced Miguel Garcia, state chairperson of Californios for Fair Representation. At the next day's Board meeting, Edelman moved to double the size of the commission in order to "allow . . . for greater opportunities for us to appoint people from the minority communities—the black, the Chicano, the Asian, and other communities—in Los Angeles County." The motion passed without recorded debate. Although the Californios group submitted lists of names from which they hoped the supervisors would pick the five additional commission members, the supervisors ignored them, choosing either insiders loyal to them or outsiders who were treated as utterly irrelevant to the redistricting process (Perkins dep., 155–57; Kousser 1991b, 658).

The best known of the five in county government circles was Robert Perkins, an African-American who had successively been chief deputy to supervisors Hayes, Burke, and Dana. Perkins could be relied on. "[T]he only way I survived three supervisors," he later noted, was to "keep my personal views out of the office . . . I sat on the [Boundary Commission] as a minority and certainly I represented my office's position, not my personal position." From his experience, he concluded that "if you expect to have boundaries drawn where all of the groups are going to be really considered, then you need an independent board rather than a board that's appointed by the Board of Supervisors." Perkins's was the only one of the five names of minority Boundary Commission members that Ron Smith, nominally Perkins's subordinate in Dana's office, could recognize in 1989 (Perkins dep., 67–68, 74; Smith dep., 200–201).

Hahn appointed Davis Lear, a black retired deputy who had served him for twenty-five years, while Edelman selected his own former deputy Jesus Melendez. During the Boundary Commission process, Melendez reportedly avoided talking to representatives of Californios. Both of these veterans apparently played roles that paralleled Perkins's on the commission, although in 1989 neither remembered any details about the 1981 redistricting at all. Antonovich tapped Frederic Quevedo, a medical doctor of Filipino origin who had first met the supervisor when he treated Antonovich's mother for an illness in 1978. As Quevedo remembers it, he never met with or received any communications from Antonovich or anyone from his office before or during his service on the commission, was never consulted on the preparation of any proposal or shown any plan prior to its formal submission to the full body, skipped the final meeting in which the only vote on any plan was taken to attend an annual convention of Filipino doctors, and was never told what the Boundary Commission ultimately decided to do. Allan Hoffenblum, Antonovich's first appointee to the commission, remembered Quevedo only as "an elderly gentleman, but I don't recall specifically who he was . . . Chinese or Filipino or someone such as that. . . . The commission was ten, but it was the five doing most of the negotiating." Like Quevedo, Lauro Neri—a politically inexperienced Hispanic printer who knew the supervisor who appointed him, Pete Schabarum, because they belonged to the same horseback-riding club—did not recall either being instructed or consulted by anyone connected with his supervisor. Although Neri claimed in 1989 that he was "in and out of his [Schabarum's] office a great deal," Schabarum at the same time denied that he recognized Neri's name (Hoffenblum dep., 329; Neri dep., 10-11, 15-16, 47, 59-60, 85-87; Quevedo dep., 21, 23, 25-27, 51-53, 80-81, 91-92, 137; Quezada dep., 71; Schabarum dep., 211).

Two county staff members from the Office of the Board of Supervisors, Richard Schoeni and Deborah Turner, facilitated the redistricting process and played larger roles in the ultimate outcome than any of the Boundary Commission members. As assistant executive officer of the Board, Schoeni served as secretary to the boundary commissions of both 1971 and 1981. In 1971, he had consulted the chief deputies of all the supervisors, had learned which areas each supervisor wanted to gain or lose, and on the basis of those consultations had actually drafted the plan formally proposed by the Boundary Commission. In 1981, at least up to the time that the Boundary Commission issued its report, he did not perform a similar middle-man role. "There was not as much informal interaction between myself and the chief deputies in 1981 . . . there was just a lot less interaction between myself and any of the offices." As for the commissioners, they rejected his office's offer of assistance, relying instead on the Rose Institute. Nor did he, as he remembers it, draw up a plan to serve as the basis for a settlement in the weeks between the report of the Boundary Commission and the final action by the Board. Nonetheless, on the last day, it was Schoeni, not Smith or Hoffenblum, who was present helping to provide staff assistance to the supervisors' final negotiations (Schoeni dep., 8-12, 36-41, 82-83, 107, 303-4, 395; Seymour dep., 524, 536).

Schoeni did earlier oversee the development of five or more plans, at least four of which, known as Plans A, B, C, and D, were presented to but ignored by the Boundary Commission. These were actually drawn by Deborah Turner, an assistant in the Board's executive office, who had neither previous redistricting experience nor a record of political activity. Working on her own with only an adding machine, maps, and aggregate population data for well-established communities within the city of Los Angeles and for smaller cities throughout the county, Turner equalized the populations of the supervisorial districts, making only slight changes in the boundaries. She then had the regional planning and data processing departments compute ethnic percentages for each of her plans. Denying that she took into account either the political or ethnic consequences of the plans that she drew—and she apparently lacked information on either—Turner seems to have performed as an efficient, nonpartisan clerk (Hoffenblum dep., 179; Perkins dep., 140; Turner dep., 41, 102–4, 106–9, 111–12, 114–16, 130–31, 136, 246–48, 260–61). Her actions prove that minor redistricting activity can be a mere clerical task.

In 1971, Latinos had not been well organized to take part in redistricting, and activists emerged from the process frustrated and angry. At hearings of the California State Advisory Committee to the U.S. Commission on Civil Rights, two Latino professors, David Lopez-Lee and Henry Pacheco, had presented maps of Los Angeles County showing that East Los Angeles was sliced into several assembly districts, but they had to rely on the assembly for statistics, they did not have the resources to draw districts themselves, and they had no data for areas outside East Los Angeles. Even more important, there was no powerful Latino inside the process, since there were only two Latino state assemblymen, neither of whom was on the Assembly Reapportionment Committee, and no Latino state senator. Traipse the legislative halls in Sacramento as they might, activists could get no firm commitments for new Latino seats, they said. Students yelling "Chicano Power" picketed and milled around, while elder statesmen such as Abe Tapia and Bert Corona of the Mexican American Political Association and Richard Calderon, who had been narrowly defeated for Congress in 1970, threatened a massive defection to *La Raza Unida* party. "The two-party system has failed the Mexican," Tapia announced. "We don't need it. We don't want it" (California State Advisory Committee to the U.S. Commission on Civil Rights 1971, 25–26, 30–33, 49 [Tapia quote]).

Although the four additional Latinos who were elected to the state assembly and state senate during the decade after 1971 probably lifted the spirits of Latino reformers, and although Latino politicians, especially Assembly Reapportionment Committee chairman Richard Alatorre, were certainly in a much better position to influence the redistricting process in the legislature in the 1980s than in the 1970s, those who had taken part in the earlier remapping did not want 1981 to be a rerun of 1971. And they were not alone. Despite Governor Ronald Reagan's veto of the Democratic reapportionment plan in the early 1970s, the Republican Party had not prospered under the lines drawn by court-appointed special masters. In 1979, Democrats enjoyed majorities of 50–30 in the state assembly, 26–14 in the state senate, and 27–16 in Congress. Even the 1980 Reagan landslide could not entirely wipe out Democratic dominance, though it did reduce it to 47–33 in the assembly, 23–17 in the senate, and 22–21 in Congress. Since Democrats would control the data and the computers in the 1981 state legislature, Republicans had to launch a private effort if they wished to compete equally in private negotiations and the battle for public opinion. Because, as they often acknowledged, Republicans stood to gain if more members of Democratic-oriented minority groups were packed into fewer seats, the Republicans might strengthen potential allies in the statewide reapportionment if Latinos were better organized for redistricting, and especially if they had access to easily manipulable machine-readable files. As Alan Heslop of the Rose Institute, a Republican staffer in the 1971 legislative redistricting, testified in a public hearing in August 1981: "This is how Republicans deal with minorities. They put them in as few districts as possible so they can waste their votes" (*LAT*, Nov. 9, 1978, I:19–20; Nov. 6, 1980, I:3, 14; Johnson 1983, 34, 60; Heslop quoted in California State Advisory Committee to the U.S. Commission on Civil Rights 1982, 8).

On November 16, 1979, and again on January 31, 1981, the Rose Institute sponsored conferences on "Hispanics and California Redistricting." Although part of Claremont McKenna College, Rose was not a typical academic entity, and these were not the usual scholarly conferences. Lacking an endowment, dependent on a constant stream of grants and contracts, Rose was firmly linked to the Republican Party. Director Alan Heslop was not the only one of the three principal officers of Rose with close ties to the Republican Party. Heslop's "alter ego," Thomas Hofeller, had worked with Heslop, Smith, Shumate, and others on the Republican reapportionment effort in the 1970s and was soon to become director of the Redistricting Department of the Republican National Committee in Washington, and Rose's chief fundraiser Dixon Arnett was a former Republican state assemblyman. The money that made the Rose REDIS software package possible and that funded the "Hispanic Reapportionment Project" at Rose came from the Republican-oriented California Business Roundtable, and its computer had been donated by former Nixon cabinet member David Packard (Navarro and Santillan 1981, 53–55; Heslop dep., 178, 270, 277–79, 360–62; Hofeller dep., 5–8; Shumate dep., 365; *LAT*, II:4).

The two Rose conferences attracted not the usual set of Ph.D.'s but groups of 50 and 150 Latino politicians and activists, respectively, from around the state. A February 7 follow-up conference at California State University at Los Angeles discussed goals and chose the name "Californios for Fair Representation." Although the acronyms and three of the four words in the names of the 1971 and 1981 organizations were the same, the contrast in the first words is instructive. Despite the fact that non-Hispanic members played important roles in the group in 1971, it called itself "Chicano," a truncated form of "Mexicano" with overtones of radicalism and ethnic nationalism. By contrast,

"Californios," a reference to the pre-1850 Mexican-American inhabitants and their descendants, exuded tradition and integration into the larger society. In 1981, however, the umbrella organization (hereinafter referred to as CFR) was simply a coalition of representatives of a number of Latino groups (*LAT,* Feb. 1, 1981, II:4; Navarro and Santillan 1981, 53–55; Meier and Rivera 1972, viii; Quezada dep., 128–30).

Shortly after the 1979 conference, Rose had hired Dr. Richard Santillan of the California Polytechnic University at Pomona as director of the Round-table-funded "Latino Redistricting Project" to help map strategy, draw districts, and serve as a spokesperson for Latinos on reapportionment issues, as well as to facilitate the free use of its computer by CFR members—during off-hours late at night. Holder of a Ph.D. in political science from Claremont Graduate School, Santillan was typical of the young professionals who led the 1981 CFR, leaders who combined ethnic activism with a demonstrated ability to work within the larger, socially pluralistic system. Of those who were most active in redistricting the county Board of Supervisors, for instance, Steve Uranga was a job training analyst with the county and an active member of the Chicano Employees' Association, while Leticia Quezada was a community relations manager for Carnation Company and a participant in numerous Latino organizations. Both had college degrees. While willing to use Rose's resources, CFR members were very conscious of wanting to maintain their political independence. Santillan, for instance, was so concerned that Rose's well-known Republican identity would compromise his position that he agreed to take on the job, he said a decade later, only on the condition that no other Rose employee would have any "involvement at all with the [Latino redistricting] project." More interested in results than in posturing, as the substitution of "Californios" for "Chicanos" symbolized, the CFR people were willing to compromise and negotiate. Activists, but not political insiders, they felt no need to protect any specific officeholder or party, and they retained the idealism, naïveté, and capacity for anger that elected office usually dulls. Lacking real political power, the CFR leaders clearly realized that they had to organize in the Latino community and, above all, that whatever their tactical disagreements in private, they had to speak with one voice in public (Huerta dep., 38, 58–59; Quezada dep., 6–18; Santillan dep., 17–24, 31–32, 66–67; Uranga dep., 9–27).

Undoubtedly recognizing CFR's sensitivity, the Republicans in the Rose leadership avoided heavy-handed pressure on the group. But whereas at the state level the drives for more Republican seats and more Latino seats were complementary, because Democrats controlled the legislature, at the county level in Los Angeles the interests of the controlling Republicans were potentially in conflict with those of CFR. In Sacramento, criticism of the procedures and plans of the state senate and assembly leadership and of the reapportionment committees was ipso facto criticism of Democrats. In Los Angeles, it was, first of all, criticism of Republicans. Unless Hoffenblum's and Smith's public and private pressure on CFR to concentrate all their attention on the districts of the incumbent Democrats succeeded, the Republicans would regret that CFR members had ever been given access to Rose's Hewlett-Packard computer (Heslop dep., 208–11; Hoffenblum dep., 70–71, 92; Quezada dep., 48–50, 60; Smith dep., 46).

THE five-person Boundary Commission first met on July 8, 1981, the minority-augmented, ten-person commission, a week later. At the initial meeting, secretary Richard Schoeni emphasized the four-vote requirement and the fact that if the Board of Supervisors did not act by November 1, the decision would be turned over to the district attorney, assessor, and sheriff. As those who followed politics closely at the time knew, the first two of these three officials, John Van De Kamp and Alexander Pope, were liberal Democrats, while the third, Republican Peter Pitchess, was carrying on a nasty feud with Supervisor Schabarum. These two provisions, the deadline and the alternative authorities, gave the Democrats a veto power that they fully realized and perhaps even provided them the upper hand. As Hahn appointee Robert Bush remarked to a reporter at the meeting, "We are not going to have a situation where three members decide the boundaries and shove them down the throats of the other two" (Bush dep., 86–87; Edelman dep., 322–27; Hoffenblum dep., 369; Seymour dep., 400–402; Schabarum dep., 341–42; *TDB*, July 10, 1981).

The commission's first meeting also demonstrated how anxious the commissioners were to make meaningless gestures of concern for the ethnic consequences of redistricting. Bush moved to recommend to the Board its expansion to seven members, a proposal that he had helped Hahn push during the 1970s in order to make it easier to elect ethnic minority members to the body. Opposed by the Republicans on the Board, as it had been during the 1970s and continued to be through the 1980s, Bush's suggestion was not seriously considered (Bush dep., 19, 31). Even more emptily rhetorical was Ron Smith's call at that meeting for "a redistricting plan that provided fair representation for the minorities in Los Angeles County," for it furnished no realistically practicable means whatever of accomplishing that objective. The commission also asked Deputy County Counsel Edward G. Pozorski to "investigate case law regarding ethnicity as a basis for redistricting to ensure the legality of the final plan," but if he did so, he never filed a written report on the matter (Pozorski dep., 60–61). At its next meeting, the commission adopted as its ninth and last guideline a goal of establishing a "fair distribution of ethnic groups," but left "fair" undefined (*LAT*, Apr. 21, 1988, II:1; July 27, 1988, II:1, 4; *LADN*, Aug. 25, 1988, 4; Kousser 1991b, 665–66).

The public meetings of the commission were a sham. As Antonovich's minority member Dr. Frederic Quevedo bleated, a month into the process, "I've been coming to these meetings for four weeks and there has only been one incident where someone has said anything about redistricting. I'm a little disturbed that everyone is just laying back. We should be determining what is acceptable to the supervisors we represent by being on the committee." Actually, although neither Quevedo nor any of the other minority commissioners seems to have been apprised of the fact, negotiations were taking place in private between Smith, Bush, and Fitch. The negotiators disregarded the staff-devised plans, as well as that presented by CFR at a public meeting of the commission on July 29. CFR's plan, its presentation, and its reception are nonetheless interesting for what they revealed about the tactics and motives of the participants in the 1981 process (*LADN*, Aug. 6, 1981; Hoffenblum dep., 69–70, 159, 177–79, 186).

As early as February 2, 1981, even before the CFR group had taken on the name "Californios," MALDEF attorney John Huerta set out a timetable and a number of goals for the organization: "The primary goal is to maximize Hispanic voter influence," Huerta announced. "[A] secondary goal is to increase the number of Hispanic elected officials" (quoted in Kousser 1991b, 667). Keenly aware of the 3–2 Republican majority on the Board and the four-vote rule for adoption of boundaries, CFR decided that to propose a plan with an overwhelmingly Hispanic district would be futile (Quezada dep., 31–32; Uranga dep., 35–36). As Prof. Richard Santillan put it, CFR realized that the supervisors "are not going to do anything that is going to jeopardize their incumbency." Consequently, even though some CFR members believed that the group should draw two seats with Hispanic population majorities of approximately 65 percent and 52 percent, they finally agreed that because the supervisors would find such percentages "very, very threatening," they would compromise. Accordingly, their plan set the Hispanic population percentages at 50 percent in District 3 and 42 percent in District 1, with the vague hope, as Santillan noted, that "we could maybe get someone elected by the end of the decade" (Santillan dep., 61–63). But while John Huerta explained that CFR "thought that by not taking a radical approach but just being very reasonable and practical and trying to incrementally improve over the existing fragmentation that there was, that we could sell that plan to this Board of Supervisors," in fact they could not. "You're talking about messing around with five kings and the way they draw their lines to keep themselves in power," Huerta reflected later (Huerta dep., 46, 58–59; similarly, see Garcia dep., 58; Quezada dep., 115–16).

CFR's public and private positions were closer to each other than those of the other participants in the process. Testifying before the Boundary Commission, Huerta declared that Latinos had little political power in Los Angeles County government because of "prior gerrymandering, our demographic profile and economic circumstances." He elaborated on how the dilution process worked:

> When one's vote is diluted, as it has been in years past, there is less of an incentive to run for office, to vote and to conduct voter education and registration drives. Once this initially happens, it creates a vicious circle that is difficult to break out of. . . . We are asking you to do this [i.e., adopt the CFR plan] without displacing incumbent supervisors. We are not seeking ethnic or racial representation. We are seeking political influence. We want the ability to elect supervisors and to have political influence with them. (quoted in Kousser 1991b, 668)

No other Latino group or any Latinos who were not part of CFR were mentioned in the Boundary Commission minutes or in newspaper reports of its meetings. No independent evidence whatsoever confirms the claims of Hoffenblum and Kathleen Crow, Antonovich's chief deputy, that the Latino community was "severely split" in public over whether to concentrate Latinos in Edelman's district or to increase the percentage in Schabarum's as well (Crow dep., 214; Hoffenblum dep., 94–99; Quezada dep., 31–32; Santillan dep., 62–63; *LAT,* Aug. 4, 1981, II:1).

CFR decided early on to disrupt Hahn's Second District as little as possible and to cooperate with any black leaders who took part in the process. Unlike Latinos, blacks, except for elected officials, seem to have paid almost no attention to reapportionment in 1981. Until Robert Perkins, Dana's chief deputy and minority boundary commissioner, got his old friend William Marshall in touch with CFR, there seems to have been no outside participation by blacks in the county redistricting. Marshall and a couple of black friends spent a day at Rose with CFR, caucused together in a corner of the room, and came up with a plan to move predominantly black Compton and northern Long Beach into the Second District in order to increase the likelihood of electing a black supervisor there if Hahn should retire sometime in the future. CFR acceded, moving these areas from Dana's Fourth District to the Second, and Marshall testified in favor of the CFR plan before the Boundary Commission. On the other hand, Compton officials, as well as some of Marshall's friends, opposed the move, believing that if they remained in Dana's district they might be able to influence his vote on some measures of health and welfare and that they might get a bigger share of construction and other funds that had traditionally been disbursed equally to each district, according to the "divide by five" principle. If they joined Hahn's district, which was already filled with poor minority communities like theirs, competition for discretionary funds would become even more intense, and the likelihood of cutbacks in government services, they feared, would grow. Or, as Hahn put it, more picturesquely, "Compton is the only thing that keeps Deane Dana from trampling over the poor" (Marshall dep., 38, 42–69, 75–76; Perkins dep., 56; Quezada dep., 38; Santillan dep., 59–61; Uranga dep., 40–41; *LADJ,* Sept. 24, 1981, II:1; *LADN,* July 30, 1981, I:4; *PSN,* Sept. 25, 1981, A:3 [Hahn quote]).

What Smith and Hoffenblum objected to about the CFR plan was not its effect on Edelman's Third District, for the Hispanic population percentage in the Third District in what became known as the Smith and Hoffenblum plans was the same, 50 percent, as it was in the CFR plan. Their real objection, as both stated directly or indirectly, was that CFR's map raised the Hispanic population percentage in Schabarum's district from 36 percent to 42 percent. CFR's design, said Hoffenblum, represented an attempt "to make the First District hard for Schabarum to hold on to" (*LAT,* Aug. 4, 1981, II:2). Smith elaborated: "What they [CFR] were interested in doing, very clearly, was overturning the results of the 1980 election [i.e., the shift from a 4–1 Democratic Board to a 3–2 Republican Board], and that was their only interest. . . . I mean their whole testimony was, 'you should draw the lines so that a majority of the districts are represented by Democrats.' " The only logic in their plan, Smith concluded, "was it would change the political configuration of the county, not change the . . . ethnic representation." He had "horrible confrontations" with CFR over the matter, he remembered (Smith dep., 102–4, 223, 227; similarly, see Quezada dep., 60).

The goals of Hoffenblum and Smith were, Hoffenblum admitted, very different from those of the Hispanic group: "We wished to create a Latino district without changing the philosophical makeup of the Board. . . . We wanted it to remain predominantly conservative. . . . We thought there was a need for an ethnic change. We did not think there was a need for a philosophical change." The Republicans could not have disliked the changes that CFR proposed for the Fourth and Fifth Districts, since the gains and losses in the CFR plan only added Republican strength to the already Republican districts. Antonovich would give up increasingly Hispanic San Gabriel, Alhambra, and San Fernando, while gaining affluent foothill communities from tony Arcadia to horsey Bradbury; Dana would tack on conservative La Mirada while sacrificing only working-class communities. There is no clearer proof of Schabarum's perceived weakness in the face of a threat from an increasingly Hispanic electorate than the Smith and Hoffenblum objections to the CFR plan (Hoffenblum dep., 70–71; Quezada dep., 48–50; Kousser 1991b, 670–72 for details).

Edelman and his aides could not afford to gloat over the Republicans' discomfort, for the CFR plan raised Edelman's Hispanic population percentage from 42 percent to 50 percent. Although Edelman and Jeff Seymour both thought that Edelman could be reelected in 1982 easily in a district that had a slight Hispanic population majority, Edelman agreed with the suggestion that eventually he might have difficulty carrying such a district. More troublesome to Edelman was that the CFR plan stripped him of many of the Westside areas that he had represented since his election to the Los Angeles City Council in 1965. "That area is the heart of the Jewish community," Seymour emphasized. Edelman had been working on programs there for fifteen years and did not wish to deplete all that political capital. Although Seymour and Edelman denied that they opposed the CFR and similar plans partly because they removed Edelman's fundraising base from his district, the *Times* reported that that was another consideration in the Edelman camp. In any case, Edelman never had to take a public stance on the CFR plan, for, as Seymour noted, Hoffenblum and other Republicans were so infuriated by it that it never came to a vote. Instead, Seymour and Edelman could meet with CFR representatives, smile sweetly, make no offer to negotiate, and go about their more serious business. Edelman shared Seymour's concern that the CFR plan robbed him of much of his home base, but neither ever conveyed their feelings to CFR, as they would have had to if they had even made a feint at considering the plan seriously (Edelman dep., 209, 240–45, 315–19; Quezada dep., 85–86; Seymour dep., 205–7, 625–28, 642, 644; Uranga dep., 61–63; *LAT,* Aug. 4, 1981, II:1).

Although a contemporary news report indicated that the redistricters looked at "two dozen" plans altogether, fairly precise descriptions of only eight have survived, only three of which—the CFR, Smith, and Hoffenblum plans—made substantial changes in the 1971 lines. Smith and Hoffenblum left to Shumate and the Rose staff the details about the tentative reshufflings that took place as a result of negotiations. To facilitate the work at Rose, everyone seems to have relied primarily on Henry Olsen, a Claremont undergraduate who knew how to operate the REDIS system and who, according to Director Heslop, had developed an encyclopedic understanding of politics in Los Angeles County. Despite the fact that Hoffenblum remembered that Shumate concocted both the Smith and Hoffenblum plans, Shumate and Smith recalled that Shumate framed only one plan, the so-called Smith plan. And while Shumate declared that almost no real work was done at Rose, Smith had memories of numerous phone calls with Rose staffers in 1981. Since the Hoffenblum plan was considerably more complex than the Smith plan, involving fifteen more unincorporated areas—clusters of census tracts that could be moved back and forth easily only on a computer—it is logical to assume that the orphan was conceived at Rose, perhaps in violation of a clause in its contract with the county that banned Rose employees from actually charting a reapportionment map for the county. As Hoffenblum later remarked, "Rose Institute was drawing the plans" (Heslop dep., 180, 186–87; Hoffenblum dep., 74–81, 110–11, 120, 153–54, 338–40; Shumate dep., 38, 58, 188, 217, 225–27, 275–76, 289, 314, 323, 361; Smith dep., 150–53, 157, 160, 163; *LADN*, Sept. 25, 1981, I:18).

The maximum Hispanic percentage in any district under either the Smith or Hoffenblum plans was 50.2 percent. The Republicans claimed to want to design a scheme that "maximized Hispanic representation." Why did they not produce a district with a higher Hispanic percentage? Surely it was possible to do so, as plans drawn for the *Garza* case made clear. Moreover, other things being equal, the fewer predominantly Democratic Hispanics there were in the three Republican districts, the more secure the Republicans would be, and the effects on the political fortunes of Schabarum, Antonovich, and Dana were certainly important to Shumate, Hoffenblum, and Smith (Hoffenblum dep., 155; Smith dep., 168).

Another possibility is that the designers were concerned with arranging district lines that looked "pretty" on a map. But this was patently untrue. The Hoffenblum plan extended a finger of Edelman's district up to the Hispanic cities of San Fernando and Pacoima and launched Dana over the Santa Monica Mountains, so that his district looked like a giant backwards J. The Smith plan broke up Dana's "beach cities" district by shifting Venice and Santa Monica to Hahn's, and repeatedly offered to transfer the Pepperdine University campus in Malibu from Antonovich to Hahn, a Pepperdine alumnus, which would have spread Hahn from the Long Beach border in the south nearly to Ventura County, on Los Angeles County's northwest edge. In fact, Los Angeles County supervisorial districts had never looked very tidy on a map. Most notorious was the "parrot's beak" in the First District, drawn to keep First District supervisor Frank Bonelli's home in his district, but this was by no means the only example. Under Debs and Edelman, the western portion of the Third District flung a tentacle over the mountains, deeper and deeper into the San Fernando Valley in 1965 and 1971, obviously to encircle more Anglo voters (see Figures 2.1 and 2.3). Aesthetic considerations were obviously unimportant (Hoffenblum dep., 151; Schoeni dep., 304–5; Smith dep., 50).

What *was* important was politics. Since the populations of each district were legally required to be equal, stuffing more Hispanics into the Edelman seat meant transferring some of his liberal Anglos to Dana or Antonovich. Beverly Hills, Hollywood, Westwood, West Hollywood, and similar areas were hardly potentially fertile grounds for a doctrinaire conservative like Antonovich or a colorless novice like Dana, and neither was so politically secure that he could afford to add such territory. Not only was Beverly Hills more than two-to-one Democratic, its citizens were also the sorts of Democrats who did not defect from the party because of racial appeals. In 1982, Beverly Hills went for Tom Bradley for governor over George Deukmejian by a percentage margin of 62–37. Likewise, Bradley got 60 percent of the vote in Hollywood, 64 percent in Westwood, and 77 percent in West Hollywood. By contrast, two-thirds of the voters in Palos Verdes, Dana's home base, and Glendale, Antonovich's, rejected Bradley.

A closer look at the Smith and Hoffenblum plans, especially at Smith's, which both men avowed was the really "serious" plan, makes clear that it was the desire to strengthen the shaky Republican hold on the Board, not their professed concern for the "empowerment" of Hispanics or a "belief in civil rights," that explained the configurations. Although Smith later contended that "there were going to be two Democratic districts and three Republican districts no matter what," in fact 64 percent of the two-party registration in the county in 1981 was Democratic, and there were plenty of possible configurations that could have changed the political as well as the ethnic composition of the Board (Hoffenblum dep., 193; Smith dep., 94–95, 150–52, 185–86).

From a partisan political standpoint, one of the key features of both the Smith and Hoffenblum plans was the shift of overwhelmingly black Compton from Dana's to Hahn's district. The clumsiness of their rationalizations of the politics behind this move demonstrates the Republican boundary commissioners' sensitivity to the issue. Dana lost overwhelmingly black Compton to Burke in 1980 by a tally of 16,118 to 711. Protesting much too much to be credible, both Smith and Hoffenblum swore that Dana expressed reluctance not only to lose the 4.2 percent of the Compton citizens that supported him but the other 95.8 percent as well. According to Hoffenblum, Dana told him, "I got a lot of support in Compton and I would really be disappointed if I would have to lose the city of Compton." Smith chorused that Dana announced to him "that he would do very well in Compton and he would be sorry if he had to lose Compton." Smith even went so far as to claim that conservative Republican supervisor James Hayes had run better in Compton than elsewhere in his district in 1972 and 1976, which Hayes denied, and that Dana had carried Compton in 1984, when Smith was again his campaign manager, when in fact the official returns give Dana only 34.6 percent of the vote against a white Democrat (Dana dep., 245, 247, 256–57, 270–71; Hayes dep., 22–23, 58–59; Hoffenblum dep., 87; Smith dep., 145, 324). Contemporary newspaper accounts painted a different picture, the *Times* reporting that Dana stalked out of Hahn's office saying, "if I don't get rid of Compton, I won't vote for anything" (*LAT*, Sept. 23, 1981, II:1). The *San Gabriel Daily Tribune* learned "that Compton was the sticking point when the five men each tried to devise districts in which they could comfortably win re-election. Supervisor Deane Dana, a conservative Republican, wanted Compton out of his district and into the district of liberal Democrat Kenneth Hahn" (*SGVT*, Sept. 23, 1981).

Of twenty-two cities wholly contained within the Fourth District, Dana carried eighteen, even though some of them were by relatively small margins. Besides Compton, the only other city that he lost in which more than 10,000 people voted was Santa Monica. Smith and Shumate moved Santa Monica, as well as the Venice area of the City of Los Angeles, which was even more of a liberal Democratic stronghold, into Hahn's district. Santa Monica was 56 percent Democratic in 1982, and Bradley polled 60 percent of the votes there in the 1982 gubernatorial race. The analogous percentages for Venice were 64 percent and 71 percent. By contrast, Downey, which the Smith plan added to his mentor's district, was 55 percent Democratic, but voted only 34 percent for Bradley, and South Gate was 65 percent Democratic and 46 percent for Bradley. As Dana later acknowledged, Santa Monica and Venice were, along with Compton, his "weakest areas." "I imagine this [the Smith plan] was his idea of the most safe possible district we could possibly have" (Dana dep., 274, 369). Of thirteen independent cities in the Fifth District, Antonovich lost only San Fernando to Baxter Ward in 1980. Antonovich's boundary commissioner, Hoffenblum, moved it into Edelman's district.

The Smith-Shumate plan reportedly served as the basis for negotiations in which Smith tried to attract either Bush or Fitch. Both Bush and Hoffenblum agreed that Bush asked to have Santa Monica and Malibu transferred into Hahn's district, and both agreed, as well, that there was little likelihood that any concession would have separated Bush from Fitch. As Bush expressed it, after the Republican victories in 1980, Hahn "had only one ally . . . Edelman. . . . To protect the interests of Supervisor Hahn's district, it was my suggestion that we—that I would not support any proposal . . . that would not also be supported by Supervisor Edelman's representatives." That pact made Fitch the linchpin of the negotiations. Smith hoped that "Edelman would have pressure [on] him [by] Hispanics, that he would have to accept a Hispanic district." The strongest attempt to apply pressure on Edelman in public was a statement that Hoffenblum made during or after the meeting at which CFR representatives addressed the Boundary Commission: "We would be remiss," Hoffenblum told the *Daily News*, truthfully but tactically, "if we did not have at least one district that was at least 50 percent Hispanic. Otherwise, it looks like we're sitting here trying to save five white supervisors." According to Hoffenblum, the "intense" discussions with Fitch centered on "how Latino [a district] . . . would he [Edelman] accept and still vote for the plan." Unlike the Hoffenblum and CFR plans, Smith-Shumate did not remove much of Edelman's Westside base from his district. Yet Edelman did not accept it, the negotiations broke down, and just to have some tangible sign of their work, the commission, by a 5-4 vote (Quevedo, who had endorsed the CFR plan, was conveniently absent) recommended not the Smith plan but the mysteriously conceived Hoffenblum plan (Bush dep., 69-74, 81-82, 84, 86-87; Hoffenblum dep., 157-59, 186, 193, 222; Smith dep., 165-66; *LADN*, July 30, 1981, I:4).

Why was something close to the Smith plan not acceptable to Edelman? At the time, Bush denounced the Republican plans for trying "to get rid of every minority they can" and "to draw a line around the inner city of Los Angeles and to give those problems to districts represented by only two supervisors." Edelman said later that these proposals "lumped Hispanics into one district and changed the boundaries in other districts to I believe weaken Democratic registered voters. I think it seemed to me like it was a Republican plan to weaken Democratic registration in certain districts." His staff, he remembered, computed the partisan percentages for each district under both the Republican plans. During 1981, before *Garza* was filed, Edelman had emphasized the ethnic, rather than the partisan, aspects of packing. Unlike the Hoffenblum plan, he told the other supervisors, the boundaries that they ultimately adopted avoided "a clumping of minorities into the central city supervisorial districts." The final report of the Boundary Commission, crafted by Richard Schoeni, admitted the packing and attempted to make a virtue out of it. The Hoffenblum plan, it reported approvingly, "increases the opportunity of Hispanics and Blacks by recognizing that a special community of interest exists for Hispanics and Blacks. Boundaries were developed to increase the electoral effectiveness of these two groups in the Second and Third Supervisorial districts" (*SGVT*, Aug. 13, 1981, A:4; *LADN*, Aug. 27, 1981, I:5; Edelman dep., 213, 223-25; Kousser 1991b, 679).

It is certainly true that the Smith and Hoffenblum plans increased the percentages of minorities in the districts of the two Democrats. Under the boundaries in place before the 1981 redistricting, 72.8 percent of the county's blacks were in Districts 2 and 3. The Smith plan raised that to 81.1 percent, largely by removing Compton from Dana's Fourth District, while the more complex Hoffenblum proposal increased it to 78.5 percent. Smith concentrated 51.2 percent of the county's Hispanics in the Hahn and Edelman districts, and Hoffenblum squeezed 55 percent of them in. To view the figures another way, Smith lifted the proportion of Edelman's district that was either black or Hispanic from 45.2 percent to 54.8 percent, while Hoffenblum stopped at 53.6 percent. What the Democratic districts gained, the Republican seats lost. Under both Smith and Hoffenblum, Dana's black percentage was cut almost in half, while under Hoffenblum, Schabarum's Hispanic percentage dropped by 13.5 percent (Kousser 1991b, 675, 680). These figures, as well as Edelman's criticisms of the Republican offers, suggest that the question ought to be what Edelman had to gain and lose from the Smith plan, not why he did not accede to it. Edelman knew that he could win the district he had by a landslide. Why subtract Eagle Rock, the Los Feliz section of Los Angeles, and Anglo parts of San Fernando Valley, and add about 100,000 new people, 78,000 of whom were Hispanic, in Pico Rivera and Huntington Park? Why allow Schabarum and Dana to pad their majorities by shifting black and Latino Democrats into Hahn's and Edelman's districts, thereby guaranteeing that many of the health and welfare policies that Edelman and Hahn had fought for, with the avid support of their constituents, would be reversed? Self-interest, partisan interest, policy interest, and, the Democrats surely assumed, their constituents' interest all pointed in the same direction—toward rejection of any aggressive Republican proposal such as the Smith or Hoffenblum plans. The wonder is that the hubristic Republican consultants ever imagined that they could induce the Democrats to swallow such a deal.

AFTER the Boundary Commission deadlocked, Allan Hoffenblum lost interest. "It was my feeling they would jiggle the lines and that would be the end of it," he said in hindsight. Ron Smith was "disgusted and discouraged" by the commission's failure, and he "didn't even think about it anymore," learning of the final settlement only through the newspaper. The executive office of the Board, which had been largely excluded from negotiations that went on under the umbrella of the Boundary Commission, became "pretty quiet" on the subject of redistricting for a time, which must have been quiet, indeed. No one remembers drawing up plans between the August 12 Boundary Commission vote for the Hoffenblum plan and the September 24 vote of the Board, but Jeff Seymour recalls seeing some plans that were conceived by either Schoeni or Turner at this time. Two otherwise unidentified "peripheral plans"—plans that made minor changes around the peripheries of the districts—may date from this period (Hoffenblum dep., 245; Schoeni dep., 392–95, 399; Seymour dep., 520–21, 524, 536; Smith dep., 43–44, Turner dep., 141, 357–58, 372–73).

Although some news reporters and CFR apparently believed that the Hoffenblum plan was a live option, in fact, as Richard Schoeni put it, "the Board set aside the Boundary Commission report and proceeded from a clean slate, if you will, with Supervisor Edelman mediating." The clean slate, of course, was not a blank map, but the lines that had been drawn in 1971. Patient negotiations between the supervisors themselves, a process reminiscent of that of the 1950s and 60s, produced occasional outbursts, such as Dana's pique over not being able to jettison Compton, and Schoeni's anger over Antonovich's seeming inability to realize that since his district had more than 20 percent of the population, he could not annex any more territory. But the negotiations went on, off the record and without leaving a paper or even much of a memory trail (*LADJ*, Sept. 24, 1981, II:1; *LAT*, Sept. 23, 1981, II:1; *PSN*, Sept. 23, 1981, A:14, Sept. 25, 1981, A:3; Schoeni dep., 374–77, 392–94).

Two days before their deadline for acting, the supervisors staged a public hearing. Although the CFR leaders asked for and perhaps got a meeting with Edelman earlier in September, they seem to have been left in the dark about the nature of the negotiations that were going on at the time. Realizing that their own plan was not under consideration, but apparently believing that the Hoffenblum plan, which they opposed because it reduced the Hispanic percentage in the First District, the one in which the Hispanic proportion was growing fastest, was still alive, CFR decided to protest. They therefore sent out a fiery handbill in an attempt to boost Hispanic attendance at the Board of Supervisors' only public meeting on redistricting. "LET YOUR VOICES BE HEARD!" the flyer announced in full capitals. "SHOW YOUR SUPPORT FOR FAIR REPRESENTATION FOR THE LATINO COMMUNITY! SHOW YOUR ELECTED OFFICIALS THAT YOU ARE OPPOSED TO MINORITY GERRYMANDERING OF OUR COMMUNITIES." The Hoffenblum plan, the broadside trumpeted, was "a blatant attempt by the conservative members of the Board of Supervisors to maintain their dominance of the liberal supervisors for the next ten years and at the expense of the HISPANIC community." At the Board hearing, an angry crowd repeatedly disrupted proceedings by shouting, and CFR leaders Leticia Quezada, Steve Uranga, Virginia Reade, and Robert Espofino denounced the Hoffenblum plan, Espofino calling it "more than an obvious attempt to maintain the present political status quo . . . unethical, immoral, unjust, and in violation of our civil rights" (Kousser 1991b, 682).

As the process that had begun in January sputtered to a close on September 24, the last day before reapportionment would be turned over to other officials, supervisors drifted in and out of the formal Board meeting that was still in session in the Board meeting room. Two by two, to avoid the sunshine law requirements of the state's Brown Act, they adjourned to an anteroom to pore over maps and discuss deals. For an hour and a half or perhaps longer, assisted by Deborah Turner and Richard Schoeni of the executive office and perhaps by a few of their personal staff members, they thrashed out details, completely ignoring the CFR plan and the other six plans that had been formally considered by the Boundary Commission. Never, so far as anyone remembered about that last day's events, did the Board members consider a plan that raised the Hispanic percentage in any district to a majority or more. Away from the public eye, they did not posture about protecting the rights of minorities, but simply went on with the business of cutting deals to protect their futures. Having earlier invested the county's money in the Rose's Institute's split-second remapping software and fancy graphics, having raised many people's hopes and wasted many people's time in both Boundary Commission and public meetings, they ended with Turner calculating and recalculating each minor boundary change on a low-tech adding machine and Schoeni tracing the barely altered lines by hand on a mylar overlay (Lewis dep., 208-10; Schoeni dep., 365–413; Seymour dep., 389–402; Turner dep., 311–412).

The plan that the Board adopted on September 24 reduced the proportion of Hispanics in Edelman's district slightly, from 42.4 percent to 41.8 percent. In the largest swap, Edelman lost 86,597 people, 74,738 of them to Hahn, of whom 56 percent were Hispanic and 8.3 percent were black. Besides this minor reduction in ethnic concentration—ironic in the light of all the attention devoted to increasing such concentration throughout the redistricting process—there were no other important changes during the redistricting. The Board's phrasemonger, Pete Schabarum, referred to it as "the ho-hum plan" (Kousser 1991b, 683).

Having raised the Hoffenblum boogeyman, Board members could seem comparatively conciliatory to Latinos by then adopting what CFR called "the status quo plan." CFR could declare a victory of sorts—at least they had avoided a substantial reduction in the Hispanic percentage in the First District—and lick their wounds privately (Quezada dep., 114, 141–44). On his way out of the room after the Board meeting on September 24, Mike Lewis, Schabarum's chief deputy, was still trying to salvage some partisan advantage from the affair. "Edelman screwed you," he told Steve Uranga of CFR. "No," Uranga replied, "the Board screwed us." Recalling the exchange, Uranga elaborated:

> Everything about it from the beginning—from the very beginning in my opinion was a farce, a show, and all these county people were participating and all of them had their little roles to play from the boundary committee to the staff of the boundary committee to the board to their aides to their appointees to the boundary committee. The whole thing was a charade or a big farce, a big show. They did a very good job of putting on a show, I thought, except . . . for those of us that were the victims of it. (Uranga dep., 67–69)

WERE LATINOS, as Steve Uranga charged, the intended victims of discrimination by the Los Angeles County Board of Supervisors? Does the evidence about redistricting, not only during 1981, but from at least 1959 on, demonstrate discriminatory motives on the part of the supervisors? To evaluate such a question fully, we cannot consider it independently, as if it encompassed the only possible explanation of the actors' behavior, for when historians or other social scientists attempt to account for or even narrate some event, they always implicitly or explicitly choose between two or more possible explanations. To say that racial or sex discrimination motivated an action is to assert that discrimination caused the action, in some sense, and that other suggested or possible rationales did not cause it, or were less important, or at least do not wholly exclude invidious discrimination as a cause. It is not enough to show that a hypothesis is merely plausible. In addition, it must be demonstrated to be better warranted than other analyses, especially those that contradict it in whole or in part.

Although they did not present a full-scale intent case themselves, the defendants in the *Garza* case, in effect, posed three fragmentary, contradictory hypotheses about the county government's motives in reapportionment. The first might be termed the "civic virtue" hypothesis, with a corollary about the constraints inherent in legal requirements. The second stressed goodwill toward minorities. The third admitted that partisan, ideological, and personal self-interest shaped the lines between supervisorial districts, but contended that Latinos were only inadvertently disadvantaged. In his relentlessly hostile treatment of Mexican-Americans in Los Angeles, Peter Skerry adopted nearly all of the arguments of the County's lawyers, largely ignoring, as those lawyers did, the arguments of presented here, which he, like they, had access to (Skerry 1993, 332–38). Are any of these hypotheses as well or better warranted than the discriminatory motivation thesis?

Campaign consultants and former supervisorial deputies averred that they were motivated in reapportionment only by a sense of civic responsibility, and that they cared less for the political welfare of the supervisors whom they represented than for that of millions of anonymous members of minority groups. Having planned for the private reapportionment effort that was secretly paid for by the newly elected three-man Republican majority on the Board, Ron Smith, Supervisor Deane Dana's appointee to the Boundary Commission in 1981, averred that his only motive in designing a redistricting plan was "to do a noble and good thing." Likewise, Supervisor Michael Antonovich declared that he selected his former campaign aide Allan Hoffenblum to the commission because he "would be able to be fair" and that his only instruction to his other Boundary Commission nominee, Dr. Frederic Quevedo was "to be fair." The chairman of the Boundary Commission, Blake Sanborn, maintained that the effect of the redistricting on the political fortunes of the supervisor who picked him, Peter F. Schabarum, "never entered [his] mind at all." On the other side of the partisan aisle, Robert Bush, Supervisor Kenneth Hahn's appointee to the commission, denied absolutely that he and Hahn ever discussed the "political implications of the configurations of the different plans," for instance, their effects on Hahn's reelection chances. And Alma Fitch, former chief deputy to Supervisor Edmund D. Edelman and his choice for the commission, claimed that the only instructions she received from her boss were to "Do the best job you can. Whatever kind of district

I have when this is over I'll be glad to run in." Common sense, the history of antiminority gerrymandering in California and elsewhere, and modern political theory, which begins with the assumption that politicians consult their self-interest first, all undermine such claims. That savvy political operatives, who must have recognized that they held their bosses' political lives in their hands, could have been indifferent or oblivious to those considerations surpasses belief. Moreover, other actions of the same people likewise belie their statements about their motives. Both Smith and Hoffenblum had directed extremely rough campaigns against prominent minority politicians, and after 1981, along with Shumate, they spearheaded the Sebastiani Initiative, a state reapportionment proposal, discussed earlier, that would have sharply reduced the number of black and Latino officeholders (Smith dep., 184; Antonovich dep., 42–43; Sanborn dep., 144–45; Bush dep., 162–64; Fitch dep., 175; Enelow and Hinich 1984, 2).

The effects of the actions of the supervisors and their appointees cast further doubt on the contention that all they wanted was "to do a noble and good thing." District lines proposed by Smith and Hoffenblum, with the assistance of Shumate, protected their Republican sponsors by ridding their districts of areas that had voted against them in previous elections, especially those that were heavily populated by African-Americans and Latinos. As the testimony of demographers in the *Garza* case demonstrated, it would have been quite possible to draw a district in 1981 that contained a much higher percentage of Hispanics than either the Smith or Hoffenblum plans did—perhaps high enough to allow Latinos a good chance to elect a candidate who was their first choice—but no official, Democratic or Republican, attempted to do so.[15] Democrats claimed to be responsive to minority concerns, but repulsed all efforts to raise the number of Hispanics in Edmund Edelman's Third Supervisorial District in 1981. Edelman made much of his friendliness toward Latinos and the fact that, as CFR asked, he opposed the Hoffenblum plan. But Edelman never took CFR's own plan seriously, even though CFR leaders rightly considered it a moderate compromise, he never negotiated with CFR, and his final proposal barely changed the status quo, which CFR had worked for months to overturn.

The historical context in 1981 also counts against the civic virtue and minority concern theses. Ideologically committed Republicans had just taken over the Board in a racially tinged campaign. Aggressive and temporarily unified, they wanted to guarantee their shaky newfound supremacy in a predominantly Democratic county in which members of minority groups overwhelmingly identified with the Democrats. By contrast, the Democrats stolidly resisted, refusing to compromise. In the partisan trench warfare, members of minority groups were cast into no-man's-land.

The defendants in the *Garza* case argued that CFR should have abandoned its own compromise proposal in 1981 and joined the Republicans in support of the Smith Plan, possibly pressuring Edelman to accept a district with a very slight Hispanic population majority. Consequently, they asserted, the Latinos themselves were responsible for the continuation of the division of Latino voters between the First and Third Districts. But in 1981, Smith and Hoffenblum were so unconcerned with conciliating CFR that they did not even inform them that it was the Smith Plan, not the Hoffenblum Plan, that they really favored, and instead of trying to negotiate with CFR leaders, they heatedly denounced them—which removed any pressure that Edelman might have felt to bend to CFR's demands. In fact, both Republican plans, by reducing the Hispanic percentage in the district with the fastest-growing Hispanic population, Schabarum's, were unattractive to Latinos, and the four-vote rule prevented their adoption anyway, since Edelman and Hahn had no reason to accept a plan that made their partisan opponents more secure. Far from showing that the Republicans acted with goodwill, this counterfactual merely displays their heavy-handed and inept attempt to conscript Latinos in their partisan war, their unwillingness to offer Latinos a winnable district, even at the expense of the Democrats, and their desire to reduce the opportunity for Latinos to influence politics in any seat currently held by a Republican.

Although legal rules did affect the outcome of redistricting, they did not prevent the supervisors or their allies from constructing a local governmental system that would have made it easier for Latino voters to elect candidates of their choice. No state law set the number of supervisors for the county, and, as Latino activists, a blue ribbon commission, and all of the supervisors recognized from at least 1970 on, expansion of the number of seats on the Board would have greatly increased the possibility of minority representation. According to the state election code, the Board may reapportion itself at any time within one year of a general election, and it did so three times in the 1950s and twice in the 1960s. Although overall population growth in the 1970s was spread relatively evenly across the districts, that was not the case during the 1980s, and the supervisors, who had authorized the establishment of a sophisticated demographic estimate unit, had the information on population inequalities and ethnic imbalance at hand. Those estimates demonstrated that by 1985, Dana's Fourth District had substantially less than the ideal 20 percent of the population, and that it was Schabarum's First District in which the Hispanic population continued to grow fastest (Kousser 1991b, 620, 644, 723). Why, in the face of massive, uneven growth, did the supervisors not take steps to equalize the districts during the 1980s? Why, if any of them really wanted to facilitate minority representation or even to undercut legal challenges, did they not propose to redraw lines before the *Garza* case was filed in 1988?

Neither the state election code's guidelines for redistricting—which emphasize geography, cohesiveness, and community of interests—nor the local criteria, which stress preserving traditional boundaries and not splitting cities, are legally binding, and all have been sacrificed in the past to the greater goals of incumbent or ideological advantage. County charter provisions that have been held to require four-vote majorities to adopt a redistricting plan and maintenance of each supervisor's residence in his new district may not have been correctly interpreted, and in any case would have allowed incumbents to draw districts more favorable to minorities. This last point is supported by the counterfactual scenario concerning what the Democrats would have done in 1981 had they won all three seats that were up for election in 1980, a thought experiment whose realism was validated by the seeming willingness of the supervisors to sacrifice the splenetic Pete Schabarum in December, 1989.

If the first two apologias fit the facts so poorly that they cannot be taken seriously, what of the third, the "unintended consequences" thesis? This view implies either that the effect of the line drawing on Latinos was not reasonably foreseeable or was unforeseen; or, even if foreseen, it was not a reason for adopting the policy, but merely a side effect. Neither contention squares with the facts in this case. In a variation of this notion, Skerry admitted that the ethnic consequences of the incumbent gerrymanders may have been foreseen but contended that intentional discrimination is not illegal as long as it is not an expression of racial hostility. That doctrine is not only legally incorrect; it also completely distorts the history of discrimination in this country and ignores the nature of evidence of officials' motives that is likely to be available, either for long past or for current actions.

As Chapter 1 demonstrated in considerable detail, American politicians who have designed electoral structures have generally understood the consequences of what they were doing, especially when these structures disadvantaged minorities. But it is the pattern of changes in the boundary lines that most convincingly undermines the inadvertency thesis. The best way to visualize the series of institutional decisions at issue in the *Garza* case is to imagine a split-screen movie showing, on one side, the demographic spread of the Hispanic core during the 1960s, 1970s, and 1980s, when it grew primarily in an easterly direction farther out the San Gabriel Valley and established a satellite population concentration in and around the city of San Fernando in the north. On the other side of the screen would be a movie of the geographic extension of the Third Supervisorial District from 1959 to 1981, an expansion in almost completely the opposite direction, away from East Los

TABLE 2.1. Every Redistricting from 1959 through 1981
"Whitened" the Third District

Year	Percentage of Hispanics in Population of Third District		Percentage of Hispanics in Population of Area Added to Third District
	Before Redistricting	After Redistricting	
1959	22.7 (1960 census)	19.8	2.6
1963	19.8 (1960 census)	17.7	2.1
1965	17.7 (1960 census)	16.9	8.3
1971	30.3 (1970 census)	27.7	13.0
1981	42.4 (1980 census)	41.8	None added

Sources: Data for 1959, 1963, and 1965 calculated from district maps supplied by Los Angeles County in the *Garza v. Los Angeles County Board of Supervisors* (1991) case and census data compiled by Prof. Dwane Marvick; 1971 data from district maps and U.S. Bureau of the Census 1970; 1981 data from calculations by Los Angeles County, supplied in *Garza*.

Angeles, into the Anglo suburbs.[16] (See Figure 2.1 above for a static representation.) Even though it would have been easier to equalize the population of the five districts by moving the Third District east, and even though such a proposal was explicitly and repeatedly considered in 1965, Supervisor Ernest Debs moved the district north, over the natural mountain barrier, into the demographically and socially distinct San Fernando Valley. Unlike the voters in the areas immediately east of Hispanic East Los Angeles, the Anglos then in the San Fernando Valley constituted what Debs's office referred to as "our kind of people." Five times from 1959 through 1981, as Table 2.1 shows, Debs and Edmund Edelman fostered boundary changes that diluted the minority population of the Third District in the most literal sense—they reduced the district's percentage of Hispanics by annexing areas that contained substantially fewer Hispanics than the rest of their district. Anglo Democrats, as well as Republicans, could preserve their power only by reshaping their districts to take in more Anglos.

To contend that ethnicity was a mere incidental consideration to the 1981 redistricters would be ludicrous. Democrats and Republicans, county computer programmers and Rose Institute mapmakers, CFR and Joseph Shumate all used ethnic data at the precinct, neighborhood, and city levels. No plan was complete without its ethnic tally, and charges of packing, stacking, or cracking the Hispanic population constantly flew back and forth. The consequences for Latinos of every proposed plan were foreseeable and foreseen. The Republican plans sought to bolster Dana and Schabarum by shifting African-Americans and Hispanics out of their districts. Democrats wished to protect their own seats and to threaten Republican seats by refusing to take more minorities. Both, it is true, wished primarily to keep their seats safe and to make trouble for their enemies. But for both, the necessary *means* to do so were minority voters. The only way to accomplish the goal of incumbent protection was through antiminority gerrymandering.[17]

Skerry has contended that to have an act declared illegal, plaintiffs should have to demonstrate that an instance of racial discrimination was motivated by "racial animus," or, to apply the principle outside the law, that to prove that racial discrimination motivated an action, a social scientist should have to show that it was pursued purely out of racial hostility. It is obvious that adopting this standard would result in a greatly diminished number of findings of racial discrimination. As Chapter 1 demonstrated, even in the nineteenth century, people favored discriminatory electoral laws or opposed efforts to dismantle them or prevent them from being put into effect more out of desires to preserve racial or partisan power than from motives of bigotry per se. More important, those who intend to discriminate rarely announce their purposes in unequivocal statements, especially if they know that blurting out such sentiments may jeopardize the legality of their actions. In fact, there were few direct statements about the patently racial intentions of the framers of the Mississippi massive resistance laws of 1967 that were at issue in *Allen v. Board of Elections* (1969), the at-large elections schemes of the 1870s overturned in *Bolden v. Mobile* and *Brown v. Mobile* (1982), or the 1901 Alabama "petty crimes provision" successfully challenged in *Hunter v. Underwood* (1985). Just as in the 1990s opponents of affirmative action or of opportunities to elect minorities to political office parade themselves as having only the true best interests of minorities at heart, the defenders of formal, legal segregation from the 1840s in Boston to the 1950s and 60s in the South proclaimed that they were acting only to protect African-Americans from violence or hostility or to promote job opportunities for blacks in their own, segregated institutions (Kousser 1988b). If expressions of malevolence are prerequisites for findings of discrimination and the saccharine sloganeering of a Ron Smith or an Allan Hoffenblum, for instance, is taken as weighty evidence against such findings, then discrimination will thrive while seeming to cease to exist, for it will never be proven.

BEGINNING in January 1990, the *Garza v. Los Angeles County Board of Supervisors* trial lasted off and on for nearly three months, taking lay and expert testimony on intent, the degree of racial polarization in elections, and estimates of the Hispanic population in the county's thousands of census tracts. Unlike the trial, politics never took a recess. On March 9, the filing date for the June primary in Supervisorial Districts 1 and 3, Supervisor Pete Schabarum shocked the public and his fellow supervisors, Republican as well as Democratic, by failing to qualify for re-election. By that time, every major Latino Democrat had either filed for re-election in another contest, which made it impossible under California law for them to run for the supervisorship, or was ineligible due to living outside the boundaries of the First District. Although Dana and Antonovich threw their support to Sarah Flores, a Hispanic Republican who had worked for Schabarum for eighteen years, Schabarum himself endorsed California Superior Court Judge Gregory O'Brien, an Anglo Republican. Flores, Schabarum declared, lacked "the educational background . . . the organizational talents . . . [and] the personal skills" required to be a supervisor. Privately, he was said to have been considerably less euphemistic. O'Brien later testified that Dana told him at the time that "if he and Mr. Antonovich backed a Hispanic candidate, Judge [David V.] Kenyon could be persuaded to dismiss the lawsuit." During the primary, Flores's campaign consultant was Dana ally Ron Smith. Only the help of Dana and Antonovich enabled Flores to raise $400,000 for her campaign in less than three months (*LAT*, Mar. 10, 1990, A:1; Mar. 16, 1990, B:3; June 7, 1990, B:1; July 26, 1990, B:1).[18]

The day before the June 5 primary, in which Flores placed first with 35 percent of the vote to O'Brien's 20 percent (*LAT*, June 7, 1990, B:1), Judge Kenyon issued a 131-page typescript opinion, ruling for the plaintiffs on all points. After a summary of the findings and claims, the first thirty-two pages of Kenyon's opinion dealt with the factual issues involved in the intent claim, essentially tracking the analysis first laid out in earlier versions of this chapter. In the years from 1959 through 1971, Kenyon found, the Board redrew its boundaries "at least in part, to avoid enhancing Hispanic voting strength in District 3, the district that has historically had the highest proportion of Hispanics and to make it less likely that a viable, well-financed Hispanic opponent would seek office in that district. This finding is based on both direct and circumstantial evidence, including the finding that, since the defeat of Edward Roybal, no well-financed Hispanic or Spanish surname candidate has run for election in District 3." In 1981, Kenyon found, "the Supervisors and their aides understood the potential for increasing Hispanic voting strength and sought to avoid the consequences of a redistricting plan designed to eliminate the fragmentation of the Hispanic population. . . . The continued fragmentation of the Hispanic vote was a *reasonably foreseeable consequence* of the adoption of the 1981 Plan. . . . [D]uring the 1981 redistricting process," he continued, "the Supervisors knew that the protection of their five Anglo incumbencies was *inextricably linked* to the continued fragmentation of the Hispanic Core." Rejecting the defendants' contention that a plausible nonracial motive trumped a racial one, Kenyon concluded: "The Supervisors appear to have acted primarily on the political instinct of self-preservation. The Court finds, however, that the Supervisors also intended what they knew to be the likely result of their actions and a prerequisite to self-preservation—the continued fragmentation of the Hispanic Core and the dilution of Hispanic voting strength" (*Garza* [1990], 1298, 1317–18, italics added).

After a predictable explosion at the judge—Antonovich called his decision a "joy ride of judicial activism" (*LAT*, June 5, 1990, A:1)—the Republicans on the Board apparently decided to treat their defeat as an opportunity.[19] The necessity of settling the federal suit, they contended, allowed them to suspend the county charter provision requiring a four-vote majority to adopt a redistricting plan, which meant that they could swap pockets of Hispanic and African-American voters in their three districts for conservative Anglos from the two Democratic districts. All through the trial, Joseph Shumate and Michael Meyers, another Republican political consultant allied closely with Schabarum, had been drawing possible five- and seven-district plans—at least twenty-two of them, according to evidence uncovered during the remedy phase of *Garza*. Both Allan Hoffenblum and Ron Smith were consulted about at least some of the plans. Each new suggestion was sent to the Rose Institute so that the demographic data could be meshed with information on party registration, as well as with data on votes in presidential and senatorial contests and those in election propositions dealing with insurance, gay rights, gun control, nuclear arms control, and education spending. For Dana aide Gaye Williams, the first question to ask about every plan was "Does it ensure a conservative majority?" But in 1990, as before, partisanship and ideology were inseparable from ethnic issues. On one list of tracts proposed to be moved from Edelman's to Antonovich's district, someone, apparently from Shumate's firm, scrawled "Move 140,000 from D3 [District 3] to D5/*All lily white*" (Kousser 1991b, 727–28, italics added).

The plan that the Republicans presented to Judge Kenyon on June 27, 1990, increased the overall Hispanic population in the Third District to 74 percent and the percentage of registered voters who were Latino to an estimated 45.5 percent (see Figure 2.5). Any attempt to move the Third District east would have strengthened Republican control of the First District—the Schabarum/Flores/O'Brien district—but potentially threatened Dana's Fourth District in two ways. Had Edelman, who lived in the extreme western end of his former district, been transferred into Dana's Fourth, he might have proven a formidable candidate. And if Dana's district, the least populous of the five by 1990, had inherited the liberal western sections of Edelman's district, Dana might have been in trouble whether or not Edelman ran against him. The consultants' clever solution to these dilemmas was to extend a tentacle, often one precinct wide, from the body of the Third District several

FIGURE 2.5. An Attempt to Turn a Legal Defeat into a Partisan Gerrymander

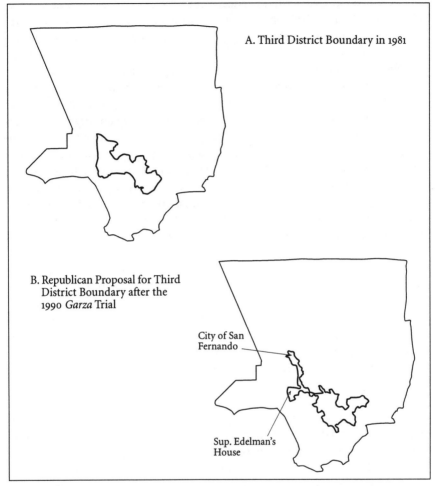

A. Third District Boundary in 1981

B. Republican Proposal for Third
District Boundary after the
1990 *Garza* Trial

City of San
Fernando

Sup. Edelman's
House

Sources: LAT, June 28, 1990, A:31.

miles west to pick up Edelman's home, and to move Hahn's Second District
north, so that it stretched, literally as well as metaphorically, from Watts to
Beverly Hills. Since another Third District tentacle reached north to wrest
Hispanic areas around the city of San Fernando from Antonovich's Fifth District,
Edelman christened this the "octopus map" (*LAT,* June 28, 1990, A:1;
LADN, June 28, 1990, 1).

Not only was the ridiculous-looking plan a blatant gerrymander designed,
as Dana publicly admitted, "to maintain conservative control of the board,"

but the NAACP, which had been largely silent during the trial, charged that the new Second District lines reduced the chances of African-Americans to elect a successor to Hahn once he retired (which he subsequently did in 1992). Although county attorneys contended that their proposal left the African-American population in the Second District stable at 36 percent, NAACP and Southern Christian Leadership Conference spokesmen pointed out that the proportion of African-American *voters* was reduced when the district jettisoned low-turnout Hispanic areas while adding wealthy high-turnout Anglo areas. Coupled with Judge Gregory O'Brien's testimony on July 25 that Dana had lied under oath and had privately appeared "fairly contemptuous of Judge Kenyon's integrity," the plan alienated Judge Kenyon, who accepted instead a MALDEF proposal to create a new First District that MALDEF's demographers estimated was 71 percent Hispanic in population and 51 percent Hispanic in registered voters. The new district alignment rendered the June election irrelevant, and Judge Kenyon ordered a primary in the new district for November (*LAT*, June 28, 1990, A:1; July 1, 1990, B:2; July 26, 1990, B:1; Aug. 4, 1990, A:1).

At the same private meeting in which they adopted the "octopus plan," the Board majority allocated $500,000 to Supervisor Schabarum as a private citizen to carry on the appeals in the *Garza* case even if a new Board decided to settle, an act that the *Los Angeles Times* termed a "cynical, secretive, ruthlessly self-interested raid on public funds" (*LAT*, June 29, 1990, B:1, 6). In their briefs to the Ninth Circuit and ultimately to the Supreme Court, counsel for the county made two major contentions on the intent issue: first, that "a 'discriminatory purpose' under the Equal Protection Clause . . . is one that reflects racial prejudice, antipathy, hostility or racism"; second, that there were "equally plausible nonracial goal explanations" for the 1959–1981 remaps, and, in particular, that partisan or ideological goals, not ethnic factors, determined the outcome in 1981. They did not contend that only "subjective" or "direct" evidence was relevant to a motive inquiry but accepted that circumstantial evidence was probative and argued that the plaintiffs had misinterpreted it (Kousser 1991b, 730).

Although most of the trial testimony in the district court had concerned the degree of racially polarized voting and whether or not a supervisorial district that contained a majority of Hispanic registered voters could be drawn, the three-judge appeals panel of Mary Schroeder, Dorothy Nelson, and Alex Kozinski rested their liability findings in their November 2, 1990 decision purely on intent. There was considerable irony in this fact, for during the arguments over the renewal of the VRA in 1981–82, many in the civil rights community had argued that *Bolden* had to be overruled because a "subjective intent" criterion was murky and difficult to prove, while statistical and other pure effect evidence was clearer and more straightforward. In *Garza*, the cumulative evidence of discriminatory intent was overwhelming, while the statistical proof of racially polarized voting and the demographic estimates of ethnic composition were more ambiguous (*Garza* [1990], 771; U.S. Senate 1982b, 24–43).

Even if it were legally necessary in non-intent cases to show that a district containing a majority of Hispanic voters could be created, Judge Schroeder ruled, for herself and Judge Nelson, that a finding of intentional discrimination relieved plaintiffs of the need to demonstrate that such a district could be drawn. Quoting extensively from Judge Kenyon's factual findings on the purposes of the reapportionments, Schroder declared them "more than amply supported by evidence in the record," and she rejected the county's proposed legal standard of "other plausible non-racial goals." "The supervisors intended to create the very discriminatory result that occurred," she concluded. "That intent was coupled with the intent to preserve incumbencies, but the discrimination need not be the sole goal in order to be unlawful" (*Garza* [1990], 769, 771).

Although Judge Kozinski, a conservative Republican appointed by President Ronald Reagan, dissented on remedy grounds, contending that the Supreme Court's language was ambiguous on the question of whether people or voters should be the basis for allocating political offices, he forcefully sustained Judge Kenyon's opinion on intent:

> When the dust has settled and local passions have cooled, this case will be remembered for its lucid demonstration that elected officials engaged in the single-minded pursuit of incumbency can run roughshod over the rights of protected minorities. The careful findings of the district court graphically document the pattern—a continuing practice of splitting the Hispanic core into two or more districts to prevent the emergence of a strong Hispanic challenger who might provide meaningful competition to the incumbent supervisors. The record is littered with telltale signs that reapportionments going back at least as far as 1959 were motivated, to no small degree, by the desire to assure that no supervisorial district would include too much of the burgeoning Hispanic population. . . . What happened here—the systematic splitting of the ethnic community into different districts—is the obvious, time-honored and most effective way of averting a potential challenge. (*Garza* [1990], 778)

To the county's proposed racial hostility criterion, Kozinski responded with a homely example. Would an Anglo who sought to keep minorities out of his all-white neighborhood for fear that their presence would erode the value of his house be guilty of ethnic discrimination? Certainly, he answered: "Your personal feelings toward minorities don't matter; what matters is that you intentionally took actions calculated to keep them out of your neighborhood." The unanimous three-judge decision on the liability issue no doubt discouraged other judges on the Ninth Circuit Court of Appeals from ordering an en banc rehearing and the Supreme Court from granting certiorari (*Garza* [1990], 763, 779–85).

Although the appeals court delayed the First District election so that they could hear full arguments in *Garza*, their favorable decision and the refusal of higher bodies to stay or overturn it allowed Judge Kenyon to order the election to take place. After a flurry of meetings of senior Latino officials, four major candidates emerged: Sarah Flores, still backed, if rather halfheartedly, by Dana and Antonovich; Gloria Molina, a liberal Democratic former CFR activist and state assemblywoman and in 1990 a member of the Los Angeles City Council; Art Torres, a liberal Democratic state senator with strong ties to organized labor and environmental groups; and Charles Calderon, a moderate Democratic state senator. No serious Anglo candidate ran. In the January 15 primary, Molina and Torres finished one-two, with Flores and Calderon trailing. Any claim that Flores had to be the representative of the Latino community collapsed along with her sponsors' fundraising efforts for her. Despite the similarity of their policy stances and the fact that Torres raised twice as much money, Molina won the February 19 runoff, becoming the first woman ever elected to the Board, as well as the first Latino in 116 years (*LAT*, Jan. 17, 1991, B:1; Jan. 23, 1991, A:1; June 19, 1990, B:7; Feb. 20, 1991, A:1, B:1). It was perhaps fitting that Molina, who had spent many hours at the Rose Institute in 1981 trying to draw boundary lines that would eventually allow Latinos to elect a candidate of their choice, should become that choice.

GLORIA MOLINA'S first major action, taken even before she was sworn into office, went some distance toward undermining the cynical contemporary commonplace that politics makes no difference, and it upheld the faith that scholarship can positively affect the lives of people outside the academy, if only marginally and temporarily.

After the Republicans took over the Board in 1980, they instituted a program that critics termed "bureaucratic disentitlement" (Lipsky 1984). Rather than openly slicing the dollar amount per recipient of "general relief," as the welfare program of last resort is called in California, the supervisors apparently directed bureaucrats to devise complicated rules and burdensome requirements for eligibility for the program, which primarily served homeless members of minority groups. For example, they required that applicants, many of whom had been living on the streets for some time and about a

third of whom had a chronic and severe mental disorder, produce such identification papers as birth certificates or drivers' licenses before they could
receive aid. Another tactic was to mail letters to the addresses given by recipients, many of whom could not afford rent for a full month on the county
stipend and who therefore spent part of the time with no settled addresses.
Those who failed to complete every question and return this monthly report form describing their efforts to obtain employment were terminated
and became ineligible to apply again for sixty days. As one high-level county
welfare bureaucrat announced in a speech in 1984, "the welfare application
process . . . was designed to be rough. It is designed quite frankly to be exclusionary" (Blasi 1987–88, 596).

Only 8 percent of the homeless who congregated in the Skid Row area of
downtown Los Angeles in 1986 managed to scale the barriers and qualify for
general relief. Jose Garcia, a homeless schizophrenic, told the Los Angeles Superior Court that "In the welfare office, I felt like an alien or a piece of meat
being pushed around. Nobody took time to help me fill the application out.
I can't read or spell very well." The thirteen-page, two-part application required one to read, in English, at approximately the twelfth-grade level. Despite a 38 percent rise in the consumer price index from 1980 through 1987, the
Republican Board majority repulsed the efforts of Edelman and Hahn to raise
the $228 per month allowance for food, clothing, and shelter paid to general
relief recipients (*LAT*, Feb. 3, 1986, II:5; Feb. 26, 1986, II:1; Mar. 12, 1986, II:1;
Apr. 11, 1986, II:1; Aug. 7, 1986, II:1 [Garcia quotation]; July 16, 1987, II:1).[20]

A human example will make the story more concrete. In 1985, Robert
Rensch was a developmentally disabled 21-year-old, single, homeless man
who could barely read at a grade-school level, who had always attended special vocational schools, and who could not hold even the simplest job without
considerable help. Rensch was lucky enough to attract the attention of a paralegal at the Legal Aid Foundation, Carl Graue, who devoted more than 100
hours trying to get Rensch qualified for general relief.

It took two months from the time of Rensch's first appointment with the
County Department of Public Social Services (DPSS) to the time when he received his first check. In those two months, Rensch had to speak to thirty
people at nine different locations. He had to complete fifteen separate forms
that contained such words as "acceptable," "permanent," "identification,"
"exhausted," "property tax," and "substantiate," none of which he understood
in context. He had to make appointments with various kinds of doctors and
follow up to make sure that they filed the appropriate forms, which they often
did not bother to do. He had to find a Department of Motor Vehicles office
five miles away from the DPSS office and get there by bus—a difficult task
for someone who had never used a phone book and who could not readily

read a map. He had to get his landlord to fill out forms, and he had to figure out for himself what to do with food stamps. When one of the five doctors whom Rensch was required to see—a doctor who had no psychological or psychiatric training—classified Rensch as able to do "light work," Rensch was supposed to figure out how to appeal this decision. Of course, Rensch could not do this, and the paralegal had to assist and guide him in everything. Most general relief clients, of course, had no helpful paralegals assigned to them.

Here is one day in Rensch's life, as reported by his paralegal, Carl Graue:

[I] accompanied Rensch to pick up the voucher. [While Rensch was waiting to be placed on the rolls, he was given a temporary housing voucher.] When Rensch and [I] arrived to pick up the renewed voucher, after a wait of one hour and twenty minutes, the eligibility worker asked about Rensch's last job. Despite [my] explanation that all of Rensch's jobs were obtained through the vocational school for the disabled and that none lasted more than seven months, the worker declared that Rensch was not eligible for General Relief and would have to sign up for Unemployment Insurance benefits, even though Rensch's type of job did not qualify him for unemployment benefits. The worker also noted that according to Rensch's evaluation, Rensch was qualified for "light work." After [I] argued that the evaluation was incorrect and pointed out the statements in the psychiatrist's letter, the worker said that Rensch would be given six bus tokens, another appointment, and another hotel voucher. Two hours later, while waiting for the tokens and the voucher, Rensch was told that his case had been terminated because his last job was not listed on the application. After another hour, [I] was able to see the supervisor who told [me] that the case was already terminated, so that Rensch could obtain another hotel voucher only by applying for General Relief again. Later that afternoon, Rensch and [I] filled out another application packet. He was given another appointment and a hotel voucher. This episode took the entire day. (Handler 1987–88, 532)

To rectify such kafkaesque practices, a coalition of poverty lawyers, the ACLU, homeless advocates, and pro bono attorneys from a major law firm sued the county ten times from 1983 to 1991, successfully attacking specific disentitlement provisions. Rensch was the named plaintiff in one such legal action. Finally, using the information that they had gained in the narrow suits about the way the county social services system as a whole worked, the lawyers, led by Gary Blasi of Legal Aid, filed a comprehensive suit seeking overall changes in the general relief program and a rise in the stipend from $312 (to which it had been raised because of the previous Legal Aid lawsuits) to $341 per month. Hiring an outside law firm at $250 per hour (Blasi received $13.75

per hour), the county stalled, paying the firm a reported $4.1 million over two years (*LAT,* Apr. 2, 1991, B:3).

The day after the U.S. Supreme Court refused to hear the county's appeal in *Garza,* and just as the campaign to elect a new supervisor in the redrawn First District was beginning to heat up, Blasi met with a representative of Molina and explained to him the problems of general relief and of the lawsuits. Molina was responsive, and when she won, she and Supervisor Edelman, bypassing the county's expensive private attorneys, met with the poverty lawyers and settled the suit satisfactorily. Although Edelman, who had fought unsuccessfully since 1980 for a more humane general relief program, was the crucial negotiator, Molina's concern and her crucial third vote made it possible for perhaps tens of thousands of people not to have to sleep in doorways, wrapped in newspapers or plastic garbage bags, for as many nights for at least a couple of winters.[21] Unfortunately, the prolonged California recession, the Proposition 13 constraints on local taxation, and huge cuts in state allocations to local governments from 1991 on eventually forced even liberal Board members to approve what one of them acknowledged were "devastating" decreases in appropriations for general relief. By March 1996, the stipend was set at $212 per month (*LAT,* Mar. 4, 1986, II:6; Mar. 12, 1986, II:1; July 16, 1987, II:1; June 16, 1991, B:1; July 16, 1991, B:3; Dec. 7, 1993, B:1; Dec. 9, 1993, B:6; Feb. 14, 1996, A:1).

Using the *Garza* case as his principal exhibit, Peter Skerry has charged that "the VRA offers illusory and even counterproductive gains" for Mexican-Americans (Skerry 1993, 332). Those Latinos who took pride in Molina's election, and those homeless people, of whatever group, who might not have ever heard of Molina or the *Garza* case or MALDEF, but who realized well enough that the County suddenly became a little less hostile to their efforts to survive in the months after the decades-long pattern of discriminatory redistricting was reversed, could well take issue with Skerry's harsh pronouncement.[22]

CHAPTER THREE

Changing the Rules to Preserve White Supremacy in Memphis

N o single piece of evidence in the Los Angeles County Board of Supervisors' case was determinative, and there were relatively few direct statements of racial motivation uncovered. Those who drew district lines often professed, at times persuasively, their sympathy for Latinos, and they acted, for the most part, out of the public eye. Rather, it was the pattern of the facts as a whole, the "totality of the circumstances," in the words of *White v. Regester* (1973), that convinced the judges of the discriminatory intentions of the supervisors and their allies and employees. By contrast, in a case from Memphis, Tennessee, which I began to research for the Justice Department exactly one year to the day after Judge Kenyon's decision in *Garza*, the number of incriminating statements and reports was so large that the problem became choosing which ones to leave out of the resulting report. There may not have been more actual discrimination in southern electoral systems, but politicians and newspaper reporters were certainly less guarded in their utterances, at least in the 1960s.

Yet one ought to distinguish the openness of expression of discriminatory motives from the actual existence of such motives. Peter Skerry conflated the two, announcing in *Mexican Americans: The Ambivalent Minority* that "the historical evidence brought to light in this litigation [the *Garza* case] revealed nothing like the treatment experienced by blacks in the South" (Skerry 1993, 333). Of course, since discriminatory districting, not societal discrimination in general, was the focus of *Garza*, there was no need in that case to stress the economic discrimination, lynching, and segregation that Mexican-Americans in Southern California, like African-Americans everywhere, have suffered (Gutierrez 1995, 21–22, 33–34; Griswold del Castillo 1979, 105–15, 141–50; Pitt 1966, 148–66; Romo 1983, 84–85, 120, 127–28, 139–40, 166; Sanchez 1993, 258–59, 267). Nonetheless, differences in the quality and quantity of evidence about discriminatory intent in the establishment and maintenance of electoral devices in the two cities should not obscure similarities in the motives for adopting them and the consequences of having adopted them. Particularly after 1965, southern electoral "reformers" became somewhat more careful than before about admitting racial purposes for their actions, and their nonracial explanations have provided fodder for judicial skepticism in other intent cases, as they did in this one. Although federal district judge Jerome Turner, on the basis of a much sketchier version of this chapter, granted a preliminary injunction against Memphis's majority-vote or runoff provisions, first adopted in 1966, he declined to do so, at least before hearing more evidence, against its provisions that most offices on the Memphis City Council and School Board would be filled by at-large elections for individually designated posts, rules that dated from 1879 and 1959, respectively.

These three provisions have been repeatedly singled out for having racially discriminatory effects. Elections conducted at-large, instead of by wards or districts, disadvantage candidates supported by groups that form minorities of a whole jurisdiction but that could form majorities of single-member districts. Even in at-large systems, if there are no designated posts, voters from minority ethnic or other groups can concentrate their ballots on one or two candidates and possibly elect their choices even if a majority group is hostile. Plurality-win systems similarly benefit minority groups because their preferred candidate may be able to avoid runoff elections with the preferred candidate of an antagonistic majority group, if the majority group splits. Nonetheless, since it is always possible that social scientific generalizations may not hold in particular cases, it is necessary to consider the events surrounding the adoption of these provisions, as well as the character and circumstances of their proponents and opponents, in order to determine whether they were adopted for racially discriminatory or nonracial reasons, or whether their consequences were not understood and therefore could not have been intended at all. What was Memphis politics like in the 1950s and 60s, what types of people fostered and fought against these "reforms," and what immediate effects did they have? Was longtime Memphis NAACP leader Jesse Turner correct when he told the U.S. Commission on Civil Rights that "the political history of this community will show that, in every instance when the Negro unity and voting strength materialized to such an extent that the chance for electing a Negro to an important post became better than average, rules for election to that post were changed in subsequent elections" (U.S. Commission on Civil Rights, 1963, 130)?

THE MEMPHIS version of the widespread southern myth of good race relations is often expressed in a particularly cloying manner. Eight years after *Brown v. Board of Education* (1954) mandated integration, Memphis responded to an NAACP lawsuit by allowing 13 of the approximately 44,000 black children in the district to attend previously white schools that were closer to their homes than any of the "colored" schools (*Northcross v. Board of Education* [1962], 820). In an editorial entitled "The Memphis Way," the allegedly more liberal of the two local newspapers commended the city for obeying court orders without violence:

> Memphis has again proved, as city schools opened, that it is a community of responsible citizens. Further change was made necessary by court orders. Three more previously all-white schools have admitted negro[1] students. This change was accepted by the public. Everyone kept their heads. This is the only right way. (*MPS*, Sept. 5, 1962, 4)

In fact, Memphis's history of legal and extralegal racial discrimination and polarization reflects more closely its informal designation as "the largest city in Mississippi" than its claim to be a progressive Border South metropolis. Its history before the doubly significant date of 1954 is relevant not only because it demonstrates how electoral rules were employed to discriminate against African-Americans in Memphis but also because the values of those who made and ratified the decisions of the 1950s, 60s, and 70s were shaped in part by the climate of racial opinion in preceding years.

UNDER pressure from national Republicans and fearing overthrow by ex-Confederate Democrats, the Republican-dominated Tennessee legislature enfranchised black Tennesseans in February 1867 (Cartwright 1976, 11). In 1868, a group of wealthy Memphians asked the state legislature to replace the system of ward elections that the city had used to choose its aldermen since 1850 with a gubernatorially appointed five-man commission. This was long before the famous yellow fever epidemic of 1878–80, along with a bonded indebtedness crisis, threw city government into chaos (Wrenn 1988, 218). The legislature at first refused to abolish or substantially change Memphis city government, and several blacks served on the Memphis City Council during the 1870s. In January 1874, a coalition of Irish-, Italian-, and African-Americans swept native-born whites from office. Despite numerous controversial calls from black leaders for school integration, blacks also served on the school board. Alfred Froman and Fred Savage, for instance, were elected in 1878 (Fraser 1975; Tucker 1972). Under the ward system, blacks, as well as lower-status whites, used their votes to obtain jobs as teachers, policemen, firemen, and other appointive city officers, in addition to a government that was willing to spend money on schools and charity services for the less advantaged.

It was not that local elections were free of racial issues or appeals in the midst of Reconstruction. Although the 1874 Republican ticket for county offices in Shelby County, where Memphis is located, included only one African-American, a local newspaper declared that the single issue in the election was to save the county from "the blight of negro rule" by voting for "the white man's ticket." The contest, it continued, was "simply a struggle for power between whites and blacks," pitting "superior capacity, intelligence and honesty" against "imbecility, ignorance and rapacity." To vote Republican was to insure "negro supremacy . . . social equality, mixed schools, amalgamation," and to guarantee that Shelby would be run by "benighted and ignorant semi-savages . . . for all time." In the eyes of the *Memphis Daily Appeal*, "Good government demands, and the necessities of the white people will enforce, the continued ascendancy of the white race." Fortunately, as whites except for some Irishmen saw it, the Democratic Party prevailed (*MDA*, July 31, 1874, 2; Aug. 1, 1874, 2; Aug. 2, 1874, 2; Aug. 5, 1874, 2; Aug. 6, 1875, 2; Aug. 9, 1874, 2).

The policies and personnel of the city government, particularly black officials and pro-black programs, led Memphis businessmen and other large property holders to move to abolish it. Declaring that "we have in our midst a large and controlling voting element, which has but little at stake in the welfare of our city," a committee of the "Protective Union" in 1875 called for the substitution of a gubernatorially appointed three-man board of commissioners for the elected government. "Popular government," a committee member announced, "has been tried since the war, and they now saw the dire results." An appointed government, they felt sure, would repeal the taxes on machinery and manufacturing property and institute the leasing of convicts to private industry. Even some Democrats opposed this "disfranchisement for the crime of *poverty*," this "blow at negro suffrage, and at our foreign born population," and the measure failed to pass the state legislature (*MDA*, Jan. 12, 1875, 1, 4; Jan. 13, 1875, 2; Jan. 15, 1875, 4, italics in original). Instead, in 1879 the legislature set up a "tax district" local government for Memphis. Elected at-large, rather than by wards, the new government changed the color and character of its elected officials and policies. Between 1860 and 1879, only 11 percent of the elected officials of the city government held property assessed at $50,000 or more, while 44 percent held less than $10,000. From 1879 to 1898, 63 percent held at least $50,000 (a very sizable fortune in those days), and only 12.5 percent held less than $10,000. Because blacks, who made up 56 percent of the population when the census takers canvassed the plague-emptied city in 1879, could still vote freely, one African-American, Lymus Wallace, a drayman, was put on a nonpartisan, ethnically balanced slate that won election in 1882. Apparently added to the slate to counter the candidacy of Robert R. Church Sr., who had the endorsement of black Republican leaders, Wallace, in the judgment of a recent historian, "had little influence" as one of five unsalaried supervisors of public works. The at-large feature of the tax district provoked frequent charges "that [the government] did not represent all groups and sections of Memphis. . . . This left numbers of black and Irish residents without effective representation" (Wrenn 1983, 110-11; 1988, 223-24). The tax district government's first budget allocated 50 percent of its funds to streets and lighting, 20 percent to fire and police, and only 10 percent to schools. It was often remarked at the time that the tax district government "left the poor folks out in the cold" (*MDAV*, Nov. 18, 1881, quoted in Wrenn 1983, 108).[2] When the tax district government was replaced in 1893, the at-large feature was retained. From 1879 to 1966, there were no district elections for the Memphis City Council.

Before 1883, the school board in Memphis was composed of two members from each of the eleven wards in the city. When a bill establishing a five-member board, to be elected at-large, was presented to the school board for its approval in 1882, the board split, rejecting the bill 8-7, with Irishmen, small businessmen, and the board's one black opposing the change, while members who were professional men or employed by large and medium-sized firms favored the smaller board. The Democratic legislature ignored the local body's sentiments and instituted the change. One black, Alfred Froman, was initially appointed, and another, Fred Savage, subsequently elected to the school board, but a violently racist campaign defeated Savage in 1886 (Wrenn 1983, 273-76; 1986).[3] In subsequent governmental reorganizations, the school board continued to be elected at large. It was eighty-three years before another black served on the board of education.

The period of unfettered black voting in Memphis came to an end in 1889-90, when the state legislature adopted measures requiring registration, a secret ballot, and the payment of a poll tax as suffrage prerequisites.[4] All of these acts, the major students of these events agree, were aimed primarily at disfranchising blacks, virtually all of whom were Republicans, and secondarily at disfranchising poor whites, and they had dramatic effects. In Memphis and Shelby County, the Republican vote dropped by over 90 percent from 1888 to 1890. Democrats swept black wards that the Republicans had carried for a generation (Cartwright 1976, 223-53; Kousser 1973 and 1974, 104-23). Even the policies of the dominant David P. Hadden faction in the tax district government were too liberal for those who proclaimed that they wished a "more vigorous, progressive leadership." The Hadden faction, said the *Memphis Daily Avalanche*, "considered it necessary to pander to the sentiment of the Negro party." In the 1889 municipal election, the paper believed, "there are no politics in it. . . . It is a question of race." Race won and Hadden's ticket, which contained a token black, lost (Wrenn 1983, 138-52).

In a word, in the nineteenth century, threats of black political power were put down most effectively by changes in electoral laws, and the at-large system worked just as it was supposed to.

IN 1905, Memphis city government was taken over by Mr. Crump. Edward Hull Crump did not merely reflect or help to shape public opinion or governmental policy in Memphis from 1905 to his death in 1954. In large part, he *was* public opinion and government. Memphis became, in effect, Crumpdom. In the four mayoral elections from 1931 to 1943, Crump-backed candidates polled almost 99 percent of the votes. In the twenty years before 1948, only two precincts in Shelby County cast majorities for candidates whom Crump opposed. The precincts were abolished shortly after the election in which they blasphemed. When Crump endorsed Gordon Browning for governor ten days before the 1936 primary, Browning polled better than 98 percent of the Shelby County vote, even though his opponent had the support of the powerful native Memphian senator Kenneth D. McKellar. Before the 1938 election, Browning broke with Crump, and his vote in Shelby fell from 59,874 to 9,315 (Capers 1947, 221; Holloway 1969, 278; Key 1949, 62–63). If a labor organizer agitated at the Ford plant, or a local reporter such as Turner Catledge, later managing editor of the *New York Times*, got too nosy, Crump or his minions had the man beaten up, often savagely (Tucker 1980, 28; Catledge 1971, 45–46; Bunche 1973, 493–502; Tindall 1967, 527–28; Honey 1991, 134–40). When a nationally known black political leader, Robert R. Church Jr., became too independent, the Crump machine had his property confiscated for unpaid taxes. When one of Church's successors, the pharmacist J. B. Martin, proved difficult to control, the city stationed policemen outside his store, stopping and questioning every customer. Both leaders fled town, financially ruined (Biles 1983; Tucker 1971, 126–30). A black Baptist minister, G. A. Long, was beaten and his church effectively confiscated for inviting a black "radical" to speak at his church in 1944. Edward Ward Carmack, a senatorial candidate who opposed Crump's ally McKellar in 1934, had his car wrecked, back damaged, jaw broken, and teeth knocked out by unknown assailants during the campaign. He was in bed and a wheelchair for four years (Tucker 1971, 142–43; Melton 1982, 212–221; Kousser 1965, 20).

Through 1927, the black community retained some independent political power. Having backed Rowlett Paine for mayor in 1923, only to see him turn against them, Bob Church and Lt. George W. Lee organized a black voter registration campaign to support Watkins Overton, whom Crump also endorsed, in 1927. Although Paine's virulent race-baiting allowed Overton to obtain most black votes without meeting their requests for such luxuries as paved streets and streetlights in black sections of the city, Lee's "Lincoln

League" could at least obtain the satisfaction of revenge on a turncoat, as
Paine's loss was at least partially attributable to black votes. Criticized for
supporting Overton, one black Memphian, Merah S. Stuart, reflected on the
race's limited power in defending the leadership's actions: "We do not divide,
in general, on most occasions . . . because the white people do not divide with
reference to us. Usually it is all one side abusing and criticizing us, and whenever we can find any group of white men that will even refrain from abuse of
us, certainly we feel that these are the men to be aligned with" (Adkins 1935,
42–44; Tucker 1971, 91–95; quote from Melton 1982, 106).

As Table 3.1 demonstrates, 1927 was the height of black voter registration in Memphis until August 1951. After 1932, when the Republicans lost the
presidency, and therefore federal patronage, Crump's control over the city
was sufficient that he could bar the vast majority of blacks from registering
while simply counting the ballots of a controllable few. Whether Crump's
dictatorship was benevolent or malevolent, honest or corrupt, "progressive"
or crassly self-interested, its character was not determined by any influence
of black voters or leaders.[5]

Crump was no racial liberal. Although his need for their votes early in his
career had forced him to give blacks control over gambling and prostitution
on Beale Street, by the 1930s, the organization was secure enough to hand
the rackets over to whites, even in the black community. As Ralph Bunche
summed up conditions in Memphis in his classic 1935 study of black politics, "Negroes now give their votes and receive nothing in return" (Bunche
[1935] 1973, 493–502). Even in his earlier days as mayor, before he perfected
his absolute control over the city, Crump issued a police order "to run every
Negro man or woman who cannot give a good account of himself or herself
out of town." For a black to state that he was as good as a white man was
to hazard arrest by Crump's police (Tucker 1971, 19). Crump never slated a
black for political office, he kept the police and fire departments lily-white—
the only offices blacks could hold in city government were janitor and garbage man—and he was a stalwart Dixiecrat in 1948, vowing that he would
stay in jail for the rest of his life rather than see blacks enjoy civil rights. No
doubt with Crump's approval, the Dixiecrats carried Shelby County for their
presidential and vice presidential candidates, Strom Thurmond and Fielding
Wright. When a "freedom train" containing copies of the Constitution and
Declaration of Independence scheduled visits throughout the nation in 1948,
Memphis officials refused to let the train stop in Mr. Crump's town because
officials of the sponsoring American Heritage Foundation required that the
exhibition be open to all, regardless of race. Some Memphis blacks had to go
to the more liberal town of Jackson, Mississippi, to view the parchment proof

TABLE 3.1. Voter Registration and Turnout
in Memphis and Shelby County, Tennessee, 1885-1991

Year	Registered Voters		Black Registration (% of total)	Total Voter Turnout
	Total	Black		
1895	10,273	3,641	35.4	—
1914	—	8,000	—	—
1916	—	10,612	—	—
1927	—	12,000	—	—
1951 (early)	—	7,000	—	—
1951 (Aug.)	104,671	19,608	18.7	25,000
1955	159,513	38,847	24.4	86,370
1959	187,541	57,109	30.5	129,286
1960	—	76,000	—	—
1962	—	77,000	—	—
1963	206,171	69,697	33.8	121,665
1964	—	93,000	—	—
1966 (July)	268,171	86,678	32.3	—
1967	235,505	80,033	34.0	146,158
1971 (June)	289,487	94,782	32.7	—
1971 (Aug.)	302,266	99,435	32.9	155,766
1975	336,287	117,000	34.8	169,646
1983	406,449	182,191	44.8	—
1987	371,644	175,407	47.2	—
1991	380,712	182,761	48.0	247,919

Sources: 1895—Roitman 1964, 136; 1914—Miller 1957, 172; 1916—Lamon 1977, 56; 1927—Adkins 1935, 42; 1951 (early)—Wright 1962, 6; 1951 (Aug.), 1959, 1963, 1967, 1971 (Aug.)—Ripy 1973, 99; 1955—*MCA*, Aug. 20, 1959; 1960, 1962, 1964—Holloway 1969, 284, 288-89; 1966 (July)—*MPS*, July 11, 1966, 1; 1971 (June)—*MPS*, June 21, 1971, 4; 1975—Daniel n.d., 54; 1983, 1987, 1991—*MCA*, Sept. 24, 1991, A:1.
Note: Blanks indicate that data is not available.

that their nation, if not yet their city, was committed to freedom (Tucker 1980, 17-18, 57; Holloway 1969, 277; Melton 1982, 254-56).

Approached to buy an advertisement in a rather timid local black newspaper, Crump exploded: "I wouldn't put an ad in that paper—you have a bunch of niggers teaching social equality, stirring up social hatred. I am not going to stand for it. I've dealt with niggers all my life and I know how to treat them. That darn paper is using communistic propaganda—we are not going to put up with Pittsburgh stuff here. This is Memphis. We will deal with them in no uncertain terms and it won't be in the dark—it will be in broad daylight. You be sure to tell them I said so."[6]

Although Crump's choices for local offices ran virtually unopposed for a generation—a record of one-man control unmatched in any large city in American history—Crump underestimated his statewide opponents, Gov. Gordon Browning and Rep. Estes Kefauver, in the elections of 1948. In a characteristic attack, Crump denounced Kefauver as a supporter of unionization, communism, and equal employment opportunity for blacks. But his bitter attack gave the relatively unknown Kefauver free publicity in his senatorial campaign, and Crump's derogation of the reticent Yale Law School graduate as a "pet coon" also backfired. Kefauver donned a coonskin cap, a symbol of the independent frontiersman, and attracted the support of a small but influential section of the Memphis elite, headed by businessman Edmund Orgill, lawyer Lucius Burch, and *Press-Scimitar* editor Edward Meeman—men too influential to attack physically and too stubborn to frighten off (Kousser 1965, 21–28; Tucker 1980, 42–57; Fontenay 1980, 137–52). Kefauver won with a plurality when Crump refused to endorse incumbent senator Tom Stewart. Had there been a runoff requirement, the future Democratic vice-presidential nominee might well have been beaten. The loss of state and federal patronage probably hurt Crump less than the loss of his reputation for invulnerability.

Symptomatic of Crump's diminished power was the campaign of Dr. Joseph Edison Walker, a black insurance company president, for the school board in 1951. Early in that year, fewer blacks were registered in Memphis than there had been in 1914 (see Table 3.1). In percentage terms, about 46 percent of the potentially eligible black population managed to register to vote in 1914, compared to only about 7 percent in 1951—more evidence of how malevolent Crump's rule had been for blacks. Aimed less at winning than at spurring black registration and organizing the black community politically, Walker's campaign was the first serious attempt by an African-American to run for local office in Memphis in seventy-one years. When Walker began, only 7,000 blacks were registered to vote; by the time the campaign ended, 19,608 (18.7 percent of the total electorate and about 20 percent of the eligible black population) were. Walker's campaign literature invited blacks to vote for him alone, while the Crump organization distributed two different brochures: in white areas, the campaign literature contained pictures of all the candidates, with Walker portrayed as unmistakably dark; in black areas, the literature did not display any photographs. Nonetheless, Walker's candidacy was a landmark in Memphis's history. When even blacks, always fair game for violence at the hands of Crump's police, dared to challenge the Mississippi-born Crump, an era was beginning to wane (Wright 1962, 6; Ripy 1973, 99; Holloway 1969, 279; Melton 1982, 316–19).

In 1954, Mister Crump died and the Supreme Court gave its blessing to integration.

UNDER THE commission form of government set up in Memphis in 1909, commissioners were elected at-large, but without running for specific offices. Often the candidates apparently ran without having decided which posts they wished to fill (*MCA*, Nov. 13, 1955, 1). The four highest vote getters of an undifferentiated group simply became the four commissioners, and they divided the administrative tasks between them after assuming office. Likewise, the four leaders in the school board contest comprised that board's members. Only the mayor was elected for a specific office, and he appointed the president of the board of education, giving the board and the commission each five members. Everyone except a few Kefauverites who fancied a council-manager form of government was perfectly satisfied with this setup until the 1955 school board election.

Black registration in Memphis rose to 38,847 in 1955, an increase of over 500 percent since the beginning of 1951. White registration grew, as well, as Crump's death promised meaningful politics. Blacks now comprised 24.4 percent of an electorate which had grown overall by more than 50 percent in only four years. And those who registered voted. The number of voters in the 1955 elections was more than triple that in 1951 (*MCA*, Nov. 5, 1955, 1; Ripy 1973, 99).

Sixteen candidates ran for the four elective school board spots in 1955, fifteen whites and black Baptist minister Roy Love. Instead of "single-shotting," however, blacks supported both Love and a sympathetic white candidate, Mrs. Frances Coe. Although Coe was successful, Love came in fifth, 5,784 votes behind the fourth-place finisher in an election in which 260,368 votes were cast. The campaign, as one student noted, "marked the beginning of white leaders' concern about the Negro vote." "The strong finish by the Reverend Love," the black *Memphis World* predicted, "will undoubtedly encourage other Negroes to seek office." To the "liberal" *Press-Scimitar*, Love's showing was less encouraging, and the paper's editorialist was fully aware of the blacks' tactics: " 'Single-shotting' in the school board race—voting for Love and no other candidates—made Love come as close to victory as he did" (*MCA*, Nov. 15, 1955, 1, 19; Wright 1962, 6; *MW*, Nov. 18, 1955, 1; *MPS*, Nov. 11, 1955, 8).

In other contests, a coalition of Kefauver Democrats and Eisenhower Republicans (both factions had disliked Crump) elected Edmund Orgill mayor. Heir to a wholesale hardware company that had been established in 1867, Orgill had married a Mississippi cotton planter's daughter and served as president of the Memphis Chamber of Commerce. A civic-spirited man of goodwill, Orgill was hardly a radical. He had been attracted to Kefauver because of the congressman's internationalist foreign policy stance and in spite of, rather than because of, Kefauver's liberal domestic views. When Orgill endorsed Dr. J. E. Walker for the school board in 1951, he did so, he said in a public statement, because "this might lessen to some extent their [i.e., blacks'] insistence upon their children attending the same schools as white children." In 1955, about two-thirds of the blacks supported Orgill, as well as Henry Loeb and Stanley Dillard, both of whom won, and both of whom turned strongly segregationist shortly thereafter. Black Republican leaders Lt. George W. Lee and attorneys Benjamin L. Hooks and J. F. Estes endorsed former Crump ally Watkins Overton, who, along with ex-Crump men Joe Boyle and Oscar Williams, lost races for mayor and commissioners.[7] The era when the Crump organization could control everything, when blacks had no choice but to accept thankless subordination, was at an end (Tucker 1980, 42–48, 65, 74–76, 81–82; Ripy 1973, 74, 80; Jalenak 1961, 13, 61, 126).

Tennessee's nationally ambitious political leaders, Gov. Frank G. Clement and Senators Estes Kefauver and Albert Gore Sr., rejected the extreme reaction to the *Brown* decision and the subsequent attacks on the Constitution that politicians in most other southern states, sometimes cynically, put forth. By 1957–58, however, white public opinion had forced the Tennessee legislature to adopt pupil placement and "parents' preference" laws and to issue a fruitless "manifesto of protest" against desegregation (Black 1976, 118–23; Graham 1967, 68–72, 84–89, 118–23, 269–74; Bartley 1969, 275–76).

In Memphis, there was no need for a reaction, for, as a historian of race relations during the first three decades of the century noted, "Memphis was almost totally lacking in white liberalism" (Lamon 1977, 223). By the 1950s, the statement was still largely true. Commenting on a 1955 U.S. Supreme Court decision that mandated the integration of public parks, golf courses, playgrounds, and swimming pools, for instance, the *Memphis Commercial Appeal* denounced the decision's "complete lack of realism"; to require public nondiscrimination by law was "of course, preposterous" to the paper's editorial writer. A white college professor who campaigned for the school board on an integrationist platform in 1955 was treated as a mere curiosity, finishing fifteenth of sixteen candidates (*MCA*, Nov. 9, 1955, 6; Nov. 11, 1955, 1). In 1956, the old Crump group, ironically calling itself "Citizens for Progress," adopted the slogan "Keep Memphis and Shelby County Down in Dixie," a barely veiled reference to segregation (Tucker 1980, 86–87; Wright 1962, 8).

When Mayor Orgill nominated the unimpeachably respectable Dr. J. E. Walker to the board of a municipal hospital that served an overwhelmingly black clientele, not a single one of the other four commissioners supported the move. The white public responded by flooding Orgill's office with adverse telegrams and sending police and fire trucks to answer false alarms at his house in the middle of the night. Although Orgill told Prof. David Tucker of Memphis State in 1973 that he had favored desegregating Memphis buses after the federal district court's opinion in the Montgomery bus case of 1956, he made no move to do so at the time. The city staunchly and successfully fought bus desegregation until it lost a court decision in 1961, and Orgill publicly stated in 1957 that he had "never advocated or desired integration." In fact, the city's bus desegregation suit started in 1956, at the same time as Montgomery's, only to be delayed on technicalities by arguments of the city's lawyers, to which district judges, but not the U.S. Supreme Court, responded favorably. The city also contested and delayed suits aimed at desegregating public libraries (filed in 1958), the zoo and other parks (1959), and schools (1960). As Orgill said at the time, "We will use all legal means to preserve segregation as it now exists. We have hired the best lawyers in the business in the bus and library integration cases. We'll continue that policy." It took eighteen months of sit-ins, perhaps the most extensive of those in any southern city, and a black boycott of downtown businesses to desegregate major restaurants, and these businesses held out until 1962, long after Nashville and other Tennessee cities had begun serving anyone with ready cash. Among the black activists arrested for sitting in at lunch counters was Mrs. Marian Sugarmon, wife of attorney Russell Sugarmon Jr. (Findlay 1975; Tucker 1980, 83–85, 118–21, 133–36; Holloway 1969, 281, 286–87; *MCA*, June 27, 1960; Aug. 2, 1961, 13; Feb. 6, 1962, 17; *MPS*, Jan. 5, 1959, 1; June 6, 1959, 1; June 27, 1960).

Orgill ran for governor in the 1958 Democratic primary, finishing a close third to two even more strongly segregationist candidates, Buford Ellington and Andrew "Tip" Taylor. Forced to defend earlier statements recommending support for the law of the land, Orgill declared in his opening campaign speech that "I have never advocated integration of our public schools and as governor I shall never do so." Local school boards, he stressed, "would rule on racial matters and no federal troops would march in Tennessee." Nonetheless, an unsigned anti-Orgill handbill, distributed widely in West Tennessee just before the primary vote, purported to tell the truth about "The NAACP, Orgill, and Segregation," and featured a picture of Orgill shaking hands with blacks at what the handbill said was "an organizational meeting of the NAACP in Memphis." Actually, it was a *Commercial Appeal* photograph of a meeting of the "Good Local Government League." In a speech at the fairgrounds in Memphis, Tip Taylor equated a vote for Orgill with a vote for the NAACP. The racial climate of West Tennessee was so torrid during the late 1950s that any suggestion of softness on segregation, any hint of sympathy for black rights, was considered devastating to a politician. Taylor carried Shelby County against favorite son Orgill (Graham 1967, 276; *MPS*, Aug. 1, 1958, 6; Aug. 5, 1958, 11; *NT*, Aug. 9, 1958, 3).

"Single shot" voting by Memphis blacks in Shepperson A. Wilbun's unsuccessful campaign for state representative in the 1958 primary election also revived fears that had been raised in 1955 and led to white calls for a designated post system to counteract potential black political power.[8] Willis Ayres Jr., chairman of the Memphis chapter of the staunchly segregationist Tennessee Federation for Constitutional Government, pressed the city commission to eliminate single-shot voting "before it provokes racial bitterness in elections." "If this single shot voting continues among this race," Ayres remarked, "it will mean that the white voters will no longer be able to split their votes trying to pick the best qualified people to serve the city. To protect themselves from minority rule, they will have to single shot their candidates."[9] In order to "prevent negroes from being elected," Ayres, in his own words, "proceeded to quietly work with our legislative delegation to see if we could copy Mississippi's anti–single shot law." Likewise, Shelby County sheriff M. A. Hinds warned a Mississippi Delta audience that "Negro voters in Memphis may soon be able to elect a Negro as city commissioner through 'single shot' voting" (*MPS*, Aug. 8, 1959, 12; *DDT*, Sept. 28, 1958). During the 1958 general election, Raymond Briggs, a Republican candidate for the state legislature from Memphis, remarked, "It is my belief that if a law is passed prohibiting single-shotting, it might curb for the time being the growing power of our colored citizens at the polls." Nonetheless, Briggs opposed such a law, he said, because it would lead to more concentration in campaigns on personalities and less on issues[10] (*MPS*, Oct. 31, 1958, 26). Whatever Briggs's reasons, his statement again reflects the widespread understanding of the connection between race and single-shotting.[11]

This explicit white fear of black single-shot voting, as well as Memphis's unbending white racism during the late 1950s, forms the context for the passage by the Tennessee state legislature in March 1959 of four private acts, introduced with the unanimous backing of the Shelby County delegation, which substituted designated posts for the free-for-all method of electing the Memphis City Commission, the school board, the Shelby County Democratic Executive Committee, and the legislative delegation. Commissioner "Buddy" Dwyer no doubt spoke for the entire commission, whose members unanimously endorsed the bill, when he said that he favored elimination of single-shot voting because, "through the practice, a minority group could get control of the government." State representative William Van Hersh was only a little less explicit: "One advantage of the arrangement," he noted, "would be to overcome inequities of 'single shot' voting, a technique in which a group votes for one candidate instead of eight" (*MCA*, Sept. 18, 1958, 42; Dec. 16, 1958, 21; June 10, 1959, 15; *MPS*, Dec. 17, 1958, 13; Mar. 20, 1959, 7).

The racial purpose of the bills was openly and unmistakably noted at the time by people other than the former Crump stalwart Dwyer. Most striking is a story on the legislation by the *Press-Scimitar*'s chief political reporter, Clark Porteous, which had the instructive title "How Anti–Single Shot Bill Would Work in Shelby—It has Racial Purpose." "The lower house bill," Porteous announced, "is frankly designed to keep minority groups—such as negroes or labor—from electing a man to the House. A Shelby delegation spokesman in Nashville admitted this. Negro leaders are aware of this threat to negroes being elected, and say it will at least postpone the day when a negro legislator or city commissioner is elected." Leaving nothing to his readers' imagination, Porteous explained that currently the top eight candidates of an unlimited field were elected to the legislature and the top four to the city commission. "As it is now, a negro candidate, running along with a number of other candidates, could get in the top eight if enough negroes voted only for one candidate. The new law would make it pointless for negroes, labor or any other minority group to concentrate on one candidate." The conventional legislative courtesy on local bills, Porteous predicted, insured their passage: "Both the lower house and the City Commission bills are local bills and will pass unless some member of the Shelby delegation blocks them." No veto was likely from the all-white Shelby delegation, which during the same month unanimously endorsed a resolution requesting the state's congressional delegation to back Senator Herman Talmadge's proposed anti-*Brown* constitutional amendment that would have vested exclusive control of public school affairs—i.e., integration—in the hands of state and local governments. The legislature passed that "massive resistance" bill (*MPS*, Feb. 11, 1959, 3; Feb. 19, 1959, 4; March 18, 1959, 26).

The *Commercial Appeal*'s reports on the bills were only slightly less explicit. "As to numbered positions, those members of the [school] board who support this act do so upon the basis that it would eliminate or at least curtail certain undesirable features of so-called 'single shot' voting." Stories on the bill providing for numbered posts for legislative positions were titled "Shelby Bill Hits Single-Shot Vote" and "Curb On One-Shot Due Before Senate," and they went to explain that "the present system makes it possible for a group to single shot—that is, vote for one candidate and ignore the others. By this means, the group is likely to insure the election of its candidate while votes for the other candidates will be scattered among the remaining contestants" (*MCA*, Feb. 18, 1959, 5; March 17, 1959, 15).

Scholars and black activists also recognized the goal of the designated post system in Memphis. "This move," William E. Wright flatly asserted, was intended to prevent Memphis Negroes from employing the voting technique of "single shotting"; i.e., of voting for only one candidate in a contest in which several candidates are to be elected. White political leaders were afraid that the Negroes would vote for a Negro candidate for the city commission or school board and withhold their votes from white candidates in the same race. In this manner Memphis Negroes would not add to the total vote of the white candidates and the Negro candidate might thereby receive enough votes to finish in the top four and be elected. (Wright 1962, 3)

Or, as Jesse H. Turner, then president of the Memphis NAACP, testified at a hearing of the U.S. Commission on Civil Rights in 1962,

> After 1955, when a Negro ran for the board of education and with Negro bloc voting the possibility came that a Negro could be elected, our officials changed the law. In 1955, of course, the four people receiving the highest—the four top votes were the ones that were selected for members of the board; but after 1955 they changed it so that the persons had to run for designated slots, which, of course, precluded Negroes from bloc voting, and, of course, this, we think, was designed for no other reason than to see to it that Negroes did not get in the administrative position of the educational system of our city here. (U.S. Commission on Civil Rights 1963, 124–25)

Other actions of the 1959 state legislature in general and the Shelby delegation in particular further buttress the hypothesis that the designated post bills had a racial purpose. People's motives in one series of actions cast light on their motives in other activities. The House, by a 73–15 margin, passed a bill exempting children from the compulsory attendance law if their schools were integrated. As finally enacted, the law delegated enforcement of compulsory attendance to local school boards. State senators Lawrence Hughes and William Cobb of Shelby introduced a bill to provide tuition grants to children who were withdrawn from integrated schools. Another bill introduced by the Shelby delegation and referred to as "a segregation bill" by the delegation's members, allowed counties to make contracts with private schools for teaching elementary as well as high schools. In the House, Herbert Moriarty Jr. of Shelby introduced a copy of the Alabama pupil placement law, which the "liberal" *Press-Scimitar* endorsed, it said, because the bill allowed gender segregation. In 1958, the paper had endorsed public payments for tuition to private schools to avoid integration. If the public schools were eventually desegregated, the paper's editorialist declared in a reflection of the oldest European racist fear, the Moriarty bill would at least keep males and females of the two races apart (*MPS*, Oct. 6, 1958, 6; Mar. 3, 1959, 1; Mar. 6, 1959, 4, 9; Mar. 11, 1959, 27; Mar. 17, 1959, 16; Mar. 18, 1959, 6).

That the free-for-all system had existed in Memphis since 1879, only to be replaced after the first election in sixty-five years to be closely contested by a black, supports the "smoking gun" statements in the newspapers, the Wright and Turner assertions, and the corroborative evidence concerning the racial purposes of other actions by the same decisionmakers. Moreover, city government functions did not suddenly become more specialized, necessitating choices by the electorate of specific persons for specific positions. And the functions of school board members, of course, were never formally specialized. Again, this fact was openly noted in the press at the time: "None of the School Board members has any specific duties not shared with the other three elected members," *Press-Scimitar* reporter John Spence noted, "but the law was passed as an effort to stop 'single-shot' voting" (*MPS*, Mar. 23, 1959, 1). Indeed, it is difficult to think of *any* other possible reason for switching to designated posts at this time. The sequence of events, logic, the many explicit statements by people at the time, and other actions taken earlier or simultaneously by the decisionmakers point unmistakably to the conclusion that the change to designated posts in 1959 was motivated by a racially discriminatory purpose.

THE DRAFTERS of the designated post bill, however, had lacked the foresight to include a provision for runoffs in the bill. According to city commissioner Henry Loeb, who had promised during his 1959 campaign to "exhaust all legal means to prevent desegregation," "No one ever brought up the matter of including a runoff requirement in the other election bills. If I had thought of it, I certainly would have recommended such a provision" (*MPS*, July 14, 1959, 7; *MCA*, June 10, 1959, 15; Wright 1962, 4). Once again, *Press-Scimitar* reporter Clark Porteous spelled out the racial purposes behind the rules explicitly:[12]

[A black candidate] is considered to have a chance of election because of the very law sponsored by the Shelby delegation in the 1959 legislature, aimed at preventing the election of a negro. The new law, aimed at stopping 'single-shot' voting, changed the city election procedure. Instead of the top four candidates being elected city commissioners, each of four city commission races, like the mayor's race, is separate. Henry Loeb, Commissioner of Public Works, has switched to the mayor's race against Mayor Edmund Orgill, leaving his position open. Thus far, six white men have entered the Public Works race, with [African-American

Russell] Sugarmon the number seven candidate. Thus if the six white
men remain in the race and divide the white vote, Sugarmon, by getting a majority of negro votes and possibly some white votes, could be
elected. (*MPS*, June 5, 1959, 5)

Because by the time of the 1959 elections an intensive black registration campaign had brought their proportion of the electorate up to 30.5 percent, the
number of white candidates did not have to be nearly so large as six to
threaten white control (Ripy 1973, 99).

Although black Republicans had long ago formed the "Lincoln League"
in Memphis and maintained membership on the state party executive committee, even in the face of numerous attempts by "lily-white" factions to exclude them from the party, African-American Democrats were only loosely
organized until 1958, when Russell Sugarmon Jr., A. W. Willis Jr., and others
formed the Shelby County Democratic Club (SCDC) to support S. A. Wilbun's
legislative campaign. To assure the support of black Republicans and the
often independent black ministers in his race for Loeb's public works commission post, Sugarmon and his group endorsed the Republican Rev. Benjamin Hooks (later executive secretary of the national NAACP) for juvenile
court judge, and Reverends Roy Love and Henry Bunton for separate positions on the board of education (Lamon 1977, 47–51, 54–58, 224; Biles 1983,
364–70; Wright 1962, 7, 9–14; Holloway 1969, 281; *JCL*, July 23, 1959).

For blacks, this was a crusade—part civil rights movement, part political
campaign. A total of $20,000 was raised from within the black community to
support the "Volunteer Ticket," and by election day, 1,200 precinct workers
had thoroughly canvassed every black precinct in the markedly segregated
city. During the last month before the August election, Martin Luther King Jr.
came to Memphis to address 5,000 blacks in the Masonic Temple on behalf
of the campaign. "We're going to pull Memphis out of the South and let segregation run down the drain," Sugarmon told the crowd at the Temple. Even
the normally apolitical black Memphis newspaper the *Tri-State Defender* en-
thused: "If ever time has been pregnant with possibilities for the Negro Memphian in politics, that time is now" (Wright 1962, 24–25; *MPS*, Aug. 1, 1959,
10; *MTSD*, July 25, 1959, 1).

Black leaders were surprised at the intensity of the adverse white reaction.[13]
After all, Sugarmon was the articulate and attractive son of an old Memphis
family, a graduate of Rutgers University and Harvard Law School, an ambitious attorney who had proved that he could make his way in white society.
Like many Memphis politicians, he had been an athlete—an All-Memphis
football center and a four-year letterman as a linebacker at Rutgers. Unlike
most, he had a reputation, according to the *Press-Scimitar*, for reading "mostly

deep stuff dealing with history, principles of democracy, sociology or economics"—not an advantage in campaigning, but usually not considered a disqualification for office either (Wright 1962, 7, 31; *MPS*, Aug. 21, 1959, 5). Hooks's competence is evident in his subsequent national position, and Love and Bunton appeared at least as well qualified for the board of education as the white businessmen, attorneys, and civically conscious women who typically served (*MCA*, Nov. 6, 1955, I:6; *MPS*, Jan. 22, 1959, 5). In Nashville, which had a city council elected by districts, two black members had served for a decade without undermining the foundations of city hall (Valien 1957, 367). The white panic at the prospect of Sugarmon's election and, to a lesser extent, at the possibility of the election of other members of the Volunteer Ticket, is the strongest indication of the white racism that pervaded Memphis in the 1950s and 60s and conditioned nearly every public action, particularly every effort to change electoral laws. The campaign also served as a glaring example for both blacks and whites of the importance of electoral arrangements. If electoral laws are ever changed unselfconsciously, Memphis after the 1959 campaign was the least likely place in which this could occur.

Since Love and Bunton each faced only one major white candidate, the predictable racially polarized voting could be expected to defeat them. The juvenile court office to which Hooks aspired was sufficiently minor that a relatively small amount of public and private pressure forced out all but one prominent white candidate.[14] The real problem for the white leadership was how to concentrate the vote on one of the four major candidates running against Sugarmon.

The first move was to remedy the oversight in the law and require a runoff. Loeb supporter Jay Biggert repeatedly called for the passage of a runoff law at Loeb-for-mayor rallies to "eliminate . . . the possibility of R. B. Sugarmon Jr., negro, getting elected Public Works Commissioner" (*MPS*, June 6, 1959, 1, 11). Loeb himself asked City Attorney Frank Gianotti to study the possibility of holding a runoff election. "My interest in bringing this matter up," stated Loeb, "is to try to see that an office-holder in Memphis is elected by the *majority* and not by any single-shotting. I am sick and tired of politicians the country over currying favor of minority groups."[15] Loeb's reference to majority rule is important, because that was to become a code word for white control in Memphis throughout the 1960s. Other statements by Loeb during this campaign render his meaning unmistakably clear: "I feel everything possible should be done to assure that the will of the majority rules in all contests." He would endorse a candidate for public works commissioner "if necessary to prevent the election of a Negro" (quoted in Jalenak 1961, 66, 69). After a meeting called "to reduce the chance of a negro candidate winning," Loeb and Commissioner Claude Armour issued a statement saying they favored election by "a majority vote," and that they wanted to "work out a solution which would make certain the winner is determined by a majority vote." Others used the concept in the same way. Arguing near the end of the campaign that one of the white candidates should withdraw, the *Commercial Appeal* said that was the only way to prevent "30% of the votes [a reference to the fact that 30 percent of the registered voters were black] from electing a candidate that 70% don't like." Likewise, the *Press-Scimitar* spoke of the pressure on white candidates to withdraw to prevent Sugarmon, "strong negro candidate, from winning on a plurality, with white candidates splitting the majority vote" (*MPS*, Aug. 13, 1959, 1; Aug. 15, 1959, 1; *MCA* quoted in Jalenak 1961, 69).

Since Gianotti concluded, after examining case law, that a runoff could not be mandated without another private act of the Tennessee legislature and since the legislature was not scheduled to meet again until January 1961, Loeb on June 16 asked Gov. Ellington to call a special session of the legislature purely to pass a runoff law for Memphis elections. News stories on the Loeb request could hardly have been more explicit about the aims of the runoff. The act, the *Commercial Appeal* said,

> would be aimed primarily at Negro candidates who enter contests where there is a large number of candidates and could win by obtaining the highest individual vote, or a simple majority. . . . Attention was directed to a runoff when Russell Sugarmon, Jr., Negro attorney, announced as a candidate for public works commissioner. There are six white candidates in the same contest. (*MCA*, June 17, 1959, 21)

Loeb pressed for a runoff law, the *Press-Scimitar* remarked,

> after the announcement that Russell Sugarmon Jr., negro attorney, would oppose the six already announced white candidates for the post of commissioner of public works. There has been wide discussion to the effect that Sugarmon's chances of winning are excellent if as many as three or more candidates do not withdraw, inasmuch as Sugarmon could be expected to draw a heavy bloc of votes from the more than 50,000 registered voters. . . . The situation which exists arose when the Shelby delegation put through a local bill designed to stop the chances of a candidate being elected by so-called single-shot voting. The bill required that candidates for City Commission and other posts must run for a specific position. However, the bill as passed has had the opposite effect from what was intended, because of the absence of a runoff provision. (*MPS*, June 18, 1959, 12)

PERHAPS mindful of the fact that he himself had been elected governor by little more than 30 percent of the vote, Ellington refused to call a special session.[16] Loeb was disappointed. "I still feel strongly we should try to assure that candidates elected to the City Commission or as Mayor should have the majority vote," the commissioner commented. "I intend to search for another legal method." White political leaders then floated the notion of holding a voluntary pre-primary for the public works position, to be financed by the city and binding by "gentleman's agreement." Only the top two candidates in this throwback to the days of the white primary would be listed on the August 20 ballot. As the *Commercial Appeal* noted in its news story on the subject, the "primary purpose of such an unofficial competition would be to remove the possibility of a Negro candidate winning the race as the result of a Negro bloc vote, over six or more white candidates." The *Press-Scimitar* was just as clear about the purpose of the unofficial white primary: "Reasoning is that if the white candidates split on a reasonably close vote, the negro candidates could get a winning vote." Three of the four leading candidates for the public works job immediately endorsed the idea. Gianotti, however, doubted whether the city could legally allocate the $40,000 needed to run this unofficial election (*MPS*, June 18, 1959, 12; June 19, 1959, 7; *MCA*, June 18, 1959, 12; Wright 1962, 14). Any contention that the ultimate adoption of a runoff or majority-vote requirement in Memphis in 1966 did not have a racially discriminatory purpose must somehow explain away these patently clear events of 1959.[17]

Without a white primary or runoff, the only option for white leaders was to force one or more of the major white candidates to withdraw and/or to organize a bandwagon for one candidate. Three facets of this process are worth emphasizing: First, private agreements proved difficult to reach and enforce, because even with the overwhelming consensus among the white political elite against the election of an African-American candidate, individual ambitions inclined each candidate to try to get others to withdraw.[18] The implication of the 1959 campaign was that a legally mandated runoff requirement was necessary, because voluntary agreements were almost unworkable. Second, all factions and every major white institution agreed on the strategy. Whatever the differences between shades of segregationist opinion, attitudes toward Crump or "reform," or allegiances in state politics, every group in Memphis's white political Establishment agreed that the election of a Harvard Law graduate who happened to be black would be an unmitigated disaster for the Memphis city government.[19] Third, although it was orchestrated privately, the bandwagon strategy was very openly discussed in the newspapers (and, no doubt, in private conversations). These discussions reflect on the motives of those who, then and later, favored at-large elections with majority-vote requirements.

"Any number of responsible citizens," the *Commercial Appeal* noted in a June 28 editorial, "are now saying openly that, while having a favorite, they would willingly switch to the candidate who apparently is out front. . . . The bandwagon development could result from several sources: Newspaper endorsement, word-of-mouth advertising, backing by influential groups, one candidate withdrawing in favor of another" (*MCA*, June 28, 1959, I:4).

Significantly, the first group of influentials to act was the "Dedicated Citizens Committee" (DCC), the outgrowth of a planned Orgill reelection committee. When a partially blocked carotid artery made it impossible for Orgill to run for mayor again, the head of the DCC, chemical corporation head Dr. Stanley Buckman, turned the committee to other purposes, calling for the establishment of a commission to rewrite the city's charter and adopt metropolitan government. A pledge to maintain segregation in Memphis was a condition for membership in the DCC (*MPS*, July 4, 1959, 1; July 6, 1959, 1; Aug. 8, 1959, 11). On July 22, Buckman's group endorsed William Farris for the public works post along with former Crump cronies Claude Armour and "Buddy" Dwyer, as well as Henry Loeb, whom the DCC had originally been formed to combat (Wright 1962, 18)![20] Endorsing segregation and the Crump remnants and spearheading the "Stop Sugarmon" campaign, the DCC invited Russell Sugarmon's sharp rebuke: "Dedicated to what?" Sugarmon asked (*MPS*, July 29, 1959, 15). The fact that Buckman's maiden effort in politics was to give the first nudge to the white bandwagon against Sugarmon throws an interesting light on his key role in the drive for metropolitan government in 1962.

Two days later, the "Council of Civic Clubs" also endorsed Farris, as did a "Veterans for Better Government" committee. Charles Cuneo, the president of the council, hoped "that this group's action last night will encourage some white candidates to withdraw, thus lessening the chance of a Negro being elected to office," according to the *Press-Scimitar* (*MPS*, July 25, 1959, 11). In the next week, both white daily newspapers backed Farris, the *Commercial Appeal* announcing patronizingly that the blacks' campaign

> can become an agency for progress rather than the calamity which it is regarded as by many. . . . At this juncture it would not be well for the Negro citizens or for community tranquility to elect a Negro public works commissioner or judge of the juvenile court. Whether a successful Negro commissioner would upset the department with wholesale replacements [which Sugarmon had specifically pledged not to do] or a Negro judge exercise close supervisory powers over broken white fami-

lies [the other way around, of course, was fine] becomes a real fear in the hearts of many in the white community.

Insultingly, the paper proposed openly to buy off the blacks with minor, segregated offices: "Why couldn't the city hall provide for an assistant city attorney, for example, or the municipal or juvenile courts set up a division for Negro problems with members of that race administering the offices?" (*MCA*, Aug. 2, 1959, I:6; *MPS*, July 24, 1959, 23 [Sugarmon pledge]). After the campaign, Sugarmon and Hooks reported that such offers had actually been made and that they had turned them down (Wright 1962, 21).

In a series of editorial statements, the *Press-Scimitar* was just as patronizing and even more forthright:

Since there is no run-off, without some concerted effort the election of a negro to an administrative position is possible and the majority of the people do not think that would make for good race relations or promote the progress of our negro citizens, not even their political progress. (July 24, 1959, 6)

Most Memphians, including many thoughtful negro citizens, realize that harmony and progress would be hard to achieve if negroes win election August 20. (July 29, 1959, 6)

R. B. Sugarmon Jr. is an able man, but surely no one can seriously believe that it would be good for either the negro or the white citizens of Memphis to elect a negro to that position. (July 31, 1959, 6)

The bandwagon proved difficult to organize. On July 25, three days after the Buckman/DCC endorsement, Farris finished fifth in a *Commercial Appeal* poll. Longtime civil servant Will Fowler, who told the DCC that he was "heartily in favor of segregation," led. By August 9th, Farris had climbed to second behind John Ford Canale, who had long been associated with the Crump faction. Fowler was third, and Sugarmon fourth. A week later, Farris finally nudged into first place, followed by Sugarmon, Canale, Fowler, and Sam Chambers, a labor candidate. Among whites, Sugarmon received less than 1 percent in the poll. In the last week before the election, commissioners Claude Armour and Henry Loeb met with the leading white candidates and proposed that the " 'weaker' candidates . . . get out of the race and let the strongest candidate face the Negro candidate." Armour told the four: "I think if this race goes to the polls as it is set up now, a minority candidate will win. I plead with you, in fact I beg you, to do something" to thin the field. Finally, Fowler dropped out, as one newspaper put it, "to lessen the vote split and the possibility of Sugarmon's election. Appeals for still others to drop out went unheeded." The day before the election, the campaign managers of Loeb and Armour endorsed Farris, an action that was treated as an endorsement by the principals themselves. Still, many white insiders were worried. "With the white candidates dividing up the white vote," Null Adams of the *Press-Scimitar* announced two days before the election, "many think a negro block [*sic*] of votes would elect Sugarmon" (*MPS*, July 15, 1959, 4; Aug. 6, 1959, 1; Aug. 13, 1959, 1; Aug. 18, 1959, 1; *JCL*, Aug. 14, 1959; Aug. 20, 1959; Wright 1962, 23).

"If the white citizens vote in high enough numbers," *Press-Scimitar* reporter Clark Porteous wrote in a front-page, election eve "news" story, "there will be no negro candidates elected." This was only the last installment in a media campaign to boost white electoral participation, the *Commercial Appeal* having earlier implored whites to register in great numbers as "protection against a minority candidate becoming the winner" (*MPS*, Aug. 19, 1959, 1; *MCA*, June 28, 1959, I:4). In the largest turnout in Memphis's municipal history up to that time, five times as large as that in the 1951 local elections, the white bloc vote beat the black bloc vote. "The intense interest stirred up by the serious threat of Sugarmon and other negro candidates," Porteous reported the day after the election, "brought out the whopping vote, even on a hot, humid day. There was no rain, and that helped." In precincts that were 95 percent or more black, Sugarmon received 94 percent of the votes; in precincts that were 95 percent or more white, 2 percent. In the most heavily black precincts, 64 percent of those registered voted; in the most heavily white, 73 percent. Sugarmon's vote total of 35,268 and Hooks's of over 32,000 would have elected them in any previous city contest. All the other black candidates also finished second in similarly polarized elections (*MPS*, Aug. 21, 1959, 1; *MCA*, Aug. 23, 1959; Wright 1962, 28–30).

In an interview the morning after the election, a white reporter asked Sugarmon "Was this the last chance for a negro candidate in Memphis? Will not the Legislature adopt a run-off law, thereby assuring defeat of negroes in future elections?" Desperately seeking a silver lining, Sugarmon responded: "I think the Legislature probably will adopt such a law—but it will make the negroes stronger. Not in the sense of being able to elect a negro to office. But the negro voting bloc will be just that much more important—actually deciding—in a run-off" (*MPS*, Aug. 21, 1959, 5).[21]

BLACK LEADERS learned two lessons from the 1959 election: avoid high-visibility campaigns, and don't trust white "liberal" politicians (Holloway 1969, 282–84). In the view of the black leadership, white liberals expected to receive their votes as a matter of course, even though they would not support black candidates or publicly renounce segregation in return. "We had worked with the so-called liberals," Lt. George W. Lee remarked, "but they never got anything done. They sold the Negro up the river" (quoted in Jalenak 1961, 92). To prove their independence from white liberals and their electoral power, to obtain some jobs for blacks, to make it impossible for white "conservatives" to say in the future that only white moderates bargained for black votes, and perhaps to gain policy concessions, the Shelby County Democratic Club endorsed candidates favored by the rural segregationist leader of the county court, Paul Barret, in 1960 and 1962. In 1960, Sugarmon's law partner A. W. Willis Jr. ran for that court (in reality, an administrative body covering the city as well as rural and suburban areas) in a campaign so quiet that it hardly stirred white fears. It did not stimulate black turnout, either. Willis lost (Wright 1962, 34–35; Sugarmon Papers, box 1, folder 3; Jalenak 1961, 76).

White leaders learned a different lesson. One spelled out the racial purpose of a runoff law in graphic terms in a letter to the editor of the *Press-Scimitar*:

> The only way to assure that public officers are elected by a majority of all votes cast is by the run-off election method. . . . Should there be a negro candidate and several white candidates running for the same public office in the first election its [the runoff law's] result would be to put in opposition, in the second election, the two candidates obtaining the highest and next highest number of votes in the first election unless one of all candidates received a majority of all votes cast in the first election and be elected then. Even a solid negro bloc which should be expected for any negro candidates in such first election could not elect the negro candidate then because the entire negro vote in Memphis would not constitute a majority of all Memphis votes—the entire negro vote being only about a third, or so, of all. Therefore, even if the negro candidate received either the highest or second highest number of votes at the first election, nevertheless, one of the white candidates for the office would also be in the second election, the run-off election, with the entire white vote of about two-thirds of all the votes in Memphis available to elect him and thus assure the election of the white candidate over the negro candidate. The run-off election method at Memphis is mandatory to preserve democracy and Southern beliefs. (*MPS*, Aug. 12, 1959, 6).

The day after the election, the *Press-Scimitar* repeated the analysis and the advice. The DCC Unity Ticket, the paper announced in an editorial, was needed

> because since Memphis has no run-off election at this time, there was danger that a negro candidate would be elected by a minority vote. The overwhelming sentiment of the white citizens—in which they were joined by some negroes—was that no matter how much one might

favor negro progress and negro participation in the government, election of a negro at this time by a minority vote would not be good for race relations in Memphis or for this city's relations with surrounding communities. . . . Negro citizens "segregated" themselves by choosing a ticket of their own, but you can hardly blame them for wanting to take advantage of the absence of a run-off to show their political strength, and they can hardly blame the white community for its determination to see that they would not succeed in electing their candidates. (*MPS*, Aug. 21, 1959, 6).

In an analytical news story the same day, the paper pointed out how important a runoff law was to whites in Memphis and why the election of even one black to the state legislative delegation would threaten the whole racial order:

Negro candidates, though defeated yesterday, stand a strong chance of being elected next year unless a special session of the Tennessee Legislature is called to enact a run-off law for Shelby County. Reason is that a run-off law, though certain to be requested by local officials, could not normally be enacted until 1961 when the next Legislature convenes. . . . Once negroes are able to elect a candidate to a legislative slot, that negro delegate could wreck any attempt to get a private bill providing for a local run-off. This is because local bills, by custom which is not recalled to have been violated, must have unanimous approval of the local delegation first. However, it is not impossible that the Legislature might throw aside custom in such an instance. . . . The only alternative for getting a runoff law would be in the form of a public (state-wide) bill. Such a bill would be subject to the actual approval of the Legislature as a whole, and has been violently opposed in previous attempts by representatives of sections where it might not be desirable.(*MPS*, Aug. 21, 1959, Y:19)[22]

Although no special session was called, the city commission proposed that the Shelby County delegation to the state legislature in 1961 push a private act providing for a runoff election in the city. Its purpose, said the *Commercial Appeal*, was "to minimize the effect of bloc voting," a well-recognized code word for organized *black* voting. For reasons that are presently unclear, state senator William S. Cobb, chairman of the Shelby delegation, seems to have opposed the runoff, and no such bill passed in 1961 (*MCA*, Dec. 26, 1960). Undismayed, the city commission prepared to ask the Shelby delegation to the 1963 legislature to work for a local runoff bill. As the *Commercial Appeal*'s story put it, in even more unmistakably racial terms, "The City Commission yesterday [Aug. 31, 1962] discussed two legislative proposals that could cut heavily into Negro bloc voting. The Mayor and four commissioners agreed unanimously to ask the Shelby County delegation—which will be elected November 6—to work for a runoff law for primaries and general elections. . . . This would probably reduce the effectiveness of bloc voting and assure majority-vote winners" (*MCA*, Sept. 1, 1962, 13).[23] Again, the effort failed.

AS EARLY as 1953, a debate on the various forms of local government drew an audience of 2,500 to Memphis State University to hear attorney Lucius Burch, Edmund Orgill, and other members of the Kefauver group call for replacement of the city commission by a council-manager government. With Orgill's election in 1955, however, the fervor to reform yielded to the necessity to administer. It was not "good government" activists, but Chamber of Commerce businessmen who initiated the movement to restructure Memphis's local government. Or, as the *Press-Scimitar* put it in an editorial that revealed as much about the editor's values as it did about historical fact, "The very heart of the drive for a new government comes from the men who mean the most to Memphis and Shelby County: its business leaders" (Morris n.d., 1; *MPS*, Nov. 5, 1962, 1).

In the spring of 1961, Memphis Chamber president Edward B. LeMaster appointed an eleven-man committee, chaired by Russel Wilkinson, an industrial real estate broker, and including former mayor Edmund Orgill and state senator Albert C. Rickey, to study the organization of local government. Two hundred miles northeast, Nashvillians had defeated a move to consolidate city and county governments into one metropolitan entity in a 1958 referendum, but after the Nashville city administration embarked on a series of controversial annexations of unincorporated suburbia, sentiment for "metro" was rekindled, and Nashville and Davidson County were preparing to vote on the issue again. After a nine-month study, the Wilkinson Committee proposed the "Shelby Unity Plan," consolidating the city and county governments and calling for governance by a mayor and a fifteen-person council, with five elected by districts from the city, five by districts from areas outside the city, and five at large from the county as a whole. District maps were painstakingly drawn (*Memphis Business*, May 1961, Oct. 1961, Mar. 1962; *MCA*, June 3, 1962, 8). Patterned largely after the 1962 Nashville metro charter, the Memphis plan as originally drafted had a much smaller number of districts (ten, to Nashville's thirty-five), and a much higher proportion of at-large seats —five of fifteen, compared to five of forty in Nashville (*Memphis Business*, Nov. 1962; Morris n.d., 1).[24] Explaining the proposal to a black meeting at the Centenary Methodist Church in the middle of April, former Mayor Orgill "said at least two of the city districts would be predominantly Negro, which would assure the election of two Negroes to the Council" (*MW*, Apr. 14, 1962, 1).

Under the state's 1953 constitutional amendments, any new consolidation charter had to be drafted formally by a joint city-county charter commission. Mayor Henry Loeb simply appointed five members of the Chamber of Commerce's Local Government Organization Committee: Wilkinson, Senator Rickey, attorney Walter P. Armstrong Jr., Southern Central president J. Thurston Roach, and former "Dedicated Citizens' Committee" head Stanley Buckman. The mayor pointedly ignored his rival Orgill. The county governing body, antagonistic to the notion of being swallowed up by the city, named five members who were less enthusiastic about civic "reform." Although the Chamber committee had apparently not consulted with blacks while drafting its plans, and the city members of the Charter Commission were all white, the county court's nominees included Lt. George W. Lee, the longtime black Republican leader (Greene, Grubbs, and Hobday 1975, 28–30; Morris n.d., 2; Wax 1969–70, 86–87). Other county members were Lake Hays, Ellen Davies Rodgers, "Old Guard" Republican David Hanover, and Holiday Inn board chairman Kemmons Wilson.[25] The supposedly more conservative county government leadership was obviously more willing to deal and work with African-Americans than the Chamber of Commerce and city politicians were.

SOMETIME during the ten private meetings of the Charter Commission from March 12 to May 17, 1962, the city members repudiated their earlier mixed district/at-large plan, which they had applied to the board of education as well as the legislative council, and committed themselves to an all at-large council. By late May, the five city members endorsed a nine-person council, most probably with three elected at large in the city, three at large in the territory outside the city, and three at large from the entire county. County appointees Hanover, Lee, Rodgers, and Hays favored a 7-7-7 plan, with the city and rural councilpersons elected by districts, while Wilson also preferred a districted proposal, but with only fifteen members. The commission deadlocked (*MCA*, May 18, 1962, 1, 5; May 19, 1962, 19; May 22, 1962, 1; June 3, 1962, 8).

The county members' pro-district position reflected another alliance of convenience between blacks and former Crump associates. County squire Paul Barret, not a member of the Charter Commission but apparently influential with the county members, pushed for an all-district 21- or 36-member council. As of the 1960 census, Memphis made up 82 percent of the population of Shelby County, and burgeoning suburbs such as Whitehaven would predictably swamp Shelby's remaining rural areas if the county members were elected at-large. The city members' plans therefore spelled political death for rural politicians like Barret. As for the blacks, the Sugarmon and

Hooks races in 1959 had proved to them that even the most respectable African-Americans had no chance under an at-large scheme. As Lt. Lee noted at a meeting of the Charter Commission, "I think districts are necessary to protect the interests of the third of the population who are Negroes" (*MCA*, May 29, 1962, 17; June 1, 1962, 25).

Stanley Buckman then proposed a two-part ploy. First, the council would be expanded to twelve persons—four elected at-large from the city, four at-large from outside Memphis, and four at-large from the entire county. Second, the Charter Commission would appoint the initial set of twelve, who would be listed by name on the charter referendum ballot and would serve from November 1962 until the normal municipal election date in August 1963. The list that Buckman drew up, with the advice of *Commercial Appeal* editor Frank Ahlgren, *Press-Scimitar* editor Edward J. Meeman, Chamber of Commerce president Edward LeMaster, County Commission candidate Jack Ramsay, and Holiday Inn chairman Kemmons Wilson, included six County Court members, two businessmen, two labor leaders, and two blacks. Notably absent were Mayor Loeb and, initially, county commission chairman David Harsh. Instead, Buckman proposed to name state senator Rickey, a member of the Charter Commission, as mayor, and Charles Baker, a member of the county court, as vice-mayor. All the current city commissioners would be appointed administrative directors of the departments that they currently headed (*MCA*, May 29, 1962, 17; May 31, 1962, 1; June 1, 1962, 25; *MPS*, May 31, 1962, 1; June 4, 1962, A:10). Anointing enough key politicians and representatives of enough potent political groups, Buckman and his coterie obviously felt, would put together majorities on the Charter Commission and in the electorate.

It was difficult to determine who was more critical of the proposition—those who were on the list or those who were off of it. Charles Baker, Russell Sugarmon, and A. W. Willis Jr., all among the chosen, immediately repudiated the offers, saying that it was up to the voters to decide who would be on the council. Mayor Loeb doubted that the Charter Commission was legally empowered to name officials and, like those whose names had been included, professed a principled devotion to voter choice (*MCA*, June 2, 1962, 13; June 3, 1962, 8; *MPS*, May 31, 1962, 1). The attempt to split Harsh and Barret from Baker, and divide Loeb from the other city commissioners, was as clumsy as it was transparent.

Most of all, the sophomorically clever stratagem demonstrates how little sympathy or understanding the Chamber and the newspaper editors had for African-Americans. Evidently, Buckman's clique had no idea how insultingly patronizing such appointments would appear or how impossible, in the civil rights era, it would be for any black to agree to serve under these conditions.

For generations, Memphis black leaders such as Bob Church, Lt. Lee, and Blair T. Hunt had had to shuffle and scratch before Mr. Crump and his sub-ordinates in order to retain their positions, and even to avoid financial and physical assaults.[26] In this historical context, any black who accepted such a job would immediately be labeled an "Uncle Tom," and any aspirations for higher office would certainly be scotched. Buckman appears to have thought that he was doing blacks a favor, perhaps making up for his launching of the steamroller against Sugarmon three years earlier. To NAACP President Jesse Turner, on the contrary, the proposal guaranteed that whites would choose blacks' leaders for them: "Since everybody is running at large, the negro doesn't have much of a chance unless he's one that the whites will accept." Or as Lt. Lee put it, the only black who could be elected in an at-large sys-tem would be "a hand picked Negro by the white group. . . . The time has not come in Memphis when white people in sufficient numbers will vote to elect a Negro. The Negro must depend upon his numbers if he wins membership or representation, otherwise he will be at the sufferance of the strong white majority" (*MPS*, May 31, 1962, 1; Sept. 6, 1962, 3; Lee to Sheriff M. A. Hinds [public letter], Sept. 27, 1962, in Hinds Papers, box 19, folder 685).

Repudiated all around, the appointment idea died without a roll call vote, and the five city members, joined by Kemmons Wilson, jammed through the all at-large plan. With staggered, four-year terms, only two positions in the city, two outside the city, and two in the county as a whole, would be elected at one time, and all would be voted on separately, so there was little possibility for a single-shotting strategy to endanger white control. Having switched to at-large for the council, the Charter Commission later shifted to at-large for the board of education. Although the Charter Commission did not include a runoff provision, Mayor Loeb and the commissioners sought to get the legis-lature to pass one, if the charter were accepted by the voters (*MCA*, June 3, 1962, 1; June 4, 1962, 15; June 6, 1962, 10; Sept. 1, 1962, 13; *MPS*, June 2, 1962, 1; June 5, 1962, 12).

The debate over the issue of whether officials should be elected at-large or by districts was subtle but illuminating. No one captured the essence of the Chamber of Commerce position better than Buckman. The at-large plan, he admitted, "is based on the principle that well-qualified professional and busi-nessmen can serve on a part-time basis and still practice their professions and maintain their businesses." That was precisely the point, opponents agreed. Only a president of his own company, such as Buckman, could blithely ignore the fact that few whites and almost no blacks could afford to take large amounts of poorly remunerated time from their everyday jobs. An at-large council, charged the Shelby County Democratic Club, would be "a rich man's council." "The cost of campaigning through the whole city, the whole county, or the county outside the city," added Charter Commission member David Hanover, "would be so great as to make it difficult or impossible for a man of small means to run" (*MPS*, May 31, 1962, 1; Sept. 6, 1962, 3; *MCA*, June 3, 1962, 1).

Seemingly oblivious to Sugarmon's defeat in 1959, and appearing to have temporarily suppressed memories of their own roles in plotting to preserve an all-white city government, the *Press-Scimitar* and *Commercial Appeal* accused black leaders, all of whom endorsed districts, of favoring "segregation." Apostrophized the *Press Scimitar*:

> To settle for a legalized segregation of voters! To stamp the most sacred democratic privilege—the privilege of voting—as black votes and white votes! Perhaps Lt. Lee and Memphis negroes could have "negro districts." But that is not good enough. Who will be the proud negro in the councils of Memphis government of the future? The negro elected from a "negro district," or the negro elected at large, by all the people of Memphis?

It was true, the *Press-Scimitar* admitted, that only in black-majority districts would blacks "be certain to elect members of the Legislative Council." But "negroes do not need the district set-up in order to gain representation in government," the newspaper asserted reassuringly, in an eerie premonition of the assertions of "colorblind optimists" three decades later. And it added, almost on the eve of the expulsion of blacks from any share in Republican leadership in Memphis, "No political group could have any lasting success in Memphis if it excluded negroes from its ticket"[27] (*MPS*, May 30, 1962, 6; June 1, 1962, 6; similarly, see *MCA*, Sept. 16, 1962, 6).

Demanding that blacks put the editorialist's conception of the "public interest" before their own interests, the afternoon daily read African-American leaders a civics lecture and claimed that those leaders misrepresented their followers, whose views only the white editorialist truly understood. "Negroes Shouldn't Ask for What's Not Good for All," the *Press-Scimitar* began:

> [C]ouncilmen elected from small districts would owe their election to only a small percentage of the voters. They would feel responsible only to please the voters of their own district, not to accomplish the common good of all the people of Shelby County, white and negro alike. At best it would be unsatisfactory; at worst it would lead to log-rolling and corruption. Only by electing councilmen at large, beholden to all, can you get the outstanding men, white and negro that we need—men who will feel they must work only for what is good for all. . . . We do not believe that the majority of our negro citizens want what is not good for

the community as a whole, and we do not believe that the negro politicians who ask for it [i.e., for districts] truly represent their sentiments.
(*MPS*, May 31, 1962, 6)

A district plan, the paper asserted, would lead to "minority rule." "Surely
there are thinking negroes who see this as clearly as we do. We would like
to hear from them." No one answered the invitation (June 1, 1962, 6; June 4,
1962, A:6).

The parallels in arguments and phraseology between the plaintiffs in *Shaw
v. Reno* (1993) and this attempt by Deep South white supremacists to bar
district representation if it gave the black community a chance to elect any
representatives of its choice might give defenders of *Shaw* some pause.

THE Chamber of Commerce termed its original proposal "The Shelby Unity
Plan." Instead, it turned out to be the disunity plan. Despite the Chamber's
optimism, the new charter, 110 pages long and issued in a formidable 176-
page pamphlet, included something to frighten nearly everybody. City teachers worried that their salaries, benefits, and working conditions would be
reduced to the level of rural areas. Old county politicians such as Paul Barret and Sheriff M. A. Hinds calculated that their bastions would be destroyed
in a government of, by, and for downtown businessmen. Suburbanites were
haunted by the specter of higher taxes. Labor unionists, never powerful in
Memphis, foresaw what influence they had ebbing away in a businessman-
dominated government. Most of all, every black organization in town, from
the NAACP to the Bluff City Council of Civic Clubs to the Shelby County
Democratic Club to whatever Republican group Lt. Lee could muster virulently opposed the charter because, as Rev. Alexander Gladney put it, "it
would be impossible for Negroes to be elected to the Legislative Council."
Or as Lt. Lee remarked, "A Charter such as is being proposed will nullify the
Negroes' voting strength" (Memphis and Shelby County Charter Commission 1962; Wax 1969–70, 86–87; *MCA*, Oct. 27, 1962, 19; Oct. 30, 1962, 4; *MPS*,
Sept. 12, 1962, A:10; Hinds Papers, box 18, folder 605; Lee to Hinds, Sept. 27,
1962, in Hinds papers, box 19, folder 685).

At a press conference at which he condemned the NAACP for pressing to
expand the city's token school desegregation plan and praised Mississippi
governor Ross Barnett's "courage" in defying a federal court order to admit
the African-American James Meredith to the University of Mississippi, Mayor
Loeb strongly backed the metro charter. He was not, however, in charge of
the pro-metro campaign, which was run by the Citizens Association (the
renamed Dedicated Citizens Committee of 1959) and the Chamber of Commerce. Insular and overconfident, the principal metro backers waited until
too close to election day in November to unveil their radio, television, and

newspaper ads (*MCA*, Sept. 17, 1962, 17; Nov. 8, 1962, 1; *MPS*, Oct. 30, 1962, 6; Edward B. LeMaster to "Members" [of the Chamber of Commerce], Oct. 12, 1962, in Program of Progress Papers, folder 120).

In a turnout that exceeded that in the Bob James–Clifford Davis race, the most closely contested congressional election in Memphis since 1888, voters solidly rejected metro. Thurston Roach, a city appointee to the Charter Commission and president of the Citizens Association, "attributed the charter's defeat to a failure to provide election of Legislative Council members by districts instead of at large." In heavily black precincts, the charter lost by votes such as 416–38 and 413–61, overall margins, according to the *Commercial Appeal*, of 80 to 90 percent. Moreover, a much higher percentage of blacks marked their ballots in the charter referendum than in the simultaneous James-Davis contest. No civically conscious Memphian after 1962 could be ignorant of the racial implications of the choice between district and at-large elections (*MCA*, Nov. 7, 1962, 17, 21; Nov. 8, 1962, 1; *MPS*, Nov. 7, 1962, 1).

THE CRUSADES of 1959 and 1962 had successively exhausted the blacks and the government reformers, and the 1963 election was to retire M. A. Hinds, one of the most successful survivors of the Crump years. Two other important forces, however, emerged between 1962 and 1966—William Ingram and the "New Guard" Republicans. By the time the next major effort was made to restructure the Memphis government, they would join the Chamber of Commerce, the newspapers, the original Kefauverites, labor union leaders, and the NAACP-SCDC crowd as key players.

THE SAME 1953 Tennessee State Constitutional Convention that had authorized metropolitan governments had allowed cities to adopt "home rule" by referendum. Under this provision, once a majority voted for home rule, the electorate could change the city charter in further referenda without going to the legislature for a "private act." Since a private act could be, in effect, vetoed by any member of a county's legislative delegation, as runoff acts had apparently been in the 1961 and 1963 legislatures, a city without home rule might be hamstrung. The City Commission therefore put a home rule amendment on the November 1963 ballot. Labor and black groups generally opposed home rule in Memphis, fearing that they would be less easily able to protect their interests than they could if all they had to do was to convince one legislator to veto a bill, but their opposition was poorly organized, and their constituencies did not rally spiritedly to this rather abstract and hypothetical cause (Greene, Grubbs, and Hobday 1975, 28–30; *MTSD*, Nov. 2, 1963, 5, 6; *MPS*, Oct. 29, 1963, 4). Home rule did not embody any specific scheme of government. Who knew, exactly, what it would bring?

Despairing of electing a candidate in an at-large race for the highly visible posts of mayor or commissioner, blacks ran no one in 1963. Had Loeb, an out-spoken segregationist who had repeatedly angered blacks during his term, run for reelection, African-Americans would have eagerly supported any opponent, as they had the hopeless Partee Fleming against Loeb in 1959. Instead, most of the black leadership, along with both newspapers and much of the Memphis establishment, endorsed Bill Farris, the white hope of 1959, but also an original Kefauverite, in his three-way contest for mayor with 62-year-old Sheriff M. A. Hinds and city judge William Ingram. Hinds received some support from minor black groups for having been the first police executive in Memphis's recent history to hire black deputies and for having opposed metro in 1962, but Willis haughtily dismissed him for having served, under the Crump regime, as the "head of the Gestapo to keep the negroes in their place" (*MPS*, Aug. 18, 1959, 21; Aug. 20, 1959, 1; Oct. 12, 1963, 12; Oct. 16, 1963, 3; Oct. 18, 1963, 28; Oct. 21, 1963, 6; Nov. 4, 1963, 21; *MTSD*, Nov. 2, 1963, 5, 6).

Ingram, a city court judge whom the black Volunteer Ticket had endorsed in 1959, was divisive and irresponsible, but he had a shrewd instinct for politics, a genius for publicity, and sufficient egotism to persevere when others would long since have given up. Since his election in 1959, he had been carrying on a highly publicized feud with the police department that had endeared him to many ordinary people, black and white, at the same time that it outraged their leaders. In a speech explaining why the black Volunteer Citizens Association was endorsing Farris, for instance, lawyer A. W. Willis Jr. said of Ingram: "I've seen him turn loose negroes who ought to have been fined, because they were guilty. And he knew it, and I knew it." Attracting few contributions or prestigious endorsements and virtually shut out of the print media, Ingram was forced to speak in parking lots with a bullhorn, and on election day he put together a bizarre coalition of some blacks, middle-class whites who were worried about higher taxes, and followers of the segregationist White Citizens' Council. Few gave him a chance to win until Hinds faded late in the campaign. The final totals showed Ingram with 48 percent, Farris with 41 percent, and Hinds with 11 percent (*MPS*, Oct. 12, 1963, 12; Nov. 6, 1963, 20; Nov. 9, 1963, 6; *MTSD*, Nov. 9, 1963, 6; Nov. 16, 1963, 1; Tucker 1980, 111–12).

When Ingram's run for higher office left his court without an incumbent, eight whites qualified, and blacks took a shot at an at-large race, running Benjamin Hooks. "With negro groups solid[ly] behind Hooks," warned the *Press-Scimitar*, "he is considered to have an excellent chance to be elected because the white vote will be divided among eight candidates." Again, panicky whites, caught without a runoff law, tried to organize an informal white primary, but this time, because of the legal nature of the post, they succeeded. They simply had the members of the bar association vote, weekly, on official voting machines, until one candidate received a majority. The others were expected to drop out, and although three did not, the winnowing process proceeded far enough that Hooks finished second to Ray W. Churchill by 1,261 votes out of more than 100,000 cast (*MPS*, Oct. 10, 1963, 23; Oct. 12, 1963, 12; Oct. 15, 1963, 4; Oct. 18, 1963, 12; Nov. 8, 1963, 1). Again, what the newspapers termed a "runoff" primary had been used to mass the white vote against a black challenger. Surely the lesson was clear to the densest political observer: the purpose of a majority-vote requirement was to keep minorities — that is, blacks — from winning.

The 1963 elections reinforced another lesson, as well. It was not possible to elect a black — *any* black — in an at-large election in Memphis at this time. In a somewhat daring departure, the *Press-Scimitar* for the first time endorsed an African-American candidate for a citywide office, one of the three blacks then running for different places on the Board of Education. Dr. Hollis Price, president of LeMoyne College since 1943, was the most bland, respectable black that could be found in Memphis. A graduate of Williston Academy and Amherst College in Massachusetts, Price held an M.A. in economics from Columbia University. Active in the Congregational Church and the Urban League (not the more desegregationist NAACP), Price had been the sole well-known African-American to endorse the metro charter (without mentioning the districting issue) in 1962. He was the only *Press-Scimitar*–endorsed school board candidate to lose, garnering less than 40 percent of the vote in a two-candidate race against a young, recently appointed white businessman (*MPS*, May 30, 1963, 6; Oct. 12, 1963, 12; Nov. 8, 1963, 1; *MCA*, Oct. 27, 1962; Board of Education Minutes, Dec. 18, 1969, b:3556).

BECAUSE three white candidates split the white vote in the Democratic primary in 1964, A. W. Willis Jr., with 36.9 percent of the vote, won an at-large nomination for the state House of Representatives from Shelby County. Immediately after the primary, there was a movement to qualify a white independent. Insurance man Jack W. Gillespie, who had lost a close race for another numbered position for the state House in the primary, was reportedly approached to run against Willis. "I believe a citizen should run as an independent candidate for Position 1, House of Representatives, who represents and is respected by a majority of the people living here, as opposed to one who represents a minority interest," Gillespie said. Even though subsequently no white independent ran, Willis was opposed by Garvin Crawford, a union member and worker at the International Harvester Company plant, whose political advertisements referred to him as the "Republican Position 1 Candidate vs. NAACP Candidates." In the ensuing November general election, Willis survived, with a bare 50.7 percent of the vote, to become the first black state legislator in Tennessee since the 1880s. The other Democratic legislative candidates received from 56 to 58.5 percent of the vote. A massive black turnout for Lyndon Johnson and a cohesive drive to get voters to simplify a long and complex ballot by pulling a single-party lever for all candidates apparently salvaged Willis's close victory (*MCA*, Aug. 9, 1964; Nov. 1, 1964, II:2; Nov. 3, 1964, 26; Nov. 4, 1964, 1, 23; Nov. 5, 1964, 14; Holloway 1969, 294–98).

In his first term in the legislature, Willis strongly supported successful bills to divide Shelby, as well as the state's other three large urban counties, into districts for election to both houses of the state legislature, as well as to split Shelby among three congressional districts. After the U.S. Supreme Court decided the reapportionment case of *Baker v. Carr* (1962), the 1963 legislature had given Shelby and other urban counties too few additional seats to satisfy a federal district court. Instead of five senators and thirteen representatives, population equality required Shelby to have six senators and sixteen representatives. Since the one-county Ninth Congressional District had the seventh highest population of any of the 435 districts in the country, the county had to be divided between at least two congressional districts, as well. Willing to deal with rural legislators who wanted to limit the increase of Shelby's overall power, the astute Willis took advantage of the necessity to redistrict to attack the at-large system and to draw a 48 percent-black congressional district that would give members of his race a chance to elect a candidate of their choice, he asserted, by about 1970.[28] Few other members of the Shelby delegation supported the move against at-large elections, and only one supported drawing congressional lines as Willis suggested. The *Press-Scimitar* was horrified that Willis favored districts instead of at-large election for the legislature "in the hope it will make easier the election of several Negro legislators in Shelby" (*MPS*, Feb. 9, 1965, 15; Feb. 10, 1965, 15, 28; May 5, 1965, 8; May 6, 1965, 8; May 11, 1965, 1, 6; May 24, 1965, 6; *MCA*, Feb. 17, 1965, 17; July 21, 1966, 49). Once again, Shelby voters were given an object lesson in the racial implications of at-large elections.

THE PASSAGE of the home rule amendment in 1963 made abolition of the city commission easier. Subsequently, instead of having to cooperate with the county government, consolidate every function, and raise fears of higher taxes to provide urban services to new areas, governmental reformers could entirely ignore the unannexed areas of Shelby County outside the city. If the number and scope of the changes in the metro charter—that book-length pamphlet—had allowed opponents to excite apprehensions about obscure provisions and the very complexity of the new arrangement, after 1963, reformers could draft short and simple amendments. Finally, they could apply the major lesson of the metro fight by making enough concessions to get the backing of every numerous group, particularly African-Americans, whose opposition was widely credited with dooming metro (Morris n.d., 4).

But many "reformers," while desiring black support, wanted to preserve all at-large elections, some wished to use the opportunity of rewriting the charter to enact a runoff law, and a few were initially unwilling even to meet with African-Americans in public (Morris undated, 4). So, while in some ways the governmental restructuring efforts of 1965–66 reflected lessons learned in the metro struggle, in other ways the conflict over the "Program of Progress" was a reprise of earlier fights over runoffs and district vs. at-large elections. Always, the underlying issue was racial. The major questions about the final product of the deliberations are these: first, whether it indicated the political strength of blacks or their weakness; second, whether it revealed the willingness of whites to share power or their desire to maintain as much of it as possible.

ALTHOUGH technically its membership was open to every voter who lived or worked in Memphis, the "Program of Progress" was actually instigated by a few men and subsequently controlled by a somewhat larger number of other men and women (*MPS*, Jan. 24, 1966, 10). What made it different was that Republican activists and black leaders were, for the first time, included in the final negotiations. Only two major forces, Democrats of the old Crump era and members of the Ingram administration or his identifiable allies, were frozen out, exclusions that nearly resulted in the defeat of the new charter in the referendum.

As early as February 1964, Lucius Burch, the original Memphis Kefauverite and longtime critic of the commission form of government, saw the constant bickering in the Ingram administration as an opportunity to remake the city charter. Burch followed up his proposal to *Commercial Appeal* editor Frank Ahlgren and *Press-Scimitar* editor Charles Schneider for the formation of a study group of people "truly representative of the power structure of the city" with a sixteen-page paper that recommended a council-manager system for Memphis. Burch's paper took no stand on the issues of district elections or runoffs. Prodded by Burch, Ahlgren assigned Jack H. Morris, a local government reporter for the *Commercial Appeal*, to write an extensively researched ten-part series of articles on the commission and other forms of local government then in use across the country. With Morris's help, Burch then brought together eight community leaders, including representatives of labor unions and blacks, to orchestrate large public meetings at which a citizen charter reform group would be given legitimacy. A slate was prepared, carefully balancing representatives of various constituencies, and in January 1966 the "Program of Progress" or "POP" committee, made up of twenty-four men and one woman, was christened, the daily newspapers serving as proud god-parents. The twenty-five included seven prominent Republicans and perhaps four others who were less open in their party persuasions but at least moving in a Republican direction; six Chamber of Commerce leaders (some Republican); six blacks, notably, Willis, Sugarmon, and Jesse Turner; two labor leaders; two Protestant clergymen and a rabbi; and one political scientist. As a student of the POP, Jonathan Wax, put it, "The leaders made every effort to keep the new movement reputable" (Tucker 1980, 112–15; Morris n.d., 3–9; *MCA*, Dec. 17, 1965, 1; *MPS*, Dec. 17, 1965; Feb. 25, 1966; Wax 1968, 48).

The two key issues in the deliberations of the POP committee, according to an unpublished insider account by Jack Morris, and certainly the two that took up the most time and generated the most published comments, were the district vs. at-large question and the runoff. According to Jonathan Wax, at-large was "the issue that several of the directors feared would destroy POP. . . . The minority groups, particularly the Negroes, favored districts in order to gain representation in the new government." Sugarmon, Turner, and Willis held out, at least partly for tactical reasons, for an all-district council, while the businessmen and clergy on the committee, loudly seconded by the newspapers, pumped for an all at-large scheme. After a series of votes in which the blacks proposed 10–3 (ten elected by districts and three at-large), 9–4, and 8–5 schemes, the directors settled on a 7–6 lineup, and detailed the drawing of district lines largely to Sugarmon; Lewis Donelson III, a prominent Republican POP member; and Cliff Tuck, the white president of the Young Democrats. Five of the six blacks voted against the 7–6 plan. In the wake of the vote, Willis threatened that black leaders might oppose the adoption of the charter (Morris n.d., 11–12; Tucker 1980, 113–15; Wax 1968, 63–64, 106–7; *MPS*, Feb. 15, 1966, 11; Mar. 1, 1966, 2; *MCA*, Apr. 8, 1966, 1; POP Minutes, Feb. 10–28, 1966, in Program of Progress Papers, folders 69–73).

Although the home rule amendment allowed the POP directors to scrap the designated post system, they decided to maintain that rule, apparently without taking a record vote on the matter. The reasons, according to Jack Morris, remained the same as in 1959: "This method is thought to sharpen issues between candidates and eliminate the possibility of 'single-shot' voting —voting for fewer candidates than seats being filled" (*MCA*, Feb. 27, 1966, II:5; *MPS*, Feb. 25, 1966, 6).

Several Republicans, as well as all of the blacks, favored districts, the former because they were not sure that they could win in at-large elections, the latter because they were certain that they could not. Republican Lewis Donelson turned the usual Chamber of Commerce argument on its head by contending that district, not at-large, elections would entice the "best possible type of citizen to run for the council." Why? Because it would take the backing of a considerable political organization to run in an at-large contest. Dr. Vasco Smith put the black view most bluntly: "We don't stand a ghost of a chance in this town running at-large. . . . Officials elected at-large tend to think of what's good for all the people or what's best for Memphis as being what's best for only 61 per cent of the people. They forget about the 39 per cent who are Negro" (*MPS*, Feb. 15, 1966, 11; Feb. 18, 1966, 3; Feb. 19, 1966, 4; *MCA*, Feb. 9, 1966, 8; Feb. 18, 1966, 21).

By this point, many whites openly admitted the black contention. Hunter Lane Jr., a reformist city commissioner and a key behind-the-scenes player in POP, agreed that "there's no doubt that Negroes generally favor election of councilmen from districts; they want a better guarantee of direct representation in city government than has proved possible with at-large elections, and I think that with over one-third of the population of the city colored this is a perfectly understandable desire. . . . Past experience indicates the practical difficulties of electing a Negro to a major office in the city-wide election." When asked why he switched from supporting an all at-large council, POP director Rabbi James A. Wax explained, "I learned that districts present the only way that a minority in the city can receive justice at the polls and representation on the council." Although understandably very sympathetic to the POP reformers in his 1968 Princeton senior thesis, Jonathan Wax, the rabbi's son, understood the issue just as his father did: "Five commissioners elected at-large made it impossible for minority groups to win representation; the Negro community, which had developed sophisticated political machinery, felt this limitation particularly keenly" (*MPS*, Feb. 15, 1966, 11; Mar. 8, 1966, 4; Apr. 14, 1966, 8; *MCA*, Feb. 2, 1966, 19; Feb. 8, 1966, 17; Feb. 27, 1966, II:5; Wax 1968, 21).

The *Press-Scimitar* denounced the compromise, underlining the racial nature of the issue and more or less openly admitting the obvious fact that no black could be elected in Memphis at that time under an at-large system: "We urge the POP directors not to succumb to opportunism—not, for the sake of assuring election of representatives of minority segments at the start, to sacrifice the long-range welfare of the community. It is understandable that minorities who are newly feeling their oats want to get quick representation on the council. . . . Let the minorities produce and put forward candidates of such quality that they can win in city-wide voting." Knowing as he had to have that every black candidate who had run for local office at-large in Memphis had been beaten, and that several were at least as well qualified for office as their opponents, the editorialist, to give him every benefit of the doubt, must have at least meant that an at-large scheme would put off the election of blacks until some halcyon time in the future and that every at-large seat in a mixed district/at-large system would go to a white (*MPS*, Feb. 28, 1966, 6).

If the *Press-Scimitar* conveniently forgot very recent history, the *Commercial Appeal* shamelessly distorted the more distant past. Electing councilpersons by district, it argued, "would restore the ward politics, log rolling, parish rivalry and private interest protection of neighborhood aldermen. Most progressive cities had to abolish aldermen by area when this century's problems of municipal business appeared. This was the method in which there flourished graft, corruption, pockets of privilege and irregular law enforcement" (*MCA*, Feb. 19, 1966, 6). This may have been the story of some other city, but it was not that of Memphis, where district elections had been ended in 1879, where Mayor E. H. Crump, elected under the commission system, was impeached and removed from office for refusing to enforce prohibition laws, and where under Crump's aegis gambling and prostitution flourished. Crump made millions selling insurance in a city in which it was rumored to be difficult to operate a business unless one employed the correct insurance broker. Crump's city had one law for Crump's friends, another for political opponents or labor organizers, and yet another, a worse one, for blacks. All of the evils that the *Commercial Appeal* attributed to district-based elections, as the editorialist must have known, were actually concomitants of at-large elections in Memphis.

In case anyone missed the racial and partisan overtones of the district vs. at-large issue during the POP debate, a state court case argued simultaneously and closely watched in Memphis would have reminded them. In 1965, the Tennessee state legislature had, for the first time, established sub-county districts for the state senate in the state's four largest counties, including Shelby. Although a three-judge federal court had sustained the apportionment, including the senate sub-districting feature, state chancellor Ned Lentz ruled that the state constitution required countywide districts for the senate, and the state supreme court upheld his decision. News stories stressed the effect of districts on the possibility of electing blacks to the senate from the urban counties. Under a banner front-page headline, for instance, the *Press-Scimitar* announced that "The division of the four big counties would apparently have assured Negroes of winning seats in the senate. Republicans also had greater hopes for electing senatorial candidates under the districting law" (*MPS*, Mar. 7, 1966, 1; Feb. 21, 1966, 6; Feb. 22, 1966, 11; Apr. 7, 1966, 11; *MCA*, Feb. 22, 1966, 17; Mar. 8, 1966, 1; Mar. 9, 1966, 22). As voters were preparing to vote on the POP as well as on a referendum on changing the state constitution to mandate sub-county districts in urban counties, the *Press-Scimitar* again reminded Memphians of the consequences of single-member districts. Noting that representatives to the state House would be elected by districts in Shelby for the first time, Null Adams pointed out that "the result is that three Negroes will be elected from districts where most voters are Negroes. The Republicans hope to win 10 seats because these districts have voted for GOP candidates in the past." Advertising in the *Press-Scimitar*'s "Voters' Guide," the Shelby County Democratic Club urged its supporters to vote for districting the state senate because districts "will enable Negroes to be represented" (*MPS*, Oct. 5, 1966, 8; Nov. 4, 1966, A:10).

HAVING negotiated a compromise of sorts on the district vs. at-large problem, the POP directors, after weeks of debate, finessed the runoff issue by suggesting that some other group put it on the August ballot separately and delaying the POP charter vote until November. As with the at-large issue, the racial implications of the runoff issue were openly discussed and widely agreed upon. At a POP directors' hearing, for instance, Rev. Alexander Gladney, a director, declared that a runoff provision "would make it hard for members of my race to ever be elected. I think the Negroes would oppose any charter which has a runoff in it." Lucius Burch, who was then testifying, "conceded that a runoff law would make it hard for a Negro to be elected." A news story by Jack Morris casually mentioned what everyone knew to be a fact, that "a runoff law has racial overtones—it makes it more difficult for a Negro to be elected." Another Morris story framed the issue and exposed the finesse even more openly: "Memphis Negroes are opposed to a runoff because they fear it would limit their chance to obtain elective office. The possibility that this opposition could be turned against the entire effort to change the city government was influential in the POP decision not to include a runoff law in its charter." In an effort to avoid outright black opposition to the POP charter, the directors voted 14–1 against including a runoff provision (*MCA*, Apr. 22, 1966, 1; Apr. 29, 1966, 27; May 13, 1966; *MPS*, Apr. 15, 1966, 1; Apr. 22, 1966, 1; POP Minutes, Apr. 21, 1966, in Program of Progress Papers, folder 84; Morris, n.d., 12).

Predictably, the *Press-Scimitar* exploded:

> "Apparently the decision was made in order to appease the Negro leaders on the committee, on the basis that Negro citizens would not vote for the new charter if it included run-off elections. . . . A great concession has already been made to the Negro leaders who are among the members of the 25-man committee. This was the provision for a majority of the 13-man council to be elected in districts instead of at-large, from the whole city—which we think would have assured better government in the long-run. Allowing seven of the 13 councilmen to be elected by districts virtually assures two or more Negro representatives on the council. (*MPS*, Apr. 25, 1966, 6)

The logic of the paper's position is that of a tightly bound syllogism, which was, in effect, repeatedly noted in Memphis during this period. If voting is racially polarized and blacks are in a minority, they will almost always lose in a runoff. That districting, rather than at-large elections, will allow blacks to elect a certain number of candidates is a recognition of racially polarized voting. Therefore, to favor at-large elections, especially with runoffs, in those races in which white voters are in the majority is virtually to foreclose the possibility of electing blacks to those seats.

WHILE MOST of the incumbent city commissioners went along with the POP charter, and the rural and suburban elected officials were not affected by it, as they had been affected by metro in 1962, the Ingram administration directed a scattershot attack on POP that nearly succeeded. Ingram first threatened to veto the commission's ordinance placing the runoff on the August ballot, not in order to prevent it from being voted on at all, but to cause sufficient administrative delay that it would have to be scheduled for November, along with the POP charter. State representative Hugh Stanton Jr. opposed Ingram's maneuver for reasons that once again underscore the racial purposes behind adoption of the runoff:

> In the November election the people will be voting on a change in the form of government. These are distinct and different issues and should be voted on in different elections. Both questions on the same ballot would confuse some. And the citizens are more apt to approve the change in the form of government if the runoff law is already in effect and they are guaranteed that majority candidates will win. (MPS, June 1, 1966, 1)

In other words, if whites knew that blacks could not win at-large or district races with pluralities, they would feel sure that the POP charter would maintain white control and would therefore accept it. In November, the black Shelby County Democratic Club endorsed the Republican opponents of Stanton and state senator Joe Pipkin because of the incumbents' efforts "in securing a runoff law in the City of Memphis" (*MPS*, May 11, 1966, 11; May 30, 1966, 2; Nov. 1, 1966, 8).

Statements during the runoff campaign echoed Stanton's sentiments. Attorney Charles Crump told the *Press-Scimitar* that he was for a majority-vote requirement because under a plurality system "any small group in a bloc vote could elect a person without a majority." In a letter to the editor, William Johnson told the *Press-Scimitar* that he opposed the runoff because it was "used only in the South, mostly to gang up on minorities, such as Jews, Catholics, Negroes and labor and other groups." Opponents of the runoff, said the *Commercial Appeal* in an election-eve editorial, "contend the runoff weakens the voice of minorities." "Negro and labor forces," Jack Morris reported, "fear that a run-off law would dilute their strength at the polls." "Opponents contend the runoff weakens the voice of minorities," the *Commercial Appeal*—

again—reminded voters on the morning of the referendum. With black organizations split in the gubernatorial and senatorial contests, and white support for runoffs in local elections overwhelming, the runoff provision passed its August test by 35,573 to 8,047, a margin of seven to one. Only 19.7 percent of the registered voters, however, expressed an opinion on the issue (*MPS*, July 11, 1966, 1; July 30, 1966; *MCA*, July 21, 1966, 49; Aug. 1, 1966, 25; Aug. 4, 1966, 59; Aug. 6, 1966, B:7).

With the runoff secured, the "reform" forces largely relaxed. Jack Morris and commissioner Hunter Lane "became appalled at the lack of campaign spirit coming from POP headquarters. No pamphlets had been printed, no copies of the charter distributed, no advertising undertaken." Lane raised money and personally staffed the office. Without a "last boost" from the Chamber of Commerce in the two weeks before the election, POP chairman Downing Pryor was convinced, the POP "would not have succeeded" (Morris n.d., 14; Downing Pryor to W. C. Mieher [president of the Chamber of Commerce], Nov. 10, 1966, in Program of Progress Papers, folder 57; Wax 1968, 111–12).

Observers disagreed on whether Ingram's blustering opposition helped more than it hurt the POP cause. Terming POP the "Program of Plunder," Ingram charged in large newspaper ads, paid for by the city, that the new charter would lead to graft, corruption, and higher taxes. Attempting to frighten the extreme segregationist part of his constituency, Ingram trumpeted: "A Majority of POP Councilmen Will Be Elected by Minority Vote from Districts"[29] (*MCA*, Oct. 17, 1966, 6; Nov. 5, 1966; Nov. 10, 1966, 67; Morris n.d., 16; Wax 1968, 90). Some former Crump organization men, including ex-mayor Walter Chandler, longtime activist and former state legislator Joseph Hanover, and ex-commissioners Buddy Dwyer and Stanley Dillard, joined Ingram in opposition, as did the black "Ministers' Independent Council of Political Leadership." In the final analysis, however, the "reformers" had learned their lesson in 1962. The POP charter, in the words of *Press-Scimitar* political writer Null Adams, was "designed in part to attract votes and it is doing just that. The election of seven of the thirteen councilmen from separate districts—instead of by a citywide vote—will bring Negro and Republican support for the proposal on the Nov. 8 ballot." The proposal carried, garnering 59.4 percent of the votes (*MPS*, Oct. 8, 1966, 4; Oct. 19, 1966, 1; Oct. 21, 1966, 2; Oct. 22, 1966, 3; Wax 1968, 91, 107, 109, 113–14).[30]

COMMENTS during the campaign demonstrate that the POP compromise on mixed district/at-large representation was a sign of black weakness, not black political strength. In a radio debate with Russell Sugarmon, Mayor William Ingram warned, "[A]fter they get this thing voted in, your Goldwater buddies can redistrict it (the council districts) so you won't have any representation whatever." Lamely, Sugarmon replied: "[N]o Southern white man can represent the Negro adequately. For ten years, we've been petitioning, with little change. We need people in government to whom the individual voter can look." Ingram riposted: "If you (Negro voters) do elect two representatives out of thirteen, what's that? One-sixth?" "That's better than none out of five," Sugarmon responded. "Since this runoff law was passed, our choice is POP or no representation at all." As if to prove that for once, Ingram was not merely scare-mongering, Henry Loeb, the former and future mayor, told the "Transportation Club" at a Claridge Hotel luncheon that although he generally favored the new charter, he opposed electing any councilpersons by district. "But," he added significantly, "under Home Rule we can correct these things as we go along." In other words, if Loeb had his way, African-Americans could not even be sure of winning any seats in the council at all in the future (*MCA*, Nov. 1, 1966, 15; *MPS*, Oct. 26, 1966, 11). In Memphis, white "liberals" were those who were willing to give blacks two or three out of thirteen seats if such a concession was necessary to obtain the white reformers' goal of replacing the city commission by a more "modern" form of government or, for Republican reformers, to assure representation for themselves. "Conservatives" like Loeb were those who were so strongly against allowing blacks to elect candidates of their choice that they were willing to renounce public bargains in order to achieve their goal of an absolutely all-white government rather than one in which blacks had at least token representation.

Were the voters who passed the POP charter in the referendum aware of the racial consequences of the district vs. at-large issue? Did they know that it was virtually impossible for African-Americans to win at-large elections in Memphis at the time? For anyone who had somehow missed all the major political events of the past decade, the *Commercial Appeal* made sure in its series of questions and answers on the POP charter in the days before the election that these effects were understood.

> Q. Would the division of the city into districts place a Negro in City Hall?

> A. Yes, two and possibly four districts could be expected to elect Negro councilmen. POP directors believe it just to provide representation on the city's lawmaking body for a group which includes one-third of the city's population. The election of officials from the city at-large, as is done with the commission, makes it harder for a Negro to win office. (*MCA*, Oct. 23, 1966, II:6)

• • •

THE MUNICIPAL elections of 1967, the first in Memphis under a mayor-council form of government in more than fifty years, might have been designed to prove the accuracy of black expectations about at-large elections and fears about the runoff. They also marked a deep split among black political leaders and derailed the political careers of three promising politicians, all of whom were casualties of Memphis's racially polarized politics and the electoral devices that had been designed to insure white control.

According to the *Press-Scimitar* and *Commercial Appeal*, which had always been hostile to him, Mayor William B. Ingram had spent four years breaking with erstwhile friends, feuding with everyone else, opposing governmental reforms, and generally making people ashamed to admit that they were Memphians. Nevertheless, Memphis had attracted job-packed industries during his term, a growing tax base had allowed him to hold the property tax rate constant, and the city had avoided serious race riots. It was no surprise that he declared for reelection or that his controversial record attracted five well-known opponents (*MPS*, Oct. 11, 1967; Oct. 20, 1967, 1; Oct. 25, 1967, 12; *MCA*, Nov. 2, 1967, 6).

Former mayor Henry Loeb, who had resigned to tend his family's laundry business shortly before the end of the term to which he had been elected in 1959, now wanted to return to government. Memphis-born but educated at Brown University, a member of Temple Israel who was careful to let it be known that he attended the Episcopal church with his wife, a World War II Navy buddy of John F. Kennedy, the handsome and charming Loeb had seemed a liberal when elected to the City Commission in 1955, but had become so identified with the segregationist cause that blacks of every faction united in opposing him (*MPS*, Sept. 30, 1967, A:24, 25).

William N. "Bill" Morris, who gained the *Commercial Appeal*'s endorsement, had been elected sheriff in 1964 and 1966. Born in Mississippi and educated in Mississippi and Alabama, the young Morris, only 34 in 1967, had graduated from Memphis State, served in the 101st Airborne, and worked as a printer and sales manager for a leasing company before his election as sheriff. His politics were as vague as Ingram's, if less volatile (*MCA*, Oct. 3, 1967, 6).

Hunter Lane was an impeccably designed moderate politician in what was, unfortunately for him, an immoderate city. Quarterback of the (white) state championship football team, as well as student body president at Memphis Central High, Lane was a magna cum laude graduate of Washington and Lee University, from which he also obtained his law degree. Returning to Memphis, he practiced law for several years, upset incumbent Buddy Dwyer for the City Commission in 1963, and worked behind the scenes for POP and the runoff in 1966. A director of the Citizens Association, vice chairman of the Better Schools Committee, and a scoutmaster, Lane was 38, earnest and hardworking, and a favorite of the newspapers, especially the *Press-Scimitar*, which endorsed him for mayor in 1967 (*MPS*, Sept. 26, 1967, 6; Sept. 30, 1967, A:24, 25).

Two years older than Lane, City Commissioner Pete Sisson almost matched Lane's resume. President of his senior class at South Side High, he was all-Memphis in basketball and graduated from Memphis State and the University of Memphis Law School. President of the Jaycees and chairman of the March of Dimes, he was active in the Citizens Association and the Chamber of Commerce and had been a Merchant Marine in World War II. Lacking newspaper and other big-name endorsements, his campaign quickly languished, finishing with a mere 2.3 percent of the primary vote (*MPS*, Sept. 30, 1967, A:24, 25; Oct. 6, 1967, 13).

A. W. Willis Jr. was the first African-American to run for mayor of Memphis, as he had been the state's first black legislator since the 1880s. Having grown up in Memphis and served in the army in Europe from 1943 to 1946, Willis did not have the option of attending white-only Memphis State or Washington and Lee, as the other future candidates did. After graduating from all-black Talladega College in Alabama, he was one of the first southern blacks to get a law degree at the University of Wisconsin. Returning to Memphis, he formed a law partnership with Russell Sugarmon, and together they prosecuted most of the city's civil rights cases and, along with other leaders of the NAACP, organized the black political campaigns in the city in the 1950s and 60s (*MPS*, Sept. 30, 1967, A:24, 25). Short and slightly built, Willis was smart and fiery, and he convinced himself that he could become the first black mayor of a large Deep South city—if not in 1967, then later.

The strategy of the almost issueless campaign was determined primarily by the existence of the runoff. In contrast to 1959, whites did not have to single out a front-runner before the election. For even if Willis made the runoff, whites, who comprised nearly two-thirds of the registered voters in 1967, could always solidify behind his opponent in the second election. Mayor Ingram's tactics in the primary brilliantly built on this fact. With no evidence that he was ever willing to make public, Ingram charged that Loeb had paid Willis $35,000 to get into the contest in order to take black votes away from Ingram. Despite the implausibility of the allegation that Willis, who had devoted long hours and received little compensation defending the black community's civil rights, would willingly assist the leading segregationist in the mayor's race, the charge stuck, and it undermined Willis's support among blacks. The black "Unity League," which endorsed Ingram, distributed a cartoon of Willis sitting on Loeb's lap counting $50 bills. That it probably hurt Loeb among whites—he had no black support to lose—is implied by the vigor with which Loeb denounced the aspersion: "I know it is a lie, you know it is a lie, and what's more disgraceful, is the fact that the current mayor knows it is a lie." Not just "an unmitigated liar," in Loeb's view, Ingram was also "a master of distortion, crafty and evasive" who heaped "abuse and humiliation" on anyone who "dared to disagree with him" (*MPS*, Sept. 9, 1967; Sept. 22, 1967, 15; Oct. 11, 1967; Oct. 28, 1967, 2).

What gave the rumor credence among African-Americans was their inability to imagine Willis beating a white candidate even if he did get into the runoff. Thus the United Baptist Churches' Association asked Willis to withdraw from the contest for mayor because "we feel it is impossible for you, or any Negro, to become mayor of our city at this time" (*MPS*, Oct. 4, 1967, 41). Since he could not expect to win in a racially polarized electorate with a majority-vote requirement, why was he running, blacks asked themselves. Ingram's unsubstantiated but constantly repeated rumor provided a ready answer.

The bandwagon effect that had undercut the campaigns of Fowler, Canale, and Chambers in 1959 and Hinds in 1963 also helped sweep Lane, Morris, Sisson, and Willis away in 1967. Lane never made many inroads into the black vote, because, although he proposed concrete programs to end racial discrimination in city jobs and build more low-cost housing, he also touted his role in the passage of the runoff in 1966, a position that was anathema to blacks[31] (*MPS*, Sept. 30, 1967, 1, 3; Nov. 1, 1967, 10). Willis's great difficulty was not attracting white votes—he never had a chance to do that and ended with fewer than a thousand—but convincing blacks that voting for him was not futile. As the Unity League put it: "It's impossible for a Negro to win the mayor's office at this time. Why waste your vote on Willis?" Willis's overblown prediction at his campaign-opening speech that he would win a majority in the primary both showed that he recognized the problem and undermined his credibility (*MPS*, Sept. 8, 1967; Sept. 16, 1967, 4; Oct. 4, 1967, 41; Oct. 23, 1967, 17).

Although his promises (for instance, to be "mayor of all the people") were much less specific than Lane's or Willis's, and although he refused to back an open housing ordinance or to abjure segregation, Mayor Ingram increasingly corralled the majority of black votes by repeating his contention that Willis could never win a runoff and that he was a bribed stalking horse for Henry Loeb. As the *Commercial Appeal* put it, black ministers "in the Ingram camp and other Ingram aides hammered away on the theme that Mr. Willis simply could not win since Negroes account for only 34 per cent of the city's registered voters. . . . Rumors that Mr. Loeb paid Mr. Willis $35,000 to enter the race were spread throughout the Negro community." Realizing that his base was being looted, Willis flailed helplessly. "Mayor Ingram campaigns in total secrecy. . . . Ingram talks like a racist to white voters and another way to Negro voters. . . . Ingram is trying to do as he did four years ago—get the segregationists as well as Negroes to vote for him" (*MPS*, Sept. 27, 1967, 1, 12; Sept. 28, 1967, 1; Sept. 30, 1967, 1, 3; Oct. 6, 1967, 1; Oct. 18, 1967, 22; Oct. 23, 1967, 17; Oct. 27, 1967, 15; *MCA*, Oct. 7, 1967, 17).

On primary day, October 5, Loeb ran first, with 33 percent of the vote, virtually all of it white. Ingram slipped into the runoff with 24.9 percent, polling an estimated 53 percent of the black vote, but only 12 percent of the white ballots. While Morris's respectable 21.4 percent showing invigorated his future political career, Lane's embarrassing 6.1 percent virtually killed his. Most humiliating of all, Willis finished a poor fourth, with only 12.2 percent of the total vote and an estimated 39 percent of the black electorate. Many blacks reportedly abstained, not wanting to vote against Willis but not wanting to help him get into a hopeless runoff, either. The *Press-Scimitar*, always anxious to point out schisms in the black community, crowed that the election marked "the destruction of the Negro bloc-voting myth" and that Ingram had broken "the back of the Shelby [County] Democratic Club." Unlike most other black politicians and groups, Willis and the SCDC refused to endorse Ingram in the runoff (*MPS*, July 17, 1962; Sept. 20, 1967, 37; Oct. 6, 1967, 1, 6, 13; Oct. 11, 1967; Oct. 18, 1967; Oct. 20, 1967, 21; Oct. 23, 1967, 17; Oct. 27, 1967, 14; *MCA*, Oct. 6, 1967, 27).

The day before the runoff election in November, *Press-Scimitar* political editor Null Adams predicted that Loeb would win because of the "white backlash" against Ingram's success in seeking black votes. In the largest total vote in Memphis's history up to that time, Loeb proved Adams an acute prognosticator, winning by a 54–46 margin. Essentially, Loeb put together his and Morris's primary votes, while Ingram added Willis's to his own in the first election. In what Adams said was a typical overwhelmingly black precinct, Ingram got 94.6 percent of the vote in the runoff, while in a typical homogeneously white precinct, Loeb received 89.1 percent. Although he had carried the conservative Frayser area "handsomely" in 1963, this time, identified as the "big Negro choice," Ingram lost it by better than two to one (*MPS*, Nov. 1, 1967, 10; Nov. 3, 1967, 1; *MCA*, Nov. 3, 1967, 1). Ingram's earlier opposition to the runoff law, which had no doubt appealed to blacks and which had kept his campaign alive through October, once again demonstrated his political sagacity. Any person, regardless of race, who was clearly marked as the candidate of choice of the black community was doomed by the runoff law.

IF THE mayor's race proved that an at-large election with a majority-vote requirement worked exactly as expected—that is, it denied minority voters an opportunity to elect a candidate of their choice—the contemporaneous at-large council races demonstrated that political devices may be so effective that they discourage anyone from seriously testing them. The "most noticeable characteristic about the city-wide council races," *Press-Scimitar* reporter Edward L. Topp remarked at the beginning of the primary campaign in 1967, "is that there are only three Negroes among the 43 candidates" for the six positions. The view that blacks could not win in such a system was so widespread that only minor black candidates ran for the at-large council seats, and the outcome—only one received as much as 12 percent of the vote—showed that the view was correct. In the runoff, the three white candidates who received the most solid black support all lost (*MPS*, Sept. 4, 1967, 17; Oct. 6, 1967, 13; Oct. 7, 1967, 17; Nov. 3, 1967, 1).

Not only were they uniformly white, the at-large winners were also much more likely to be of upper-class status than their district counterparts. Three were major businessmen and three attorneys, while the district winners included a housewife and a minister. At-large members were likely to belong to upper-crust churches, Presbyterian and Episcopalian, whereas district representatives were usually drawn from the more déclassé Church of Christ or the Baptist Church. All the at-large councilmen lived in the relatively prestigious Midtown or East Memphis areas, while district councilpersons represented not only those but working-class Frayser and black Orange Mound as well (Ripy 1973, 91–94). The Chamber of Commerce and the Citizens Association had known exactly what they would get when they pushed to maintain at-large elections for the Memphis city government.

The district elections basically followed party and racial lines. Lyndon Johnson had carried four of the seven districts in the 1964 presidential election, and Democratic candidates for the council won four. In the two majority-black districts, only three of the fifteen primary candidates were white, and they were eliminated in the first round. In the one marginal district (47.3 percent black among registered voters), the runoff pitted a black, Fred L. Davis, who was endorsed by the *Press-Scimitar,* against a white, Elmer B. Vaughn. Shortly before primary day, Vaughn's sound truck had toured the district "telling the voters that they had a choice between voting for him or having a Negro council representative." In a slight upset, Davis, who also had the backing of the AFL-CIO and the Citizens Association and benefited from the Ingram organization's intense get-out-the-vote effort in Orange Mound, won the runoff with 53.2 percent of the vote. Only one serious black candidate ran in any of the "whiter" districts. In the first district, which was 38 percent black in voter registration, Rev. Alexander Gladney, a POP director, finished third in the primary (*MPS*, Sept. 29, 1967, 8; Oct. 6, 1967, 13; Oct 17, 1967, 10; Oct. 19, 1967, 21; Oct. 28, 1967, A:12; Nov. 3, 1967).[32]

As a whole, the council almost perfectly reflected the POP designs—indeed, two of the most prominent POP directors, Downing Pryor and Lewis Donelson III, were elected to at-large seats. Instead of the white Democrats, mostly conservative, who had filled the City Commission, the new council consisted of five Republicans, four independents, and only four Democrats, three of whom were black (*MPS*, Nov. 3, 1967, 1). The election returns alone should quash any notion that the POP directors were service club amateurs or that they were unsure or unconscious of the political implications of any action that they took.

TWO BLACK candidates were among the fourteen for the five at-large school board seats in 1967: Rev. E. W. Williamson, who had run unsuccessfully in 1963, and Rev. James M. Lawson, a close adviser to Martin Luther King Jr., and one of the principal proponents and organizers of Gandhian nonviolence throughout the South during the civil rights movement (Beifuss 1989, 137–42; McKnight [1984] 1989, 645–46). Neither got as much as 30 percent in his three-person contest, and all five of the incumbents were reelected without runoffs (*MPS*, Sept. 30, 1967, A:27; Oct. 6, 1967, 13). Despite the fact that a majority of the students in the public schools were African-Americans, the school board, elected at-large with numbered posts and a majority-vote requirement, had not had a black member since the 1880s. Excluded from office by racial bloc voting and an electoral structure that denied minorities any representation at all, the black community had no alternative after 1954 but to file seemingly endless desegregation cases before notably unresponsive federal district judges. The school board's tactics of discuss, delay, and appeal were captured perfectly in a 1965 page-one headline in the *Commercial Appeal*: "Board To Fight Racial Change" (*MCA*, May 28, 1965, 1).

In the aftermath of the 1969 sanitation workers' strike, which brought Martin Luther King Jr. to Memphis and an early death, the NAACP and other groups called a series of "Black Monday" school boycotts that kept as many as 60,000 students away from the public schools. The Board's response was to propose that it temporarily add two nonvoting black "advisers," LeMoyne-Owen College president Hollis Price and 30-year-old local attorney George H. Brown Jr., and that it work with the legislature to change the method of election so that it would be possible to elect some African-Americans to the body. The Board's leading racial hard-liner, Hugh Bosworth, raged: "The white majority not only in Memphis but across the nation is getting fed up with the placating, milk-sop approach being taken here in Memphis." When the majority of the Board settled on a proposal that called for seven board members to be elected by district and four at-large, Mayor Loeb and conservative city councilman Wyeth Chandler successfully led a fight to include a runoff provision. Unless runoffs were guaranteed, Chandler asserted, "I think it's going to give the NAACP control of the school board." Two black city councilmen agreed with Chandler's analysis, if not his policy preferences. "The only reason that you had a runoff in the first place," noted Fred L. Davis, "was to stop black single-shotting." James L. Netters added: "You know a black man will never get elected at large with a runoff" (Memphis Board of Education Minutes, July 25, Sept. 26, Oct. 24, Dec. 18, 1969, 3396, 3492, 3517, 3556; *MCA*, Nov. 7, 1969, 1, 6; Nov. 17, 1969, 1, 9; Nov. 18, 1969, 11; Dec. 19, 1969, 1; Jan. 21, 1970, 15).

Hugh Bosworth of the Board opposed any districts at all:

> The primary reason for districts, is to guarantee the election of one or more Negro board members. . . . It is interesting that some supporters of districting are not really supporters of the majority vote at all. Rather they oppose election by position and want election by plurality rather than majority. Such a position undermines rather than strengthens our democratic form of government. This is minority rather than majority rule. We need to eliminate the possibility of a plurality from school board elections rather than to weaken the democratic process further. And last but not least the very Negroes [who] would benefit supposedly by districts should, I think, consider themselves insulted by the proponents of districting. After all, what are these supposedly benevolent people really saying? At best they are saying that no Negro can be elected on the basis of merit alone. They are saying that no Negro can run on a non-racial basis. They are saying that the white voters will never allow any Negro to be elected. These people would deny the Negro an equal opportunity to be elected on an equal basis.

What was at stake in maintaining the at-large, numbered-post system, Bosworth announced, was nothing less than "American liberty" (Memphis Board of Education Minutes, Mar. 14, 1969, 3206; *MCA*, Mar. 15, 1969, II:1). After a bitter, public struggle that forced the state legislature to abandon its decades-old unit method of proceeding in local legislation, under which any House or Senate member of a county delegation could veto any proposed local law, the legislature set up a new system of seven single-district members and two at-large members with runoffs for each seat on the Memphis school board. Only the refusal of Republican and conservative Democratic legislators to support any change unless it contained a majority-vote provision forced African-American House members to accede to what one termed a "disenfranchisement gimmick" (*MCA*, Nov. 14, 1969, 6; Jan. 4, 1970, VI:4; Jan. 11, 1970, VI:4; Jan. 13, 1970, 1; Jan. 14, 1970, 6; Jan. 19, 1970, 6; Jan. 21, 1970, 1; Feb. 1, 1970, 1; Feb. 2, 1970, 23; Feb. 5, 1970, 1; Feb. 8, 1970, 1, 3; Feb. 9, 1970, 1; Feb. 11, 1970, 1;

Feb. 13, 1970, 1; Feb. 15, 1970, 1; Feb. 17, 1970, 1; Feb. 20, 1970, 1, 21; Feb. 21, 1970, 6; Kousser 1992, 67–76).

WHAT DOES the evidence add up to? Were the at-large, designated post, and runoff laws just "disenfranchisement gimmicks" or were they adopted for nonracial reasons? Although only one scholar seems to have published an explanation of any of the events considered in this paper, similar happenings in other places have been studied, and various alternative explanations have been put forth about those instances (Tucker 1980, 100–117). The first might be termed the "civic virtue hypothesis": Electoral laws are framed by disinterested reformers who merely want to "do good" or achieve some abstract ideal, such as a more democratic or efficient polity, or the election of people with a "community-wide viewpoint." In this case, newspaper editorialists and such people as Henry Loeb and Hugh Bosworth claimed that it was a devotion to "majority rule" that caused them to favor at-large elections or runoffs. In a letter of protest against the filing of the case of *U.S. v. City of Memphis,* Jack H. Morris, a key participant as well as a newspaper reporter for the *Commercial Appeal* during the period when the POP Charter was framed, retrospectively saw the POP as resulting "from the tireless efforts of a number of good men and women, both black and white, to create a fairer and better government" (Morris to Attorney General Dick Thornburgh, Mar. 17, 1991, in Morris 1991).

The second, closely related thesis stresses that compromise is necessary in an imperfect world, especially a world less enlightened than our own. In 1966, when the runoff and POP charter were instituted, for example, was it not a triumph to desegregate Memphis officeholding at all, even with two or three members out of thirteen? Jack Morris's 1991 letter also puts forward this thesis, which he does not distinguish from the pure civic virtue hypothesis. One of the POP Commission's "objectives from the start was to provide a system of government in which blacks *could* hold elective office. . . . It was always recognized, and supported, that districts would bring blacks into city government for the first time." Again, in 1970, was it not a progressive step to add district seats, a few of which would certainly be filled by blacks, to the Board of Education? Could these changes, which allowed blacks to share political power for the first time in Memphis, have been motivated by racially discriminatory purposes?

A third, less starry-eyed explanation, the one favored by lawyers for Los Angeles County in the *Garza* case, admits that self-interest often motivates rule-makers but claims that, at least in particular cases, they wished only to preserve their own political careers or to assist those of members of their political party or social class. They were, in this view, indifferent to the race of their opponents. Another familiar contention, the unintended-consequences hypothesis, is that the effects in question were unforeseen and therefore necessarily unintended. Designated posts might have been adopted for reasons of efficiency, for instance, without their framers meaning for blacks to be adversely affected by the change. The runoff might have been inspired by William Ingram's 48 percent margin in 1963 and the temporary consternation that more settled souls felt about the disorderly wrangling that marred city government during the Ingram administration.

Let us consider the "do-gooder" explanation first. Was the "majority rule" phraseology employed by the proponents of at-large elections and runoff requirements in Memphis in the period after 1955, for instance, just decorative rhetoric, a euphemism for *white* majority rule? In the only scholarly book on Memphis politics during this period, David Tucker devotes a paragraph to the decision of the 1962 Metro Charter Commission to substitute at-large elections for the originally proposed district elections for the council and school board. While admitting that blacks believed that the decision was "anti-Negro," Tucker contends that it

> represented the chamber [of commerce]'s abstract political theory, shared by reformers such as Lucius Burch, that at-large elections would avoid corrupt ward politics and insure the election of men who would never put the needs of their own district above the welfare of the entire community. To be sure, at-large campaigns were expensive and more likely to elect financially able candidates from the Chamber of Commerce, but *not all chamber representatives sought to exclude blacks from office.* (Tucker 1980, 108, italics added)

Tucker does not discuss the purposes of designated posts or the runoff in his book, and he might well admit that such provisions were racially discriminatory in purpose, even if he thought that the at-large scheme was not. After all, the principal theme of his book is "the central role of race" (Tucker 1980, xi). Moreover, it is difficult to imagine how numbered posts or runoffs would discourage corruption or parochialism. Therefore, whether or not avoiding corruption or parochialism were the goals of reformers, these objectives can at most explain the maintenance of at-large elections.

Even more important, Tucker admits indirectly that at least *some* Charter Commission members wanted to exclude blacks from office. Among those who did not, he mentioned only Stanley Buckman, who proposed that the Charter Commission temporarily appoint "acceptable" blacks to two of the twelve positions on the council. Since the Charter Commission vote to substitute at-large for district elections was 6–4, the switch of one of the Chamber appointees would have resulted in a tie vote, and the switch of two would have resulted in a proposal with at least ten districts. Even if racial concerns moved only a few of the Chamber members, then, their role was pivotal, tipping the decision toward at-large elections. Under commonsensical notions of causation,[33] then, racially discriminatory intentions caused the maintenance of at-large elections in this instance, even if Tucker's contention is fully accepted.

But the stances of even the most liberal of Memphis's reformers, such as Hunter Lane, Stanley Buckman, and Lucius Burch, led inexorably to racially unequal political outcomes, as they were fully aware. All three realized, as did every political observer in Memphis at the time, that except in the most unusual cases, whites would fill every at-large seat, and that majority-vote requirements and anti–single shot arrangements disadvantaged black candidates. "The Negro electorate is justifiably suspicious and distrustful of the degree to which their interest will be protected by the general constituency," Burch told a POP hearing. As the *Press-Scimitar* summarized Burch's views: "In order to obtain Negro support, which is absolutely necessary for the approval of the charter, there must be some representation by districts. . . . Burch conceded that a runoff law would make it hard for a Negro to be elected" (*MPS*, Apr. 14, 1966, 8; Apr. 15, 1966, 1). The reformers knew that few whites in Memphis would vote for a black, however well qualified. Indeed, Buckman had taken a leadership role in the "Stop Sugarmon" campaign of 1959, and neither Lane nor Burch had spoken out against this effort. Thus, even if they acted out of some "abstract idea," they were fully mindful of the fact that one consequence of that idea was to deny blacks an equal opportunity to elect their most preferred candidates.

And the "reformers" did not act alone. Indeed, they were not the chief actors. Burch, Lane, and Edmund Orgill never served on a charter commission or as POP directors, and Burch never held important elective office at all. The major actors were politicians such as Henry Loeb, Wyeth Chandler, and Hugh Bosworth, and they were more open about their racially discriminatory motives in pushing for numbered posts, the runoff, and the continuation of at-large elections. All three built their careers on the "white backlash," and their statements make clear that when they spoke of "majority rule," they explicitly meant *white* majority rule (Beifuss 1989, 55–56, 80; *NYT*, Nov. 15, 1979, A:24).

Along with the most staunchly segregationist politicians and at least some of the white liberals, the *Press-Scimitar* and *Commercial Appeal* and their editors avidly participated in the campaign against Sugarmon, Hooks, and the other blacks on the "Volunteer Ticket" in 1959, and, of course, neither paper endorsed Willis for mayor in 1967. The *Commercial Appeal* was especially vocal in its support for the school board's foot-dragging on integration. Both papers laced their editorials on the subjects of at-large elections, designated posts, and runoffs with patronizing lectures to blacks advising them to abandon their insistence on electing candidates of their choice for the good of the (white) majority in Memphis. Both explicitly recognized, time and time again, that designated posts, at-large elections, and runoffs disadvantaged black candidates, and they distorted history or ignored the facts of recent elections, of which they must have been keenly aware, in order to reach the predetermined conclusions of their editorials. When considered in the context of the elections and other events during the period, the newspaper editorialists' rhetorical devotion to "majority rule" does not provide evidence for the importance of nonracial motives in the adoption or maintenance of the electoral devices in question.

A similar argument dooms the "compromise" or "progressive step" hypothesis. If the racial opinions of elites or the white public were so conservative during the 1950s and 1960s in Memphis that only small steps toward racial equality could be taken, then the maintenance of at-large elections for six city council and two school board seats must logically have been the result of white racial concerns. Suppose that former *Commercial Appeal* reporter Morris and the POP charter group had been as perfectly virtuous in 1966 as he asserted, in the midst of a voting rights case twenty-five years later, that they had been. Even so, if those men and women kept six seats at-large knowing the racial consequences of their act, at least partially because of a belief that less racially tolerant leaders or members of the public would oppose the POP charter if it allowed blacks "too much" power by adopting a plan with a higher proportion of districts, then their actions were taken because of racial considerations. In fact, there is overwhelming evidence from statements of the time by both whites and blacks that at-large elections were continued with the expectation that they would be filled exclusively or nearly exclusively by whites, and that many white leaders favored them *because* of that understanding. Proponents of this thesis cannot have it both ways: If districts were introduced to allow blacks some representation, then, unless there was some other compelling, nonracial reason to do so, at-large seats must have been maintained to reinforce white control of the vast majority of the seats.[34]

The purpose of the detailed analyses in this chapter has been to place the consideration or adoption of particular electoral rules in a historical context that would illuminate the motives of the framers. A brief overview casts severe doubt on the unintended-consequences hypothesis as well as on the suggestion that the laws reflected politicians' self-interest but that this self-interest was not inextricably intertwined with racial considerations. The at-large system was first instituted in 1879 after a twelve-year campaign to end district elections in order to combat "a large and controlling voting element, which has but little at stake in the welfare of our city," a reference to African-Americans and perhaps some foreign-born citizens. The barely token representation of blacks in Memphis politics during the 1880s gave way after 1890 to solidly white government without noticeable black candidacies for office for the ensuing sixty years. Roy Love's near victory in 1955 and S. A. Wilbun's legislative campaign in 1958 raised expectations in the black community, which led to the "Volunteer" campaign, and fears in the white community, which led to designated posts and attempts to institute runoffs. The 1959 elections reaffirmed the push for runoffs and showed that even outstanding black candidates could expect few white votes and little chance in at-large elections. The defeat of metro in 1962 forced reformers to involve blacks in the POP, to agree to at least some districts, and to disconnect the runoff issue from the more general charter change. Blacks opposed maintaining at-large elections, as they opposed runoffs, because recent experience and simple political logic taught them that these schemes, when employed in a racially polarized electorate such as Memphis's, made it impossible for them to elect candidates that they really preferred. The 1967 elections completely fulfilled expectations, as the widely understood futility of African-American candidacies in majority-white constituencies in Memphis discouraged any serious black candidates for city council from running at-large at all and lent credence to the otherwise preposterous charge that the city's principal civil rights lawyer had conspired with its foremost segregationist. The 1969 sanitation strike and school boycott so traumatized city leaders, black and white, that whites finally agreed to add districts to the school board. Everyone fully realized that blacks could not win even token representation on the board as long as all of the seats were elected at-large and that even the 1970 revisions would result in no more than three black seats out of nine.

Putting events in their proper historical context makes clear that the individual or group self-interest thesis admits too much and ignores too much. It admits that white political leaders and electoral law reformers wanted to protect their individual, partisan, or class interests (e.g., Buckman's desire for a part-time council of affluent businessmen and professionals) but denies that such protection required discrimination against blacks. In a racially polarized polity, however, the careers of individual white politicians would surely be endangered if blacks enjoyed equal political opportunities. Very few blacks met Buckman's criterion of affluence and free time, and those who did, especially if they attained their positions by being anointed by whites, were hardly likely to be the choices of the black community. Most of all, the explanation asks us to overlook the major political, social, and economic fault line in the community, to blind ourselves to the fact that racial conflicts dominated the politics of the time in Memphis, to believe that politicians who had to be precisely attuned to racial nuances to survive in office entirely ignored racial considerations when drafting electoral laws.

The unintended-consequences hypothesis is the least plausible alternative. When newspapers, black leaders, and other white politicians were constantly stressing the racial consequences of changing or maintaining electoral laws, how could the framers of those laws (who were usually politicians themselves) have been ignorant of these implications? At best, the politicians could have considered those consequences and decided to go ahead for other reasons. But, as shown above in the discussion of the civic virtue hypothesis, every other reason that the framers may have had for acting included racial considerations on the part of crucial decisionmakers.

In sum, none of the four alternative hypotheses about changes in or maintenance of electoral laws in Memphis during the years from 1959 through 1970 accords nearly so well with logic and facts as that of racially discriminatory purpose.

THE 1991 Memphis elections began by looking like a rerun of nearly all those of the previous generation. In 1975, 1979, and 1983, African-Americans had united behind the mayoral candidacy of W. Otis Higgs Jr., a criminal court judge and former member of the same racially integrated law firm as Russell Sugarmon and A. W. Willis Jr. In the first two elections, Higgs lost to Wyeth Chandler, who used unsubtle racial appeals to the white majority in order to win runoffs, after barely finishing ahead of Higgs in the preliminary contests. In 1979, for instance, Chandler led Higgs by only 2,200 votes in the primary but won the runoff more comfortably, by 14,000 (*NYT*, Nov. 16, 1979, A:20). But when Chandler resigned to accept a judgeship in 1982, a younger and much less ideological white politician, Dick Hackett, won a special election and then defeated Higgs in 1983 in a racially polarized but less divisive campaign. Running for reelection in 1987, Hackett reportedly received nearly a fifth of the black vote; by 1991, six of his thirteen "cabinet" officers were African-Americans, and he presided over the most integrated administration in the history of Memphis government up to that time. Realizing that they could not hope to elect a black candidate against a white incumbent if their vote was divided, African-American politicians spent the first half of 1991 trying to cull the list of hopefuls, which included Higgs, Congressman Harold Ford, City Councilman Shep Wilbun, former national NAACP executive secretary Benjamin Hooks, and twelve-year school superintendent Willie Herenton. An innovative educator who had never before sought elective office, the superintendent was controversial because of a sexual harassment suit settled out of court in 1988 and because, despite great energy, he had not been able to turn the troubled Memphis schools completely around. Nonetheless, the neophyte Herenton emerged from two rather disorganized popular meetings as the anointed candidate of the black community (*MCA*, June 12, 1991, A:8;

June 13, 1991, B:1; June 15, 1991, A:1; June 16, 1991, A:1; June 17, 1991, A:1; June 20, 1991, B:1; Sept. 30, 1991, B:1; Oct. 1, 1991, A:11; Oct. 4, 1991, A:1; Pohlmann and Kirby 1996, 31–50, 74–193; Wright 1996).

The only other person to declare was Robert "Prince Mongo" Hodges, a white pizza parlor operator and perennial joke candidate, who appealed to alienated young white voters by appearing in outrageous costumes, claiming to be "a spirit from the planet Zambodia," and promising to end taxes and to hold public hangings, probably beginning with current elected officials. Even though 55 percent of the overall population of Memphis was black and black registered voters outnumbered whites by more than 10,000, there were over 21,000 registered voters who checked the "other" box on the racial question, and observers believed the vast majority of them were actually white. If turnout was equal for members of both races, or if white participation exceeded black, as it almost always did in Memphis, the whites would compose a majority of the electorate. The contest appeared to be headed for a runoff or an outright primary victory for the experienced Hackett, who raised three times the campaign funds that Herenton did (*MCA*, June 17, 1991, A:1; June 18, 1991, B:1; Sept. 27, 1991, A:9,B:1; Oct. 1, 1991, B:6).

But on July 26, 1991, a month after the candidate lineup was settled, federal district judge Jerome Turner shocked the city, as well as attorneys for all sides of the lawsuit challenging at-large elections, numbered posts, and runoffs by issuing a preliminary injunction against runoffs in at-large contests in Memphis, making his prohibition effective for the October 1991 contests.[35] The judge's action; union discontent with Hackett's opposition to raises for government workers; the anti-Establishment campaign of "Prince Mongo," who drew votes from Hackett; overconfidence that led the incumbent to refuse to debate his opponent, to eschew polls, and to spend only slightly more than half of the money he had raised; and, most important, the seemingly unbridgeable gulf between the black and white communities in the city produced a major upset. Despite his record as the most racially progressive white mayor in the history of Memphis and the backing of Higgs and the remnants of the Shelby County Democratic Club, Hackett, according to the most detailed study of the election, received only about 1 percent of the African-American votes. Congressman Ford and the visiting Jesse Jackson helped to turn out huge numbers of African-American voters for Herenton and other black at-large candidates. Despite the fact that Herenton's white support was even less than the black crossover votes received by the incumbent, Herenton won by 142 votes or 49.44 percent to Hackett's 49.38 percent, with Prince Mongo's 1.18 percent preventing either from carrying a majority of the 247,955 votes. Four of the six at-large City Council winners and one of the two at-large

Board of Education winners also polled less than a majority of the votes but avoided runoffs because of the injunction. In all, blacks doubled the number of their seats on the City Council to six of thirteen, and actually controlled a majority of the nine Board of Education positions (the schools were by then 80 percent black) for the first time ever (*MCA*, Oct. 4, 1991, A:1, 8, 16; Oct. 5, 1991, A:1; Pohlmann and Kirby, 1996, 121–93). As evidenced by their relatively low turnout, whites were much less enthusiastic about the racially conciliatory Hackett than they had been about his much more confrontational predecessors, Henry Loeb and Wyeth Chandler.

Perhaps it was inevitable that racial moderation would fail in Memphis, that a talented, seeming progressive like Henry Loeb would turn hard right, that the careers of promising moderates like Russell Sugarmon, A. W. Willis Jr., and Hunter Lane would be stillborn in those tense times, that hardier souls who tried to move toward the conciliatory center, like Otis Higgs and Dick Hackett, would be less successful than more brittle representatives of their races like Willie Herenton and Wyeth Chandler. Perhaps public opinion was just too polarized, the population was too equally split between the races, the Deep South plantation heritage was too much for either side to forget or overcome. Perhaps Memphis was just another instance of the intractability of race relations in America.

But the political structure, the three devices that were all initiated or maintained in the years from 1958 to 1966 in an effort to preserve the supremacy of the white majority, clearly did not help. Instead of encouraging moderation and cross-racial appeals and policies among both racial communities, they rewarded intransigence and a concentration on rallying one's segregated tribe. Instead of providing some influence for the minority, they guaranteed that the citywide majority winner would take all. Instead of healing divisions and eroding stereotypes, the electoral rules exacerbated both. Unlike the parallel assertions of Justice O'Connor in *Shaw v. Reno* (1993, 2827) about the deleterious consequences of race-based districting, these conclusions about the effects of the antiminority rules employed in Memphis are based on a close analysis of actual evidence.

Events in the Memphis black community in 1991 encapsulated forty years of bitter struggle, but with an ironic twist. As African-Americans were engaged in a winnowing that resembled the organization of the white bandwagon in 1959, the NAACP, which had opposed at-large elections for at least thirty years, reversed its stance. Since the 1990 census had shown a black population majority in the city, the local chapter of the NAACP decided, African-Americans were finally in a position to take advantage of the at-large system. Undercutting the stance of the group's national organization and of the Department of Justice, the Memphis NAACP asked the federal court to preserve the at-large system (*RCA*, May 30, 1991, B:1). Applying the lesson that Memphis whites had taught them over and over again, that in a jurisdictionwide system, the minority had no right to representation, the NAACP concluded that it was blacks' turn to shut the minority out.[36]

CHAPTER FOUR

Controlling the "Bloc Vote" in Georgia

M emphis was not the only southern jurisdiction that, in the shadow of continuing or increasing black political participation, adopted a majority-vote requirement or other election "reforms." In fact, southern states were the first to embrace unofficial and, later, statutory primaries for the nomination of party candidates in the late nineteenth and early twentieth centuries, and they were the only states to pass statewide runoff requirements. Racial considerations clearly played a major part in the adoption of primaries in the South, and probably in the passage of runoffs during that period, although much less research has been done on the purposes of majority-vote schemes (Kousser 1974, 72–82; 1984d).

In 1964, the state of Georgia wrote a sweeping majority-vote clause into its election code, and despite attempts in the legislature and the courts to eliminate or modify it since then, the provision remains. In a sense, determining the intent of this law was much simpler than the corresponding tasks in Los Angeles or Memphis. The Los Angeles decisions involved district boundaries drawn by a changing group of supervisors and their confederates over a 22-year period. Those in Memphis concerned actions by legislatures, city governments, and an unofficial commission, as well as the city's electorate, over a span of eighty years. By contrast, in Georgia, the behavior to be explained was the motivation of the framer and supporters of a single bill, incorporated after it had passed one house of the legislature into a section of a more extensive statute. As in Memphis, there were plenty of open or slightly coded contemporary statements about the racial purposes of the majority-vote prerequisite. But even more so than in the litigation in the Tennessee city, attorneys for the state of Georgia challenged my account of the origins of the law and produced lay witnesses who, thirty years later and in the context of a legal case that promised to tinge their historical reputations with racism, denied that considerations of race had had anything whatsoever to do with the passage of the runoff law. To understand why the legislature adopted the requirement and to choose between competing explanations of that action, one must examine the historical context and relevant aspects of the careers of the major actors and take a close look at the events surrounding the passage of the statute. A few statements by witnesses, quoted against a vague context colored by the passage of time, are not sufficient to decide the question of motivation.

THE BARE narrative is simply stated. On January 25, 1963, Representative Denmark Groover Jr. of Bibb County introduced in the Georgia House of Representatives H.B. 117, which required a majority vote to elect any candidate to a local or state office in both primary and general elections. Referred to the House Judiciary Committee, it was reported favorably by committee chairman and future governor George Busbee on February 19, without amendment. That same day, the House considered the bill, rejected amendments that apparently would have excluded some counties from the bill's coverage, adopted an amendment changing the effective date of the measure, and, after some controversy, passed the bill by a vote of 133 to 41 (Georgia House of Representatives *Journal* 1963, 301, 352, 549, 645–48). Leading the debate, Groover was quoted or paraphrased by newspaper reporters as saying that a runoff requirement would reduce the influence of "the bloc vote or special interest groups in elections," or "bloc groups," or "the Negro bloc vote," or "Negroes and other minorities." Rather than act on the bill in the few remaining days of the 1963 legislative session, the Senate in effect passed the issue along to the Election Law Study Committee (hereinafter ELSC), an advisory body that had been authorized by the legislature at the same time that the majority-vote bill passed the House. The ELSC was to recodify the state's election laws because the "county unit" system for electing statewide officers—which required that winners receive a majority of "county units," which were proportional to the grossly malapportioned seats in the state legislature—had been ruled unconstitutional in *Gray v. Sanders* in 1963 (*AC*, Feb. 20, 1963, 8).

The ELSC's proposed recodification, which the legislature considered in a two-month special session called by Gov. Carl Sanders in 1964, included a majority-vote provision that was in substance identical to Groover's measure. Neither the ELSC nor any legislative committee issued a report setting out its reasons for favoring runoffs, and there was no debate on the provision in 1964 in either house of the legislature reported by the newspapers or in official publications. On March 31, 1964, between the time that the ELSC made its recommendation and the beginning of the special session on May 2, the all-white State Democratic Executive Committee voted unanimously to require candidates for local office in Democratic primaries to be elected by majority vote. Previously, the question of requiring a majority or a plurality had been left to local party committees, and there was no uniformity from county to county or even, in some counties, from election to election. On May 22, the Senate, without taking a separate roll call on the provision requiring a majority vote in primaries and general elections, adopted it as Section 34-1514 of the election code. By a 30–8 margin, the Senate refused to postpone the effective date of the majority-vote requirement until January 1, 1965 in Fulton County, a refusal that had the effect of destroying the chances of African-American Atlanta lawyer Donald Hollowell to win a superior court judgeship. The House likewise passed the bill with no separate discussion or roll call on the majority-vote section (*AC*, Apr. 1, 1964, 1; *RoN*, Apr. 1, 1964, 1; *AJ*, Apr. 1, 1964, 1; May 28, 1964, 1; *ABH*, Apr. 1, 1964, 1).

This anemic narrative raises many more questions than it answers: What role did African-Americans play in the politics of Georgia, and how and why was that role changing in the 1950s and 60s? What did the phrase "bloc vote" mean in the state at the time? Why did certain politicians bemoan the demise of the county unit system? Did the rise and rapidly changing character of the Republican Party in Georgia affect political calculations that might relate to runoffs? Who was Denmark Groover, what was his place in the state's politics, and what experiences led him to propose a majority-vote requirement? How did white politicians—notably Groover, various governors, and members of the state legislature and of the ELSC—respond to the civil rights movement, especially to its political aspects? Whatever Groover's positions on contemporary issues, were Gov. Carl Sanders and his allies such staunch racial liberals and Groover so uninfluential in the legislature at the time that his motives were irrelevant? Were the framers of the majority-vote requirement aware of its racially discriminatory consequences? Did they favor it as part of a consistent, long-term commitment of the state to majority rule? Was it simply an anti-fraud, "good government" measure, or perhaps an informational device to insure that voters knew who was backing whom? Was it merely passed as part of an "election reform package"? Or was it perhaps part of a subtle Democratic Party effort to disadvantage Republicans, a matter of partisan jockeying that had nothing to do with race?

THE RACIALLY discriminatory, one-party political system that had constrained southern politics since the 1890s began to crumble in 1944, with the outlawing of the white Democratic primary in *Smith v. Allwright*. The next year, Georgia abolished the poll tax, an action endorsed by both "liberal" governor Ellis Arnall and arch-reactionary Eugene Talmadge, who assured white Georgians that blacks would not vote so long as the white primary continued

(Henderson 1991, 89–92). Talmadge's statement when he announced his candidacy for governor in 1946, six months after a district court had struck down Georgia's white primary, illustrates the rhetorical tone of the state's politics at the time:

> The most important issue of all now faces the people of Georgia and of the Southland—the Democratic white primary. Alien influences and communistic influences from the East are agitating social equality in our state. They desire negroes to participate in our white primary in order to destroy the traditions and heritages of our Southland. . . . They want negro policemen, negro office holders, negro tax assessors and many other offices, federal, state and local that are held by the white people of this state. If elected governor, I shall see that the traditions which were fought for by our grandparents are maintained and preserved. I shall see that the people of this state have a Democratic white primary unfettered and unhampered by radical, communistic and alien influences. (*HS*, Apr. 11, 1946, 1)

Georgia's effort to evade *Allwright* through the transparent sham of repealing its primary laws failed, and as Figure 4.1 shows, black voters quickly inundated the state's voter rolls, at least compared to their proportions since the 1908 passage of the state's disfranchisement amendment, which had provided for a cumulative poll tax and a literacy or property test, with "understanding" and grandfather-clause exclusions for whites (*King v. Chapman* [1945]; Lawson 1976, 49; Henderson 1991, 141–45; Kousser 1974, 209–23). In 1949, after campaigning "To Oppose the Civil Rights Program [and] To Curb Bloc Voting in Georgia" (*AC*, Sept. 5, 1948, B:7), the administration of Gene Talmadge's son Herman successfully pushed through the legislature a simple but easily manipulable literacy test and abolished permanent voter registration, which allowed the periodic purging of black voters.[1] The Associated Press story on the bill's passage in the House commented, "The House measure was designed to carry out the governor's pledge to end bloc voting. Talmadge has said Negroes are the only group in Georgia to bloc vote" (*AuC*, Jan. 26, 1949, 1). Such laws, which facilitated discriminatory practices, kept the African-American voting proportion down to practically nothing in some counties, but in others, it rose at times perilously close to a majority (*AC*, June 7, 1957, 13).

The national test case on the constitutionality of the 1957 U.S. Civil Rights Act, *U.S. v. Raines* (1960), illustrates how the literacy test worked in parts of rural Georgia. Terrell County, a 65 percent black county in the southwestern corner of the state, was defended by Charles Bloch, a frequent witness against federal civil rights laws in congressional hearings and the law partner of Denmark Groover. Bloch was assisted by Peter Zack Geer, another key figure in

FIGURE 4.1. Percentage of Eligible Blacks Registered to Vote in Georgia, 1940–1969

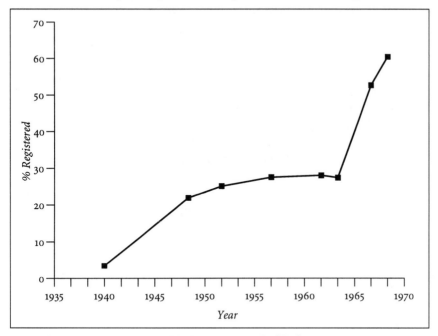

Sources: Lawson 1976, 134, 284, 331; U.S. Commission on Civil Rights 1968, 222-23.

election law "reform," who was lieutenant governor and leader of the Senate during 1963-64 (MN, Mar. 23, 1958, 1; June 27, 1960, 1; U.S. Senate 1965,
251; Groover dep. 1984, 26-28; Lawson 1976, 206-9).[2] Continuing long after
the U.S. Supreme Court decision that upheld the constitutionality of the Civil
Rights Act, the Terrell case proved repeatedly how ludicrously the Georgia
literacy test was administered. Testimony in 1960, for instance, revealed that
only 35 of the county's 5,036 eligible black adults had even dared to take the
test, and that only 4 of them had passed. A college-educated schoolteacher
was flunked because, according to the white registrar, a graduate of Harvard Law School, the schoolteacher mispronounced the word "equity," while
another teacher, who had a master's degree from New York University, was
not only declared illiterate but fired from her job. Bloch denied that there was
any racial discrimination whatsoever in voting registration in Terrell County
(MN, June 27, 1960, 1; June 28, 1960, 1). In 1962, when Sheriff Z. T. Mathews
and a group of armed deputies from "Terrible Terrell" broke up a peace-
ful voting rights meeting, the sheriff announced, according to an account in
the New York Times, "We want our colored people to go on living like they

have for years." By 1963, even after the appointment of voting registrars by a federal judge, only 128 blacks, less than 3 percent of those eligible in the county, had managed to register (Student Nonviolent Coordinating Committee 1962 [Mathews quote]; *MN*, June 9, 1960, 24; *AC*, Apr. 29, 1963, 7).

The prospect of federal activity on voting rights also stimulated the state to rewrite its literacy test in 1957, a task entrusted to the first ELSC. The number of questions that a prospective registrant had to complete to the registrar's satisfaction was raised from 10 to 20, out of a total of 30, and the difficulty and degree of subjectivity of the questions were substantially increased, both raising the standard and facilitating discriminatory administration. New questions asked the voter, for instance, to define a "republican form of government," to explain the difference between the way the federal and Georgia constitutions treated the suspension of the writ of habeas corpus, to name the counties in the voter's judicial district, and to indicate the official who succeeded to the governorship if both the governor and his successor died in office. As the political writer for the *Atlanta Constitution* wrote, in an article carefully cut out and deposited in the files of the ELSC, "The new test is one of several committee proposals which are aimed frankly at making it more difficult for Negroes to register in the future" (*AC*, Nov. 22, 1957, 21).

But the scandal of ridiculous and obviously discriminatory suffrage provisions like these in the South attracted increasing national attention. Seeking black votes in the 1960 presidential election, both John F. Kennedy and Richard M. Nixon endorsed the abolition or standardization of literacy tests. When the Democrats won, the Kennedy and Johnson administrations backed various civil rights proposals, several dealing with voting. A ban on the arbitrary administration of literacy tests, the chief bulwark of racial discrimination in voter registration in Georgia at the time, failed to survive a U.S. Senate filibuster in 1962, but it was revived in 1963 and passed as part of the Civil Rights Bill of 1964. As the state legislators ploughed through the election code in May and June of 1964, the U.S. Senate was debating, imposing cloture, and passing the first truly far-reaching civil rights bill in nearly ninety years. By the provisions of the new national law, anyone with a sixth-grade education would be presumed literate, and slight errors on forms would not invalidate someone's registration. Almost simultaneously, the U.S. Supreme Court ruled in *Reynolds v. Sims* that both houses of every state legislature had to be apportioned on a population basis. Four days later, a three-judge federal court held that *Reynolds* applied in Georgia (Lawson 1976, 291, 299; *AC*, May 12, 1964, 13; June 9, 1964, 4; June 11, 1964, 1, 19; June 16, 1964, 1; June 20, 1964, 1; June 29, 1964, 1).

THE LITERACY test was not the only device buttressing white political supremacy in Georgia that was removed in the early 1960s. Many states were badly malapportioned at the time, and the rural politicos in charge tended to be less favorable toward African-Americans, who were disproportionately concentrated in urban areas, than were more cosmopolitan white representatives. But only Georgia had the notorious county unit system, and the state's leading politicians boasted of the system's connection with white rule. Appealing for Georgians to write the county unit system into the state constitution in 1950, for example, Gov. Herman Talmadge charged that the opponents of the system were led by "the anti-segregation, pro–civil rights crowd who seek to destroy the County Unit System so they can control elections to state offices by manipulating the bloc vote centered in Atlanta. They reason, and rightly so, that any governor they might elect under these conditions would not lift a finger to preserve our traditional pattern of segregation in Georgia. . . . the very future of our entire pattern of segregation in Georgia is tied closely and inseparably to our County Unit System." Defeated, he tried again two years later, if anything more shrilly, arguing that there were potentially "over 100,000 bloc voters over the age of 18 in the Atlanta metropolitan area. . . . Without the protection of the County Unit System to diffuse political initiative over the entire state, the huge bloc vote concentrated in the Atlanta metropolitan area would reduce all of the other six-unit counties from their present co-equal status to that of mere vassalage." The amendment, he insisted, should be passed "in order to beat [Atlanta Mayor William] Hartsfield, [Atlanta black leader A. T.] Walden, and their bloc vote." In other speeches, he added to the list of enemies of the county unit the Communist Party, the NAACP, the Southern Regional Council, "the notorious Rosenwald Foundation," and those who "frequently participate in [racially] mixed meetings and mixed social gatherings." Talmadge's successor as governor, Marvin Griffin, called segregation and the county unit system the state's "two great traditions." Other defenders, according to historian James Bonner, termed the county unit system a barrier against the "bloc vote" and "race mixing" and a foundation of "the Southern way of life" (*HS*, Oct. 26, 1950, 1; Sept. 11, 1952, 1; Oct. 23, 1952, 1; Pajari 1988, 89–90; Pyles 1988, 150; Roberts 1988, 8; Bonner 1963). Was the connection between these two traditions merely rhetorical, race-baiting to keep power in the hands of a rurally dominated faction of rustics and corruptionists? Or was there truth beneath Talmadge's demagoguery?

Mandated by a 1917 state law that declared that statewide offices in the Democratic primary would be decided by a majority of the county units won, rather than by the number of popular votes, the county unit system clearly disadvantaged urban areas. This disadvantage was the major reason Talmadge's proposals to amend the constitution to include the county unit system lost in the referenda, where every vote counted equally. By 1960, the eight counties with the largest populations had 41 percent of the population but only 12 percent of the members of the state House of Representatives, and thus 12 percent of the number of county units. By contrast, the 121 smallest counties (there were 159 counties in the state) contained 32 percent of the population, but accounted for 59 percent of the county unit votes. In 1960, the ratio of population to unit votes in the largest county was nearly 100 times as high as that in the smallest county. In 1960, 39 percent of the state's voting-age African-American population lived in the six largest counties, and they were the most politically active and assertive of their race in the state. The counties they lived in were accorded only 9 percent of the 410 county unit votes. By contrast, in many of the less populous counties, which were massively over-represented by the malapportionment and county unit systems, blacks found it very difficult to register, and those who managed to do so usually had little choice but to pay deference to the traditional, white, plantation-style leaders (Henderson 1991, 223; Bernd 1972, 297, 305, 337). This was true in such counties as Burke, which later earned notoriety in *Rogers v. Lodge* (1982),[3] where in 1962 84 percent of the white and only 6.5 percent of the black adults were registered to vote; Miller, home of 1964 lieutenant governor and long-time ELSC member Peter Zack Geer, where over 100 percent of the whites and less than 1 percent of the blacks were registered; and Telfair, lair of the Talmadges, where the percentages were 80 and 16, respectively. While urban white representatives occasionally opposed racist measures in the state legislature, those from the rural areas that contained large proportions of blacks very rarely did. Thus, the malapportionment of the legislature and the county unit system did in fact bias the choice of governmental officers and, in turn, policy against African-Americans (U.S. Commission on Rights Civil 1968, 234–39; Bernd 1972, 299; *South v. Peters* [1950], 277–78).

Any politician with statewide ambitions had to pledge fealty to the county unit system. Thus, in his successful 1958 gubernatorial campaign, Ernest Vandiver, in the words of historian Charles Pyles, "claimed that he was best qualified to preserve segregation and the county unit system. The two issues were connected in his mind, and he argued that the county unit system maintained the people's control of their government and thus guaranteed they would never be dictated to and controlled by the NAACP." Two years later, the urbane Senate president pro tem Carl E. Sanders of the major city of Augusta, who would succeed Vandiver, "declared that the abolition of the county unit system would abandon control of state government to 'pressure groups or bloc votes.' Sanders added that the system is 'Georgia's greatest protection for keeping representative government, maintaining conservative government and keeping liberals and radicals from taking over' " (Pyles 1988, 146; *MT*, June 10, 1960, 7).

When the Supreme Court in *Baker v. Carr* (1962) spelled the doom of the county unit system and its legislative counterpart by ruling that apportionment was justiciable, something had to be done to keep "liberals and radicals" and the "bloc vote"—a phrase that Sanders clearly used, just as Herman Talmadge had, to refer to African-Americans—from taking over. Two hours after the March 25 filing of the Supreme Court's decision in *Baker*, Atlanta businessman James O'Rear Sanders sued state Democratic Party chairman James H. Gray in an effort to overturn the county unit scheme. Within five weeks, Gov. Ernest Vandiver had called a special session of the legislature, which adopted a plan that reduced the difference in the ratio of population to unit votes between the largest and the smallest counties from 100:1 to "only" 14:1, a three-judge federal court had heard the case, and the judges had rejected the compromise and for all practical purposes eliminated the county unit system entirely. The split in the legislature was between those who wished to bend under the authority of the federal courts and those who held out defiantly, such as longtime Marvin Griffin supporter Rep. John Sheffield of tiny Brooks County, where 61 percent of the whites but only 12 percent of the blacks were registered to vote in 1962. Attacking Gov. Vandiver for reneging on his promise to preserve the county unit system, Sheffield "charged that changes in the county system will lead to other compromises with the NAACP on the integration question and to consolidation of counties. 'Personally,' Sheffield concluded to a scattering of House members, 'I like the old guard in Georgia—the crowd that speaks out against integration' " (*MN*, Mar. 27, 1962, 4, 5; *MT*, Apr. 3, 1962, 1; Apr. 17, 1962, 6 [Sheffield quote]; Apr. 27, 1962, 1; Apr. 30, 1962, 1; May 4, 1962, 1; Pyles 1988, 151).

The three-judge court's ruling against the county unit system in *Gray v. Sanders* (1962) caused one immediate problem: What should be the basis for the 1962 Democratic primary campaigns? The rules of the Democratic Party in effect in April 1962 provided for a runoff only for governor or U.S. senator, and then only in the very unlikely event that there was a tie in the grossly malapportioned county unit votes and that no candidate had received a majority of the popular vote. For all other statewide offices—lieutenant governor, secretary of state, comptroller general, commissioner of agriculture, attorney general, commissioner of labor, treasurer, superintendent of schools, public service commissioner, and judges of the state appeals and supreme courts—a plurality of the popular vote, not a majority, was the tiebreaker after county unit votes were tallied (Georgia Democratic State Executive Committee 1962, Section X). Even apart from the county unit system, before 1962 the state could hardly have been said to have had a policy in favor of "majority rule."

In more practical terms, what mattered in the Democratic State Executive Committee's adoption of new rules to govern the first purely popular statewide election since 1908 was its effect on current candidates. In the governor's race, there were three: former Gov. Marvin Griffin, a blustering racist whose administration had been credibly accused of a startling level of corruption; Lt. Gov. Garland Byrd, a comparative moderate on the race issue, who was said to be close to Gov. Vandiver; and state senator Carl Sanders, another moderate segregationist who was Vandiver's Senate leader and who had originally expected to join the crowded field of nine candidates for lieutenant governor. Before Sanders announced for governor, friends of Byrd and Vandiver had said repeatedly that they feared a third candidate "would take votes away from Byrd in the more populous areas and insure the nomination of Griffin . . . [who] has a record of garnering votes in the small counties." Even though other rumored candidacies did not develop, Vandiver was too torn between Byrd and Sanders to endorse either (Bartley 1983, 161–62, 166; Bass and DeVries 1976, 140; Dubay 1988, 108–10; Cook 1988, 171; *MT*, Apr. 22, 1962, 1 [quote]; Apr. 25, 1962, 1; *DKNE*, Apr. 26, 1962, 1).

The answer to how to beat Griffin was for Vandiver to use his control of the Democratic State Executive Committee to require that the winner had to get a majority, not just a plurality, of the popular vote. Griffin, who had won in 1954 on a county unit basis despite garnering only 36 percent of the popular votes, favored a plurality-win system, and Vandiver's decision was said to be "a sharp setback" to his campaign. As the political editor of the *Atlanta Constitution* explained, "Griffin's bid for getting the primary onto a plurality basis was interpreted at the Capitol as an attempt to win on the first ballot in a split field and forestall the possibility of a head-to-head runoff against one opponent." When a heart attack forced Byrd out of the contest on May 5, before Vandiver's decision was formally ratified by the State Executive Committee, an *Atlanta Journal* news story noted that the majority-or-plurality question was "not such a burning issue" as it had been when all three men were running (*MT*, May 1, 1962, 1; May 2, 1962, 5; May 4, 1962, 1; *AC*, May 1, 1962, 1; *AJ*, June 18, 1962, 1).

Because of another federal court ruling in *Toombs v. Fortson* in May 1962, the winner of the Griffin-Sanders race would face a newly constituted legislature when he took office, one in which one house had to be apportioned on a population basis while the other remained overwhelmingly dominated by small rural counties (*ATR*, May 26, 1962, 1). Altogether, with the county unit system and legislative malapportionment dead or dying, the task of drawing new electoral rules comprehensively could not be avoided during the administration of the next governor.

As THOUGH the outlawing of the literacy test and the county unit system and the reapportionment of the legislature to give more power to cities and suburbs were not enough dislocation, white Democrats in Georgia in the early

1960s faced a suddenly revived and radically changing Republican Party. Because the Democrats had so zealously guarded white supremacy in Georgia since the Civil War, the tiny Republican party had traditionally attracted a fair number of African-Americans, especially in Atlanta, as well as a few white moderates. In 1956, so many blacks had voted Republican in response to Earl Warren's *Brown* decision that a year later, state senator James S. Peters proposed to the ELSC that party registration be instituted and that Republicans be banned from Democratic primaries in order to decrease the number of blacks voting in the primaries. "Negroes in Georgia," the *Constitution*'s article on the move explained, "shifted in large numbers to the Eisenhower banner in last November's election. They also voted overwhelmingly for the GOP congressional candidate in the Fifth District. These voters—as well as whites who vote Republican in national elections—are the ones Peters would like to keep out of the Democratic primaries." The first serious black candidate for alderman in Atlanta in the twentieth century, Theodore M. Alexander, who had lost a nonpartisan runoff election with a white segregationist just two weeks before Peters's proposal, was a Republican. As late as 1962, Atlanta Republicans nominated two African-Americans for the state senate, one winning his party's honors only when a judge ruled that the votes should be tabulated by districts rather than countywide. In the same year, the GOP candidate for Congress in Fulton County ran as the racially moderate alternative to the conservative Democratic incumbent (*AC*, May 23, 1957, 1; July 19, 1957, 11; Oct. 22, 1962, 1; *ADW*, Oct. 16, 1962, 1; *MT*, Oct. 20, 1962, 1; Sept. 12, 1964, 3).

But the complexion of the Republican party changed dramatically when a "New Guard" faction used the regionally popular candidacy of Barry Goldwater to take over the party from "Old Guard" cultural moderates. The New Guard shunned those blacks whom they did not entirely alienate. Moderates and new conservatives differed not only on ideology but also on the best way to build the Republican Party, new state chairman Joe Tribble of Savannah declaring that the increase in whites for the GOP would more than offset any loss in black votes caused by denying blacks places in the national convention delegation. Outside of Atlanta, another New Guard leader remarked, "Negroes vote Democrat by block [*sic*]. . . . Republicans in various parts of the state feel that they can get along without the block [*sic*]." In response, moderate state senator Dan McIntyre of Fulton County and Atlanta aldermen Rodney Cook and Richard Freeman contended that "the only real growth in the Republican Party in Georgia has come from policies of moderation and common sense." Old Guard Republican National Committeeman Robert B. Snodgrass remarked forlornly, "There are some Republicans who want to read the Negroes out of the party. I do not agree with this. I feel Negroes should participate in party activities and I think the Republican party wants the Negro vote" (*MT*, May 3, 1964, 1; *BN*, May 9, 1964, 2; *RoNT*, May 6, 1964, 15; *AT*, June 29, 1964, A:4).

The presidential election that year proved Snodgrass wrong and Tribble right, as a Republican presidential candidate won Georgia for the first time since Ulysses Grant in 1872. Carrying approximately two-thirds of the white vote, Goldwater was the first Republican to crack the Black Belt in the state, running especially strongly in rural counties where there were few blacks registered (Bernd 1972, 336–37). For conservative Democratic leaders in such counties, the predictable upsurge, which scholars agree was largely a response to the civil rights push by President Lyndon Johnson and the national Democrats, lent an extra dose of urgency to election law reform (Carmines and Stimson 1989; Huckfeldt and Kohfeld 1989; Edsall and Edsall 1991). It was particularly important to conservative Democrats that backlash Republicans stay within the Democratic party during nonpresidential elections and that the party not be too closely associated with blacks or with white candidates who reached out to blacks. Two means of accomplishing these ends were open primaries (i.e., those in which Republicans were allowed to vote in the Democratic primary) and the majority-vote requirement which, as a *Valdosta Times* story on Groover's H.B. 117 noted, "will dim the chances of the Republican Party in many local elections" (*VT*, Feb. 21, 1963, 1). If blacks or liberal whites won Democratic primaries, Republicans would be able to grow by appealing to white conservative voters. A majority-vote requirement that kept African-Americans or liberal whites from gaining Democratic nominations, therefore, might stifle the Republican party.

THAT THE majority-vote requirement would be helpful in containing the Republican party was, for white Democrats in 1963–64, only a hypothesis. That it would disadvantage African-Americans was a reality that had been demonstrated repeatedly, before a statewide audience, in the state's capital city. Since 1871, when the state legislature had replaced a ward system with at-large elections, Atlanta had not elected a single black member to its city council, even though African-Americans had registered with few restraints since the 1940s. In 1957, Theodore M. Alexander ran for an open seat against one "moderate" and one "conservative" white. Reminding supporters of the history of black exclusion from local government, Alexander declared that he was running not "for myself but for the voice of a people which has had no voice on this board since 1871." As whites split in the primary, Alexander polled more than a third of the votes, and the *Atlanta Constitution*'s lead paragraph on the day after the election emphasized that "Alexander, Negro" had forced a runoff. The prospect of the first black in an important elective position in the state since 1907 so frightened extreme racists that Gov. Marvin

Griffin took the unprecedented step of intervening in a local election, publicly urging "my friends and all friends of segregation" to engage in "bloc voting" against Alexander. Distributed by Alexander's opponent Jack Summers, who, the *Constitution* noted, bore "a striking resemblance to the late Eugene Talmadge," the statement was credited with stimulating an unprecedentedly high turnout in the runoff and insuring that enough whites voted in the strikingly racially polarized contest to keep the 16-member Board solidly white. In homogeneous black precincts, Alexander received more than 99 percent of the votes in the runoff, while in homogeneous white precincts, Summers polled more than 98 percent. Although little more than a quarter of Atlanta's registered voters in 1957 were black, Alexander's 35 percent showing in the primary demonstrated the importance of the majority-vote requirement, because if there had been another serious white candidate and no majority-vote provision, Alexander would have won. And a mandatory runoff provision would not have prevented an Alexander victory if there had been a district instead of an at-large system of electing members of the Council; the county was so heavily segregated that if districts were fairly drawn, at least some of them would have had black majorities of the voters (*AC*, May 3, 1957, 8; May 8, 1957, 3; May 9, 1957, 1; May 18, 1957, 1, 3; May 23, 1957, 1; Walker 1963).

A local election in 1964, just at the time when the legislature was considering the majority-vote requirement, spotlighted the racial consequences of the runoff provision even more dramatically. Unlike many other contests in Georgia at the time, in which local or state Democratic committees could decide whether pluralities or majorities were necessary for election, judicial elections in Fulton County, under a special 1925 law, had to be controlled by pluralities. Two days before the special session of the legislature called to consider election law changes, and only ten seconds before the qualification deadline, the state's most prominent civil rights lawyer, Donald Hollowell, filed for the highly visible office of superior court judge of Fulton County. According to the *Atlanta Inquirer*, Hollowell's entrance "jolted" politicians, black as well as white, who had expected a two-man race between the staunchly segregationist incumbent, Durwood Pye, and "moderate" white attorney Paul Webb Jr. The prominence of Pye and Hollowell guaranteed an attentive public audience and drew attention to the connection between racial politics and the struggle against segregation in the larger civil rights movement (*SMN*, May 3, 1964, A:7; *AC*, May 6, 1964, 21; *AI*, May 6, 1964, 1).

To preserve school segregation after the *Brown* decision in 1954, Gov. Marvin Griffin had appointed Durwood Pye to head the "Georgia Education Commission," which was charged with coming up with a strategy for the state. Working with Griffin, the governor's House floor leader Denmark Groover, and others, Pye proposed and the legislature adopted measures to close white schools if courts mandated integration and to pay white students' tuition at "private" schools, in addition to resolutions endorsing state "interposition" and declaring the *Brown* decision null and void. According to Griffin, Pye fought against integration with "determination, vim, vigor, and steel-trap acumen." Pye also supervised extensive interstate spying on integrationist organizations. In recognition of Pye's contributions to maintaining the "southern way of life," Gov. Griffin appointed him to the most important superior court judgeship in the state, personally administering the oath of office. Pye did not disappoint. When sit-ins came to Atlanta, Pye insisted on trying them himself, although he did not usually handle misdemeanors, and he sentenced violators of the state's trespass law to as much as 18 months in jail. When Hollowell, representing most of the demonstrators, got federal judges to remove 100 of their cases to federal courts on the grounds that Pye was too racially biased to try them fairly, Pye cited Hollowell for contempt (Bartley 1969, 54–55; Dubay 1988, 111; *BPS*, Oct. 25, 1962, 3; *AC*, June 8, 1964, 16; *AI*, May 6, 1964, 1; *GDN*, Sept. 10, 1964, 1; *AT*, Sept. 24, 1964, 1).

Hollowell's campaign strategy, it was widely reported, was predicated on winning a plurality when the two white candidates split the white vote. As the *Constitution* put it, Hollowell "is gambling that the law allowing a simple plurality victory in the judgeship primary will not be amended." Or as the *Atlanta Daily World*, a black Republican paper, asserted, "Mr. Hollowell does not stand a chance of winning a race based on a majority vote." Within three days of his entry into the contest, Fulton County legislators were rumored to be preparing a bill to repeal the 1925 law in order to insure Hollowell's defeat by requiring a majority vote to win—a special action that became unnecessary with the adoption of the statewide majority-vote requirement. In a final effort to make it possible to elect Hollowell, black state senator Leroy Johnson moved unsuccessfully to exempt Fulton County from the majority-vote requirement until January 1, 1965, and Republican state senator Dan McIntyre moved to delay the operative date of the majority-vote requirement throughout the state until the new year. News stories explicitly linked the Johnson and MacIntyre amendments to Hollowell's chances. The United Press International story remarked, "The Negro Senator from Fulton County tried to get an amendment adopted that would have put a Fulton judgeship race on a plurality basis. . . . This directly affects a Fulton superior court judge, Durwood T. Pye, who has two opponents, one of them a Negro." The article in the *Constitution* noted that "although he did not mention his name, Johnson made reference to a three-man race for a Superior Court judgeship in Atlanta involving Negro attorney Donald Hollowell." A piece in the *Atlanta Journal* on MacIntyre's amendment reported, "The specific judge's race he said he was referring to is one involving efforts by a white lawyer and a Negro lawyer to unseat Superior Court Judge Durwood T. Pye." Recognizing the effect of the measure on the black candidate's electoral chances, the Senate rejected Johnson's motion by a vote of 30–8 and McIntyre's by 32–8 (*AC*, May 6, 1964, 21; May 15, 1964, 4; May 28, 1964, 10; June 8, 1964, 16; *ADW*, May 13, 1964, 1; *AJ*, May 18, 1964, 7; May 27, 1964, 1; May 28, 1964, 1; *CE*, May 28, 1964, 17; *ABH*, May 28, 1964, 1; *MN*, May 25, 1964, 1).

His chances diminished after the electoral law changed, Hollowell's black support splintered, with several old-line black politicians joining the *Atlanta Constitution*, which had from the beginning opposed Hollowell's candidacy on the grounds that the prime task was to defeat Pye and that a viable Hollowell campaign would only siphon votes from Webb and unite whites behind Pye. The parallel with the predicament of A. W. Willis Jr. in Memphis in 1967 is instructive. After Hollowell finished third in the primary, he immediately endorsed Webb, who lost to Pye by a 51–49 margin when Pye, according to newspaper reports, solidified the white vote behind him by making strong segregationist appeals. The *Atlanta Times*, which backed Pye, headlined its story on the runoff "Judge Pye defeats bloc vote" (*ADW*, May 7, 1964, 1; May 13, 1964, 1; May 24, 1964, 1; Sept. 25, 1964, 4; *AI*, May 9, 1964, 1; May 16, 1964, 2; Sept. 5, 1964, 1; Sept. 12, 1964, 1; Sept. 26, 1964, 1; *AC*, May 15, 1964, 4; *AJ*, May 18, 1964, 7; *VT*, May 23, 1964, 1; *CE*, May 28, 1964, 17; *AT*, Sept. 10, 1964, 1; Sept. 24, 1964, A:10; *WJH*, Sept. 25, 1964, 4).

Between December 1962 and May 1964, black registration rose from 167,000 to 275,000, according to the *Atlanta Constitution* and the Georgia Voters' League. Nearly half of the state's counties had a black voter registration campaign during the spring of 1964. In every campaign in which black candidates ran, and even in some campaigns that involved white moderates and where no race issue was ostensibly raised, election returns and newspaper reports showed very marked racial polarization. Combined with the increasing voting rights activity in Congress and the federal courts, the homegrown civil rights movement threatened the security of the white political monopoly in Georgia. But from 1871 on, and continuing with high-profile campaigns that took place just as the legislature was considering the "reformed" election code, the repeatedly tested antidote to substantial black registration was a change in electoral rules, particularly from district-based, plurality systems to at-large elections and a majority-vote requirement (*AC*, May 9, 1957, 1; May 23, 1957, 1, 5; June 7, 1957, 13; May 15, 1964, 20; Hornsby 1977).

THE GEORGIA legislature in 1963–64 had so many members and so few with much experience, so much to do in such a limited time with so few staffers to help, that the few leaders were even more important in shaping legisla-

212 The "Bloc Vote" in Georgia

tion than leaders usually are. Thus, savvy and knowledgeable legislators like Denmark Groover, advisory bodies like the ELSC, and the governor and his numerous executive assistants played especially crucial roles in these pivotal legislative sessions. To determine the intent of the legislature in passing the majority-vote section and other provisions of the election code, we must devote considerable attention to these key individuals. It is true that almost anyone could easily have determined that a majority-vote requirement would make it more difficult for black voters to be able to elect candidates of their choice, for there were numerous earlier examples of such laws stretching back at least to 1907, when the disfranchising legislature passed a majority-vote law for primaries in Fulton County (Georgia House of Representatives *Journal* 1907, 1063; Georgia Senate *Journal* 1907, 712; Georgia *Laws* 1907, 98).[4] But not just anyone could have gotten such an electoral change on the legislature's agenda and managed its passage. In fact, since the legislature was split between a predominantly rural House and a Senate that gave urban areas the same weight as their populations, the whole election code, and especially its chief provisions, could not have passed without support from both the predominantly rural, faction led by Groover and the predominantly urban faction led by Carl Sanders.

DENMARK GROOVER proudly claimed credit for the passage of H.B. 117. He wrote it, he introduced it, and he guided it through. "I got a majority," for the bill, he crowed in 1984. When Mitchel House, a more urban-oriented Bibb County legislator, attacked the bill on the floor, rural solons rallied to support Groover and H.B. 117. "[T]hey resented Mitchel House trying to whip me, and they weren't going to let it happen," Groover continued. "I don't know that the bill would have passed on its merits in the House, based on the rural attitude that they were better off, some of them, with the political machines, with the plurality, than they would have been with a majority" (Groover dep. 1984, 43–44).[5] What role had Groover played in state politics that enabled him to command such loyalty?

As Marvin Griffin's floor leader in 1955–56, Groover had been the chief framer or spokesman for the administration's array of segregationist bills. Praising a measure to replace what he termed the "meaningless" red and white stripes on the state flag, stripes that resembled those on the nation's symbol, with the stars and bars of the Confederate battle flag, Groover told the solons that the secessionist flag "has deep meaning in the hearts of all true Southerners. . . . [A]nything we in Georgia can do to preserve the memory of the Confederacy is a step forward." That the pro-slavery "deep meaning" of that symbol might be repugnant to black southerners did not concern the representative from Macon. The author of the state's interposition statute declar-

ing the *Brown* decision inoperative in Georgia, Groover also pushed bills to require the closing of public schools that courts ordered desegregated; to allow
the sale or lease of schools, parks, golf courses, and swimming pools to private
groups to prevent them from being integrated; to require segregated waiting
rooms for both interstate and intrastate common carriers; and to authorize
the state attorney general to defend any local official or employee charged
with violating a federal law. Most of these laws passed almost unanimously,
the interposition bill, for instance, flying through the House by a 178-1 margin, with Groover, as the *Constitution*'s story had it, "carrying the ball for
the administration, as usual." Despite doubts as to its constitutionality, the
plan to close and privatize the public schools if integration threatened, which
Groover termed "the best plan yet offered to maintain segregation," swept
through the House by a vote of 174-13. Among the 174 school closers who followed Groover's lead was a freshman from Augusta, Carl Sanders (*AC*, June 1,
1955, 1; Jan. 25, 1956, 1; Feb. 7, 1956, 1; Feb. 9, 1956, 1; Feb. 10, 1956, 1; *AJ*, Jan. 28,
1956, 12; Georgia House *Journal* 1955, 380; 1956, 351-52, 670, 745, 782-83).

Despite his statewide prominence, in 1956 Groover was beaten for reelection to the House by the comparatively moderate Ed Wilson and, after having
toyed with the idea of becoming the Griffin faction's candidate for governor
in 1958, instead attempted to return to the state House (*MT*, Mar. 26, 1958, 1).
To understand why Groover lost that contest and why he introduced and
fought so hard for the majority-vote requirement in 1963-64 requires a short
journey to his hometown, Macon.

With a voting age population that was 31 percent black in 1960 but a voting registration only 16 percent black in 1962, Bibb County may have seemed
fairly typical of Middle Georgia, but it was not. Even after the disfranchisement amendment passed in 1908, significant numbers of African-Americans
in Bibb continued to vote. In 1920, 30.5 percent of the registered voters in the
county were black, and though this had dwindled to 9.3 percent in 1944, it
shot up in 1946 from under 1,000 to over 10,000, which was about a third of
the total registration. Since Bibb's polling places were segregated until a 1962
federal court suit forced integration, statistical techniques are not needed to
uncover voting patterns. In 1946, 99.6 percent of the blacks who voted in the
Democratic primary chose James V. Carmichael over Eugene Talmadge (U.S.
Commission on Civil Rights 1968, 234-39; *MN*, June 8, 1960, 1; *U.S. v. Bibb
County Democratic Executive Committee* [1962]).

The emergence in Macon of black political organizations, which distributed candidate slates to black voters shortly before elections and sometimes
advertised in the segregated "colored pages" of the *News* and the *Telegraph*,
and the fact that segregated polling places demonstrated their sway over the
black community soon attracted white politicians. In 1947, Lewis B. Wilson

won the mayoralty with 51 percent of the white vote, but 84 percent of the black. In 1948, E. Julian Peacock received 53 percent of the white vote and 83 percent of the black in his race for sheriff. At other times, the black vote split more evenly, but the power of the vote usually sent comparatively moderate whites to the legislature and bought attention from local elected officials. In the early 1960s, for example, Mayor Ed Wilson cooperated with black leader William P. Randall to desegregate most public services without violence, and, compared to many Georgia cities, with little disruption. The contrast between the tenacity of segregation in areas of Macon's life that were subject to political influence and those that were not is instructive. Public schools in Bibb County were governed by a countywide board of education over which Macon African-Americans had less influence than they did over the city government. Requests from black leaders for moves toward school integration in 1954, 1955, 1961, and 1963 were filed and brusquely repulsed, and it took a court order to bring about school integration. The integration of city buses required a boycott and a lawsuit, but opening up public accommodations came about much more easily. Indeed, the *News* reported that "integration has been achieved so smoothly here that opponents have charged the city gave in by default." Both the integration and the *News*'s story were testimony to black political power (*MN*, June 9, 1960, 1; June 10, 1960, 1; Mar. 14, 1963, 1; Mar. 15, 1963, 1; Mar. 26, 1963, 1; Georgia Government Documentation Project 1989, 14, 43–44).

Among the candidates who received little black support was Denmark Groover. In an at-large election for the legislature in 1952, Groover got 17 percent of the black votes; in two-man races in 1956 and 1958, 26.6 percent and 16.4 percent, respectively. Although his upset loss in 1956 to racial moderate Ed Wilson came at the hands of a majority of white, as well as of black voters, his defeat by Taylor Phillips in 1958 was demonstrably a product of the black "bloc vote," for Groover's white majority fell 189 votes short of offsetting the landslide of black votes for Phillips. It was hardly surprising that African-Americans opposed Groover. As Groover commented in 1984, "I was a segregationist. I was a county unit man . . . And I was raised in a country county and I had many prejudices, and I don't mind admitting it. . . . If you want to establish that some of my political activity was racially motivated, it was. . . . It would have been a major miracle, or taken a modern case of absolute blindness, for blacks to have supported me in 1958." Summing up his racial views at the time, he described them as "reactionary" (*MN*, June 13, 1960, 1; June 15, 1960, 1; June 17, 1960, 1; Groover dep. 1984, 22–23, 26–28, 48–49).

The direct origin of the majority-vote law may well have been Groover's reaction to his 1958 defeat at the hands of black slatemakers. As his loss became clear on election night, Groover launched an attack on "Negro 'bloc voting,'" and called for a recount of all of the voting machines in the segregated black precincts. After this, his second consecutive election defeat, Groover seemed to become obsessed with "bloc voting," attempting to amend the election code in 1964 to prevent persons from taking slate cards into the polling places with them, and expatiating at length on slates and "bloc voting" during a 1984 deposition (*MT*, Sept. 11, 1958, 1; Groover dep. 1984, 16–20, 21, 23–26, 28, 43–44, 66).[6]

Others with similar views in Macon shared Groover's obsession. In 1960, superior court judge Oscar Long charged the Bibb County grand jury to investigate "Negro Bloc Voting," launching what Macon newspapers, which heavily reported the investigation, termed the "bloc voting probe." Condemning "an inane and inexplicable pattern of Negro bloc voting," Long charged that black bloc voting "could ultimately destroy this country and its system of government." He ignored polarized white voting and black disfranchisement entirely. Acting under the umbrella of a universally violated law that prohibited any payments to election canvassers, which Long, himself, had broken during his own election campaigns, Long certified to the grand jury the following questions: "Was the Negro vote delivered in [*sic*] bloc to any candidate or candidates? If so, who delivered it and how was it done? What contact did the candidates or their supporters have with the Negro group or its leaders? What money was involved, if any? How was the money used? What workers were employed? What promises did the candidates make, if any, in order to obtain the bloc vote?" When Sheriff James Wood condemned Long's investigation as "a crude attempt at judicial intimidation of Negro voters and leaders," and pointed out its connection with the election campaign then in progress, the Ku Klux Klan called for the sheriff's impeachment, Judge Long held him in contempt, and the case finally ended with Wood's vindication by the U.S. Supreme Court. Mayor Ed Wilson, like Wood elected with heavy support from African-Americans, also publicly denounced Long's crusade. Although the grand jury indicted no one, Groover testified, and the only election mentioned in the grand jury report as possibly raising any suspicions of unethical conduct was the Groover-Phillips race of 1958 (*MN*, June 6, 1960, 13; June 7, 1960, 5; June 9, 1960, 1; June 13, 1960, 11; July 1, 1960, 14; July 5, 1960, 1, 12; July 21, 1960, 1; Mar. 22, 1962, 1; Mar. 23, 1962, 20).

Considering Groover's previous reputation, the *Macon News* called his failure "to flail the 'block [*sic*] vote' openly" in 1962 the "surprise of the local campaign." The paper went on to note:

> Groover's friends have not neglected, however, to work the segregationist vote in his behalf. A letter from Groover to Bill Stallings urging that "unless the majority stick together, our affairs will be run by a hand-

ful of persons who control large numbers of voters" is being mailed to some white voters with notes calling attention to Groover's poor showing among Negro voters in 1956 and 1958 and saying "Truly he is a poor Negro vote getter." The vote [by segregated precincts] in his 1958 loss to his present opponent, J. Taylor Phillips, is reprinted from a newspaper clipping on the back of the letter.

Fortunately for Groover, Phillips had disappointed his black supporters, the leading black politician terming him a "renegade" and "pseudo-liberal," and while few blacks supported Groover, they largely abstained from voting for Phillips in 1962 either (*MN*, Sept. 11, 1962, 11; Sept. 13, 1962, 22; Sept. 14, 1962, 11; Georgia Government Documentation Project 1989, 14, 91). Thus, Groover returned to the legislature in 1963, less outspokenly segregationist than during the 1950s, but determined to rein in black political power.

Implicitly recognizing that Groover's outspokenly racist views in the 1950s and 60s supported contentions that the majority-vote requirement was passed with a racially discriminatory purpose, witnesses for the State of Georgia in *Brooks v. Harris* were extremely anxious to minimize Groover's role in the 1963–64 legislature. According to former Governor Carl Sanders, Groover "had no influence, so far as I was concerned . . . other than him being sort of a gadfly and picking at things and trying to spoil things, he was not influential at all." Former House Speaker George T. Smith contended that Groover "didn't have any power at all. . . . He had absolutely no influence. He was not a party to the Sanders team. He was not consulted. . . . Denmark was never asked, to my knowledge, by anybody for advice or input. . . . He never did talk to me. I never did talk to him" (*Brooks v. Harris* trial transcript, 4:189 [Sanders quote]; 5:74–76 [Smith quote]).[7] While it is true that Groover was not part of the Sanders administration leadership, the recollections of Sanders and Smith a generation later were not in accord with either their own or other politicians' documented behavior during the 1963–64 legislative session.

Two pieces of evidence, while largely symbolic, cast some doubt on the later sweeping dismissals of Groover's importance. One is a photograph distributed by United Press International and run on page 1 of the *Atlanta Times* of Groover, Sanders, and Sanders's Senate floor leader Julian Webb during the May–June 1964 special session in apparent close conversation. The caption reads "Georgia Senate floor leader Julian Webb (left) and Gov. Carl Sanders listen to Rep. Denmark Groover discuss the court-ordered reapportionment of the General Assembly." A second is that, as the session ended, Groover's friends and supporters threw him a party in Atlanta attended by 150–200 people. When Gov. Sanders, who was scheduled to introduce Groover to the crowd, had to go out of town on business, Speaker George T. Smith stepped in to do the honors (*AT*, June 21, 1964, 1; *MT*, June 19, 1964, 1).

In the 1963–64 legislature, Groover was recognized as the "Leader of the Loyal Opposition" and a potential gubernatorial candidate in 1966. Sanders administration loyalists were said to watch him "like hawks." Although they had wanted to adopt rules that required votes from only 52 of the 205 House members to pass an article of the revised state constitution, administration leaders reportedly "yielded to pressure from Rep. Denmark Groover of Macon and agreed to require a so-called 'constitutional majority' of 105 votes to adopt any entire article." To get the House to adopt a new apportionment for itself in the state constitution, Sanders floor leader Arthur Bolton had to compromise with Groover, the two agreeing on and cosponsoring a scheme, thereafter thrown out by a federal court, to keep rural power intact. Along with Bolton and Frank Twitty, Groover was named by Speaker George T. Smith to the conference committee on changes in the new state constitution, the other subject, besides the election code, considered at the special session of the legislature. The constitutional provisions that required counties to obtain the legislature's approval for changes in many local laws could not have passed, a newspaper reporter declared, without Groover's help. "The Sanders men gave Groover credit for turning the tide on county home rule." A House resolution termed him "truly one of the most wise, able, and just legislators who has ever served in the General Assembly of Georgia," which was hyperbolic even for end-of-session puffery. As a testimony to his power in the session—as well as to his lack of attachment to political "reform"— the encomium probably ranks below the fact that the powers of the State Election Board, the principal anti-corruption facet of the revised 1964 election code, were severely curtailed expressly to make the bill "acceptable to Rep. Denmark Groover" after "administration forces . . . negotiat[ed] with Representative Denmark Groover of Bibb County in pursuit of some kind of compromise" (*MN*, Mar. 11, 1963, 4; May 28, 1964, 34; June 8, 1964, 1; June 19, 1964, 8; *MT*, May 5, 1964, 1; May 30, 1964, 1; June 9, 1964, 1; June 11, 1964, 8; *AJ*, May 19, 1964, 1; June 5, 1964, 1; June 9, 1964, 1; *AC*, May 19, 1964, 3; June 4, 1964, 12; June 9, 1964, 1). Groover's move to emasculate the Election Board, the centerpiece of whatever anti-fraud motives there were in the struggle for election law "reform," undercuts any notion that he was motivated by "good government" impulses in his actions concerning election laws.

Groover could lead rural politicians in the malapportioned House not only because of the force of his intellect and character, but also because, for a politician from an urban area, he had been extraordinarily supportive of the county unit system and its companion, the malapportioned legislature. "Nobody in this House," he remarked in 1964, "is more interested in having one branch of the General Assembly based on pure geography than I." When, during the session, the U.S. Supreme Court ruled that both houses of a state legislature had to be apportioned on a population basis, it was Groover who successfully pushed through a resolution requesting that Georgia's U.S. Senators Richard Russell and Herman Talmadge introduce legislation stripping the Court of the power to hear such suits. The day of that decision, Groover's resolution stated, was "the saddest day in American history." The passage in the regular session of a congressional redistricting plan for the state that allocated members of Congress on an equal population basis so angered Groover that he literally tore the official House clock off the wall. When Congress threatened to regulate the literacy test in federal elections, Groover proposed to revert to a late-nineteenth-century southern subterfuge by holding primaries for state and local elections separate from those for national elections. His amendment, Groover announced, would prevent the "onerous burdens which advocates of the civil rights bill want to put on federal elections, from slopping over on our local elections" (*MN*, May 19, 1964, 1; June 22, 1964, 4; *MT*, June 3, 1964, 2; June 19, 1964, 6; *AJ*, June 16, 1964). No legislator was more concerned with election laws or more clearly aware of their consequences than Denmark Groover, and no one outside the Sanders leadership was more influential.

THE SAME day that Groover's majority-vote bill passed the House, the Senate unanimously endorsed the creation of a partially legislative Election Law Study Committee, the fourth such ELSC since 1957. Since the demise of the county unit system and the prospect of federal legislation undercutting the state's literacy test invited a wholesale rewriting of the election laws, which had never previously been integrated into one coherent system, Groover's bill was temporarily shelved. As he remarked in 1984, "I think it was fairly well understood at that time that [the majority-vote measure] would wait for the election code." Because the election code that was ultimately enacted was drafted for the ELSC by assistant attorney-general Paul Rodgers, it is important to consider the nature and probable intent of that body (*AC*, Feb. 20, 1963, 8; Groover dep. 1984, 38–39; *AJ*, May 14, 1964, 2).

The ELSC was no blue-ribbon, civics-textbook commission. First established in 1957 by a legislature that both called for the repeal of the Fourteenth and Fifteenth Amendments and, paradoxically, declared them "null and void and of no effect," the ELSC took its main task during its first year to be counteracting the surging black registration and the threatened passage of the first federal voting rights law since the 1870s. Thereafter, the ELSC was revived before nearly every legislative session, drafting and reviewing bills and making recommendations. Chaired throughout the 1950s and 60s by veteran secretary of state and chief elections officer Ben Fortson, the committee included Attorney General Eugene Cook, varying numbers of state legislators, some local officials, and one or more "public" members. Until he was elected lieutenant governor in the 1962 election, Peter Zack Geer was a vociferous and active member (Georgia *Laws* 1957, 348; ELSC 1968). A sense of the committee's character may be gleaned from a look at its highest ranking, longest serving members.

An exchange of correspondence illuminates Ben Fortson's view of black voting. In October 1963, the ELSC floated a proposal to abolish the Georgia literacy test altogether and to substitute a more subtle means of disfranchising illiterates that would not be affected by the current attempts to ban literacy tests by federal law. Assisting people in marking their complicated ballots would simply be made a crime. When it was pointed out that voters might bring sample ballots with them into the booth and follow the pattern printed or written there, the ELSC sought to outlaw sample ballots as well. Publicity about these measures misled many who wished to keep blacks largely disfranchised into thinking that Fortson and his colleagues had endorsed a "revolutionary step," as the ordinary (the principal executive officer) of the notoriously discriminatory Burke County, John J. Jones, suggested in a letter to Fortson. Did Fortson, as Jones put it, want "to throw the flood gates wide open to the ignorant and uninformed"? Fortson's reply to Jones explicitly outlined the manner in which his sophisticated means were aimed at the same racially discriminatory end as the literacy test. The change proposed by ELSC and state House member Joe Underwood, wrote Fortson, was made

> in order to help the registrars and election officials of this state. I hesitate to go into the question of Federal courts, but I am sure you realize as well as anyone that all of these questions are being carried into the Federal courts every day. Mr. Underwood's proposal was a sincere attempt to try to set up something that would help us protect ourselves. I understand your feelings about the matter and I respect your point of view. It is my own. I would not be for the proposal at all if the penalties attached would not result in an honest election honestly counted and if it would not prevent block[*sic*]-voting by any group.

Still unconvinced, Jones replied that the more subtle literacy test would not work because "bloc voters would be well coached in advance, and unqualified people should not be registered at all" (Jones to Fortson, Oct. 17, 1963; Fortson to Jones, Oct. 25, 1963; Jones to Fortson, Oct. 28, 1963, all in ELSC Files, Correspondence). Continuously reelected secretary of state since 1946, Fortson was certainly in a position to know what the point of view of the chief executive of Burke County was. His identification with that point of view ("It is my own") and his explanation to Jones of the crafty mechanism of keeping a literacy test while avoiding legal liability shows that he wished the election code to continue to disadvantage blacks—just less obviously.

Attorney General Eugene Cook was another holdover from the Talmadge era. In the early 1950s, Cook had campaigned across the state for a Talmadge-backed state constitutional amendment that would have allowed the legislature to turn the public school system into a private school system and to institute tuition payments for students in those private schools, a transparent effort to avoid integration. In a later, widely circulated speech, "The Ugly Truth about the NAACP," Cook, whom Prof. Numan Bartley has called "the South's most vociferous critic" of the NAACP, charged that "either knowingly or unwittingly, it [the NAACP] has allowed itself to become part and parcel of the Communist conspiracy to overthrow the democratic governments of this nation and its sovereign states." Its leaders had no real interest in black welfare, he charged, but had merely seized on the racial issue "as a convenient front for their more nefarious activities and as one with which they could dupe naive do-gooders, fuzzy-minded intellectuals, misguided clergymen and radical journalists to be their pawns." They were, he warned, "delivering this nation into the hands of international communism." When, despite a law prohibiting state-supported schools from participating in interracial athletic events, the Georgia Tech football team accepted a postseason bowl bid in 1955 even though one member of the opposing team was African-American, Cook decried the unwillingness of the school to stand up for law and principle: "For segregation to remain an integral part of Georgia's social customs and traditions, it must and will be practiced 24 hours a day, seven days a week, and 365 days a year." In line with that practice, Cook announced in the same year that if an African-American were admitted to the state's law school, that school would be closed. In 1962, Cook was endorsed for reelection by the Ku Klux Klan and refused to repudiate the Klan's support (Bartley 1969, 185–86, 213, 236; Dyer 1985, 311; *MN*, Sept. 8, 1962, 4).

Peter Zack Geer was an unblushing segregationist who inherited his views from his ancestors. His grandfather, William I. Geer, had been a member of the 1907 disfranchising legislature and had cosponsored a substitute constitutional amendment that would have disfranchised blacks and mulattoes explicitly, instead of through a facially neutral literacy or property test. Peter Zack's father, Colquitt superior court judge Walter I. Geer, once threatened to jail any FBI agent who dared to investigate voting rights discrimination in Terrell County. In 1961, after white students rioted against integration at the University of Georgia, Peter Zack, then chief aide to Gov. Ernest Vandiver, issued a statement praising the rioters for having "the character and the courage not to submit to dictatorship and tyranny." Two years later, Geer as lieutenant governor also chaired the Senate Judiciary Committee, which oversaw the election code, and the day before the House passed the majority-vote bill he successfully repulsed an attempt to water down the state's anti-integration, private school subsidy policy (Georgia House *Journal* 1907, 927–29; *AC*, Oct. 14, 1963, 18; *MN*, Sept. 6, 1958, 1; Feb. 8, 1963, 1; Mar. 1, 1963, 1).

In 1957, Geer was the principal author for the ELSC of a tougher literacy test intended to inhibit blacks from registering.[8] At the ELSC hearings and meetings on the law, Geer, according to the *Constitution*, "made no secret of his desire to bar 'illiterate Negro bloc voters' from registering." The new questions were so difficult that only seven of twenty-two white women from the elite Atlanta Voters' Guild who arranged to take the test passed. Naturally, the questions were not supposed to be asked of the already registered, largely white voters. Geer made clear his concerns on this score in a private letter: "[I]t seems to be the desire of the whole committee to perpetuate the existing registration list, and I can foresee that upon prospective negro voters being disqualified under the new law, that they might then challenge on [*sic*] masse the registered and qualified voters on the list, and attempt to subject the old voters to the new examination. This would be catastrophic, indeed." The expansion of the list of disqualifying crimes was another means to the same end, for, according to Geer, "90% of the Negroes in my section could be convicted of adultery and bigamy . . . [I] would rather see a few white persons inconvenienced than be faced with several hundred bloc voters." With some minor amendments, the new literacy test passed both houses of the 1957 legislature (*AJ*, Dec. 15, 1957, 2; Apr. 17, 1958, 2; *AC*, Nov. 22, 1957, 21; Dec. 13, 1957, 25; Geer to Frank Edwards, Nov. 29, 1957, in ELSC Files, "Edwards Correspondence" folder; Georgia House *Journal* 1957, 1137–38, 1151, 1177–80).

Although other members of the 1963–64 and earlier ELSCs were less well-known and generally less active on the Committee than Chairman Fortson, Cook, and Geer, there is no reason to believe that the racial views of the vast majority of them differed from those of whose opinions we have clear evidence. The ELSC's vote for the substitution of a secret ballot with no assistance for the endangered literacy test in 1963 was unanimous, and committee members apparently voted with a full knowledge of its import, since Fortson told correspondents directly that the discussion within the ELSC on the issue reflected his understanding of it. The committee was also likely the source for the *Atlanta Constitution*'s story on the subject, which said that the purpose of the measure was to "eliminate possible federal civil rights suits . . . [and] negate the current proposals before Congress to say that anyone who has a 6th grade education or higher would be presumed literate for purposes of registration" (*AC*, Oct. 17, 1963, 1). Passed by the ELSC on the same day that it endorsed the majority-vote requirement, over the objection of the Committee's sole Republican, the subtly discriminatory secret ballot proposal undermines any view that the ELSC was indifferent to or less than fully supportive of the necessity to protect white political supremacy.

The one shred of evidence of ELSC liberalism on the majority-vote issue offered at the preliminary injunction hearing in *Brooks v. Harris* was almost comically weak. Five months *after* the ELSC had firmly decided to include a majority-vote requirement in its recommendations, Ms. Melba Williams, a white Democratic Party activist from DeKalb County, was appointed to the committee by Gov. Carl Sanders. It is not surprising that Ms. Williams testified that she heard no discussion of any racial or other purpose behind the majority-vote requirement while she was on the committee (*Brooks v. Harris* 1990 trial transcript, 5:138–39). Whatever discussions there had been—and there are no transcripts of the ELSC meetings—were over long before she was placed on the committee and could attend their meetings. That is, her testimony that she heard no discussion of a racial purpose for the provision by no means implies that there was no such discussion, much less no such purpose on the part of the actual decisionmakers on the issue.

IN HIS testimony in 1990 in *Brooks v. Harris,* Carl E. Sanders represented himself an a staunch opponent of racial discrimination who as governor controlled the legislature and would never have favored any election law that he thought had a racially discriminatory purpose. "I did everything that I could in every way that I could to show that there was no first or second class relationship between blacks and whites while I was governor of Georgia," he asserted (*Brooks v. Harris* trial transcript, 4:175). Sanders's record from the 1950s and 60s was very different from his recollections thirty years later.

In his first term in the Georgia House in 1955–56, Sanders voted for all of the following: a bill authorizing the governor to close public schools, an interposition resolution by Denmark Groover and others declaring the *Brown* decisions "null, void, and of no effect," a bill by Groover requiring segregation for both interstate and intrastate passengers in the waiting rooms of common carriers, one authorizing the state police to enforce segregation laws, and another allowing the sale of public parks to private parties to prevent their integration. As president pro tem of the Senate in 1959, he was the lead sponsor of bills to allow the governor to close public schools and universities, to rewrite the admissions rules for the University of Georgia, and to authorize the hiring of counsel in integration challenges. In 1960, he sponsored two barratry[9] bills, described in Associated Press stories in Sanders's hometown newspaper as "segregation bills," which, the story explained, were "designed to curb school integration suits where plaintiffs usually are represented by attorneys of the National Assn. for the Advancement of Colored People." In the same session, he also favored a measure aimed at those who sat in at lunch counters and other places to protest segregation by making it a misdemeanor to refuse to depart from public premises after being requested to do so. In 1961, Sanders sponsored a bill to provide tuition grants to students who attended private schools and voted for one to repeal compulsory education. Although in the 1950s and 60s, it was widely noted that such laws were attempts to subvert integration, Sanders in 1990 denied that his purpose in sponsoring the 1961 tuition bill had anything to do with integration (Georgia House *Journal* 1956, 365–66, 782–83, 656, 1366–67; Georgia Senate *Journal* 1959, 65–67; *AuC*, Feb. 16, 1960, 1; Feb. 19, 1960, 1; *AC*, Jan. 26, 1956, 1; Feb. 2, 1960, 1; Feb. 9, 1960, 13; Feb. 15, 1960, 1; Feb. 16, 1960, 1; Georgia *Laws* 1960, 1135–37; *MT*, Feb. 21, 1963, 1; Bartley 1969, 54–55; *Brooks v. Harris* trial transcript, 4: 202–6).

Like Ernest Vandiver, who had promised during his 1958 campaign for governor that "neither my child nor yours will ever attend an integrated school during my administration—no, not one," Sanders weakened his position on school closing once absolute defiance proved unable to preserve white-only schools. Vandiver acceded to the court-ordered integration of the University of Georgia by Charlayne Hunter and Hamilton Holmes in January 1961 and successfully pushed the legislature to repeal laws requiring state funds to be cut off from integrated schools. Later that year, Sanders and Frank Twitty, Vandiver's House floor leader, who had filled the same role in Herman Talmadge's administration, "made a state-wide tour under sponsorship of the Georgia State Chamber of Commerce and . . . made it clear to their audiences that they were steadfastly for segregation. And at the same time, they reassured their listeners, they would not let their public schools be closed" (Vandiver 1988, 159; Pyles 1988, 149–50; *AuCH*, July 8, 1962, B:3).

Perhaps the best summary of Sanders's record is in the words of the "Segregation" section of his own platform in the 1962 governor's race:

> My record in support of legislation over the years to maintain segregation is long, continuing, and well-known. It is not one of empty oratory, but concrete results. It rests upon law and order and the consent of the governed. As your governor, every legal means and every lawful recourse available will be utilized to the fullest to strengthen and to maintain Georgia's traditional separation, sponsored by the responsible leadership of the state, and passed almost unanimously by the General Assembly. Legal attacks against Georgia's institutions in the federal courts will be resisted, and with every available defense. (*AJC*, July 1, 1962, 46)

Sanders's stance was certainly not as shrill as that of his opponent Marvin Griffin, whose advertisements framed the issue as "Will you vote White [i.e., for Griffin], or will you vote Black?" But it was far from showing any sympathy whatever with integration. Sanders hotly denied Griffin's charge that he was supported by such integrationists as *Atlanta Constitution* editor Ralph McGill or Martin Luther King Jr., and he bracketed King and his colleague Ralph Abernathy with Citizens' Council head Roy Harris and Marvin Griffin as "race-baiters and hate-mongers." On the contrary, the Sanders campaign touted advertisements from such well-known extreme segregationists as Bill Bodenhamer, the executive director of the States Rights Council, a Baptist minister and state legislator who had declared segregation "the will of God" and who had run an especially strident campaign against Ernest Vandiver in the 1958 governor's race. "Carl is a segregationist," Bodenhamer announced, "just as I am a segregationist!" "What Did Marvin Griffin Do About This Integration?" a Sanders campaign ad asked. "NOTHING. What will He DO If Re-Elected? Nothing." Endorsing Sanders, the *Macon Telegraph* remarked that Sanders "knows the vast majority of Georgians are in favor of segregation, just as he is. His approach to the problem will do far more to preserve the Southern pattern of life than Mr. Griffin's bombast, agitation and ultimatums" (*MN*, Sept. 11, 1962, 7; *MT*, June 12, 1962, 1; Sept. 9, 1962, 4; Sept. 11, 1962, 9; *BPS*, June 7, 1962, 8; Black 1976, 68; *AC*, Jan. 26, 1956, 1; Bernd 1972, 330–31; Vandiver 1988, 158–59; *AH*, Sept. 9, 1962, A:13, 14).

Sanders's attitudes and actions on racial discrimination in electoral rules closely paralleled his attitudes and actions on segregation. Not only did he defend the county unit system, but as governor-elect, he led the state legislature in an almost successful effort to evade the state constitution in order to block the election of the first African-American to the Georgia legislature in fifty-six years. The incident casts doubt on any contention that Sanders's support of the majority vote had nothing to do with race.

In May 1962, a federal court ruled that one house of the Georgia legislature had to be apportioned on a population basis by January 1, 1963. Since every county had at least one House member and many would have none by themselves if the House were reapportioned along population lines, a consensus quickly developed to make the smaller Senate the one-person, one-vote body, and Gov. Vandiver called a special session to meet after the September primaries to enact the needed legislation. The most controversial question in the session, which was completely dominated by governor-elect Sanders, was whether senators from counties that were accorded more than one senator would run at-large or by districts. Although the state constitution clearly mandated district elections, the legislative leadership decided to require them to be held at-large. Apparently recognizing the unconstitutionality of its actions, the legislature hedged its decision in two ways—requiring candidates to live in separate, equally populous geographical districts within multiseat counties and drafting an amendment to the state constitution, to be voted on in a referendum in November (after the election of the new senators), that specifically authorized at-large elections in multiseat jurisdictions (*ATR*, May 26, 1962, 1; Oct. 5, 1962, 1; *MT*, Oct. 1, 1962, 1; *AC*, Oct. 3, 1962, 1; Oct. 8, 1962, 1).

The new residency districts and the prospect that the state constitution might be at least temporarily adhered to encouraged the first serious campaigns by African-Americans for the state legislature since the early part of the century. In Atlanta, Leroy Johnson ran against four whites for the Democratic nomination in one seat, and T. M. Alexander was unopposed on the Republican side to run for the same seat in the general election. Another black Republican, Rod Harris, was a candidate for a second senate seat. As a newspaper columnist pointed out, dividing the large counties into senatorial districts "would assure that there would be one or two Negro senators from Fulton County, and perhaps some from others, inasmuch as the large concentration of Negro population in some Fulton areas would make it impossible to district in such a way as to avoid having one or two districts with very predominantly colored population." The Sanders-sponsored at-large elections in these majority-white counties would, it was widely recognized, virtually eliminate the possibility of electing black candidates (*ADW*, Oct. 7, 1962, 1; Oct. 13, 1962, 1; *DKNE*, Oct. 4, 1962, 1; *MT*, Oct. 4, 1962, 1; *AC*, Oct. 8, 1962, 1).[10] What was the legislature's intent?

On the senate floor, the discreet Sanders apparently contended only that countywide elections were necessary "to get agreements on local legislation." But according to a United Press International report, Rep. Guy Rutland of DeKalb County, who claimed to be speaking for Sanders, "has said Sanders wanted the provision to avoid the possible election of a Negro senator from Fulton." Frank Twitty, the Vandiver floor leader in the House, was even more blunt. Referring to a proposal to require all senators to be chosen by districts, Twitty told his colleagues in a floor debate, "I'm not going to vote for anything that would automatically put a member of a minority race in the state Senate." Other newspaper articles containing statements or sentiments that were not attributed to particular legislators made the same point repeatedly, insuring that any political observer at the time could not miss the racial concerns of the legislators or the racial consequences of at-large elections. The *Macon Telegraph*'s story, for instance, noted that "some supporters of the county-wide election provision regard it as an obstacle to the election of Negro senators from those districts," while the *Atlanta Journal*'s remarked that "the argument was frankly used that countywide electing would be less likely to produce Negro senators than letting citizens of only a specific district do the voting" (*MT*, Oct. 1, 1962, 1; Oct. 4, 1962, 1; Oct 5, 1962, 1; *CD*, Oct. 4, 1962, 1; *AC*, Oct. 2, 1962, 1; Oct. 5, 1962, 1; Oct. 8, 1962, 1; Oct. 9, 1962, 1; *AJ*, Oct. 9, 1962, 6).

Mrs. Edward Vinson, president of the Georgia League of Women Voters, which had opposed at-large voting for senators, called the racial argument an "open invitation to [a] court suit." In fact, it was immediately challenged in both state and federal courts. Although the federal court refused to rule in time to enjoin the elections, which took place within ten days of the passage of the reapportionment act, Fulton County Superior Court judge Durwood Pye, after listening to arguments that the at-large system was intentionally racially discriminatory and that it violated an express provision in the state constitution requiring districting, declared it void. A staunch segregationist and supporter of Marvin Griffin, Pye said that his ruling on state grounds obviated the need to reach the federal question of racial discrimination. Pye's ruling changed the results. If the votes had been counted at the county level, Johnson would have faced a runoff against white racist activist Ed Barfield. Counted at the district level, in a black-majority district, Johnson beat the other four candidates combined. In the Republican primary held on the same day in Atlanta, the substitution of district-level for county-level returns reversed the victory of a white candidate over a black. Griffin, still bitter at his defeat by Sanders a month and a half earlier, swiped at Sanders: "The Atlanta newspapers and Governor-nominate Sanders have been using the Negro bloc vote for personal gain and political power. Neither wanted Johnson in the Senate and both contrived to prohibit by law his election to that body. These people are not sincere" (*AJ*, Oct. 9, 1962, 6; *ADW*, Oct. 9, 1962, 1; Oct. 16, 1962, 1; *MT*, Oct. 14, 1962, 1; Oct. 18, 1962, 1; Oct. 21, 1962, 1; Oct. 20, 1962, 1; *AC*, Oct. 19, 1962, 1; Oct. 22, 1962, 1; Barfield to Ben Fortson, June 13, 1963, in ELSC Papers, Correspondence; *BPS*, Oct. 25, 1962, 3).

Perhaps Sanders was more sincerely committed to segregation, at least, than Griffin charged. In 1963, when Charlayne Hunter and a Georgia white man that she had met at the University of Georgia married in New York (the marriage would have been illegal in Georgia), Gov. Sanders felt called upon to denounce the union publicly as "a shame and a disgrace." In 1964, when Congress was considering whether to ban segregation in public accommodations, Sanders testified against it as a violation of private property and states' rights (*CE*, Sept. 6, 1963, 8; Cook 1988, 180).

Carl Sanders's record before and during his administration as governor indicates that he would be likely to have favored racially discriminatory electoral rules not merely in spite of but because of their discriminatory purpose.

IN SOME newspaper reports of Denmark Groover's remarks in February 1963 before the House and the Senate Rules Committee, he is quoted as saying that the majority-vote requirement would eliminate the "bloc vote" or would prevent "bloc vote groups" from controlling elections. Other reports have him referring to "Negroes and other minorities" or "Negro bloc voting" (*VT*,

Feb. 20, 1963, 1; Feb. 21, 1963, 1; *MT*, Feb. 21, 1963, 1; *MO*, Feb. 21, 1963, 2). Does the usage of the phrase "bloc vote" in Georgia at that time indicate that Groover was unambiguously referring to African-Americans and that his audience would have understood him to be doing so, or does it show that he could equally well have been referring to any other cohesive group, such as a "labor bloc vote"?

As we have seen above, Herman Talmadge popularized the phrase "bloc vote" in his gubernatorial campaign in 1948, and there is no question at all that he meant it as a reference to *black* voting. Two years later, he argued that writing the county unit system into the state constitution was necessary to overcome the "Bloc Vote Menace." In a rerun of the referendum in 1952, Talmadge assailed "the bloc voters league in Atlanta" which threatened the entire state because it had recently "issued a call for 40,000 newly registered bloc voters there before the next general election." In an article on a 1957 ELSC report, Peter Zack Geer is quoted as saying that the stiffened literacy test was aimed at "illiterate Negro bloc voters. . . . If it is the Negroes that fall into the class of bloc voters, I can't help it." In Macon in 1960, superior court judge Oscar Long's "bloc voting probe," at which Groover testified, was unmistakably aimed only at blacks. In 1962, two of Groover's enemies in Macon politics were accused of making deals to get "the Negro bloc vote" (*HS*, Oct. 26, 1950, 1; Sept. 11, 1952, 1; *AC*, Dec. 13, 1957, 25; *MT*, Sept. 9, 1962, 26).

Perhaps the phrase reached the height of its use in the 1962 gubernatorial campaign of Marvin Griffin, whom Groover supported. At an organizational meeting of a Griffin for Governor club in Wilkinson County, Judge Hubert C. Morgan of DeKalb County declared that "The negro bloc vote in Atlanta controls the activities of the city public officials. . . . Total integration is wanted by 'Rastus' McGill, Martin Luther King and the negro bloc vote in Atlanta."[11] In one advertisement run in newspapers shortly before the primary, Griffin warned that "This Big 200,000 Bloc Vote Can Control Georgia," and before the word "Bloc," he placed a black square. In the text of the ad, he assailed the "200,000 Negro Bloc Vote . . . controlled by King and his NAACP" that would "undoubtedly go to Carl Sanders." A vote for Sanders, Griffin announced, would "risk turning the State of Georgia over to control by The Big [black square] Bloc Vote." In another ad, Griffin's Bibb County managers denounced "the self-serving bloc vote of the colored race." Sanders, they charged, "has sought and will receive this same colored bloc vote." Griffin apparently used the same phrase in speeches across the state. After the campaign was over, Griffin announced that "95% of the Negro vote is under the domination of the NAACP and Sanders received this 95% Negro bloc vote" (*BPS*, June 7, 1962, 8; Sept. 27, 1962, 1; *MV*, Sept. 6, 1962, 3; *MT*, Sept. 11, 1962, 9; *AH*, Sept. 12, 1962, 1).

The same usage continued after 1962. During the debate in 1964 on a provision to prohibit voters from bringing to the polls printed facsimile ballots or lists, assistant senate floor leader Julian Webb and floor leader Milton Carlton, both members of the Sanders administration team, favored the controversial proposal as a means to "stop block [*sic*] voting" or "cut down on bloc voting." Unmistakably referring to African-Americans when he commented on the same section of the bill, Groover "said that the problem was not that bloc voters took memos into the polls, but that they got them at 'big church meetings the night before.' " Even less ambiguously, an Associated Press story on the subject reported that advocates of the memo provision said it "was intended to curb what they called bloc voting by Negroes." And every two years in Macon, there would be another charge that one or more candidates had "bought and paid for the Negro bloc vote" or granted "favors" to obtain the "bloc vote" in a superior court race. In light of this overwhelming contemporary evidence, it is no wonder that in his 1984 deposition, even Denmark Groover admitted that "bloc vote" was a "euphemism" for "blacks voting in a bloc, that's what it meant" (*AJ*, May 18, 1964, 7; *AC*, May 26, 1964, 7; June 11, 1964, 1; *MT*, June 11, 1964, 8; Sept. 13, 1966, 14; *MTN*, Sept. 6, 1964, 22; Groover dep. 1984, 19–20).

THERE WERE three short periods during 1963–64 when important action on the majority-vote provision took place: February 19–28, 1963, when the House passed H.B. 117 and the Senate Rules Committee first shelved, then revived it; September 1–October 15, 1963, when the ELSC made decisions on both the majority vote and the secret ballot literacy test; and May 3–June 10, 1964, when the House and Senate considered election code revisions recommended by the ELSC (Georgia House *Journal* 1963, 301, 352, 645–48; Georgia Senate *Journal* 1964 Extra Sess., 234; Georgia House *Journal* 1964 Extra Sess., 781–82, 791–98). What additional light can the events of those periods throw on the purposes of those who framed and passed the majority-vote requirement?

H.B. 117 was identical in substance with the election code section adopted by the ELSC, which passed the legislature with relatively minor amendments on unrecorded votes. All three versions required a majority vote in primaries and general elections for all, or nearly all, local and state offices. Only on H.B. 117 has a discussion of the purposes of the majority vote survived, and it was the only version that produced a roll call, which may yield inferences about the motives of those actors who did not speak.

When the House considered the majority-vote requirement on February 19, 1963, Denmark Groover's Bibb County colleague and political enemy William F. Laite Jr. contended that the provision was antidemocratic. "I sincerely feel that a majority vote eliminates or excludes competition and would discourage new blood from seeking political office to a large degree," Laite announced. "A majority vote bill would increase election and candidate-election costs and these costs are already substantially out of reason. This fact alone would restrict competition. . . . Runoffs draw a substantially decreasing number of voters which I feel does not reflect the will of the majority of the people." Against these strong arguments, Groover played the race card, saying that the provision's main purpose was "to prevent special interest and bloc groups from controlling elections." Other reports noted that Groover connected the provision with the county unit system: "The Bibb County legislator explained a majority vote would again provide protection which he said was removed with the death of the county unit system, indicating it would thwart election control by Negroes and other minorities" (*MT*, Feb. 21, 1963, 1; *VT*, Feb. 21, 1963, 1; *MO*, Feb. 21, 1963, 2).

After the House passed the bill by a vote of 133–41, the Senate Rules Committee initially voted a "do not pass" resolution. Some members of the committee, which was chaired by Lt. Gov. Peter Zack Geer, were concerned about the increased expense of runoffs, while others voted to shelve it "partly because of a feeling that the proposed ELSC would consider this and other election reforms before the next session of the General Assembly." To revive his bill, Groover appeared before the Rules Committee in a public session and used an explicitly racial argument. "We have a situation," Groover told the committee, "when the federal government interceded to increase the registration of Negro voters. One-third of the Negroes in my county will not vote without an endorsement sheet gotten up the night before. It would be true of any other bloc vote group, regardless of race or color." Although the Rules Committee withdrew its negative report, the bill did not come to the floor during the remaining two weeks of the session (*CD*, Feb. 28, 1963, 1; *AC*, Mar. 1, 1963, 20 [Groover quote]; *MN*, Mar. 3, 1963, 1; Mar. 12, 1963, 4).

Examination of the roll call vote on H.B. 117 in the House suggests that the same racist motivations that drove Groover underlay the actions of most other legislators. Table 4.1 presents an ordered probit analysis of that roll call, which evaluates differences in characteristics of the home counties of the proponents, opponents, and abstainers on the roll call with a view to answering the following questions:[12] Were the proponents more likely than the abstainers to come from counties with low levels of black voting registration, where there was apparently a greater level of discrimination in the administration of voting qualifications? Were the opponents of the majority-vote requirement more likely than either proponents or abstainers to represent counties with relatively high levels of black registration, where African-American voters by 1962 already enjoyed some influence? The negative and highly statistically significant coefficient on the variable "Blackreg" in Table 4.1 (the percentage of black adults who were registered to vote when the legislators were elected in 1962) confirms the hypotheses underlying these first two questions: supporters of H.B. 117 were in fact disproportionately likely to come from the most racially discriminatory counties, opponents from the least discriminatory, and abstainers from counties with relatively moderate discrimination.[13] Another question addressed by the ordered probit analysis is the effect of county population size on representatives' responses to H.B. 117. During the debate on the bill, Groover stated that it would "prevent local Democratic committees from shifting elections back and forth between a majority and a plurality basis" (*AC*, Feb. 21, 1963, 1). Presumably, such shifts would cause less consternation in smaller counties than in large urban centers, where many citizens and politicians would be discomforted and the news media could be expected to denounce self-serving tricks. And indeed, the coefficient on the variable "Size" in Table 4.1 shows that legislators from small counties were somewhat less likely than more urban representatives to vote for the bill, though the relationship overall is not statistically significant at conventional levels. Nevertheless, 70 of the 121 legislators from counties that had only one representative in the malapportioned House voted for H.B. 117, while only 26 opposed it (25 abstained or were absent). That is, by nearly three to one, small county legislators voted for the bill *in spite of* the constraints that it placed on their ability to manipulate elections. The implications of these coefficients are consistent with the discussions on the floor: legislators voted for the bill *because* of its racial impact and would have opposed it but for its racial impact. The racially discriminatory purpose of H.B. 117 was not only the predominant reason for its passage but an absolutely necessary condition.

As an ad hoc committee, the ELSC left less direct evidence of its motives than did the legislature. Although Assistant Attorney General Paul Rodgers used the Pennsylvania election code as a guide, he did not adopt its plurality-vote standard, and he never explained his reasons for failing to do so. The principal recorded opposition to the majority vote within the ELSC came from state senator and Democratic Party chairman J. B. Fuqua, Gov. Sanders's "innermost political counsel," who sent Fortson the following message on September 7, 1963: "As a practical matter, the present practice of plurality rather than majority vote has not resulted in widespread inequities or dissatisfaction. I would prefer to stay on the plurality basis, or, as an alternative, require a run-off provided no candidate received more than, say, 35% of the vote cast in a primary." At an ELSC hearing three days later in Atlanta, Fuqua publicly announced his preference that Georgia elections, as a newspaper summarized it, "stay on a plurality basis," and several witnesses agreed "that a 40% plurality be accepted as conclusive in order to avoid expensive runoff elections." Sanders, however, immediately announced that he favored a ma-

TABLE 4.1. Did Georgia House Members Favor the Majority-Vote Requirement for Racial Reasons? Ordered Probit Analysis of House Vote on H.B. 117

Independent Variables	Dependent Variable: Vote on H.B. 117 (Yea, Abstain, Nay)
Constant	1.03 (6.47)[a]
Blackreg (percentage of eligible blacks registered to vote, 1962)	−0.74 (−2.24)
Size (voting-age population of county, 1960)[b]	1.06 (1.50)

Sources: Georgia House of Representatives 1963, 645–48; U.S. Commission on Civil Rights 1968, 234–39.
[a] t statistics are shown in parentheses; t values greater than 1.96 are statistically significant at the conventional 0.05 level.
[b] Calculated as a proportion of the voting-age population of Fulton County, 1960.

jority vote, and although he left it up to the citizens of the state to express their preferences at public ELSC hearings, he suggested that what Fuqua really meant was that localities should be free to adopt plurality elections. By the time that he wrote Fortson another letter a month later, Fuqua was marching to the same drummer as others in the administration, even though his about-face lacked grace: "Incidentally," Fuqua wrote, "I very strongly favor the majority rule in State primaries, and some recent reports that I favored a return to the plurality rule is [sic] a complete misrepresentation. Comments that I have made regarding this referred only to local primaries. I would like to see majority rule apply in local primaries, but just do not see how it is practical to finance it within the framework of the present organization of the local Democratic committees" (Minutes of ELSC Subcommittee Meeting, Aug. 27, 1963, in Fortson Papers; Purdon 1930, 363, 568; AJC Magazine, Mar. 3, 1963, 9; AC, Sept. 12, 1963, 14; AJ, Sept. 11, 1963, 2; Fuqua to Fortson, Sept. 7, 1963 [first Fuqua quote], Oct. 14, 1963 [second Fuqua quote], in ELSC Files, Box 34, classification nos. 4519–25; Sanders press release, Sept. 13, 1963, in ELSC Files).

The Fuqua reversal illustrates three points: dissent within the administration was quickly smoothed over; there was no public discussion of the purposes of the majority-vote measure at this time, even when its addition to the code was contested; and the later stress by witnesses in Brooks v. Harris on the runoff as a means of countering manipulations of the rules for local elections was by no means widely discussed in 1963–64 (for the witness's stress, see Brooks v. Harris trial transcript, 4:170 [Sanders]; 5:22–23 [Carlton]; 5:81–83 [Smith]). Some knowledgeable observers who were part of the administration team did not think such problems were grave at all. Like Fuqua, State Democratic Party Secretary George D. Stewart denied that fraud was a problem. Georgia, Stewart said, had "the cleanest 15-year primary record in the nation," noting that there had been "only one occasion of questionable results in a county and two actual contests of primaries" (*AC*, Apr. 10, 1964, 14).

On October 15, 1963, all but one member of the ELSC, William J. Schloth, the only Republican on the committee, voted to add to the code a majority-vote requirement for all elections. There were no position papers, no recorded discussion, and no committee report giving even nominal reasons for the ELSC's choice. But actions by the ELSC taken the same day on the collateral issue of substituting a subtle literacy test for a blatantly discriminatory one and public reactions to that often misunderstood move shed additional light on the purposes of the majority-vote section. As discussed above, the ELSC proposed to abolish the 30-question test that was given to anyone whom registrars decided to challenge and to substitute a law making it a felony to provide assistance to a voter, unless he or she were physically disabled. An editorial column in the *Atlanta Constitution* explained the rationale: "The key lies in the side proposal to make it a felony for anyone to help the citizen vote. Without help, an illiterate cannot read or mark the ballot properly— and therefore the ballot itself becomes his literacy test." Another article in the *Constitution* on the same day noted that the change would "raise our image tremendously on the national level because nobody could accuse Georgia of using the literacy tests to block qualified Negro voters from registering. . . . Committee members estimated the change would result in perhaps a 10% increase in voter registration and perhaps a 10% increase in ballots thrown out for being improperly marked" (*AJ*, June 4, 1964, 2; *AC*, Oct. 17, 1963, 1, 4). In other words, the committee thought that the change would insulate the racial status quo in politics from attack in Congress and the federal courts.

But many whites did not fully understand the subtle shift. Referring to what she supposed was the abandonment of the literacy test, Mrs. J. J. Smith of Macon wrote Ben Fortson: "Would you mind telling me if you are any part negro? Also why you think Georgia people should submit to negro government." The mayor of Montezuma, Dr. C. P. Savage, declared that African-Americans there "are not responsible as good voting citizens even yet and these several hundred we have voting are the best ones of the lot. Lord knows what would happen if we turned the general rabble of their race loose at the polls."[14] Calvin F. Craig, Grand Dragon of the United Klans of America, protested what he considered a change that was aimed at "getting tens of thousands of illiterate negroes registered to vote in the State of Georgia . . . to create a State Bloc Vote." The president of a network of five "Johnny Reb" radio stations editorialized that the ELSC action represented "a deliberate attempt to give suffrage to people who don't know how to vote." Even the *Atlanta Journal*, located in the enlightened metropolis that advertised itself as "too busy to hate," misunderstood and protested what it called "a surprising display of voting generosity. . . . But will the country relish the kind of democracy it's likely to get if too many voters are completely ignorant of what to do with their ballots, or show no hesitancy in making them available to the highest bidder?" And Governor Carl Sanders himself "advised extreme caution about eliminating literacy tests"[15] (Smith to Fortson, Oct. 7, 1963, in ELSC Files, Box 34, classification nos. 4519–25; Savage to Fortson, Oct. 17, 1963; Craig to Fortson, Oct. 21, 1963; Allen M. Woodall to Fortson, Oct. 23, 1963, in Fortson Papers; *AJ*, Oct. 17, 1963, 34; *CE*, Nov. 15, 1963, 21).

Even those who understood the stratagem sometimes doubted its efficacy. In November, Attorney General Eugene Cook reversed his earlier stand in the ELSC, protesting:

> Blind subservience to some false and illusory "democratic ideal" can not be permitted to elevate ignorance to such a favored station. . . . It was our thought originally that this gesture would insulate us against federal court suits. . . . Upon further study, however, I perceive that it takes no great degree of sophistication to discern that this is a mere play on words. . . . [T]he proposal we have made would only shift the discrimination to the vote-counting stage, always the most fertile field of sharp practices. (Cook to Fortson, Nov. 20, 1963, Fortson Papers)

Citing Supreme Court case law, Cook feared that federal courts would declare it unconstitutional for a state that had allowed an illiterate voter to register to make it impossible in practice for him or her to vote. A further difficulty was that, as an editorial in the *Columbus Enquirer* put it, the ELSC proposal "would not keep a person from coming to the poll with a ballot already marked for him." This difficulty provoked a fight that had to be settled on the floor of the legislature. In the end, the ELSC's proposed code and changes in the state constitution contained the "no assistance" provision and eliminated the 30-question test but required the proposed State Election Board to draw up a new test, which the ELSC expected would contain ten questions, all more objective than those from the earlier test (*CE*, Oct. 18, 1963, 4; Georgia House *Journal* 1964, 2360–63).

The ELSC's actions on the literacy test and the public response have two implications for arguments about the purposes of the majority-vote requirement. First, the ELSC was clearly interested in substituting sophisticated for simple tools of electoral discrimination. The majority vote, which could be presented as a move toward "democracy," just as the abolition of the literacy test was, might well have been another example of that impulse. Second, the public mood of interested whites, from those in the Klan to those in the editorial offices of major metropolitan dailies, was extremely adverse to any electoral rule that would be likely to increase African-American political power. If the ELSC or the legislature felt it necessary to be responsive to expressed white public opinion in Georgia, it would frame measures that would contain black electoral potency.

ON MAY 3, 1964, newspapers reported that the legislature's special session on the election code and the constitution had opened, that African-American civil rights lawyer Donald Hollowell had qualified to run for the superior court in Atlanta, and that the Goldwater forces had taken over the state Republican Party (*AJ*, May 3, 1964, 1; *SMN*, May 3, 1964, A:7; *MT*, May 3, 1964, 1). The recurrent news stories on the Hollowell-Pye-Webb contest and the exclusion of blacks from the GOP insured that no politically conscious legislator or other observer at the time could have missed the racial significance of the majority-vote provision or the alienation of blacks from the Republican Party. The majority-vote provision was noncontroversial because, in a legislature containing only one black and very few really sympathetic whites, its widely understood racial purpose was agreed upon.

By contrast, both houses of the legislature went through seemingly capricious reversals over facets of literacy tests because of the fear that for the first time federal supervision might require electoral regulations to be applied in the same way to members of both races. As Senator Hugh Gillis realized, the nonassistance policy would disfranchise illiterates who were already on the rolls, most of whom, he did not have to remind his peers, were white. Presumably responding to such arguments, but without explaining its reasons, the Senate Rules Committee amended the code to allow assistance to illiterates, but passed a further provision to prohibit a voter from carrying into the polls a marked facsimile of the ballot. The motive behind this "anti-slate card" section, according to Sanders's Senate floor leaders Julian Webb and Milton Carlton, was "to discourage bloc voting." Debate over what the Associated Press story termed the "bloc vote curb" consumed an entire day in the Senate and passed by the minimum constitutional majority. Opponents, the story reported, "argued that everyone knew the intent of the section was to prevent an 'organized bloc vote,' but that it would have the effect of preventing voters who legitimately use facsimile ballots such as [those] in newspapers as an aid in voting." Worried that the law would either turn innocent housewives and businessmen who tore sample ballots out of newspapers into criminals or that it would be enforced selectively against "colored people who join together to oppose a candidate," the *Macon Telegraph* condemned the Senate action. But what the *Telegraph* condemned was exactly what some legislators wanted. When Mitchel House of Macon tried to delete the anti-slate card section in the House Rules Committee, Roy McCracken of Jefferson County admitted that it was unenforceable but said he thought that it would discourage "bloc voting" just by appearing on the books and therefore always being a threat to organized bloc groups. On the floor, the House first deleted the anti-slate section "even though the fact that it was aimed essentially at putting a brake on Negro bloc voting gave it some appeal." It then reconsidered that vote, rejected moves to prohibit the publication of slate cards for seven days before the election, then voted to keep the section. Finally, a House-Senate conference committee dropped the anti-slate provision, which even Denmark Groover condemned as forcing poll officials "to ask a little old lady to open up her pocket book to see if she had some memoranda in there" (*AJ*, May 7, 1964, 2; May 27, 1964, 1; *AC*, May 15, 1964, 1; May 26, 1964, 7; May 27, 1964, 1; June 3, 1964, 1; June 11, 1964, 1; June 16, 1964, 3; *AuH*, May 26, 1964, 1; *MT*, May 27, 1964, 1; May 28, 1964, 4; June 11, 1964, 1, 8).

The legislature was similarly conflicted about the multiquestion test. Thus, the Senate barely defeated a move to restore the number of questions on the literacy test to thirty and then voted overwhelmingly to limit them to six specified and straightforward ones. A motion in the House Rules Committee to restore the thirty questions "and any others we can think of" failed by only two votes, and the House finally agreed to fix the number of questions at twenty, but to increase the passing grade from 67 percent under the former constitution to 75 percent under the new. Eventually, the conference committee settled on the House version, thus essentially preserving a test that the ELSC had proposed to eliminate altogether (*AC*, May 21, 1964, 1; June 3, 1964, 1; June 16, 1964, 3; *AJ*, June 4, 1964, 2).

The contrast between the confused battles over variations on the literacy test and the great silence over the majority-vote provision in 1964 is instructive. The potential effects of the quasi-literacy tests on black and white voters were ambiguous and depended on the extent of federal supervision that all knew was coming. The effect of the majority-vote requirement was as clear as the contemporaneous contest for superior court judge in the state capital.

THE CASE FOR the proposition that the majority-vote requirement was adopted for a racially discriminatory purpose can be briefly summarized. The historical context in which it was framed was one in which the structure of segregation and political discrimination erected around the turn of the century was collapsing. The county unit system, malapportionment, and the overt literacy test had just been overthrown; segregated schools and public accommodations were under siege; the civil rights movement, with its voter registration drives, had spread throughout Georgia; and the Republican

Party had revived itself by pushing its African-American adherents into the Democratic Party and competing with the Democrats for the most racially conservative whites. In the last legislature in which either house was severely malapportioned, Denmark Groover, the leader of the Griffin faction in the House, a legislative wizard and self-described racial "reactionary" who was still transfixed by his defeat at the hands of the black "bloc vote" in Macon in 1958, wrote and drove through the House a majority-vote bill. When self-interest or more principled concerns threatened to derail his bill in the House and in the Senate Judiciary Committee, Groover used explicit or barely veiled racial arguments to pass and revive it.

The provision was incorporated in a comprehensive election code that was sponsored by an all-white Election Law Study Committee that had been dominated since its beginning by staunch defenders of racial discrimination in voting and which made every effort in 1963–64 to frame more subtle replacements for the literacy test, a test that had become the principal safeguard of white political supremacy in the state. The Sanders administration was committed to as little racial change as was feasible in the circumstances. Gov. Carl Sanders himself had always been and continued to be a steady proponent of segregation and literacy tests, and after he was safely elected governor, he had led an effort, which was obviously contrary to the state constitution, to institute an at-large election system for urban counties in an effort to keep the legislature lily-white. Fostering and supporting changes in election laws that had racially discriminatory purposes and effects was entirely consistent with other actions of Sanders, as with those of Groover and the ELSC.

A statistical analysis of the one legislative roll call taken on the provision shows that legislators from counties in which the disparities between black and white voter registration were largest and where the black registration percentages were smallest were those most likely to support the majority-vote bill, which implies that their motives were consonant with those articulated by their leaders. Two other statistical facts are also significant. First, in 1960 only 9.2 percent of the African-American and 2.4 percent of the white voting-age population lived in the 21 counties in the state that had black majorities. Second, in December 1962 only 13 percent of the state's registered voters were black (U.S. Commission on Civil Rights 1968, 234–39). Consequently, if voting continued to be as racially polarized as it had been every time a black candidate had run in the state, then a majority-vote requirement, along with at-large voting for many local offices, insured that almost nowhere in Georgia would African-Americans be able to control political outcomes (Walker 1963; Hornsby 1977; *AC*, May 9, 1957, 1; May 23, 1957, 1; June 7, 1957, 13).

FOUR ALTERNATIVES to the hypothesis that it was racial discrimination that motivated the legislators and other officials in Georgia are variations of unintended-consequences theses. First, any differential racial effect might conceivably have been an unintended consequence of a provision adopted for purely philosophical and progressive reasons. Majoritarianism, announced Ben Fortson after the ELSC's adoption of the requirement, is "a very deep and abiding principle." Governor Sanders offered two versions of this theme, saying twenty-seven years later (but not publicly in 1963–64) that he had favored the majority-vote provision because it imposed uniformity on the helter-skelter election system of the state and that "in American politics . . . you ought to have the majority of the people voting for you when you went in if you considered yourself to have a mandate to do anything that was going to be beneficial for the people to begin with" (*AC,* Oct. 16, 1963, 1; *Brooks v. Harris* trial transcript, 4:180–81, Sanders statement). Framers or their defenders often represent themselves as pure, disinterested, good government reformers who were unconcerned with the consequences of their reforms on anyone's interest (*Brooks v. Harris* trial transcript, 5:144–47, Melba Ruth Williams statement). At one point, even Denmark Groover attempted to cast his actions in this guise, contending that the majority-vote provision was purely an informational device, designed to insure that voters knew who was backing whom, at least in a potential second stage in a multicandidate election (Groover dep. 1984, 16–26, 66).

Second, some framers later contended that in 1963–64 they had been entirely unaware of any possible racial consequences of a majority-vote requirement. Testifying in *Brooks v. Harris,* for example, 1963–64 House Speaker George T. Smith was asked whether "any member of the General Assembly had thought there was going to be a discriminatory effect on black candidates through majority voting?" "No, I did not," Smith answered, "because it was not the purpose for it, nor have I ever heard it expressed. I never heard one person ever mention that was the purpose of it or was involved in it." According to Smith, there were no "facts that would have been before the General Assembly . . . in 1964, upon which any of them [the members] could have even thought that majority voting would have discriminated against black candidates" (*Brooks v. Harris* trial transcript, 5:113–15).

Third, it might be asserted that the framers were aware of the racial consequences and that that counted against the change, but that they went ahead in spite of those consequences (*Personnel Administrator of Mass. v. Feeney,* 1979). Perhaps a crisis of political corruption, somehow involving plurality-win rules, demanded action, even though a runoff would have what decision-makers viewed, according to this hypothesis, as the unfortunate side-effect of disadvantaging African-Americans.

A fourth, more self-interested twist to the unintended-consequences view, and one specific to this situation, would be that in light of the growth of the Republican Party in the Deep South in the mid-1960s, the majority provision represented an attempt to inhibit the Goldwater-inspired emergence of a viable two-party system.

A fifth hypothesis would combine facets of the other four, granting that racial purposes were important but denying that such purposes were necessary for the adoption of the law. In his opinion in *Brooks v. Miller* (1996), district court judge Richard Freeman contended that before 1964, "Georgia's elections were marked by corruption and manipulation" (4). While admitting that "Georgia's efforts at election law reform from 1957 to 1964 grew in large part from a desire to maintain a segregated and discriminatory status quo in the face of rising black voter registration and heightened scrutiny by the federal government," Freeman asserted that the majority-vote provision "would have been enacted even in the absence of those reasons" because "Sanders and other supporters of the majority-vote requirement had ample 'good government' reasons for advocating the measure" (26–27).[16]

None of these five alternative explanations will bear even the most gentle scrutiny.

The state whose greatest political innovation was the county-unit system was hardly a hotbed of majoritarianism, and before 1964, primaries had been decided by pluralities approximately as often as by majorities, insofar as anyone could tell (*SEP,* Apr. 1, 1964, 1). There was no tradition or current practice of any state policy favoring majority rule in Georgia in 1964. The rhetorical concern with the desirability of majority rule expressed by a few of those who had previously stoutly defended the rule of a minority of whites over the majority of whites and blacks—which included Sanders and, even more vehemently, Groover—is simply not credible. Moreover, it is obvious that in the presence of racially polarized voting any electoral structure that rewards majority groups penalizes minority groups. An adverse effect on minorities is then just the logical implication of majoritarianism, and to embrace the latter is therefore necessarily to will the former. Far from being disinterested reformers, Groover and the other legislators, Speaker Smith, Gov. Sanders, and nearly all the members of the ELSC were white politicians who had long pledged their fealty to segregation and discriminatory voting practices and who were forced to abandon the system of racial exclusion only by the strong hand of the federal government. The fact that the only "reformer" who had any role whatsoever in the decisions to adopt the majority-vote requirement whom the State could cite on its side was a person who was not appointed to the ELSC until five months after the majority-vote section was agreed upon provides a vivid testimony to the weakness of the State's case on this point.

The contentions that no one in 1963–64 mentioned the racial consequences of the runoff and that there were no examples of its discriminatory effect that legislators of the time would have noticed are clearly false. Newspapers all

across the state reported the racially charged reasons that Groover and anonymous legislators adduced in advocating the passage of the majority vote, as
they did the consequences of replacing a plurality with a majority rule for
the closely watched Atlanta Superior Court judgeship contest between segregationist Durwood Pye, civil rights lawyer Donald Hollowell, and white
moderate Paul Webb. Whatever anyone said three decades later in the heat of
a trial, no minimally attentive legislator, much less the speaker of the House,
could have been unaware of such statements and events.

The racial views of the supporters of the majority-vote provision and the
fact that they acted at a time of political crisis in the southern racial system
make it extremely unlikely that if they realized the racial consequences of
what they were doing, those considerations played no role in their decisions.
The most charitable interpretation of this hypothesis is that they were responding to an outburst or continuing condition of political corruption. Yet
according to Sanders administration leaders, there was little current political
corruption in the state, much less a scandalous amount of manipulation of
the pre-1964 majority or plurality option feature of local or state elections. In
any event, this was hardly a reformist legislature; rather it was one that sav-
aged the chief anticorruption features of the ELSC's proposed code and fought
as hard as it could to preserve a malapportioned legislature. Referring to the
court decisions instituting the rule of one person, one vote, Rep. Johnnie
Caldwell of Upson County pleaded for quick adoption: "It behooves all of us
to remember we will never have the opportunity as a rural-dominated House
to pass another election code. You and I know there are some things written in this code purely for rural areas. It's harder to change something that's
already written. Let's go ahead and pass this thing" (*AJ*, June 23, 1964, 1).

While the partisan hypothesis is inherently plausible—self-interested motives for election laws always are—there is little actual evidence to support it,
and in any event it is inextricably interwoven with racial purpose. Although
the sole Republican member of the ELSC did oppose the runoff, there was
almost no mention of the effect of that rule on the Republican Party during
the time of its consideration. Compared to the plentiful expression of racial
reasons, this is quite thin evidence. It is certainly true that Democratic legislators and members of the Sanders administration had reason to worry about
the rise of a second party of white supremacy. To compete with the GOP for
their traditional conservative white constituency, Georgia Democrats needed
to avoid primary nominations being determined by minority liberals. To prevent defections from disaffected supporters of losing primary candidates,
they needed to make sure that the primary continued to be THE election
for the overwhelming majority of voters. A majority-vote requirement that
kept conservative white Democrats in control and minimized the influence

of the rapidly growing number of African-American voters in the Democratic party might, therefore, inhibit the advance of the party of Goldwater. But, of course, that is precisely the problem with the anti-Republican thesis as an alternative to the racial motivation explanation. Republicans could be disadvantaged only by disadvantaging blacks. Even if the number of statements indicating partisan reasons for adopting the majority-vote requirement were much higher than they in fact were, the hypothesis would not be a proper alternative, because if it were true, foreseen racial purposes and consequences would have to have been true as well.

In *Brooks v. Miller*, Judge Freeman granted that for Denmark Groover and others, the majority vote had a primarily racial purpose. The judge saved the provision from unconstitutionality, however, through three moves: First, he portrayed Sanders as a racial "pragmatist," not a politician with a long and consistent record of support for segregation and for racial discrimination in electoral arrangements, and asserted that Sanders supported the majority-vote requirement for nonracial reasons. Sanders's nonracial purpose, never publicly mentioned by anyone connected with his administration in 1963–64 but brought up during the trials during the 1990s, was that the governor believed that plurality rule facilitated election tricks. Second, Judge Freeman assumed that only the motives of the Sanders administration counted, and that Groover and the 1963 House passage of the majority-vote requirement had no influence on its 1964 inclusion in the comprehensive election code. Third, the judge downplayed the connections between other, patently racially discriminatory actions of the ELSC both before and after 1964 and their adoption of the majority vote, and he portrayed the 1963–64 ELSC as entirely a creature of the Sanders administration, rather than one led by holdovers from the Talmadge and Griffin eras. Freeman also, without explanation, discounted the importance of racial reasons for imposing the majority vote, alone among the fifteen sections of its chapter of the election code, in time to have a dramatic effect on the 1964 Hollowell/Pye/Webb contest; ignored the 1963–64 House's many anti-reformist actions and the plentiful evidence of Groover's importance in that body; and fully credited such witnesses as Sanders and Speaker Smith, whose testimony in the 1990s, as pointed out above, was sharply at variance with what they did and said in the 1950s and 1960s, and former *Atlanta Constitution* editor Eugene Patterson, whose statements during the 1996 trial repeatedly contradicted what he had told historian Steven Lawson in a taped interview in 1991.[17]

The nonracial reason for the majority-vote requirement, Judge Freeman concluded, was that local courthouse "rings" sometimes entered "stalking horse" candidates to split the vote of their factional opponents, counting on the core of "ring" supporters to carry a plurality of the vote. Such chicanery, the argument went, would be defeated by a runoff requirement, which would guarantee that one "anti-ring" and one "ring" candidate would face each other in a second round. The attorney for the State of Georgia and Judge Freeman emphasized that in 1962, Peter Zack Geer was rumored to have planned to induce one Carl F. Sanders to run for lieutenant governor, which, they concluded without examining any evidence, caused Carl E. Sanders to drop out of that contest and run for governor. But Carl E. Sanders had other reasons for jumping from the nine-person field for lieutenant governor into the much less crowded gubernatorial field, and it is impossible to know whether, except for Garland Byrd's fortuitous heart attack, Sanders would have qualified for a potential runoff in either the lieutenant governor or the governor's race. In fact, in 1962, Geer ended up in a runoff, not with a "moderate segregationist" like Sanders but with the rabble-rousing Lester Maddox. As the example indicates, the calculations in this and other hypothetical cases were extremely uncertain, particularly at a time and place of such political upheaval as Georgia in the 1960s.

More important than such hypotheticals was the actual example of the Hollowell/Pye/Webb contest. In an editorial presumably written by Eugene Patterson, the *Atlanta Constitution* condemned Donald Hollowell for running because he might split the vote opposed to Marvin Griffin–ally Durwood Pye. Hollowell might win in a plurality contest, the *Constitution* thought, but only by "some long shot" in a runoff (*AC,* May 15, 1964, 4). Every wire service report or metropolitan newspaper story on the successful effort to move up the date of the majority-vote requirement to cover the 1964 elections emphasized its adverse effect on Hollowell (*ABH,* May 28, 1964, 1; *AC,* May 23, 1964, 1; May 28, 1964, 1; *AJ,* May 27, 1964, 1; *CE,* May 28, 1964, 17; *VT,* May 23, 1964, 1). This example throws light on the only mentions of the "stalking horse" argument for the majority vote in the public record in 1963–64, one in a *Constitution* editorial, and the other in a speech by Groover. The editorial—in a newspaper heartily disliked by the rural segregationists who still controlled Georgia House—praised the runoff provision of the election code for ending "the old trick of entering vote-splitting candidates for the purpose of assuring minority victories by others" (*AC,* June 24, 1964, 4). Groover also argued for the majority vote as a device to counter manipulations and, revealingly, attributed the manipulations to be curtailed not to courthouse rings but to "special interests and bloc groups," who might control elections by entering "several candidates to split the field" (*MT,* Feb. 21, 1963, 1; *VDT,* Feb. 20, 1963, 1). Even the supposedly nonracial reason attributed, without any contemporaneous evidence whatsoever, to the Sanders Administration in the 1960s, then, vibrated with racial overtones.

To imagine a nonracial world in Georgia in 1963–64, one without a civil rights movement, a burgeoning black vote, a crisis in the conservatives' control of electoral structures, and an old rural segregationist order still very potent in the legislature, is to invent a fantasy of convenience. The real history, detailing the real motives and actions of key actors of the time, before those motives were whitewashed for a court case in the 1990s, was suffused with racial purpose. In short, all five alternative hypotheses are either without evidentiary support or inextricably linked with racial purpose, or both. The majority-vote requirement was passed in Georgia in 1963–64 to preserve the rule of the white majority against the growing "bloc vote."

CHAPTER FIVE

A Century of Electoral Discrimination
in North Carolina

*T*he saga of litigation that produced the Supreme Court cases of *Shaw v. Reno* (1993) and *Shaw v. Hunt* (1996) began after the state of North Carolina, which had not sent an African-American to Congress since 1898, drew two bare-majority black congressional districts in 1991–92. The rural First District sprawled over a good deal of eastern North Carolina, while the urban Twelfth tracked Interstate 85 for 160 miles from Charlotte to Durham. In each district 57 percent of the people and 51–54 percent of the registered voters were African-Americans. Termed an example of "political apartheid" by Justice Sandra Day O'Connor in her majority opinion in *Shaw v. Reno* (1993, 2827), the districts were in fact the least segregated, most nearly racially balanced congressional districts in the state in the twentieth century. The redistricting plan was challenged in federal court by Robinson Everett, a Duke University law professor who was both chief attorney in the case and, along with his son, a plaintiff, and three other white people from Durham. Three of the five plaintiffs lived in neither the First nor the Twelfth District, and the two who resided in the Twelfth District voted for the Democratic nominee, Mel Watt, who was black, in the 1992 general election. Claiming to speak for all North Carolinians of every race, the plaintiffs charged that the legislature, under pressure from the U.S. Department of Justice, had perpetuated a "racial gerrymander" that infringed their right "to participate in a process for electing members of the House of Representatives which is color-blind and wherein the right to vote is not abridged on account of the race or color of the voters" (Everett 1993, 15, n. 9; *Shaw v. Barr* 1992, 470; Speas 1995, 31).

In his 1993 brief to the Supreme Court, Everett claimed, "No court or agency has determined that racial discrimination has ever occurred in the creation of congressional districts in North Carolina. Indeed, it is clear that none has taken place; and so there was no constitutional violation to be remedied by establishing two majority-minority districts." To set up districts with majorities of African-Americans voluntarily, his statement implied, would be illegal. Not only was the drawing of such districts not constitutionally necessary, he continued, it was an insult to citizens of both races. Whites, he asserted, suffered an "impression of injustice" because the Twelfth District was constructed to allow black voters to elect a candidate of their choice, who, Everett surmised, would "consider his primary duty to be the representation of blacks." Yet paradoxically, he argued, African-Americans would gain no benefit from having a responsive representative. Indeed, he characterized the action as "an implicit affront to blacks because it implied that they are incapable of organizing coalitions to elect favored candidates of whatever race" (Everett 1993, 19, 42–45, 58).

How do Everett's contentions, for which he offered no evidence whatsoever, square with the facts? Was the 1990 redistricting the first time that race had been taken into account in redistricting North Carolina? Were districts before that time constructed by following what the state's leading newspaper declared were the "basic criteria [that] haven't changed in 200 years: to make each district as compact as possible, as contiguous as possible, and as reflective as possible of common interests" (*RNO*, June 1, 1991, A:12)? Did the 1991–92 line drawings represent radical changes from past practices, unprecedented corruptions of a previously unbroken devotion to the principles of civics textbooks? Was there a single, pervading racial motive for the reshuffling of district lines in 1991–92, one so readily apparent from their geography that there was no need to do more than to glance at a map to determine it? Or does a more detailed consideration of the evidence suggest that other purposes played important, even dominant, roles in the way lines were finally drawn? How did the state's redistricting experiences fit into its politics? Had whites in the state before 1991 demonstrated that they would readily support qualified African-American candidates for office? Were the whites who had been elected before 1992 equally responsive to their constituents, regardless of race? Was the redistricting of 1991–92, in sum, an unnecessary special privilege for blacks—unnecessary because they could compete and be represented equally without it, and special because no white politicians had ever received districts tailored for them and had never considered the race of the voters when deciding how to separate them into districts?

ANY KNOWLEDGEABLE, longtime political observer in North Carolina could have informed Robinson Everett that the racial and partisan gerrymandering of congressional districts in North Carolina did not begin in 1991, and that the 1990s were not the first time that the shape of congressional districts in the state had attracted widespread adverse comment. Anyone familiar with the state's nineteenth-century politics could have added that racial gerrymandering began more than a century earlier. As noted in Chapter 1, North Carolina Democrats from 1872 through the disfranchisement of blacks in the state in 1900 packed African-Americans into the "Black Second," the only congressional district in the South during that era to have its own published biography (Anderson 1981). Blacks did benefit in some respects from the creation of this district, for it provided access to patronage and a goal for aspiring local and state legislative officeholders. More than fifty blacks from counties of the Second District sat in the state legislature from 1872 to 1900, and four African-Americans represented the district in Congress, including George White, elected in 1898, the last black from the South to serve in Congress for 72 years. From time to time, Democrats, members of what was then called "the party of white supremacy," conciliated black voters in the Second. Up to 85 percent of potential black voters in the state as a whole participated in elections during the 1890s, and local services were distributed fairly equally between the races during this period. The disfranchisement amendment of 1900 changed all that and made it safe for the Democrats to reduce the Second District's population and especially the number of blacks in it (Kousser 1974, 182–95; Kousser 1980a). What distinguished the redistricting of 1991–92 was not that it was motivated by race or partisanship, for these motives had determined the composition of districts 120 years before; it was not that it created districts that were noncompact or that their ungainly shapes attracted attention, for the Second District over a century ago was considered "grotesque." What was different in 1991–92 was that for the first time in the long history of racial and partisan gerrymandering in North Carolina it was blacks, not whites, who benefited, and some whites concluded that now the rules needed to be changed.

FOR A STATE in the "Rim" or "Border" South with a cherished progressive self-image, North Carolina suppressed black political activity thoroughly during the period of the "nadir" of race relations in the first half of the twentieth century and only slowly, grudgingly, and partially liberalized its policies thereafter. Only 15 percent of the state's blacks—less than the percentage in Georgia—were registered to vote in 1948, and only 36 percent in 1962. Because of low overall voter registration and continued use of a literacy test, forty of North Carolina' counties were subjected to Section 5 of the VRA in 1965. A year later, black registration finally surpassed 50 percent for the first time since 1900. While Tennessee elected its first black of the century to the General Assembly in 1964 and abolished multimember districts in urban counties in 1965 on the grounds that they discriminated against blacks,

North Carolina did not elect a black state legislator until 1968, and it re-fused at that time to abolish multimember districts for the state legislature, even though it was advised that they might be challenged in court on the grounds of racial discrimination. It simultaneously passed a numbered-post system with an anti-"single shot" provision over the protests of blacks and white Republicans, who charged that it would have a discriminatory impact. A federal court subsequently struck down that law as racially discriminatory (*Dunston v. Scott* 1972). The same legislature that adopted the multimember-district/numbered-post system also refused to add heavily black, activist Dur-ham County to the Second Congressional District, reportedly to prevent a rise in black influence in that district (Harry Watson trial testimony, 242, 255, 300–307, in *Gingles v. Edmisten* [1984]; Plaintiff-Intervenor's Exhibit 25 in *Shaw v. Hunt* [1994]).

Marking the political reemergence of North Carolina blacks, 1968 was the year Henry Frye of Greensboro became the first African-American elected to the General Assembly, black Charlotte dentist Dr. Reginald Hawkins received 129,808 votes for the Democratic nomination for governor, and Eva Clayton became the first black since 1898 to run a serious campaign for Congress. When Clayton, who had never previously held public office, began her cam-paign, blacks made up approximately 40 percent of the population of the Sec-ond District but only 11 percent of the voters. Although her poorly financed and rather amateurish campaign lost 70–30 to eight-term incumbent L. H. Fountain, the most conservative Democrat in the state's congressional dele-gation, Clayton and her cadre of black activists managed to raise black regis-tration to 26 percent of the district's voters (*RT*, Sept. 4, 1970, 4; *RNO*, Mar. 13, 1972, 5).

Four years later, in 1972, Howard Lee became Fountain's second and much more serious black challenger. The son of a Georgia sharecropper, Lee had come to Chapel Hill to attend graduate school in social work at the Univer-sity of North Carolina in 1961 and stayed on in a job at Duke University. In 1969 he had been narrowly elected to the largely ceremonial office of mayor of the majority-white town of Chapel Hill. He was reelected in 1971. As the first black mayor in the state during the twentieth century, he had been named vice-chairman of the state Democratic party in 1970. An impressive speaker with an ability to appeal to whites, he had flirted with the idea of running for lieutenant governor, but when the legislature added his home county of Orange to the Second District in its principal change in congressional dis-trict boundaries in 1971, Lee decided to follow in Clayton's path. Expecting to capitalize not only on increased black registration but on an appeal to white youths newly able to register after the institution of the 18-year-old vote, Lee hoped that whites would look beyond his race. Blacks in politics, he declared, needed to be "concerned about people on the basis of character rather than skin color." "I have been working awfully hard," he said on another occasion, "to establish a relationship between myself and members of the white community" (*RNO*, Apr. 29, 1970, 5; July 16, 1970, 4; Sept. 6, 1970, 1; May 5, 1971, 20; Sept. 21, 1971, 1; Jan. 11, 1972, 1; Feb. 20, 1972, 4; Mar. 13, 1972, 5; *RT*, Sept. 4, 1970, 4; Nov. 16, 1970, 30).

Optimistically, Lee proposed a budget of $75,000 for his campaign and aimed at raising black registration from 26 percent to 35 percent of the total eligible to vote in the district. For the first time since his initial election in 1952, L. H. Fountain appointed campaign managers in every county in the district, ran radio and television advertisements, and handed out bumper stickers. Termed by Tom Wicker of the *New York Times* "an archetypical Southern conservative, whose large black constituency has had little if any effect on his unyielding position on racial and social issues," Fountain still wore white linen suits and white shoes on the floor of Congress in 1972 and had no blacks on his staff. Despite Lee's vigorous campaign, which represented the "toughest challenge" of Fountain's career, the mayor succeeded in raising the black registration percentage only to 30 percent, and he lost in the primary, 59 percent to 41 percent. According to Daniel C. Hoover of the *Raleigh News and Observer*, "Although [Lee] got some white votes, especially in his own traditionally liberal Chapel Hill area, the balloting generally was along racial lines." Being "a highly skilled campaigner with strong appeal not only to blacks but to liberal urbanites as well" was not enough to win an overwhelmingly rural Second District in which voting was widely understood to be markedly racially polarized. Lee's failure apparently discouraged other potential African-American candidates, as no serious black candidacy for Congress emerged in the state for the rest of the decade (*RNO*, Mar. 31, 1972, 6; Apr. 9, 1972, A:12; Apr. 19, 1972, 4; May 8, 1972, A:9; May 11, 1972, 5; Mar. 2, 1976, 1; *RT*, May 8, 1972, A:10).[1]

THE 1981 congressional redistricting is worth studying in detail because it illustrates four important facts. First, before 1991, white congressmen openly manipulated redistricting to buttress their positions against candidates who might appeal to black voters. Second, racial, partisan, and incumbent-protecting goals interacted, often producing unlikely coalitions because of the "ripple effects" of changes in one district on the shape of another. Third, the VRA, as interpreted at the time by the Department of Justice, constrained racially discriminatory legislative actions—but not very much. Fourth, although committees paid lip service to the value of compactness, legislators did not hesitate to sacrifice it to what they obviously considered the more important ends of protecting racial, partisan, and incumbent interests. This represented no change from previous de facto state policy. As Republican congressman James T. Broyhill commented, "One only has to look at the outline of the North Carolina congressional districts to know that compactness has not been a consideration in the past"[2] (Broyhill to Helen R. Marvin and J. P. Huskins, Feb. 20, 1981, in North Carolina Joint Redistricting Committee Files, hereafter referred to as "JRC files"). During the 1950s and 60s, the state's congressional districts were derided as "bacon strips" with "tortuous" boundaries. The Fourth District in 1966 was contiguous only at a pinpoint (Orr 1970, 55, 63–64, 69–70).

Unless the standards of redistricting, the population distribution, partisan control, or the number of seats in the body shift markedly from one decade to the next, redistricting begins with the status quo and generally ends close to it. It was a sign of how much was at stake in relatively small changes that it took six months to reach agreement on how to revise the state's eleven districts in 1981. During the bitter, protracted conflicts, a joint committee collapsed, a "super subcommittee" came to nothing, an agreement on a plan by five Democratic congressmen was ignored, committees of both houses stalled and reversed themselves, a committee-endorsed proposal was shelved on the floor, the majority party lost control of the process, and the final plan was then vetoed by the Department of Justice (Terence D. Sullivan to Alex K. Brock, Sept. 11, 1981, in JRC files). Basically, the controversy involved three districts. In the Second, L. H. Fountain's friends sought to protect him against adding activist blacks and some liberal whites in Durham to his rural district and even sought to reduce the black percentage in order to diminish any potential challenge from someone whose political views resided in the ample space to Fountain's left. In the Sixth District, Democrat Richardson Preyer's allies wanted to overturn his 1980 upset by Republican Eugene Johnston and return the state's most liberal congressman to Washington. But since increasing the proportion of Democrats in Preyer's district would inevitably reduce that in the adjoining Fifth District, where fellow Democrat Stephen L. Neal never had an easy contest, Neal's backers attempted to forge an alliance with Republicans to bolster the Democratic majority in his district by shifting Republican areas into the Sixth and Democratic counties into the Fifth. The desperate Preyer ended up trying to arrange a tacit agreement with Fountain, the state's most conservative Democrat (*RNO*, May 16, 1981, B:5; May 31, 1981, 1).

The principal controversy in 1981 was over whether to move Durham County into Fountain's Second District or to move Orange County out of it and join Durham, Orange, and Wake Counties together into a new "Research Triangle" district. (Although there was no legal necessity to keep counties intact in drawing congressional districts, the state did so by convention before 1981.) For several months, nearly every newspaper discussion of redistricting reminded readers, who naturally included congressmen and state legislators, that "the likely political impact" of including Durham in the Second District "would be to assure Fountain of tough Democratic primary opposition from Durham Democrats, including black candidates" (*RNO*, May 14, 1982, 35).

The first preference of African-American leaders who testified in hearings as well as that of two of the three black legislators who served on the Joint Redistricting Committee—Daniel T. Blue Jr. (D-Wake), Kenneth Spaulding (D-Durham), and Henry E. Frye (D-Forsyth)—seems to have been to keep Orange County in the Second District and to add Durham County to it.[3] When black activists Willie C. Lovett and Lavonia Allison of Durham testified in favor of such an arrangement, *Raleigh News and Observer* capital correspondent A. L. May noted that "while Lovett and Ms. Allison didn't mention it, black leaders have said that a new district with Durham and liberal-voting Orange might give blacks a good chance to elect a black congressman." Spaulding drew up a map that contained both Durham and Orange but not Fountain's home county of Edgecombe, in the Second District (*RT*, July 2, 1981, A:13; *RNO*, Apr. 17, 1981, 38; JRC files, May 15, 1981).

Many white legislators and congressmen agreed with the move to add Durham to the Second District because of the ripple effects elsewhere. In fact, four of the first five major plans that the Joint Committee on Redistricting considered placed Durham in Fountain's bailiwick. Putting Durham in the Second would have necessitated shifting rural territory to Walter Jones's First District, a prospect that he liked, and would probably have pulled the Sixth District east or south, enabling Stephen Neal's Fifth District to pick up Democratic areas, especially Rockingham County, from the Sixth. Early attention thus centered on a plan by Neal ally Rep. Ted Kaplan (D-Forsyth), which gained the endorsement of Jones and Neal and picked up that of three more southeastern congressmen, Bill Hefner, Charles Rose, and Charles Whitley, by changing their districts as little as possible. "From the outset," noted the *News and Observer*'s capital insider column, "Kaplan's purpose was to protect the interest of his congressman, Stephen L. Neal, a Winston-Salem Democrat." To break the momentum of the Kaplan Plan, which reportedly had solid commitments from majorities of both the Senate and House members on the Joint Committee, Sen. Dallas L. Alford Jr. (D-Nash) proposed to join Durham, Orange, and Wake in a Research Triangle district and to stretch Fountain's Second halfway across the top of the state from Caswell County in the middle to Dare County on the coast. Kenneth Spaulding protested that this violated one of the subcommittee's criteria, compactness. As A. L. May noted, "Alford is one of several lawmakers from Fountain's district who is trying to protect the congressman's interests. The major fight is over whether to put Durham in the Second and probably placing strong Democratic primary opponents, including black candidates, against the conservative Fountain" (Walter Jones, Charles O. Whitley, Stephen L. Neal, Charles Rose, and W. G.

Hefner to Sen. Helen Marvin and Rep. J. P. Huskins, May 13, 1981, in JRC files; *RNO*, May 14, 1981, 35; May 16, 1981, B:5; May 19, 1981, 23; May 31, 1981, 1).

As the Joint Committee on Redistricting and its various subcommittees sputtered, Fountain's staff drew up a proposal to abandon the state's long tradition of not splitting counties, and Preyer and his allies joined in the effort. When the cochair of the Joint Committee, Sen. Helen Marvin (D-Gaston), submitted a plan liberalizing the Sixth District by adding Orange to it, thereby increasing Preyer's chances to regain the seat, even the Republicans, who controlled 20 percent of the seats in the legislature, began considering alliances with the different Democratic factions. With Kaplan's plan drawing support from Republicans and from Democrats outside the Second and Sixth Districts, House Speaker Pro-Tem Allen C. Barbee (D-Nash), a Fountain supporter, took advantage of the illness of the committee chairman to adjourn a May 28 meeting before Kaplan's plan could be voted on, thereby so angering the Senate members that they completely abandoned the Joint Committee, leaving each house to draw its own plan (*RNO*, May 20, 1981, 25; May 29, 1981, 37; May 31, 1981, 1; *RT*, May 21, 1981, A:5; May 27, 1981, C:1; May 28, 1981, A:14; June 2, 1981, A:11; Richardson Preyer to Sen. Helen Marvin, May 29, 1981, in JRC files).

When the Senate committee five days later approved the Kaplan Plan over the objection of Fountain ally Alford, the *Raleigh Times* explained Alford's objections: "Fountain's supporters in the House want counties split so the Second can avoid being lumped in with Durham's large black population. Legislators from the area have said privately that they're afraid a black candidate could defeat Fountain in the Democratic primary. They say that would lead to defeat in the general election, however." On the Senate floor, Majority Leader Kenneth C. Royall Jr. (D-Durham), another Fountain friend, blocked acceptance of the committee proposal. "Not only would urban Durham disturb the rural nature of the Second District," A. L. May remarked in the *News and Observer*, "but the Fountain supporters are worried the county would present Fountain with serious Democratic primary opponents, including strong black candidates." As the newspaper stories, based on interviews with often unidentified legislators, made clear, race, partisanship, incumbent protection, and preserving a rural community of interest inspired Royall and Barbee to propose a plan removing Orange from the Second District, keeping Durham out, and shifting more Republican voters into the Sixth District to attract Republican legislators and followers of Fifth District Congressman Neal. Explicitly noting that their scheme reduced the black population proportion in the Second to 37 percent, Royall contended that such a change was not large enough to count as "retrogressive" (*RT*, June 2, 1981, A:11; *RNO*, June 2, 1981, 1; June 4, 1981, 44; June 5, 1981, 1; June 6, 1981, 7).[4]

A directly parallel process took place in the House. After a long deadlock and rejection of several split-county plans, the Redistricting Committee reported a plan that put Durham into the Second District and buttressed Democratic support in the Sixth District, only to be overcome on the House floor by a coalition of supporters of Democratic congressmen Fountain, Neal, and Hefner and all the Republicans. The final proposal was similar enough to that of the Senate that slight compromises in a conference committee brought the six-month struggle to what legislators hoped was an end (*RNO*, June 7, 1981, I:30; June 12, 1981, 40; June 16, 1981, 1; June 18, 1981, 26; June 19, 1981, 26; June 26, 1981, 14; June 27, 1981, 6; July 1, 1981, 8; July 2, 1981, 1; *RT*, June 10, 1981, B:12; June 17, 1981, 30; June 23, 1981, A:6; June 30, 1981, A:1; July 2, 1981, A:13; July 3, 1981, A:9; July 8, 1981, A:1; House Subcommittee on Congressional Redistricting Minutes, June 15, 17, 1981, in JRC files).

Since the Second District favored by Fountain's defenders curved northward up around Durham County then circled back southwest again to pick up Alamance and Chatham Counties, it became known as the "fishhook" district. Metaphorically, the whole purpose of "Fountain's fishhook" was to avoid snaring a black fish. Rotated ninety degrees, the Second bore a striking resemblance to the original 1812 Massachusetts district that made Elbridge Gerry's name notorious, as the *News and Observer* pointed out in an editorial criticizing the district as "clearly not compact": "It shows that in drawing districts for a specific political purpose, 20th century North Carolina legislators are not much different from their counterparts in 19th century Massachusetts." "The Legislature," the paper noted in another editorial a few days later, "has given the state districts that are hooked, humped, and generally ungainly—in a word, gerrymandered—to protect incumbents." But the solons, including most especially the Republicans, rejected calls from House members Patricia S. Hunt (D-Orange) and Daniel T. Blue to create more compact districts that crossed county lines, and they voted down Hunt's plan to do so in a manner that would assist Richardson Preyer in regaining his congressional seat. As finally passed, the bill was a bipartisan gerrymander which, the *News and Observer* noted, "helped [Eugene] Johnston, a conservative Republican, and Fountain, an old-time conservative Democrat who frequently votes contrary to the Democratic majority in the House." In a report on redistricting in thirty-two states, the citizens' watchdog group Common Cause named the North Carolina Second District as one of the two "infamous gerrymanders" of the year (*RNO*, June 6, 1981, 4; June 19, 1981, 26; July 10, 1981, 4; Sept. 13, 1981, 1; *RT*, June 23, 1981, A:6).

To REMOVE the fishhook, the NAACP's Legal Defense Fund (LDF) sued the state and lobbied the Department of Justice. In the name of Ralph Gingles, LDF local counsel Leslie Winner charged the legislature with adopting a congressional plan that had both the purpose and the effect of diluting black political strength. In addition, the suit challenged the degree of population inequality in both the congressional and legislative plans and the continued use of multimember districts on the state level. Asked why the body had allowed population variations of up to 24 percent between the largest and smallest districts in the General Assembly, Daniel T. Liley (D-Lenoir), cochair of the House Legislative Redistricting Committee, replied, "We were simply hoping nobody would challenge it" (*RNO*, Sept. 9, 1981, A:10; Sept. 17, 1981, 1; Sept. 18, 1981, 46; Oct. 9, 1981, 1; Oct. 10, 1981, 1).

In December 1981, before the *Gingles* suit could be heard by a three-judge panel, the U.S. Department of Justice rejected the congressional plan. In his "Section 5 objection letter," assistant attorney general for civil rights William Bradford Reynolds declared that the Justice Department "received allegations that the decision to exclude Durham County from Congressional District No. 2 had the effect of minimizing minority voting strength and was motivated by racial considerations—i.e., the desire to preclude from that district the voting influence of the politically-active black community in Durham." Reynolds found "particularly troublesome the strangely irregular shape" of the Second District and was also disturbed by the pattern of decreasing black population in the Second District, from 43 percent in 1970 to 40.2 percent after the 1971 reapportionment to 36.7 percent in the plan submitted in 1981— this despite a rise in the black population percentage over that period in the state as a whole (*RT*, Dec. 8, 1981, A:1).[5]

Editorially chiding the legislature for its long record of racial discrimination in redistricting, the *Raleigh Times* remarked:

> From here on, legislators will be prudent to include, among their standards for drawing districts, not only fair population representation but a fair chance for racial representation. That change is overdue. Until now, districting plans' impact on minority political clout and vice versa has been a behind the scenes concern of the powerful people who draft the plans—but rarely an on-the-record one.
>
> For example, legislative protectors of Second District Congressman L. H. Fountain said privately they backed a "fishhook" district (now thrown out) because they feared a more compact one including heavily black Durham County would boost black candidates' chances. In public, they merely said they wanted to keep the Second District rural. (*RT*, Dec. 14, 1981, A:4)

Rejecting calls to sue the Justice Department to overturn its denial of preclearance, the legislature decided to redraw its plans. The all-but-formally-declared black candidate Mickey Michaux, reported the *Raleigh Times*, "has drawn a map that puts Durham and Orange into the Second District. It's a district he believes he'd win." Black leaders in Durham constructed three other similar maps, which were introduced, along with Michaux's, by Rep. Kenneth Spaulding. But the legislature rejected these efforts of Spaulding's, as well as his repeated attempts to require single-member districts in urban areas that contained large black populations. Spaulding correctly predicted that the federal courts would reject the legislature's refusal to remedy the discrimination in the General Assembly completely (*RT*, Dec. 28, 1981, C:1; Feb. 6, 1982, A:8; *RNO*, Feb. 4, 1982, 39).

Although it did not go as far as black leaders wanted—it did not keep Orange County in the Second District or eliminate Edgecombe County from it—the legislature did add Durham County and eliminate the district's un-gainly projection through Alamance and Chatham Counties. As House Redistricting Committee cochair J. P. Huskins put it, "We have taken the hook off the fishhook" (*RNO*, Feb. 9, 1982, 4; Feb. 11, 1982, A:1). But the struggle was not easy. As *News and Observer* reporter Daniel C. Hoover noted,

> [W]hite, conservative eastern legislators fought tenaciously to preserve the traditional 2nd district . . . .
>
> Unspoken publicly by some of the legislators were these fears:
>
> —That when Fountain retires, a black Democrat will be nominated, triggering a white backlash that will deliver the 2nd to the Republicans and form the nucleus for gradual erosion of the Democratic power base there.
>
> —That Durham's black political activists will fan out over the district and begin registering heretofore apathetic rural blacks, kindle their political awareness and upset the district's grassroots sociopolitical balance. (*RNO*, Feb. 14, 1982, A:32)

In other words, even if it were unsuccessful, a black campaign for Congress might result in the overthrow of the racial and political status quo. The stakes in the redistricting decision could hardly have been higher.

Why, then, did the legislature, which after all included only 4 blacks, elected through single-shot voting and apparent private agreements on slates,[6] and 34 Republicans among its 170 members, take the action it did? Pressed explicitly by the Justice Department either to justify its decision to exclude Durham or modify its plan, legislators had no choice, since they knew that a working majority of them had intended to keep Fountain safe from a challenge and since they had so often been reminded of the racial effect of their plan for the Second District. Because changes could be made to Fountain's district without affecting other incumbents' chances significantly, it was easier and less potentially disruptive to comply than to fight. Some were also angry at the tactics of Fountain's confederates. As Joint Redistricting Committee cochair Helen Marvin put it, "Time after time it was Congressman Fountain who was trying to dictate to us" (*RNO*, Feb. 10, 1982, A:18).

Although the Department of Justice precleared the new plan, which met the criticisms of the fishhook scheme that were specifically raised in Reynolds's objection letter, the NAACP-LDF did not immediately move to dismiss the congressional portions of the *Gingles* suit. "It's a lot better," commented Leslie Winner, "but it's not good enough." The plan, she said in papers filed with the federal court, perpetuates "the effects of past discrimination against black citizens." Only reluctantly did the LDF two months later drop its challenge to the Second District, contending that although "the districts as apportioned do not allow the black citizens of North Carolina to select representatives of their choosing," the plan "does not appear to violate the United States Constitution or the VRA as currently construed" (*RNO*, Feb. 12, 1982, D:4; Mar. 12, 1982, 1; Mar. 18, 1982, A:19; *RT*, Mar. 12, 1982, C:6; "Motion for Partial Voluntary Dismissal," *Gingles v. Edmisten*, Apr. 21, 1982). Although Winner did not discuss the case law that led her to this conclusion, it is not difficult to reconstruct what her reasoning must have been. The principal Section 5 precedent at the time, *Beer v. U.S.* (1976), would have denied relief unless there was demonstrable "retrogression" in potential black political influence, and the legislature had carefully designed the Second District to have the exact same percentage of blacks, to a tenth of a percentage point, in its population in 1982 as in 1971. The 1980 *Mobile v. Bolden* plurality opinion, under strenuous attack in 1982 but not formally modified as of April, required plaintiffs in VRA or constitutional challenges to prove that the statute in question had been adopted with a racially discriminatory motive; more important, the opinion seemed to adopt an unprincipled and incoherent approach to evaluating evidence of such intent (see Chapter 7 below). The renewed VRA with its anti-*Bolden* amendment to Section 2 was signed into law only on June 29, and the Supreme Court's opinion in *Rogers v. Lodge*, which regularized standards for proving intent, was issued two days later. In April 1982, however, the statutory and judicial precedents were considerably less promising. Therefore, dropping the congressional redistricting complaint from the first *Gingles* case did not signal either that the LDF approved the 1981 districts or that they believed them in accord with the VRA and the Constitution. Rather, the LDF decision was a matter of legal strategy that might well have been different if it had been made seventy-five days later.

ASKED FOR comment about the Justice Department's rejection of the "fishhook" plan in December, L. H. Fountain's spokesman Ted Daniel denied that the congressman had exercised much influence on the legislative decision. "The congressman said repeatedly that he would have been happy with any district—including Durham or not." For a month and a half after the legislature turned down his desperate followers' final move to suspend the new plan for thirty days and ask the Department of Justice to reconsider the old one again, Fountain continued to go through the motions of running. Six days after the formal announcement of what promised to be a vigorous and well-funded campaign by Mickey Michaux and the Durham Committee on the Affairs of Black People, however, the 15-term congressman announced his retirement. An unidentified colleague of Fountain's summed up his reasons: "He sort of felt he was let down by (the Legislature) putting Durham County in his district, which he had a lot of apprehension about" (*RT*, Dec. 8, 1981, A:1; Feb. 11, 1982, A:1; *RNO*, Feb. 20, 1982, 1; Mar. 15, 1982, 1; Mar. 18, 1982, 1; Mar. 22, 1982, C:1; Mar. 28, 1982, A:1).

After a brief shakeout of prospective candidates, the contest settled down to a two-white-man race to determine who would face Michaux in the run-off, which, as one candidate put it, "has been the name of the game since day one." Former state House Speaker James E. Ramsey positioned himself in the middle, between the liberal Michaux and Tim Valentine, who had been a state legislator in the 1950s and state chairman of the Democratic party in the 1960s and who sought and won most of the Fountain supporters. Neither Ramsey nor Valentine raised race as an issue in the first primary (*RNO*, Mar. 28, 1982, A:1; June 27, 1982, A:27; July 19, 1982, C:4).

Michaux, who said from the beginning that he "hoped race would not be an issue," acted as though he knew better, deciding not to use billboards with his picture on them and putting most of his early effort into a drive to register black voters. With blacks running for local offices in every county in the Second District, the percentage of the registered voters who were black rose from 27.6 percent to 30 percent. The son of an affluent businessman from a well-known Durham family, Michaux had run for the legislature three times in "liberal" Durham County from 1964 to 1968 before finally winning a seat in 1972. After three terms in the legislature, he was rewarded for his early support for Jimmy Carter for president with appointment as U.S. Attorney. Raising more money from labor unions than any other congressional candidate in the state and eventually loaning his own campaign $69,000, Michaux had a sizable staff as well as assistance in preparing speeches from such notables as Duke political scientist James David Barber (*RNO*, Mar. 22, 1982, C:1; May 23, 1982, A:29; June 27, 1982, A:38; July 16, 1982, D:12; July 17, 1982, C:4; Nov. 26, 1983, C:1). Highly visible and personable, experienced in campaigning among and cooperating with whites, Michaux was as promising a candidate as black North Carolina could produce. To the vast majority of whites in the Second District, however, only one of his characteristics—his race—made any difference.

Turnout in the first primary was high and voting was racially polarized. Although noting that Michaux's campaign had been geared not only to register more blacks but to "appeal to white liberals and moderates," A. L. May of the *News and Observer* suggested that the candidate received "a share of the white vote" only in Durham. Statistical analysis by Prof. Richard Engstrom substantiated contemporary newspaper accounts. According to Engstrom, Michaux received 88.6 percent of the black vote but only 13.9 percent of the white vote in the first primary. As Jesse Jackson publicized during his presidential campaign in 1984, which challenged runoff laws as racially discriminatory, Michaux finished first with 44.1 percent of the vote, compared to 32.9 percent for Valentine and 23 percent for Ramsey. Overall Democratic turnout in the Second District was 53 percent, quite high for a primary (*RNO,* June 30, 1982, A:1; July 1, 1982, A:20; Defendant-Intervenor's Exhibit 13, Table 1, *Shaw v. Hunt* 1994 [Engstrom analysis]).

There was only one issue in the runoff. "The veteran politicos tell it simply," A. L. May reported. "Get a black candidate against a white in a runoff primary in rural Eastern North Carolina, and the white will win every time." A dozen Democratic leaders whom he interviewed told May that "the July 27 runoff will boil down to racial bloc voting throughout the district." "I'm afraid it's going to be straight down racial lines," May was told by a Wilson County Democratic leader who, May said, "asked not to be identified." But the conservative Valentine, who had pledged on the evening of his first primary victory not to make race an issue in the runoff, left nothing to chance. Using the code words "bloc vote," a phrase made famous throughout the South by Georgia's Herman Talmadge in his 1948 gubernatorial campaign, Valentine sent a letter to white voters, over his own signature, that warned: "If you and your friends don't vote on July 27, my opponent's bloc vote will decide the election for you." Another target-mailed letter, employing another code word, coyly noted, "My opponent will again be busing his supporters to the polling places." Whites got the message. As one said, leaving the polls, "There wasn't but one choice, Valentine, because he is white" (*RNO,* July 11, 1982, A:25; July 23, 1982, A:4; July 25, 1982, A:25; July 28, 1982, 1; *RT,* Feb. 20, 1984, A:7).

With turnout at 57 percent, even higher than in the first primary, Valentine won by a 53.8–46.2 percent margin, the voting "strongly following racial lines," according to the *News and Observer.* Prof. Engstrom's statistical analysis confirmed newspaper impressions of "widespread bloc voting," as he estimated that 91.5 percent of the blacks but only 13.1 percent of the whites voted for Michaux. Angered by his opponent's resort to a racial appeal, Michaux grudgingly endorsed him a month after the runoff, remarking that Valentine's "only single qualification is that he's a Democrat." Even less conciliatory, the Durham Committee on the Affairs of Black People urged its supporters to write Michaux's name in on the November ballot, rather than voting for the Democratic nominee. Michaux received 14.6 percent of the votes (*RNO,* July 28, 1982, 1; July 29, 1982, A:4, C:1; Aug. 11, 1982, 1; Aug. 28, 1982, C:4; Oct. 5, 1982, C:3; Oct. 31, 1982, A:42; Nov. 4, 1982, A:24; *RT,* Sept. 18, 1982, B:5; Defendant-Intervenors' Exhibit 13, Table 1, *Shaw v. Hunt,* 1994 [Engstrom analysis]).

IN THE legislature in 1973, Michaux had cosponsored a bill to eliminate run-off elections as costly for the state and unfair to blacks. The bill failed. In the wake of Michaux's loss in 1982, Rep. Kenneth Spaulding, another young black lawyer from a prominent Durham family, renewed the effort in a way that was typical of his more moderate and conciliatory stance. Instead of trying to abolish the runoff completely, which he favored but was sure wouldn't have a chance of passing, Spaulding proposed to require a candidate to obtain only 40 percent, instead of 50 percent, to become the nominee for a statewide or federal office. When a subcommittee killed this bill, he modified it again and again, requiring in one version that any first-place finisher who got less than 50 percent had to beat the second-place finisher by more than five percent to avoid a runoff, and then that the winner had to get 41 percent and beat his closest opponent by three percent. Both of these alternative measures died too (*RNO,* July 11, 1982, A:25; Feb. 10, 1983, A:20; Feb. 22, 1983, C:12; Mar. 16, 1983, C:4; Mar. 18, 1983, A:14; Mar. 25, 1983, B:6; Apr. 1, 1983, D:4; *RT,* Feb. 18, 1983, A:2; Feb. 22, 1983, A:15). It was symbolic of Spaulding's fate. No matter how moderate he tried to become, no matter that he was not as flamboyant as Michaux, no matter that he stressed "fiscal conservatism" in his legislative career and his 1984 congressional campaign, to most whites in the Second District, he was merely another black candidate.

When he opened his campaign against the freshman Valentine in November 1983, Spaulding made "a plea for biracial support," urging, "Minorities side by side with non-minorities should lead this state in a meaningful, open manner." By March 1984, he was still pushing "an appeal to whites to ignore color. . . . I think the voters, black and white, have moved forward, beyond flesh tone." But like Michaux, Spaulding knew that he could not expect to get many white votes and that the keys to success lay in registering and turning out black voters. Although less well known and less well financed than Michaux and facing an incumbent instead of running for an open seat, Spaulding had one huge advantage that Michaux had not had: he was on the same ballot as Jesse Jackson. The first black candidate for president in American history with any chance to win a major party nomination, Jackson made a prodigious effort to register enough new black voters to carry the North Carolina primary, especially emphasizing the Second District (*RNO*, Nov. 30, 1983, C:1; Mar. 19, 1984, A:1; Apr. 18, 1984, A:1; Apr. 21, 1984, C:5; May 6, 1984, A:49). White Democrats in the state were less enthusiastic than blacks in choosing between Jackson and two white Yankees, Walter Mondale and Gary Hart.

Up through 1982, a markedly smaller proportion of blacks than whites registered to vote in both the First and Second Congressional Districts. Although the proportion of blacks in the population in the Second District in 1972 was 40.1 percent, the African-American population was disproportionately young, so the percentage of the voting-age population that was black was only 34.2 percent. Whether because of the lingering effects of past discrimination or apathy, the estimated proportion of blacks among registered Democrats was even lower—30.5 percent.[7] Over the years, the proportion of blacks who were registered slowly increased and the proportion of whites who were Democrats slowly declined, but the largest jump before 1992 took place in 1984, especially in the Second District. During Michaux's campaign, only an estimated 32.9 percent of the Democrats in the Second District were black; during Spaulding's, the estimated figure was 40.6 percent.

The major effort that went into registering 13,000 new black voters moved Spaulding only 1.7 percent closer to Valentine than Michaux had been. With no third candidate in the contest, Valentine's 52.1–47.9 percent victory was enough to guarantee his nomination and easy election in November. The first sentence of the *News and Observer*'s election story emphasized racial bloc voting: "U.S. Rep. I. T. 'Tim' Valentine, in voting that generally followed racial lines, turned back a strong challenge from state Rep. Kenneth B. Spaulding." Again, Engstrom's statistical analysis confirmed observers' reports. He estimated that Spaulding received 89.7 percent of the black vote and 14.1 percent of the white, percentages that are nearly identical to Michaux's two years earlier. As a Raleigh business lobbyist, V. B. "Hawk" Johnson, summed it up, "That's the story, there are still more whites than blacks"[8] (*RNO*, May 10, 1984, A:9; Defendant-Intervenor's Exhibit 13, Table 1, *Shaw v. Hunt* 1994 [Engstrom analysis]).

With considerable foresight, *News and Observer* reporter Daniel C. Hoover predicted as soon as the 1984 primary results became known that "the latest victory could serve to deter future black opponents, leaving Valentine generally secure from serious primary challenges." Announcing that he would not challenge Valentine in 1986, Michaux echoed Hoover, saying that "many black voters have lost their enthusiasm for another primary challenge against Valentine after having worked hard in losing causes in 1982 and 1984" (*RNO*,

May 10, 1984, A:9; Dec. 27, 1985, A:1). Valentine had no primary opponents from 1986 through 1992.

IF THE members of the North Carolina legislature in 1991 had contemplated drawing districts that were essentially similar in their racial composition to those of the 1980s, they could not have expected to prevail if an intent case had been filed against them under Section 2 of the VRA and the Fourteenth and Fifteenth Amendments.[9] First, the history of past discrimination would have counted against them — the racial and partisan concerns that so notoriously underlay the formation of the "Black Second" and the well-known history of other discriminatory electoral devices such as the poll tax, the literacy test, at-large voting for the state legislature, and the anti–single shot law. Second would have been the immediate historical context to the 1981 redistricting. Howard Lee's somewhat surprising showing in the 1972 Second District congressional race and his first-place finish in the first primary for lieutenant governor in 1976 (he lost in the runoff) suggested that a better funded black candidate might be a threat, especially if Durham were added to white-crossover-prone Orange in the Second District. Michaux's open ambition to run for Congress in 1982 put a dark face on those fears, which were patently shared by Congressman Fountain and his friends in the legislature (*RT*, July 21, 1980, 32). Even though the legislature was forced by the Department of Justice to adopt a non-retrogressive plan in 1981, the members' clear preference for the fishhook and their continuation of at-large elections for the state legislature, both of which were widely acknowledged to be attempts to preserve racial discrimination, would have added to the suspicion that the state could not be trusted to treat African-Americans fairly if left to its own devices. The deviation in 1981 from the traditional state policy of not splitting counties, which was forced not by population equality concerns but by the desire to preserve Fountain from challenge by a candidate favored by the black community, and the numerous discussions of racially discriminatory motives during the lengthy struggle would have added significantly to the state's difficulties. Third, the widely publicized failure of black political candidates for Congress in the state since 1900 (e.g., *RNO*, Jan. 12, 1972, 1) and the universally understood pattern of racial bloc voting in election campaigns would have shown an awareness of the consequences of refusing to draw majority-minority districts. In essence, the repeated efforts by highly qualified black candidates in the Second Congressional District, the district with the highest proportion of African-Americans, served as experiments about the conditions under which black candidates could be elected to Congress in the state. Could they beat an entrenched incumbent? Clayton's and Lee's campaigns against Fountain in 1968 and 1972 settled that negatively.

Could they win an open seat? Michaux's campaign against Valentine in 1982 settled that negatively. Could they win with the aid of a massive registration effort and by running at the same time as a primary campaign by a serious, statewide African-American candidate? Spaulding's campaign against Valentine in 1984 settled that negatively. Could they win with a rural candidate, an urban candidate, a liberal candidate, a moderate candidate, a candidate backed by labor unions or not identified with labor, a grassroots candidate, a well-financed elite candidate, a candidate riding the coattails of a charismatic leader, a candidate independent of other politicians? If the candidate was black, the answer to every question—any question—was negative. After 1984, it was clear that blacks needed more, probably considerably more than 40 percent of the population in a congressional district to be able to elect a candidate who was their first choice. A deliberate refusal to draw such a district in 1991–92 would certainly have fueled a lawsuit, and the evidence of the four campaigns would bolster both intent and effect cases. North Carolina spent half of the 1980s in an unsuccessful effort to stave off racial change in the state legislature, ultimately losing the *Gingles* case in the Supreme Court in 1986. The almost certain prospect of defeat in another such case gave the state a considerable interest in remedying past discrimination by drawing one or more districts in which African-Americans would have a fair opportunity to elect a candidate of their choice.[10]

Legally and politically, the context for redistricting in North Carolina in 1991 differed a great deal from that of 1981. Nationally, the 1982 amendments to Section 2 of the VRA, as elaborated in the Supreme Court's decision in *Gingles*, had been interpreted to mandate the drawing of minority opportunity districts wherever possible, but the definition of "possible" was vague and unsettled (Congressional Quarterly 1993, xiii). Furthermore, the Supreme Court in *Rogers v. Lodge* (1982) and lower federal courts in such cases as the remand decision in *Bolden v. City of Mobile* (1982) and the mixed-motive case of *Garza v. Los Angeles County Board of Supervisors* (1990) had shown that it was possible to prove a racially discriminatory purpose to the satisfaction of many judges. Even before the 1990 elections, then House Speaker Josephus L. Mavretic, D-Edgecombe, warned his colleagues of the likelihood of legal challenges to the upcoming redistricting, including suits under the VRA, and indicated his desire to avoid them if possible. In part, no doubt, to circumvent such litigation, the House Redistricting Committee hired Leslie Winner, the *Gingles* lawyer, as its consultant. Along with her brother, State Senator Dennis Winner (D-Asheville) chair of the Senate Redistricting Committee, Leslie Winner would be inside the tent this time (*RNO*, Oct. 14, 1990, C:1; Jan. 8, 1992, B:1; Jan. 14, 1992, A:1).

Not only had the *Gingles* litigation cost the state money and pride, it had also added to the number of African-American and Republican legislators, as at-large systems in several counties gave way to single-member districts. In 1981, only 20 percent of the legislators were Republicans, whereas in 1991 31 percent were: 14 of the 50 state senators and 39 of the 120 members of the House. While in 1981 there had been only 4 blacks in the legislature, by 1991 there were 19, a full 11 percent, or half of their proportion in the state's population. Their presence was larger, but still much too small to allow them to dictate to anyone. It was true that blacks occupied important leadership positions in the legislature, as Dan Blue ascended to the speakership in that year and Milton F. "Toby" Fitch became one of three cochairs of the House Redistricting Committee, but with power went partisan responsibility. Blue, Fitch, and the others owed their positions to the support of a predominantly white party, with the good fortune of which their own fortunes were inextricably intertwined. Moreover, any aspirations that they had for higher office were subject to the will of an electorate that was three-quarters white. Their positions eliminated any possible use of the "balance of power" strategy that members of minority groups have often been urged to employ in redistricting efforts, particularly in the recent past. As people who shared power in the Democratic party, they could not make deals with Republicans or use the threat of doing so to pressure white Democrats for more black seats (*RNO*, Jan. 7, 1992, A:1). Thus, until the Justice Department's refusal to preclear the legislature's first congressional plan, Speaker Blue and the other black legislators firmly supported a proposal to create only one black-majority congressional seat out of twelve.

Perhaps even more than the increased power of African-Americans in the legislature, the increased number of Republican legislators changed the conditions in which the battle over redistricting was fought. From the beginning to the end of the 1990s cycle of redistricting in North Carolina and, indeed, through the *Shaw v. Hunt* suit, the partisan warfare was bitter and brutal.[11] At one of the first meetings of the House Redistricting Committee, Republican members proposed a guideline that "would prohibit the drawing of new districts that would dilute the voting strength of political parties or that are designed to protect incumbent legislators"—a rule so obviously impossible to achieve that its suggestion could only have been meant to embarrass the majority party. Every plan produced on the legislature's computer instantaneously linked partisan registration data as well as returns from three recent statewide elections to population and racial percentages for each district, giving unmistakable cues to all participants and observers about the partisan and racial consequences of any plan or proposed changes to it. Newspaper articles pointed out that the first Democratic proposal decreased Republican percentages in four districts, possibly endangering one or two Republican incumbents and strengthening Democrat David Price in the Fourth District. When the plan was made fully public, the *News and Observer* summarized the purposes of its authors as "to simultaneously equalize district populations, turn 11 districts into 12, protect incumbent Democrats, inflict maximum carnage on most incumbent Republicans and construct one district with a black majority" (*RNO*, May 2, 1991, B:3; May 29, 1991, B:1; June 1, 1991, A:12).

Republicans retaliated by playing the race card in a manner different from that of the famous Jesse Helms "white hands" television commercial of 1990.[12] State House member David Balmer proposed a plan with two districts that, he contended, contained a majority of minorities, not in an effort to convince his colleagues to adopt it but in an attempt to get courts to intervene. As he said on the floor of the House when he offered it, "We would hope that if it is possible to draw two congressional districts with high minority percentages that the federal courts would come in and encourage the North Carolina legislature to draw two minority congressional districts. This district simply shows that it can be done." Even before the legislature officially adopted a plan, the state's four Republican congressmen sent a letter to assistant attorney general for civil rights John Dunne asking the Justice Department to intervene in the process on the grounds that the legislature had not adopted the Balmer plan. A skeptical Mickey Michaux, now returned to the legislature, remarked in coy street language, "I ain't never known no Republican trying to help anybody black,"[13] while African-American state senator Frank W. Ballance Jr. (D-Warren) commented that "when people who have been kicking me all over town propose a plan, it raises questions" (*RNO*, May 30, 1991, B:1; June 14, 1991, B:3; June 19, 1991, B:1).

The rise in the number of Republicans in the legislature and the expectations of African-Americans that the amended VRA and the increased power of black legislators would make black voices more audible than in 1981 simplified and structured the redistricting process. No longer would intraparty strife such as that between L. H. Fountain and five more moderate Democratic congressmen determine the agenda and endlessly deadlock the legislature. Democrats could afford few defections, because the Republicans might take advantage of them to force through one of their own plans. Just as important, it was no longer possible to insist on preserving county, city, town, township, or even precinct boundaries, because the absolute population equality interpretation of the U.S. Supreme Court opinion in *Karcher v. Daggett* (1983) required that all of these give way (Joint Senate and House Committees on Congressional Redistricting, "Redistricting Criteria For Congressional Seats," Apr. 17, 1991, Plaintiff's Exhibit 14, *Shaw v. Hunt* 1994). Two probably unintended consequences of this emphasis on precise population equality were to give more power to the technicians, who had to fix up every plan in order to reduce population deviations to nearly zero, and to prevent people from adamantly refusing to transfer a well-recognized entity, a whole county, from one district to another. Taken together, all these developments removed the focus of redistricting from geography and local attachments and put it instead on partisan politics and social groups that transcended localities. In this sense, 1991–92 was the first "modern" redistricting in the history of North Carolina.

A process run by lawyers seeking to avoid legal missteps or obvious bias, the redistricting effort of 1991 was comparatively short and predictable. There were public hearings at which everyone could speak and where perhaps the most notable calls were those from black citizens and representatives of the NAACP and ACLU for more seats for minorities, including one or two in Congress. Computers with efficient redistricting software were made available to all members, along with training on how to use them (Cohen dep., 45–57). Both Republicans and African-Americans were well represented on the redistricting committees and at the hearings. Plans were developed quickly and offered for public discussion. Within a few weeks of its public unveiling, "Congressional Base Plan #1," or "CB1" for short, had evolved into CB6 and been passed by both houses of the legislature, which rejected proposals by Republican representatives David Balmer of Charlotte and Larry T. Justus of Hendersonville. Balmer's 6.2 plan, which contained one black majority district and another approximately equally divided between blacks and whites of voting age, with Lumbee Indians holding the balance of power, attracted the most attention of any of the non-Democratic plans.[14] On the day the House took its final vote, Balmer introduced another plan, known as Balmer 8.1, which did not rely on black-Indian cohesion for a majority, but the legislature never fully considered this proposal. CB6, passed as Chapter 601 of the 1991 Session Laws, contained a single black majority district centered in the northeast rural and small-town section of the state but stretching into the city of Durham (*RNO*, June 14, 1991, B:3; June 26, 1991, B:3; June 27, 1991, B:1; July 9, 1991, B:3; Sept. 28, 1991, B:4; Cohen dep., 198).

The addition of a twelfth congressional seat and the announcement of the retirement of the 77-year-old Walter Jones of the First District allowed CB6 to fulfill two goals without inconveniencing any Democratic incumbents. Territory from the previous First and Second Districts could be joined to create a district with a small majority of African-Americans, 51.3 percent, in the voting-age population. Legislative opinion reflected the widely shared belief among voting rights lawyers that states and localities that could create majority-minority districts had the legal responsibility to do so, and that the indicator of such a district in the minds of judges was the presence of a voting-age population majority (Cohen dep., 75–77). The new district, which could be conceded to the Republicans and located in the central Piedmont section of the state, could be made useful to the Democrats if it absorbed troublesome Republicans from marginally Democratic districts in the area. The only district with a majority of registered Republicans in the state, the CB6 Twelfth was in fact a landslide Republican district, since Republican percentages typically ran 15–30 percent ahead of the party's registration in congressional contests.

When the Department of Justice on December 18 rejected the state's congressional plan and suggested the possibility of drawing a second majority-minority district in the southeast, seeming to hint at Balmer's Charlotte-to-Wilmington formulation that gutted the districts of Democrats Charles Rose and Bill Hefner, the Democrats' first reaction was, as Speaker Blue put it, that "the entire thing is political." This impression was not reduced when Republican state chairman R. Jack Hawke Jr. boasted that any new plan would give Republicans a majority of the congressional delegation, which then stood at 7–4 Democratic. Within a week, five Democratic congressmen urged Blue and the state to file a Section 5 appeal in the District of Columbia federal court. But before the end of the year Congressman Rose's aide John Merritt was in Raleigh shopping a new plan that he hoped would avoid both court and a party debacle, particularly for his boss. Starting from the Republican "Balmer 8.1," the scheme had been modified by a legislative staff member at the request of State Rep. Thomas C. Hardaway, a black Democrat from Halifax County, which was in Rose's district, to make the plan less favorable to the GOP. Hardaway brought what was by then called the "Optimum II-Zero" plan to Merritt's attention, and Merritt immediately took the concept to the nearby office of the National Committee for an Effective Congress (NCEC), a liberal political action group with a well-known competence in the technical aspects of redistricting and politics. At NCEC, a complete map was drawn over a weekend with the help of people from the staffs of other Democratic congressmen. Merritt, who had good contacts in the legislature, then took thirty copies of the plan to Raleigh, where he met with Leslie Winner and Gerry Cohen, the chief legislative staffer on reapportionment, as well as a number of legislators. He also talked in person and by phone with state and national leaders of the NAACP in an ultimately successful effort to interest them in the plan. On January 8, ten days after Merritt had come to Raleigh, Mary Peeler of the North Carolina NAACP presented something very close to Merritt's plan at a legislative hearing (*RNO*, Dec. 20, 1991, A:1; Dec. 31, 1991, A:1; Jan. 9, 1992, B:1; Jan. 10, 1992, A:1; Jan. 20, 1992, A:1; Cohen dep., 264–65; Merritt dep., 21–34).

Reaction to the Merritt-Peeler plan from Republican politicians and the media was harsh, but for somewhat different reasons. Republicans at first ignored the plan's racial aspects, while newspapers focused on them. Thus, Republican state chairman Hawke charged the Democrats with "trying to get rid of Republicans and protect Democratic incumbents." The *News and Observer*, however—utterly ignoring the state's long history of racial and partisan gerrymandering, discrimination, and disfranchisement—denounced every congressional plan that contained a majority-black district as based on a "profoundly un-American principle" that will "radically change our system of government" (*RNO*, Jan. 13, 1992, A:8; Jan. 17, 1992, B:1). Instead, the state's leading political newspaper seemed to favor a new plan proposed by the League of Women Voters (LWV), a plan that did not contain a single district that African-Americans had a reasonable chance to win. In northeastern North Carolina, the LWV plan drew a district that was approximately 45 percent black in population and no doubt contained a smaller proportion of the voting-age population and registered voters. The Michaux and Spaulding contests proved that racial bloc voting was too strong to allow the election of a black candidate in such a district.[15] The LWV southeastern district, with a combined black and Indian population of 43.7 percent, was even farther from offering minorities an opportunity to elect candidates of their choice. Although it looked compact when drawn on an undetailed map, the LWV proposal was technically quite flawed, lacking contiguity in some areas, failing to assign others to any district at all, and consequently not properly balancing the census population figures (Cohen dep., 270–76). Moreover, LWV state president Claudia Kadis's comments in a newspaper column pushing the LWV plan make clear how far fair representation for African-Americans was from her organization's concerns. The Merritt-Peeler proposed First District, she sneered, "consists mainly of rural areas with little in common but minority populations and poverty." In Kadis's view, the poor and minorities apparently did not deserve representation because they did not qualify as "communities of interest." In fact, the only examples she gave of communities of interest were "television markets, newspaper delivery areas, highway and rail networks, [and] chambers of commerce." When it endorsed the LWV proposal while denouncing the legislators for being "driven by wrongheaded determination to protect incumbent Democratic congressmen," the *News and Observer* did not go so far as to argue that the LWV plan gave blacks a fair opportunity, noting only that it "improves blacks' victory chances" (*RNO*, Jan. 23, 1992, A:15; Jan. 24, 1992, A:16).

There were two motives behind the relatively minor but numerous changes made to the Merritt-Peeler plan before it was adopted as CB10 (or "Chapter 7," in the official parlance of state law). One was to make District 12 more consistently urban and therefore more of a homogeneous community of interest; the other was to accommodate various political and idiosyncratic wishes of influential politicians. As Gerry Cohen, the legislative technician who actually performed the changes noted, parts of two cities, Winston-Salem and Gastonia, were added to District 12, and rural parts of four counties were deleted, in a successful attempt to raise from 60 percent to 80 percent the proportion of the district's population living in communities of more than 20,000 people. Democrats in the legislature began referring to the proposed Twelfth as "the urban black district," one that would have "a strong urban agenda" (*RNO*, Jan. 19, 1992, A:1; Jan. 21, 1992, B:1). Politically, modifications were made in District 1 that aimed, Cohen said, at "improving the chances of incumbent congressmen in the Second, Third and Eighth Districts to be elected." John Merritt simply sent Cohen faxes of precincts to be moved. In the Piedmont, Cohen received a similar list from a staffer of Congressman Steve Neal, and he moved predominantly Republican Randolph County from the Fourth to the Sixth District in an effort to benefit both Fourth District Democrat David Price and Sixth District Republican Howard Coble. Other alterations improved the reelection chances of Eleventh District Republican Charles Taylor; moved the home of Rep. Walter Jones Jr., who wished to succeed his father in Congress, into the new First District; and shifted lines marginally to put staff aides or campaign managers of various members of Congress in their bosses' districts. The legislature adopted the plan in a largely party-line vote. Before the vote, Sen. Frank W. Ballance Jr. endorsed CB10 as a "remedial piece of legislation," saying, "There may come a time when we can come back here and do away with these black districts and elect people based on their qualifications" (Cohen dep., 171, 177–84, 211–24, 230, 240; *RNO*, Jan. 24, 1992, B:3; Jan. 25, 1992, A:1). But the time, as the history of black attempts to elect candidates of their choice to Congress in the 1980s proved, had not yet arrived.

DESPITE the fact that participants in the North Carolina reapportionment of 1991–92 were more open about discussing the partisan aspects of their handiwork than is often the case in redistricting episodes, they did disagree publicly about the effects of the very numerous proposed plans. To make sense of the process, it is useful to have a standardized and objective means of assessing the partisan effects of the various plans. Although predicting future elections is a somewhat inexact process because voters may shift their behavior, economic and other socioeconomic conditions may change, and different candidates may run for office, it is possible to make fairly precise estimates based on patterns from the immediate past for the offices at issue. In a 1995 analysis of congressional and state lower house elections in California from 1970 through 1994, I showed that a very simple statistical technique can account for nearly 90 percent of the outcomes in those elections; it does equally well predicting outcomes of congressional elections in Texas (Kousser 1995a).

Essentially, one performs an ordinary least squares regression of the percentage of the total vote for each party on the percentage of the total number of voters who are registered with each of the major parties, or on some other index of core partisan voting strength. The resulting estimates can be used for two purposes. First, by multiplying the registration proportions in each district by the coefficients taken from the regression equations, determining the victor in each district in this hypothetical election, and then comparing the hypothetical with the actual results, one can test how well the model predicts winners and losers. Second, once the method is validated, it can be applied to plans that were not put into effect, in order to determine the likely outcomes if they had been adopted. The advantage of using data based on congressional elections to predict the results of future congressional elections is that there may be different dynamics operating in elections for different offices. Naturally, as with any other index, there are problems with this one, the most important being that it assumes that voters from each party defect to the other party at the same rate throughout the state. However, the index is useful at giving outsiders a sense of the political consequences that insiders know of but seldom discuss in public in full candor.

The estimated regression parameters for all contested congressional elections in North Carolina from 1980 through 1992, as well as various measures of goodness of fit, are given elsewhere (Kousser 1995c, 701–2). Overall, the equations predicted about 80 percent of the contests correctly, generally missing only in the marginal contests concentrated in the Fifth, Sixth, and Eleventh Districts. In 1992, the equations called eleven of the twelve contests correctly, slightly underestimating Democratic strength in the Fifth District in what was a very good year for the Democrats. Table 5.1 applies the same technique to nineteen redistricting plans proposed in 1991–92 that were never put into effect and the one that was, CB10. In order to indicate what legislators, members of Congress, and their staffs expected the partisan effects of their plans to be, predictions from equations relating to the two immediately succeeding elections, one a presidential year and one an off-year, are included. The last column suggests what might have happened under the conditions of the 1992 election.

The most obvious conclusion that can be drawn from the table is that the partisan effects of a plan are easy to predict once one knows the party of the person or persons who drew it. The nine Republican plans almost uniformly split the twelve-person congressional delegation in half no matter which party is favored by overall trends in a particular election year. In fact, the vast majority of the districts in the Republican plans were, by this measure, uncompetitive—landslides for one party or the other. If the Flaherty Plan had

TABLE 5.1. Partisan Effects of Redistricting Plans Proposed in 1991 and 1992

Plan Name	Predicted Democratic Seats Based on Regressions from Election of		
	1988	1990	1992
Democratic Plans			
Congressional Base Plan 1 (CB1)	7	9	7
CB2	7	8	7
CB3	7	8	7
CB4	7	7	7
CB5	7	7	7
CB6 (1991 Final)	7	9	7
Merritt/Rose/NAACP	8	8	8
CB7	7	7	7
CB8	7	7	7
CB9	7	8	7
CB10 (1992 Final)	7	8	7
Republican Plans			
Justus, 1991	6	6	6
Justus, Compact 2-minority	6	6	6
Balmer 6.2	6	6	6
Balmer 7.8	6	6	6
Balmer 8.1	6	6	6
Balmer 9.1	6	7	6
Balmer 10.1	6	7	6
Flaherty	6	6	6
Hofeller	6	6	6

Source: Kousser 1995c, 703.

been in place in 1992, for instance, the smallest predicted margin of victory in any district would have been 6.5 percent. In the same 1992 election, only three of the races in Thomas Hofeller's proposed districts would have been closer than 10 percent, with the closest of them being a 4.7 percent victory for a Republican. By contrast, all of the Democratic plans were estimated to produce from seven to nine Democrats in the twelve-person delegation, and more of the contests would be expected to be somewhat closer. Had CB9 been adopted in 1992, for instance, the estimate is that two of the races would have been decided by less than 4 percent. Looking at the table and imagining that the Democrats projected the most recent patterns of voter behavior, those from 1990, into the future, it is easy to see why they were dismayed when the Department of Justice rejected CB6; why Republicans, who hoped that the action of the Justice Department would force the legislature to adopt one of their plans, were jubilant; and why Democrats welcomed the proposal worked out by John Merritt and presented to the legislature by Mary Peeler. This table suggests more graphically than any district map possibly could why the Democratic majority in the legislature chose to respond to the Justice Department's call to establish two majority-minority districts by adopting CB10, instead of one of the Republican alternatives. As State Republican Chairman Jack Hawke stated at the time, and as my statistical analysis reaffirms, the stakes were two Democratic members of Congress (*RNO*, Dec. 20, 1991, A:1).

A CLOSE study of the activities of legislators in North Carolina in 1991–92 shows that they adopted the districts they did for many reasons. The first was to satisfy an extremely precise definition of the equal population standard that legislators believed was implied by *Karcher v. Daggett* and other cases. If the solons had believed that districts only had to be within 5 percent of the ideal population size, as they assumed was the standard for state legislatures, they could have drawn much more compact districts with political effects similar to those that they drew. The second reason was to satisfy the standards of the VRA, as interpreted by the Department of Justice. Third was to protect Democratic incumbents and, more generally, the interests of the Democratic party. As Gerry Cohen commented during the *Shaw v. Hunt* trial, "All lines drawn in this case were politically driven." Or as the cochair of the Redistricting Committee, Toby Fitch, put it, "Politics [is what] redistricting is all about" (*GNR*, Mar. 30, 1994, F:2; *RNO*, Apr. 1, 1994, A:3). A fourth reason was to make it possible for African-Americans, for the first time this century, to elect one or two candidates of their choice to Congress from the state, an action that remedied nine decades of discrimination. Fifth was to avoid the litigation that legislators knew would certainly otherwise ensue, litigation similar to that which had embroiled the state in a half-decade of turmoil, expense, and embarrassment during the 1980s.[16] A sixth reason, relevant to the case of what became the Twelfth District, was to construct an urban district that would share similar problems and proclivities and would be relatively easy to traverse. In sum, just as in 1981, the motives of the legislature were mixed.

There is no question, and, indeed, the State openly acknowledged that the First and Twelfth Districts were drawn with a consciousness of race. No one would seriously suggest, as defendants did in Los Angeles, Memphis, and Georgia, that the racial composition of the First and Twelfth congressional districts was merely an unintended consequence of an attempt to achieve other, nonracial ends. But a desire to comply with federal court decisions and those of the Justice Department in a manner that obviously does not disadvantage protected minorities can hardly be seen to have a racially discriminatory intent, although it obviously does take race into account. As I argue in

Chapter 8 below, taking race into account for remediation and compliance is compatible with Justice O'Connor's *Shaw v. Reno* opinion, and it is the central holding of the majority of the three-judge lower court panel in *Shaw v. Hunt.* If the shape or placement of districts is of particular importance, then the principal question is why the legislature chose to draw the First, and particularly the Twelfth, as it did and not elsewhere or in a manner that some might consider more aesthetically pleasing. And the answers—as Table 5.1, contemporary comments, John Merritt's deposition, the Republican suit in *Pope v. Blue* (1992), and a good deal of subsequent comment in journals and news articles all agree—are partisanship and incumbent protection. If the legislature could have drawn the Twelfth District in other ways that would have made it possible for blacks to elect a candidate of their choice and it chose this way because the I-85 district hurt no Democrats, then the decision to draw the "ugly" Twelfth District could not logically have been taken for racial reasons at all.

FORMALLY or informally, precisely or approximately, redistricting authorities will always be conscious of racial cleavages, because they are the single most salient social and political facts in contemporary America, as they have been in much of the nation's past. Redistricting cannot be race-unconscious until the country ceases to be, and pretending that society or politics has become colorblind can only allow discrimination to go unchecked. Like Robinson Everett, who presented to the Supreme Court a nondiscriminatory political history that bore little relation to the reality of his state's experience, the majority of that court in *Shaw v. Reno* invented social and political "facts" to justify its radical decision. One way to demonstrate the consequences of denying African-Americans a fair opportunity to elect candidates of their choice is to contrast what economists would call the "stylized facts" relied on by Justice O'Connor with the actual facts of political opinion and behavior in North Carolina.[17]

Noncompact minority opportunity districts, Justice O'Connor announced, in a public policy argument that might well have been addressed to a legislature, reinforce the stereotype "that members of the same racial group—regardless of their age, education, economic status, or the community in which they live—think alike, share the same political interests, and will prefer the same candidates at the polls." They also "may exacerbate . . . patterns of racial bloc voting." Finally, they make elected officials "more likely to believe that their primary obligation is to represent only the members of that group, rather than their constituency as a whole." Putting all three together in a quotable conclusion, O'Connor suggested that "Racial gerrymandering, even for remedial purposes, may balkanize us into competing racial factions"

(*Shaw v. Reno* 1993, 2827, 2832). Rather than conventional legal or constitutional arguments, these are essentially empirical, social scientific generalizations, which might in principle be true in some instances and false in others. Neither Justice O'Connor, nor the plaintiffs, nor any of the numerous defenders of the "racial gerrymandering" decisions have actually examined any evidence for these generalizations, apparently assuming them correct a priori. How do they square with the evidence for North Carolina?

Fortuitously, in 1993, just as the Supreme Court justices were composing their opinions in *Shaw v. Reno*, the Z. Smith Reynolds Foundation of Winston-Salem was conducting an extensive survey of the attitudes of black and white North Carolinians. Table 5.2 presents the answers given to nineteen of the questions asked and lists the percentages of each race holding the indicated attitudes. Panel A shows that whites and blacks differed widely in their beliefs about the extent of prejudice and racial discrimination in North Carolina in 1993. One in five blacks but only one in twenty whites considered race relations or discrimination to be one of the most important problems facing the state. More than twice as many blacks as whites considered racial discrimination in the state very serious and increasing. Nearly twice as high a percentage of blacks as whites agreed very strongly that most whites in the state are prejudiced, and nearly three times as many thought most whites "want to keep blacks down."

Panels B and C reveal even wider racial differences concerning the degree of private and public discrimination in North Carolina in the early 1990s. African-Americans were three to four times as likely as whites to believe that there was antiblack discrimination in jobs, housing, education, public accommodations, scholarships, local government, and law enforcement. Whites were more likely than blacks, by nearly a seven-to-one margin, to perceive anti*white* discrimination in jobs and scholarships and to think that the federal and state governments have done "too much to help blacks achieve equality," the latter attitude being held by 30 percent of whites but only 1 percent of blacks. Five times as high a proportion of blacks as whites considered "equal justice for minorities in North Carolina" to be a major problem. Panel D shows that members of the two races also differed markedly in their views of important governmental policies such as banning housing discrimination, affirmative action in college admissions or employment, and busing schoolchildren for integration. In sum, in North Carolina in 1993, as in the nation as a whole, whites and blacks saw entirely different worlds (see Sigelman and Welch 1991; Tate 1993; Dawson 1994; Kinder and Sanders 1996 for national racial attitudes). In the white view, there was little remaining prejudice or public or private discrimination and consequently little need for government

TABLE 5.2. Differences in Attitudes by Race in North Carolina, 1993

Survey Item	Percentage Agreeing With Statement	
	White	Black
A. *General Beliefs about Prejudice*		
Race relations and racial discrimination are important problems	5	20
Racial discrimination and prejudice in N.C. are very serious	17	37
Prejudice and discrimination against blacks in N.C. are more prevalent in 1993 than they were in 1980	17	36
Agree very strongly that most whites in N.C. have prejudiced views	38	70
Most whites in N.C. want to keep blacks down	13	40
B. *Degree of Private Discrimination Today*		
Whites in N.C. have a better chance than blacks to get		
— any job they are qualified for	19	70
— any housing they can afford	13	54
— a good education	9	38
Blacks are often treated more slowly or less politely in N.C. restaurants or retail stores	8	45
Qualified blacks are denied jobs, scholarships	20	74
Qualified whites lose out on jobs, scholarships	40	6
C. *General Bias in Government Programs*		
Local governments in N.C. favor whites over blacks	13	52
Law enforcement in N.C. is tougher on blacks	19	64
Equal justice for minorities in N.C. is a major problem	15	65
In the past ten years, federal and state governments		
— have done too much to help blacks achieve equality	30	1
— have done too little	23	76
D. *Policy Preferences*		
Prefer local housing ordinances that permit discrimination	44	15
Strongly oppose giving blacks preferred treatment in college admissions or employment	52	24
Strongly favor busing schoolchildren for racial integration	4	26

Source: Telephone sample survey of 403 whites and 409 blacks in North Carolina, conducted September–October 1993 by Howard, Merrell and Partners of Raleigh, sponsored by Z. Smith Reynolds Foundation.

programs to do anything to counteract them. In the black view, prejudice and discrimination were pervasive, and governments at all levels should act to remedy this serious plight.

While it is true that both communities generally agreed on such issues as crime and that whites in 1993 rarely assented to statements that blatantly displayed traditional white supremacist or segregationist beliefs, the gulfs between blacks' and whites' perceptions of discrimination and bias and the resulting differences in policy preferences were dramatically wide. Observers, including legislators and judges, may decry the separation of attitudes and deplore or disagree with the differences in perception, but it is surely not irrational to act as if the differences existed (*Shaw v. Reno*, 2845, n. 2 [Souter, dissenting]).[18] These are not stereotypes, but very real disparities of view. Could anyone seriously suggest that any two other "communities of interest" in the state at the time would have had more deep, broad, and consistent differences of opinion related to major concerns of public policy? If these do not count as distinct communities of interest deserving of representation in politics, which ones would, and on what grounds?

Justice O'Connor's second assertion, that minority opportunity districts may exacerbate racial bloc voting, is wrong for three reasons. First, racial bloc voting in congressional elections was already extremely high. In the Mickey Michaux and Kenneth Spaulding contests against Tim Valentine in 1982 and 1984, over 90 percent of African-Americans voted for the black candidates, while 86–88 percent of the whites voted white. There was not much room left for further exacerbation. Second, in the 1992 contests, there was less racial polarization in the primary election in the Twelfth District, because no major white candidate ran, and somewhat more in the primary and runoff in the First, where almost no voters at all seem to have crossed the racial divide. Once Mel Watt and Eva Clayton got the Democratic nominations in their districts, however, they gained appreciably more white support in the general election. Clayton, who had garnered virtually no white votes in the runoff, picked up an estimated 34 percent in the general election in the First District against a white Republican (*Shaw v. Hunt* 1994, Exhibit 13, Table 1). Whether drawing minority opportunity districts increased or decreased the already very sharp racial polarization, therefore, depends on which election one chooses to look at. Third, it seems legally and morally questionable to preserve intentionally discriminatory electoral setups because whites refuse to vote for the preferred candidates of minority communities. Lee, Michaux, Spaulding, and perhaps Clayton devoted considerable attention to obtaining white support in their congressional campaigns in the Second District, and Harvey Gantt made heroic efforts to do so in his U.S. Senate campaign against Jesse Helms in 1990. When Valentine and Helms race-baited, however, white voters overwhelmingly supported them. Under Justice O'Connor's logic, the equal protection clause of the Fourteenth Amendment apparently means that the punishment for the black failure to break down white prejudice is the continuation of structural barriers to black success, while the reward for intolerant white behavior is the maintenance of districts that only white-preferred candidates can win.

Justice O'Connor's third supposition, that politicians elected from districts controlled by African-American or Latino voters will be especially responsive to those constituents is not so much wrong as unreflective.[19] First, one major purpose of election by districts has always been to give groups that do not compose a majority of the whole population a chance to have their voices heard. Politicians are supposed to represent the largest groups in their constituencies, and if there are unbridgeable divisions of opinion within their districts, they cannot possibly represent their "whole constituencies" (Grofman 1982). Second, because as we have seen, black and white opinion diverged markedly in North Carolina in the 1990s, it seems fair to ask whether the converse of Justice O'Connor's observation was true as well: Did white politicians in North Carolina reflect black interests so well that blacks did not need black faces to represent them, as Prof. Carol Swain has suggested is sometimes true in the nation as a whole (Swain 1993)?[20]

The most easily accessible and comprehensive index of ideological patterns of behavior in congressional roll calls is *Congressional Quarterly*'s annual compilation "Conservative Coalition Scores," based on legislators' votes in 60–100 roll calls per session on a wide range of subjects. The scale varies from 0 to 100, with 100 being the most conservative, as *CQ* determines it.[21] Figure 5.1, which summarizes twenty-seven years of data succinctly, demonstrates that black and white members of Congress from North Carolina did *not* vote similarly.

The members of Congress from the state have been grouped into three categories—Republicans, Democrats from the two most heavily black districts (Districts 1 and 2 from 1970 to 1992, Districts 1 and 12 from 1993 on), and Democrats from other districts—and the scores for each category have been averaged. The pattern is striking. Republicans consistently scored about 90 percent conservative. Democrats from districts other than the two "black" ones averaged around 70 percent but varied from the low 60s to the low 80s in particular years. The two white Democrats from Districts 1 and 2 acted like Republicans until 1980 and then somewhat more like other Democrats.[22] The huge anomaly in the figure appears when two black Democrats, Eva Clayton and Mel Watt, replaced whites in the two "black districts" after the 1992 election. Suddenly, a conservative index that had been nearly 90 percent in 1991 and 60 percent in 1992 dropped to 11 percent.[23] Although the scores for the

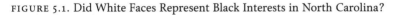

FIGURE 5.1. Did White Faces Represent Black Interests in North Carolina?

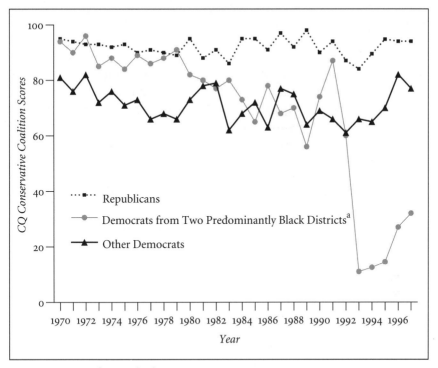

Sources: Congressional Quarterly Almanac, 1970–97.
Note: The scores shown are the average scores of members in each category. Because not all members were present for all the relevant roll calls, each member's conservative score was divided by the sum of his conservative and anticonservative scores. For instance, a congressman who joined the Conservative Coalition on 80 percent of the total roll calls, opposed it on 5 percent, and was absent on 15 percent was given a score of 94 (80/85 = 94). These scores were then averaged over the number of members in the category.
[a] Before 1992, these two districts were 60 and 65 percent white.

African-American members of Congress rose somewhat after the Supreme Court's decision in *Shaw v. Hunt* (1996) threatened to move them into heavily white districts, the gap between their scores and those of white members of Congress, regardless of party, remained striking. In North Carolina, the color of the member of Congress seems to make a major difference in roll call voting.

Blacks who have run for Congress in North Carolina have often denied that they would be responsive only to other African-Americans. In a 1983 article with the title "Black lawmakers don't want to be just spokesmen for minority group," for example, Kenneth Spaulding, then head of the Black Caucus in the state legislature, declared, "The benefit minorities have in the General Assembly is they can express views for people, black or white, who have not had opportunities to be a part of the American dream. . . . When you represent a district, you represent everyone in that district" (*RNO*, Jan. 30, 1983, A:28). But even if this was mere rhetoric, even if aspiring African-American politicians in a state that was three-fourths white catered only to their small minority constituency, Figure 5.1 suggests that Justice O'Connor's conjecture applies at least as strongly to whites as to blacks. As observers noted and as their roll call behavior indicates, white politicians in North Carolina have overwhelmingly considered their "primary obligations" to be to whites, while they have largely ignored the opinions of the black members of their constituencies, opinions that the Reynolds survey showed were very different from those of the white electorate. To substitute a "colorblind" map with twelve decidedly white districts for the color- and party-conscious map drawn in 1992 is to exclude the voices of North Carolina's black community from Congress.[24]

CHAPTER SIX

Traditional Districting Principles, Texas-style

*I*n her prevailing opinion in *Bush v. Vera*, issued the same June day in 1996 as the opinions in *Shaw v. Hunt* from North Carolina, Justice Sandra Day O'Connor declared that the Supreme Court would not have examined Texas's congressional redistricting of 1991 so closely "if race-neutral, traditional districting considerations [had] predominated over racial ones." Later on in that opinion, she contended that since the Supreme Court's first *Shaw* decision in 1993, legislators and district courts had "reembraced the traditional districting practices that were almost universally followed before the 1990 census," practices that, she said, "acknowledge voters as more than mere racial statistics" (*Bush v. Vera* [1996], 1954, 1964). The shapes of three minority opportunity districts that were at issue in *Vera* did not by themselves, according to O'Connor, render them unconstitutional. Rather, the threshold question was whether racial or other considerations, such as protecting incumbents or politicians with major influence over redistricting, had been the "predominant reason" for the contorted shapes of three minority opportunity districts in Dallas and Houston. A review of parts of the evidence—not all of the evidence, which is presented in this chapter—convinced O'Connor and four "conservative" colleagues, but not four dissenting justices, that race predominated in the legislators' minds.

O'Connor's unsupported assertions about the race neutrality of previous districting practices may conceivably hold for some states, but they certainly do not for Texas. And to the extent that her opinions in the whole series of redistricting cases decided by the Supreme Court imply that before 1991 boundary lines were regular, districts were compact, and communities of interest were carefully preserved, she was incorrect. If O'Connor had reviewed the history of Texas redistricting, moreover, she not only would have had to abandon her misty-eyed view of tradition but would also have comprehended what happened and why it happened in Texas in 1991 much more clearly, and she should then have had to reverse her conclusion about the predominance of racial reasons for the boundary lines of the crucial districts. Unfortunately, neither the opinions in the Supreme Court nor that in the district court reviewed the historical facts, and all of the opinions, from the dissenters as well as the majority, left out crucial aspects of the battles of 1991. Focusing on the politics of redistricting in Texas from 1971 through 1992, this chapter provides a fuller view of the actions of legislators and members of Congress and allows a deeper understanding of the reasons for the redistricting decisions made in Texas in 1991.

THREE aspects of the demography of Texas—its size, ethnic diversity, and urban agglomerations—distinguish it from all other southern states except Florida. The second largest American state, in population as well as in area, Texas in 1990 had two and a half times the number of people of North Carolina and was much more urban. In fact, the two consolidated metropolitan statistical areas of Dallas/Fort Worth and Houston/Galveston by themselves contained 17 percent more people than the entire state of North Carolina. While North Carolina's one substantial ethnic minority, African-Americans, accounted for 22 percent of its population, Texas had *two* major ethnic minorities—Latinos constituted 26 percent of the population and blacks 12 percent (U.S. Department of Commerce 1993, Tables 31, 32, 42). Since blacks were concentrated predominantly in Houston and the Dallas/Fort Worth "Metroplex," it was easy, in principle, to draw congressional and state legislative districts that urban black voters could control while keeping districts within the same metropolitan areas. The rural Latino population in South Texas was so overwhelming in numbers that it required considerable craftsmanship *not* to draw several rural Latino congressional districts. In Houston, however, the high proportion of noncitizens among Hispanics, the dispersion of the population in the unzoned city, and the fact that Hispanics and African-Americans lived interspersed with each other made it difficult to establish congressional districts that gave both fair opportunities to elect candidates of their choice. Yet while such demographic realities provided the raw human material for the 1991 redistricters to shape, they did not by themselves determine the result. It was the Lone Star State's incomparably brutal politics and shockingly frank political discourse that determined which hands would be given a chance to craft outcomes, which would dominate, and what evidence they would leave of the intentions of their actions (see Davidson 1990 for an introduction to recent Texas politics).

PRIOR TO the U.S. Supreme Court's 1962 decision in *Baker v. Carr*, rural conservatives in the state maintained power by denying urban areas anything close to the representation that their population proportion merited and even by refusing to reapportion altogether. There was no reapportionment of the state legislature from 1921 until 1951 and no congressional reapportionment between 1933 and 1957. Since 1962, the state has been in court almost continuously over issues of population equality, multimember districts, charges of partisan gerrymandering and antiminority racial discrimination, and, in the 1990s, over issues of compactness and allegations of discrimination against Anglos (Bickerstaff 1991). In 1966, for example, the redistricting of the state House of Representatives was challenged on the grounds not only of unequal population but also, according to a standard account, because of "the political and racial gerrymandering that was evident in the new plan, the disenfranchisement of Negroes, and the overall crazy-quilt irrationality of the apportionment" (Claunch, Chumlea, and Dickson 1981). Since courts in Texas have perhaps plunged much more headlong into the "political thicket"[1] than have courts in any other state, the normal pressures of political compromise have been relaxed. No agreement is final until every court says it is, and each line has been drawn, each justification offered, with attention to what might attract the critical eye or ear of a judge. Until recently, lawsuits have protected the rights of discrete and insular ethnic and racial minorities much more than the normal political process has. In the legislature during the 1960s and 70s, for instance, "proposals by minorities to shape districts to their liking were generally rejected in redistricting committees or after floor challenges to committee reports" (Claunch, Chumlea, and Dickson 1981). Before the 1991 legislative session, it was only the courts that moved Texas minorities toward equal access to the political process—a deeply ironic observation in light of judges' actions after 1991.

THE 1971 redistricting in Texas was like a Renaissance melodrama: deeply flawed and Machiavellian leading characters, complicated and noisy intrigues, and a sanguinary finale. As at performances of Elizabethan plays, the poorer sort were largely confined to being spectators in the "pit," and in Texas the real players worked hard to continue the separation. Although African-Americans, Latinos, Republicans, and liberal Anglos in the state had long contended that multimember state House districts discriminated against them, and although the U.S. Supreme Court mandated single-member districts for Mississippi in the midst of the Texas legislature's consideration of its own plans, the conservative Lone Star State body adamantly refused to abolish multimember plans in the large urban counties (*HC*, June 4, 1971, 1). The state senate plan substituted conservative whites for liberal whites in the only district that had elected an African-American in this century, insuring retrogression in minority representation in the upper house (Texas House Study Group 1981, 30–31). Abjuring elaborate pretense about committee hearings or open consideration of alternatives, House Speaker Gus Mutscher, caught up already in what became known as the Sharpstown Bank scandal; Lt. Gov. Ben Barnes, soon to be tainted by a loan from the same bank; and a few of their allies drew the lines. Besides disadvantaging African-Americans and Hispanics, the plans were also designed to punish Mutscher's critics, a vociferous but outvoted coalition known as the "Dirty Thirty," made up of twenty liberal Democrats and the 150-member House's ten Republicans (Calvert and De Leon 1990, 395–97; *AAS,* May 20, 1971, 10; June 1, 1971, 1; *HC,* June 1, 1971, 1). On the regular session's last day, a raucous gallery cheered as one of the House's two blacks, "Dirty Thirty" leader Curtis Graves of Houston, blasted Mutscher. At least fourteen of the thirty, including the only announced challenger to Mutscher's speaker post, found themselves paired against other incumbents in the new districting arrangement. Announcing a suit demanding single-member districts in the state House the day after the passage of the reapportionment scheme, State Republican Party chairman Dr. George Willeford declared, "We will no longer stand idly by while a clique of political demagogues doles out the state's 150 House seats to suit its own vested interest" (*AAS,* May 27, 1971, 1; May 28, 1971, 1; *DMN,* June 1, 1971, 1).

Personal, ideological, racial, and partisan motives also played major roles in the 1971 redistricting for Congress, a task too full of conflict to be completed during the legislature's regular session. In West Texas, the Mutscher plan pitted Republican Bob Price against Democrat Graham Purcell in order to save the underpopulated seats of three other Democrats—Omar Burleson, Clark Fisher, and Abraham Kazen—while Redistricting Committee chairman Delwin Jones wanted to sacrifice any or all of them to protect his friend and fellow Democrat George Mahon. In East Texas, the bribery indictment and illness of Congressman John Dowdy left him defenseless against a move to combine much of his district with that of a stronger incumbent, Wright Patman, in order that the legislature could create a new, open seat. Two legislators who were on the conference committee that was trying to reach final agreement on congressional lines, Rep. Clyde Haynes and Sen. Charles Wilson, sparred over which one of them the new district would be tailored for (*AAS,* May 13, 1971, 2; June 5, 1971, 1; *HC,* June 1, 1971, 1; June 3, 1971, 1). In burgeoning Houston, Barbara Jordan, the first African-American to serve in the Texas State Senate in this century, a forceful woman who somehow always managed to stay in the good graces of the party and legislative leadership, was allowed to draw her own congressional seat. She subsequently won the 1972 Democratic primary, defeating the more stridently reformist Curtis Graves, and easily swept the general election to become the state's first black member of Congress in the century. A third new district, the Twenty-fourth, spanning Dallas and Tarrant Counties, was so contorted in shape that it was widely ridiculed. Republican Rep. Fred Agnich described it as "preposterous," liberal Democratic representative Dick Reed termed it a "kind of monster," and the ever-colorful state senator Oscar Mauzy declared that "a 1-eyed 1-legged justice of the peace in Langtry would know more than to draw something up like that." All agreed that it was not "compact," and many noted the jagged edge caused by shifting ten black precincts in the South Oak Cliff area of Dallas County from the adjacent Fifth District, a move apparently designed to preserve conservative control of the Fifth. Reflecting the rural conservative dominance of the process, the underpopulated districts of rural congressional and state Senate incumbents were preserved by adding small parts of the urban counties, severely fraying the boundaries of Harris, Bexar, Dallas, and Tarrant Counties (*HC,* June 1, 1971, 24; June 5, 1971, 1; *HP,* May 9, 1971, A:6; *DMN,* June 6, 1971, A:6; June 6, 1971, A:1,6; *AAS,* May 23, 1971, 9; Black and Hispanic Members of the Texas State Legislature 1981a, 4).

Race-conscious, discriminatory motives; personal, partisan, ethnic, or ideological purposes that produced oddly shaped districts; and covert designs and closed processes permeated the 1971 redistricting in Texas. These traditional Texas districting principles, motives, and means would continue to be followed and elaborated on over the next two decades.

ALTHOUGH in 1965 a Texas state court had refused to overturn multimember districts on the basis of their being racially discriminatory per se, Curtis Graves carried his legislative attack on such districts into federal court as soon as the redistrictings for both houses had been completed in 1971 (*Hainsworth v. Martin* 1965). In a suit targeting Lt. Gov. Ben Barnes, Graves's lawyers succeeded in convincing a federal court to outlaw multimember State House districts in Dallas and Bexar Counties. When *Graves v. Barnes* (1972) was appealed to the U.S. Supreme Court, it became the landmark *White v. Regester* (1973), still the fountain of vote dilution law in the United States. Nonetheless, the state did not submit willingly. Another *Graves* decision in 1974 was necessary to impose single-member districts in seven more Texas counties, and even though the legislature in 1975 acceded to abolishing the remaining multimember seats, it drew what the U.S. Department of Justice ruled were racially discriminatory lines in Tarrant, Nueces, and Jefferson Counties.[2] It was not until 1978 that an unchallenged election was finally held in the state (Bickerstaff 1991, 2–4).

The 1971 congressional arrangement was also challenged in court and significantly amended. Finding a constitutional violation in a variation of 4.1 percent between the most heavily and least heavily populated districts, a federal court attempted to order into effect a set of lines that differed markedly from those that the legislature had adopted. After the U.S. Supreme Court scolded the three-judge panel for not showing sufficient deference to the legislative will, however, the panel adopted a scheme that more closely tracked the state's choices (Bickerstaff 1991, 3–4; *White v. Weiser* [1973]). One of its most important changes moved ten black Dallas precincts from the Twenty-fourth District back to their original home in the Fifth before the 1976 elections, a change that led directly to the replacement of Fifth District Republican congressman Alan Steelman by liberal Democrat Jim Mattox and indirectly to the principal controversy of the 1981 redistricting.

BY ENDING the career of the heir apparent of the conservative John Connolly wing of the Democratic party, Ben Barnes's entanglement in the Sharpstown Bank imbroglio created a vacuum in Texas government. After Barnes finished third in the 1972 Democratic gubernatorial primary and Connolly bolted the party altogether, the colorless Dolph Briscoe did not so much fill as personify the empty space left by the departure of the state's strong men. State legislator and "Dirty Thirty" member Frances Farenthold's effort to substitute a strong woman for a strong man fell short in the 1972 Democratic runoff, as the premature feminist lost to Briscoe. Into that gulf in 1978 marched Dallas businessman William Clements, a staunch conservative, even by Texas standards, who eked out a bare margin over Democratic nominee John Hill, who had beaten Briscoe in that year's Democratic primary (Calvert and De Leon 1990, 435–36). The veto power held by Clements, the first Republican governor in Texas since Reconstruction, radically changed the game of redistricting in 1981.

The most visible symbol of the rise of the GOP in Texas, Clements was not the only Republican to influence redistricting in the 1980s. Instead of ten Republicans in the lower house of the legislature, as there had been in 1971, there were thirty-eight in 1981. Although most of the additional twenty-eight replaced conservative Democrats, that wing of the party, led by House Speaker Billy Clayton and Lt. Gov. Bill Hobby, was still dominant in both houses of the legislature, and conservative Democrats still filled most congressional seats. But the liberal wing, personified by John Bryant, chairman of the House Study Group, could not be ignored, and the Democrats as a whole organized a party caucus, a tactic that had not been necessary since the days of Populism in the 1890s. Thus, 1981 was the first redistricting of the twentieth century in which more than one partisan interest played an active role (*HC*, Aug. 9, 1981, I:12; Harmel and Hamm 1986).

Paralleling developments in the legislature were party and ideological bifurcations in the congressional delegation. In Dallas, liberal Jim Mattox of the Fifth District was joined in 1978 by moderate-liberal Martin Frost in the adjacent Twenty-fourth, while in the Houston area, Republican Ron Paul's 1978 victory was followed by that of Jack Fields, who rode Ronald Reagan's 1980 coattails to defeat perhaps the most liberal Anglo Democratic congressman from the South, Bob Eckhardt. In Corpus Christi, moderate Democrat Bill Patman enjoyed strong Hispanic support in his successful campaign to replace his conservative fellow party member Joe Wyatt in 1980. The principal objectives of the coalition of Republicans and conservative Democrats during the 1981 redistricting were to strengthen Fields, to weaken Patman and Paul (who had by far the most liberal voting record of any Texas Republican in the 1981 Congress),[3] and to destroy Frost and Mattox.

The feisty Clements, still inexperienced in Texas state government after a couple of relatively unproductive years in office, held two major weapons besides his veto and his de facto alliance with Speaker Clayton and Lt. Gov. Hobby: wealthy lobbyists and the VRA. An organization of big businessmen formed the morning after a $2.8 million Clements fund-raiser, "Texans for a Conservative Congress" spent $76,000 organizing many of the chief patrons of Texas legislative campaigns to lobby the objects of their past donations to vote for districts that helped Republicans in particular and conservatives in general. Bankers, perhaps half-jokingly, threatened to call in the loans of legislators who did not cooperate. In light of the committee's antagonism toward minorities, one Hispanic leader, Reuben Bonilla, quipped that the organization should be named "Texans for a Bigoted Society." Another group, the "Texans for Fair Redistricting Committee," reportedly a front for oil and business political action committees, sent a letter to legislators promising to base future contributions on whether legislators supported the redistricting plan that Gov. Clements favored (*CCCT*, June 26, 1981, B:1; Attlesey 1981; *AAS*, Aug. 9, 1981, B:13). Money may well have determined the outcomes of a series of extremely close votes in July and August of 1981 in both houses of the legislature.

At the same time that Republicans in Congress were scathingly attacking "proportional representation" for minorities during the debate over the renewal of the VRA, Republicans in Texas were insisting on proportional representation of minorities in Dallas in an effort to weaken white liberal Democratic congressmen. This patently opportunistic Republican support for such a "minority" district precipitated what might be termed "the first battle of Dallas." Noting that the total black population of Dallas County amounted to 54.6 percent of that of an ideal congressional district and that if all were put into one district—a difficult task, for despite continuing prejudice and discrimination, not all Dallas blacks were segregated into a compact area— they would drain enough Democratic votes from Jim Mattox's Fifth District to make it solidly Republican, Gov. Clements professed a conversion to black empowerment, promising to veto "any plan that did not create a minority district in Dallas county and restrict all of Democratic Congressman

Jim Mattox's Fifth District to the county." Clements's insistence on confining the district to Dallas County is another sign of his use of race as a proxy for other aims, for the Democrats' obvious counterploy to an attempt to carve an African-American district out of Districts 5 and 24 was to extend each into rural and small-town Democratic areas in surrounding counties. "The black community of Dallas wants its own representative and they are not better served by two liberal white Democrats," Clements announced (*DTH*, June 1, 1981, A:1; *DMN*, Nov. 5, 1981, A:31; *HP*, March 2, 1982, C:22).

Although the governor testified under oath to his devotion to the election of a black member of Congress and his lack of involvement in the details of the process, and although he once assured skeptical reporters that he had never calculated the political effect of any changes in congressional districts, he refused to support a plan that would possibly have created a minority opportunity district in Dallas without turning another district Republican, declaring that the choice "comes down to whether the conservatives will hang together and do what's right for Texas, which is a conservative state, or whether we're going to let the tail wag the dog and let these liberals carry the day." This was tantamount to an admission that it was ideological and partisan conservatism, not racial liberalism, that explained Clements's stance. Dallas African-American leader Isaac Johnson echoed the charges of many other Democrats, white as well as black, when he contended that Clements "does not care about blacks and browns in Dallas, only about the political fortunes of the Republican party" (*HP*, Dec. 5, 1981, A:6; *FWST*, Aug. 12, 1981, A:8; *HC*, July 15, 1981, I:18; July 21, 1981, I:8; Aug. 7, 1981; I:12; Loe 1981, 222; *DMN*, July 16, 1981, A:34; July 27, 1981, A:13; *AAS*, Aug. 6, 1981, B:5).

The African-American community in the state was deeply split over whether to attempt to create a "black congressional district" in Dallas in 1981 (NYT, Dec. 20, 1981, 15).[4] An ad hoc "Coalition for Minority Representation"—led by former Dallas city councilwoman Lucy Patterson, former state House member Eddie Bernice Johnson, Progressive Voters League officers Jesse Jones and John Wiley Price, and Dallas city councilman Fred Blair—contended that it did not matter how liberal the voting records of Jim Mattox and Martin Frost were or how much effort they devoted to their black constituents. They should be replaced because, as whites, they were incapable of truly representing African-Americans.[5] "Congressman Mattox is Anglo, and Congressman Frost is Jewish," declared Lucy Patterson, and therefore "cannot fully understand the needs of the black community" (*DMN*, July 14, 1981, A:19; Ehrenhalt 1983). Chris Reed Brown of Dallas told a meeting of the Democratic State Executive Committee that Frost owed it to blacks to leave the district, move to College Station, and run against conservative Democrat

Phil Gramm. Brown and her fellow Coalition members joined Gov. Clements, Speaker Clayton, Lt. Gov. Hobby, and House Redistricting Committee chairman Tim Von Dohlen (D-Goliad) in backing S.B. 1, a bill carried in the Senate by conservative Democrat John Wilson of La Grange. Somewhat unselfconsciously, Coalition members, who had drawn their map with the help of the Dallas County Republican chairman, accused African-Americans who disagreed with them of "selling out to the white power structure" or, more picturesquely, of being "water boys" for "political slave traders"—that is, white moderate and liberal Democrats.[6] Disagreements became so heated once that a security guard had to restrain a "Coalition" member from assaulting a minority legislator (*DMN*, July 20, 1981, A:19; Aug. 2, 1981, A:29; Ehrenhalt 1983; Loe 1981, 215).

Thirty-three of the thirty-four minority state legislators disagreed with most black leaders in Dallas and backed instead the approach of the principal contending bill, S.B. 3, sponsored by senators Oscar Mauzy (D-Dallas) and Peyton McKnight (D-Tyler) but principally drafted by Democratic congressmen Jim Wright of Fort Worth and Martin Frost. S.B. 3 preserved the districts of Frost and Mattox and split Dallas blacks at the Trinity River, as they had been split in the *White v. Weiser* court-ordered plan in 1973. Although Sen. John Wilson charged that S.B. 3 was "only based on protecting incumbents," its black and white defenders, led by the chairman of the legislative Black Caucus, Rep. Craig Washington (D-Houston), combined high principle with practical politics in pressing for it (*DMN*, July 14, 1981, A:19; *HC*, July 15, 1981, I:18; July 16, 1981, I:9). Articulating that principle, Washington declared that "Anything that packs blacks to guarantee that a black is elected while minimizing black political influence is patronizing and we should fight it." "The ultimate goal," he said in a deposition, "is not to elect black and brown faces but to insure whoever is representing those black and brown people who vote represents their best interests." Challenging S.B. 1 with an elaborate analysis that showed stark differences between the voting records of Anglo members of Congress from Texas whose districts contained significant percentages of minorities and those who did not, black and Hispanic members of the legislature concluded in a letter to the Justice Department that "a Congressman does not have to be Black or Hispanic in order to be responsive to the needs of minority communities" (*DTH*, June 1, 1981, A:1; Washington dep., 66; Black and Hispanic Members of the Texas State Legislature 1981, 6–7).[7]

But it was not just that minority legislators were more interested in substantive than in symbolic representation. They also knew, as Paul Ragsdale, a black state representative from Dallas and a member of the House Redistricting Committee in 1981, pointed out, that it was virtually impossible to draw a congressional district in Dallas that would have an actual majority of black voters. the "black district" of S.B. 1 was less than 47 percent black in population and no doubt even less in voting-age population.[8] Blacks registered and turned out to vote at disproportionately low levels, compared to Anglos, and minority legislators showed in a letter to the Justice Department that Hispanics did not generally support black candidates against Anglos in Democratic primaries in Dallas. "You can't get a majority black district in Dallas County even with gerrymandering," contended Ragsdale, who had drawn the state House districts for the county. "If you could do it, I'd already have done it," he concluded. What good did it do, asked minority legislators who opposed S.B. 1 on final passage, to draw a 47 percent black district containing the homes of Frost and Mattox when Frost, who had already collected $200,000 in campaign contributions and who had long carefully cultivated black support, would almost certainly beat any black opponent (*DMN*, July 27, 1981, A:13; *HP*, Dec. 6, 1981, D:6; Black and Hispanic Members of the Texas State Legislature 1981, 12–15)?[9] If Frost won, all the bitter struggle would have accomplished would be the substitution of a conservative Republican for Mattox, whose views were far closer to those of the vast majority of blacks, and increased antipathy between blacks and their day-to-day white allies—another reason, of course, for Clements and other conservatives to support S.B. 1.

When S.B. 1 passed, "Coalition" African-Americans cheered, Frost prepared to run for Congress in the "black district" anyway, Mattox bounced into the race for state attorney-general, and minority legislators and their allies lobbied the Justice Department and sued in federal court. The campaigns in the S.B. 1 "black district" proved the sagacity of the minority legislators, as highly visible black candidates Lucy Patterson and Eddie Bernice Johnson, who had joined Clements and the Republicans in agitating for the new district, trailed Frost in November 1981 by approximately 2–1 in trial runs in public opinion polls (*DMN*, Nov. 5, 1981, A:31). The suits were also partially successful, as a three-judge court restored virtually the S.B. 3 boundaries in Dallas in time for the 1982 election. In 1983, the legislature adopted nearly the same lines as the federal court had (*Seamon v. Upham* 1982–84; *DTH*, June 27, 1983, A:10). In the 1982 contest, Frost crushed Patterson, who switched parties to run against him as a Republican. Patterson is estimated to have received only about 6 percent of the black votes in overwhelmingly African-American precincts (Ehrenhalt 1983; Prof. Larry Carlile testimony before Texas House, May 16, 1983, cited in John W. Fainter Jr. to William French Smith, July 21, 1983, in Texas 1983). Frost and John Bryant, whose voting record closely paralleled Mattox's, filled the Twenty-fourth and Fifth District seats for the rest of the 1980s. But what Paul Ragsdale called a "blood bath" within the black community and between blacks and liberal Anglos, re-verberated into the next decade (Transcript of Floor Debate in Texas House of Representatives on S.B. 480, May 26, 1983, 5, in Texas 1983). In 1991, Republicans would try again to divide liberals along racial lines, and Democrats would attempt not to make the same mistakes twice.

THE SHOOT-OUT over Dallas was not the only reason for the long, bitter, and closely contested struggle over congressional reapportionment in 1981. Because of population growth during the 1970s, Texas gained three new congressional seats after the 1980 census. Everyone agreed that one of the three should be a safe Republican seat in the Dallas suburbs and that another should be located somewhere in Harris County, with a district in the northern suburbs helping the Republicans, one in the southern part of the county probably Democratic, and one in the center city possibly endangering the only district held by an African-American, Mickey Leland, who had succeeded Barbara Jordan when she retired from office in 1978. Latinos wanted the third to be in South Texas, and during the Special Session, Hispanic legislators Matt Garcia and Al Luna unsuccessfully pressed for a plan that balanced the Hispanic percentages between the existing Fifteenth District, represented since 1964 by the conservative Mexican-American Eligio De La Garza, and a new district, the Twenty-seventh, instead of packing Hispanics into the Fifteenth. Under S.B. 1 and S.B. 3 (both of which were patterned after an earlier MALDEF proposal), the Hispanic population proportion in the Fifteenth District would be 81 percent, while that in the Twenty-seventh would be 55–56 percent—the latter probably not enough for Mexican-Americans to elect a candidate of their choice. The Garcia-Luna amendment, which was in effect later adopted by the three-judge federal court in *Seamon v. Upham* (1982) after the Justice Department had objected to the packing in District 15 under S.B. 1, made the percentages 71 and 65, respectively (William Bradford Reynolds to David Dean, Jan. 29, 1982, in Texas 1981, Section 5 Files, U.S. Dept. of Justice; *HC*, Jan. 30, 1982, I:1; *NYT*, Feb. 28, 1982, 28). The point is that neither the Republican S.B. 1 nor the Democratic S.B. 3 was fully responsive to expressed Hispanic interests in South Texas. Both parties' unresponsiveness contributed to a record that might be used in a Section 2 or constitutional challenge against a 1991 plan if redistricters in the latter year again brushed Hispanic demands aside. That record increased the legal pressure on the 1991 redistricters to insure that minorities had a good opportunity to elect candidates of their choice.

Instead of inserting a new district in South Texas, House Redistricting Committee Chair Tim Von Dohlen split the city of Corpus Christi and twisted the Fourteenth District into a shape that reminded state House member

Hugo Berlanga (D-Corpus Christi) of a dragon, retaining only 40 percent of the population from the previous Fourteenth District. One of the reasons that the relatively moderate Bill Patman had won the Fourteenth District contest in 1980 was that the minority percentage in the district was 45.4 percent. S.B. 1 reduced that to 31.6 percent, halving the proportion of Hispanic voters, who had, observers claimed, so strongly supported Patman. That was not enough for Von Dohlen, who reportedly planned to run against Patman if the new district were suitable, or for the Anglo businessmen of Corpus Christi, who argued and lobbied the legislature long and hard to divide their city along ethnic lines, putting Anglos into one congressional district and Mexican-Americans in another. According to Ruben Bonilla, the past president of the League of United Latin American Citizens (LULAC), what he termed this "malevolent scheme to promote selfish personal economic vested interests" had been proposed because Patman and Sen. Carlos Truan, rather than the candidates favored by the "Anglo establishment" in Corpus Christi, had won in 1980. Appearing at a Redistricting Committee meeting to oppose Von Dohlen's scheme, three Democratic lawmakers—Berlanga, Craig Washington, and Bob Bush, an Anglo—wore bright yellow T-shirts emblazoned with a dragon and the words "Dragon Slayers" (Comacho et al. 1982, 30, n. 5; *DTH*, June 1, 1981, A:1; Texas House Committee on Regions, Compacts and Districts 1981, 1–226; *DMN*, June 26, 1981, A:22; *AAS*, July 23, 1981, B:4; *HC*, July 24, 1981, I:9; July 28, 1981, I:9).

An opponent of Republican congressman Ron Paul, as well as of Patman and the Hispanic community's interests, Von Dohlen eventually abandoned his effort to split Corpus Christi and came up with the scheme of shifting Democrats into Paul's marginal district and Republicans into Patman's, attacking both congressmen with a simple swap that even moved Paul's house into Patman's district, forcing Paul either to run against Patman or to leave his Brazoria County home.[10] If Paul refused to move, either he or Patman would lose; if Paul followed his old district into Fort Bend County, that would open up the Fourteenth for Von Dohlen's Republican friend, state House member Brad Wright, who would then, Von Dohlen hoped, eliminate Patman, whose district had been weakened. (Earlier, Von Dohlen had proposed to tailor a new district for Brad Wright, but the Brazoria switch threw more stones and promised to knock off a pair of hated birds.) By alienating both Paul's and Patman's friends in the lower house, however, Von Dohlen had overreached himself. The House rejected his stratagem, 81–64, on the day that it finally adopted a congressional plan. Emphasizing Von Dohlen's failure to insure Patman's immediate defeat by himself or one of his friends, House Democratic Caucus chairman Bob Bush asserted that Von Dohlen had "won the battle, but lost the war" (*HC*, July 17, 1981, I:11; July 28, 1981, I:9; July 29, 1981, I:12; July 30, 1981, I:10,23; July 31, 1981, I:3; *AAS*, July 24, 1981, B:2; July 28,

1981, B:2; July 31, 1981, B:6; *DMN*, July 29, 1981, A:28; July 30, 1981, A:1; July 31, 1981, A:22).

BECAUSE Speaker Billy Clayton put five members of minority groups on the House Redistricting Committee (Bob Valles of El Paso and Reby Cary of Fort Worth, as well as Washington, Ragsdale, and Berlanga), the State might have argued in later court cases that minorities could not have been discriminated against in the 1981 redistricting, because their presence on this key committee guaranteed them influence. Did it? Not according to the minority legislators' comment on the plan to the Justice Department, which argued that minorities were "run over at every turn by the conservative White majority, the presiding officers of the House and Senate, and the Governor." Assessing the outcome of their involvement, they concluded, "We had little real impact on the final plan. We understand the sham that took place. The State systematically attempted to create the impression of minority legislators' participation when the truth is that there was none" (Black and Hispanic Members of the Texas State Legislature 1981a, 1).

The facts support the contentions of the 1981 "Comment." There were no blacks and only four Latinos in the Senate in 1981, and none played a role in framing S.B. 1. Nor were the five minority House members on the Redistricting Committee consulted until Von Dohlen presented his plan. In fact, they did not receive data on the ethnic composition of the proposed districts until the day before the committee was first scheduled to vote on plans. When Ragsdale tried to make a motion for delay, to allow time to review the data, Von Dohlen ignored him, and minority members stalked out in order to break the committee's quorum. When the amended S.B. 1 reached the floor, Ragsdale offered an amendment basically restoring the balance of the black population between Districts 5 and 24, and when this lost, he joined Carlyle Smith (D-Grand Prairie) in offering an amendment that designated District 5 as the majority-minority district and extended District 24 south into rural counties in an effort to preserve it for the Democratic party, if not for a moderate like Martin Frost. These proposals and a similar one by Craig Washington lost on the House floor by identical three-vote margins (Black and Hispanic Members of the Texas State Legislature 1981a, 23; *DMN*, July 29, 1981, A:28).

At this point, for the only time in the session on the redistricting issue, Gov. Clements and Speaker Clayton lost control. In a decision described by an observer as "potentially devastating" for the conservative leadership, a momentarily unified Democratic caucus sent the reapportionment issue back to Von Dohlen's committee, apparently hoping that the group would amend the bill in line with the Ragsdale-Smith amendment, the effect of which would be to create the majority-minority district that Gov. Clements claimed to want but to prevent Republicans from winning another seat in Dallas County. Demonstrating that partisan concerns really motivated him, Clements promised to veto Ragsdale-Smith. As a reporter put it, "The battle over congressional reapportionment reached full-scale partisan warfare." After both sides lobbied intensely, Speaker Clayton extracted the bill from the committee by threatening to refer it to another committee, amended S.B. 1 to punish moderate Democrats even more, and, after minority and other Democratic caucus members absented themselves to break a quorum, sent out sergeants-at-arms to arrest members in lobbies and hotel rooms, bring them back to the House at 4:45 A.M., and count enough of them as present to pass the congressional redistricting bill (*DMN*, Aug. 4, 1981, A:1 ["potentially devastating"]; Aug. 5, 1981, A:21; Aug. 6, 1981, A:30; Aug. 8, 1981, A:40; Aug. 10, 1981, A:20; *HC*, Aug. 4, 1981, I:6; Aug. 6, 1981, I:12; Aug. 7, 1981, I:12 ["warfare"]; Aug. 8, 1981, I:13; Aug. 10, 1981, I:8; *AAS*, Aug. 6, 1981, B:5; Aug. 10, 1981, A:1; Black and Hispanic Members of the Texas State Legislature 1981, 29). The arrests were a classic exercise of strong-arm tactics by a powerful Texas speaker out to preserve conservative control at practically any cost, and an exercise that came, as before, at the expense of moderate Anglo Democrats and over the vehement protests of black and Hispanic legislators.

As passed, S.B. 1 was a severe blow to minority influence on the congressional delegation. As Tony Bonilla, president of LULAC, put it, picturesquely, "We've been raped again. The Republicans who ran under the Democratic banner have joined forces with the other Republicans to do a hatchet job on four of our fine progressive congressmen and have diluted and minimized the Hispanic vote" (*FWST*, Aug. 12, 1981, A:8). During the 1980s, approximately 90 percent of blacks and 72 percent of Hispanics in Texas were Democrats. On the other hand, 90 percent of the Republican voters were Anglo (Vedlitz, Dyer, and Hill 1988, 49). Thus, any actions that substantially reduced the probability that a Democratic member of Congress could be elected disproportionately damaged the almost certain choices of minority voters.[11] In Dallas, the minority percentage in the Fifth District was reduced from 29 percent to 12 percent, and the Democratic party's prospects in the district became hopeless. In Houston, the minority percentage in the Eighth, which had been represented for more than a decade by the extremely liberal Bob Eckhardt, dropped from 40 percent to 29 percent, effectively guaranteeing the seat to the Republicans for the foreseeable future. In the Fourteenth, Patman had not been damaged as much as Von Dohlen threatened to do, but the reduction in his minority percentage by nearly a third allowed Republicans to defeat him in 1984. The Twenty-second, the seat that Ron Paul had won after seesaw battles with moderate Democrat Bob Gammage during the 1970s, also saw a decline in the minority percentage from 31 percent to 23 percent and a consequent shriveling of Democratic chances. Overall, as black and Hispanic members of the legislature pointed out in a comment to the Justice Department, under the court-ordered plan from the 1970s, minorities could control three of the twenty-four seats and influence nine others; under S.B. 1, they still could control no more than three, but they could influence only seven of the expanded total of twenty-seven. This, they said, was retrogressive (Black and Hispanic Members of Texas State Legislature 1981b, 1–2).

TEXAS politicians ritually repeat "good government" rhetoric less during redistricting than officeholders in other states do, and they lack conviction when they do. Like the 1971 experience, the 1981 reapportionment only further demonstrated that the raw struggle for partisan, personal, and ethnic power rarely lies far below the surface of Texas politics. The attempt by the conservative Anglo legislature, only partially reversed by the courts in *Seamon v. Upham,* to buttress the electoral strength of conservative congressmen and reduce that of moderates, the half-hearted and unconvincing use of the VRA ploy by Governor Clements to cover a partisan power play, the strenuous efforts by Democratic incumbents Frost and Mattox to save their seats at the expense of principle or party, the dogged and partially successful effort by Von Dohlen to savage Patman and Paul, the blatant packing of Hispanics into the district of a well-established Hispanic incumbent, the exclusion of minority legislators from the real power to shape plans—all of these facts might tilt the judicial scales even more against the State if the legislature were not more sympathetic to minority concerns in 1991.[12] From the beginning of the 1991 districting, then, politicians who had either participated in earlier redistrictings or, as political activists, surely knew about them must have anticipated a legal challenge from minorities if they failed to afford them real opportunity and influence. And the challenge would be buttressed not only by an amended VRA but also by a long record of discrimination in redistricting in Texas itself. With the substantial increase during the 1980s of the Hispanic population in Houston and South Texas and the lesser but still appreciable rise of the black percentage in Dallas, minorities had an even stronger case for more seats in 1991 than they had had in 1981. The Republican strategy of forming a temporary alliance of convenience with minorities so as to weaken Democratic strength in adjacent districts had been so well rehearsed that by 1991 everyone knew their lines perfectly. All that was required for a revival of the stage production was an expected Republican victory in the 1990 gubernatorial election and an uncontroversial count in the 1990 census.

•   •   •

BUT NEITHER happened. Instead of holding the governorship, enjoying a de facto alliance with the conservative Democratic legislative leadership, and facing a loosely organized opposition, Texas Republicans in 1991 confronted a newly elected and partisan Democratic governor, Ann Richards, and more moderate and less fractionated Democratic legislative and congressional delegations. Republican gains in Texas during the 1980s—a rise in state House members from thirty-eight to fifty-seven and in congressmen from five to eight—had the paradoxical effect of increasing Democratic cohesion and power during the 1991 reapportionment. The Texas legislature became much more partisan during the 1980s (Harmel and Hamm 1986). The jump in Republican membership in the legislature also meant that African-Americans and Latinos made up a larger proportion of the Democrats—34 percent of the 181 members of the two houses, as opposed to 26 percent in 1981. More than ever, Democrats could not ignore their minority group members, and blacks and Hispanics appeared to be ever more tempting targets for Republican deal makers. As in 1981, some minority politicians seemed receptive. "The best friend that minorities have," announced Houston city councilman Ben Reyes, "is the Republican Party" (*HC*, Feb. 3, 1991, C:4).

Activists who were less concerned than Reyes was with tweaking erstwhile Anglo Democratic allies believed minorities' best friend was the VRA. Many people on all sides of the political spectrum interpreted the 1982 amendments to require creation of majority-minority districts whenever possible. Thus, during debates over redistricting, Sen. Teel Bivins (R-Amarillo), one of the Republican leaders on the issue, remarked "If it is possible to create a minority district, the [Voting Rights] act requires that one be drawn." In an article on Texas redistricting, Thomas B. Edsall of the *Washington Post* said: "Under amendments to the [Voting Rights] act in 1982 and Supreme Court rulings since then, legislatures drawing district lines in areas with histories of racially polarized voting are effectively required to create districts giving blacks and Hispanics voting majorities whenever reasonably possible." During the *Terrazas v. Slagle* trial in 1991 before a three-judge federal panel, Sen. David Sibley (R-Waco) asked Sen. Eddie Bernice Johnson (D-Dallas), who had chaired the congressional districting subcommittee of the Senate Redistricting Committee, whether she had repeatedly told colleagues during the session "If you can draw a minority district, you must draw a minority district." Agreeing that she had, she justified the statement as reflecting her understanding of the VRA (*ASNG*, Aug. 18, 1991, A:1; *WP* [NWE], June 3–9, 1991, 12; trial transcript, *Terrazas v. Slagle*, Dec. 12, 1991, 253).

The results of the 1990 census and the development of computer technology interacted with politics and legal developments to set the stage for reapportionment in 1991. For one thing, the burgeoning of the state's population added three seats to the congressional delegation, which made it possible to satisfy new demands while maintaining incumbents. But since most of the population growth occurred either in Republican-leaning suburbs or among Hispanics in Houston and South Texas, the new seats could go in two very different demographic, political, and geographical directions. For another, the widely noted undercount, which was especially concentrated among minorities, and the decision by political appointees of the Bush administration not to correct or update the results of the original census heightened the alienation of minority activists from the GOP. A third important factor was that rapid, frequent, and inexpensive redrawing of boundaries became possible and virtually inevitable during the consideration of district lines because of the extremely fine-grained population information made available by the Census Bureau, because hardware and software developments facilitated the recalculation of linked political and ethnic statistics with every major or minor boundary change, and because the U.S. Supreme Court's decision in *Karcher v. Daggett* in 1983 that every population deviation between congressional districts was constitutionally suspect meant that a very large number of city and county boundaries would have to be breached. As the chairman of the House Redistricting Committee noted, "because of the tight [population] tolerance the courts have approved, there is no way that we can avoid county cuts" (*HC*, Mar. 21, 1991, A:1; Mar. 23, 1991, A:30; Mar. 24, 1991, C:2; *DMN*, Apr. 15, 1991, A:1; Aug. 25, 1991, A:41; Texas House Floor Debates, transcript, Aug. 21, 1991, 7, in Texas 1991). Technical progress and inflexible legal rules, in other words, inevitably increased the conflicts in and the complexity of the redistricting process.[13] A fourth factor was the numerous successful minority voting dilution cases during the 1980s—particularly the massive documentation of racially polarized voting and discrimination in *Williams v. City of Dallas* (1990), issued on the eve of reapportionment—which surely reminded the legislators of their potential liability if their plans failed to allow Hispanics and African-Americans an equal opportunity with Anglos to elect candidates of their choice (Brischetto, Richards, Davidson, and Grofman 1994).

Anglo Democrats had also learned certain lessons from the 1981 experience. Not only were they better organized this time, but they did not ignore finances. In 1981, only the conservative Democrat-Republican coalition had brandished promises of campaign money before legislators during reapportionment. A decade later, the Democratic congressmen most obviously threatened by the redrawing of lines, Martin Frost of the Twenty-fourth and John Bryant of the Fifth, had made 1990 campaign contributions of $56,700 to state legislators. Frost alone contributed to nineteen of the twenty-three Democratic winners in the state Senate and forty-five of the ninety-two in the House, gifts that probably at least assured him an audience to plead his case. Moreover, early in the process Democrats decided to make minorities a better offer than Republicans could afford to tender. Republicans initially hoped that one or two of the three new congressional seats would be located in the suburbs, and both leaders and followers pushed for this. Hoping to head off a minority-Republican coalition, knowing that except in extraordinary circumstances every minority seat was a Democratic seat, and realizing that they would be able to craft districts to accommodate both new minority and incumbent Democratic positions, the Democrats announced that all three of the new districts should go to minorities—Latino districts in Houston and South Texas and a black district in Dallas (Alston 1991; *HC*, Mar. 24, 1991, C:2; *DMN*, Apr. 7, 1991, A:42; *AAS*, Apr. 21, 1991, B:1).

WITH DEMOCRATS in control of the legislature and the executive office, with both political parties and all of the pertinent leaders at least rhetorically committed to a new African-American congressional district in Dallas, with a Dallas County black population now amounting to 65.3 percent of the ideal congressional district, with extremely detailed ethnic and general population statistics available, and with a black state senator, Eddie Bernice Johnson, as chair of the relevant subcommittee, it should have been relatively painless to agree on congressional district lines in the Metroplex. As Martin Frost put it optimistically when he endorsed the principle of a black Dallas district nearly a year before census data became available, "The minority population exists in Dallas County to create a majority-minority district. It's just a matter of drawing the lines" (*DMN*, July 14, 1990, A:35). Had the process taken place behind closed doors, without any necessity for public posturing and no premium on disagreements, instead being conducted through a relatively open process with plenty of opportunity for comments, criticisms, and redraftings, consensus would no doubt have come more quickly. Messiness is often a by-product of reform.

The Frost and Bryant strategy was simple. There were two keys to electing a black member of Congress: first, make sure that no strong Anglo candidate ran in the district by giving potential candidates other winnable districts; second, make sure that the black population of the district comprised a comfortable majority of a probable Democratic primary electorate, and that the district contained enough reliable nonblack Democrats to blunt any likely Republican campaign. The first principle, conveniently enough for the Anglo Democrats, suggested keeping Frost in his Oak Cliff base, letting him retain some South Dallas blacks, and cannibalizing Republican Joe Barton's Sixth District, which stretched south from Dallas and Tarrant counties all the way to the Houston suburbs, to include enough Anglo Democrats to send Frost back to Washington. Bryant's Fifth District would head south and east from its starting point in Dallas County. As the fourth-ranking Democrat on the influential Rules Committee in the House and the new chairman of "IMPAC 2000," the national redistricting arm of the Democratic party, Frost's growing national power and proven fundraising ability would enable him to do well in a substantially redrawn district. Bryant, a practiced campaigner, would also survive. The second principle suggested that the proportion of minorities did not have to be overwhelming, certainly not at the much mentioned 65 percent target, if a large number of the Anglos in the district could be expected to vote in the Republican primary. In other words, if the Dallas black district, early on given the number 30, went north into the affluent "Park Cities," Highland Park and University Park, it could be fairly compact in shape and still leave enough blacks outside its southerly edge to keep Frost and Bryant happy and reelected. These principles were implicit in the proposal agreed on by the Democratic members of Congress, which made District 30 a 61 percent combined-minority district, 43 percent black and 19 percent Latino, and which, a historian hired by Frost contended on the basis of a statistical analysis of Dallas elections, could be carried by a black candidate. The keys to victory by a black candidate were black and Anglo turnout in the primary, the level of Anglo Democratic support for a black candidate in the general election, and the relatively high percentage of Republicans in the district—40 percent for President Bush in 1988 and 45 percent for Senator Phil Gramm in 1990—which meant that even with only 43 percent of the population, blacks alone might comprise two-thirds or more of the normal Democratic vote (*HC*, Dec. 23, 1990, A:1; Apr. 16, 1991, A:11; *AAS*, Dec. 23, 1990, B:1; Apr. 21, 1991, B:1; *DTH*, May 1, 1991, A:1; May 5, 1991, A:23; *DMN*, Apr. 16, 1991, A:17; Glasser 1991; Lichtman 1994).[14]

But the black percentage of the Democratic primary electorate was not the key for Sen. Johnson, who astonished her colleagues by announcing her candidacy for the seat even as its boundaries were being debated and who had more power to set its limits than anyone else did. For her, the key was to make the district black enough to satisfy demands for a district that African-Americans could win without coalescing with anyone else—demands that had festered since the days of the "Coalition for Minority Representation" in 1981, of which she was a leading member—but not black enough to elect someone else, particularly her chief rival, Dallas County Commissioner John Wiley Price. At first, Johnson proposed a District 30 that was 45 percent black and 21 percent Hispanic (*DMN*, May 16, 1991, A:1; Aug. 9, 1991, A:1; Aug. 10, 1991, A:24; Aug. 12, 1991, A:50; *HC*, Aug. 19, 1991, A:1; *AAS*, Aug. 22, 1991, B:1; *DTH*, Aug. 22, 1991, A:31; Fred Blair [D-Dallas], in Transcript of Texas House

Floor Debate, Aug. 21, 1991, 196–97, in Texas 1991; Texas Congressional Redistricting Staff 1991, 2, in Texas 1991; transcript of trial testimony, Sen. Eddie Bernice Johnson, *Terrazas v. Slagle*, Dec. 12, 1991, 237–38, 242; Glasser 1991).[15]

The response to Johnson's plan is worth considering in some detail, because it demonstrates the widespread understanding among Republicans as well as Democrats, Anglos as well as African-Americans, that the shape of the Thirtieth District would be determined by personal and partisan factors as well as by racial ones. If the justices of the Supreme Court, dissenters as well as those in the majority in *Bush v. Vera* (1996), ignored the influence of competition *within* the black community on the final positioning of the district, observers in Texas at the time certainly did not. As Tom Pauken, then a radio talk show host and columnist for the *Dallas Times-Herald* and later State Chairman of the Republican Party, noted, the argument was not over establishing a black district, but over whether to include in it *Anglo and Hispanic* precincts currently in Frost's district in the Grand Prairie area "in order to give her [Johnson] an advantage over John Wiley Price in a Democratic primary race. Price has very little political support outside the black community." Frost agreed, telling the national magazine *Roll Call* that "the argument at this point is not over the minority content of the Dallas district. The argument is over white Democrats in Grand Prairie and Pleasant Grove." Sen. Johnson herself noted that she'd gotten considerable support in her 1986 state Senate contest from Anglos in Grand Prairie, where her sister was assistant superintendent of instruction in the public schools. She was interested in extending the Thirtieth District in that direction (*DTH*, Feb. 17, 1991, A:25; Glasser 1991; *WP* [NWE], June 3–9, 1991, 12–13; transcript of trial testimony, Sen. Eddie Bernice Johnson, *Terrazas v. Slagle*, Dec. 12, 1991, 246).

The fact that most of the major newspapers covering the Metroplex reported that jockeying by politicians within the black community helped to shape the lines of the Thirtieth District indicates how widespread that view was, if not before the appearance of the articles, then certainly afterwards.[16]

> While Ms. Johnson will have a hard time cutting many of the commissioner's [i.e., Price's] present southern Dallas County constituents out of the district, she no doubt will try to draw it to include more white precincts in Oak Cliff and Grand Prairie. Such voters would consider Ms. Johnson far more acceptable than the combative Mr. Price. (*DMN*, Jan. 20, 1991, I:9)

> Johnson is expected to draw a district somewhat less dominated by minority residents than Price's precinct. (*FWST*, Mar. 17, 1991, A:1)

> Ironically, they [Johnson and Frost] are battling not over black Democrats, but over white ones in Grand Prairie and Oak Cliff. Johnson wants

the white Democrats in the district because as a moderate Democrat, she fears a challenge from her left if the district becomes too minority-dominated. Frost wants them to be sure he can win the general election against a Republican. (*AAS*, Apr. 21, 1991, B:1)

In the end, however, the choice of a black representative could boil down to which white voters are used to supplement the new district's minority core. If northern Dallas County Republicans are included in the district, black voters would dominate the primary, perhaps helping a more liberal candidate. If Democratic voters in Grand Prairie or Irving are included in the district, the Democratic primary would be split between blacks, Hispanics and whites, assisting a more centrist candidate or enhancing a white candidacy. As one Dallas Democratic strategist put it, "Go north and help John Wiley. Go west and you help Eddie Bernice." (*DTH*, May 5, 1991, A:23)

Driving the Thirtieth District west to pick up Anglo Democrats from Frost's Twenty-fourth and south to try to attain the symbolically important 50 percent black population goal, which became a popular slogan that no politician could ignore, however meaningless it was in practical electoral terms, had two consequences that largely determined the shape of congressional districts in Dallas and Tarrant Counties. First, the borders of the part of the Thirtieth District outside the black population core had to be drawn with some care in order not to take in too many Anglos and Hispanics. In a sense, this had nothing to do with race. To win the Thirtieth District, Johnson needed reliable Anglo Democratic votes from her Senate district, but if she did not produce a district that blacks could indisputably control, she risked losing black voters to John Wiley Price or to Texas House member Fred Blair. It was not because Sen. Johnson wanted a segregated constituency or a segregated district that she drew irregular lines on the map, but precisely because she was trying to protect an interracial coalition that would send her, and not another, more radical politician, to Washington.[17] To anonymous critics in the legislature and Congress, it appeared that "her only interest was in creating a district that she could win" (*FWST*, Dec. 16, 1991, A:13). It is ironic that the courts would later rule that the Thirtieth District was not "narrowly tailored," for, as congressional districts had been in Texas throughout this century, it was tailored narrowly and quite precisely to elect the person who drew its outlines. Second, the more Democratic voters, black and white, that Johnson took from Frost, the more he had to look for substitutes. Eventually, he found them in Tarrant County in part of a complicated three-way swap in which Frost gained black areas from Fort Worth Democratic congressman Pete Geren, Geren acquired white Democrats from the proposed Thirtieth, and Frost gave up South Dallas black areas to the Thirtieth (*FWST*, Aug. 22,

1991, C:1; Aug. 23, 1991, A:11; *AAS,* Aug. 22, 1991, B:1). The trade made all of the politicians and, arguably, their constituents better off, and it certainly forwarded the goal of interracial coalitions: The ideological balance of the Twenty-fourth did not shift so much as to endanger the moderate Frost, who continued to represent a black influence district; the comparatively moderate Johnson [18] got close enough to the magic number of 50 percent, which had the effect of deterring more racially militant challengers; and the more conservative Geren retained enough minority constituents to keep the district from turning Republican immediately but not enough to encourage Anglo liberal opposition to himself.

WHAT MADE moderate Democrats happy made Republicans apoplectic, and they charged Democrats not with a racial purpose but with a partisan one. "These lines are very logical and very rational," state House member Kent Grusendorf (R-Arlington) said of the proposal that the House passed. "The lines have been drawn, dissecting communities very creatively in order to pack Republicans and maximize Democratic representation. . . . This plan was drawn with only one thing in mind, and that is to protect Democratic incumbents, period." His colleague Fred Hill (R-Richardson) specifically denounced the final plan for placing African-American districts in southern Dallas County in District 24 "simply for the single purpose of assuring his [Martin Frost's] re-election because those are Democrat voters." The boundaries of the Thirtieth District, Hill went on, had "nothing to do with minority representation because if we were really concerned about minority representation, we would have drawn this map in such a way that minorities were considered and not simply to elect Democrats" (*FWST,* Aug. 22, 1991, C:1; Transcript of Texas House Floor Debate, Aug. 21, 1991, 190, 195, Aug. 25, 1991, Audiotape 10-B, 27–31, in Texas 1991). It is significant that in considering whether the "predominant reason" for the actions of the Texas legislature in drawing the Thirtieth District was racial, Justice O'Connor did not directly confront this "smoking gun" evidence of a nonracial purpose.

Republicans were no more consistent in their dedication to compact shapes and municipal and county boundaries than were Democrats. Thus, they vehemently protested the move to reduce Joe Barton's Sixth District from an elongated Dallas-to-Houston district to a less lengthy and more socioeconomically homogeneous Metroplex suburban seat. The old Sixth, often referred to as "the most gerrymandered district in Texas," had been designed for conservative Democrat Olin Teague during the late 1960s and had survived to become first Phil Gramm's in 1978 and then, when Gramm left for the Senate in 1984, Joe Barton's. It was the subject of a much-quoted description by state senators Oscar Mauzy and "Babe" Schwartz, which was later misrepresented as applying to the North Carolina Twelfth District: "If you left from the north," Mauzy and Schwartz solemnly pronounced, "and went down Interstate 15 from Dallas in a four-door sedan with all four doors open, and you drove all the way south to Houston, you would kill or seriously maim half the population in the district." [19] Barton, the chief Republican congressional liaison on redistricting, insisted that he should be allowed to keep his district much as it was because it contained College Station and he was a Texas A&M alumnus and his children were then attending that university, which is located in College Station. Nor did Democrats object to the lack of compactness of the Sixth District. They just needed to chop parts of it off, as *Houston Chronicle* reporter R. G. Ratcliffe put it, "so they can create a black congressional district in Dallas while maintaining the security of two districts held by liberal Anglo Democrats." Moreover, Republicans, who in 1981 had staunchly favored splitting Corpus Christi along ethnic lines, just as strongly protested when in 1991 Democrats split several West Texas cities in the same manner (*DMN*, Apr. 21, 1991, A:43 ["four-door sedan"]; *HC*, Dec. 23, 1990, A:1 [Ratcliffe quote]; *AAS*, Apr. 21, 1991, B:1; Transcript of Texas House floor debate, Aug. 21, 1991, 136–40, in Texas 1991). Neither party held closely to such principles when partisan or other advantage conflicted with them.

Indeed, partisan advantage, not surprisingly, best explains the overall differences between congressional redistricting plans offered by Republicans and Democrats. Although Texas had no partisan registration during this period, Republican consultants paid special attention to the patterns in "down-ticket" races such as that for the Court of Criminal Appeals. Despite substantially lower participation, perhaps particularly among minority voters, compared to that in contests for governor, senator, or attorney-general, the votes in these lower visibility races, insiders thought, gave one the best estimate of the core partisanship of each district (Testimony of Jim Duncan, Trial Transcript, *Terrazas v. Slagle*, Dec. 11, 1991, 60–63, 96–100, 120). The 1992 results provide considerable support for that view. Candidates from the same political party carried both congressional and Criminal Appeals Court contests in twenty-eight of the thirty congressional districts.[20] In other words, in all but two districts, the Criminal Appeals Court returns accurately predicted the congressional winner.

Democrats carried twenty-one of the thirty congressional seats in 1992, and their candidate for the Court of Criminal Appeals prevailed in twenty-one as well.[21] If the votes are reaggregated to determine who would have carried each congressional district in the Criminal Appeals race had other plans been in effect, every major Democratic plan gave the same number—twenty-one Democrats; by contrast, all Republican plans gave the Democrats between fifteen and eighteen seats.[22] Using regression techniques similar to those used to produce Table 5.1 above, an expert witness for the State of Texas in *Vera v. Richards* estimated that under the plan proposed by the plaintiffs in that case, Democrats would have carried only seventeen seats in 1992 (Lichtman 1994, 11). If the 1990 governor's race is taken as an indicator, Democratic plans would have produced seventeen to nineteen Democratic victories, while Republican plans would have produced from thirteen to fifteen. The chief difference between Republican and Democratic control of Texas reapportionment, by these measures, was four to six seats in Congress.

In private, where they did not need to posture for the press, Republicans admitted that they did not care much about ethnic minority interests in redistricting. Responding to the Texas Legislative Survey, a poll run by University of Texas–Dallas government professor Greg Thielemann and funded by three newspapers, most Republican members of the state House ranked "helping minorities" last of their four priorities. On a scale of 1 to 4, with 4 being least important, the average Republican score for "helping minorities" was 3.46; "helping your party" ranked first, at 1.66. Democratic House members ranked "helping minorities" at 2.06, just behind "protecting yourself" at 2.03, as their most important goal (*SAL*, Mar. 11, 1991, A:1).

In public, Republicans claimed, as they had a decade earlier, to be the erstwhile best friends of African-Americans and Hispanics, and they appropriated the slick title used by business political action committees in 1981, calling themselves the "Texas Fair Redistricting Committee," which they referred to interchangeably as the "Republican Redistricting Committee" (transcript of trial testimony, Mary Ann Wyatt, *Terrazas v. Slagle*, Dec. 10, 1991, 15–16). "When you draw minority districts," Kent Grusendorf explained in April 1991, "you enhance Republicans. Redistricting is a time when Republicans and minorities have a great deal of common interest." Stripped of Grusendorf's euphemisms, the Republican strategy, noted Dave McNeely of the *Austin American-Statesman*, "was to help minority group members pack as many blacks and Hispanics as possible into some inner-city congressional districts—and to create suburban districts friendly to the GOP" (*AAS*, Apr. 21, 1991, B:1). As McNeely suggested and Republican redistricting consultants made explicit, packing the most reliably Democratic voters was most efficient for Republicans if African-Americans and Latinos could be treated as unitary and cohesive. Then, all one had to do was to set and reach some artificial target to create a "minority district," whether it contained enough actual minority voters to elect anyone or not. One Republican consultant even contended that minority candidates would do better in combination minority districts than in black or Hispanic districts alone (transcript of trial testimony of Henry Flores, *Terrazas v. Slagle*, Dec. 11, 1991, 138–65).[23]

People in Dallas and Houston knew that minority cohesion could not be so blithely assumed. In 1983, the only Hispanic on the Dallas City Council, Ricardo Medrano, lost a runoff to Paul Fielding, an Anglo, in a district that was approximately a third black, a third Latino, and a third Anglo. Although African-Americans had supported Medrano, a member of a prominent Hispanic political family, in his first election in 1979, black political leaders refused to back him in 1983 because many felt that he had been tardy in taking action to abate pollution from a lead smelting operation, because he declined to support efforts to draw a third black-majority district in 1981, and because he refused to pledge to endorse a black for the position in the future. At a press conference after his defeat, Medrano exploded. Progressive Voters League leaders John Wiley Price, Mattie Nash, and Jesse Jones, he charged, "have torn the foundation [of the black-brown coalition] down. Judas got 30 pieces of silver—they got more than 30. Money, that's always been the bottom line" (*DMN*, Apr. 17, 1983, A:20,21; *DTH*, Apr. 17, 1983, A:1; *Williams v. City of Dallas* [1990], 1323).

Houston in 1991 suffered an even more high-profile example of the breakdown of minority cohesion, as black state House member Sylvester Turner lost a bitter mayoral race to Anglo Bob Lanier. Although ugly personal rumors circulating about Turner may have damaged his campaign, Hispanic support for Lanier was public and overwhelming and may have cost Turner election as the first African-American mayor of a major Texas city. "We turned out our voters for Lanier in the mayoral election," Lisa Hernandez of Southwest Voter Registration Education Project later boasted (trial testimony of Robert Eckels, *Terrazas v. Slagle*, Dec. 10, 1991, 119–26; *HC Texas Magazine*, May 3, 1992, 10). If African-Americans or Latinos were to have real opportunities to elect candidates of their choice in Houston, they would have to be separated into different congressional districts. Pooling them by drawing an aesthetically pleasing "minority district" in the middle of Houston would only perpetuate the already boiling ethnic strife—just what Republicans needed to disrupt the Democratic coalition.

THE FIRST PLAN presented by Sen. Eddie Bernice Johnson for a "Hispanic congressional district" in Houston made the district only 44 percent Hispanic in population and excluded the home of the principal Latino on the House Redistricting Committee, Roman Martinez. Widely rumored to covet the seat for himself, Martinez was said to have been furious about Johnson's move. Without naming names, Johnson remarked that the Houston situation was complicated by the fact that some Hispanic leaders wanted to cut the homes of other Hispanics out of the prospective district (*HC*, May 1, 1991, A:26). That was only a small part of the complexity.

The census of 1990 found 644,935 persons of Hispanic origin in Harris

County, a more than sufficient number to form a congressional district of 566,217, the ideal size for Texas. Whether enough of them could be united without damaging the chances of blacks, who had held the Eighteenth District since 1972, and without alienating surrounding Anglo incumbents was more problematic. Craig Washington's Eighteenth District actually contained more Hispanics than blacks, 37 percent of its voting-age population, compared to a black proportion of just 34.5 percent. Extracting the fairly interspersed Hispanic population and adding blacks from three adjacent districts, each of which was about 20 percent black, would somehow have to be accomplished, everyone assumed, in order to avoid charges of retrogression under Section 5 of the VRA (*AAS*, Apr. 21, 1991, B:1).[24] Since only 30–45 percent of the Hispanics of voting age were then registered to vote in Harris County,[25] and since blacks could hardly be assumed to be certain to back a Latino candidate in a primary, the total population would have to be substantially more than 50 percent Hispanic in order to assure the Hispanic community of a good chance to elect a candidate of its choice.

There were essentially two ways to get that population—go northeast and take it from Republican Jack Fields's Eighth District, which would please Democrats and make it impossible to create another suburban Republican district north of Houston, or go southeast and take it from Democrat Mike Andrews's Twenty-fifth District, which would alienate Democrats. Republicans proposed a plan that gutted Andrews's district to create a seat that was 47 percent Hispanic and 15 percent black, and therefore, with approximately equal numbers of black and Hispanic voters, a district of maximum potential interethnic conflict. Andrews's house was carefully placed several miles outside the line of the Republicans' proposed Twenty-fifth (*HC*, Apr. 30, 1991, A:21). There was no way to avoid mixing partisanship with the attempt to create a new Hispanic district.

In Houston as in Dallas, the jockeying of potential candidates for personal advantage combined with partisan factors to affect the shape of the new congressional district. Since the number of state senators in Texas in 1991, thirty-one, was almost the same as the number of members of Congress, thirty, many state senate districts overlapped considerably with congressional seats. With experience in running campaigns in large, similar districts, state senators became the natural predators of congressional incumbents. Sen. Gene Green, a labor union–oriented, Anglo, Democratic state legislator from Houston for twenty years, was an obvious candidate for the new Houston seat, designated early on as the Twenty-ninth. In his position as the principal line-drawer for Harris County congressional districts in the state House, Roman Martinez's "chief aim," according to one report, was "to draw a district that would exclude the home of state Sen. Gene Green." Since Green's home was in the northern part of Houston, this consideration tilted Roman Martinez and his mentor, City Councilman Ben Reyes, who was also interested in going to Congress, toward the pro-Republican option of moving the district south to attack Andrews (*HP*, Apr. 30, 1991, A:11 ["chief aim"]; *HC*, Feb. 3, 1991, C:3; *DMN*, Apr. 15, 1991, A:1).

Sen. Johnson's redrafted plan, which raised the Hispanic population percentage in the Twenty-ninth to 56 percent, was thus not enough to satisfy Rep. Martinez, because Green's home was left in the district. In August, Martinez unveiled a plan that excluded not only Green's house but also Baytown, which was the home territory of longtime LULAC activist Tony Campos, whose son Marc was supporting Al Luna, a bitter rival of Reyes and Martinez, for Congress. The percentages and shapes seemed to matter less than the personalities. "We've got that thing so close now," commented Democratic State Chairman Bob Slagle, who took an active role in the reapportionment, that "it's just a matter of everybody playing for an angle." Finally, Green and Martinez met and agreed that neither would draw the other, or any other prospective Democratic candidate or even campaign consultant, out of the district. As finally meticulously drawn with help from Southwest Voter Registration Education Project, which ironically had acquired its redistricting software without cost from the Republican National Committee earlier, when the Republicans were trying to woo minority activists in Texas, the Twenty-ninth was 60.6 percent Hispanic and 10.2 percent black in population, though only 55.4 percent Hispanic in voting-age population and 26.3 percent in registered voters (*HC*, Feb. 18, 1991, A:11; Aug. 6, 1991, A:11; Aug. 19, 1991, A:1; Aug. 24, 1991, A:26; Dec. 22, 1991, C:1; *HP*, May 15, 1991, A:17; May 16, 1991, A:24; Aug. 6, 1991, A:13; Aug. 25, 1991, A:31; registration and population statistics from Texas Legislative Council).

Partisanship, the desire to protect Anglo as well as black incumbents in adjacent districts, and the personal struggles for power that are an inevitable concomitant of democracy combined with a desire to establish an ethnic district to shape its lines. To represent the complex story as if it were wholly determined by ethnicity would be to misunderstand it fundamentally. And as if to prove that the Twenty-ninth was not a "segregated district," its representative solely dedicated to a single group's undifferentiated interest, three Latinos—Ben Reyes, Al Luna, and Chief Municipal Judge Sylvia Garcia—contested the Democratic primary with Gene Green. After two bitter, racially polarized runoffs with Reyes, Green—with a combination of National Rifle Association and labor union financing and backed by a coalition of Anglos, many blacks, and even a few Mexican-Americans—became the congressman from the "Hispanic district" (*HC*, Jan. 31, 1992, A:21; Feb. 15, 1992, A:26; Feb. 29, 1992, A:1; Mar. 1, 1992, "Voters' Guide" section, 1; Mar. 4, 1992, A:16;

Mar. 5, 1992, A:1; Mar. 11, 1992, A:1; Mar. 27, 1992, A:26; Mar. 31, 1992, A:10; Apr. 15, 1992, A:1; July 25, 1992, A:28; July 29, 1992, A:1; July 30, 1992, A:17). When Reyes entered the race for Congress, Roman Martinez dropped out, deciding instead to contest incumbent state senator John Whitmire, an Anglo, whose seat, designed by a federal district court, was 57 percent Hispanic in population. Putting together a coalition of Anglos and blacks but getting only about 20 percent of the Latino vote, Whitmire eked out a 52–48 percent victory in a nastily fought runoff primary with Martinez (*HC*, Feb. 15, 1992, A:26; Mar. 11, 1992, A:25; Mar. 12, 1992, A:14; Apr. 18, 1992, A:23; Burka 1992). The tidier but almost as large Twenty-ninth district imposed by the district court after the Supreme Court decision in *Bush v. Vera* (1996) cut the Hispanic portion of the population by a quarter, insuring that the Hispanic community in the state's largest city will not be able to elect a candidate of choice in the foreseeable future (*HC*, Aug. 7, 1996, A:6).

HISPANIC population growth in South Texas was so great that there was little controversy over whether to draw a new district there. Nor was the state about to repeat its 1981 decision to pack one district with Hispanics while leaving a next-door district with less than a working majority of Latinos, a decision of which the Justice Department and a federal court in the 1980s had emphatically disapproved. And the presence in the state senate of an ambitious and popular legislator, Frank Tejeda, made the third minority congressional district in the state, the Twenty-eighth, noncontroversial. Drawn by and for Tejeda, the Twenty-eighth provided him with virtually uncontested victories in both the primary and general elections (*SAE*, Apr. 28, 1991, M:2; *AAS*, Mar. 2, 1992, A:1). With markedly less controversy than Eddie Bernice Johnson or Roman Martinez but with just as specific intent to create a minority opportunity district, Frank Tejeda was given a district of his own. Because the edges of the Twenty-eighth were not as ragged as those of the Eighteenth, Twenty-ninth, or Thirtieth, it was not successfully challenged in the district or Supreme courts.

ATTORNEYS for the plaintiffs in *Vera v. Richards* (1994) introduced two novel legal theories that bear on the general question of determining the motives for drawing the subset of districts—the Eighteenth, Twenty-ninth, and Thirtieth—that were at issue in the Supreme Court. In one theory, the attorneys seemed to recognize that the legislature was moved by partisan and personal impulses as well as by desires to allow African-Americans and Latinos to have equal opportunities with whites to elect candidates of their choice, which everyone agreed could be accomplished in Texas in the 1990s only in substantially minority districts. Although in the chief precedent at the time,

Shaw v. Reno (1993), Justice O'Connor had repeatedly stated that race had to be the *sole* reason for district lines for them to be ruled unconstitutional,[26] the plaintiffs announced the theory that *any* use whatsoever of knowledge about where people of different races lived would render a redistricting unconstitutional.[27] It did not matter what the percentages of minorities in the resulting districts were or whether race was employed merely as a means to some other, nonracial end, such as incumbent protection (Hurd 1994a, 1–4). Thus, they challenged not just the three new majority-minority districts, or even the nine total majority-minority districts, but all thirty districts in the state.

Paradoxically, the evidence that the plaintiffs used to infer racial purposes would have required the state to be hyperconscious of race to avoid allegations of racial motives. Completely abjuring any research into the actual process by which the redistricting plan was drawn or into previous redistricting efforts in the state, the plaintiffs merely compared ethnic and district maps and calculated ethnic percentages of split counties and Voter Tabulation Districts ("VTDs"). Unless the ethnic percentages in parts of counties or VTDs in different congressional districts were exactly the same, the plaintiffs, ignoring geography and social patterns entirely, inferred that they had been intentionally split on racial lines (Hurd 1994b, 4–10). To take perhaps the most egregious example, the plaintiffs inferred a racial intent in the split of Johnson County because the part located in Congressional District 6 was 7.8 percent black and Hispanic while that in District 12 was 11.3 percent. They did not consider alternative explanations of the demographic and geographic composition of districts. How the racial balancing needed to get the percentages to come out approximately equal could be accomplished without race-conscious design the plaintiffs did not explain, and their calculus ignored the obligation that the redistricters had felt to minimize population deviations between districts, which had necessitated cutting across county, city, and VTD boundaries. Moreover, if Section 5 is construed as allowing no retrogression in the ethnic percentages of minority opportunity districts in states where Section 5 applies, as Justice O'Connor suggests in *Bush v. Vera* (1996, 1963), then redistricters cannot possibly avoid drawing boundaries in a race-conscious fashion. Finally, this proposed (and rejected) standard would invalidate virtually every redistricting in the country during the twentieth century, at least in states that had significant ethnic conflict or differentiation, and it would open up nearly every conceivable plan in the future to judicial supervision. This seems a bit extreme.

In a second, less developed but apparently deeply felt companion theory, the *Vera* plaintiffs attacked any *politically* conscious redistricting as unconstitutional under *Reynolds v. Sims* (1964) because it discriminates against voters whose candidates lost. It is not clear how seriously this proposal to enable all-powerful courts to "take politics out of redistricting" was meant; the three-judge panel only flirted with it, and the Supreme Court did not consider it (*Vera v. Richards* [1994], 1334). Under the plaintiffs' doctrines, any congressional or legislative district that somehow managed to escape challenge as race-conscious would fall to political consciousness. Among other consequences of such a wildly unrealistic standard would be that arguments about the connections between or comparative weight of ethnic versus incumbent-protecting or partisan factors in redistricting would be legally irrelevant. That turning redistricting over to judges might not remove politics is suggested by the experience of *Terrazas v. Slagle* (1991), in which a brazenly partisan former Texas Republican legislator, Judge James Nowlin, was caught allowing his 1981 redistricting committee colleague, George Pierce, to draw part of the state senate district in which Pierce subsequently ran. Despite Nowlin's self-righteous avowal that his only purpose was to empower ethnic minorities, his plan only slightly amended the Republican party's proposed arrangement of lines. Representatives of minority groups bitterly attacked his scheme, which paired seven Democratic incumbents against each other but fostered no Republican fratricide, and the 1992 outcome produced one less Latino and four fewer Democratic senators than the plan that the legislature had adopted almost certainly would have. The election's casualties included the Democratic senate majority leader and the Democratic chairman of the Redistricting Committee. After an outcry over Nowlin's provable misdeeds, the Fifth Circuit Court of Appeals appointed a committee that conducted a short investigation and slapped the judge on the wrist. Still, it took more pressure to get Nowlin to recuse himself from the case (*DMN*, Dec. 25, 1991, A:1; Jan. 15, 1992, A:1; Feb. 13, 1992, A:36; *TCT*, Dec. 26, 1991, 1; *HC*, Jan. 6, 1992, A:1; Jan. 8, 1992, A:17; Jan. 9, 1992, A:1; Jan. 11, 1992, A:1; Feb. 8, 1992, A:1; Nov. 5, 1992, A:1; Nov. 8, 1992, A:2; *HP*, Jan. 11, 1992, A:1; Jan. 17, 1992, A:11; *AAS*, Jan. 11, 1992, A:1; Jan. 21, 1992, B:1; May 19, 1992, A:9; May 24, 1992, B:2; *FWST*, Jan. 15, 1992, 13; Jan. 16, 1992, 21; July 23, 1992, A:19; *SAL*, Feb. 7, 1992, A:1; Aug. 30, 1992, A:1; *SAE*, Feb. 11, 1992, A:5; *NYT*, Jan. 26, 1992, 14; Politz et al. 1992).[28]

BESIDES generating fanciful legal theories, the *Vera* trial afforded an overview of the 1991 redistricting process that threw considerable light on the motives of those who drew the Houston and Dallas districts, and it suggests that some of the standards that the Supreme Court has erected may be circumvented by mere rhetorical or technical shifts. Evidence brought out during the *Vera* litigation undermines the map's-eye view advanced by the plaintiffs and district court judges that the process of redistricting had one pervasive or overriding purpose. It reveals, first, the decentralization that allowed incumbents and influential prospective candidates to shape their own districts and therefore maximize their election or reelection probabilities free of most top-down constraints; second, the degree to which facts about partisan and racial geographic concentrations could be used interchangeably as predictors of electoral behavior; third, the extent to which elected officials wanted their districts to include or, sometimes, to exclude voters whom they had represented or had had contact with before, characteristics that were often more important to the politicians than the ethnicity, class, or party of voters who might be included in their districts; and fourth, the importance that arbitrary numbers—50 percent, 60 percent, 65 percent, 80 percent—took on, goals that forced those actually drawing the lines to increase the irregularity of districts for reasons that only appeared to be concerned with race or ethnicity.

Asked during her deposition what her involvement was in drawing District 18 in Houston, Eddie Bernice Johnson, chair of the State Senate subcommittee on congressional redistricting in 1991, replied "None." She put Sen. Gene Green in charge of arranging districts for Harris County and Sen. Frank Tejeda in charge of those in South Texas. The correlation between which senators had charge of drawing each new congressional district and the ultimate victors in those districts was exact. Questioned as to why a line was marked at a particular place in Brazos County, Johnson responded: "Frankly I don't know, because on this part of the plan the incumbents did most of the architecture." "Incumbents," she remarked later, "came in and worked the parts of the map that they desired and if it worked in the total picture that's what we did. We basically attempted to satisfy these incumbents." Nor were Democratic incumbents the only ones accommodated, she claimed. "Are you telling me now that what drove this was a friendly bipartisan incumbent protection plan?" a lawyer asked. "Exactly," Sen. Johnson responded. "I was open to everyone who came to see me and it was not all [D]emocratic influence in this plan." "It was bipartisan, there was no attempt to prefer and maximize the [D]emocratic representation?" the lawyer continued. "It was an effort to protect those incumbents because there was no way I could survive without doing it in this process," the senator replied (Johnson dep., 47–48, 74–75, 101, 121).

Legislative redistricting technician Christopher Sharman, who observed and helped craft many of the details of the maps as he sat at a computer terminal and assisted elected officials and their staff members in drawing districts, reflected the same view. "There were very few people that were involved in the whole districting map," he remarked. "It mostly was regional. . . . Dallas/Fort Worth was a region; Harris County was a region; the [Rio Grande] Valley was a region; Bexar County [San Antonio] was a region. . . . East Texas was certainly a region." Although El Paso congressman Ron Coleman was designated by the Democrats in the delegation as their liaison on redistricting with the legislature, Coleman and his staffer Paul Rogers, according to Sharman, "just kind of observed the process and tried to play mediator for certain conflicts." Unlike Speakers Mutscher and Clayton or Lt. Governors Barnes and Hobby in 1971 and 1981, Lt. Gov. Bob Bullock was only a mediator in 1991, and House Speaker Gib Lewis's principal role, said Sharman, was to throw "a wrench, so to speak, into the works" at the last moment because of a parochial concern with his hometown, Fort Worth. Strikingly unlike Gov. Bill Clements in 1981, Gov. Ann Richards barely rated any mention at all in connection with congressional redistricting in 1991. Only in the final negotiations did Richards threaten to veto any plan that paired Congressmen Bryant and Frost (Sharman dep., 82–84, 104–5, 116; *DTH*, Sept. 1, 1991, A:1). Although individual Republican congressmen directly or indirectly made their wishes known to the Democrats who were in charge of redistricting, and although the party, through its "Fair Redistricting Committee," produced a comprehensive plan, there was no mention of comprehensive negotiations between leaders of the two parties in the newspapers or depositions. Such high-level interparty negotiations, had they taken place, would have been another means of providing authoritative control.

The combination of a lack of overall direction and the necessity to satisfy incumbents of both parties produced both bitter conflicts and the resolution of those conflicts by the drawing of irregular lines. The fact that this happened in areas containing few minority voters as well as in those with many minority voters, suggests that the irregularities reflected the particular interests of politicians more than they did racial interests. Sharman described a meeting in Lt. Gov. Bob Bullock's office on a Sunday, apparently August 20, 1991, at which staffers presented a tentative map to congressmen Mike Andrews, John Bryant, Jim Chapman, Chet Edwards, Martin Frost, "Kika" De La Garza, Pete Geren, Ralph Hall, Greg Laughlin, Solomon Ortiz, Bill Sarpalius, and Charles Wilson—twelve of the nineteen Democratic incumbents. There were "numerous conflicts that arose when they saw what their districts actually looked like, and then the process went on from there." Bullock "basically went congress member by congress member asking them what it was that they needed changed with their districts in order to be happy." A typical example was in East Texas. Congressman Charlie Wilson in the Second District managed to rid himself of those parts of Nacogdoches County that had voted against him, which produced a ripple effect in Congressman Jim Chapman's First District. Since Chapman did not want Smith County, where he had not been successful in the past, and Congressman Ralph Hall did not want to give up what was for him good territory in Hunt County, Gregg County ended up being split. One of the several splits made to Denton County came because a minor newspaper editor "just hated Congressman Hall and wrote very nasty things about him," and Hall wanted to jettison the editor's community. Congressman Bill Sarpalius didn't want to give up an airport in Lubbock, while Eddie Bernice Johnson wanted her district to include Dallas/Fort Worth International Airport. Other seemingly anomalous extensions to Johnson's district were the results of her desires to pick up areas where she could raise campaign funds from Jewish voters and from middle-class blacks who had moved into Collin County, some distance from central Dallas, and her effort to include an overwhelmingly white but liberal area in Grand Prairie that had provided her margin of victory—over a black opponent—in the 1986 State Senate race. In San Antonio, Democrat Albert Bustamante and Republican Lamar Smith insisted on having areas containing their houses included in their districts, and Smith was pleased to have communities where key campaign contributors lived within his district's perimeters (Sharman dep., 53, 106–9, 116–20, 124–26, 181–84, 193–95; Johnson dep., 136–41, 162–65; *SAL*, Aug. 8, 1991, B:1).

Having sponsored the armed forces base closing bill, Republican Dick Armey received so much opposition when the Carswell Air Force Base in Tarrant County was slated for closure that he moved his home from Tarrant to Denton County and made sure that his new Twenty-sixth Congressional District excluded as much of Tarrant as he could manage. " 'He's getting as far away from Carswell as possible,' said state Rep. Jim Horn, R-Denton" (*DRC*, Aug. 8, 1991, A:1). The home of a Republican legislator who was a possible opponent of Armey's conveniently ended up in another district. In overwhelmingly Hispanic South Texas, splits or proposed splits in the towns of Harlingen and Kingsville involved a prospective 1994 contest between Congressman Solomon Ortiz of Corpus Christi and State Senator Eddie Lucio Jr., of Brownsville, both Democrats and both Hispanics. Lucio told the *Harlingen Valley Morning Star* that Ortiz's Twenty-seventh congressional district was being shaped " 'to ensure Solomon gets elected time and time again' " (Johnson dep., 151; *PSC*, Aug. 28, 1991, A:1; *HVMS*, July 17, 1991, A:1).[29]

Naturally, in more ethnically mixed areas, ethnicity was used by both Democrats and Republicans as an index of voting behavior—what Justice O'Connor referred to in her principal opinion in *Bush v. Vera* (1996), 1956) as using "race as a proxy." The principal dividing line in Texas society since the days of the Republic, race could hardly be ignored in politics. As Teel Bivins (R-Amarillo), the chief Republican spokesman on redistricting in the Senate, put it: "We started first with minority communities in the state and tried to draw every minority district that we could. Now I will be the first to admit to you, as I've stated on this floor previously, that when you take that approach and you create the ability for minorities to elect one of their own, that there is clearly an indirect benefit to Republicans who are going to seek to run in other districts." Republicans were at least as self-conscious about using racial and ethnic characteristics to help their party and their incumbents as Democrats were. It was just, as Bivins's statement clearly sets out, that Republicans wanted to pack minorities and make sure that there were too few minority voters outside the packed districts to elect Anglo Democrats, whereas Democrats, as the depositions of Johnson and Sharman reaffirm, wanted to include enough reliably Democratic minorities in their districts to protect them from Republicans (Transcript of Texas Senate Committee of the Whole, Aug. 24, 1991, Tape 2, 5 [Bivins] in Texas 1991; Johnson dep., 117–20; Sharman dep., 78).

But the same depositions underline the fact that even in Dallas and Houston race was not the only index, and that if it had not been available, proxies would have been nearly as efficient in spotting voters useful to incumbents and other prospective candidates. Just as ethnicity can be a proxy for political proclivities, those proclivities can likewise serve as proxies for race or, in some cases, religion. Thus, an overwhelmingly Republican area is very likely to be white, extremely wealthy, and/or fundamentalist Protestant. As a practical matter, redistricters can use figures on several variables interchangeably, and they will choose whichever one is most convenient or is available at the most detailed level. Since in the 1990 census, ethnicity was recoverable below the VTD level, while voting records were generally kept at the VTD level or higher, technicians chose to focus on race. It would have been possible, however, to draw districts with nearly the same minority proportions simply by choosing the most Democratic areas, and analogously, to draw a white fundamentalist Protestant district by choosing the most Republican precincts.

Thus, to determine which voters best fit her conception of the Thirtieth District, Sen. Johnson used results of referenda on rapid transit and school bonds, as well as race, other election returns, and personal observations. "[W]hat we also looked at is voting patterns, and voting patterns were just as easy to get [on the legislature's 'Red Apple' computer system] as ethnic background." Frost and Bryant, she said, did not ask to have minority voters per se put into their districts, but they did ask for Democrats. "They were fighting over those blue voters [Democrats, in Red Apple's code]. They wanted blue voters, the voting patterns that showed up blue on the computer screen. . . . Traditionally, minority voters vote [D]emocrat[ic] overwhelmingly, 97, 98, 99 percent, so when you're looking for [D]emocrats you're looking virtually for the same population" (Johnson dep., 85–86, 117, 144).

Nor did Johnson want every black in the Thirtieth. Chris Sharman's deposition confirmed newspaper reports that Johnson wished to avoid African-American areas in Dallas that might support County Commissioner John Wiley Price, and added the information that Johnson preferred to bypass

Duncanville because it was the territory of Royce West, a prominent black lawyer who had run a high-visibility campaign for district attorney a few years earlier, and who was another potential candidate for Congress against her. Johnson also wanted to exclude a small black area north of downtown Dallas because she knew, not from the census, but presumably from personal observation, that it was filled with noncitizen, transient, nonpolitical Haitian apartment dwellers. As this example emphasizes, even if there were no detailed census, politicians would still be able to rely on their own rough knowledge of the sociopolitical traits of various areas to tailor districts for themselves (Sharman dep., 59–60, 79–80; *DMN*, Aug. 8, 1991, A:1; Aug. 9, 1991, A:1).

Just as Johnson picked and chose among both blacks and whites, Bryant and Frost and, in Houston, Green and Martinez did not cast their ethnic nets blindly. Politics was the end, and race not always the means. More than just raising their black percentages, Bryant and Frost, according to Johnson, "mostly wanted people they had represented before that they thought would be familiar with their name[s]." Sharman's instructions in building District 30 for Johnson were to find Democrats, especially black Democrats, "that were not old constituents of" Frost or Bryant, because the congressmen were "very interested" in keeping people who knew them. Gene Green, who had long represented heavily Latino Baytown and Hispanic areas north of downtown Houston, wanted them in the Twenty-ninth Congressional District, and for the same reason, Roman Martinez did not. As Sharman put it, "Roman Martinez was trying to include Hispanics that lived in the southern end of the county that had never been represented by Gene Green, didn't know who Gene Green was." And while Green favored including in the Twenty-ninth District the middle-class black area of Pleasantville that he represented in the State Senate as well as parts of Houston dominated by Central Americans, who might not follow the Mexican-American lead, Martinez disagreed and won out. On the other hand, Martinez asked to include his whole State House district within the Twenty-ninth, in spite of the fact that 10 percent of its population was black, and he pushed to take in areas, whatever their ethnic percentages, that previous elections had proven to be "not racially polarized" against Latinos (Johnson dep., 82, 146; Sharman dep., 51, 55, 60–63, 160–61, 169; Martinez dep., I, 33–34; II, 16, 36–37; III, 17; *HP*, Aug. 20, 1991, A:9; Aug. 24, 1991, A:23; *AAS*, Aug. 12, 1991, A:4).

Judge Edith Jones for the district court and Justice O'Connor for the Supreme Court made a good deal of statements by Sen. Eddie Bernice Johnson in the 1992 *Terrazas v. Slagle* trial and statements by the state government in Texas's VRA Section 5 submission to the Justice Department that emphasized racial motives underlying the boundaries of these districts. Asked whether the shape of the Thirtieth District reflected in part an effort "to aid Congressman Bryant or Congressman Frost," Johnson replied that "I wouldn't do anything but look out for Black voters." In its Section 5 narrative, the State declared that "throughout the course of the Congressional redistricting process, the lines of the proposed District 30 were constantly reconfigured in an attempt to maximize the voting strength for this black community in Dallas County." While it were trying to convince the Justice Department to preclear its congressional plan, the State never mentioned incumbency protection, the effort to fine tune the Thirtieth District for Johnson alone, or any other explanations for the lines. Is this good evidence for Judge Jones's conclusion that Johnson's "*sole* focus in drawing the district" was racial (*Vera v. Richards* [1994], 1320, 1339; *Bush v. Vera* [1994], 1956–57)?

There are three reasons not to put much weight on such evidence in this case and, by analogy, in others. First, as Justice John Paul Stevens pointed out in his dissent, the focus of a Section 5 inquiry is whether the electoral change under consideration had the purpose or effect of disadvantaging minorities, particularly whether it left them in worse shape than they would have been without the law. Other reasons for action are simply irrelevant to the purpose of such a document (*Bush v. Vera* [1996], 1985, n. 24 [Stevens, dissent]). Second, Johnson, who was at the time running for election and who wanted to protect herself from the well-founded public perception that she had designed the district to hurt potential black opponents and that she had compromised with white moderates and liberals in drawing the lines, the same criticism that she had joined in so vociferously during the 1981 redistricting, had overwhelming self-interested reasons for dissimulating about her conduct. Third, Johnson's statements and those of the State in this instance were contradicted by the weight of evidence from contemporary newspapers, which was not produced in the context of a trial or by people with an obvious interest in the outcome of a legal case and was therefore more believable. Even "smoking gun" statements need corroboration and interpretation.

A detailed examination of the redistricting process also emphasizes the importance of arbitrary percentages in determining boundaries. Black leaders in Dallas insisted on a district that was 50 percent black in population and loudly threatened to protest to the Justice Department and to sue if a district that was only 47 percent black was approved (*DMN*, Aug. 8, 1991, A:1; Aug. 9, 1991, A:1; Aug. 19, 1991, A:13; Aug. 22, 1991, A:1; *AAS*, Aug. 20, 1991, B:1; *AN*, Aug. 20, 1991, C:3; *HP*, Aug. 22, 1991, A:37; *DTH*, Aug. 22, 1991, A:31; Sept. 1, 1991, A:1; Fred Blair, in Transcript of Texas House Floor Debate, Aug. 21, 1991, 39–42, in Texas 1991). Roman Martinez agreed that Gene Green could draw his own house, which was in a majority-Anglo area, into the Twenty-ninth

District only if the district's Hispanic percentage remained over 60 percent, which probably not coincidentally was the same percentage as that in Martinez's State House district. The only way to include Green's neighborhood and keep the Latino percentage over that symbolic threshold was to divide a great many voter tabulation districts. Republican Teel Bivins predicted that the Justice Department and federal judges would prefer his plan over that adopted by the legislature because the GOP plan contained a district that was 65 percent combined minority, failing to note that the 40 percent of the district that was Hispanic in fact constituted only 25.6 percent of the voting-age population and only 11.1 percent of the registered voters. Despite producing the magic number of 65 percent, Sen. Johnson noted, the Bivins plan only constructed another influence district. And late in the process of redistricting, Rep. Pete Geren insisted that 80 percent of the population in his district be located in Tarrant County, which caused ripple effects in adjacent districts and county splits in rural counties close to the Metroplex. Geren, according to Sharman, wanted his district to encompass "[R]epublican and suburban . . . areas that he felt he would run better in or would do better in than most [D]emocrats" (Martinez dep., I, 28–31; Texas Senate Committee of the Whole, transcript of debate, Aug. 24, 1991, Tape 2, 3, 9–11, in Texas 1991; Sharman dep., 86–90; statistics from Texas Legislative Council). In other words, the conservative Geren, who had replaced the much more liberal Jim Wright, wished to design his district to protect himself from a liberal challenge in a Democratic primary.

All these details give substance to the generalizations of Dave McNeely of the *Austin American-Statesman,* who had closely attended the redistricting story:

> Drawing those new districts, while still seeking to protect Democratic incumbents like Martin Frost and John Bryant, who have enjoyed strong support from minorities, has brought some awesomely illogical district lines. . . .
>
> The districts they have drawn are largely at the behest of the 19 incumbent Democrats in Congress, with new minority districts in Houston, Dallas and San Antonio.
>
> The Democratic incumbents also seek to lop off unwanted territory that is infested with Republicans, and give it to Texas' eight Republican congressmen.
>
> While some of the Republican congressmen complain about that, most are privately happy, because it means their districts become so Republican that they are in no danger from pesky Democrats. And under

the current Republican ethic, Republican incumbents are almost always left free of serious challenge in the GOP primary. (*AAS*, Aug. 15, 1991, A:17)

Republican editorialists agreed. Decrying the bifurcation—along county lines —of Amarillo, the *Amarillo News* declared that "the only people of Texas who will truly benefit from this plan appear to be the two incumbent congressmen. The redrawn districts gives [*sic*] [Larry] Combest [R-Lubbock] the part of Amarillo that is considered a Republican stronghold, while [Bill] Sarpalius [D-Amarillo] gets areas that are more entrenched with Democratic voters." The cities were split, according to Delwin Jones (R-Lubbock), vice-chair of the State House Redistricting Committee, because " 'Sarpalius [is] hunting for every Democratic vote he can find.' " Even the *Wall Street Journal*, decrying the shape of the Thirtieth District, admitted that "it would have been easy to draw rational minority districts, but then several white Democratic incumbents would have been in political jeopardy with the loss of minority voters" (*AN*, Aug. 7, 1991, A:4; Aug. 26, 1991, A:1; *WSJ*, Oct. 18, 1991, A:14).

Although the legislative leaders on redistricting did not broadcast the messy details in public, they did quite forthrightly represent the results of those often idiosyncratic boundaries and the process that produced them. Addressing the House on the day that the almost-final plan passed, Redistricting Committee chair Tom Uher (D-Bay City) remarked:

> Because of the flexibility that we had due to the fact that we had three additional seats, we were able to try to design districts that would recognize each incumbent and how that incumbent might be able to win in a district, having a reasonable chance to win in that district. In each of the new districts, we attempted to draw districts that would permit certain candidates who wanted to run to be elected from those new districts. (Texas House, Transcript of Floor Debate, Aug. 21, 1991, 141–42, Texas 1991)

WHILE NO ONE doubts that the Texas redistricting of 1991 was race-conscious and that race played a role in fashioning the boundaries, no one who has reviewed the evidence laid out in considerable detail in this chapter can reasonably conclude that race was the *sole* factor in shaping the Eighteenth, Twenty-ninth, and Thirtieth districts. Once it was decided to create two new minority opportunity districts in Houston and the Metroplex, the actual boundaries, the zigs and zags and protrusions that attracted critics' eyes and without which the Supreme Court apparently would not have found them unconstitutional, were more the products of partisan, personal, and idiosyncratic considerations than racial ones.

It would have been possible to draw districts that scored higher on an index of compactness if legislators had not desired to enable African-Americans and Latinos to have an opportunity to elect candidates of their choice, as the solons thought the VRA, the Constitution, and, for some, their consciences required. Of course, had partisan, personal, and incumbent-protecting considerations somehow been ignored, it would have been possible to draw much more compact majority-minority districts. Not to have drawn majority-minority districts would have risked having the Justice Department refuse to preclear the plan under the VRA; what federal courts had condemned as the discriminatory records of the 1971 and 1981 legislatures could have been counted against the 1991 legislature in a constitutional challenge based on discriminatory intent; and many legislators stated, and some no doubt genuinely believed, that to establish such districts was simply the right thing to do.

It would have been possible to sketch boundaries that looked "prettier" on a flat, featureless map if legislators had not been concerned about protecting incumbents Frost and Bryant in the north and Andrews and Washington in the south. As all the previous reapportionments, particularly that of 1981, demonstrate, legislators always pay close attention to the effect of redistricting on the fortunes of incumbents.

It would have been possible to draw districts with shorter perimeters and with much less controversy if legislators with power over redistricting, senators Eddie Bernice Johnson and Gene Green and Rep. Roman Martinez, had not been concerned with guarding themselves against rivals, often rivals from their own ethnic group. District lines in America have always reflected struggles for power, in Texas as elsewhere, as the 1971 redistricting starkly illustrates. Should anyone be surprised that minority politicians do not act very differently from majority politicians, that they followed the same real—not cosmetic and rhetorical—"traditional districting principles" as everyone else? Are such practices only unconstitutional if minority politicians or moderate or liberal Anglo Democrats follow them? If not, why have the courts discovered only lately that noncompact districts are objectionable, and then only if they bound minority opportunity districts?

It would have been possible to avoid much heated controversy and many lawsuits if there had been no question of partisan or ideological advantage connected with the establishment of majority-minority districts in 1981 and 1991. Republicans and conservative Democrats wanted to pack undifferentiated minorities into central-city districts in order to replace liberal and moderate Anglo Democrats with people with whom they were more ideologically compatible. The targeted Democrats wanted to retain their seats at the expense of conservatives if possible but at the expense of minority candidates if necessary. Many of the irregularities in district lines were the consequences of efforts to produce certain outcomes not in the majority-minority districts but in the adjacent districts where African-Americans or Latinos were distinctly in the minority.

It is conceivable that there are instances in which a desire to create districts for separate racial or ethnic groups is the only explanation for all the twists and turns of legislative boundaries. The 1991 Texas congressional plan, which, as an analysis of the 1971 and 1981 redistrictings so clearly shows, closely followed the state's real "traditional districting principles" of partisan, ideological, personal, and racial advantage, was not such an instance.

CHAPTER SEVEN

Intent and Effect
in Law and History

*L*ike historians, judges perch on the edge of social science. Historians explain particular events or sets of events by invoking, usually implicitly, generalizations about human behavior that could be formulated as explicit social scientific laws. A historian trying to account for the fact that in 1972 Barbara Jordan became the first African-American member of Congress ever elected from Texas would note that as a state senator on the redistricting committee, she had the ability to shape her eventual congressional district, and the historian would rely on a generalization such as the one that politicians typically act in their own self-interest, or even that humans in general do, to flesh out the explanation.[1] Because the generalization seems so commonsensical, at least to Americans of the late twentieth century, the historian would probably not refer to it explicitly or even decide for himself at what level of generality he meant to couch it. In a similar fashion, judges decide particular cases, usually invoking previous cases as precedents and not bothering to make fully explicit the general principles that they are invoking. Indeed, because they are developed case by case, those principles may only become apparent long after particular cases are decided. Contradictory precedents and principles often give judges leeway to choose different outcomes of cases, just as clashing generalizations about human behavior give historians and other social scientists room to explain different outcomes of events. Neither judges nor historians customarily set out in detail exactly what methods they have used or what generalizations they have appealed to. In many instances, discussions of methods or principles may be unnecessary, but not at this time in voting rights law. As this chapter and the next will show, the Supreme Court since at least 1976 has required plaintiffs in racial equal protection and Fifteenth Amendment cases to prove that the laws or practices that they allege discriminate against them were adopted with a discriminatory purpose; moreover, in the 1995 case of *Miller v. Johnson,* the Court ruled that plaintiffs in "racial gerrymandering" suits must prove that the "predominant motive" for the challenged district lines was racial.[2]

The Supreme Court in *Miller* set out no standards for proving "predominance," or even "motive," "purpose," or "intent.[3] If the law of intent in voting rights cases is to become fair and predictable and if historians and others who contribute their analyses to such cases or judge them afterwards are to be consistent, it is imperative to try to establish explicit criteria for determining motives. In such essentially empirical inquiries, judges and legal scholars have no particular advantages over historians of electoral rules and behavior, whose normal business is analyzing large amounts of qualitative and quantitative information in order to determine the causes and effects of particular actions (e.g., Kousser 1974; Kleppner 1982; Argersinger 1992).[4] Indeed, historians who specialize in a subject area, who are often aware of analogous circumstances and relevant scholarship and who are likely to be able to put particular events into their full historical context, may be better qualified for such tasks than many judges, who are necessarily generalists, concerned with myriad legal questions in diverse areas of the law. Chapters 2 through 6 of this book provide sample analyses of the motives for adopting various electoral rules or boundaries, from which implicit organizing principles can be extracted. Logic, conventional historical practices, and the pronouncements of various federal courts yield additional insights into how one should go about proving intent, especially in voting rights cases. Such a discussion may also be useful to historians and political scientists in inquiries that have nothing to do with legal cases, for neither discipline has spawned many discussions of how to analyze qualitative evidence systematically.

It will be instructive first to retrace the steps that the Supreme Court took in deciding that establishing motives was necessary in equal protection cases, for they reveal the arguments for and against effect and intent tests and introduce many of the issues related to their application to voting rights cases. How have the justices treated these issues in classic cases such as *Plessy v. Ferguson* (1896) and *Brown v. Board of Education* (1954)? To what extent are the concepts of intent and effect separable? Is effect or impact a simple, objective notion, while motive is necessarily subjective and ill-defined? What patterns of impact has the Court taken to be necessary to prove discrimination? What sorts of evidence of purposes have courts demanded and how have they weighed it? Have judges been consistent in requiring the showing of intent, and even if they have not, have they followed the same steps in assessing intent in each case where they held that it was required? Is analyzing motives a hopelessly irregular, disorderly task, or is it possible to spell out a fairer, more systematic methodology for determining intent than judges or commentators previously have?

THE U.S. SUPREME COURT made its first pronouncements on intent in racial discrimination cases more than a century ago.[5] In its 1884 and 1885 terms, three cases challenging San Francisco's regulation of laundries raised the issue directly, and the Court's resolution of them has interesting implications for more recent history (*Barbier v. Connolly* [1884]; *Soon Hing v. Crowley* [1885]; *Yick Wo v. Hopkins* [1886]). Hardworking Chinese dominated the laundry business in San Francisco during the 1870s and 80s. Popular nativist agitation led the city government to pass a series of regulations, impartial on their face, that mandated health and fire inspections, banned night work, and required special licenses for laundries operated in wooden structures, on the pretext that they represented fire hazards (Saxton 1971, 113–56; Issel and Cherny 1986, 125–30; McClain 1994, 43–76, 98–132). The purpose of these and other related ordinances, the Board of Supervisors announced—though not in the text of the laws—was to "drive [the Chinese] to other states" (quoted in Daniels 1988, 39). In cases in 1874 and 1876, two local court judges in San Francisco struck down a license tax on laundries on the grounds that its fee schedule discriminated against the poor, but they disagreed on whether it was proper for judges to consider the Board of Supervisors's anti-Chinese motives for passing the ordinance. While Judge John Stanly declared that "this Court has nothing to do with the secret [i.e., not expressly mentioned in the text of the law] motives or intentions of the body which passed the order," Judge Samuel B. McKee announced that such an inquiry was altogether proper, but unnecessary in this instance, because the "unequal, unreasonable and unjust" effect of the law was enough to void it under general principles of common law (McClain 1994, 52–54).

It was a decade before a San Francisco laundry case reached the U.S. Supreme Court, but the opinions in two of the three cases that the justices heard touched the same questions of intent and effect that Stanly and McKee had discussed. Two of the lawsuits, *Barbier v. Connolly* and *Soon Hing v. Crowley*, challenged the anti–night work provision, the first charging it was an unreasonable infringement on the rights of anyone, no matter what his race, to labor and to acquire property, the second impugning it as a subterfuge for racial discrimination. Sustaining the ordinance against the first challenge as a standard exercise of the police power, Justice Stephen J. Field distinguished in the second case between the purposes and the prejudices of legislators and rejected evidence about their prejudices as improper for judges to consider:

The motives of the legislators, considered as to the purposes they had in view, will always be presumed to be to accomplish that which follows as the natural and reasonable effect of their enactments. Their motives, considered as the moral inducements for their votes, will vary with the different members of the legislative body. The diverse character of such motives, and the impossibility of penetrating into the hearts of men and ascertaining the truth, precludes all such inquiries as impracticable and futile. And in the present case, even if the motives of the supervisors were as alleged, the ordinance would not be thereby changed from a legitimate police regulation, unless in its enforcement it is made to operate only against the class mentioned; and of this there is no pretense. (*Soon Hing v. Crowley* [1884], 710–11)

The logic of Field's position was that the judiciary would consider the intent of the legislators as possibly probative but instead of seeking direct evidence[6] of intent would deduce what motivated them from the likely effects of the law. Moreover, in Field's view, intent by itself was insufficient to determine a decision. Plaintiffs had to prove that the effect of the regulation harmed them in order to overturn it. This "reasonable foreseeability" standard, so long established, is of course particularly pertinent to election laws, shaped as they are by politicians whose self-interest could hardly be more involved.[7]

Fourteen months after *Soon Hing,* the Court, in the third unanimous opinion of this trilogy, issued its decision in the more famous case of *Yick Wo v. Hopkins.* What apparently moved the Court to decide for the plaintiffs in this case, but not in the previous two, was that the ordinance on its face gave the Board of Supervisors the power to discriminate between whites and Chinese in granting licenses to laundries in wooden buildings and that it was demonstrated that the power had been used in precisely this fashion. The ordinance had been adopted, Yick Wo's lawyers contended, "for the purpose of discriminating against him and his countrymen," and it was "enforced so as to accomplish that result" (McClain 1994, 116). Quoting from U.S. Circuit Court Judge Lorenzo Sawyer's opinion in a companion case, which referred to "the notorious public and municipal history of the times" and declared that the anti-Chinese purpose of the ordinance "must be apparent to every citizen of San Francisco," Justice Stanley Matthews emphasized not only the fact that every Chinese applicant, but only one Caucasian, who applied for the necessary license was turned down but also that the ordinance evidenced by its very terms a discriminatory "necessary tendency." An elementary cross-classification table demonstrates dramatically the overwhelming effect that so impressed the Court, making plain that the discretion open to the supervisors was employed in a biased manner (see Table 7.1). But no matter how

TABLE 7.1. Laundry License Approval
and Race of Ownership in San Francisco, 1880s

| | Race of Laundry Operator | |
License Decisions	Chinese	Other
Granted	0	80
Not Granted	201	1

Source: *Yick Wo v. Hopkins*, 118 U.S. 356 (1886).

necessary proof of effect was to sustaining the claim that rights had been violated, evidence not available on the face of the ordinance was obviously also important. Otherwise, how did the Court distinguish between the impartial "tendency" of the health and fire inspections, which foreclosed a legal attack, and the "opportunities . . . of unequal and unjust discrimination" in the administration of the wooden building ordinances, which facilitated a successful lawsuit (*Yick Wo v. Hopkins* [1886], 362-74)?

One soaring sentence in Matthews's opinion invited further litigation:

> Though the law itself be fair on its face, and impartial in appearance, yet, if it is applied and administered by public authority with an evil eye and an unequal hand, so as practically to make unjust and illegal discriminations between persons in similar circumstances, material to their rights, the denial of equal justice is still within the prohibition of the constitution. (*Yick Wo v. Hopkins* [1886], 373-74).

This invitation was taken up by an obscure black lawyer from Greenville, Mississippi, Cornelius J. Jones, who was trying to overturn the state's notorious 1890 "disfranchising" constitution by asking Congress to unseat representatives elected under its voting provisions. Jones's African-American client, Henry Williams, was convicted of murder before an all-white jury drawn from the voter rolls. Pointing to the discretion granted to registrars to discriminate against blacks through the "understanding"[8] and other clauses in the constitution and quoting from newspaper reports of the debates at the constitutional convention, whose delegates repeatedly avowed their racist purposes, Jones asked the Court to void Williams's conviction and overturn the Mississippi constitution at the same time (*Williams v. Mississippi* [1898]; Kousser 1991b, 687, n. 451). Ignoring the guarantee of racially impartial suffrage in the Fifteenth Amendment, Jones relied solely on the equal protection clause of the Fourteenth. Although the relevant state constitutional provision was at least as suspicious on its face as the San Francisco laundry ordinance thrown out in *Yick Wo* and although the Mississippi Supreme Court had, in a companion case, admitted the racist intent of the convention (*Ratliff v. Beale* [1896], 865), Jones had failed to show that blacks were actually disfranchised by the constitution. Perhaps Jones thought that demonstrating their absence from the jury panel was sufficient and more relevant than their exclusion from the state's voter rolls, which would have been difficult to prove anyway, since no official records of registration by race were kept in Mississippi at that time. The Mississippi constitution and associated laws "do not on their face discriminate between the races," intoned Justice Joseph McKenna disingenuously, "and it has not been shown that their actual administration was evil; only that evil was possible under them" (*Williams v. Mississippi* [1896], 225).

Although historians have sometimes treated *Williams* as a more positive endorsement of the "Mississippi Plan" than it was, strictly construed, contemporary disfranchisers gave it a more circumscribed reading and feared its apparent implication that proof of a racially discriminatory effect would invalidate southern electoral laws and administrative practices (Woodward 1951, 322–23; Kousser 1991b, n. 458). The legal threats were particularly acute in Louisiana and Alabama, which adopted versions of the "grandfather clause" to allow illiterate and propertyless whites to assume that they, but not blacks, would be able to register to vote once the new constitutions went into effect. Delegates to the Alabama constitutional convention of 1901 were so openly racist and the registrars' subsequent discrimination was so flagrant, that black educator Booker T. Washington had no trouble secretly raising and disbursing the money to finance a legal challenge (Kousser 1974, 58–62, 162–71; Kousser 1991b, 688, n. 460; Meier 1957, 111). Appending several speeches from the constitutional convention debates to his briefs as direct evidence of intent, African-American lawyer Wilford H. Smith demonstrated the requisite effect in two ways. First, the lead plaintiff, literate federal courthouse janitor Jackson W. Giles and twelve other black Alabamians swore that they were qualified to vote under the law but had been denied registration solely because of their race. Deprived of their previous sport of making up election returns, officials turned to inventing preposterous questions. For instance, Elbert Thornton, a Barbour County African-American, swore that he was able to answer all of a series of questions about government except the following: "What are the differences between Jeffersonian Democracy and the Calhoun principles as compared to the Monroe Doctrine?" Second, Smith presented extensive newspaper reports on the comparative numbers of blacks and whites who registered under the new constitution in numerous localities around the state. According to figures published in the state's leading newspaper, 75 percent of the whites but only 1 percent of the blacks in Alabama were allowed to register to vote in 1902. Similar suits were filed in Louisiana and Virginia (Kousser 1974, 61; 1991b, 689 nn. 462–63).

Faced with compelling direct proof of intent, prima facie evidence in the terms of the constitution, and both individual and collective documentation of the overwhelmingly racially discriminatory effects of the law, U.S. district court Judge Thomas G. Jones, a former Alabama governor who had been a delegate to the 1901 state constitutional convention, invoked the "political questions doctrine," arguing that this was not the sort of question courts could deal with. While seeming to admit the sufficiency of evidence of both intent and effect, "liberal" Supreme Court Justice Oliver Wendell Holmes, writing for a six-man majority, declared the courts unable to counter the power of a state that was so adamant in passing and administering its laws in a discriminatory fashion. Furthermore, if the Court granted Giles's wish to throw out the whole scheme of suffrage regulations as unconstitutional, Holmes continued, in a sophomorically clever argument, under what provisions could Giles then be registered to vote (*MDA*, Oct. 13, 1902, 18; *Giles v. Harris* [1903])?[9]

Just as Holmes blatantly ignored both substantive and jurisdictional precedents, which the dissenters in *Giles v. Harris* vigorously pointed out, the Supreme Court a decade later utterly ignored the precedent of *Giles*. *Guinn and Beal v. U.S.* (1915) was originally brought by Oklahoma Republicans who feared the loss of their black supporters and reluctantly carried on by the national administration, as part of William Howard Taft's successful effort to gain renomination as the Republican presidential candidate in 1912, and more avidly by the just-organized NAACP. In its decision in *Guinn*, the Supreme Court overturned a 1910 amendment to the Oklahoma state constitution that allowed illiterates to register to vote if they were descended from men enfranchised before the passage of the Fifteenth Amendment. No direct evidence of intent or of more general effects than the denial of a few blacks' right to vote was presented, and Louisiana-bred Chief Justice Edward Douglass White's opinion in this and a companion case from Maryland did not cite *Yick Wo*, *Williams*, or *Giles*. Doubtless recalling his own "conservative" political faction's opposition to the grandfather clause in the 1898 Louisiana constitutional convention, White ruled similar clauses from Oklahoma and Maryland unconstitutional because the provisions revealed their intent on their faces. Apparently neither of the states made an effort to provide any nonracial justifications for the clauses (*Giles v. Harris* [1903], 489–504; Bickel and Schmidt 1984, 927–49; *Guinn and Beal v. U.S.* [1915], 363–64; *Myers v. Anderson* [1915], 379; Kousser 1974, 164–65).

Moving from intent and effect in *Yick Wo*, to effect alone in *Williams*, to political questions in *Giles*, to intent and effect with an emphasis on the former in *Guinn*, the turn-of-the-century Supreme Court followed a confusing and contradictory path on its rulings on occupational and voting rights. In

324 Intent and Effect

its decisions in cases involving segregation and discrimination in public accommodations and education, the Court's opinions on motives and impact became even more tangled.

THE COURT'S justices sometimes assumed that good faith and a nondiscriminatory intent lay behind challenged laws. Most notoriously, in *Plessy v. Ferguson* (1896), Justice Henry Billings Brown declared, "We consider the underlying fallacy of the plaintiff's argument to consist in the assumption that the enforced separation of the two races stamps the colored race with a badge of inferiority." A distinction *between* people on the basis of race, in other words, was not necessarily a discrimination *against* one group, and only the latter was unconstitutional, in Brown's view. Government action, Brown believed, could have no effect, discriminatory or otherwise, on the natural order of society: "If one race be inferior to the other socially, the constitution of the United States cannot put them upon the same plane." In his most famous dissent, the first Justice John Marshall Harlan scornfully answered Brown: "Every one knows that the statute in question had its origin in the *purpose*, not so much to exclude white persons from railroad cars occupied by blacks, as to exclude colored people from coaches occupied by or assigned to white persons. . . . The thing to accomplish was, under the guise of giving equal accommodation for whites and blacks, to compel the latter to keep to themselves while traveling in railroad passenger coaches. No one would be so wanting in candor as to assert the contrary." That is, Harlan did not disagree with Brown that it was only discrimination *against* African-Americans that was unconstitutional, that it was only *harm against a group* that violated the equal protection clause; the dissenter merely saw through what he called "the thin disguise" that the segregation law was intended to treat people of both races equally. It is instructive to note that neither in the trial nor in the briefs for Plessy, the *gen de couleur* who challenged the Louisiana railroad segregation statute, was there any discussion of what the legislators said about why they passed the law (*Plessy v. Ferguson* [1896], 551, 552, 557, italics added; Kousser 1980b; Lofgren 1987, 44–60, 148–73; Fiss 1993, 364–65).

Three years later, when the Supreme Court considered the question of whether it would enforce the "equal" part of *Plessy*'s "separate but equal" in the Georgia case of *Cumming v. Richmond County Board of Education* (1899), Harlan reversed course. A former slaveowner whose speech and behavior, according to his most recent biographer, often reflected contemporary white supremacist patterns, Harlan was as inconsistent in his devotion to color-blindness in his Supreme Court opinions as he had been in his opposition to slavery and racial discrimination in his campaigns for elective office (Kousser 1980b; Beth 1992, 92–93, 226; Yarbrough 1995, x–xi, 84, 228).

Augusta, Georgia, had supported two high schools for whites and one for blacks for many years before 1897. Faced with an overflowing black elementary school population, the Board of Education in that year decided to close Ware High School, which at the time was the only publicly supported high school for African-Americans in the state, and to convert the building into elementary classrooms and hire four elementary teachers for the same total amount as they had paid Ware's two teachers—which was itself only half of what they paid the principal of the high school for white girls (Kousser 1980b). To buttress their defense in potential litigation, the all-white Richmond County Board of Education responded to the resultant storm of minority protest by holding a public hearing at which those discriminated against were allowed to present their grievances before the Board politely rejected minority criticisms.

Augusta whites also asserted their good faith. It would have been "unwise and unconscionable to keep up a high school for sixty pupils and turn away three hundred little [N]egroes who were asking to be taught their alphabet and to read and write," the Board's lawyers announced. At the same time that they played upon the judges' heartstrings, the lawyers tried to obscure the facts, detailed in the plaintiffs' briefs, that the school board could have shifted the money for black elementary schools from the much larger funds devoted to white schools in this majority-black county, or that they could have used part of the 23 percent increase in state funds for education for the year to continue operating Ware (Kousser 1980b).

In a decision that no one has ever been able to explain satisfactorily and that has long been recognized as a terrible blot on his reputation, Justice Harlan ruled, for a unanimous Supreme Court, in favor of Richmond County (Kluger 1975, 83; Kousser 1980b). To sustain a contention of discrimination under the Fourteenth Amendment's equal protection clause, Harlan announced, blacks had to demonstrate that the Board of Education had "proceeded in bad faith," that they had been motivated by "hostility to the colored population because of their race." Using public funds to provide high schools for whites but not for blacks, he thought, was not "a clear and unmistakable disregard of rights secured by the supreme law of the land" (*Cumming v. Richmond County* [1899], 545).

Harlan's opinion in *Cumming* and comments on it expose two of the chief difficulties with impact tests of equal protection: What is the right comparison, and what is the right criterion? There were four possible comparisons of potential legal interest in the Ware case. First, the Court could have paid attention to the extent of *change* in the situation of black students. But there were two kinds of changes to consider. What the Court apparently focused on was the amount of money spent on *black education per se* before and after the elimination of Ware. Since it was approximately the same, the justices concluded that there was no retrogression and therefore no denial of equality. But if the justices had spotlighted the change in black expenditures *in relation to those on whites,* they might have come to another conclusion. Because the huge increase in state expenditures on education went wholly to whites in Richmond County, the ratio of black to white expenditures on teachers' salaries per child in the relevant age group actually decreased from 35.0 percent in 1897 to 29.2 percent in 1900. Spending on buildings and administration was not detailed by race but was no doubt even more biased in favor of whites. By this comparative measure, blacks retrogressed. Second, the Court could have scrutinized the absolute level of expenditures itself, not just the change. The fact that Richmond County spent only a third as much on educating the average black child as on educating the average white child might itself have been considered a sufficiently discriminatory impact to invalidate the system and, indeed, several such school equalization suits had been filed and won before *Cumming,* including one in Harlan's home state of Kentucky (Kousser 1980b, 25; Kousser 1986, 23-26). Third, the Court could have concentrated, as the plaintiffs asked, on the simple fact that the Board subsidized two high schools for whites but ended the subsidy for blacks. The opportunities for public schooling were simply not the same for both races. Fourth, as Andrew Kull has suggested, the Court might have emphasized that there was no publicly supported high school for white *boys* in Augusta in 1897, and thus closing Ware merely put all black children on the same plane as white boys (Kull 1992, 128-30). Discrimination among whites by gender, in this view, excused discrimination by race. So long as white boys had no public high school, race was not the sole dividing line between those with and without public opportunities, and Kull apparently believes that unless race is the only distinction made between people in the challenged law, there is no violation of the equal protection clause.[10]

In addition, there are three possible criteria against which to assess inequities: strict proportionality, rough proportionality, and absolute inequality. If equality is construed strictly, then perhaps a court would have to rule that expenditures for black and white schools had to be precisely equal. If a looser construction is allowed, then a school system that offered approximately the same advantages—instruction in the same grades, more or less equivalent teacher and building quality, etc.—could be held constitutional. If absolute or almost absolute inequality is required to prove a constitutional violation, then if the emphasis were on high schooling alone, *Cumming* would parallel *Yick Wo* and *Giles,* where the impact was also radically disproportionate. If the comparison were on whether there were any schools at all available to black children, then of course the plaintiffs would lose. The point is that impact in itself is not a mere objective fact, for without further argument, it is not obvious which aspect of impact is relevant, or what criterion is appropriate.

Harlan's opinion in *Cumming* also added a radical "racial hostility test" of intent. Perhaps this might have been satisfied by a sufficiently disproportionate impact, but it is difficult to imagine what plaintiffs could have done to convince the justice that theirs was the proper definition of discriminatory effect. If evidence other than impact was possibly probative, did Harlan really expect Board members to admit under oath that their sole, principal, or even minor purpose had been discriminatory, rather than asserting a soothing beneficence, as they in fact did? Surely asking for such evidence would have been unreasonable. But if mere verbal assertions of good faith sufficed to defeat an allegation of discrimination, why would this passage from the opening address to the Louisiana constitutional convention of 1898 by its president, Ernest Kruttschnitt, not serve?

> My fellow-delegates, let us not be misunderstood! Let us say to the large class of the people of Louisiana who will be disfranchised under any of the proposed limitations of the suffrage, that what we seek to do is undertaken in a spirit, not of hostility to any particular men or set of men, but in the belief that the State should see to the protection of the weaker classes; should guard them against the machinations of those who would use them only to further their own base ends; should see to it that they are not allowed to harm themselves. We owe it to the ignorant, we owe it to the weak, to protect them just as we would protect a little child and prevent it from injuring itself with sharp-edged tools placed in its hands. (quoted in Kousser 1974, 164)

Demonstrating the complexity of an effect test, the difficulty of a racial hostility test, and the superficiality of the "colorblind" hero Harlan's commitment to nondiscrimination, *Cumming* deserves a more central place than it has usually received in discussions of equal protection law.

BEGINNING in 1915 with *Guinn*, courts began to chip away at the edifice of discrimination that they had helped to buttress. That often-told story need not be recounted here, for all of the intervening developments of the courts' thinking about intent and effect can be subsumed in a discussion of *Brown v. Board of Education of Topeka, Kansas* (1954). Since *Brown* is the *ur*-precedent, the keystone of judicial interpretation and power in the post-1937 era of the Supreme Court, it is no wonder that the struggle for control of its meaning, which began even before it was issued, is far from subsiding more than forty years after Chief Justice Earl Warren's opinion came down. Three questions have dominated the discussion: What harm did *Brown* identify, how did it identify it, and what measures were governments allowed and/or required to take to remedy those evils? If *Plessy* disingenuously assumed a beneficent intent and a nondiscriminatory effect, and *Cumming* adopted an impact standard that defendants could hardly fail and demanded proof of a malevolent motive that only the clumsiest of defendants would divulge, *Brown* held that if one could demonstrate that school segregation had deleterious consequences for African-American children, then the reasons for adopting that policy were either irrelevant or presumed to be invidious (Seidman and Tushnet 1996, 104–5).

For over a hundred years of litigation on segregation and racial discrimination in schools, judges had always assumed that plaintiffs had to demonstrate that African-American students were harmed by segregation (Kousser 1986). In the immediate precursor to *Brown, Sweatt v. Painter,* the NAACP-LDF went to great lengths to show that the hastily established "colored law school" in Texas offered black students a grossly inferior education compared to that available to whites at the University of Texas. During *Brown* and its companion cases, the NAACP-LDF paraded psychologists, anthropologists, and sociologists, some of whose work was enshrined in *Brown*'s famous footnote 11, to prove that segregation harmed black children (Kluger 1975, 256–84, 315–45). The difficult point in the research was to isolate the effects of schools per se—and, even more particularly, of schools governed by explicitly state-sanctioned segregation—on the mental and psychological development of African-American children. Although the Court or various plaintiffs might have arrayed evidence that segregated institutions or practices were in fact currently unequal in many tangible respects, that the pattern was so strong that they were very likely to remain unequal for the indefinite future, and that therefore integration was the only feasible near-term relief possible, the decision to make a frontal assault on segregation discouraged this line of argument. Instead, Chief Justice Warren stretched a point considerably when he asserted that the scholars that he cited had conclusively demonstrated a connection between strict school segregation by law and black children's feelings of inferiority.

Yet once Warren had decided to ignore tangible inequities, the formalistic alternatives to relying on social science were even less satisfactory. When racist critics of the decision argued that it should be reversed because its social scientific underpinnings were either wrong or exaggerated by the Court, a few friendly law professors asserted that all would be well if the social science were abandoned and the justices merely assumed the social fact that enforced segregation harmed blacks. Yet for the justices to declare social facts by ukase, as Justice Brown had done in *Plessy,* would have been to rest the Court's legitimacy on a frailer foundation than social psychology, stripping the opinion of any extrajudicial justification on the basis of social "facts" that large segments of the white public have never believed (Newby 1969; Graglia 1976, 26–29; Wilkinson 1979, 31–37; Tushnet 1987, 119). To take judicial notice that the purpose of segregation was to stigmatize and subordinate African-Americans without investigating evidence for such a motive would also have amounted to a judicial assumption of a social fact that white segregationists, at least in the context of a legal action, would no doubt have denied (Lawrence 1980, 50–52).

Perhaps even more important, to reimagine *Brown* as resting on an unstated principle was to throw its meaning open to a variety of contradictory claims. Thus, Prof. Lino Graglia, a prominent critic of mandatory integration, declared that because *Brown*'s social science did not convince him and because the Court simultaneously outlawed segregation in schools of the District of Columbia, which were not subject to the equal protection clause, the Court's decisions "did not turn on a finding of educational harm to black children" (*Bolling v. Sharpe* [1954], 499; Graglia 1976, 29). Graglia ignored the fact that Warren had specifically given the due process clause an equal protection interpretation in *Bolling v. Sharpe,* in effect "incorporating" equal protection standards into its sister clause. In any event, Graglia's move allowed him to approve Judge John J. Parker's opinion in the remand case of *Briggs v. Elliott* (1955), one of the four cases that had been consolidated with *Brown* by the Supreme Court, which held that *Brown* merely banned segregation, instead of requiring integration or the dismantling of dual school systems. If African-Americans were not harmed by segregation, then integration could not help them and was irrelevant, so long as states stopped designating schools as racially separate. "Freedom of choice" plans, in which a few stalwart black children in the South asked to be admitted to white schools, were all that *Brown* required or, indeed, allowed.

A defender of the Supreme Court's recent decisions on "racial gerrymandering," Prof. James Blumstein, has gone farther in reinterpreting *Brown,* which, he asserts, "embodies the idea that race-dependent decisions are unacceptable except in the most unusual and compelling circumstances."[11] When *Brown* and other cases referred to "discrimination," Blumstein has declared, they meant only racial *distinction,* that is, they referred to the use of race as "a criterion of selection" and not to racial *harm.* "Discrimination must be distinguished from disadvantage. A fair system free of deliberate racial bias may result in racial disadvantage," according to Blumstein (Blumstein 1995, 529). Another defender, Prof. Katharine Butler, has characterized the "evil" in school segregation, and the only harm that *Brown* was concerned with, as "racial sorting." It was irrelevant to the Constitution, she thought, whether the percentage of whites in each school was 0 percent, 25 percent,

50 percent, or any other number, if the individuals had been assigned by race (Butler 1996, 323, 356). Presumably, all that the NAACP-LDF had had to do in *Brown*—if the decision meant what Blumstein, Butler, and other neoconservatives said it did—was to point to statutes requiring racial segregation, and the trivially easy case would have been won. In fact, in their oral arguments before the Supreme Court, NAACP counsel Robert Carter and Thurgood Marshall focused on what Marshall called the "actual injury" to African-American children. "I have yet to hear anyone say that they denied that these children are harmed by reason of this segregation," the future justice insisted. "I know of no scientist that has made any study, whether he be anthropologist or sociologist, who does not admit that segregation harms the child. . . . It is our position that any legislative or governmental classification must fall with an even hand on all persons similarly situated" (quoted in Davis 1997, 31, 38). Yet paradoxically, all that the southern school boards could have done in response to the decision in *Brown*, if the Blumstein/Butler view is correct, would have been to pull down the "colored" and "white" signs at the respective schools and eliminate separate attendance zones. No action to compensate for ninety years of suddenly illegal state-sponsored segregation was constitutionally necessary or permissible. Any attempt to remedy past racial wrongs, Butler announced, was "folly" (Butler 1996, 598). Impact was irrelevant and intent so readily apparent that one hardly needed judges to enforce such blatantly obvious constitutional rights, which had unaccountably been overlooked by judges for a century.

But for distortion, Blumstein and Butler are no match for Justice Clarence Thomas. In a bitter and misleading attack, in the guise of an interpretation of *Brown*, Thomas declared that it had been legally incorrect to base *Brown* on social scientific evidence, that the decision rested entirely on an individualistic notion of injury, that *Brown* did not ban segregation, and that integration was inherently racist.[12] Saying that judges did not need "the unnecessary and misleading assistance of the social sciences" or those fields' "easy answers,"[13] he argued that judges could and should decide on the basis of their own common sense that segregation is not wrong per se, for, continued this graduate of Yale Law School, "if separation itself is a harm, and if integration therefore is the only way that blacks can receive a proper education, then there must be something inferior about blacks." The Warren and Burger Courts' dismantling of school segregation, he argued, had been based on "a theory of black inferiority." All that the Fourteenth Amendment required, in Thomas's view, was that government not "discriminate *among* its citizens on the basis of race" (*Missouri v. Jenkins* [1995], 2064–66, emphasis added).

Thomas's view of the Fourteenth Amendment—so far from those of Justice Warren's statement in *Brown* that segregated educational facilities were "inherently unequal," so contradictory to the Court's actions in destroying segregation "root and branch" in *Green v. County School Board* (1968) and many other cases, so intolerantly dismissive of other professions and points of view—refuted itself. If judges disagreed so completely with each other, how could they rely on *common* sense? Which answers were "easier"—those that could be rigorously assessed and possibly falsified or those that merely reflected personal preferences? *Brown* had been based on harm not to individual African-Americans but to blacks as a group, not on judges' arbitrary value judgments alone but on the best evidence presented to them on the effect of explicitly mandated segregation on black students, not on racist assumptions—a charge that defamed the memory of Thomas's predecessor on the bench, Thurgood Marshall, the black lawyer who tried *Brown*—but on the belief that government could and should act to guarantee equal educational opportunity for all Americans (Seidman and Tushnet 1996, 106–7). Thomas's radical revision of history was as incorrect as it was illogical.

While it is true that during the consideration of *Brown*, Justice William O. Douglas claimed to want to outlaw all racial classifications, the Court as a whole did not share his view. Chief Justice Warren certainly did not enshrine it in *Brown*, in which he spotlighted what the Kansas court had called the "detrimental effect [of segregation] upon the colored children." Over the next twenty years, the Court, in opinions joined by Douglas, required school boards to take affirmative action to dismantle previously segregated schools and, if Douglas and his liberal brethren had had their way, would have mandated efforts to alleviate de facto school segregation (*Brown v. Board of Education* [1954], 494; Tushnet 1991, 1906; *Green v. County Board of Education* [1968]; *Swann v. Charlotte-Mecklenburg Board of Education* [1971]; *Milliken v. Bradley* [1974, Marshall, dissent]).[14] Neither *Brown* nor its integrationist progeny in schools and other areas of American public life barred considerations of race and especially not considerations of racial disadvantage, as Blumstein has contended. Such segregated facilities as public parks and publicly owned or regulated restaurants or transportation systems excluded blacks without offering an alternative or stigmatized them by forcing them into subordinate positions. Even if some modern commentators disingenuously ignore the fact (Blumstein 1995, 552–53), no one from the 1860s to the 1950s needed to be told that separate railroad or street cars and seats in the back of the bus symbolized black racial subordination. Anti-miscegenation laws were based on racist theories and were employed, the Court rightly noted, to further "white supremacy." Because in these cases disadvantage was too obvious to need social scientific examination, they do not support the view that *Brown* banned all notice of race or was unconcerned with actual injuries (e.g., *Muir v. Louisville Park Theatrical Assn.* [1954]; *Mayor of Baltimore v. Dawson* [1955]; *Holmes v. City of Atlanta* [1955]; *Gayle v. Browder* [1956]; *New Orleans Park Improvement Assn. v. Detige* [1958]; *Watson v. City of Memphis* [1963]; *Loving v. Virginia* [1967]). This was particularly clear when the Court first entered the thicket of racial politics in *Gomillion v. Lightfoot* (1960).

Despite massive continued discrimination against black registrants in the black university town of Tuskegee, Alabama, African-American voting registration had steadily risen and threatened to surpass white registration. To prevent any blacks from being elected, a local act of the Alabama legislature in 1957 snipped the previously square boundaries of the city of Tuskegee into what the Court termed "an uncouth twenty-eight-sided figure," which had the "effect" of removing from the city's boundaries "all save four or five of its 400 Negro voters while not removing a single white voter or resident" (*Gomillion v. Lightfoot* 1960, 340–41). Actually, the impact of the deannexation was much more dramatic than the Supreme Court's statement indicated. In 1950, Tuskegee's population of 6,712 had been 80.4 percent black. Because the redrawn boundaries reduced the population to only 1,750 in 1960, the U.S. Census Bureau did not print population figures by race for the town, but it was probably nearly 100 percent white. The statute had turned an overwhelmingly African-American town, whose politics whites surely could not have controlled much longer, into a white homeland, a true example of apartheid in America. The nearly lily-white town was surrounded by a county, whose government controlled fewer significant powers, that was over 80 percent black.

Faced with a Fourteenth and Fifteenth Amendment challenge, Tuskegee offered no nonracial justification for its action, merely claiming an absolute right to regulate its own political affairs. Reaching beyond the justiciability issue that he began by terming "the sole question" before the Court, Justice Felix Frankfurter deduced that an "unlawful end" had motivated Tuskegee representatives. He based his deduction on the "unconstitutional result," which he thought was evidenced partly by demographic statistics and partly by a before-and-after map that made the gerrymander obvious. In a brief opinion, Justice Charles Whitaker concurred on the grounds that the state's "purpose" was to segregate black from white voters, and that under *Brown*, such a segregative purpose violated the Fourteenth Amendment (*Gomillion v. Lightfoot* [1960], 340–42, 347–49). Thus, *Gomillion* involved both effect and intent, both the Fourteenth and Fifteenth Amendments, both redistricting and disfranchisement.[15] For a case about maps, it certainly charted few clear doctrinal boundaries (Ely 1970, 1252–53; Norrell 1985, 119, 124).

Indeed, it was this doctrinal confusion that made *Gomillion* the origin of contradictory lines of precedent. Courts took two roads out of Tuskegee. The pure effect road led through *Baker v. Carr* (1962) and *Reynolds v. Sims* (1964) to all of the apportionment cases and at least to the neighborhood of the "political gerrymandering" case of *Davis v. Bandemer* (1986). In these cases, plaintiffs were not required to show any desires on the part of, say, rural legislators to discriminate against the urban or suburban population of their states in apportionment. The fact of numerical inequality of representation was, by itself, necessary and sufficient to demonstrate a violation of equal protection, and proportional representation of every geographically based group was necessarily accepted as an absolute, since every person was to be equally represented.[16] It was not only illegal to deny individuals the vote, Chief Justice Warren announced in *Reynolds*; there was also a constitutional violation if some people's votes were, in his words, "effectively diluted," and he particularly mentioned "diluting votes on the basis of race" as unconstitutional (*Reynolds v. Sims* [1964], 557, 562; Blacksher and Menefee 1982, 14–18).[17]

At first it appeared that the same standard that the Court had established for the white suburbanites in Birmingham and Mobile, Alabama, who brought the *Reynolds* suit, would be applied to racial minorities. In a 1965 Georgia case, Justice William Brennan wrote for a 7-2 majority that "it might well be that, designedly or otherwise, a multi-member constituency apportionment scheme, under the circumstances of a particular case, would operate to minimize or cancel out the voting strength of racial or political elements of the voting population" (*Fortson v. Dorsey* [1965], 439). Yet when this and related issues were properly presented to the Court, it set off on a different road than the one it had followed in the apportionment cases. The path to the minority vote dilution cases was full of detours, but eventually plaintiffs were compelled to demonstrate racially discriminatory intent, often a more difficult task than showing impact. In contrast to the apportionment cases, proportional representation was explicitly outlawed as a standard in minority vote dilution cases, though courts irresistibly fell back on it in practice.

The first detour concerned draft cards and swimming pools. In *U.S. v. O'Brien* and *Palmer v. Thompson,* majorities of the Supreme Court looked over the precipice of intent and swerved toward an absolute effect standard. (See Eisenberg 1977, 43–45, for other cases.) Antiwar student activist O'Brien challenged his conviction for burning his selective service card on the grounds that Congress had been motivated by a desire to suppress dissent when it amended the selective service law in 1965 to prohibit the mutilation of draft cards. Although the sparse comments on the amendment on the floor of Congress and in the House and Senate reports buttressed O'Brien's contention, Chief Justice Warren rejected the antiwar student's First Amendment defense. Requiring men to possess draft cards, Warren concluded for an 8-1 majority, was the most narrowly drawn means of administering the selective service system, which was incident to the warmaking power. Possession precluded mutilation. And since Congress clearly had the power to enact the amendment, its motive was irrelevant (*U.S. v. O'Brien* [1968], 381–84, 386–88). The effect of the law may have been to remove one dramatic way of protesting, and it presumably had no impact at all on supporters of the Vietnam War, but Warren neglected disproportionate impact entirely.

The *Palmer* case arose from the closing of all publicly owned swimming pools by the city of Jackson, Mississippi, in the face of federal court–ordered integration. Contending that courts would have difficulty determining motivation, especially the "sole" or "dominant" motivation of a group of legislators; that an injunction would be futile, because a legislature could merely repass the regulation without an incriminating motive; and that judicial inquiry into legislative motives would overstep the proper separation between the powers of the two branches of government, Justice Hugo Black, speaking for a bare 5–4 majority, unequivocally rejected the notion that an equal protection violation could rest solely on intent (*Palmer v. Thompson* [1971], 218–19, 227). Curiously, two weeks later, in a 7–1 decision, the Supreme Court, with no mention of *Palmer* and no justification of its holding, announced that aid to parochial schools constituted an establishment of religion unless the legislation authorizing it had a "secular purpose" and met two other criteria (*Lemon v. Kurtzman* [1971]). If purpose was so easy to discern, so unproblematic, in religion cases, why not in racial discrimination cases?

Dissenting justices and commentators raked Justice Black's *Palmer* opinion, although they largely ignored parallel arguments in *O'Brien*. In a statement that was nearly four times as long as Black's majority opinion, and which in form resembled an opinion of the court more than a dissent, Justice Byron White declared that previous cases contained an "invidious purpose or motive" standard. His detailed examination of "the circumstances surrounding this action and the absence of other credible reasons for the closings" convinced White that the city's motive was to stop integration in public services, a motive that he considered unconstitutional per se (*Palmer v. Thompson* [1971], 240–43).

Professor Paul Brest answered Black's points about difficulty, futility, and impropriety more directly. While weighing motives might be hard, it was unnecessary, Brest contended, to determine the sole or dominant reason for behavior, because an illicit motive, even if comparatively unimportant, might tip the balance toward action—for instance, by moving a pivotal member or group in a legislative body. Nor was direct evidence of intent necessary, for here, as elsewhere in the law, circumstantial evidence, such as the sequence of events that led to the decision, the terms of the regulation themselves, or the placement of election district lines, often gives a clear enough indication of motivation, as it had in *Gomillion*. As for futility, it would be a credulous court, indeed, that would wipe from its memory a prior ruling of illicit motivation when considering a reenacted law. Finally, every invalidation by a court of a law or an administrative practice intrudes on legislative or administrative powers, often in the pursuit of individual constitutional rights. Why is it more of an imposition to question the *motive* for a decision than to upset the decision itself (Brest 1971, 119–20, 125, 128–30)?

As if to underscore the Court's inconsistency about purpose and effect, a week before *Palmer*, five Justices, among them four members of the *Palmer* anti-motivation majority (Justice Black, Justice Harry Blackmun, Chief Justice Warren Burger, and Justice Potter Stewart), had joined an opinion by Justice White in *Whitcomb v. Chavis*. In 1960, 14.4 percent of the population of Marion County, Indiana, was black, but because all members of the state legislature from the county had long been required by the state constitution to be chosen in at-large elections, and because Republicans usually won every seat from the county, only three of the 115 members from the county who served between 1960 and 1968 were black Democrats. The six black Republicans during the period apparently won in spite of the opposition of most African-American voters. In other words, black voters received about one-fifth of their proportionate representation. Nonetheless, the Court decided, this disproportionate impact was not enough to demonstrate that the at-large system was discriminatory. Since all Democratic candidates, white as well as black, lost every election except 1964, in which the entire Democratic slate won, the discrimination was partisan, not racial.

Even though all the evidence in the case concerned impact, Justice White treated it as an intent case, asserting that the Reconstruction Amendments protected "the civil rights of Negroes" against "purposeful devices to further racial discrimination." In addition to announcing an intent standard for minority vote dilution cases, *Chavis* was notable for declaring that it would have been a violation of equal protection if "ghetto residents had less opportunity than other Marion County residents to participate in the political processes and to elect legislators of their choice," language that would echo through all subsequent minority vote dilution cases (*Whitcomb v. Chavis* [1971], 149). Overall, as in most of Justice White's numerous voting rights opinions, this case turned on facts, not abstract principles, and White's analysis closely resembled that which a social scientist might perform, arraying statistics, discussing mathematical models of representation, assessing causes, and introducing such "control variables" as party. After *Chavis*, the question was more whether the Court would establish a method for assessing the evidence of discrimination than what the legal doctrines would be.[18]

Two years later in *White v. Regester*, Justice White, speaking for a unanimous Court, provided the outlines for such a method in an opinion that overturned multimember legislative districting schemes in Dallas and San Antonio, Texas, as unconstitutionally racially discriminatory against blacks and Mexican-Americans. What distinguished the situation in Texas from that in Indianapolis was not open statements of racially discriminatory intent, but the presence of factors that "enhanced" the effect of at-large elections on minorities—a history of official and unofficial racial discrimination, language barriers to Spanish speakers, majority-vote and numbered-post requirements, and a lack of access to a slating group.[19] The "totality of the circumstances," Justice White announced, proved that members of minority groups "had less opportunity than did other residents in the district to participate in the political processes and to elect legislators of their choice" in multimember districts in Texas. Again stressing the factual nature of a vote dilution inquiry, the Court specifically approved the findings of the district court because they represented "a blend of history and an intensely local appraisal of the design and impact of the Bexar County [San Antonio] multimember district in the light of past and present reality, political and otherwise." Indeed, the facts were so important that Justice White did not bother to make clear whether this case turned on impact or intent, and he left it to readers to determine just why each of the factors enhanced the effects of the electoral structure and how to weigh them. Later that year, *White v. Regester* was reduced to a formula by the Fifth Circuit Court of Appeals in *Zimmer v. McKeithen*, and the "factors" became known as the "*Zimmer*" or "*White-Zimmer*" factors (*White v. Regester* [1973], 766, 769; *Zimmer v. McKeithen* [1973]).

The replacement of three justices allowed the Supreme Court to sidestep *Palmer* and adopt an intent standard for all racial equal protection cases. But in the very case that announced the standard, the Court relied primarily on effect evidence to assess motivation. Under the equal protection clause, said Justice White for a 7–2 majority in *Washington v. Davis* (1976), "a law claimed to be racially discriminatory must ultimately be traced to a racially discriminatory purpose." It would not be unconstitutional "*solely* because it has a racially disproportionate impact." Otherwise—this was the slippery slope on the effect side—all sorts of tax, welfare, regulatory, and other policies that bore more heavily on members of one race than of another would be drawn into question. Nonetheless, White concluded, "an invidious discriminatory purpose may often be inferred from *the totality of the relevant facts,* including the fact, if it is true, that the law bears more heavily on one race than another." Lest it be thought that the blurring of the concepts of motive and impact was careless or inadvertent, Justice John Paul Stevens's concurrence underscored the point that intent could be proven by indirect evidence: "Frequently the most probative evidence of intent will be objective evidence of what actually happened rather than evidence describing the subjective state of mind of the actor. For normally the actor is presumed to have intended the natural consequences of his deeds. . . . My point in making this observation is to suggest that the line between discriminatory purpose and discriminatory impact is not nearly as bright, and perhaps not as critical, as the reader of the Court's opinion might assume" (*Washington v. Davis* [1976], 230, 240, 242, 248, 253-54, italics added).

In the next term after *Washington v. Davis,* Justice Lewis Powell outlined some of the ways to prove purpose in racial discrimination cases, drawing heavily on Brest's critique of *Palmer.* A racially disproportionate impact, wrote Powell, "may provide an important starting point" for the inquiry into motive, and could be determinative where the effect was as stark as that in *Yick Wo* or *Gomillion.* In cases where the pattern was more ambiguous, plaintiffs had to show only that race was "*a* motivating factor," not that it was "dominant" or "primary." At that point, the burden of proof switched to the defendants to demonstrate that "the same decision would have resulted even had the impermissible purpose not been considered." Only if nondiscriminatory motives were insufficient to account for the municipality's decision would that decision be subject to "strict scrutiny" by the courts, requiring an especially strong justification. In addition to impact, Powell explained, intent could be deduced from "the historical background of the decision," the sequence of events that led up to it, especially whether there were departures from normal procedures, the legislative or administrative history, and statements from officials. In this instance, the Court concluded, an overwhelmingly white Chicago suburb's effort to exclude low-cost housing and the minorities that the inexpensive dwellings would attract was part of a longstanding effort by the community to bolster real estate prices (Brest 1971; *Village of Arlington Heights v. Metro. Hous. Dev. Corp.* [1977], 265-68, 270-71, italics added).

A sex discrimination challenge to the Massachusetts veterans' preference for state employment (*Personnel Administrator of Massachusetts v. Feeney* [1979]) elicited the last major doctrinal discussion of intent from the Supreme Court during the 1970s. The concept of discriminatory purpose, announced Justice Potter Stewart's opinion for the court, means "that *the* decisionmaker . . . selected or reaffirmed a particular course of action at least in part 'because of,' not merely 'in spite of,' its adverse effects upon an identifiable group." Exactly how this criterion applied to a legislature, which is not a unitary decisionmaker, Stewart did not explore, but it is significant that Stewart stressed discrimination *against a group,* rather than merely *distinctions between individuals.* Until the Rehnquist Court, this was standard equal protection doctrine.

Like Powell and Stevens before him, Justice Stewart rejected the necessity

TABLE 7.2. Percentage of Massachusetts Residents Appointed
to State Jobs, 1963–1973, Who Were Veterans, by Gender

Status	Gender	
	Male	Female
Veteran	54	2
Nonveteran	46	98
Total	100	100

Source: *Personnel Administrator of Mass. v. Feeney*, 442 U.S. 256 (1979).

of establishing intent only by direct statements: "Proof of discriminatory intent must necessarily usually rely on objective factors." And as in *Yick Wo*, the Court was moved by facts that can be encapsulated easily in a 2×2 table, such as Table 7.2. Both the majority and Justices Stevens and White in a concurring opinion seemed to rest their opinions in this "intent case" largely on the bottom left cell of the table. The fact that nearly half the males who won jobs in the state government were nonveterans was a clear indication to seven members of the Supreme Court that the veterans' preference was not a mere subterfuge for gender discrimination. The district and appeals courts had focused instead on the contrast between the two columns. For the lower courts and for Justices Thurgood Marshall and William Brennan in dissent, it did not matter so much that a minority of men were disadvantaged, for 98 percent of women were.[20] What may have tilted the outcome for the Supreme Court majority was their conclusion that the legislative history and "all of the available evidence" besides impact gave no indication of a discriminatory intent and that veterans' preferences had "always been deemed to be legitimate" (*Personnel Administrator of Massachusetts v. Feeney* [1979], 270–71, 279, italics added; *Anthony v. Commonwealth* [1976]).

City of Mobile v. Bolden (1980) applied the intent standard developed in constitutional cases to those brought under Section 2 of the VRA, which the prevailing opinion equated with the Fifteenth Amendment. Although none of the confused set of opinions commanded a majority, Justice Stewart—speaking for a plurality made up of Chief Justice Burger, Justice Powell, Justice William Rehnquist, and himself—declared that it was necessary to prove intent, even if a case involved a fundamental right like voting rather than privileges such as housing and government jobs, which had been the issues in *Washington v. Davis, Arlington Heights,* and *Feeney*.[21] Despite the fact that the Fifteenth Amendment stated that the right to vote could not be "abridged" on account of race, Stewart announced that that amendment and therefore Section 2 of the VRA were not violated unless individuals were completely disfranchised. (Contrast *Nevett v. Sides* [1978], 236 [Wisdom, concurring].) He ignored the fact that in the leading Fifteenth Amendment cases, the white primary cases and *Gomillion*, blacks had not lost their rights to vote but had been deprived of opportunities to influence the outcomes of the most important elections. There was a constitutional right to cast an undiluted vote, Stewart acknowledged, but it rested wholly on the Fourteenth Amendment, and it was purely an individual right, not a group right, for otherwise it would inevitably lead to proportional representation. Substantively more important than these somewhat arcane theoretical considerations, the plurality believed, was the fact that the evidence that had convinced District Court Judge Virgil Pittman and the Fifth Circuit Court of Appeals was insufficient to prove intent. Four other justices (White, Blackmun, Marshall, and Brennan) were satisfied that the evidence in *Bolden* had proved a discriminatory intent, although Blackmun agreed with the city of Mobile that Judge Pittman's single-member district remedy was too extreme. Justice Stevens sided with Mobile on the grounds that the evidence had not shown a discriminatory impact, which was what he, Marshall, and Brennan believed to be the proper standard (*City of Mobile v. Bolden* 1980).

Justice Stewart's plurality opinion was subjected to perhaps the most vociferous protest of any Supreme Court civil rights opinion since *Brown*. According to Prof. Avi Soifer, Stewart required an "overwhelming demonstration of the most blatant form of discriminatory motive . . . proof far stronger than the standard of causation generally used in the common law . . . proof akin to that required in a criminal context . . . a smoking gun." Civil rights lawyer Frank Parker believed that Stewart had rejected the "foreseeability standard" and had "implied that circumstantial evidence of discriminatory purpose would not suffice to prove discriminatory intent." Laughlin McDonald of the ACLU charged that *Bolden* demanded proof of "subjective racial intent." Similar glosses on Stewart's opinion fueled the struggle over the renewal of the VRA in 1981–82 (Soifer 390, 1981, 400, 404; Parker 1983, 737–46; McDonald 1989, 1263–64; Boyd and Markman, 1983, 1390, 1404–5; *Rogers v. Lodge* [1982], 643–44, Stevens dissent). Was *Bolden* so extreme? Did it establish, unequivocally, not only an "intent" standard, but one that required direct, not objective or circumstantial, evidence? In short, what was *Bolden*'s intent?[22]

One consideration that undercuts this extreme reading is that Stewart began by interpreting *Guinn* and *Gomillion* as "purpose" cases, despite the fact that, as shown above, no direct evidence of intent was presented in either case. A second is that he recognized the potential relevance of discriminatory impact, merely stating that impact "*alone* cannot be decisive . . . of discriminatory purpose."[23] A third is that the plaintiffs had not contended that the at-large system of the Mobile city government had been established with a discriminatory purpose, and they had not pointed to particular officials or events that indicated that it had been maintained for a discriminatory purpose. Stewart specifically reserved the question of discriminatory maintenance and did not rule out the possibility that objective evidence might be sufficient to prove it (*City of Mobile v. Bolden* [1980], 63–64, 70, 74–76, italics in original).

The difficulty with Stewart's opinion was not that it embraced a direct or subjective intent criterion but that, as Justice White pointed out in dissent, it established no standard at all. Ignoring White's "totality of the circumstances" or "totality of the relevant facts" approaches in *White v. Regester* and *Washington v. Davis*, Stewart considered four factors, which he rejected as "sufficient proof" of discriminatory purpose one by one, without discussing whether they might be adequate if weighed together or specifying what sort of additional evidence might tip the scales in the plaintiffs' direction.[24] The fact that no black had ever been elected to the Mobile City Commission, if considered "alone," was only evidence of normal political defeat. Proof of racial discrimination in municipal employment and public services provided, by itself, only a "tenuous and circumstantial" indication of the invalidity of the electoral system. The history of past official racial discrimination in Mobile, unless specifically related to the establishment or maintenance of the Commission, was only "of limited help" in the purpose inquiry. The numbered-post and majority-vote requirements disadvantaged any minority but did not prove an intent to discriminate against blacks specifically (*City of Mobile v. Bolden* [1980], 96, 74–75).

Some commentators' interpretation of Stewart's opinion, especially in light of the trenchant criticisms in the dissents of Justices White and Marshall, was that a result-oriented, anti–civil rights faction on the Supreme Court had narrowed the inquiry to make it as difficult as possible for minority litigants to prevail and had then captiously rejected whatever evidence was offered (Parker 1983, 742–45; Weinzweig 1983, 322–29). The more optimistic gloss was that all the plurality required was greater specificity and care in argument. According to this view, the relations of general trends to particular decisions that established or maintained the electoral systems in question had to be demonstrated explicitly, and either direct or circumstantial evidence of the racially discriminatory intent of such acts was acceptable. This sort of careful hypothesis testing of causal explanations was just what political historians had been doing for years. When *Bolden* and the companion school-board case in Mobile were reargued before the district court on remand in 1981, the plaintiffs brought in historians as expert witnesses and concentrated on motivation. Once again, they prevailed, and this time, Judge Pittman's new decisions, full of lessons on Reconstruction and "Progressive Era" history, were not overturned on appeal (McCrary 1984; *Bolden v. City of Mobile* [1982]; *Brown v. Board of School Commissioners of Mobile County* [1982], [1983]).

Besides the *Bolden* remand's empirical proof that it was possible to establish the intent of the original framers of an aged electoral scheme in a court, 1982 brought two other relevant events. In a case in which the evidence seemed almost indistinguishable from that in the original *Bolden* case but where lower court judges had phrased their decisions in terms of intent, rather than effect, a 6–3 majority of the Supreme Court ruled that the at-large system for electing county commissioners in Burke County, Georgia, had been maintained for racially discriminatory reasons. Joined in the majority by *Bolden* dissenters Brennan and Marshall, as well as by Chief Justice Burger, who had been part of the plurality in *Bolden*, Justice Blackmun, who had concurred with the outcome in *Bolden* because of the remedy ordered, and Justice Sandra Day O'Connor, who had replaced Stewart, Justice White triumphantly led the retreat from Mobile back to Dallas and San Antonio. Transmogrifying the *White-Zimmer* factors from gauges of effect into indicators of intent, Justice White enumerated a series of considerations that, he asserted, proved that Burke County whites had racial motives for maintaining their government's at-large system: racially polarized voting and the failure to elect black candidates; past official discrimination in education and voting regulations, which inhibited blacks' current registration and political participation; exclusion from Democratic Party posts until 1976; property qualifications for some offices; hiring discrimination in the county government; the unresponsiveness of the county government to the particularized concerns of African-Americans; blacks' depressed socioeconomic status; the refusal of representatives to the state legislature, who by tradition controlled local legislation, to introduce bills requiring single-member districts; the large geographical size of Burke County, which made it difficult for poor candidates to campaign; and the majority-vote and numbered-post requirements for election (*Rogers v. Lodge* [1982], 624–28).

The other event was the debate over and amendment of Section 2 of the VRA, which made absolutely explicit, contrary to the plurality opinion in *Bolden*, that Congress meant to allow plaintiffs in voting rights cases to prevail if they demonstrated *either* intent *or* effect.[25] According to the Senate Judiciary Committee's report on the bill, a plaintiff who chose to prove intent under the amended Section 2 might rely on "direct or indirect circumstantial evidence, including the normal inferences to be drawn from the foreseeability of defendant's actions." Paraphrasing *White v. Regester* and *Zimmer v. McKeithen*, the report also outlined nine factors that might be relevant to proving a case of discriminatory *effect*, only two of which—a candidate slating process from which minorities were excluded and racial appeals in campaigns—were not considered by Justice White in *Lodge* as indicators of *intent*. The seven others that he had mentioned were a history of discrimination, racially polarized voting, the use of such "enhancing devices" as majority-vote requirements, the continuing effects of past discrimination, the extent of minority officeholding, a lack of responsiveness, and a tenuous policy underlying the challenged regulation—unresponsiveness and tenuousness being designated by the Senate Report as less important than the other factors. Although the Senate Report criticized the intent standard on the grounds that it was "unnecessarily divisive" involving charges of racism, that proving it was "inordinately difficult," and that it asked "the wrong question"—why the law was first passed, rather than what its current effect was—the line that Congress drew between intent and effect seemed as thin and wavy as the distinction made by the Court. Indeed, the conjunction within two days of the publication of the *Lodge* opinion and the passage of the amended VRA made clear that it mattered less whether the standard in voting rights cases was referred to as "intent" or "effect" than what sorts of evidence were counted as probative and how they were weighed (U.S. Senate 1982, 27-31; 36-37; McDonald 1989, 1265; *Rogers v. Lodge* [1982], 624-28). The only partial defeat for the civil rights forces in 1981-82 was the amendment to Section 2 that stated that Congress did not mean to establish a right of minorities to proportional representation.

The patchwork of intent and effect discussions in other Supreme Court decisions of the 1980s formed a crazy quilt whose doctrinal pattern was strikingly irregular (Weinzweig 1983, 322-35; Ortiz 1989, 1134-42). In 1981, for instance, the same four justices who had formed the plurality in *Bolden* joined in another plurality opinion in *Michael M.*, a case in which California's statutory rape law was challenged on two grounds: first, that its effect was to discriminate against males; and second, that its adoption in the nineteenth century was tainted by now-outmoded sexual stereotypes of young women. But whereas in *Bolden*, Burger, Powell, Rehnquist, and Stewart had demanded proof of intent, in *Michael M.* they returned to the intent-irrelevant view of *O'Brien* and *Palmer v. Thompson*! An "impermissible motive," Rehnquist intoned, would not void an "otherwise constitutional statute." Yet four years later, this time speaking for a unanimous court, Rehnquist rejected a provision of the 1901 Alabama Constitution that disfranchised people convicted of various petty or more serious crimes largely on the ground that it would not have been adopted "but for" a racially discriminatory motive. This time, motive was not only relevant, but the presence of a "permissible motive," the state constitutional convention's desire to disfranchise poor whites, did not "trump" its racially discriminatory motive [26] (*Michael M. v. Superior Court of Sonoma County* [1981], 472, n. 7; *Hunter v. Underwood* [1985], 228).

In the most important case to interpret the 1982 VRA amendments, *Thornburg v. Gingles* (1986), Justice Brennan ignored intent altogether in tossing out certain districts adopted in the 1981 North Carolina legislative reapportionment. The 1982 amendments rendered effect evidence sufficient, and two of the "Senate Report factors," minority electoral success and racially polarized voting, seemed to Brennan more important than the others. To it, he added that in at-large election cases the minority group had to be sufficiently large and geographically compact to form at least one district. The anti-intent character of the opinion is captured in the fact that Brennan explicitly rejected the use of control variables such as party in the measurement of racially polarized voting on the grounds that causation was "irrelevant to [a] Section 2 inquiry" (*Thornburg v. Gingles* [1986], 50–51, 62). Seemingly uncomplicated, this "three-pronged *Gingles* test" became the fulcrum of voting rights cases for the rest of the decade and strongly influenced the 1990s round of redistricting, being interpreted by people of nearly all political persuasions as mandating the drawing of minority opportunity districts wherever possible. Although minority plaintiffs continued to introduce intent evidence, they and most judges in minority vote dilution cases put much more emphasis on effects. Under the *Gingles* standard, minorities had unprecedented success in court, even with the judiciary increasingly dominated by judges appointed by Presidents Reagan and Bush (Grofman, Handley, and Niemi 1992; Davidson and Grofman 1994).

On the same day that it announced *Gingles*, a 6–3 majority of the Supreme Court ruled in *Davis v. Bandemer* that partisan gerrymanders were justiciable. In a striking parallel to *Brown*, Justice White's opinion for a four-person plurality of Justices Blackmun, Brennan, Marshall, and himself essentially waived the intent requirement, explicitly assuming, citing the work of social scientists, that redistricters always designed districts with partisan consequences in mind. If a partisan impact was demonstrated, the plurality was willing to infer a partisan intent. But the plurality demanded more than intent. As in the minority vote dilution cases, the plurality thought, it was necessary in partisan dilution cases to show a partisan effect. The difficulty was how to gauge that impact. Plaintiffs argued that if, in a single election, their party received a smaller proportion of seats than of votes in the state as a whole, then the courts should redress the balance. In a parallel to *Washington v. Davis*, Justice White feared that setting an impact threshold so low "would invite an attack on all or almost all redistricting plans." Consequently, he ruled that the true test of impact was an electoral system "that will consistently degrade a voter's or a group of voters' influence on the political process as a whole." Since Indiana's gerrymander had not been shown, in White's view, to disadvantage the Democrats' chances irreparably, it did not violate the equal protection clause (*Davis v. Bandemer* [1986], 127–33).

Justice O'Connor concurred in the result, but not in its reasoning. Joined by Chief Justice Burger and Justice Rehnquist, she distinguished political from racial gerrymandering and opposed judicial intervention in purely political redistricting cases. In words that ring with heavy irony when placed

next to her opinion seven years later in *Shaw v. Reno,* O'Connor said she
would deny standing to members of the major parties because they "cannot claim that they are a discrete and insular group vulnerable to exclusion
from the political process by some dominant group." Individual voters deserved protection against gerrymandering or intentional dilution only if they
were members of "racial minority groups" who were "vulnerable to exclusion
from the political process. . . . As a matter of past history and present reality,
there is a direct and immediate relationship between the racial minority's
group voting strength in a particular community and the individual rights of
its members to vote and to participate in the political process." That is, only
for racial minorities were individual and group rights intimately related, and
only those whom history proved so vulnerable to political harm that they
could not effectively defend themselves deserved redress from the courts. The
plurality's test, she thought, would inevitably eventually lead to proportional
political representation. Along with Justices Powell and Stevens, O'Connor,
Burger, and Rehnquist believed the plurality's "consistently degraded" test
was unmanageable (*Davis v. Bandemer* [1986], 151–62, 184).[27]

Although it did not have the force of a majority or plurality behind it, the
Powell/Stevens focus on intent in gerrymandering cases, racial or political,
is of obvious relevance to *Shaw v. Reno* and succeeding cases. Drawing upon
but extending earlier opinions, Powell pointed to six features that he thought
needed to be examined in order to distinguish unconstitutional gerrymandering from the usual effort to gain partisan and personal advantage through
line-drawing: compactness; contiguity; the degree of congruity of districts
with lines of political subdivisions; the process by which the law had been
adopted and the law's legislative history; population disparities; and statistics on vote dilution. Severe departures from compactness, contiguity, population equality, or the preservation of county and township lines in redistricting were indications of an intent to disadvantage opponents, as was a closed
process that gave neither opponents nor the public any influence. Legislative
histories might reveal the proponents' goals, and statistics on the dilution of
out-party votes might provide a measure of the achievement of those goals.
Most of these factors were manifestly objective, and population disparities
and vote dilution were clearly measures of impact. Indeed, Powell agreed
with the plurality that plaintiffs in such cases had to demonstrate a discriminatory effect in order to prevail, and it might be argued that his discussion,
like that of Justice White in *White v. Regester* (1973), did not make a hard and
fast distinction between intent and effect. In any event, it is significant for
Shaw that Powell quoted part of the district court opinion that pointed out
the incongruity of submerging largely black townships in districts dominated
by white suburbs (*Davis v. Bandemer* [1986], 165–77).

In the last major redistricting case before *Shaw v. Reno*, then, the Justices stood 4–2 (the plurality vs. Powell and Stevens) on whether impact, rather than intent, should be the chief focus; 6–0 (the plurality, plus Powell and Stevens) on whether dilution was an important element of a gerrymander that violated the Fourteenth Amendment; and 7–2 (the plurality and the O'Connor group) on whether the barriers to gerrymandering suits by whites and political parties should be considerably higher than those to members of groups that had traditionally been discriminated against in American politics and society. Seven years later, *Shaw* would reverse each of these conclusions and it would convince many commentators that the whole framework of minority vote dilution—from *White v. Regester* through the 1982 amendments to the VRA to *Gingles*—was in danger of being scrapped.

WHAT DOES this review of a century of Supreme Court opinions tell us about effect and intent? The Supreme Court has never followed a consistent line about whether it is possible or desirable to uncover legislative motives, and it does not now (Binion 1983, 434). Broadly speaking, intent is currently required in racial discrimination and religious establishment cases, it is irrelevant in free speech cases, it is sometimes relevant and sometimes irrelevant in gender discrimination cases, and the Court has never explained why (Klarman 1991, 303–8, on other gender cases). It has also been inconsistent in ruling whether to consider effects as evidence of intent, in specifying the degree to which courts should defer to elected bodies, and in weighing different kinds of evidence in both intent and effect cases.

Court opinions have also revealed difficulties with the notions and operationalization of both effect and intent. The problems with impact include which of several possible comparisons to use, as illustrated above in the *Cumming* and *Feeney* cases, and whether to rest equal protection on relative comparisons, such as whether blacks and whites are elected in the same proportions, or to insist that plaintiffs have to be nearly excluded from the right or benefit claimed in order to establish a constitutional violation, as they were in *Yick Wo* or *Gomillion*. Justices have feared, for example, in *Washington v. Davis*, that an impact standard might sweep too wide, calling into question any governmental program or even any aspect of society in which results were not equal for every group. And if impact is used as an element of intent, there are always the problems of determining whether it was foreseen and, if so, whether it was desired, problems best illustrated in *Feeney*.

The basic problems with intent are deciding what evidence is necessary, what evidence is available, and how it is to be assessed. If only direct evidence of the subjective purposes of framers or administrators, such as sworn confessions of racially hostile motives, is sufficient, then few violations will be found (Miller 1977, 733; Weinzweig 1983, 299–300, 318–19). Even slaveholders might have testified, in racist arguments that many antebellum judges would have found credible, that they were acting from essentially benevolent impulses in giving previously benighted Africans the benefits of Christian civilization and American prosperity. How much less ludicrous was the claim of Los Angeles County redistricters in 1981 to have acted toward Latinos only out of the most beneficent motives? Any reasonable intent standard, therefore, must allow circumstantial evidence and reject a requirement of proof of hostility.[28] This leaves the difficulty of how strong the motive must be shown to be: sole, dominant, necessary, or merely contributing. The Court has been inconsistent here as well, adopting a variation of a "necessary" standard in *Arlington Heights* and, as I will show in the next chapter, a "sole" standard in *Shaw v. Reno* and a "predominant" standard in *Miller v. Johnson*.[29] An even graver practical consideration is what evidence is available. If important decisions were made long ago, as in the Mobile cases, the evidence is likely to be quite sparse; if they are made closer to the present, judges may balk at forcing officials to testify about their actions and feelings, and officials may be reticent or worse about revealing them.[30] Where there are large numbers of actors, for instance, in a state legislature, it will be impractical to examine all the members, and usually only the few who were deeply involved in a piece of legislation will remember much about even very recent events. If the decisions took place over a series of years and were made by a shifting set of members of a governmental body, then it will often be more difficult to assign a single purpose to them, and the number of people and decisions to be analyzed may be unwieldy (Ely 1970, 1219–21). In such instances, rules of thumb in gathering and assessing evidence of their purposes will become even more important than they are in uncovering the reasons for a single decision. However strong the evidence, judges may hesitate to convict officials, in effect, of racism, and the outcomes of cases may turn on different judges' different values (Karst 1978, 1165; *Nevett v. Sides* [1978], 233 [Wisdom, concurring]). Finally, the quality and quantity of information available in each instance will vary so much that no mathematical formula for weighing preassigned categories of it will be practicable. In cases like that in Memphis, the direct evidence of intent was plentiful; in Los Angeles, scarce. In both, I believe, the argument for a racially discriminatory motive was persuasive, but no mechanical test based on one case could fit the other, and a test based on both would be too loose to be of any real use.

WHAT IS possible is to set out factors that ought to be taken into account in any inquiry into the intent with which an electoral rule was adopted or maintained, that is, a framework for organizing the totality of the evidence. Based on Supreme Court and lower federal court opinions, as well as on law journal articles and my experience in analyzing such questions in normal scholarship and in conducting research for trials, such a list, with the rationale for each factor spelled out and illustrative examples supplied, may help to guide future inquiries and may provide criteria against which to assess their adequacy and objectivity.[31]

TEN INTENT FACTORS
1. Models of human behavior
2. Historical context
3. Text of law or lines of districts
4. Demographic facts
5. Climate of racial politics
6. Background of key decisionmakers
7. Other actions of key decisionmakers
8. Statements by important participants
9. State policies and institutional rules
10. Impact

Models of Human Behavior

Underlying every causal explanation in history is an implicit or explicit model of human behavior, a theory, often inchoate, of how people typically act in certain kinds of situations. Sometimes based on empirical generalizations, sometimes on rough analogies, sometimes on common sense, these frameworks should not mechanically determine conclusions—if they do, why bother about the evidence? But they do establish baselines of initial plausibility for different possible interpretations, and the thinner the available evidence in any instance, the more determinative of conclusions the theory is likely to be. Three examples drawn from the voting rights arena illustrate, respectively, the systematic, commonsensical, and analogical foundations of models. At-large elections have repeatedly been found to disadvantage political or racial minorities (Engstrom and McDonald 1981, 1987; Davidson and Korbel 1981). Politicians who desire election or reelection care quite a lot about electoral laws and changes in them (Argersinger 1984, 489). In the first instance in American history in which a large number of members of an ethnic minority were able to vote, during the post–Civil War era in the Deep South, politicos immediately demonstrated both the willingness and the ability to gerrymander district lines in order to crack, stack, and pack African-American voters (see Chapter 1 above).

Judges, as well as historians, have frequently made such models important parts of their reasoning. In *Feeney*, for instance, Justice Stewart stressed that both federal and state governments had long given military veterans special hiring privileges, which implied that there was nothing special about Massachusetts' actions, no unusual animus against women that needed to be explained. In his plurality opinion in *Bolden*, Stewart claimed—ignoring contrary scholarly findings, even in one of the works he cited—that an at-large system of elections "was universally heralded not many years ago as a praiseworthy and progressive reform of corrupt municipal government" (*City of Mobile v. Bolden* [1981], 70, n. 15, citing Banfield and Wilson 1963, 151 but not 307-8). In *Whitfield v. Democratic Party of Arkansas* (1988), Judge G. Thomas Eisele placed considerable emphasis on the presence of a runoff requirement in France and its absence in South Korea in 1988 and in Chile before 1973 as evidence that "there are compelling, obvious reasons, completely unrelated to race, for states to opt for runoff elections" (*Whitfield v. Democratic Party of Arkansas* [1988], 1373-74). The logic behind the judge's deduction was that if governments sometimes adopt or, in his view, should adopt majority-vote requirements for nonracial reasons, then one could straightforwardly apply this generalization to explain the decisions to enact a runoff requirement in Arkansas in the 1930s and its extension to municipal general elections in 1983.[32] As the examples suggest, the strength of the inferences from literature reviews or analogies should depend on how solid the finding is in the literature and how close the analogy is. If a full review of the scholarship establishes that the type of law at issue is almost always adopted for a certain reason, or if the analogy is very close, such as the adoption of literacy tests and poll taxes in one southern state after another between 1890 and 1908, then the amount of additional evidence needed to establish the case will be less than if the scholarship is thin or contradictory or the analogy strained.

Whatever their validity in particular instances, such generalizations are significant because they provide keys to what one can expect that political actors know and foresee and because they affect the degree of skepticism with which analysts approach each possible explanation. If one expects politicians never to be interested in reelection or to be ignorant of how to draw district lines or shape other electoral rules for their advantage or their enemies' disadvantage, as attorneys for the State of Georgia purported to believe in cases involving the majority vote, then one might accept at face value statements of civic virtue and be genuinely surprised when electoral systems had the effect of disadvantaging minorities. Differences over such expectations always make "unforeseen consequences" notions obvious alternative hypotheses to racial or partisan intent. Because of their background importance in shaping reasoning, psychological or sociological models ought to be adopted self-consciously, and they ought to be based on the best available empirical evidence. There is no easier way to construct a biased "law office history" than to begin with one's conclusions, basing them on little more than unexamined individual experiences and values. The first factor, models of behavior, then, is meant to be partly prescriptive, for analysts of electoral rules and structures ought to be aware of relevant scholarly literature about parallel instances; partly descriptive, for expectations based on one's reading and experience will inevitably affect one's assessment of evidence; and partly cautionary, for awareness of possible unconscious biases may help one avoid them.

Historical Context

The second factor to review is the historical context, especially the sequence of events, which is important for what it reveals about the general attitudes and interests of decisionmakers (*Green v. County School Board* [1968]; *Village of Arlington Heights v. Metro Hous. Dev. Corp.* [1977], 267; *Rogers v. Lodge* [1982], 625; *Seamon v. Upham* [1982], 972–76; *U.S. v. Marengo County Commission* [1984], 1567). In the remand portion of the Mobile cases, for instance, the plaintiffs demonstrated that the at-large election systems for the Mobile city government and school board originated not in 1911 or 1919, as everyone had assumed at the time of the first *Bolden* case, but in the 1870s, a time of violent racial turmoil, when the vast majority of blacks were still able to vote, and when they had been appointed and elected to offices in Mobile. Mobile decisionmakers had run ward-based Democratic primaries from 1872 to 1906, designing the electoral structure to let whites settle their battles first in largely segregated primaries and then solidly confront blacks in at-large general elections, an electoral structure guaranteed to disadvantage minorities (McCrary and Hebert 1989, 107). The adoption of a numbered-post system in Memphis after the first serious black candidate for the legislature in the twentieth century nearly won election, the institution of a majority-vote requirement in the wake of the Sugarmon campaign, and the statewide adoption of a majority-vote requirement in Georgia in the midst of the threatening upsurge of black voters inspired by the civil rights movement constitute virtually dispositive evidence of the racial purposes behind the enactments, even if nothing else were known about the instances.

Hunter v. Underwood challenged a suffrage provision, Section 182 of the 1901 Alabama constitution, which had been framed by a convention whose chief purpose, openly and widely advertised, was to disfranchise as many blacks as possible (Kousser 1974, 165–71). A contention that any of the suffrage provisions was free of the white supremacist zeal that animated that convention was too incredible even for the defendants, who merely argued that the convention delegates had wished to disfranchise poor whites too (*Hunter v. Underwood* [1985], 231–32). *U.S. v. Dallas County, Ala.* involved a county government at-large election scheme that had been passed in 1901 between the time that the disfranchising convention was authorized and the time that it met (McCrary and Hebert 1989, 109–12). White politicians from Dallas County, the county seat of which is Selma, were among the leaders in the 1901 constitutional convention, and the plaintiffs successfully stressed that the same motives underlying the convention lay behind the county's at-large election provision.

In *Taylor v. Haywood County, Tenn.* ([1982], 1127–28), it was held to be significant that the county switched to an at-large mode of electing its road commission at its initial opportunity after the election of the first black ever to sit on that board. In *Garza v. Los Angeles County Board of Supervisors,* the 1959 redistricting, coming just after the closest election for supervisor in the postwar era and the only one in which a Latino candidate launched a major campaign and taking place just before new census data would be available, raised considerable suspicion. Any local or state election laws enacted shortly after the invalidation of practices such as the white primary (*Elmore v. Rice* [1947]; Lawson 1976, 49–52; *McMillan v. Escambia County, Fla.* [1981], 1245–46; *NAACP v. Gadsden County School Board* [1982], 982), during the turmoil after the *Brown* decision (*U.S. v. Marengo County* [1984]), after a serious contest by a significant minority candidate (*Zimmer v. McKeithen* [1973]; *Robinson v. Commissioners Court* [1974], 679–80; *McMillan v. Escambia County* [1981], 1247–48; *Jeffers v. Clinton* [1990], 594), after the passage of the Voting Rights Act (*Smith v. Paris* [1966]), or coterminous with a minority voter registration campaign or a racially charged election (*City of Port Arthur, Texas v. U.S.* [1981]) come into court bearing a heavy burden of doubt. Judges in each of the cited cases emphasized these contexts in their opinions.

Text of Law or Lines of Districts

The third factor to consider should be the text or provisions of the law or regulation or, in the case of alleged racial gerrymandering, the pattern of the lines drawn compared to the ethnic geography of the area (*Rogers v. Lodge* [1982], 645, n. 28 [Stevens dissent]; *Buskey v. Oliver* [1983], 1483). Does either the grammar or the substance of a law, analyzed carefully in the light of facts that can be assumed or demonstrated to have been known at a time, reveal one or more purposes? Analogously, do the twists and turns of district boundaries, compared with other proposed plans, correlate most strongly with partisan, personal, or ethnic advantage? The law at issue in *U.S. v. Dallas County,* for instance, tacked an at-large scheme on in an illogical and syntactically clumsy way at the end of a section that had clearly established a ward system

(Alabama Serial [1901], 890, Section 6). This fact raised the suspicion that the method of election was a last-minute thought, an insurance scheme to preserve white supremacy in case the constitutional convention did not go as planned, or in the event that the courts invalidated the resulting constitution (Trial Transcript, *U.S. v. Dallas County* [1982], 3326, 3659, McCrary and Kousser testimony). In another example, the addition of some but not other misdemeanors to the list of felonies for which men were disfranchised by Section 182 of the 1901 Alabama constitution was taken to be an indication of racially discriminatory intent by the Supreme Court in *Hunter v. Underwood,* especially since one of the misdemeanors appended was miscegenation, a racist "crime" for which white men were never convicted in the South (*Hunter v. Underwood* [1985], 226–28). Likewise, numbered-post, majority-vote, anti-"single shot," and staggered-terms provisions of at-large election systems can all be viewed as indicators of motivation because all are well understood to disadvantage minorities (*Nevett v. Sides* [1978], 223; *Rogers v. Lodge* [1982], 627). Similarly, secret ballot acts that denied illiterates any assistance at the time of widespread illiteracy, especially among African-Americans, broadcast their purpose. The "uncouth 28-sided figure" was enough to convince the Supreme Court in *Gomillion,* and the East Los Angeles Wall between the first and third supervisorial districts supported the same inference of ethnically discriminatory desires in *Garza.*

Basic Demographic Facts

The fourth variety of evidence to be evaluated is the basic demographic facts. A fast-growing and/or concentrated minority population, the existence of unusually populous or geographically spread-out districts that magnify the disadvantages of representatives of relatively impecunious groups, and populations whose depressed educational and economic levels reflect the vestiges of past and present racial and ethnic discrimination are all facts that politicians can be expected to observe and that, therefore, should be assumed to affect their design of electoral structures. For example, in the four single-member residency districts detailed in the 1901 Alabama law at issue in *U.S. v. Dallas County,* literate, adult male blacks constituted 78 percent of one of the districts and slight majorities of two other districts (Trial Transcript, *U.S. v. Dallas County* [1982], 3588–3600, Kousser testimony). Had courts ordered the literacy test in the 1901 Alabama constitution to be fairly administered, therefore, African-Americans would almost certainly have been able to elect at least one commissioner in Dallas County under a ward system. No one, of course, doubted that politics in Selma in 1901 was racially polarized or that whites at that time considered black political power threatening. Plaintiffs argued that these facts and the hypothesized outcome under single-member districts strengthened the case that the at-large system was adopted with a racially discriminatory intent (McCrary and Hebert 1989, 109–12). In Los Angeles County, the demographic information and discussion that comprised such a large proportion of the redistricting files, especially in 1981, showed unmistakably that all participants were aware of the gigantic size of the districts and the ethnic facts of the county's life and that they took these into account in drawing lines between supervisorial districts. In Georgia, the dramatic shrinkage in the number of majority-black counties before 1960 made the majority-vote requirement a much more attractive tool for maintaining white supremacy than it would have been two decades earlier. And the unprecedentedly detailed ethnic data released in time for the 1990s round of redistricting, together with the strictures of the 1982 VRA amendments, as interpreted in *Gingles,* made all redistricters aware of the racial consequences of every movement of lines.

Climate of Racial Politics

The fifth factor is the climate of racial politics, which is usually indicated by two basic political facts: the number of minority candidates elected and the approximate extent of racial polarization among voters. Such facts must be assumed to condition the expectations of officials who frame or maintain electoral arrangements (*Solomon v. Liberty County* [1988], 1572). In the Alabama Black Belt during Reconstruction, blacks and their white allies dominated elective offices. Although little direct evidence survives about the reasons for moves to substitute appointive for elective local governments in Dallas and other counties, historians have never doubted that racially discriminatory purposes underlay such laws. That all of the officers subsequently appointed were white—a dramatically disproportionate racial effect—is, of course, what primarily convinced historians of the racist intent of the provisions. In Sumter County, South Carolina, in a 1978 referendum on whether to switch from at-large to single-member districts for the county commission, a newspaper advertisement arranged by the incumbent white commissioners touted the easier election of minority-favored candidates as one of the "advantages" of single-member districts and, for anyone who missed the racial cue once, as one of the "disadvantages" of the at-large system. The one black among the seven county commissioners was not informed of the meeting that authorized the advertisement (*SDI,* Nov. 3, 1978; Kousser Declaration, *County Council of Sumter County, S.C. v. U.S.* [1983], 25–26). In Chattanooga, Tennessee, during the 1970s and 80s, only one black candidate for the city commission attracted a substantial white crossover vote—a fact evident even without statistical analyses of voting, since he was the only black in that one-third black city to win. It is logical to assume that projections from such past experience conditioned opinions about the consequences of changing to a single-member district system during a referendum on the subject in 1988, voting that was, as usual, racially polarized (Plaintiff's Exhibit 461, *Brown v. Board of Commissioners of the City of Chattanooga, Tennessee* [1989]).

Similarly, in Los Angeles, everyone who dealt with county government knew that no supervisor in the postwar era had been Latino, and there was a widespread understanding that, given a viable and otherwise attractive choice, Latinos usually preferred Latino candidates, but Anglos did not. In North Carolina, no legislator could have been unaware of the fact that before 1992, no African-American had been elected to Congress in the twentieth century, and no political activist who had been in the state during the 1980s could have missed the polarized Michaux and Spaulding congressional campaigns. Anyone who had been paying the least attention to political news in 1981 would have noticed the racial causes and consequences of the six-month-long fight over redistricting. While it is true, as Chief Justice Rehnquist remarked in *Shaw v. Hunt*, that there was in 1991–92 no report neatly summarizing all these facts for the legislators, they did not need such a report to realize that there had been a historical pattern of racial discrimination in redistricting in the state, that no black had been elected to Congress for ninety-two years, and that voting was racially polarized. In addition, there was a good deal of discussion of such facts in newspapers and in the legislature itself during the session (*Shaw v. Hunt* [1996], 1903).

Background of Key Decisionmakers

A sixth factor is the background of key decisionmakers, because it may reflect on their motives in particular instances (*Hendrix v. McKinney* [1978], 630–31; *Rogers v. Lodge* [1982], 645, n. 28 [Stevens dissent]). The principal framer of Section 182 of the 1901 Alabama constitution, John Fielding Burns, was a planter and longtime magistrate in Dallas County, which was at that time 80 percent black, and he presided over a court where most defendants were black (McMillan 1955, 275, n. 76). Burns's experiences reduced the plausibility of the argument made by the defendants that the section was aimed principally at poor whites (*Hunter v. Underwood* [1985], 231). James Nunnellee, who introduced the Dallas County Commission bill into the state senate in 1901, was the editor of the *Selma Times*. In 1895, he had written:

> The *Times* is one of those papers that does not believe it is any harm to rob or appropriate the vote of an illiterate Negro. We do not believe they ought ever to have had the privilege of voting. This right was given

or forced upon them and the white people by the bayonette [*sic*], and the first law of nature, self preservation, gives us the right to do anything to keep our race and civilization from being wiped off the face of the earth. (quoted in McMillan 1955, 225 n. 49)

Although their sentiments were no doubt a good deal tamer than Nunnellee's, the key roles of Ron Smith and Allan Hoffenblum of Los Angeles in campaigns against prominent minority politicians undercut arguments that they were sincerely concerned only to create districts where blacks or Latinos would have a fair chance to elect candidates of their choice. In Georgia, the radical segregationist backgrounds of majority-vote framer Denmark Groover and influential Election Law Study Commission members Peter Zack Geer, Eugene Cook, and Ben Fortson, and the moderate but still strongly segregationist words and actions of Gov. Carl Sanders cast doubt on assertions that they were unconcerned with racial issues when they fostered the majority vote requirement.

Other Actions of Key Decisionmakers

The seventh factor, other actions of key decisionmakers, like their backgrounds, may be indirect indicators of their general attitudes toward minority groups. There are two broad classes of such indicators: process indexes and output indexes. The former includes everything from imposing voting restrictions such as poll taxes or literacy tests to holding hearings and appointing minority representatives to decisionmaking bodies. A legislature that restricted the suffrage in a manner that disproportionately affected members of minority groups or that won office from such an electorate may well have been motivated by the same bias when it designed an electoral structure. Thus, in *Hunter v. Underwood*, Justice Rehnquist's quotation of parts of the white supremacist opening speech of John B. Knox, the president of the 1901 Alabama constitutional convention, and his references to other discriminatory actions of that convention were pertinent to the motives of the convention in adopting Section 182 (*Hunter v. Underwood* [1985], 230). A Georgia legislator's introduction of a manifestly racist white primary law, according to an Eleventh Circuit opinion, tainted his sponsorship of a local bill that reduced the number of county executive officers from three to one, thus making it more difficult for African-Americans in a majority-white county to elect candidates of their choice (*Carrollton Branch of* NAACP *v. Stallings* [1987], 1551–52).

Similarly, the purportedly beneficent objectives of an official body that does not provide minority group members with a forum to express their views or that creates only an appearance of listening are suspect (*Karcher v. Daggett* [1983], 2674–75 [Stevens concurrence]; *Seamon v. Upham* [1982], 1019). No Los Angeles County supervisorial redistricting plan adopted from at least 1953 through 1981 was unveiled before the meeting at which it was voted upon, and the appointment of minority boundary commission members in 1981 and the opening of commission meetings to presentations by the Californios group were mere shams. African-Americans and Latinos who were appointed to the redistricting committees in North Carolina and Texas in 1981 had little actual power. The fact is, as every previous chapter of this book has shown, that racial discrimination has been ingrained in American political institutions for so long and the stakes are so high in matters of electoral arrangements that the normal give-and-take between politicians that sometimes protects minority interests in other areas of policy is much less often sufficient when it comes to electoral rules. Courts and other observers should therefore view such processes with heightened skepticism.

The term "responsiveness" is typically applied to output measures, such as gauges of equality of services. If ghettoes or barrios have unpaved streets, no sewers, parks and schools badly in need of repair, inadequate police, fire, and medical services, few appointments to boards and commissions, etc., while Anglo areas enjoy excellent public benefits, then one suspects that electoral structures designed or maintained by the same government may be deliberately discriminatory (Defendant's Exhibits 109–110, in *County Council of Sumter County, S.C. v. U.S.* [1983]). But responsiveness is often difficult to determine precisely, for two reasons: first, records are often not available by race or ethnicity or for areas that correspond closely to ethnically distinct districts; and second, measures of different services may give different results. However accurate or unequivocal the measures, responsiveness is not the same as representation but only an indirect indicator of it. Mussolini made the trains run on time, but dispensed with elections (Note 1982a, 985). To make an intent case hinge on responsiveness, as the Fifth Circuit Court of Appeals did in *Lodge v. Buxton* (1981), is to substitute one's judgment of what government ought to be doing for the voters' right to select candidates of their own choice (*Rogers v. Lodge* [1982], 625, n. 9).

Statements by Important Participants

The eighth factor, statements by important participants, which are referred to as "smoking gun" evidence if they are sufficiently incriminating, are difficult to come by and must be interpreted with due caution and skepticism, but they may, in some cases, be significant as an indication of intent (*Village of Arlington Heights v. Metro Hous. Dev. Corp.* [1977], 268). It is certainly too strong to say that they constitute "no test of intent at all" (Weinzweig 1983, 333). The only direct evidence of the intent of the framer of Section 182, or of the views of other delegates to the 1901 Alabama Constitutional convention on the matter of Section 182, is a newspaper interview with John F. Burns, in which he stated his belief that the wife-beating provision of the section alone would disfranchise 60 percent of the adult male blacks in the state (Gross 1969, 244). The chief sponsor of a 1962 Mississippi law requiring all cities with a mayor-council form of government to adopt at-large elections urged its passage in order "to maintain our southern way of life" (quoted in McCrary and Hebert 1989, 105). The Memphis record overflows with statements of racial purpose, and those of Denmark Groover during the 1963 debate on the majority vote could not be explained away, no matter how frantically attorneys for the State of Georgia tried.

But statements from participants may be misleading because people may distort the expression of their intentions in four ways. First, they may simply forget, or say they forget, why they acted. In the depositions in the *Garza* case, the single most common response by protagonists, sometimes prompted by their counsel, was "I don't recall" (e.g., Smith dep., 98). Second, people may have, or say they have, several motives for acting, and they may retrospectively weigh one sort of intention differently than they actually did when they acted. In a 1984 deposition, Denmark Groover, who had announced in 1963 that the purpose of the runoff requirement was to contain the "bloc vote," tried to cast its purpose as merely informational, allowing voters in a second stage of the elections to know which candidate had gained certain endorsements in the first stage—an extremely strained interpretation, at best. Third, people may try to appear to be lambs when they are, or were, actually wolves. The repeated attribution to themselves of the most civic-minded, selfless motives by people whose actions belie their words is one of the perverse delights of the *Garza* record, while Georgia Gov. Carl Sanders's retrospective self-transformation into a staunch supporter of integration and black rights in *Brooks v. Harris* (1990) was rather less amusing.

As these examples make clear, there is generally much less reason to trust sworn statements made after, sometimes long after, the events, statements generated as part of a judicial process aimed at discovering whether people acted with racially discriminatory purposes or not, than there is to trust statements and evidence of behavior gathered at the time when the events took place, which are often recorded only in newspapers. It is not that reporters always get stories right or capture them in sufficient detail. But they do not usually have the same biases as politicians or their helpers, especially when those politicians' motives or reputations are on trial. Political historians conventionally rely heavily on newspapers. Used with care, they are no less essential in legal cases and as a rule are more rather than less reliable than statements carefully spun for a trial.

Fourth, sometimes sheep perversely wish to seem to be wolves, or at least they attempt to hide a bad motive behind a worse one. When they passed poll taxes, literacy or property tests, and white primary laws around the turn of the nineteenth century in the South, upper-class white Democratic disfranchisers often concealed their desire to rid the electorate of poorer whites, especially Republicans and Populists, behind a cloud of racist rhetoric. To be sure, their principal aim was to exclude most African-Americans from the polls, but they hoped simultaneously to eliminate all partisan and class opponents—objectives that they rarely paraded (Kousser 1974, 238–65). Since sophisticated and well-counseled politicians such as those in Los Angeles are unlikely to litter the area with smoldering guns, the absence of smoke should not be taken to imply that no infraction has been committed.

State Policies and Institutional Rules

State policies and formal and informal institutional rules constitute the ninth general category of relevant evidence (Miller and Packman 1987, 25). If every city or county in a particular state has exactly the same electoral structure, it is difficult to argue that one locality adopted that structure for a different purpose than the rest did. If there is no variation, in other words, there is no variation to be explained, though, of course, one could investigate why the state as a whole adopted the policy in the first place. On the other hand, if there are diverse electoral setups from place to place, then one may possibly have been chosen for racially discriminatory reasons (Trial Transcript, *U.S. v. Dallas County* [1982], 3529–42, Kousser testimony; *Dillard v. Crenshaw Co., Ala.* [1986]; McCrary and Hebert 1989, 118–21). If legislatures act inconsistently—such as by packing minorities in one area while fragmenting them in others, as Texas did in 1981—an inference of racial discrimination is logical (*Seamon v. Upham* [1982], 998–1008; *Village of Arlington Heights v. Metro. Hous. Dev. Corp.* [1977], 267). Formal rules, such as the requirement to obtain four out of five votes to adopt a redistricting plan in Los Angeles County, and informal rules, such as legislative deference to local Democratic delegations in South Carolina in 1967, also help to shape explanations. In Los Angeles County, the existence of the four-vote rule implied that one should discount much of the pro-Latino rhetoric of supervisors and their operatives in 1981 as mere posturing, because everyone realized that the final plan adopted would have to satisfy incumbents of both political parties. The tradition of legislative deference in South Carolina suggested that the analyst in the Sumter County case could concentrate on the intent of the local legislative delegation, ignoring that of other legislators, which made the problem of discerning the intent of the legislature in adopting an at-large election law for the Sumter County government more tractable (McCrary and Hebert 1989, 113).

Impact

Regardless of whether elections have been held under the system being evaluated, there is a tenth factor, the impact of the adopted rule, that overlaps with several of the previous nine (*Hendrix v. McKinney* [1978], 630–31; *Personnel Admin. of Mass. v. Feeney* [1979], 279, n. 25, 283; *Seamon v. Upham* [1982], 976–79). In vote dilution cases, the number of minority or minority-favored candidates elected is the basic measure, but one might also look at changes in the behavior of elected officials and in the demography of any redrawn districts. There are two reasons for differentiating impact from other factors. First, it may be considered prospectively, that is. the expected impact of a proposed law can be evaluated even before it goes into effect or even if it initially fails. Second, the climate of racial opinion may be changing or evidence of it at the time that the law was passed may be ambiguous, and the results of elections after the law's enactment may throw light on the way that those who voted for the law understood the nature of public opinion and behavior. The rationale for using effect as a measure of intent is that, especially with electoral rules, framers may be assumed to be aware of and to calculate the consequences of their actions carefully and to be quite good at such calculations. Often, the legislative record, official or unofficial, will make clear that the impact in question was fully foreseen, as in Memphis in 1959, where a newspaper dispatch announced that the bill mandating numbered posts "has [a] racial purpose," or in Los Angeles County in 1981, where the meeting at which the Board of Supervisors adopted a redistricting plan featured a virtual protest rally by Latinos who objected to the splitting of the Latino community between two supervisorial districts. Even when they err, as Memphis officials did when they neglected to add a runoff provision to their numbered-post system in 1959, the reaction may provide strong indications of the intent of the original law. The impact of the at-large election laws in Dallas County, Alabama, or Atlanta, Georgia—no African-Americans elected for four or five generations—buttresses other evidence of their predominant purpose.

ONCE THE evidence is organized, how should it be assessed and weighed? When historians attempt to explain an event, they implicitly or explicitly choose between two or more possible explanations. To say that racial or gen-

der discrimination motivated an action is to say that discrimination caused
the action, in some sense, and that other suggested or possible rationales did
not cause it, or were less important, or at least do not wholly exclude invidious discrimination as a cause. Explanations cannot be assessed independently but only in relation to other explanations. To appraise the evidence for
a racially discriminatory motive, arrayed under some or all of the ten rubrics
discussed above, then, one must also examine the arguments for other possible motives. How is this to be done, and what weight must be attached to
a "bad" motive for it to be sufficiently important to be illegal, or, conversely,
how powerful an influence does a "good" motive have to be to wash away
possible stains of a bad one? Listing the difficulties with explanations of purposes—as, for example, Justice Stevens did in his dissent in *Rogers v. Lodge*
(1982)—is now out of bounds, because for at least two decades solid majorities of the Supreme Court have required plaintiffs to prove racial intent.

One clear, but clearly wrong, answer to the question of what constitutes an
illegal intent would validate the actions of any government that had inventive
lawyers. In the words of Prof. John Hart Ely, the chief proponent of this approach to racial discrimination law, which amounts to what is usually termed
a "rational basis test," "it will be next to impossible for a court responsibly
to conclude that a decision was affected by an unconstitutional motivation
whenever it is possible to articulate a plausible legitimate explanation for the
action taken." Applying this principle, Ely endorsed the 1959 Warren Court
decision upholding the North Carolina literacy test adopted in 1900 as part
of what its proponents termed the "white supremacy campaign." Yet no historian who has examined the passage of that provision has ever doubted that
it was adopted primarily for a racially discriminatory purpose (Ely 1970, 1215,
n. 31, 1275–79; 1980, 138; *Lassiter v. Northampton Election Board* [1959]; Kousser
1974, 182–93). Depending on what different judges considered "plausible" or
"legitimate," such a standard would either ratify nearly every action or provide no guidance at all. Justice Brown in *Plessy* implicitly accepted the argument that mandatory segregation on railroads was a mere incidental regulation, which lacked any discriminatory intent, while the first Justice Harlan
swallowed the Augusta school board's line that by closing the only black public high school in the state, it was merely trying to take better care of black
elementary school students. A standard that might fail to rule out disfranchisement, segregation, and racially unequal exclusion from public services
cannot be acceptable. When offered to protect black rights, moreover, such
explanations have recently been treated with scorn. In the post–*Shaw v. Reno*
cases, plaintiffs' efforts to bring together and systematize facts or arguments
made during the consideration of a redistricting have been enough for courts
to reject them on the grounds that they were only post hoc rationalizations

(*Hays v. Louisiana* [1993], 1203; *Shaw v. Hunt* [1996], 1903). In matters of race, the Rehnquist Court has been much less deferential to state legislatures than was the supposedly activist Warren Court.

Even if a nonracial argument was first offered in debate or reports at the time a statute or regulation was adopted, it is unreasonable to approve just any such rationale, however compelling it might seem. From the 1840s on, proponents of school segregation claimed that blacks learned in a different manner than whites did, and that segregation was therefore beneficial for children of both races. Others contended, often plausibly, that racial separation would inhibit violence (Kousser 1988b, 941, 973–74; Fischer 1974, 138–39). Accepted at face value, both arguments are based on unquestionably legitimate and important governmental ends.[33] It follows immediately that if a court is serious about considering intent, it must pursue the quest beyond simple assertions of beneficent or neutral purposes, whenever they were made. To allow one motive, however worthy, to excuse another motive, however harmful, without further attempts to weigh their importance is to abandon a fair and honest search for intent, and to countenance policies that nearly everyone would now condemn.

While judges have seldom specified how significant a racial motive has to be to invalidate an action, they have sometimes used the terms "sole" or "predominant" or spoken of standards that may be characterized as "necessary" or merely "contributing." Except for the "sole" and "contributing" standards, two kinds of mixed motives complicate any attempts to apply these criteria in practice—mixed motives between persons and mixed motives within persons. Different people may have different goals in voting for a particular bill, for example, and one person may have more than one reason for doing so. Furthermore, differences in the power or strategies of members of a legislative body may either complicate or simplify the analyst's task in attributing causes. Some people—because of the offices they hold, such as committee chairs, or their interest in an issue, or because a legislature is closely divided and they choose to form part of a pivotal group—may be more important than others to a particular decision, and their intentions should matter more to the observer.[34]

The "sole" test is so easy to pass that it is applicable only where defendants argue just that courts ought not to decide an issue, as in *Gomillion*, because refuting an assertion that race was the sole cause of an action requires merely that a nonracial purpose be a contributing cause of one participant's assent to the action. More useful are the "necessary" and "contributing" standards of *Arlington Heights* and *Feeney*, respectively. In *Arlington Heights*, Justice Powell ruled that once discriminatory purpose had been shown to be "*a* motivating factor," the burden shifted to the agency to prove "that the same decision would have resulted even had the impermissible purpose not been considered." In other words, it had to disprove the hypothesis that a favorable disposition toward racial discrimination was a necessary condition of its action. The formula in Justice Stewart's opinion in *Feeney* not only swapped the burden of proof, but was more favorable to those alleging racial discrimination. "Discriminatory intent," according to Justice Stewart, "is simply not amenable to calibration. It either is a factor that has influenced the legislative choice or it is not" (*Village of Arlington Heights v. Metro. Hous. Dev. Corp.* [1977], 270–71, n. 21; *Personnel Admin. of Mass. v. Feeney* [1979], 277).

The *Arlington Heights* standard is asymmetric, often unrealistic, and can sometimes lead to paradoxical results. Under *Arlington Heights,* once plaintiffs show that race is a factor in a decision, all the defendants have to do is to convince a judge that any combination of nonracial factors would have produced the same result had race not been considered. Race might have been the principal motive of every member of a majority of the legislature, and a judge might rule that it was, but if she decided that the majority would have voted the same way if racial concerns had been irrelevant, then she would rule under the *Arlington Heights* standard that the legislature did not act for a racial purpose. *Arlington Heights* asks us to construct a counterfactual world in which racial matters, which quite often have been an integral part of the actual world in America, do not exist. A South without a history of slavery, segregation, and pervasive political, social, and economic discrimination against African-Americans, for instance, would be a different country — not just a convenient fiction, but a specious fantasy.

That *Arlington Heights*'s diversion from what actually happened to what might have happened is an invitation to subjectivity is illustrated in Judge Richard Freeman's decision in *Brooks v. Miller,* discussed above in Chapter 4. Although Judge Freeman admitted that race played a significant role in the Georgia legislature's adoption of the majority-vote law in 1963–64, he ruled that the legislature and Gov. Carl Sanders also had "good government reasons" for acting — the desire to avoid election tricks, such as a county machine's switching between majority and plurality requirements, depending on who was expected to run in each election. As pointed out earlier, this explanation was largely a rationalization prepared for a trial that took place thirty years after the events in question, a rationalization that had been barely mentioned during the 1960s and which was a much less plausible motive in the context of the times and for the major actors involved than was a desire to protect white supremacy. But civic-conscious intentions appealed to Judge Freeman, as they do to many judges, who may take up *Arlington Heights*'s invitation as a way of excusing the actions of legislators and governors whom they hesitate to convict of racist acts. A standard more securely tied to reality would reduce the influence of personal opinions in such cases, or at least force the judges to give better reasons for their decisions.

Even aside from the difficulty of constructing a race-free thought experiment, *Arlington Heights* can lead to paradoxes whenever legislators have mixed motives and differences in power. Suppose that on a particular issue a legislature were divided into two extreme groups of roughly equal numbers and one set of moderates, a set that could, in fact, consist of only one member.[35] Suppose also that the members of a group that favored a proposal had both racial and nonracial reasons for supporting it, that the pivotal member had no racial motivation whatsoever, and that the measure passed. Then despite the fact that race significantly motivated nearly a majority of the members, *Arlington Heights* would not find a racially discriminatory purpose, because if racial motives had been excluded, the same decision would have been made. By contrast, suppose that neither of the large groups favored or opposed the bill out of any racial concerns at all, but that the pivot had mixed racial and nonracial motives, with racial concerns inclining him toward supporting the proposal, but his other, less important values tugging him the opposite way. If race were eliminated from consideration, therefore, the proposal would lose, which would prove, according to *Arlington Heights*, that the law was actually adopted for a racially discriminatory motive. Yet the way the examples were constructed, the bill passed each time, but a racially discriminatory purpose was found when only one person was moved by race, and no racially discriminatory purpose was pronounced when a near-majority was. By not taking account of the complexity of human beings' preference functions, a complexity that everyone realizes through introspection, *Arlington Heights* can mislead. The blunter tool of *Feeney* would find discriminatory intent in either case.[36] Neither *Arlington Heights* nor *Feeney* explicitly takes into account institutional peculiarities, which might make people with certain views or holding certain institutional positions more powerful than they would be under other rules. In this respect, *Feeney*'s bluntness is potentially a defect, while *Arlington Heights* might be interpreted to include institutional details in particular cases.

The "predominant" criterion has some of the same difficulties as the *Arlington Heights* standard, but in addition it is unclear how it would treat the case of a differentially powerful legislator who pushed through a bill. If he did so for racial reasons, but other legislators followed him out of loyalty or partisanship, would this demonstrate a racial purpose? What if he were indifferent to racial concerns, but the others in his coalition, perhaps a vast majority, were not? Can "decisive" substitute for "predominant"? Although it would seem strange for an observer to ignore the motives of an overwhelming number of legislators and to call the motive of one particularly powerful member the "predominant" reason for the law's passage, that is possible in this example.[37]

Although mixed motives may pose difficulties for arguments about causation, they can sometimes be disentangled, and at other times the fact that they cannot be separated should be taken to indicate that both are necessary, for otherwise, a violation is excused by assumption (Brest 1971, 119; *McMillan v. Escambia County, Fla.* [1981], 1244–45; *Rybicki v. Board of Elections* [1982], 1109–10; *Buskey v. Oliver* [1983], 1483). The key to untangling two or more motives is to find a situation in which the actors did not have to choose both together. In 1965, for instance, the Los Angeles County Board of Supervisors could have accomplished the goal of equalizing population among districts by drawing lines that simultaneously increased the Latino proportion in the Third District, but instead it chose a more complicated series of swaps that reduced the Latino percentage in that district. In North Carolina in 1992, the legislature could have created more compact minority opportunity districts but instead chose "uglier" lines that helped Democrats. In Dallas in 1991, the Texas legislature could have drawn a "prettier" minority opportunity district, but opted to accommodate white Democratic incumbents and to disadvantage potential black opponents of the chairwoman of the state senate congressional redistricting subcommittee. The Los Angeles example strengthens the case for racial purpose; the North Carolina and Texas examples, that for partisan and personal motivations.

UNLIKE PHILOSOPHERS, who are free to speculate abstractly about what it means to say that an act was intended (e.g., Davidson 1980; Mele 1992), historians, other social scientists, and judges are limited to the available evidence, and they must do the best they can with what they have. In most instances relating to election laws, there will be multiple actors; they will be absent, uncommunicative, or of doubtful credibility by the time a legal challenge is filed; and the circumstantial evidence will be both imperfect and voluminous. Because the amount of evidence that may be arrayed under the ten different rubrics will vary from case to case, no general weighting scheme is possible. The Supreme Court has never erected clear standards or given much guidance as to how to determine intent, and to the extent that it has tried—for example, in *Arlington Heights*—its rationale has been incomplete and its criteria flawed. Both intent and effect standards are subject to manipulation and may lead to widely disparate results, depending on judges' preconceptions and the inconsistency in their treatment of evidence. Thus, judges and those who must appeal to them are in as difficult circumstances as historians are in their normal scholarship. Methodological practices, therefore, should be the same as they would be if none of the activity had anything to do with ongoing litigation (Kantor and Kousser 1993).

The basic precept of scholarship or argument, which I owe to Prof. Donald McCloskey, is "Put your thesis at risk." Applied to analyses of the intentions behind the adoption of electoral laws, this commandment implies five rules. First, clarify exactly what decision is at issue and explain why that decision is the relevant one. It may make quite a lot of difference whether the analyst focuses on the initial adoption of an electoral structure, its maintenance, or its extension to an additional area. For instance, if an at-large system or a run-off was established long ago and efforts to substitute districts or pluralities were recently rejected, which event more clearly reveals the provision's intent (*Whitfield v. Democratic Party of Arkansas* [1988])? If a runoff system was extended to a number of newly created judgeships, does any discriminatory purpose proven about the initial adoption of the runoff infect the judgeships (*Georgia v. Reno* [1995])? If a legislature chooses to draw a district to assist a particular incumbent or party or ethnic group, and then does so in a way to accommodate other redistricting interests, is it the decision to draw such a district in the first place or the actual shape of the resulting district, pushed and pulled by multiple interests, that is in question?

Second, articulate and justify your assumptions, models, and standards, or at least adopt them self-consciously. Whose intentions must be explained? How much weight must racial discrimination have had to render those intentions illegal? How do people like these, making decisions like these, generally act? In the given circumstances, how credible and how critical are various types of evidence likely to be?

Third, specify the racial discrimination hypothesis and all significant alternative hypotheses as clearly and completely as possible. In general, there will be two types: claims that the racial effect was unintended and assertions that other goals were more important. Like all hypotheses, they should be stated in ways that are potentially falsifiable, and the analyst should try to formulate definitive tests between rival theories.

Fourth, look at all of the evidence and openly confront any evidence that appears to weigh against each thesis. Psychologically, this is perhaps the most difficult rule to follow, but the potential embarrassment awaiting anyone who breaks it provides strong incentives to comply.

Fifth, choose the explanation that best accounts for the evidence and give the audience an indication of how strong the case is. A "sole intention" standard is too strong, a "contributing" standard is too weak, and a "necessary" standard is too difficult to apply in practice. If "predominant" is taken to mean "most important for those actors about whom we have telling evidence" rather than "more important for every actor" or "more important than all other causes put together," then the "best explanation" maxim is equivalent to a "predominant" standard.

In general, the analyst should make every step of her argument clear, set out the relevant facts in sufficient detail that a reader can evaluate how strongly they support her conclusions, and avoid letting preconceived notions drive the result—simple rules too often broken by judges and scholars but necessary if a particular determination of intent is to stand up to the inevitable criticism. If expert witnesses, judges, and other analysts followed these tenets, not all controversy in intent cases would be eliminated, but explanations would be more open, explicit, and comprehensive, and it would be much easier to determine when standards had not been applied uniformly. While these precepts do not furnish a magic formula, they do provide for a more regular, transparent, and therefore potentially fairer process of evaluating motives, and they undermine summary dismissals of motive-based inquiry as posing unintelligible questions (Pildes 1997, 2540).

CHAPTER EIGHT

Shaw and Postmodern Equal Protection

*C*ulture is fragile. Institutions are tough. Reformers and revolutionaries of all political stripes know this, which is why they strive so hard to demolish or transform their opponents' institutions and to solidify their own. Only by passing the Thirteenth Amendment in 1864 could abolitionists make sure that slavery, the strongest economic and social institution in the nation's history, would never revive. To try to insure that the states would guard the rights, privileges, and immunities of every person, particularly the former slaves, and to prohibit racial discrimination in the political process, the crusaders passed the Fourteenth and Fifteenth Amendments. The majority of southern whites opposed all of these enactments; their leaders were willing to use any means necessary to evade them; northern Democrats did all they could to facilitate the former rebels' schemes; and the federal protective structures were relatively weak and were further weakened by the Supreme Court. Still, it took two generations to shred the largely paper promises of the Fourteenth and Fifteenth Amendments, and slavery never rose again. In the Second Reconstruction, which rebuilt and extensively remodeled American institutions on the basis of foundations laid in the First Reconstruction, the new abolitionists dismantled mandatory segregation, strengthened the guarantee of equal participation in politics, and attacked public and private discrimination in public accommodations, housing, employment, and other areas. As understanding of the processes of discrimination grew, antidiscrimination institutions were elaborated—or often, after 1969, undermined—through executive, legislative, or judicial actions. In voting, the most important mechanism was the VRA, and the most significant changes made to it after 1965 were the 1982 amendments, which unequivocally applied it to electoral structures everywhere in the country and which allowed suits based solely on effects. As interpreted in *Gingles*, the amended VRA insured African-Americans, Latinos, and other minority citizens a strong voice in the reapportionments of the 1990s and an active ally in the Department of Justice. For the first time ever, ethnic minorities throughout the nation enjoyed real power during redistricting—and the Supreme Court bristled.

The rightward lunge of the Rehnquist Court, especially after the retirements of Justices Marshall and Brennan, is best appreciated by setting its record against those of its immediate predecessors. Although sometimes termed "revolutionary," the Supreme Court under Earl Warren in fact moved rather slowly and tentatively to expand the role laid out for it in the famous footnote 4 of *U.S. v. Carolene Products Company* (1938), 152–53, chiefly by using the equal protection clause to protect what the footnote called "discrete and insular minorities" and to insure that the political process was open, fair, and inclusive. Carving out some rights—such as voting, jury service, education, and interstate travel—as fundamental, the Warren Court gave them special attention, but it allowed white southerners fourteen years of latitude after *Brown* to take significant action against school segregation, and it hastily retreated when subjected to attacks on its early civil liberties decisions. That its reapportionment jurisprudence developed much more rapidly only proves how uncontroversial the ideal of "one person, one vote" was in an overwhelmingly urban/suburban society (Wilkinson 1979, 61–127; Murphy 1962). Although the Burger Court did cut back on the fundamental rights branch of equal protection, rejecting the view that governments had to insure equality in the benefits that they provided because that might mean subsidizing benefits for the poor, it expanded the reach of the equal protection clause to cover middle-class women. Its record on school segregation, affirmative action, and voting rights was quite mixed. While it ordered extensive desegregation in Charlotte, North Carolina, and Denver, Colorado, it disapproved cross-district busing in Detroit, Michigan. Remedial, very carefully designed, or congressionally sanctioned affirmative action programs passed its muster, and though it reined in Section 5 of the VRA in *Beer* and Section 2 in *Bolden*, it read the Constitution and the revised Section 2 expansively in *Lodge* and *Gingles* (Klarman 1991, 282–310; Burns 1987; Williams 1987). By contrast, the Rehnquist Court, like the Waite and Fuller Courts in the nineteenth century, employed the equal protection clause to overturn policies with which the justices merely disagreed, nonchalantly upsetting or blithely ignoring inconvenient precedents, discarding any pretense of following the original intent of the constitutional framers, a popular conservative slogan of the 1970s and 80s, and threatening a return to the conservative activism of the pre-1937 era (Kay 1980; Maltz 1990). Nowhere was the Rehnquist reaction more striking than in the area of minority voting rights, where a supportive and nearly universal consensus had seemed to reign when Rehnquist replaced Burger as chief justice in 1986.

A Guide to a Long Chapter

Overviews of judicial opinions on particular subjects may have different purposes. For example, decisions may be taken as indicators of public opinion or policy, in which event discussions of particular cases may be brief or skeletal (e.g., Kousser 1986). A more familiar approach skims opinions to extract the common principles that they embody. Assuming that there is some shared meaning, some rational coherence, some logical strand of ideas, the analyst who takes this approach merely seeks to uncover that meaning. In this long, continuing, and obviously useful tradition, inconsistencies between and within cases are to be ignored, smoothed out, or perhaps condemned, and opinions must be discussed rather summarily (e.g., Cooley 1868; Pildes 1997). A third approach, the one pursued here, is to describe the legal developments, to seek to explain why particular judges decided as they did, and to offer logical and factual evaluations of their arguments. Where opinions are complex and contradictory, and where they are at considerable variance with facts, as is the case in recent voting rights law, this third approach, unlike the first two, requires extensive and detailed treatment of a large number of opinions—perhaps more detailed than some readers will appreciate.

There is another reason for the length of this chapter. While praise can be expressed sparely, serious criticism requires the meticulous marshaling of evidence. My conclusions are that *Shaw v. Reno* and its successors are revolutionary, contradictory, and incoherent; that they are infected with racial and partisan bias; and that they have turned the intent of the Fourteenth and Fifteenth Amendments on their head and deliberately distorted history and language in an effort to stamp out the embers of the Second Reconstruction. Much more than a quick glance at the evidence is necessary to sustain such charges.

Signposts, in the form of subheadings throughout the chapter, and a basic road map may help. The Supreme Court considered racial gerrymandering cases in the 1960s and 70s, but rejected challenges to districts that had apparently been designed to make it possible for minorities to elect preferred candidates. Neither the prevailing opinions nor the dissents, I argue, provided any unambiguous support for the 1993 case of *Shaw v. Reno*. Instead, *Shaw* was a radical departure, granting standing to plaintiffs who could not show specific injury; inventing largely fictitious harms to society; exalting a vague, open-ended, and factually unwarranted category of "traditional districting principles," especially aesthetically pleasing district shapes, over the original egalitarian intent of the Fourteenth Amendment; and appropriating heightened, egalitarian language from the civil rights movement in an effort to undermine some of the chief gains of that movement. The next year, after the initial barrages against *Shaw,* the five-person *Shaw* majority of the Supreme Court seemed hesitant and divided. Two of the five, Justice O'Connor and Chief Justice Rehnquist, joined in reaffirmations of the Court's commitment to the VRA and to race-conscious baselines for evaluating legal and constitutional matters, while two others, Justices Scalia and Thomas, called for the reversal of twenty-five years of Supreme Court decisions that applied the VRA to election structures.

In the wake of historic Republican victories in the 1994 elections, the *Shaw* majority once more came together in *Miller v. Johnson* (1995), an even more radical opinion that deemphasized the shape of districts, substituted a "predominant motive" standard for *Shaw*'s "sole factor" criterion, and opened up to constitutional challenge every district in which a "significant" number of minority voters had been "placed," in which redistricters had used "race as a proxy" for political behavior, which threatened not only every minority opportunity district in the country but every district in which minorities enjoyed substantial influence. The same term, the Court also created an ad hoc, conceptually illogical solution to the puzzle of who had standing to bring a racial gerrymandering suit by ruling in *Hays v. Louisiana* that only those who lived in the confines of the challenged district could sue.

In 1996, the five *Shaw* justices fragmented again in the Texas case of *Bush v. Vera,* O'Connor reemphasizing compactness as both a necessary and sufficient condition for minority opportunity districts, a view directly challenged by Kennedy, Scalia, and Thomas. Taking the extremely unusual step of filing a concurring opinion in a case in which she herself had written the prevailing opinion, O'Connor also hinted that her four erstwhile allies stood ready to declare Section 2 and perhaps Section 5 of the VRA unconstitutional. However, the five justices agreed in both *Vera* and *Shaw v. Hunt,* the second iteration of the *Shaw* case from North Carolina, that neither race-conscious efforts to comply with the VRA nor attempts to correct past discrimination and combat present discrimination were acceptable justifications for creating the particular minority opportunity districts at issue. Not only was the VRA stripped of its ability to protect minority voters during redistricting, it was interpreted by Justice O'Connor in a way that patently discriminated against minority voters. While majority white districts could assume even the most convoluted shape and could contain any percentage of whites, Section 2 of the VRA, in O'Connor's formulation, required that any minority opportunity district be as compact as a hypothetical judge might draw it, and Section 5 prevented any increase in the minority group proportion of any district with that contained a large number of minority voters.

The *Shaw* majority did not apply the same standards to Republican-drawn plans from California and Ohio as it did to Democratic plans from North Carolina, Georgia, and Texas. In California, the author of the redistricting plan admitted that he deliberately drew minority opportunity districts and that they were not geographically compact. The Supreme Court summarily affirmed a district court decision sustaining the plan (*DeWitt v. Wilson* [1995]). In Ohio, a Republican redistricting board openly packed blacks into as few state legislative districts as possible, claiming that the VRA required such packing, which also conveniently maximized the number of Republican seats. When a district court ruled that the Ohio plan diluted African-Americans' overall influence in state politics by raising their percentages in a few districts to unnecessarily high levels, the Supreme Court, in an O'Connor opinion issued shortly before *Shaw v. Reno*, sustained the Republican plan, praising Ohio for relying on an interpretation of the VRA, however erroneous that interpretation, instead of on such traditional standards as compactness, which were set out in the state's own constitution (*Voinovich v. Quilter* [1993]). After *Miller*, Ohio Democrats sponsored a racial gerrymandering challenge to the legislative plan, and they had no trouble convincing the district court to rule that racial motives had predominated in the drawing of the heavily black districts in the state. But without comment, the Supreme Court remanded the Ohio case back to the district court, implying that the lower court's opinion was somehow inconsistent with *Miller* and *Vera* (*Voinovich v. Quilter* [1996]).

Why was the Supreme Court so inconsistent from opinion to opinion? In particular, why did Justice O'Connor, seemingly the pivotal voter in many of the cases, insist on a vague compactness standard that had no grounding in the Constitution or in federal law? Why did O'Connor not go all the way toward a standard of absolute colorblindness in redistricting, paralleling her strong stances in affirmative action cases, as "colorblind" lawyers and scholars such as Abigail Thernstrom pressed for? With O'Connor's vote, a five-person majority could almost surely have been formed to rule the VRA unconstitutional and to outlaw every minority opportunity district and every attempt to preserve or increase minority group influence in politics. After examining a series of hypotheses, I conclude that the best explanation is the Republican partisanship of the only Supreme Court justice on the Rehnquist Court ever to have served in major elective office, former Arizona State Senate majority leader Sandra Day O'Connor.

After identifying a series of questions and contradictions in the racial gerrymandering cases that the Court must answer and clarify if the opinions are ever to serve as a guide to practitioners, I turn to the effect of the decisions on the redistricting of 2001. The redistricting cycle of the 1990s was the most open to the public and the fairest to racial minorities in American history, and it was based on the most detailed and precise social and political information ever. Legal guidelines were clear and well understood, both the law and the Department of Justice provided active protection for racial minorities, and the vast majority of redistricting decisions were made, at least initially, by elected officials and their employees, not by judges. Because of the vague and contradictory *Shaw* line of decisions and the broad invitations to judicial activism that they contain, the next redistricting cycle is likely to be closed to the public, the information actually used to draw lines is apt to be hidden, the negotiations between representatives of minority groups and their normal Democratic allies will probably be either nonexistent or deeply secret, and regardless of what legislatures or other elected bodies accomplish, federal judges, the vast majority of whom will be Reagan-Bush appointees, are nearly certain to make most of the important redistricting choices in any state containing an appreciable number of minority group members. The *Shaw* cases have largely expelled minority group representatives and even elected officials from the political thicket of redistricting and left white "conservative" Republican judges in charge. And in a savage irony, the opinions that led to this result were said to be based on the Fourteenth Amendment, an amendment that sought above all to protect the recently freed slaves from hostile governmental action led by members of political parties opposed to them.

Racial Gerrymandering in the Supreme Court before *Shaw*

The 1990s were not the first time that the Court confronted the question of racial gerrymandering. Despite the immense number of racial gerrymanders *against* minorities during and after the First Reconstruction and during the Second, *Gomillion* was the only antiminority racial gerrymandering case that the Supreme Court heard before 1993, a fact that prompted a leading voting rights attorney to describe winning such cases before any court as "well-nigh impossible" (Derfner 1982, 66). But in the 1960s and 70s, the Court had twice rejected pleas that it was illegal to take race into account in redistricting in ways apparently meant to assist minorities in electing candidates of choice. Both cases came not from the South but from New York City, and the first had more political overtones than the Court's opinion revealed.

Population shifts cost New York State two congressional seats after the 1960 census, and the Republican-controlled legislature took both of them out of overwhelmingly Democratic Manhattan, reducing the island's districts from six to four. To retain the one Republican seat, the predominantly upper-class, "silk-stocking" Seventeenth District, which the party had barely won in 1954 and 1956, Republicans underpopulated it by 10 percent compared to the average Manhattan district, paired two sets of liberal Democratic incumbents, and packed African-Americans and Puerto Ricans into the 86 percent nonwhite Eighteenth District. The packing insured the reelection of Adam Clayton Powell, the black congressman who had endorsed Dwight Eisenhower for president in 1956 and feuded with Tammany Hall in 1958. Powell later told a prominent Democratic Party lawyer that he had personally negotiated the lines of his Eighteenth District with a representative of Republican Governor Nelson Rockefeller. The New York state redistricting attracted considerable national attention at the time, Democratic National Committee chairman John M. Bailey denouncing it as "an example of political larceny in the robber baron tradition." In policy terms, however, black interests were well served by silk-stocking Republican congressman John V. Lindsay, a principal draftsman of the 1957 and 1964 civil rights laws (Martis 1982, 195, 197; Congressional Quarterly 1961; Hamilton 1991, 254, 266–75, 301–8, 422–23; Hentoff 1969, 60–62).

A 2–1 majority of a federal district court ruled that the maps and statistics presented by those who challenged the districts as drawn with the purpose and effect of "ghettoizing the Island of Manhattan" did not prove their case. Judge Leonard Moore focused on the plaintiffs' failure to show through anything other than district appearances that political or racial considerations had motivated the redistricters. While Judge Wilfred Feinberg believed that segregating people in different districts solely because of race was unconstitutional, he held that nonracial purposes outweighed racial ones in this instance, since the district lines were fairly straight, the populations between districts were not grossly unequal, and the new boundaries built on the old ones in a fashion that he found "logical." In dissent, Judge Thomas F. Murphy was persuaded merely by the percentages of racial groups in each district— 86 percent nonwhite in the Eighteenth, 5 percent in the Seventeenth—that the redistricting law was "solely concerned with segregating" voters by "fencing" nonwhites out of the Republican district and into Powell's. Seven members of the Supreme Court, in a five-page opinion written by Justice Hugo Black, accepted the lower court's findings on the facts without discussing why and without explicitly considering whether pro-minority redistricting was unconstitutional and, if so, under what circumstances (*Wright v. Rockefeller* [1962]; [1964], 54–58).[1]

Justices William O. Douglas and Arthur Goldberg dissented, Douglas in a flowery denunciation of "racial boroughs" that dwelt on ethnically separate voting lists in India, Cyprus, and Lebanon, and concluded that "no State could make an electoral district out of any racial bloc unless the electoral unit represented an actual neighborhood."[2] He did not, however, spell out any means of determining what constituted a neighborhood, though his description of the district boundaries in New York seemed to indicate that he thought a neighborhood was always something delineated by long straight lines. Goldberg's discussion was the most theoretical, declaring that under *Brown* any state-sanctioned segregation was unconstitutional per se and that neither an actual motive nor harm to individuals need be proven. Since Goldberg thought that once a prima facie case of racial effects was made, the State should be given a chance to rebut "the inference that racial segregation was a purpose of the districting," he did, in fact, embrace what I refer to in Chapter 7 as an intent standard, albeit a very weak one (*Wright v. Rockefeller* [1964], 59–74).

There are four things to note about the case. First was the widely rumored alliance between the Republicans and Powell, and the mixed motives that that alliance represented. Since Republicans rammed the redistricting bill through just a day after it had been introduced in the legislature, holding no public hearings and carefully pairing only Democratic incumbents against each other throughout New York state in a reported effort to change the balance of the state's congressional delegation from 22–21 Democratic to 25–16 Republican, it seems likely that a full analysis would show that partisan and personal, not racial, motives predominated (Congressional Quarterly 1961).[3] Second, the district was really quite segregated, much more so than any drawn in the South after the 1990 census. If segregation was the constitutional and moral evil to be combated, what would Douglas or Goldberg have said about districts like those in North Carolina in 1992 that were only 50–65 percent black, not "racial registers" but much more integrated than nearly any other social, economic, or political institution in America? Third, seven members of the Court expressed no opinion on the standards proposed in Douglas's and Goldberg's dissents, possibly accepting them and just disagreeing on whether the facts made a convincing case or possibly rejecting the criticisms of taking race into account in redistricting. Fourth, despite their rhetoric, neither Douglas nor Goldberg would have banned race-conscious districting altogether. Douglas made an exception for what he called "neighborhoods," which in less populated states would have to stretch across many counties. Goldberg would have allowed the State to rebut the charge of racial purpose even though the Eighteenth District was overwhelmingly nonwhite and even though New York openly admitted that it had considered race in designing its districts (*Wright v. Rockefeller* [1964]). The dissenting opinions in *Wright* provide only uncertain precedents and complicated analogies for the "racial gerrymandering" cases of the 1990s.[4]

Thirteen years later, the Supreme Court squarely faced the issue of racial gerrymandering in *United Jewish Organizations of Williamsburgh v. Carey* (1977), thereafter known as *UJO*. The 1970 amendments to the VRA brought three counties in New York under the coverage of Section 5. When a plan to redistrict the state legislature was submitted to the Justice Department, the department objected to the packing of African-Americans and Puerto Ricans into a few overwhelmingly nonwhite districts in the Bedford-Stuyvesant section of Brooklyn, commenting that there was no apparent reason why these groups could not be spread out into a larger number of districts. In fact, there had been a solid tradition of racial gerrymandering—against people of color— since the Brooklyn ghetto began to expand in the 1950s. The 1961 redistricting plan, for instance, sliced the ghetto into five congressional districts, and it took a 1967 federal district court decision and a subsequent redistricting to unite the black neighborhood, making possible the first ever election of a black member of Congress from Brooklyn (Connolly 1977, 162–80; *Wells v. Rockefeller* [1969]).[5] In redrawing the state legislative districts in 1974, after the Justice Department's objection, New York split an area dominated by Hasidic Jews, who had previously been concentrated in single state assembly and senate districts. Implicitly assuming that they formed a politically cohesive group themselves by asserting that the new plan would cut the "effectiveness" of their votes in half, members of the conservative sect also contended, contradictorily, that they had been assigned to the two new electoral districts solely because of their white race. Their attempt to enjoin implementation of the plan was summarily dismissed by a federal district court in New York, which ruled that racial considerations could constitutionally be employed in an effort to correct past discrimination, and that Hasidic Jews had no right to recognition as a separate minority group during redistricting. Since the case never went to a full trial, neither side presented any substantial evidence that there had been previous discrimination against nonwhites in Brooklyn, that voting was racially or religiously polarized, or that their groups were politically cohesive. A divided appeals court affirmed the lower court decision, the majority of James L. Oakes and Robert J. Kelleher ruling that the state's responsibility to comply with Section 5 necessitated taking race into account and pointing out that whites were overrepresented in Kings County's legislative delegation. Dissenting judge Marvin Frankel decried the effort to shape districts that were approximately 65 percent nonwhite, in order to maximize the number of districts in which nonwhites had an opportunity to elect candidates of their choice, instead of establishing districts that had higher or lower percentages (*UJO* [1974]).

Although they could not agree on a single opinion, seven of the Supreme Court Justices firmly rejected the plaintiffs' contention that taking race into account in redistricting was always unconstitutional.[6] In the simplest opinion, Justice Stewart, speaking for himself and Justice Powell, held that the state's purpose was to comply with Section 5, not to disadvantage whites, and that the plan lacked a discriminatory effect because whites still composed majorities in 70 percent of the districts, even though only 65 percent of the county's population was white. Since the plan lacked a discriminatory purpose or effect, it was constitutional. More elaborately, and like an attorney offering alternative bases for finding for his client or a legislator engineering a logroll, Justice White attracted three votes (Stevens, Blackmun, and Brennan) for the proposition that compliance with Section 5 validated race-conscious redistricting and two votes (Stevens and Rehnquist) for the view that even if the VRA had not existed, the use of race in redistricting did not violate the Fourteenth or Fifteenth Amendments so long as it did not represent a "racial slur or stigma with respect to whites or any other race."[7] By passing Section 5, White said, Congress meant to substitute a speedy administrative procedure for lengthy judicial review of electoral changes in states or counties where there was a pattern that suggested racial discrimination in voting rules. After 1965, minorities in these areas did not have to go to court to prove discrimination in order to stop the institution of new laws relating to voting, including new redistrictings. Unless the Court was willing to overturn *Allen, Beer,* and other precedents and to rule Section 5 unconstitutional, covered jurisdictions had to have the right to draw race-conscious districts, with whatever percentage of minorities the state and the Justice Department could agree on, in order to comply with national law.[8] The part of White's opinion that Rehnquist, but not Blackmun or Brennan, joined treated this as a typical vote dilution case. Applying the dilution standard from *White v. Regester,* Justice White noted that the plan did not prohibit any white voter from participating in the political processes of the county or "unfairly cancel out white voting strength," which was apparently a euphemism for proportional representation. "Intentional reduction of white voting power" by shifting lines to insure that minorities had a better chance to elect candidates of their choice was constitutional, Justice White concluded, and he noted, without explicitly making it a necessary condition, that the state had employed "sound districting principles such as compactness and population equality." He did not explain what he meant by compactness or what its link to the constitution was, or what other districting principles might be "sound" (*UJO,* [1977], 155–68, 179–80).

In a dictum to his concurring opinion, Justice Brennan, speaking for himself alone, raised cautions about the constitutionality of race-conscious redistricting outside of areas covered by Section 5. While he approved "benign" or pro-minority affirmative action, he noted that some Puerto Rican and black intervenors in the case opposed the plan at issue, which showed that it was not always easy to tell which policies were favorable to minorities. He also worried that the explicit use of race in redistricting might "stimulate our society's latent race consciousness," stigmatize beneficiaries by implying that they needed special protection, or leave whites with an "impression of injustice," especially if a "coherent group like the Hasidim," rather than more heterogeneous white communities, were split. Such considerations, Brennan implied, might have to be balanced against the benefits of greater influence for minorities in jurisdictions not subject to Section 5. Because it would be so difficult, Brennan asserted, to disentangle the motives for the inevitable reliance on race during redistricting, it was appropriate to analyze it under an impact standard, which Section 5 allowed. On that score, Brennan was perfectly in accord with the other six justices that the plan was constitutional because it had no discriminatory effect (*UJO* [1977], 168–79).

Only Chief Justice Burger dissented, accepting the propositions, without citing any evidence, that racial bloc voting was a thing of the past and that a political melting pot was constitutionally required—except in the case of Hasidic Jews, whom he thought had a right not to be split between districts for the purpose of benefiting blacks and Puerto Ricans. What bothered him most, as it had Judge Frankel, was very equivocal evidence that the Justice Department had used a 65 percent nonwhite level as a rule of thumb in deciding whether a district allowed minorities, who typically registered and voted at lower proportions than whites did, a fair opportunity to elect candidates of choice. In an interpretation that stood *Gomillion* on its head, Burger read the Tuskegee case as expressing the principle that redistricting could not set a "quota" of members of a particular race, when, in fact, the district in *Gomillion* was ruled unconstitutional because Alabama had removed nearly all the blacks from the town limits with the purpose and effect of severely reducing their political power. Since there was no evidence in *UJO* that the influence of whites or even of the Hasidim was unfairly diminished by the redistricting, *Gomillion*, properly understood, did not support their case. The Chief Justice also contended that if, as the lower court had found, the redistricting was partly designed to rectify historical discrimination in redistricting against nonwhites in Brooklyn, the proper remedy was to redistrict "along neutral lines." How to determine such lines or why 90–95 percent nonwhite districts were more "neutral" than 65 percent districts, Burger did not say (*UJO* [1977], 180–87).

The Supreme Court did not hear another racial gerrymandering case for sixteen years. The prospect of winning such a case, particularly for whites seeking to dismantle minority opportunity districts in areas subject to Section 5, did not seem high. The two previous challenges had attracted only one or two votes, and it might be embarrassing for a "conservative" court to ignore or overthrow such well-established recent precedents. Chief Justice Rehnquist, the leading "conservative," was on record in *UJO* as approving race-conscious districting even if the VRA had never been passed. Justice O'Connor, the leading "moderate," had denied in her dissent in *Davis v. Bandemer* (1986) that anyone except disadvantaged ethnic minorities could claim discrimination against them in a redistricting case. Outside the judiciary, Democrats throughout the country had no alternative but to support greater representation for two of their core constituency groups, African-Americans and Latinos, while Republicans in the 1980s and early 1990s gleefully dangled alliances of convenience before minority leaders, hoping that packing them into minority opportunity districts would translate into more Republican seats elsewhere (Kelly 1995).[9] The Republican-controlled Department of Justice and every minority public interest law group—particularly the NAACP, the NAACP-LDF, the ACLU, and MALDEF—mobilized vigorously to expand minority opportunity districts and met little resistance from politicians. Despite Republican dominance of federal judgeships and several Supreme Court decisions overturning affirmative action programs, the legal consensus on voting rights seemed firm. Even the Thernstroms admit that at the time, "it was scarcely an exaggeration to say that race-conscious action in the electoral sphere had only adherents" (Thernstrom and Thernstrom 1997, 481). At celebrations of the twenty-fifth anniversary of the VRA in 1990, most voting rights activists saw no dangers looming.

Then came *Shaw*.

The Basic Questions in the Racial Gerrymandering Cases

Shaw v. Reno (1993) and its successors over the next three years—*Miller v. Johnson* (1995), *U.S. v. Hays* (1995), *Shaw v. Hunt* (1996), and *Bush v. Vera* (1996)— were confused and inconsistent because they invented "facts" and distorted history, using the Reconstruction Amendments to protect powerful whites rather than much less politically potent minorities, employed the language of equality and integration to promote inequality and exclusion, and established racial and partisan double standards while pretending to be colorblind and nonpartisan. In a theoretical sense, the cases foundered on four fundamental questions.

First, what was the nature of the constitutional harm? In minority vote dilution, reapportionment, segregation, employment discrimination, and affirmative action cases, a law or practice disadvantaged someone—a minority or suburban voter, a black or Latino pupil, or someone who lost a job, a contract, a promotion, or admission to a school allegedly because of his or her race or gender. Who was hurt by pro-minority redistricting, and how? Was white political power unfairly diminished, and if so, what was the standard of fairness? Were whites or minorities stigmatized by it, and if so, how was that stigma to be measured and how was it to be balanced against benefits of the redistricting? If they were not stigmatized, were some people stereotyped, and if so, did it make any difference whether or not the stereotypes were true? Was there a harm to the polity itself, an "expressive harm," and if so, how was it to be identified and how was it to be connected to any constitutional provision (Pildes and Niemi 1993)? Was the problem one of illicit influence over or bias in the redistricting process, and if so, why was this a problem only when minorities exercised that influence, not when whites did?

Second, what was the connection between previous cases and whatever harm was at issue here? Was *Shaw* the obvious and natural successor of *Brown* and *Reynolds v. Sims*, as its academic defenders claim (Blumstein 1995; Butler 1995; O'Rourke 1995)? How was it connected to the VRA and to minority vote dilution cases? Did it implicitly repeal Section 2 and Section 5 and reverse all of the minority vote dilution cases, as some of its celebrants apparently believed, or could the two strands of law coexist, separate and unequal? Since at least *Washington v. Davis* (1976), racial equal protection cases had required proof of intent. Would the *Shaw* line of cases adopt an intent standard, and if so, which one? During the Burger and Rehnquist years, the Court had repeatedly denied standing to bring a case to plaintiffs who merely wished to air a public policy issue, often delivering stern lectures to environmentalists or people who wished to challenge racially discriminatory actions on the propriety of settling such disputes in the legislative branch. If the harm in *Shaw* was merely to the polity in general, what private person had standing to speak for the "public interest," and what differentiated racial gerrymandering cases in this regard from the earlier standing decisions?

Third, what was the baseline against which to measure racial gerrymandering, what role did that baseline play in the analysis, and what was the constitutional or other justification for that baseline? Two reasons that *Reynolds v. Sims* (1964) was so easily and widely accepted were the close linguistic and philosophical link between the equal protection clause and equal population in each district and the fact that virtually all numerical indexes of population equality gave nearly identical results on actual redistricting plans (Altman 1998, chap. 6). How would one know if a constitutionally suspect racial gerrymander had taken place? If there were some numerical standard, such as a measure of compactness, which one should it be, since more than thirty had been proposed and they gave extremely different results (Altman 1998, chap. 2)? Was noncompactness, however measured, merely an indication of a suspicious purpose, or was it somehow a violation itself, and if a violation, why were noncompact white districts not unconstitutional? Were there any other characteristics besides compactness, that helped to define a baseline for distinguishing illicit from licit districts, and if so, why were they constitutionally necessary or relevant?

Fourth, what was the proper relation in these cases and the issues that they raised between the courts and other branches of government? In *UJO*, the Court had deferred to Congress and the Department of Justice as declarers and executors of public policy, more specialized and better able to seek out information in framing voting rights policy and to carry it out affirmatively, instead of having to wait for cases to be brought, sporadically, as the judicial branch did. In *Wright v. Rockefeller* and in reapportionment cases such as *Gaffney v. Cummings* (1973) and *Davis v. Bandemer* (1986), the Court had allowed state legislatures considerable leeway in their goals in designing districts, approving protection of incumbents and, within limits, purposeful disadvantaging of partisan opponents. Would the courts be as deferential to other branches of government in *Shaw*-type cases?

Shaw v. Reno: The Preliminaries

As after every round of redistricting since 1961, the 1991–92 reshuffling of lines sparked immediate and massive litigation in which losers tried to gain in the courts what they had failed to secure in the legislatures, commissions, or local governments, while enterprising lawyers and often quirky ideologues trotted out new legal theories or refurbished old ones (Karlan 1993b, 1727–29). The plaintiffs in *Shaw v. Reno* offered a variety. Their most fundamental argument was that the legislature, under pressure from the Department of Justice, had perpetuated a "racial gerrymander" that infringed the rights of every North Carolinian, under the equal protection clause and the Fifteenth Amendment, "to participate in a process for electing members of the House of Representatives which is color-blind and wherein the right to vote is not abridged on account of the race or color of the voters." But they also added much less orthodox claims that no judge during the litigation deigned to address. Their lawyer, Robinson Everett, claimed that mention of "the people" in Article I, Section 2 of the U.S. Constitution implied that "the people" could not be divided on racial grounds, that the grant in Article I, Section 4 of control over the "times, places and manner of holding elections" to state legislatures implied that all federal control was illegal, and that colorblind voting was a "privilege" guaranteed by the privileges or immunities clause of the Fourteenth Amendment (Everett 1993, 15; *Shaw v. Barr* [1992], 470).

Everett was unlucky enough to draw two judges with considerable experience in voting rights, J. Dickson Phillips Jr. and W. Earl Britt, two of the three judges who had heard the *Gingles* case. These two Democrats treated Everett's seemingly quixotic theories rather brusquely, dismissing claims against both federal and state defendants on the grounds that the plaintiffs had proven neither a discriminatory purpose nor a discriminatory effect and that therefore, according to previous vote dilution precedents, they had failed "to state a claim under which relief can be granted."[10] Not only did *UJO*, in Phillips's view, squarely decide the issue, but the fact that blacks comprised only a small proportion of the legislature virtually foreclosed a case of invidious racial intent, for how could they have controlled that body? The fact that even if they were to win two of the twelve seats African-Americans would have less than proportional statewide representation in Congress made it impossible to demonstrate a discriminatory effect (*Shaw v. Barr* [1992], 462–73).

Although agreeing with the majority that the case against the federal defendants should be dismissed and that race-conscious districting was not unconstitutional per se, Judge Richard Vorhees, a Republican, thought that *UJO* allowed such districting only if lines followed what he characterized as the "time-honored, constitutional concepts . . . such as contiguity, compactness, communities of interest, residential patterns, and population equality." Plaintiffs might, he thought, be able to prove at a full trial that there had been discrimination against black voters who had not been included in the First or Twelfth Districts or white voters who had not been excluded from them—that is, that the districts were not segregated enough.[11] Operating fully within the tradition of vote dilution litigation, Vorhees called for a trial to give plaintiffs a chance to prove "invidious discrimination against majority race voters." The rough statewide proportionality between the percentage of blacks in the population and the percentage of minority opportunity districts in Congress had to be balanced against what he asserted to be the facts that blacks and whites who lived in the same areas "share the same interests and concerns" and that there was no racially polarized voting, enabling them to "elect a mutually agreeable Representative, irrespective of race" (*Shaw v. Barr* [1992], 473–81). Vorhees presented no evidence for any of these assertions, which, as Chapter 5 has shown, were all false.

The spectrum of arguments broadened when *Shaw* was first appealed to the Supreme Court.[12] Stealing a phrase from Justice Brennan's opinion in *UJO*, Everett asserted that North Carolina whites had suffered an "impression of injustice" because the Twelfth District was drawn to allow black voters to elect a candidate of their choice, who, Everett claimed, would "consider his primary duty to be the representation of blacks." Yet in a curious racial double standard, he contended that African-Americans would gain no "benefit"—not even an "impression of justice," to reverse his phrase—from having a responsive representative. Indeed, he argued, the action "was an implicit affront to blacks because it implied that they are incapable of organizing coalitions to elect favored candidates of whatever race" (Everett 1993, 42–45). Unlike the NAACP in *Brown*, Everett made not the slightest effort to prove his psychological allegations, and he and every observer of North Carolina politics during the 1980s knew that the Michaux and Spaulding congressional campaigns disproved his dreamy-eyed statement about coalitional possibilities.[13] An utterly speculative "impression of injustice" might not have seemed a sufficiently grave harm to merit much attention from the Supreme Court.[14]

Not only were his facts untrue and his injury dubious and innocuous,[15] but Everett's constitutional arguments and those of groups that filed amicus briefs in *Shaw*—the Republican National Committee, North Carolina senator Jesse Helms, and the conservative Washington Legal Foundation—also contradicted each other. For example, Everett believed that the Constitution prohibited any race-conscious districting at all, whether performed by the state on its own or under the rubric of the VRA, and he sought to prohibit the use of racial statistics to aid in drawing minority opportunity districts (Everett 1993, 15, 27). On the other hand, Republicans, who unsuccessfully challenged both the North Carolina and Texas congressional redistrictings as *partisan* gerrymanders in which Democrats had allegedly paraded a concern with racial minority interests to cover their real, partisan motives, favored allowing some race-conscious districting (*Pope v. Blue* [1992]; *Terrazas v. Slagle* [1991]). As their actions in Ohio made clear, Republicans were perfectly willing to pack blacks into minority opportunity districts (*Voinovich v. Quilter* [1993]; Karlan 1993a). What bothered them was allocating minority voters who were not necessary for control of a district to nearby districts in order to increase the number of legislators that minorities could influence and Democrats could elect. Simply put, the Republican National Committee favored race-conscious districting if it hurt Democrats but opposed it if it hurt Republicans.

The two allies also differed on the importance of compactness and similar limiting principles. Everett asserted that any districts drawn "because of compactness, contiguousness, geographical boundaries, community of interest, or other factors" could not have had a discriminatory intent, whatever the racial effects of the lines (Everett 1993, 42–45, 75–76). Why racial communities of interest did not qualify, how compactness might be measured, what the other factors might be, or why they validated or constitutionalized race-conscious districting, Everett did not explain. Furthermore, he would have imposed a compactness requirement only on minority opportunity districts, because only a *race*-based criterion, he believed, offended the Constitution.[16] By contrast, the Republicans were more concerned to assure Republican opportunity districts than to deny minority opportunity districts. Thus, the Republican National Committee's *Shaw* briefs recycled the political gerrymandering claims from *Pope v. Blue* and reused the arguments with which the Bush administration had failed to convince Congress to pass a mandatory compactness bill to apply to the 1990s round of redistricting. Unlike Everett, the Republicans wanted compactness imposed on every congressional district, whatever its racial proportion and regardless of whether racial considerations played any role in setting its boundaries (Hess 1993, 1–10, 23–24).[17]

Predictably, the amicus brief filed by the Washington Legal Foundation, the Equal Opportunity Foundation, and North Carolina senator Jesse Helms stood for white rights. Whites who lived in black-majority districts, the brief declared, "have effectively been disenfranchised," and since the number of congressional districts that white voters in the state could absolutely control had dropped from eleven to ten, whites throughout the state had also been damaged. In other words, Helms and his allies read *Beer*'s non-retrogression principle as a grandfather clause, a guarantee that white power could never be decreased. Nor could the State legally claim to have drawn minority opportunity seats on the grounds that it would otherwise have faced a Section 2 or equal protection clause suit. *Gingles* made the ability to draw a compact minority opportunity district a condition for replacing at-large with single-member districts under Section 2. Turning its principles on their head, the conservatives suggested that if majority-white districts were compact, by some unstated definition, then they would be "largely immune" to a Section 2 or constitutional challenge, even if the state had deliberately drawn twelve majority-white districts. In practice favoring policies that preserved power in the white hands featured in Helms's most famous television commercial in his notoriously racist 1990 campaign against African-American Harvey Gantt, the brief straight-facedly purported to embrace egalitarianism: "Racial gerrymandering," it intoned, "by placing the state's stamp of approval on the notion that people of different races are inherently different from one another—is a giant step backward from our goal of a color-blind society" (Popeo and Samp 1993, 2, 15–16, 20–21).[18]

The State of North Carolina, the Justice Department, and various amici also focused on injury to whites, but they found none. Reading *Feeney* as imposing a "racial animus" standard, the state contended that since it had not meant to hurt whites by drawing two majority-minority districts, whites had no basis for an equal protection claim. Moreover, whites could freely participate in politics and could dominate elections in ten out of twelve seats, which was more than their population percentage in the state (83 percent vs. 77 percent). Complying with the VRA, trying to insure equal opportunities for minorities, and remedying generalized past discrimination, the State argued, were legitimate reasons for race-conscious districting. Imposing a special burden of justification on minority opportunity districts would not only contradict numerous lower federal court and Supreme Court decisions, but it would also undermine the VRA, impose a racial double standard, and treat racial groups differently from other "communities of interest" (Powell

1993, 7, 17, 44–45, 49; Katzenbach et al. 1993, 4–5, 8; Arden and Wice 1993, 23; Bryson et al., 22–23, 26; Verrilli 1993, 5–6, 17; Jones 1993, 3).

Shaw v. Reno: The Supreme Court's Decision

The Supreme Court's decision in *Shaw v. Reno* shocked specialists in voting rights and attracted more attention in the serious popular media and in law review articles and symposia than any voting rights decision since *Bolden*, and perhaps since *Baker v. Carr*. Why did it come as such a surprise? First, in racial equal protection cases since *Washington v. Davis* (1976) and Section 2 intent cases since *Bolden* (1980), plaintiffs had had to demonstrate not only a discriminatory intent but also a discriminatory effect, usually proved in vote dilution cases by a lack of proportional representation.[19] (See, for instance, *Washington v. Davis* [1976], 239; *Village of Arlington Heights v. Metro Hous. Dev. Corp.* [1977], 265; *Washington v. Finlay* [1981], 925; *McMillan v. Escambia County* [1981], 1248; *NAACP v. Gadsden County School Board* [1982], 981; *Gingles v. Edmisten* [1984], 352, n. 8; *Irby v. Fitz-Hugh* [1989], 1355–56; *Garza v. Los Angeles County* [1990—Appeals Court], 771; *Turner v. Arkansas* [1991], 583; Note 1982b, 976–78.) As Chief Justice Rehnquist expressed it, in an opinion signed by the same five justices who formed the majority in *Shaw* and the other "racial gerrymandering" cases, the " 'ordinary equal protection standards' " required one who challenged a government policy to prove that it " 'had a discriminatory effect and that it was motivated by a discriminatory purpose' " (*U.S. v. Armstrong* [1996], 1487, quoting *U.S. v. Wayte* [1985], 608). Because whites in North Carolina and every other state where a *Shaw*-type case was eventually filed were able to elect equal or higher proportions of members of Congress than their percentage in the population, the Supreme Court had to waive the requirement of showing discriminatory effects in order for white plaintiffs to win. Second, under the "case or controversy" provision of Article III of the U.S. Constitution, courts were not supposed to hear cases that merely asked them to decide abstract questions of general public policy, and during the years of the Burger and Rehnquist courts the Supreme Court had often interpreted that provision very strictly. In 1992, for instance, Justice Scalia had announced that a plaintiff had to demonstrate as an "irreducible constitutional minimum of standing," that he has "suffered an 'injury in fact'—an invasion of a legally-protected interest which is (a) concrete and particularized . . . and (b) 'actual or imminent, not "conjectural" or "hypothetical." ' . . . We have consistently held that a plaintiff raising only a generally available grievance about government—claiming only harm to his and every citizen's interest in proper application of the Constitution and laws, and seeking relief that no more directly and tangibly benefits him than it does the public at large—does not state an Article III case or controversy" (*Lujan v. Defenders of Wildlife* [1992], 2136, 2143). Three other justices who a year later joined Scalia in the *Shaw* majority signed his opinion in *Lujan*. In a case in which African-American parents challenged federal tax exemptions for private segregated schools, Justice O'Connor, speaking for a six-person majority, denied the parents standing because they merely claimed what she called an "abstract stigmatic injury" (*Allen v. Wright* [1984], 3327). *Shaw* plaintiffs could no more show a particularized "injury in fact" than could environmentalists, opponents of the Vietnam War or of the Central Intelligence Agency, or supporters of school integration, and for the Supreme Court to grant the *Shaw* plaintiffs standing without either overruling the previous cases or saying why they were inapplicable would subject the Court to withering criticism for ideologically driven inconsistency (Karlan 1993b, 278–81; Pildes and Niemi 1993, 130–34; Parker 1995, 11–18, for the criticism). Third, as suggested by the only question that the Supreme Court submitted to parties arguing the case,[20] the Court knew that *UJO* stood directly in the way of the *Shaw* plaintiffs, and this near-unanimous decision would have to be overruled or largely ignored in order to decide in their favor. Fourth, the drawing of minority opportunity districts had been largely uncontroversial in the 1990s round of redistricting. Other racial issues, especially those concerned with employment and contracts, might be matters of agitation, but voting rights seemed settled. Only radicals would rip apart this consensus. Fifth, as Prof. Daniel Hays Lowenstein emphasizes, North Carolina had drawn a second minority opportunity district under Justice Department pressure. Why should the state's action in obeying what was widely believed to be the correct interpretation of the VRA be unconstitutional (Lowenstein, personal communication)?

The "conservative" majority on the Supreme Court was, in fact, radical. In a sharply divided 5–4 decision issued on the last day of the 1993 term, Justice O'Connor—speaking for a majority that included Chief Justice Rehnquist and Justices Anthony Kennedy, Antonin Scalia, and Clarence Thomas—granted, or perhaps answered, Robinson Everett's prayer. Implicitly recognizing that white plaintiffs could not prove the sort of discriminatory effect that had been required in vote dilution cases and could not demonstrate that they had been harmed, much less singled out for injury, because they were white, Justice O'Connor in *Shaw v. Reno* recognized a new, "analytically distinct claim," a generalized injury to the political system itself, a "lasting harm to our society," that "white voters (or voters of any other race)" could assert—that the way the state had drawn district lines amounted to a "racial classification."[21] Never mentioning in her opinion that the congressional districts in question were only 57 percent black—not almost zero percent, as the reshaped Tuskegee city limits had been, or exactly 100 percent black, as "colored" southern public schools had been before *Brown*—O'Connor laced her opinion with misleading, heavily freighted phrases purporting to describe the legislature's purposes in drawing such districts. The new districts were, in her words, attempts "to segregate the races for purposes of voting . . . to classify and separate voters by race . . . to segregate voters into separate voting districts . . . [to] balkanize us into competing racial factions"; they resembled "political apartheid" (*Shaw v. Reno* [1993], 2819–32 [O'Connor, majority]; 2840 [White, dissent] for immediate criticisms of this language). But no one would have called schools in the pre-*Brown* South "segregated" if a race-conscious process of assigning children to schools had resulted in a few districts that were racially balanced, many that were overwhelmingly, but not entirely white, and none that were two-thirds or more black—the pattern that described the southern congressional districts created in 1991–92.[22] Justice O'Connor was playing language games using Humpty Dumpty's rules.[23]

In striking contrast to Chief Justice Warren's opinion in *Brown*, which emphasized the harm that segregation visited on African-American children, O'Connor glossed the equal protection clause as preventing "discrimination *between* individuals on the basis of race," not merely discrimination *against* individuals or members of a group (*Shaw v. Reno* [1993], 2824, italics added; Note 1993, 200–204; Goldstein 1994, 1154). Under this new cause of action— that is, different from that in vote dilution cases—plaintiffs could proceed if there was some unspecified correlation between racial and district lines in minority opportunity districts and if the boundaries of such districts were, in O'Connor's precise phrases, "bizarre," "irregular," or "egregious." No proof of injury or of discriminatory impact was necessary. In effect, O'Connor had classified the equal protection clause racially—people of color had to show that they were hurt by some action; whites, only that government appeared to have made some racial distinction.

In addition to her two linguistic sleights of hand with segregation and discrimination, O'Connor represented "compactness, contiguity, and respect for political subdivisions" as "objective factors" or "traditional districting principles" that might refute a contention of racial gerrymandering. She did not, however, choose among the many possible numerical measures of compactness, which gave very different results for real as well as for simulated districting schemes (Altman 1998, chaps. 2, 6). The fact that she casually termed the principal Republican alternative to the second black-majority district "reasonably compact," even though it was thirty miles longer and much more difficult to traverse than the district actually adopted by the North Carolina legislature, indicated that she meant a district's ugliness to remain entirely in the eye of whatever judge beheld it.[24] She also made no effort whatsoever

FIGURE 8.1. Two Congressional Districts in Texas, 1992

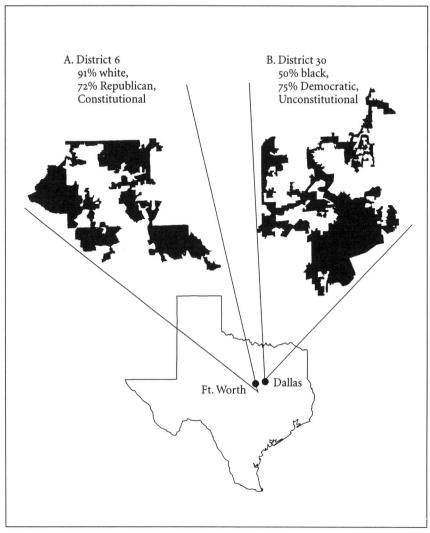

A. District 6
91% white,
72% Republican,
Constitutional

B. District 30
50% black,
75% Democratic,
Unconstitutional

Ft. Worth   Dallas

Source: A—*Bush v. Vera* (1996), 1995; B—ibid., 1965.

to show that such principles really were "traditional," and as I have demonstrated in Chapters 1, 5 and 6, they are not.[25] Nor did O'Connor explain how congressional districts could fit perfectly into political subdivisions and still attain the exact population equality demanded by *Karcher v. Daggett* (1983). Cities, counties, suburbs, wards, precincts, census tracts, school districts, etc.

are all often defined rather arbitrarily and without any relation to present-day social or economic patterns. Which political subdivisions were infrangible, and why? In what became a public relations embarrassment for the Court, O'Connor did not require that compactness or any other specific principles govern the drawing of majority-white districts, despite being urged to do so by the Republican National Committee's brief in *Shaw*. Dissenting justices in later cases, as well as black members of Congress whose districts were expunged by courts, had no trouble finding examples of white-majority districts that looked at least as irregular on a flat, featureless map as the overthrown minority districts (see Figure 8.1). On television or in newspapers, the contrast graphically belied the phrase "equal protection of the laws" (*LAT*, June 30, 1995, A:20; *Bush v. Vera* [1996], 1994–97).

Shaw v. Reno: Compactness and Cultural Studies

Why did the Court put so much emphasis on compactness, and why did it apply different standards to majority-white districts than it did to those containing heavy proportions of minorities?[26] In perhaps the most widely cited academic commentary on *Shaw v. Reno*, Prof. Richard Pildes tied Justice O'Connor's vague stance on compactness to the idea that the injuries that she identified in the case were "expressive." The principle that underlay *Shaw*, Pildes wrote, was that "government cannot redistrict in a way that conveys the social impression that race consciousness has overridden all other, traditionally relevant redistricting values. In the Court's view, certain districts whose appearance is exceptionally 'bizarre' and 'irregular' suggest that impression" (Pildes and Niemi 1993, 145).[27] O'Connor posited three psychological harms to society to justify her proclamation of a new constitutional right. First, she surmised, noncompact minority opportunity districts reinforce the stereotype "that members of the same racial group—regardless of their age, education, economic status, or the community in which they live—think alike, share the same political interests, and will prefer the same candidates at the polls." Second, such districts also "may exacerbate . . . patterns of racial bloc voting." Finally, they make elected officials "more likely to believe that their primary obligation is to represent only the members of that group, rather than their constituency as a whole." In Chapter 5, I presented empirical evidence from North Carolina on each of these claims, and showed that the first was misleading, because blacks in fact were politically cohesive and attitudinally quite different from whites; the second was simply false; and the third concealed a racial double standard.[28] It is also worth pointing out that the three generalizations are mutually contradictory. If there already is racial bloc voting, then, as Justice David Souter noted in his dissent in *Shaw* (2845,

n. 2), treating members of each racial group as having systematically different preferences is facing reality, not creating stereotypes. The proposition that an African-American or Latino member of Congress may feel herself responsive only to members of her group, and not to whites, presumes that her group has distinctive preferences, again contradicting the stereotype argument. Finally, if the stereotypes are not true, then racial bloc voting will not occur, no member of Congress will think herself particularly beholden to any group, no constituent will be left out, and, more generally, no antidiscrimination principle would ever have arisen in constitutional law (Seidman and Tushnet 1996, 96–97).

In effect conceding that there is no empirical support for O'Connor's position, her academic ally Prof. Katharine Butler (1996, 357) has declared that "supplanting standard districting criteria with racial ones is inherently harmful." This seems the only possible defense for O'Connor's assertion about stereotypes. It is certain that the numerous social psychological studies of the development, maintenance, and alteration of stereotypes and behavior based on them do not endorse O'Connor's position. Thus, the dominant cognitive perspective on stereotypes sees them as easily formed, ubiquitous, and persistent simplifications of reality that are necessary for human beings to function and harmful only if they are erroneous (Tajfel 1969; Rothbart and John 1993). More affective approaches to white stereotypes about African-Americans view them as reflective of basic personality or political orientations, such as ethnocentrism and political conservatism, and find that "negative stereotypes of blacks' character are widely diffused through contemporary American society . . . racial prejudice remains the same old racism at its core" (Sniderman and Piazza 1993, 51, 53). Approaches derived from information processing separate almost universally held and automatically accessible stereotypes from prejudiced attitudes, which are less common, and separate both from prejudiced behavior, which is even less usual, though still common. If the goal is to decrease prejudiced behavior, according to this school, then the method is to reduce prejudice and, in less prejudiced persons, to make the conflict between the stereotype and their egalitarian attitudes conscious (Devine 1989). None of these, or a wide range of other studies, suggests that governmental action in the post-legal segregation era is necessary, sufficient, or even important in creating stereotypes, and none suggests that the invocation of true stereotypes can cause prejudiced behavior. Moreover, studies of the reduction of prejudice suggest that contact between members of the majority group and high-status members of minority groups, such as members of legislatures or Congress, may reduce majority prejudice (Amir 1976). As the reelection success of African-American incumbents, even those in districts that have become majority white, implies, the creation of opportunities for minority candidates to prove their worth to whites seems to reduce, not increase, racially prejudiced behavior. And as the overwhelming burden of social scientific evidence demonstrates, such chances almost never take place, at least in the South, outside minority opportunity districts (Davidson and Grofman 1994). The scholarly evidence on O'Connor's proposition about stereotype reinforcement, then, offers no support for her position.

In *Brown*, Chief Justice Warren had asserted that specific legal mandates for segregation imposed greater psychological harm on black children than neighborhood segregation did, thereby putting off for awhile the question of whether allegedly de facto segregation was unconstitutional. Although *Shaw* presented an analogous issue, Justice O'Connor did not assert that the harms that she predicated were peculiar to noncompact districts, and it is difficult to see why they should be. When almost identical public policy arguments were made to Congress—and rejected by it—during the hearings on the renewal of the VRA in 1982, their proponents applied them to districts of every shape, not just noncompact ones. Current defenders of *Shaw* often echo the 1982 comments, Butler remarking, for example, that the harm to whites that *Shaw* sought to remedy "is being placed in a district drawn for a group to which the voter does not and cannot belong," an injury, if it is one, that would seem to apply whatever the shape of the district.[29] Thernstrom, who favored elimination of all minority opportunity districts, explicitly asked "Why are less irregular lines necessarily less race-driven?" (U.S. Senate 1982a, 662, 745, 1328, 1449; McDonald 1995b, 16; Butler 1996, 341; Thernstrom 1994, 41). Why should voting in a district with smooth edges be less racially polarized than in another district with the same racial makeup, but with jagged boundaries? Why don't majority-white districts of whatever shape reinforce racial stereotypes, since they almost never elect black or Latino representatives in the South and only rarely do so outside it? Why should representatives from square or circular districts be any less responsive to their core constituencies, whatever their class, religion, race, party, etc. than those from districts whose boundaries meander? Surely former state senator O'Connor could not believe that representatives need the cue of an oddly shaped district to discern their most loyal supporters. What evidence is there that representatives from "pretty" districts treat constituents as individuals devoid of social or political traits, while those from ungainly districts view their voters as merely bundles of stereotypical qualities (Aleinikoff and Issacharoff 1993, 614-15)? The harms that O'Connor used to justify the outcome in *Shaw*, then, would seem potentially to threaten districts with every shape and every racial composition. Indeed, popular as well as academic observers have predicted that *Shaw* will eventually lead to the outlawing of all consciously drawn minority opportunity districts, however compact (Toobin 1997, 32). And if the completely subjective and entirely unevidenced concept of expressive harms were to be applied to areas of governmental policy besides districting, it would be quite dangerously open-ended. If any government recognition of racial distinctions encourages stereotypes and private or public race-tinged behavior, then aren't any efforts to remedy current or past racial discrimination in voting, employment, contracts, housing, or criminal justice, or even to collect information that uses race as a category constitutionally suspect (Karlan 1996, 295, n. 52)?[30] Carried to this extreme, a prohibition on "discrimination between," under what Kenneth Karst has termed the "model of formal racial neutrality," would make it impossible for any governmental body in America to take action to alleviate "discrimination against" (Karst 1993, 74–77).

That O'Connor was unwilling to go so far casts doubt on parts of Pildes's interpretation of *Shaw*'s ambiguities and suggests that it ought to be viewed not as a "district appearance" case but as a more conventional intent case, in which the evil to be avoided is a distinction made purely on the basis of race (Pildes and Niemi 1993, 118).[31] On this reading, the difference between *Shaw* and earlier cases was not that irregular lines in themselves flaunted racial differentiations to officials and the public, instructing them in the propriety of racial border lines and exacerbating private tensions, but that whites did not have to prove injury. District shapes were merely indications of a forbidden intent. Shape was a limiting principle for O'Connor, a triggering condition, though perhaps not the only one, that was similar to the compactness prong of *Gingles*, allowing minorities to have districts drawn for them only if their geographical concentration was, by some rough measure, sufficient (*Miller v. Johnson* [1995], 2486; *Quilter v. Voinovich* [1995], 1016–17). Thus, O'Connor's emphasis on shape as a symptom of intent might prevent *Shaw* from threatening to overturn every governmental program that recognized societally accepted categories or sought to remedy past or present disadvantages. Whether other explanations for the district lines might ultimately prove more satisfying than the first impression based on the district's twists and turns, *Shaw v. Reno* did not determine. Even if the other causes were deemed to have been subordinated to race, *Shaw* did not decide whether the state's reasons for charting its districts along racial lines could be deemed compelling.

The evidence for this gloss is, first, that although Justice O'Connor rejected Everett's plea for race-unconscious districting, she left the question of whether " 'the intentional creation of majority-minority districts, without more' [presumably, more evidence of an intent to harm] always gives rise to an equal protection claim" to be decided in future cases. If any district, whatever its shape, might be unconstitutional, then *Shaw* could not have meant to make "bizarre" shapes a necessary element of the harm that the

majority posited. The dividing line—impossible to operationalize, I believe—
was between awareness and intent, not between compact and noncompact
minority opportunity districts. In O'Connor's words, "This Court never has
held that race-conscious state decisionmaking is impermissible in *all* circumstances. . . . [R]edistricting differs from other kinds of state decisionmaking
in that the legislature always is *aware* of race when it draws district lines, just
as it is aware of age, economic status, religious and political persuasion, and a
variety of other demographic factors." Since redistricters will always have the
information and since the knowledge may be crucial to their political careers
and policy goals, it would be naïve to assume that they will avoid using it and
pointless to spend time and effort proving that they do so. Second, O'Connor
noted that while it might be difficult to determine "from the face of a single
member districting plan that it *purposefully* distinguishes between voters on
the basis of race," an irregular shape was a tangible and immediate indication
of such a purpose, or, as Justice Stevens remarked in his concurring opinion
in *Karcher v. Daggett* (1983), in a passage that O'Connor quoted approvingly
in *Shaw*, "dramatically irregular shapes may have sufficient probative force to
call for an explanation." Third, if the shape of the districts at issue in *Shaw*
had been meant to be determinative of whether a racial classification had
taken place, then the case would not have been remanded to the district court
with an invitation, twice stated, to the State to contradict the "allegations of
a racial gerrymander" (*Shaw v. Reno* [1993], 2824, 2826–32, italics added). A
bizarre shape was, therefore, neither a necessary nor a sufficient condition to
force the State to show that a strong, legitimate interest justified the redistricting.

If *Shaw* was an intent case, how much did race have to count in the decisions about boundaries? Sometimes quoting from previous cases, O'Connor
stated *fifteen times* that it must be the single reason: [32]

> What appellants object to is redistricting legislation that is so
> extremely irregular on its face that it rationally can be viewed *only* as
> an effort to segregate the races for purposes of voting . . . (2824)

> Classifications of citizens *solely* on the basis of race . . . (2824)

> . . . "unexplainable on grounds other than race" . . . (2825)

> . . . could not be explained on grounds other than race . . . (2825)

> . . . "*solely* concerned with segregating white and colored
> voters" . . . (2825)

> . . . obviously drawn for *the* purpose of separating voters by
> race . . . (2826)

... could "be explained *only* in racial terms" ... (2826)

... not so bizarre as to permit of *no other* conclusion. (2826)

... anything other than an effort to "segregat[e] ... voters" on the basis of race. (2826)

When a district obviously is created *solely* to effectuate the perceived common interests of one racial group ... (2827)

... rationally cannot be understood as *anything other* than an effort to separate voters into different districts on the basis of race ... (2828)

... cannot be understood as *anything other* than an effort to classify and separate voters by race ... (2828)

... rationally could be understood *only* as an effort to segregate voters by race. (2829)

... rationally cannot be understood as *anything other* than an effort to segregate citizens into separate voting districts on the basis of race ... (2830)

... a reapportionment scheme so irrational on its face that it can be understood *only* as an effort to segregate voters into separate voting districts because of their race ... (2832)

Presumably, then, if states could show that another motive contributed to the drawing of the districts in question, then the Court would have to declare them legal. Since there are virtually always somewhat mixed motives involved in redistricting, this standard would have to be abandoned unless *Shaw* was to be entirely toothless. Its repeated statement in O'Connor's opinion is a sign of just how unthoughtful the opinion was.

After *Shaw*, lower courts differed as to whether noncompact minority opportunity districts were automatically subject to "strict scrutiny." What is strict scrutiny and why does it matter? Beginning in *McLaughlin v. Florida* (1964), the Supreme Court gradually and sporadically adopted a formula for dealing with alleged racial classifications. Courts would first determine whether or not the law in question did in fact classify people by race. If it did, the law would be considered much more skeptically or, in the formulaic phrase, subjected to strict or heightened scrutiny. The relevant government would then have to produce one or more "compelling state interests" to justify its decision, and it would have to show that its scheme was "narrowly tailored" to accomplish this end (*Wygant v. Jackson Bd. of Educ.* [1986], 1847).[33] Thus, "strict scrutiny" and related concepts require, in equal protection and other areas of the law, a particularly careful balancing of rights against interests (Gottlieb 1993).[34]

Although formally, *Shaw v. Reno* ruled only that plaintiffs might go ahead and try to prove that the districts did in fact represent racial classifications, O'Connor gave some indications of how the Court might treat possible justifications of compelling state interest that were based on Sections 2 and 5 of the VRA as well as on past discrimination. If the legislature claimed that it was trying to comply with Section 2, then it would have to demonstrate that the minority or minorities were politically cohesive and that there was racial bloc voting in the jurisdiction.[35] More disturbingly, O'Connor hinted that she accepted Jesse Helms's grandfather clause interpretation of Section 5: "A reapportionment plan would not be narrowly tailored to the goal of avoiding retrogression if the State went beyond what was reasonably necessary to avoid retrogression." If there were no minority opportunity districts in North Carolina before 1991, O'Connor seemed to be saying, Section 5 could not require any after 1991, regardless of whether the districting scheme had, in the words of the VRA, the "purpose" or "effect" of denying or abridging the right to vote on account of race.[36] Moreover, a history of past discrimination in voting—O'Connor did not consider that there might have been a particularized history of past discrimination in redistricting itself—would justify remedial actions only if the districts were drawn on "sound districting principles," including that of compactness (*Shaw v. Reno* [1993], 2830-32).[37]

In a decision that threatened the only seats that African-Americans had won in North Carolina in the twentieth century, O'Connor finished with a seemingly egalitarian peroration: "Racial classifications of any sort pose the risk of lasting harm to our society. They reinforce the belief, held by too many for too much of our history, that individuals should be judged by the color of their skin. . . . Racial gerrymandering, even for remedial purposes, may balkanize us into competing racial factions; it threatens to carry us further from the goal of a political system in which race no longer matters—a goal that the Fourteenth and Fifteenth Amendments embody, and to which the Nation continues to aspire" (*Shaw v. Reno* [1993], 2832). But the history was of discrimination *against* blacks, and remedies would be needed only if racial factions already existed and many whites were not committed to color-blindness. The irony of the statements may not have been so unintended as it seemed on first glance.[38]

At least the four dissenters—Justices White, Stevens, Blackmun, and Souter—were not amused. In his last opinion before retirement, Justice White, the author of more voting rights opinions than any other justice during his three decades on the Court, denied that district shape made any constitutional difference at all, and he focused relentlessly on the lack of injury suffered by whites.[39] Obviously displeased that the Court had decided to "sidestep" *UJO*, which he contended was indistinguishable from *Shaw* in all but what he called "surface differences" such as compactness, White lambasted the notion that whites were harmed in this case as a "departure from settled equal protection principles." In his view, the question was not whether voters were classified by race during a redistricting, for that was inevitable, as O'Connor had admitted. "Rather," he insisted, "the issue is whether the classification based on race discriminates against *anyone* by denying equal access to the political process." Likely problems with putting *Shaw* into practice, White concluded, "illustrate the unworkability of a standard that is divorced from any measure of constitutional harm." Justice Stevens, who, along with Justice Blackmun, had joined White's opinion, pointed to the irony that under the majority's view, "it is permissible to draw boundaries to provide adequate representation for rural voters, for union members, for Hasidic Jews, for Polish Americans, or for Republicans," but not "for members of the very minority group whose history in the United States gave birth to the Equal Protection Clause" (*Shaw v. Reno* [1993], 2834–45, italics in original).

Only slightly less outraged in tone than White's opinion, Justice Souter's dissent differentiated voting from other areas in which affirmative action had been struck down, questioned O'Connor's use of precedents, and ridiculed her notion of diffuse cultural injury. Besides relying on Douglas's dissent in *Wright v. Rockefeller* (1964), on a minor part of *UJO*, in an interpretation that the author of the opinion, Justice White, disavowed, and on a distorted analogy with *Gomillion*, O'Connor connected her *Shaw* opinion to a set of recent affirmative action and jury selection cases. Souter argued that they were inapplicable. In the affirmative action cases, favoring a minority contractor or employee, for instance, necessarily disadvantaged a white contractor or employee. In criminal cases, peremptory challenges of jurors of one race might bias the process against a particular defendant. By contrast, in voting, placing a person in one district as opposed to another did not deprive her of a vote, and so long as the political power of the group to which she belonged was not diluted, she could not prove a discriminatory impact. Moreover, to comply with the VRA, race had to be taken into account in districting in areas where there was evidence of racial bloc voting. In other words, Souter argued, federal law demanded classification by race, and if the Court did not mean to invalidate the VRA, which it did not hint at in *Shaw*, then states were faced with the choice of obeying the law passed by Congress or the contradictory interpretation of the Constitution mandated by the Court. It was for these reasons, according to Souter, that the Court had never before applied strict scrutiny in racial districting cases. In other areas of the law, any discrimination between was necessarily a discrimination against, but not in voting.

Racial classification simply did not mean the same thing in voting as in previous types of cases, and therefore the precedents that O'Connor cited were irrelevant. Finally, argued Souter, the harms that O'Connor invoked were in no way similar to those in cases of disadvantage. It was "utterly implausible" to contend that the psychological impact of "this strangely-shaped majority-minority district" was comparable to what *Brown* had referred to as "a feeling of inferiority as to [African-Americans'] status in the community that may affect their hearts and minds in a way unlikely ever to be undone." "As for representative democracy," Souter said, he had "difficulty seeing how it is threatened (indeed why it is not, rather, enhanced) by districts that are not even alleged to dilute anyone's vote" (*Shaw v. Reno* [1993], 2845–49).

Justice White termed the injury that O'Connor postulated in *Shaw* a "fiction" and accused her of "imagining a heretofore unknown type of constitutional claim" (*Shaw v. Reno* [1993], 2836, 2838). If he had been an academic, rather than a judge, White might have called the opinion "postmodern," which it was in four respects. First, *Shaw* treated facts as pure "social constructions," to use the jargon, or, in simpler terms, as things the postmodernist should feel free to make up as he chooses. "Reality" and "truth" are always to be used in quotation marks. Thus, the French postmodernist Jean Baudrillard denied in 1991 that it was possible to know whether the Gulf War had taken place or whether it was merely a fabricated television extravaganza. How much less fanciful was Justice O'Connor's invention of "traditional districting principles" that America has not, in fact, followed and "injuries" that either hurt no one, did not exist, or were no greater than harms under any other system? Second, as in much postmodern literary criticism, *Shaw* was full of language games, of the distortion of familiar words in order to undermine the current "hegemonic discourse." Thus, the words "segregation," "apartheid," and "discrimination" were employed, with changed meanings, to reverse the integration of electoral districts and legislative bodies and to restore racial inequities. As has often been charged, postmodernism shrouds fundamentally reactionary or at least nihilistic impulses behind clouds of trendy rhetoric (Palmer 1990, 189–98; Norris 1992, 11–15, 52–85, 126–58; Rosenau 1992, 62–91, 155–66). Likewise, O'Connor and the revolutionary-conservative majority on the Rehnquist Court have tried to hide their inegalitarian objectives behind a facade of equality-talk. Third, while previous equal protection and voting rights law was aimed at real deprivations of power—such as unequal opportunities in education, politics, housing, and jobs—*Shaw*, as if it were an essay in literary theory, was concerned only with symbolic harms to an amorphous "society." *Brown, White v. Regester,* and *Gingles* were essays in practical political science; *Shaw*, in cultural studies. Fourth, the opinion suggested the beginnings of what might be named "postmodern equal protection theory." Traditional equal protection asked only whether laws were reasonably related to a proper governmental end. "Modern" equal protection theory applied heightened scrutiny to discrimination against people based on race and established special protections to keep political processes flowing freely and fairly (Kay 1980; Klarman 1991). In contrast, *Shaw* and succeeding cases seemed to threaten to ban governmental distinctions between people, with the effect of facilitating discrimination against the very "discrete and insular minorities" that the Reconstruction Amendments were passed to protect and of insuring that one interest—the heretofore least powerful interest—would not be equally represented in bargaining over changes in political structures and processes. Indeed, several scholars have suggested that what bothers "conservatives" on the Court about affirmative action or racial gerrymandering is the use of civil rights statutes or remedies to accomplish aims usually identified with interest groups (Strauss 1995, 26-28; Aleinikoff and Issacharoff 1993, 600). O'Connor and her allies contend that they are leveling the playing field, when what they are really doing is barring the weakest players from using the same strategies as all of the other contestants, making them, as one brief aptly stated it, "redistricting pariahs" (Butler 1996, 363; Rumbaut and Hair 1995a, 57).

The 1994 Cases: A Retreat from *Shaw*?

Some observers feared, while others hoped, that postmodern equal protection would immediately be applied thoroughly and across the board. Several noted the contradictions between the vra and *Shaw*—the vra requiring race-conscious districts, *Shaw* cautioning against them. The dissenting justices and various observers also criticized O'Connor's vague compactness standard as unworkable. Briffault questioned the viability of a doctrine that, as glossed by Pildes, meant that it was not the reality but the appearance of a racial classification that offended the Constitution, not the harm but its expression (Butler 1996, 342; Karlan 1993a, 287; Fletcher 1994, 247-49; Parker 1995, 47-54; Briffault 1995, 45). One seeming way out of these dilemmas was to ban race-conscious districting altogether and to declare the vra unconstitutional, at least to the extent that it was incompatible with the absolute ban.[40] There were some indications that the majority justices were sympathetic with that position. *Shaw* and other opinions of the Court in the early 1990s had raised but refused to decide the question of whether Section 2 of the vra was constitutional, and *Shaw* had implied that the Justice Department's expansive interpretation of Section 5 was incorrect, if not unconstitutional (*Shaw v. Reno* [1993], 2831; *Voinovich v. Quilter* [1993], 1157; *Chisom v. Roemer* [1991], 2376 [Kennedy, dissenting]; Aleinikoff and Issacharoff 1993, 639, 650). But the next

Supreme Court term's two major voting rights decisions only confused the issues further, and they inadvertently pointed to the fatal flaw in applying *Shaw* as it was usually interpreted at the time—its indeterminant benchmark.[41] In earlier times, *Johnson v. De Grandy* (1994) and *Holder v. Hall* (1994) would have been considered serious losses for liberals. But after *Shaw,* mixed news was good news (Wright 1995, 100–105, 122).

In *De Grandy,* the failure of the state of Florida to create as many black and Cuban opportunity districts for the state legislature as possible had been challenged by the NAACP and a Cuban group led by Republican legislator Miguel De Grandy. Six of the seven justices who agreed that Florida's actions were valid joined all of Justice Souter's opinion ruling that states need not maximize the number of minority opportunity districts so long as they provided approximately proportional representation and did not discriminate against minorities in other aspects of the electoral system. Since redistricting is not an automatic process, Souter's position endorsed race-conscious districting, and it used the most obvious baseline, the result that one would expect to find in sufficiently large, repeated samples of a population if the sampling process was unbiased—proportional representation of subsets of the population.[42] Plaintiffs in Section 2 cases, Souter went on, not only had to satisfy the three "*Gingles* factors," which he termed preconditions for such suits, but they also had to offer evidence on the rest of the "*Zimmer-White* factors" in a "totality of the circumstances" inquiry. Even though this seemed more in accord with the intent of Congress in 1982, it did represent an important, if silent, reversal of the *Gingles* standard that had bred so much minority success (McDonald 1995a, 282–83). Souter also seemed to indicate, without explicitly deciding, that the first *Gingles* factor required that to qualify for possible relief, minorities had to comprise a majority of the voting-age population, not the citizen or total population, in a hypothetical district. This was somewhat favorable to Latinos, many of whom were noncitizens, but not to minorities in general, because the ratios of adults in their populations were generally lower than the ratio among whites. Interestingly, Justice O'Connor and Chief Justice Rehnquist joined three of the *Shaw* dissenters—Souter, Blackmun, and Stevens—and Justice White's replacement, Ruth Bader Ginsburg, in the *De Grandy* majority. Even more strikingly, Souter's opinion never mentioned *Shaw,* a fact underlined by Justice Kennedy's concurrence, which discussed *Shaw* at length. And while Kennedy implied that if the issue of race-conscious districting per se had been properly raised, he would have overturned the Florida districts on *Shaw* grounds, O'Connor, in a brief separate concurrence, stressed that proportional representation, a quintessentially race-conscious measure, was probative evidence, though not by itself dispositive evidence, that votes had not been diluted. Possible fissures within the *Shaw* majority were also suggested by the fact that Justices Scalia and Thomas dissented because they interpreted Section 2 not to apply to electoral structures at all (*Johnson v. De Grandy* [1994]).

The second 1994 voting rights case, *Holder v. Hall,* reinforced the impression of fragmentation and further emphasized benchmarks, as the *Shaw* majority split into three groups, the prevailing opinion by Kennedy being joined entirely only by Rehnquist. O'Connor agreed with most of Kennedy's opinion, while Scalia signed onto Thomas's radically revisionist history of the VRA, discussed above in Chapter 1. The four *Shaw* dissenters, with Ginsburg substituted for White, dissented again in two principal opinions—one criticizing Kennedy's views, the other Thomas's.

Holder concerned a tiny Georgia county. Bleckley County, 22.4 percent African-American, has been governed since 1912 by a single official, who has always been white, as have been all the rest of the countywide elected officials in that county. During the 1980s and 90s, ten other Georgia counties substituted multimember county commissions, elected by districts, for the single-commissioner form of government, and the local grand jury repeatedly recommended steps toward such a change in Bleckley County. Nonetheless, in a 1986 referendum, 57 percent of the county's voters turned down a proposal to raise the number of commissioners to five. Blacks sued under Section 2 and the Fourteenth and Fifteenth Amendments and expected to win because the case was practically identical to the Carroll County case of *Carrollton Branch of NAACP v. Stallings* (1987), a circuit court decision that the Supreme Court had declined to review.[43] As predicted, the circuit court decided in the plaintiffs' favor on the basis of the *Gingles* factors, ignoring constitutional issues, since it was not necessary to go so far to reach a decision. This time, however, the Supreme Court reversed the circuit court, the prevailing opinion holding that there was no natural benchmark by which to determine, under the first prong of the *Gingles* test, whether African-Americans could constitute the majority of a district in a single-member districting system. Despite the fact that a five-member county commission was the most common size in Georgia, that the Bleckley County School Board was elected from five single-member districts, that the Georgia state legislature had authorized the 1986 referendum on a five-member commission for the county, and that other Georgia counties that dropped single commissioners had expanded to only three to six members, Justice O'Connor raised the specter of plaintiffs demanding that the number of members of legislative bodies be multiplied tenfold or contending that the proper comparison was to a huge commission in another state. Since there were no universally applicable comparisons in challenges to the size of an electoral body, realistic or actually proposed alternatives could apparently be ignored. Justice Thomas went further, contending that there could never be a benchmark in any minority vote dilution case, because specifying one would require a choice, unguided by the Constitution, among "an infinite number of theories of effective suffrage, representation, and the proper apportionment of political power in a representative democracy." None of the dissenters noted the stark contradiction between the insistence of O'Connor, Kennedy, and Rehnquist on a knife-edged, theoretically derived benchmark in *Holder* and their promulgation of a baseline in *Shaw* that somehow involved an undefined compactness standard and a vague, ahistorical reference to "traditional districting principles." Nor did any comment on the failure of Justice Thomas to require the same impossible philosophical precondition before the Supreme Court acted in *Shaw* (McDonald 1995b, 62–73; Karlan 1996, 298; *Holder v. Hall* [1994]). Two contentions of Thomas in *Holder*—that voting involves individuals, not groups, and that political participation is largely symbolic, not instrumental—may not be true, but they are certainly propositions in political theory.

Miller and *Hays*: The "Predominant Motive" Test and Standing

The appearance of disunity and hesitation within the *Shaw* majority in *De Grandy* and *Holder* was replaced in 1995 by ideological bloc-voting achieved at the expense of theoretical coherence and consistency.[44] The Court heard appeals concerning congressional redistricting in Louisiana (*U.S. v. Hays*) and Georgia (*Miller v. Johnson*) in cases that, in contrast to *De Grandy* and *Holder*, had been decided by lower courts after *Shaw*, rather than before. While *Hays* yielded only an opinion on the standing issue, *Miller* made courts the nation's regular redistricting authority and decreed, in effect, that disadvantaged minorities were the only interests that hereafter could not normally be recognized during redistricting (Karlan 1995, 103). The harsh rhetoric, strong anti–Justice Department tone, and unequivocal intent standard of Justice Kennedy's majority opinion brought into question all minority opportunity districts in the country and perhaps all districts with a "significant" minority population. The opinion did not, however, invalidate all minority opportunity districts outright or automatically subject them to scrutiny that was "strict in theory, fatal in fact" (Gunther 1972, 8), as Scalia, Thomas, and possibly Rehnquist and Kennedy seemed to desire. By contrast, O'Connor apparently thought *Shaw* applied only to very ugly districts, and she, at least, did not want to overthrow the VRA completely. O'Connor's half-hearted effort to remove the inconsistencies in the "conservatives'" treatment of standing in *Shaw*-type cases and in other cases that had liberal plaintiffs ended up only reemphasizing the larger disparities.

Louisiana and Georgia not only had long histories of racial discrimination against African-Americans in electoral laws but also well-documented recent instances of antiblack racial gerrymandering of congressional districts. From 1898 through 1983, black voters were in the minority in every Louisiana congressional district. In 1981, the legislature cracked the black population in New Orleans, placing it in two congressional districts, a decision overturned by a federal court, which established one black-majority district of the eight in the state (*Major v. Treen* [1983]). Until 1990, however, the Second District continued to elect white incumbent Lindy Boggs, placing African-American William Jefferson in the seat only when Boggs retired (Days et al. 1994, 2–3). Similarly, in 1971, Georgia split the black population of the Atlanta area into three congressional districts and removed the homes of two prominent black politicians from the most heavily African-American district, the Fifth. Only when the Justice Department refused to preclear the plan did the legislature draw a 44 percent black district, which sent Andrew Young, one of five blacks ever elected in majority-white congressional districts from the South, to Congress for two terms, after which he was replaced by Wyche Fowler, a liberal white.[45] By 1980, the Fifth was 50 percent black in population, but considerably less than 50 percent in voter registration, and the legislature proposed to increase its black population to 57 percent, which would have raised its black voter registration to 46 percent. Observers agreed that this was not a high enough percentage to elect an African-American candidate against an entrenched white incumbent. The chairman of the House Reapportionment Committee, Joe Mack Wilson, refused to raise the black percentage further, commenting "I don't want to draw nigger districts."[46] The Department of Justice objected, not because of retrogression but on grounds of discriminatory purpose; when the State sued in the district court of the District of Columbia to overturn the objection, that court sustained the Justice Department (*Busbee v. Smith* [1983], 498–517; McDonald et al. 1994, 10–13).[47]

The 1990s round of redistricting was a different story because of the 1982 VRA amendments, the *Gingles* ruling, a more aggressive Justice Department, and larger black caucuses in both states. Population changes expanded Georgia's congressional delegation from ten to eleven seats, but reduced Louisiana's from eight to seven. This simple fact made Georgia's redistricting task much simpler than Louisiana's and enabled it to draw much more compact districts and still protect incumbents, while accommodating African-Americans. With a black population of 27 percent, Georgia black leaders believed that they deserved three seats, which would have given them exactly proportional representation, but the legislature created only two. When the Justice Department objected, the State twice redrew the districts, finally arriving at a plan with three majority-black districts. The controversial Eleventh District, which connected black communities in three of the state's major cities, scored much higher on both perimeter and area measures of compactness than the North Carolina minority opportunity districts, and respondents to a *Shaw*-type suit brought by disappointed Democratic office-seekers argued that the Eleventh was insufficiently bizarre to violate *Shaw* and that many of its irregularities were the result of partisan and personal considerations (McDonald et al. 1994, 13–23).

Louisiana, 30 percent black and with much less regular state boundaries than Georgia, drew a much more contorted second minority opportunity district, nicknamed "the Zorro district" because it was shaped like a jagged Z. But when, after the *Shaw* decision, white plaintiffs successfully challenged the plan in a three-judge federal court, the legislature redrew it, creating a new black-majority district patterned on the former Eighth District, which had originally been drawn in 1967 and persisted in modified form through 1991. If the Court was demanding "traditional districting principles," the Louisiana legislature apparently thought, why not give them something that closely resembled an actual traditional district? Since the district court, in its initial decision, had declared that the Zorro district was not narrowly tailored because it was insufficiently compact and had an unnecessarily high proportion of African-Americans, the legislature drew a much tidier district with a total population that was only 54 percent, rather than 63 percent, black (*Hays v. Louisiana* [1993], 1207–9; Days et al. 1994, 3–7, 30; Spears 1994, 25).

The Georgia district court in *Miller* and the Louisiana district court in *Hays*, two *Shaw*-type racial gerrymandering cases brought by white plaintiffs, were palpably hostile to the outside agitators from the Justice Department. The Georgia judges were also outraged that that state's legislature had accepted suggestions from an ACLU attorney and that Justice had communicated with what the court termed "partisan 'informants' " and "secret agents." Judges in both courts were aghast that the states' black caucuses finally got their way in the congressional redistricting. In parallel decisions, both district courts overthrew the redistrictings and tossed out the new minority opportunity districts. Both courts brushed aside contentions that *Shaw* applied only to extremely noncompact districts, that under *Shaw* the sole motive for drawing a district had to be racial, and that it was illegal under the VRA for lower courts other than the District Court of the District of Columbia to overrule a Justice Department Section 5 ruling.[48] The Georgia court interpreted *Shaw* to mean that race had to be the predominant motive in drawing a district, while the Louisiana court ruled that race need be only an "important factor" either in the decision to draw a minority opportunity district at all or in the shape of the district. Neither court made any attempt to determine what each state's traditional districting principles actually were or to compare the degree of compactness of the challenged districts with any objective measure. Both rejected out of hand the suggestion that black communities in different areas might share interests, at least any that a post-*Shaw* court could legally take note of. However, Judge Jacques L. Wiener Jr., who wrote the 1994 *Hays* district court opinion, was certain that "English-Scotch-Irish," "Continental French-Spanish-German Roman Catholics," and "sui generic Creoles" formed communities of interest that redistricters could legitimately recognize. The Louisiana legislature's wholesale revision of its map after *Shaw* and the 1993 *Hays* decision did nothing to satisfy the district court judges, who for good measure also overruled *UJO*. In the two cases, only dissenting Judge J. L. Edmondson in Georgia compared any minority opportunity districts to white districts or used any mathematical index of compactness, and he declared the Eleventh District relatively compact (*Hays v. Louisiana* [1993], esp. 1196–97 n. 21 and 1201; *Hays v. Louisiana* [1994]; *Johnson v. Miller* [1994]).

Justice Kennedy's opinion in *Miller,* speaking for the same five-person majority as in *Shaw,* tied up some of the earlier opinion's loose ends but unraveled many others. If judicial self-restraint and careful craftsmanship were the hallmarks of conservative jurisprudence, as they had been for Justice Felix Frankfurter and his influential academic followers, this was not a conservative opinion. Kennedy began by declaring that the "central mandate" of the equal protection clause was "racial neutrality in governmental decisionmaking," a criterion that was so general as to exclude no legal position except perhaps that of slaveowners. Segregationists, for instance, had claimed that government was neutral when it did not interfere in private racial discrimination and when it provided "separate but equal" public programs and facilities (Lofgren 1987, 52, 170–71; Kousser 1988, 972–75). Voting rights liberals, on the other hand, believed that neutrality meant that the federal government should ban only those laws or structures that had a racially discriminatory purpose or effect on members of groups that history showed had less ability than others did to protect themselves from unfavorable governmental action. Misleadingly, Kennedy quoted language from Justice Powell's opinion in *Bakke* in which Powell stated that "racial and ethnic distinctions of any sort are inherently suspect." His quotation was misleading because the *Bakke* case had involved a challenge to discrimination *against* white applicants to the University of California at Davis Medical School, not just to distinctions *between* students. As Powell remarked later in his *Bakke* opinion, "When a classification denies an individual opportunities or benefits enjoyed by others solely because of his race or ethnic background, it must be regarded as suspect." The redistricting involved in *UJO,* Powell said, was legal because it deprived no one of "meaningful participation in the electoral process." No more helpful to Kennedy's argument were other affirmative action and segregation cases that he cited, because they overturned either exclusion of African-Americans from public accommodations open to whites or disproportionate burdens on members of one or another race. In the first case that Kennedy referred to, for example, the 1967 challenge to a Virginia law against interracial marriages, the Supreme Court overturned the statute not merely because it distinguished between persons on the basis of race, but because, in the Court's words, it was "designed to maintain white supremacy." As with the majority opinion in *Shaw*, Kennedy's twisting of precedents did not fool the dissenters, as Justice Stevens convincingly dispersed Kennedy's legalistic fog (*Regents of the University of California v. Bakke* [1978], 305; *Miller v. Johnson* [1995], 2482-86, 2497-98; *Loving v. Virginia* [1967], 11).

In the other dissent, Justice Ginsburg carefully detailed Georgia's history of discrimination in electoral practices, including the 1981 redistricting, and drew on trial testimony to show that many of the irregularities in the Eleventh District had to do with partisan or personal advantage or preference, not race. Kennedy ignored all this evidence, as the majority on the district court largely had, which made it easier to conclude that race primarily accounted for the shape of the Eleventh. Kennedy also abjured any systematic test of compactness or comparisons with previously or contemporaneously drawn white-majority districts, and he announced that the black communities in Atlanta and Savannah were "worlds apart in culture"—a curious judgment, irrelevant to electoral politics even if true, because by the time Kennedy made the announcement, both communities had enthusiastically supported African-American congresswoman Cynthia McKinney in two elections (*Miller v. Johnson* [1995], 2483-85, 2500-2504).[49]

In *Shaw*, Justice O'Connor had described three injuries to the nation that, she asserted, racial gerrymandering embodied or produced: stereotyping, exacerbating racial bloc voting, and cuing elected minority representatives to ignore their white constituents. In *Miller*, Kennedy dropped the last two, connecting racial gerrymandering only with stereotyping. The advantages of this move were that it eliminated the contradictions among the three harms, pointed out earlier in this chapter, and that it appeared to tie the alleged injury to the individualized notion of the equal protection clause and of politics that the *Miller* opinion embraced. It had seemed paradoxical in *Shaw* that the notion of politics was purely individual, while the harms cited were ones that applied to the society as a whole, but that did not especially burden any single person. Stereotyping, as Kennedy apparently saw it, was that individual injury. What the justice failed to note was that strictly individual stereotyping was inapplicable to redistricting, for in a geographical arrangement, no single person was placed in a district. Everyone, no matter what their race, gender, party, etc., who lived in a particular area, was assigned to the same district. Thus, whatever generalizations were used to separate people into legislative districts were applied only to those in the group that lived in a particular area, not to single individuals. In any event, Kennedy was by no means ready to abandon the notion of collective injury. Instead, he insisted that race-conscious districting not only symbolically damaged individuals but also "cause[d] society serious harm." Henceforth, Kennedy announced, governments would have to act not just neutrally with regard to race but as if there were no racial differences in politics at all. To do otherwise was to engage in unconstitutional stereotyping or the use of "race as a proxy" (*Miller v. Johnson* [1995], 2486–87).

The disadvantages of Kennedy's position were three: First, it completely ignored the political history and current reality of racial cleavages in politics, to which Kennedy paid no attention (McDonald 1995a, 288). Second, far from objecting to what Kennedy termed the "offensive and demeaning assumption" that they formed political communities, African-Americans, the most politically unified group in the nation, and, to a lesser extent, Latinos clearly wanted the right to elect candidates of their choice, as they proved whenever they got a chance to vote in minority opportunity districts. In any event, Kennedy hardly allowed minorities to speak for themselves, to say whether they felt stigmatized or demeaned. The conservative white Republican knew best how African-Americans and Latinos should feel, and he had the power to write his conception of reality into the Constitution. Third, Kennedy's retrenchment from *Shaw*'s fictive harms did not entirely get rid of the contradictions, for how could race be used as a proxy for anything else if voters' behavior did not correlate highly with race (*Miller v. Johnson* [1995], 2486–88)?

Without noting its divergence from the "sole factor" standard of *Shaw*, Justice Kennedy adopted the Georgia court's "predominant force" or "dominant and controlling rationale" criterion, and he declared that that motive could be proven by facts other than the circumstantial evidence of shape.[50] Noncompactness was neither necessary nor sufficient to prove a constitutional violation; compactness provided no absolute defense against charges of racial gerrymandering. In a passage that breathtakingly extended *Shaw*'s reach, Kennedy declared:

> The plaintiff's burden is to show, either through circumstantial evidence of a district's shape and demographics or more direct evidence going to legislative purpose, that race was the predominant factor motivating the legislature's decision to place a significant number of voters within or without a particular district. To make this showing, a plaintiff must prove that the legislature subordinated traditional race-neutral districting principles, including but not limited to compactness, con-

tiguity, respect for political subdivisions or communities defined by actual shared interests, to racial considerations. (*Miller v. Johnson* [1995], 2488)[51]

Significantly, Kennedy neither mentioned nor excluded partisan or incumbent advantage, the most traditional districting principles of all. But by his statement, a *Shaw* claim was no longer limited to "bizarre" districts, or even, seemingly, to minority opportunity districts. Any time an undefined "significant" number of minority voters were assigned to any district, someone could challenge the district in court. Thousands of local, state, and federal districts might be subject to such suits (Rumbaut and Hair 1995b, 10). But districts do not exist, like some Platonic ideal forms, apart from human actions. On the contrary, every time districts are drawn in states containing "significant" numbers of minority voters, those voters have to be "placed" somewhere. If these statements of Kennedy's take on an independent life, as words in Supreme Court opinions often do, shedding the facts and analysis of a case like a chrysalis, then any districting plan whatsoever in such states might end up in court. Despite Justice O'Connor's plaintive concurrence, stating that the test was "a demanding one" that did not "throw into doubt the vast majority of the Nation's 435 congressional districts," and that it did not "treat efforts to create majority-minority districts *less* favorably than similar efforts on behalf of other groups," in fact it did exactly these things. Justice Ginsburg's dissent seemed the better prophecy: "Only after litigation—under either the Voting Rights Act, the Court's new *Miller* standard, or both—will States now be assured that plans conscious of race are safe. Federal judges in large numbers may be drawn into the fray" (*Miller v. Johnson* [1995], 2497, 2507).

Rejecting "blind judicial deference to legislative or executive pronouncements," Kennedy also made it much harder for redistricters to rely on the VRA, which had potentially served either to deflect strict scrutiny or to constitute a compelling interest. Proponents of minority opportunity districts had asserted that if a state or locality had the choice of drawing such a district and decided not to do so, that choice was evidence of an intent to deny minorities an equal chance to participate in politics and to elect preferred candidates, thus violating the Fourteenth and Fifteenth Amendments and the purpose provisions of Sections 2 and 5 of the VRA.[52] The choice was illegal, however, only if it produced a discriminatory effect, which nearly everyone measured, as in *De Grandy*, by less than proportional representation for minorities. Under Section 2, such an effect by itself was a violation, assuming that a potential district met the *Gingles* test (Gray and Moore 1995a, 28; Days et al., 1995c, 8). Since Department of Justice regulations from 1986 until 1997 declared that any law that violated Section 2 or the Constitution could not be precleared, states or localities had strong incentives to adopt any feasible minority opportunity districts, up to a number that would give minorities proportional representation. They could then claim, correctly, that their motive in doing so was to comply with federal law, which was also surely a compelling interest. Although *UJO* strongly supported the argument that adherence to Section 5 provided a nondiscriminatory motive for race-related districting, Kennedy, moving beyond the "sidestepping" of *Shaw*, ruled that *UJO* to the contrary notwithstanding, any race-conscious redistricting would be subject to "our strictest scrutiny." He simply ignored the Section 2 justification (*Miller v. Johnson* [1995], 2487–91).

Nor could compliance with Section 5 provide a compelling interest, Kennedy averred, because the Department of Justice had extended its meaning beyond pure retrogression. Since according to Kennedy, there could be no discriminatory purpose in refusing to draw a race-based district, the Department should not have denied preclearance of the initial Georgia plan on the basis of Section 5's purpose component. The state of Georgia should not have believed that it had to comply with the Department's rulings, Kennedy's argument went on, and it therefore had no compelling interest in drawing more than one or possibly two minority opportunity districts. If Section 5 were to be interpreted to require race-based districts, then the VRA might be unconstitutional according to the Fourteenth Amendment. But despite much evidence in the 1981–82 congressional hearings and reports that Congress meant to allow race-based districting, evidence that Kennedy entirely ignored, he avoided deciding explicitly whether the VRA was constitutional by ruling that Congress had no such intention (*Miller v. Johnson* [1995], 2491–94; McDonald et al. 1994, 40–41).[53] This may well have been one of a series of compromises necessary to obtain the wavering O'Connor's vote. Kennedy never explained how, if race could not constitutionally be the predominant factor in districting, a state or local government could be required to draw the same number of minority opportunity districts, perhaps with the same minority percentages, as it had previously drawn, an exercise that obviously required it to take race predominantly into account. Nor did he specify or justify what the appropriate baseline for retrogression was, though virtually everyone seems to have assumed that it meant the previous redistricting. As for Section 2 as a compelling interest, Kennedy ignored it, as he had in the previous sections of the opinion, perhaps a compromise to keep Scalia and Thomas, who thought Section 2 did not apply to electoral structures at all, from writing separately. Or perhaps Kennedy believed that the choice to draw a minority opportunity district, if required by Section 2, was unconstitutional in itself, since in drawing such a district, the state had to "place" voters in districts according to their race (Briffault 1995, 59–63). In that case, ignoring Section 2 was probably necessary to secure O'Connor's vote. Getting a majority to sign on to one opinion is often said to lead to clarity in the law. *Miller* was not one of those occasions.

Like O'Connor in *Shaw*, Kennedy ended *Miller* with a paean to "eradicating invidious discrimination" against "minorities' right to vote." But no remedy that required invoking "stereotypes," he said, was legal under the Fourteenth Amendment. If it was necessary to ignore the history of discrimination, the continuation of racial bloc voting in Georgia and elsewhere, and the real world of interest, partisan, and personal jockeying in redistricting, and to undermine or overlook parts of the VRA in order to affirm a principle recently discovered and tied only very tenuously to any constitutional language or larger purpose, the *Shaw-Miller* majority was up to the task.

WHEN THE Louisiana legislature redrew the state's congressional districts after the first district court decision in *Hays*, it left none of the residences of the original plaintiffs in either of the state's two minority opportunity districts. This fact allowed Justice O'Connor, speaking for the five *Shaw* Justices, to create a "standing" doctrine that formally had something to do with an injury. As explained above, *Miller* had not mentioned two of *Shaw*'s injuries, and that excision had been integral to the decision, since the ruling applied not just to minority opportunity districts, but to any districts in which someone "placed" a "significant number" of voters because of race or used "race as a proxy" for some other political trait. There could be no signal to a representative to be inattentive to a white minority in his constituency if whites in fact composed a majority and African-American or Latino voters had been included in his district, using race as a proxy for Democratic proclivities, in order to make his victory more likely. Without noting any inconsistency, O'Connor rescued the "representational harm" proposition from the dustbin into which *Miller* had cast it, and used it to deny the *Hays* plaintiffs standing to sue. In *Shaw v. Reno* (1993), 2827, O'Connor had stated that "when a district obviously is created solely to effectuate the perceived common interests of one racial group, elected officials are more likely to believe that their primary obligation is to represent only the members of that group, rather than their constituency as a whole." Whites who lived outside such a district presumably had representatives who were responsive to them and thus individually suffered no harms. Case dismissed (*U.S. v. Hays* [1995], 2433–37).

Of course, the dismissal was trivially circumvented by recruiting new plaintiffs who did live in the district, the district court instantly ruled the revised districts unconstitutional, and the Supreme Court declined to review the lower court decision (Spears 1996, 11). Basing its 1995 decision on standing alone and then not writing an opinion about the district court's ruling on remand allowed the *Shaw-Miller* majority to finesse the question of whether in drawing a plan based on a former district, the legislature had adhered to "traditional districting principles." In any event, it was doubtful as an empirical matter that representatives elected from districts with different shapes actually differed in their behavior, as the *Shaw* majority and its defenders asserted. According to the Thernstroms, "congressional districts that were deliberately drawn to be overwhelmingly black invited the sort of ideological militance that became the model for the black legislative candidate" (Thernstrom and Thernstrom 1997, 483). But in fact, the only systematic study of the topic showed that representatives from the less compact, post-1990 black majority districts were less likely than their counterparts from more compact districts to consider themselves representatives of "black interests" and more likely to adopt a "politics of commonality" (Canon 1995).[54]

Nor did it seem even-handed for the Court to surmise that whites suffered when they lived in integrated but majority-minority districts while minorities experienced no harm when they were submerged in majority-white districts, whether compact or not (Karlan 1996, 292–94). Whites did not have to prove representational harm, for the Court merely assumed it, and blacks had no recourse to such a claim, for the Court was sure that blacks had no group interests deserving of protection. As Justice Stevens later pointed out in *Shaw v. Hunt,* such "speculative assertions of injury" were themselves "based on a stereotypical assumption about the kind of representation that politicians elected by minority voters are capable of providing" (*Shaw v. Hunt* [1996], 1911–12). *Hays,* then, granted standing to the plaintiffs by inflicting precisely the injury, a public governmental imprimatur on stereotypical thinking, that *Miller* purported to correct. It also cast further doubt on the "expressive harm" interpretation of these cases, for, as the *Shaw II* plaintiffs forcefully maintained, it is difficult to see why people who lived just across a district line or even in another part of the same state would be less likely to receive the message that the government had classified citizens by race than those who lived in the districts at issue (Everett 1995a, 2–3). Indeed, even Pildes, the principal academic explicator of O'Connor's voting rights jurisprudence, found the justice's standing doctrine in *Hays* unjustifiable. He suggested that anyone in a state and perhaps anyone in the country should be granted standing to overturn any minority opportunity district that they believed to be noncompact![55] Nevertheless, the use of "representational harm" as a threshold condition for lawsuits suggested that the other two harms, stereotyping and racial bloc voting, might be thresholds in future cases. Perhaps the Court might consider empirical evidence on whether racial differences in political opinions and behavior were real or merely prejudiced illusions and whether minority opportunity districts really did increase racial bloc voting or ill will. Some even held out the hope that representational harm was an empirical issue, rather than an assumption, for the Court (Briffault 1995, 67–82; Hodgkiss 1994, 23–24; Gray and Moore 1995a, 47–49; Rumbaut and Hair 1995a, 60–63). In *Miller* and *Hays*, every strand bound off loosened another (Karlan 1996).

Partisan and Racial Motives in the Texas and North Carolina Cases

Partisan and racial concerns were intertwined in redistricting in the 1990s more than they had been in a century. Republican opportunities were the mirror images of Democratic problems. The 1982 VRA amendments, as interpreted in *Gingles* and Department of Justice regulations, required jurisdictions to create minority opportunity districts when they could or face Section 5 preclearance difficulties or Section 2 or constitutional lawsuits. As a consequence, Republicans throughout the nation followed the same strategy as Texas Republicans had in 1981 and Los Angeles Republicans had in their settlement motion in *Garza* in 1990, proposing to pack minorities into as few seats as possible and to turn white and minority Democrats against each other by making gains for one group come at the expense of the other. The alternative Republican strategy—followed successfully in Alabama, California, Florida, Illinois, New York, and South Carolina—was to deadlock redistricting efforts and throw redistricting to Republican-dominated state or federal courts. The courts or special masters appointed by them virtually always followed the policy of creating the maximum number of minority opportunity districts, just the strategy that the Supreme Court so strongly condemned when, the justices charged, the Department of Justice carried it out (Congressional Quarterly 1993a, 19, 55–57, 166, 234, 496, 667–69; Spears 1992; *Wilson v. Eu* [1992], 714–15). The Supreme Court was much more deferential to plans drawn by lower courts in *Growe v. Emison* (1993) and *Johnson v. De Grandy* (1994) than it was to legislatively drawn maps from North Carolina, Louisiana, and Texas.

Responding to this widely understood Republican strategy, Democrats, especially in the South, sought to craft plans that simultaneously satisfied minority politicians and white Democratic incumbents. Technical and legal factors aided Democrats in this effort. Because the absolute population equality standard of *Karcher v. Daggett* (1983) made it impossible to preserve county, municipal, and even precinct boundaries; because racial census data was available on the unprecedentedly detailed level of city blocks; because the Census Bureau tailored its other population data to existing precinct boundaries, making the combination of political and demographic data much easier than ever before; and because of the speed and inexpensiveness of computer hardware and redistricting software by the 1990s, the opportunities for manipulating district boundaries were greater than ever. The result was a swirl of lines drawn with the purpose and effect of extracting minority voters from Republican districts to create both minority opportunity districts and districts that were as favorable as possible, under the circumstances, for white Democrats (Congressional Quarterly 1990, 28–29, 40–43; 1993a, 19; 1993b, 1–8; 1993c, xii–xv, 105–6, 355–57). As Richard Pildes has noted, the proportion of blacks in southern congressional districts that had Republican incumbents in 1990 declined by 6.6 percentage points in the new 1992 districts, while that in constituencies that had been represented by white Democrats in 1990 decreased by only 1.6 percentage points. Seventy-three percent of the black voters in the South who ended up in new black-majority districts in 1991–92 came from Republican districts. That some of the resultant Democratic margins were insufficient to survive continuing Republican trends among white southerners in 1992 and 1994 is significant politically, but it does not undercut the point that only by drawing districts with complicated perimeters did Democrats have a chance of surmounting the dilemma that the Republican strategy had placed them in (Pildes 1995, 1385 n. 117, 1389–90). Whether or not the degree of compactness of districts usually has a strong effect in favor of one particular party, which is an unresolved empirical question, it certainly did in the redistrictings of the 1990s. Noncompact districts in the vicinity of minority areas helped Democrats; housing was sufficiently segregated in many urban areas that Republicans could pack minorities and still draw districts that would seem compact to a sympathetic judge.

The opinions in the *Bush v. Vera* (hereafter *Vera*) and *Shaw v. Hunt* (hereafter *Shaw II*) cases that the Supreme Court decided in 1996 can be understood only if placed against the background of the intense partisan and personal infighting analyzed in Chapters 5 and 6. Justices did not have to be redistricting experts or even be acutely attuned to partisan nuances to understand the political as well as the racial and ethnic consequences of every facet of their decisions in these cases. Republicans seem to have largely financed both cases, and legal papers produced by the states, the Department of Justice, and various organizations that filed "friend of the court" briefs recounted the partisan and incumbent maneuverings explicitly and in considerable detail. The Democratic National Committee filed a brief in the Texas case, and the North Carolina Republican Party, assisted by the chief counsel of the Republican National Committee, filed a brief in *Shaw II*. The plaintiffs' redistricting proposal in *Vera*, as the briefs noted, was estimated to yield the Republicans a seven-seat gain in Congress and was designed, said the expert who drew it, "to provide a fairer distribution of the seats based on what we know about the *partisan* divisions in the state" (Hair 1994, 7–10; Speas 1994, 3–5; Gray and Moore 1995a, 9–15; Days et al. 1995a, 7–11, 43–45; Rumbaut and Hair 1995a, 29; Smith 1995; Farr 1995a, italics added). The district court opinion in *Vera* had a partisan tinge that perhaps only Judge Edith Jones, former chief counsel to the Texas Republican State Committee, could have given it. And the prevailing opinion in *Vera* at the Supreme Court level was written by the only member of the Court to have sat in a state legislature during a redistricting, former Arizona Republican Senate Majority Leader Sandra Day O'Connor. These were thoroughly political cases from beginning to end.

Numerous statements demonstrate the justices' complete awareness of the partisan causes and consequences of the redistricting.

> O'CONNOR: [T]he incumbents of the adjacent *Democratic* Districts 5 and 24 exerted strong and partly successful efforts to retain predominantly African-American *Democratic* voters in their districts. (There was evidence that 97% of African-American voters in and around the city of Dallas vote *Democrat*.) (*Vera* [1996], 1956, italics added)

> KENNEDY: District 30 also involved the illicit use of race as a proxy when legislators shifted blocs of African-American voters to districts of incumbent *Democrats* in order to promote partisan interests. (*Vera* [1996], 1972, italics added)

> STEVENS: Texas's entire map is a political, not a racial, gerrymander. . . . Johnson's plan transferred many of Frost and Bryant's most reliable *Democratic* supporters into the proposed district. . . . The real problem is the politically motivated gerrymandering that occurred in Texas." (*Vera* [1996], 1975, 1980, 1990, italics added).

In *Shaw v. Reno* (hereafter *Shaw I*), Justice O'Connor had referred to *UJO* as a "highly fractured decision" (*Shaw I*, 2829). Compared to *Vera*, however, *UJO* was a model of unity and clarity. In *Vera*, O'Connor wrote the prevailing opinion, in which she was joined by Chief Justice Rehnquist and Justice Kennedy. Not only did Kennedy then write a concurring opinion, dissenting from two of O'Connor's major points, but quite extraordinarily, O'Connor wrote another opinion concurring with her own prevailing opinion, expressing views that apparently no other justice fully shared and announcing that on one major issue she and the four dissenters now formed a majority. As one wag put it, "At last, O'Connor has found a justice she can agree with" (Rosen 1996, 6). In addition, Justice Thomas, joined by Justice Scalia, wrote an opinion concurring in the judgment but not in the prevailing opinion, and Justices Stevens and Souter wrote separate dissents, in both of which Justices Breyer and Ginsburg joined, though neither Stevens nor Souter joined each others' dissents. With four opinions among them, the five majority justices looked less like a bloc than a herd of cats.

O'Connor began her *Vera* opinion by granting most of the original plaintiffs standing on the grounds that each lived in one of the three minority opportunity districts that the district court had found unconstitutional, and that *Hays* had decided that anyone living in an allegedly racially gerrymandered district had standing to sue. She did not discuss the question of representational harm explicitly, which would have been embarrassing since, as briefs pointed out, the "Hispanic district" had elected an Anglo who in the 1992 Democratic primary was the choice of only 1 percent of Latino voters in Houston (Hicks and Hair 1994, 7; Days et al. 1995c, 6). This indicated that any signal to officials elected from "bizarre" minority opportunity districts to ignore white constituents had not been accurately received. Moreover, the only representational harms that any of the plaintiffs could think of when deposed was that they were Republicans and the elected officials in the districts were Democrats (Gray and Moore 1995a, 47-49). It was convenient for O'Connor that once a principle such as automatic standing for district residents is established in a Supreme Court opinion, it never has to be argued again, but can merely be cited. Having once served the function of smoothing over the "conservative" justices' contradictory doctrines of standing in racial gerrymandering cases and in those with liberal plaintiffs, "representational harms" could be relegated to the shadows of argument again.

When states or localities subject to Section 5 submitted districting laws and accompanying documents to the Department of Justice in the 1990s, or when legislative committees or courts in states that contained enough minorities to form one or more districts reported to their colleagues or the public, they nearly always spotlighted their creation of minority opportunity districts (e.g., *Wilson v. Eu* [1992], 714-17, 744-53). Otherwise, they would have risked denial of preclearance, an increased likelihood of liability under Section 2 or the Constitution, or public accusations of racism (Rumbaut and Hair 1995a, 46-54). But *Vera* showed that for at least three of the Court's "conservatives"—Justices Kennedy, Scalia, and Thomas—such admissions were enough to satisfy *Miller*'s "predominant motive" test, thereby triggering strict scrutiny. A desire to comply with the VRA or the Constitution or to rectify specific past discrimination might possibly provide compelling state interests, but they could not be nonracial motives for acting, presumably because they could not be pursued without using racial means. For these three justices, "racial classifications" were always illegal, whether they were means or ends, and a purpose test, which all three had endorsed in *Miller* as the centerpiece of racial gerrymandering cases, was relevant only when considering ends. Moreover, since in *Vera* they focused only on the decision to draw such districts in the first place, the shape or other "traditional" principles involved in drawing them were irrelevant. Thus, whether the districts took the forms they did because legislators wished to protect incumbents, to promote their party's interests, or out of pure racial hostility, was inconsequential. Unless there was no other evidence that race had been used in forming district lines, the majority of the *Shaw I* majority rejected O'Connor's oft-quoted statement in that case that "reapportionment is one area in which appearances do matter." For Thomas, Scalia, and Kennedy, only if a minority opportunity district was unintentionally created—an impossibility, since no district is ever unintentionally created—would it avoid heightened scrutiny. Their academic ally, Prof. Katharine Butler (1996, 350, 355), would permit what she has called "naturally occurring" minority opportunity districts, those that "emerge as a result of following standard districting criteria," as if districts were immanent Platonic forms with a natural preexistence that only awaited the neutral application of universally followed principles. This conception could hardly be more divorced from Anglo-American practices that predate the American Revolution (*Vera* [1996], 1971–74; *Shaw I* [1993], 2827; Rumbaut and Hair 1995b, 5–6). In *Miller*, Kennedy had accused the Justice Department of requiring states to maximize the number of minority opportunity districts. Now in *Vera*, along with Scalia and Thomas, he was insisting, in effect, that the states minimize them. In light of his concurrence, it was difficult to understand why Kennedy aligned himself with the opinion written by O'Connor and signed by Rehnquist, rather than that by Thomas and Scalia.

In this case, at least, Justice O'Connor and Chief Justice Rehnquist seemed to believe that any compact, contiguous minority opportunity district was constitutional, whatever the legislature's intent in drawing it, thereby undermining a different aspect of the *Miller* "predominant motive" test than the other three *Shaw* justices had.[56] Over the vehement protests of Kennedy and Thomas, O'Connor relied for precedent on this point on the Court's 1995 summary affirmance of a challenge to the California Supreme Court's redistricting of that state's legislative and congressional seats. Despite the fact that the California special master had repeatedly admitted and clearly carried out his intention to maximize the number of minority opportunity districts in the state, a fact strongly emphasized by plaintiffs who challenged the redistricting after the decision in *Shaw I*, a federal district court rather unceremoniously dismissed the case and the Supreme Court refused to grant the appeal a full hearing (*Wilson v. Eu* [1992], 733, 769–70; Smith 1994, 15–16; *DeWitt v. Wilson* [1994, 1995]). Kennedy had ever so fleetingly mentioned *DeWitt* in his *Miller* opinion, with the curious reference "but see *DeWitt v. Wilson*," as if he were a scholar seeking to minimize the rancor of an opponent by at least citing her, with a locution such as "for a contrary view, see" (*Miller v. Johnson* [1995], 2487). Although the Court never openly examined the compactness of the California districts or their adherence to "traditional districting principles," and although the special master had not claimed that the districts were geographically compact but only "functionally compact," O'Connor in *Vera* interpreted the Court's actions in *DeWitt* as firmly establishing the proposition that compact districts were always legal (*DeWitt v. Wilson* [1994], 1414; *Wilson v. Eu* [1992], 749; *Vera*, 1951).[57]

The defenders of the Texas minority opportunity districts took heart from Kennedy's emphasis in *Miller* on the fact that the Eleventh District in Georgia connected widely separated communities, the residents of each of which, he seemed to assume, shared common interests, and from a statement of O'Connor's in *Shaw I*: "[W]hen members of a racial group live together in one community, a reapportionment plan that concentrates members of the group in one district and excludes them from others may reflect wholly legitimate purposes" (*Shaw I*, 2826; Rumbaut and Hair 1995a, 22–23). Because all three districts were in single metropolitan areas, they shared media coverage, they were small and quickly traversable, and many residents in them participated in the same social institutions, their defenders argued that they were legal under the Court's precedents (Hair 1994, 10–13). In *Vera*, however, O'Connor ignored such inconsistencies with earlier cases. As viewed on an enlarged map, the boundaries were squiggly. She therefore turned from maps to other evidence in order to determine whether heightened scrutiny should be applied. The fact that she examined a great deal of evidence indicated clearly that the State's admission that it had intended to draw three minority opportunity districts was not determinative for her and Rehnquist, as it was for Thomas, Scalia, and Kennedy.

The State and its allies had argued that a desire to protect incumbents insulated the 1991 Texas redistricting from a racial gerrymander challenge for three reasons. First, they argued, Texas had always protected incumbents during redistricting, so that in designing districts to facilitate the election of minority incumbents or power-brokers, it was merely adhering to its own traditional districting principles.[58] Second, since many white-majority districts in Texas were, by the most common measures, approximately as noncompact as the minority opportunity districts were, and since they were made so in order to facilitate incumbents' reelection chances, there was nothing special that needed to be explained about the three districts and thus no reason to spotlight the importance of race in shaping them. To require that minority opportunity districts had to be very compact while overwhelmingly Anglo districts did not have to be, they argued, would discriminate against both minority voters and minority incumbents. Plaintiffs in *Vera* actually agreed with defendants on this point; all noncompact districts, they asserted, "interfere with or preclude effective political representation" (Hurd 1995, 29). Third, many of the particular irregularities in the Eighteenth, Twenty-ninth, and Thirtieth districts were produced by efforts to foster the election of white Democrats. The Eighteenth in Houston and the Thirtieth in Dallas had both been pushed north so that white Democrats could capture reliably Democratic African-American voters in the southern parts of both cities, forcing the Eighteenth and Thirtieth to become less compact than other alternatives that the legislature explicitly considered. The Twenty-ninth splayed out partly because of a tug-of-war between two prospective candidates, one white and one Latino, whose political bases lay in different parts of Houston. As one brief put it, "The essence of this case is political 'gerrymandering,' not racial 'gerrymandering'" (Hair 1994, 16–17; Gray and Moore 1995a, 5–15; Rumbaut and Hair 1995a, 3–5, 26–45; Smith 1995). If minority vote dilution claims could be defeated by "controlling" for party, and thus undercutting the case for racial intent—as had happened in *Whitcomb v. Chavis* (1971) and in the recent Texas case of *LULAC v. Clements* (1993)—then, by analogy, controlling for party and incumbent protection ought to demonstrate that race was not the predominant motive in *Vera*. A precisely similar argument was made by North Carolina and its allies in their briefs in *Shaw II* (Speas 1995a, 16–17; Hodgkiss 1995, 16–21).

Because of the length of time that litigation consumes, the district court judges in both *Shaw v. Hunt* and *Vera v. Richards* had had to issue their opinions before the Supreme Court had announced the "predominant motive" standard in *Miller*. The North Carolina judges interpreted *Shaw I* to have established a requirement that every noncompact minority opportunity district be subjected to strict scrutiny, leaving the discussion of competing explanations for the drawing of such districts to the "compelling state interest" sections of their opinions (*Shaw v. Hunt* [1994], 427–34). But in her district court opinion in *Vera*, Judge Edith Jones had in effect answered all three of Texas's arguments. First, she ruled out a consideration of incumbency or partisanship as potential motives for explaining the shape of the districts on the grounds that they had not been mentioned in *Shaw I* as "traditional districting principles." Second, white majority districts were irrelevant to racial gerrymandering cases unless their compositions were influenced by attempts to place minorities in them in order to help particular white candidates. Third, using "race as a proxy" to craft white districts was just as unconstitutional as creating irregularly shaped minority opportunity districts, Jones ruled, and she teetered on the edge of granting the plaintiffs' motion to throw out twenty-four of the thirty Texas congressional districts that contained appreciable numbers of minorities, or at least some of those districts, before settling for tossing out only the three most urban minority opportunity districts (*Vera v. Richards* [1994], 1326–28, 1333–36).

The partisan, racial, and theoretical consequences of Jones's move, which preceded and complemented the parallel section of Kennedy's opinion in *Miller*, were potentially momentous. If it were applied very strictly, Democrats could not include minority voters within any district that they hoped to carry without hazarding a racial gerrymandering suit, especially not if the boundary around them might appear irregular (Rumbaut and Hair 1995b, 10–11). Attempts to establish minority "influence districts" self-consciously would be equally illegal, thereby undercutting the position of those who have contended that minority influence might increase if minority voters were arrayed in districts so as to be able to elect fewer "descriptive" or minority representatives, but more "substantive" or sympathetic white representatives (Swain 1995, 1996).[59] Finally, the "race as a proxy" point undermined all of the alleged injuries and the inflamed rhetoric of *Shaw I*. Race would work as a proxy only if political behavior were truly strongly correlated with race and some other trait, such as partisan proclivity, not if it were an irrational or demeaning stereotype. Furthermore, once placed in a majority-white district, the blacks and Latinos were expected to coalesce with white Democrats, and the resulting behavior of members of the coalition of two or more races could not be characterized as fitting a racial stereotype.[60] Racially polarized voting in a state would be decreased by placing more minorities in Democratic districts where race was used as a proxy, since the point of including a minority of minorities in a district was to get them to join whites in voting for candidates that substantial numbers of members of all races desired.[61] Representational harm could not take place, since elected candidates in such districts could hardly devote themselves exclusively to responding to the concerns of their minority constituents. While it would be true that "segregation" or "apartheid" might be increased, compared to creating minority opportunity districts that were approximately racially balanced, that is clearly not the comparison that O'Connor had in mind in *Shaw I*, and in any event, it would seem bizarre to consider a district that was 15–35 percent minority as a "segregated" minority district. All this is to say that to broaden *Shaw I* from an attack on racial gerrymandering to one on partisan Democratic—but not Republican—gerrymandering, as Jones did in *Vera*, required destroying the persuasive and theoretical structure of *Shaw I* itself (Smith 1995, 4–6).[62]

While O'Connor overruled her fellow former Republican activist on the first point by considering incumbency protection a traditional districting principle, she agreed with Jones on the second and third points. Examining the Dallas district in considerable detail and those in Houston much more summarily, O'Connor concluded that race was more important than incumbent protection by citing two types of evidence.[63] The first type consisted of statements made in an earlier political gerrymandering case and in documents submitted to the Department of Justice to obtain preclearance of the redistricting changes. In those forums, Eddie Bernice Johnson and other Democrats had contended that the reasons for those changes were racial, not partisan, incumbent-protecting, or self-interested. O'Connor ignored Republican testimony in the same cases, spotlighted in the briefs in *Vera* and *Shaw II*, that the motivation behind redistricting was purely partisan, as well as some contrary testimony by Senator Johnson, all of which Justice Stevens quoted at length in his *Vera* dissent (Gray and Moore 1995a, 9–11; Rumbaut and Hair 1995, 28–29; Speas 1995, 16; *Vera* [1996], 1984–85, n. 23). Although O'Connor did note that some of the Democrats reversed their emphasis when trying to defend against racial gerrymandering charges, she did not systematically compare their statements made before legal activity influenced their content, or examine their actual actions, rather than just their words, and she was much less skeptical of the validity and importance of contradictory "smoking gun" statements than Justice Stevens was in his dissent.

The second type of evidence stressed the fact that racial data was available on the city block level, while political data was measured only on the precinct level, and precincts were often split, indicating to O'Connor that the redistricters had stressed race more than partisanship. This was a very curious judgment, because O'Connor accepted statisticians' findings that, in Dallas at least, 97 percent of blacks generally voted in the Democratic primary. If the correlation between race and party was nearly perfect, then any redistricter who was not constrained to follow precinct boundaries and who sought the most efficient disposition of Democratic votes would split off the black portion of any precinct in which Democratic support was much below 100 percent, distributing the most reliable Democrats to the most marginal districts and leaving the less reliable in Republican or already safely Democratic districts. Of course, something like that is exactly what happened in Dallas, as black Democrats were sheared off of the Thirtieth Congressional District, the minority opportunity district, in order to help white Democratic incumbents in the Fifth and Twenty-fourth Districts survive.

Seeming to recognize that these two arguments were not convincing, O'Connor threw in a third argument that seemed to make the first two superfluous: "race as a proxy." If blacks were assigned to the districts of incumbent white Democrats, she argued, that did not count as an incumbency explanation but as a racial one. "[T]he fact that racial data were used in complex ways, and for multiple objectives," she pronounced, merging means and motives in a slightly different way than Thomas and Scalia did, "does not mean that race did not predominate over other considerations. The record discloses intensive and pervasive use of race both as a proxy to protect the political fortunes of adjacent incumbents, and for its own sake in maximizing the minority population of District 30 regardless of traditional districting principles" (*Vera* [1996], 1958). Revealingly, O'Connor did not mention the fact, stressed by Judge David Hittner's concurrence in the district court, that some of the irregularities in the district came about because Eddie Bernice Johnson wanted to add a Jewish area where she enjoyed significant support (*Vera v. Richards* [1994], 1346–47). The shape of the heavily Republican Sixth District, which Justice Stevens harped on in his dissent, was irrelevant for O'Connor, even if it was designed to protect right-wing incumbent Joe Barton, because its boundaries had not been determined by race. (See Figure 8.1 above.)

Thus, incumbency protection worked for Justice O'Connor in an even more partisan way than for Judge Jones. It protected white Republican incumbents but not white Democrats, who generally, at least in the South, needed minority votes to remain in office. For black or Latino Democrats, incumbency protection did not even count, at least in this part of O'Connor's inconsistent opinion, as a "traditional districting principle." Whatever *Miller* said, the real motives for irregular boundaries around minority opportunity districts were made entirely irrelevant by *Vera*. For O'Connor and Rehnquist, race and shape were all that mattered, at least in this case; for Thomas, Scalia, and Kennedy, a decision to draw a minority opportunity district, which was necessarily made every time such a district was drawn, was sufficient to require strict scrutiny. Whether all five justices would invalidate the use of race as a proxy when it did not result in any minority opportunity district at all but was merely employed to buttress the prospects of white Democrats remained to be determined in subsequent cases.[64]

For O'Connor, the "bizarre, noncompact shape" of the Thirtieth district and the "intricacy of the lines" of the Eighteenth and Twenty-ninth virtually decided the level of scrutiny (*Vera* [1996], 1958–59). But compactness also undermined the defenses that the State of Texas offered under Section 2, and it was determinative of narrow tailoring as well. A judge-created principle, not mentioned in either the Constitution or the VRA, compactness, as employed in *Vera* and *Shaw II*, made a mockery of the slogan of color-blindness, because it not only applied only to minorities, it blocked them at every turn. Without a clear definition (O'Connor approved both Jones's "eyeball" usage and an ad hoc combination of diverse different mathematical indices from a law review article), without empirical support for its status as a "traditional districting principle," without legal or constitutional warrant in national law, compactness had become the all-purpose antidote to minority political power (Pildes and Niemi 1993; *Vera* [1996], 1952; Altman 1998, chap. 3).[65]

Judges in equal protection and similar cases often truncate parts of their inquiries. If the law or practice at issue is a narrowly tailored response to a problem that a government has a compelling state interest in attacking, then it does not matter whether it is considered under strict scrutiny or the less stringent "rationality" standard, and the intent question may be skipped or severely compressed.[66] Conversely, if it fails the narrow tailoring question, one need not consider compelling state interests and vice versa. Thus, in the district court opinion in *Vera*, Judge Jones essentially skipped compelling state interests, because she believed that every minority opportunity district "must have the least possible amount of irregularity of shape, making allowances for traditional districting criteria" (*Vera v. Richards* [1994], 1343). Since these districts did not have the shortest possible perimeters, they failed to be narrowly tailored, in Jones's view. Because Justice Kennedy in *Miller* had concluded that Georgia did not have a compelling state interest in drawing the Eleventh District, he had avoided explaining what narrow tailoring meant in the context of redistricting, and no one could be sure whether Jones's literal interpretation—that narrow tailoring meant geographically minimal borders—was correct or not (*Miller v. Johnson* [1995], 2490–93). Justice O'Connor, however, went out of her way to decide against minorities on both compelling state interests and narrow tailoring—yet more evidence that these cases were not exercises in judicial conservatism.

Defenders of the Texas and North Carolina districts argued that the states had three compelling interests that should satisfy strict scrutiny: complying with Sections 2 and 5 of the VRA and remedying historic discrimination. The sticking point under Section 2 was the nature of the compactness required under *Gingles*.[67] The states contended that all *Gingles* implied was that they had to show that a compact minority opportunity district could hypothetically be drawn. After that, states could take into account other interests, such as the desire to protect incumbents or to provide urban representation, in drawing actual districts. In Texas, everyone conceded that compact black opportunity districts could have been drawn in Dallas and Houston, although there was less consensus about whether, in addition, a compact Latino district could have been drawn in Houston. In North Carolina, O'Connor's discussion in *Shaw I* seemed to indicate that she believed that the two African-American opportunity districts proposed by the Republicans were sufficiently compact to satisfy her. If a state drew enough minority opportunity districts to guarantee minorities the same opportunity as whites to elect candidates of their choice, there would be no discriminatory effect, regardless of the shape of the districts, and therefore no Section 2 violation, the states contended. Did states not have a discretion to set the boundaries of minority opportunity districts as they wished, just as they had for white districts (Days et al.

1995a, 38–45; Days 1995, 3–5; Gray and Moore 1995a, 28–35, 43–46; Speas 1995, 41–45; Rumbaut and Hair 1995a, 56–69)?

While paying lip service to federalism concerns, O'Connor's answer was negative. Minority opportunity districts did not have to be as compact as possible, as Judge Jones had announced, because that would lead to "endless 'beauty contests'" with other proposed districts that were, by some measure, more compact than the districts actually adopted. But they did have to be "reasonably compact." And incumbency could not excuse irregularly shaped districts if part of the reason that they were irregular was that race had been used as a proxy to draw lines to protect incumbents (*Vera* [1996], 1960–61). Thus, for O'Connor and Rehnquist, the same evidence that proved that a district deserved strict scrutiny, the coexistence of an irregular boundary and minority racial concentrations, also undermined the argument that compliance with Section 2 was a compelling state interest. According to their position, if a district as actually drawn was not *required* by Section 2, it could not be *justified* by Section 2, even if drawing it would have served as an ironclad defense against a Section 2 suit. In *Gingles*, compactness had been merely one element in a formula for assessing whether a violation of Section 2 had occurred, and the relevant question was whether a minority opportunity district could be drawn (*Thornburg v. Gingles* [1986], 38, 50, n. 17; *Johnson v. De Grandy* [1994], 2655). In *Vera*, compactness became a requirement for minority districts but not for white districts, and the relevant question was whether the district actually drawn was sufficiently compact to please a majority of the justices. States were free to take other interests or goals into account only in drawing white-majority districts, and they might perhaps not be able to consider race even in setting those boundaries. Apparently, every state had such a strong interest in drawing compact districts—no matter that they might disavow that interest—that no other interest, such as partisanship or incumbent protection, could outweigh it, if the boundaries accommodated the interests of minorities. The Supreme Court would decide what public purposes the states might pursue and what weight they might attach to them. For O'Connor and Rehnquist, federalism was for whites only.

Not satisfied to hobble Section 2 as a compelling state interest, O'Connor next turned to narrow tailoring. Before *Shaw I*, the leading Supreme Court explication of narrow tailoring came in *U.S. v. Paradise* (1987), 171, in which Justice Brennan set out four principles. An affirmative action program to increase the number of African-American officers in the Alabama Highway Patrol was considered narrowly tailored to fit the compelling state interest of remedying previous discrimination against blacks in hiring and promotion in the Patrol because no alternative, effective remedy was available, because the plan was not a rigid quota and it had a limited duration, because its numerical goals were reasonably related to the number of minorities in the relevant labor market, and because it minimized the effect on innocent third parties. In *Vera* and *Shaw II*, defenders of the districts argued that *Paradise* implied that districts should be considered narrowly tailored if (1) the proportion of minority opportunity districts (which, unlike quotas, did not guarantee minority success[68]) drawn by the state was as small as or smaller than the percentage of minorities in the population; (2) if the level of racial bloc voting showed that districts with smaller proportions of minorities would not give minority populations chances to elect candidates of their choice that were equal to the chances available to Anglos; (3) if the state did not pack a larger proportion of minorities into minority opportunity districts than was necessary to elect a candidate of choice, thus diluting their influence in other districts; and (4) if the state were allowed to accommodate nonracial interests in its districting arrangements, which meant that districts would probably be less compact than if only race had been taken into account. If a state could not consider other interests, that would not only discourage voluntary compliance with Section 2, but it would also heighten the disadvantages faced by minorities and increase the concentration on race in the districting process, because minorities would have to convince redistricters to subordinate every other value in order to maximize the compactness of the minority opportunity districts (Hair 1994, 21–22; Days et al., 1995b, 35–45; Days 1995, 11–12; Rumbaut and Hair 1995a, 54–55, 59; Speas 1995, 45–49).

O'Connor ignored the first three arguments, reiterated that the process was unconstitutionally tainted if racial means were employed for political ends and explicitly rejected Justice Kennedy's statement in *Miller* (1995), 2486, that the shape of a district was relevant only as an indication of motive. Noncompact minority opportunity districts—but not majority-white districts, of whatever shape—"convey the message that political identity is, or should be, predominantly racial," she announced, and that was a violation of narrow tailoring. Why it was unconstitutional to convey a message that politics was racially polarized, if that was the case, and how such a doctrine comported with Section 2, which could be invoked only if this message were proven to be true, O'Connor did not explain. Did not a government document, such as O'Connor's opinion itself, that announced that 97 percent of African-Americans in Dallas voted Democratic, or any judicial opinion that documented racially polarized voting "convey the message that political identity is . . . predominantly racial"? How was one to know which expressions of the truth a majority of the Supreme Court would deem harmful? As an "example" of this expressive harm, O'Connor moved from cultural psychology to political sociology. Cutting across precinct lines to draw a minority opportunity district—but not a white majority district—"disrupts nonracial bases of political identity and thus intensifies the emphasis on race" (*Vera* [1996], 1961–62). Yet this was not an instance of a symbolic message, but a description of the practices of precinct-walking campaigners. Furthermore, O'Connor here neglected to mention the fact, pointed out in the State's brief, that precinct boundaries in Texas were conventionally redrawn after every redistricting (Gray and Moore 1995b, 17). Precincts did not track any "natural or traditional divisions" in society, as O'Connor asserted, but were mere lines of administrative convenience, which were repeatedly reshaped as population or other political boundary lines shifted.

Although evidence of racial discrimination in past redistricting, in the form of an earlier version of Chapter 6, was presented as evidence in *Vera*, Judge Jones, who must have been personally aware of the facts of the 1981 redistricting, since she was chief counsel of the Texas Republican State Committee during the litigation over that redistricting, sidestepped it. The record of specific, identified discrimination was thus barely perceptible on the printed record, and the appeal briefs from the State of Texas and the U.S. concentrated primarily on racially polarized voting as a present indication of present and past discrimination. But no amount of evidence of past discrimination, however specific and however strong the proof that the legislature acted on it, would have made any difference to O'Connor, because the districts had to be compact to be narrowly tailored (*Vera* [1996], 1962–63). For O'Connor, no interest was sufficiently compelling to allow "ugly" minority opportunity districts.

In her concurrence to her own plurality opinion in *Vera*, O'Connor stated that she and the four dissenters formed a majority for the proposition that states should continue to act as though Section 2 was constitutional until the Supreme Court ruled otherwise—an alarming statement, since it implied that Kennedy, Rehnquist, Scalia, and Thomas, who signed onto her majority opinion, but not her concurrence, all agreed that Section 2 was unconstitutional. For herself, O'Connor, in a striking divergence from her views in *Shaw I* about what Section 2 required, announced that an intent to comply with Section 2 would be deemed narrowly tailored only if the resulting district "does not deviate substantially from a hypothetical court-drawn Section 2 district for predominantly racial reasons," and she made clear that what particularly bothered her was the effect on the lines of "the misuse of race as a proxy" (*Vera* [1996], 1970). In other words, a state could constitutionally decide to draw a minority opportunity district, but once it did so, it had to intuit exactly where a judge concerned only with compactness and preserving other existing political boundaries would draw that district. No other state goals could affect the boundaries if they added or subtracted minorities from those that the hypothetical judge would have included. In *Johnson v. De Grandy*

(1994), 2661, Justice Souter had remarked that under the Constitution, "minority voters are not immune from the obligation to pull, haul, and trade to find common political ground." With regard to redistricting, O'Connor, who had signed onto Souter's *De Grandy* opinion, now announced, in effect, that minority politicians and their Anglo allies not only had no *obligation* to pull, haul, and trade, they had no *right* to do so. Any other standard, O'Connor announced, would constitute an "unjustified and excessive" and therefore unconstitutional use of race (*Vera* [1996], 1970). But the effect of her "narrow tailoring" doctrine was in fact quite the reverse, and it contradicted her opinion in *Shaw I* starkly. In *Shaw I*, O'Connor had stated that if race were the sole reason for district boundaries, the plan was subject to strict scrutiny, and she had implied that it was probably unconstitutional. In *Vera*, she decided, in effect, that if drawing a minority opportunity district were *not* the sole reason for those boundaries, the plan could not be narrowly tailored and was therefore unconstitutional. In the first case, there was too much emphasis on race; in the second, not enough. Such contradictions and the deep divisions in the Court's "conservative" majority put future redistricters of goodwill, who, like the Texas legislators, wished to alleviate past discrimination, adhere to the VRA, or overcome the current prejudice that produces widespread racial bloc voting, in an impossible bind.

BECAUSE the Eighteenth District in Houston had been represented by an African-American since Barbara Jordan was elected in 1972, the State also claimed that drawing it was justified by an intention to comply with Section 5. Plaintiffs countered with the novel argument that because the Eighteenth was less than 50 percent black, Section 5 did not apply to it, an argument that O'Connor did not consider (Hurd 1995, 45). As explained above, in *Shaw I*, O'Connor had indicated that the non-retrogression interpretation of Section 5 would not justify going beyond the status quo in minority seats. Now, she used the concept of narrow tailoring not to mean compactness, as she had interpreted it in connection with Section 2 and the consequences of past and present discrimination, but to tighten her grandfather-clause reading of Section 5. Because of an outmigration of African-Americans and an influx of Latinos, the black proportion of the Eighteenth District, which had been 40.8 percent in 1980, had dropped to 35.1 percent by 1990. In redrawing it, the legislature strengthened black control by raising the African-American percentage to 50.9. O'Connor, however, declared that Section 5 required only that the district be 35.1 percent black and that even if African-Americans could not subsequently elect their candidate of choice with a low and perhaps further declining percentage of the population, no higher percentage could be justified. The State could not voluntarily draw the district so as to raise the black percentage at all and still claim that doing so was mandated by Section 5 (*Vera* [1996], 1963). Non-retrogression put a ceiling not only on the number of minority opportunity districts that could be drawn legally but on the percentage of minorities in each district, at least if the districts did not meet O'Connor's aesthetic criteria. The justice made no effort to support this extreme interpretation of Section 5 by referring to the text of the law or to the congressional hearings or reports, both of which seemed clearly to contradict it (U.S. Senate 1982b, 12 n. 31; McDonald 1989, 1288–91, for citations to hearings and case law). It is also hard to see how to constrain this intensely race-conscious stance. If non-retrogression applies to any district with any number of minorities, and it is violated by raising a 35 percent minority percentage, why not a 20 percent minority percentage, or 10, 5, or 1? How could a legislature comply with this hyper-Helmsian reading of Section 5 and not violate *Miller*'s predominant motive test? [69]

O'Connor's ruling was perfectly tailored to promote maximum conflict among two of the Democrats' most loyal constituencies in the 2001 reapportionments, for Houston's demographic trends were mirrored in major cities such as Los Angeles, Chicago, New York, and others throughout the country. Unless redistricters were allowed to follow African-Americans to the near suburbs and restore the black percentages lost to legislative districts by black flight and Latino in-migration, the two groups would be locked in a zero-sum game for representation that would result in a loss of minority representation, a shattering of coalition and Democratic party politics, and an exacerbation of racial hostility between the most disadvantaged ethnic groups, save Native Americans, in American society. O'Connor did not have to speculate about these effects of her ruling, for they were already on the record in Houston, and they spice her opinion (*Bush v. Vera* [1996], 1958–60, 1963). She therefore could not have been unaware that her opinion would heighten such interethnic and intraparty tensions.

In their concurrences, Justices Kennedy and Thomas, who was joined by Scalia, did not discuss narrow tailoring, and Thomas downgraded while Kennedy denigrated compactness as a necessary and sufficient proof of racial gerrymandering. Both concurrences would allow even noncompact minority opportunity districts so long as they were not drawn on purpose. As Thomas put it, quoting *Feeney*, to be constitutional, the districts in question had to be constructed "in spite of" race, not "because of" it. For Kennedy, what was prohibited was "gratuitous race-based districting or use of race as a proxy for other interests." Any consciously drawn minority opportunity districts, whatever their shape, were, the three judges believed, unconstitutional per se. And Thomas explicitly disavowed O'Connor's compactness interpretation of *De Witt v. Wilson* (1995). Since districts don't just fall from the sky, the Kennedy-

Thomas standard, as Justice Stevens noted in his dissent, threatened every minority opportunity district in the country (*Vera* [1996], 1972–74, 1977, n. 8; *Personnel Administrator of Massachusetts v. Feeney* [1979], 279).

THE DISSENTS of Justices Stevens and Souter in *Vera* were partly complementary and partly contradictory. Stevens accepted the *Miller* predominant-motive standard, at least for purposes of argument, but showed, through a much more rigorous evaluation of the evidence than Justice O'Connor engaged in, that race was not the predominant factor in the drawing of District 30. Critical of compactness standards, he also concluded that even if the Houston districts were subject to strict scrutiny, they survived it, because compliance with the VRA provided a compelling state interest, and the districts were designed to meet that objective. More fundamentally, Stevens, who as early as *Bolden* had declared that "racial, religious, ethnic, and economic gerrymanders are all species of political gerrymanders," accused the *Shaw-Miller-Vera* majority of adopting a roundabout means of confronting political gerrymanders, while pretending to discuss only race. Although Stevens, a Republican, was willing to outlaw political gerrymandering, at least in some circumstances, he was unwilling to use race as a subterfuge for doing so, and he strongly criticized the Court's "unnecessary intrusion into the ability of States to negotiate solutions to political differences while providing long-excluded groups the opportunity to participate effectively in the democratic process" (*Vera* [1996], 1975 n. 2; 1988 n. 29, quoting *City of Mobile v. Bolden* [1980], 88; 1993).

By contrast, Justice Souter's dissent was wholly theoretical, and he was much cooler toward the predominant-motive test and warmer toward compactness than Stevens was. Despite Stevens's demonstration that the predominant-motive criterion could be employed fairly and could separate other factors from strictly racial considerations, Souter condemned "*Miller*'s impossible obligation to untangle racial considerations from so-called 'race-neutral' objectives." The majority therefore had four choices: completely outlaw the intentional creation of minority opportunity districts, entirely eliminate the practice of districting, adopt some quantitative standard of compactness, or abandon *Shaw*-type causes of action altogether. The first two he condemned as too radical, because they were likely to lead to much more minority vote dilution, a declaration that Section 2 was unconstitutional, and/or complete upheaval in the political system. The harm to society purportedly expressed by ungainly minority opportunity districts was insufficient to justify the degree of intervention into the traditional redistricting process that a quantitative compactness requirement, to be applied only to minority districts, would necessitate.[70] These objections, the confused and illogical standards of the *Shaw-Miller-Vera* line of cases, and their inconsistency with the Court's other equal protection decisions, led Souter, in what amounted to a plea to his sometime ally Justice O'Connor, to call for the Court's "withdrawal from the presently untenable state of the law." Whereas O'Connor in *Shaw I* had cited no evidence to justify the injuries that she claimed racial gerrymandering caused, Souter drew explicitly on studies of past and present racial and ethnic politics to hold out the hope "that if vote dilution is attacked at the same time that race is given the recognition that ethnicity has historically received in American politics, the force of race in politics will also moderate in time" (*Vera* [1996], 1997–2013). Souter's optimistic, nonpartisan moderation, his deference to states and legislatures, and his and Stevens's care in facts and argumentation could hardly have contrasted more with the majority's partisan radicalism, scorn for nonjudicial bodies, inconsistency, and carelessness.

Shaw II and the Court's simultaneous remand of an Ohio case demonstrated how the vague and contradictory standards of *Shaw I, Miller,* and *Vera* could be selectively used to facilitate a logrolled majority and how an unprincipled application of the notions of purpose and compactness could block or validate any minority opportunity district, as the judges wished. Chief Justice Rehnquist united all five of the *Shaw* justices on one majority opinion by subjecting the North Carolina Twelfth District to strict scrutiny for two distinct reasons.[71] To attract Justices Kennedy, Scalia, and Thomas, he ruled that the State's admission that it had meant to draw two minority opportunity districts satisfied *Miller*'s intent standard. Unlike Justice O'Connor in *Vera*, Rehnquist made no pretense of systematically weighing the importance of the alternative explanations offered by the State—that is, that redistricters had sought to establish districts around rural and urban African-American communities of interest and that they had placed the Twelfth District where they did, instead of stretching it across rural southeastern North Carolina, to protect white Democratic incumbents in the southeast—and merely mentioned those reasons dismissively. "That the legislature addressed these interests," the chief justice remarked curtly, "does not in any way refute the fact that race was the legislature's predominant consideration" (*Shaw II* [1996], 1901). To attract Justice O'Connor, Rehnquist switched the focus from the motive for the decision to establish the Twelfth District to the shape of the district, which was long and narrow (though shorter and much easier to traverse than the Republican-proposed alternative that O'Connor had precipitantly declared to be compact in *Shaw I*). Since for O'Connor, any noncompact minority opportunity district was suspect, Rehnquist did not have to spend any time discussing the reasons for the placement and actual boundaries of the Twelfth district. Thus, Rehnquist cobbled together his majority by two tactics: suppressing inconvenient details and treating two decisions—to establish the district and to draw its boundaries—as one (*Shaw II* [1996], 1899–1901).

Having obtained a majority consensus for subjecting the district to strict scrutiny, Rehnquist turned to the three reasons offered by the State as compelling interests.[72] First, the chief justice repudiated the notion that an intent to alleviate the effects of specific past discrimination in redistricting, as detailed in an earlier version of chapter 5, justified the drawing of minority opportunity districts. Without examining any of the evidence presented, Rehnquist asserted that such a notion could have motivated only "some" of the legislators because that report and other, similar evidence was not prepared before the legislature adopted its redistricting plans. He paid no attention to proof, detailed in the briefs, that people whose business was politics were well aware of the previous decade's discrimination in redistricting, as well as of racially polarized voting and racial appeals in elections that had quite recently taken place in their state (Speas 1995, 11–13; Days et al. 1995b, 8; Hodgkiss 1995, 36–38). Perhaps if the 1991 legislature had prepared a "*Croson* study," the name given to reports on past specific discrimination that have been compiled by states and municipalities since the 1989 case of *City of Richmond v. Croson* in order to justify the adoption of affirmative action programs in employment and contracts, Rehnquist would have found it more difficult to decide this point so summarily. By allowing for the possibility that previous actions could justify remedial districting, Rehnquist implicitly rejected the extreme view of the Pacific Legal Foundation that past discrimination in redistricting or previous elections could never excuse race-conscious districting because, according to the Foundation, "Each time a governmental entity redistricts its jurisdiction, the slate is cleaned," or the even more extreme position of Prof. Katharine Butler that past discrimination could never validate race-conscious action in any circumstance whatsoever (La Fetra 1995, 15; Butler 1995, 616).

Second, Rehnquist argued that Section 5 was insufficient to justify the final North Carolina plan because any change that increased the number of minority opportunity districts could not have had a retrogressive effect. As for the purpose prong of Section 5, the chief justice blithely credited the reasoning that the State had offered to the Justice Department to justify its initial decision to draw only one majority-minority district, reasoning that the Justice Department had rejected as merely "pretextual." But it was inconsistent, as Justice Stevens pointed out in dissent, to accept North Carolina's justification for refusing to draw a second district at face value while offhandedly dismissing its explanation for having later changed its mind. Furthermore, instead of treating the purpose inquiry seriously, Rehnquist made no attempt to review any other evidence of the State's real motives for either decision (*Shaw II* [1996], 1904, 1919). And the chief justice went even further beyond the ne-

428 *Postmodern Equal Protection*

cessities of this case to suggest in a footnote that the remedy for a plan with a racially discriminatory purpose could not be race-conscious itself. If such a hint were followed in future decisions, then courts could not order race-conscious remedies for even the most egregious intentional discrimination.[73]

Finally, like O'Connor in *Vera*, Rehnquist rejected an intent to comply with Section 2 or to avoid a lawsuit based on that provision as a compelling interest, on the basis that a court establishing a remedy for a successful Section 2 challenge would not have drawn a district that looked like the Twelfth. Only "reasonably compact" districts could satisfy Section 2, according to Rehnquist, which raised the intriguing and dismaying possibility, suggested by Justice Stevens in dissent, that someone could employ Section 2, and not just *Shaw*, to challenge a plan containing a certain number of minority opportunity districts on the grounds that it was possible to propose a plan with *fewer*, but more compact, districts. Rehnquist also undermined a Section 2 defense by asserting that the right not to have one's vote diluted was a purely individual right and that therefore a district that was partially shifted away from a compact area in which a minority population was highly concentrated did not satisfy all of the people whose votes had been diluted. Instead, it granted relief to some other members of the same race, who had no right to redress, because in their area there were not enough minority group members to form a compact district. Thus, a district other than the one a court would have drawn was not narrowly tailored to remedy a potential Section 2 lawsuit, and the legislature had no discretion to consider values or interests other than racial ones.[74] Although he conceded in a footnote that successful minority plaintiffs in Section 2 cases gained no individual right to be included in a new minority opportunity district, thus undercutting his individualist view of dilution, Rehnquist did not confront the much more serious point that minority vote dilution law as a whole—whether derived from the VRA, as in *Gingles*, or the Constitution, as in *White v. Regester* (1973)—was based on the concept of discrimination against a *group*, not just an individual. Otherwise, the notions of racial bloc voting, a history of discrimination, and all the rest of the "totality of the circumstances" inquiries long recognized by the Supreme Court and Congress made no sense (Karlan 1995, 84–89; Karlan and Levinson 1996, 1204–8). Smoothing over such points to keep his majority together, Rehnquist nonetheless provided another citation for those advocates of "colorblindness" who would like to nullify minority vote dilution law altogether (*Shaw II* [1996], 1902–7; La Fetra 1995).

Although the North Carolina redistricting was just as partisan as that in Texas—as the scholarly opinion by the 2–1 Democratic North Carolina district court made clear, albeit in less strident tones than the 3–0 Republican Texas district court—Rehnquist in *Shaw II* virtually ignored partisanship and incumbent protection as motives for the decisions to draw two minority opportunity districts and to place them where the legislature did. Whereas Texas legislators carefully carved the urban districts from adjacent ones occupied by white Democrats, leaving the incumbents enough faithfully Democratic minority voters to win reelection, North Carolina legislators sculpted the Twelfth District out of largely Republican territory, displacing the district away from areas represented by white Democrats. This contrast may have deflected attention from Rehnquist's omission of a discussion of partisanship in *Shaw II*. But Justice Stevens, in the only written dissent in the case, restored its real partisan context. Charging that "the amorphous nature of the race discrimination claim recognized in *Shaw I*" made it inevitable that such claims would be employed "for partisan ends," Stevens noted that the North Carolina Republican Party had intervened in *Shaw II*, even though, he asserted, their "real grievance is that they are represented in Congress by Democrats when they would prefer to be represented by members of their own party." In his view, the Republicans' participation in the suit, together with the long and narrow shape of the Twelfth District, constituted evidence that the predominant motive of the legislature in drawing the Twelfth District was partisan, not racial. If the Democrats had been interested chiefly in race, he argued, they would have accepted the more compact Republican plan mentioned in the attorney-general's Section 5 objection letter. "Party politics," Stevens concluded, "explain the district's odd shape" (*Shaw II* [1996], 1908, 1916). Thus, under the *Miller* predominant-motive test, the State's action should not have been subjected to heightened scrutiny at all.

Because none of the plaintiffs alleged that they suffered differential treatment but only that they shared with other North Carolinians an affront because the State had not acted in a colorblind manner, Stevens further declared that their case should not have been brought under the equal protection clause, which "protects against wrongs which by definition burden some persons but not others" or "stamps persons of one race with a badge of inferiority." *Shaw* claims were not about equal protection, Stevens asserted, but about "substantive due process," a phrase that conjured up the activist, policy-oriented, "conservative" jurisprudence of the pre-1937 Supreme Court. If the generalized harm to the polity was merely "expressive," Stevens went on, what constitutional principle established "whether the message conveyed is a distressing endorsement of racial separatism, or an inspiring call to integration of the political process" (*Shaw II* [1996], 1908–10)?

Stevens also criticized the majority opinion's artificial dichotomy between motives and interests and its conduct of the inquiries into compelling interests and narrow tailoring. Although North Carolina claimed that an intent to comply with the VRA and to avoid litigation had both motivated its decision to draw a second minority opportunity district and served as a compelling state interest for that decision, Rehnquist did not even consider the possibility that compliance with Sections 2 or 5 could have been a purpose of the legislature. Perhaps, as Stevens suggested, the chief justice believed that using a race-conscious means of complying with a federal law fatally compromised an otherwise race-neutral motive. Indeed, Rehnquist may have accepted the plaintiffs' even blunter position that a desire to comply with the VRA was not a justification but a confession of having acted with unconstitutional color-consciousness (Everett 1995c, 10).

When he had turned to compelling interests, the chief justice had dismissed the State's assertion that it was reasonable to comply with the Justice Department's interpretation of Section 5 and to expect that it might lose a Section 2 case if it had not created a second minority opportunity district. Stevens, however, pointed out that the facts that the district court had accepted both assertions and that the Justice Department was the principal designated interpreter of the VRA gave North Carolina's assertion considerable credibility. He also contested Rehnquist's dismissal of the intent to remedy past discrimination as unimportant because it allegedly affected only "some" legislators. As the plaintiffs had put it, any factor that was not "sufficient" by itself to have moved the legislature was "irrelevant" to its actions (Everett 1995c, 12). Stevens did not accept this logic, taking the view that something can be "a legitimate and significant additional factor supporting the decision" without explaining the actions of all or even a majority of legislators (*Shaw II* [1996], 1917–20). Rehnquist's stance seemed to imply that a state must be absolutely positive of its own guilt and absolutely certain of the outcome of a lawsuit and that it must issue a detailed public confession before adopting an electoral change that would ameliorate the position of minorities—conditions, explicitly endorsed in the Republican briefs, that would provide strong incentives for inaction and continued discrimination (Farr 1995b, 8–17).

On Rehnquist's view that a district would not be narrowly tailored to satisfy Section 2 unless it was the precise district that a judge would propose as a remedy in a successful Section 2 case, Stevens was scathing, calling it "a pure judicial invention" and "judicial creativity rather than constitutional principle." However elongated, District 12 helped to insulate North Carolina from a potential Section 2 challenge from African-American plaintiffs because it gave them nearly proportional representation. Unlike some affirmative action remedies—for instance, ones used in employment or government contracting cases—noncompact districts injured no one. Thus, argued Stevens, the means precisely fit the end and harmed no third parties, which was what narrow tailoring had meant prior to *Vera* and *Shaw II* (*Shaw II* [1996], 1920–22).

Finally, requiring judicial or judge-like remedies,[75] instead of deferring to "conscientious" congressional and state legislative efforts "to resolve difficult questions of politics and race that have long plagued" the country, was "seriously misguided," Stevens concluded, unless there was convincing evidence "that voters are being denied fair and effective representation as a result of their race." There was none here, the dissenter believed, but only "a majority's attempt to enable the minority to participate more effectively in the process of democratic government." That attempt "should not be viewed with the same hostility that is appropriate for oppressive and exclusionary abuses of political power" (*Shaw II* [1996], 1907, 1922).[76]

Republican Racial Gerrymandering Is Constitutional: *Voinovich v. Quilter*

Eleven days after the Court issued its Texas and North Carolina opinions, it took the seemingly minor action of remanding a case from the Supreme Court to a federal district court. The Supreme Court's actions in this and their earlier consideration of the same case, *Voinovich v. Quilter,* can be deemed consistent with *Miller, Vera,* and *Shaw II* only if *Quilter*'s partisan consequences are taken into account. In 1991, the 3–2 Republican Ohio Apportionment Board, claiming that Section 2 required it to maximize the number of majority-minority districts regardless of the degree of white crossover voting in the state, packed African-Americans into a small number of state legislative districts, reducing their influence on elections in adjacent, potentially Democratic districts. The plan was actually drawn by James R. Tilling, the executive director of the Republican Caucus in the Ohio State Senate, who had also been the chief fundraiser of the state Republican party, and who apparently followed a strategic plan that advised Republicans to "pack black minorities" and force Democratic incumbents of all races to run against each other. As in the country as a whole, 85 percent or more of African-American voters in Ohio regularly supported Democratic nominees. Under the Democratic-drafted 1981 plan, black legislators had won more than two-thirds of the vote between 1984 and 1990 in districts that ranged from 38.5 percent to 53.2 percent African-American in population. An average of 57 percent of whites had voted for black legislative candidates. The 1991 plan increased the black percentages in these districts by from 7.7 to 13.7 percentage points. Although the Republicans claimed to be increasing the black percentages, in Tilling's words, to "ensure" the continued election of African-American candidates if the black incumbents should die or retire, the Republicans' statistical expert witness estimated that even nonincumbent black candidates would receive a minimum of 68 percent and an average of 78 percent in the redrawn districts. This was more than an *opportunity* to elect candidates of choice; it was what

Tilling called a "guarantee," but one extracted at the price of diminishing blacks' influence in surrounding districts. Overall, the 1991 plan increased the number of majority-minority districts in the state from four to eight, but decreased the number of districts that were between 10 percent and 50 percent black from twenty to twelve. Although the state branches of the NAACP and an organization called the "Black Elected Democrats of Ohio" endorsed some or all of the Republican plan, the state Democratic Party, which almost invariably carried districts that were 13 percent or more black, sued under Section 2 and the Fifteenth Amendment, claiming that the packing diminished black influence in the state as a whole (*Quilter v. Voinovich* [1992]; Gilliam 1992, 19–21; Gilliam 1996a, 3, 28a).

A 2–1 Democratic federal panel that included Nathaniel R. Jones, former general counsel of the NAACP, ruled against the Republicans. Packing blacks into some districts diluted their influence elsewhere, the majority reasoned, and the State could not engage in such dilution unless it proved that Section 2 had been violated and that voting was sufficiently racially polarized that blacks needed majority-minority districts to elect their preferred candidates. In response, the Apportionment Board reduced the number of majority-minority districts to five, with two more over 49 percent black. Without engaging in any statistical analysis or conducting more public hearings, the Board adopted official findings that the state's politics was racially polarized and that the totality of the circumstances showed the state to be in violation of Section 2, and it proclaimed, as similar bodies in other states had, that it had been careful to emphasize the racial characteristics of voters in drawing districts. The Board ignored the fact that since 1970, only one district that was more than 35 percent black in population had elected a white representative. After the district court again ruled against the Republicans, this time adding a Fifteenth Amendment intent finding to its Section 2 grounds, the State appealed, emphasizing that the support of the Ohio NAACP made it "inconceivable" that the plan had a racially discriminatory purpose.

The State's (Republicans') position on Section 2 seemed paradoxical. On the one hand, it claimed that Section 2 required it to maximize the number of majority-minority districts, whether such districts were necessary to elect minority-preferred candidates or not, and it admitted that such packing did not maximize "minority voting strength" or influence. On the other hand, it objected to having to determine whether Section 2 had been violated in the past or would be violated in the 1990s if the State adopted a plan with somewhat lower percentages of minorities in the most heavily black districts. Later, it asserted, even less logically, that the threat of a suit challenging the packing of blacks into a few districts justified precisely that packing. The Ohio Republicans' arguments made legal sense only if Section 2, as interpreted in *Gingles,* was merely a formalistic rule, universally applicable, whatever the degree of past or present discrimination or racial polarization, that equated dilution with failing to maximize the number of districts that were more than half minority in population. Thus, in hearings throughout the state, Tilling repeatedly said that he understood the VRA to require the maximization of the number of majority-minority districts, and in notes compiled while he was actually drawing districts, Tilling remarked that he had, for instance, "start[ed] with majority-minority districts" in Cincinnati, that he had drawn a heavily black district in Columbus carefully to "avoid primarily white" areas, and that he had tried "to maximize the minority voters" in a district in Akron. In other words, he admitted racial gerrymandering and denied that failing to maximize minority voting power could amount to a dilution of minority votes. Even though blacks could demonstrably win seats in Ohio with considerably less than population or voting-age majorities, they still had to be crammed into majority-minority seats, he asserted. The partisan political sense of the formalistic rule—pack the most reliable Democratic voters as much as possible—was transparent (*Quilter v. Voinovich* [1992]; Goodman 1992b, 10–17, 23; Goodman 1992a, 2–3; Goodman 1996b, 23, ; Gilliam 1996a, 4; Gilliam 1996b, 4–5).[77] Never did the Ohio Republicans make the "colorblind" arguments that they had engaged in partisan gerrymandering, that voting was not markedly polarized by race in Ohio, and that African-Americans therefore deserved no special protection.

In a short, unanimous opinion delivered by Justice O'Connor three months before *Shaw I,* the Supreme Court accepted the Justice Department's position that unless voting was racially polarized, there could be no Section 2 violation, and therefore no dilution. Even though the State's interpretation of the VRA as requiring maximization of the number of majority-minority districts was incorrect, at least where voting was not polarized, the fact that it had seemingly acted on this interpretation shielded it from an accusation of discriminatory motivation. Indeed, disregarding the districting principles written into the Ohio Constitution in order to obey the VRA, O'Connor remarked, "does not raise an inference of intentional discrimination; it demonstrates obedience to the Supremacy Clause of the United States Constitution"—a difficult sentiment to square with her paeans to "traditional districting principles" in her opinions in *Shaw I* and *Vera.* If the actions of Democratic legislators in North Carolina and Georgia could be declared intentionally discriminatory even though they followed the Justice Department's interpretations of Section 5, which the Court later ruled incorrect, how could Republican legislators in Ohio, who had followed a bizarre interpretation of Section 2—mandatory packing—that was blessed by no authority, escape the same judgment? Even assuming that "influence district" claims were valid, the Supreme Court ruled, the district court's opinion that Section 2 and the Fifteenth Amendment had been violated was erroneous (Starr 1992, 10–13; *Voinovich v. Quilter* [1993]).[78]

Because the only equal protection claim by the plaintiffs, one concerning population inequalities between districts, had not been fully considered by the district court, the Supreme Court remanded the case for further examination of that question. But after the decision in *Shaw I*, the district court allowed the Democratic plaintiffs to amend their suit to transform it into a "racial gerrymandering" claim. The subsequent district court decision by Judge Nathaniel Jones, handed down after the Supreme Court decision in *Miller*, sought to hoist the "conservatives" on their own petard.[79] Interpreting *Shaw I*'s references to bizarrely shaped districts as mere indications of intent, as Justice Kennedy had in *Miller*, Jones concluded that strict scrutiny should be imposed, even if the State had largely followed its traditional districting principles, because race was admittedly its predominant motive for drawing the majority-minority districts. He did not assess the Democrats' charges that the Ohio districts were less compact than the Ohio Constitution seemingly required, because he believed that *Miller*'s predominant-motive standard meant what it said. Although charges of partisan considerations danced around the edges of Jones's opinion, receiving somewhat less attention than in the district court's 1992 opinions, Jones did not systematically consider whether Republican partisanship, rather than race, motivated the redistricters in Ohio, and he did not discuss the use of race as a means or a proxy. Once strict scrutiny was imposed, the case was practically over, for all Jones had to do was to cite the evidence that there was no racially polarized voting, and Section 2 was eliminated as a possible compelling state interest. Because there was no overwhelming pattern of past discrimination in the state, because Ohio was not covered by Section 5, and because Justice O'Connor in the first *Quilter* case and other judges in other cases had ruled that adherence to the state constitution did not give a state a compelling reason for failing to observe federal statutory or constitutional law, no other interests justified Ohio's actions, either (*Quilter v. Voinovich* [1995], 1011–37).

By the time the Supreme Court considered Ohio's appeal of the 1995 *Quilter* decision, the justices had no doubt largely written their opinions in *Vera* and *Shaw II*. The parallels were striking, and seven of the nine justices, at least, should have had no trouble making up their minds. For the dissenters, there was no more reason to impose strict scrutiny for Ohio's acts than for North Carolina's, Georgia's, or Texas's, and the case should have ended there. For Kennedy, Scalia, and Thomas, the statements of the Ohio redistricters should have been at least as revealing of racial purpose as those of redistricters in other states, and that was all that had been needed to get them to invoke strict scrutiny before. Although the lower court had, unaccountably, not considered the issue, using race as a proxy to assist Republican partisan gerrymandering in Ohio ought to have been no less unconstitutional than using race as a proxy to help Democratic partisans in Georgia and Texas had been declared to be. And as explained above, *Gingles'* requirement that one show racial bloc voting, as interpreted in *Vera* and *Shaw II*, ruled out all potential compelling interests in Ohio. Rehnquist's position is more difficult to discern, but in *Shaw II*, he stressed that under *Miller*, an adherence to "traditional districting principles" did not automatically rescue a redistricting from strict scrutiny. If the predominant motive was racial, Rehnquist said, then *Miller* dictated that strict scrutiny be applied (*Shaw II* [1996], 1901). Because the evidence of partisan motivation in Ohio was no stronger or weaker than that in North Carolina or Texas, Rehnquist ought to have decided that Ohio's actions were also subject to heightened scrutiny and, because of the lack of racial bloc voting, were unconstitutional.

That left the enigmatic O'Connor. In her principal opinion in *Vera*, she remarked that "for strict scrutiny to apply, the plaintiffs must prove that other, legitimate districting principles were 'subordinated' to race. By that, we mean that race must be '*the predominant* factor motivating the legislature's [redistricting] decision.'" But she also glossed the remand in the California redistricting case, *DeWitt v. Wilson* (1995), as standing for the proposition that "strict scrutiny did not apply to an intentionally created compact majority-minority district." And in her concurring opinion, O'Connor asserted that "only if traditional districting criteria are neglected *and* that neglect is predominantly due to the misuse of race does strict scrutiny apply" (*Vera* [1996], 1951–52, 1969, italics in original, citations omitted). In the last two sentences, which contradict *Miller*'s predominant-motive standard and entirely sever the link between the racial gerrymandering cases and all other equal protection cases since 1976, districts that some judge subjectively termed "compact" could be 100 percent minority, drawing them could severely disadvantage minority voters, and redistricters could openly avow their discriminatory desires, as they did in Ohio, and minorities would still have no remedy. Since the Democratic majority on the lower court had not believed that compactness might save districts that were drawn, in Tilling's words "to guarantee the election of a black candidate," the record available to the Supreme Court did not clearly show whether compactness and other "traditional principles" had been adhered to or not (*Quilter v. Voinovich* [1995], 1024).[80] It is conceivable that that is what the opaque remand order of the Supreme Court in *Quilter II* meant for the lower court to do. But the very imprecision and illogic of O'Connor's position, one that requires an undefined compactness of minority opportunity districts and none at all of white districts and that gives no constitutional justification whatsoever for imposing the standard on either, allows her, as the pivotal justice, free rein to condemn partisan redistrictings as racial in North Carolina and Texas and to bless equally partisan redistrictings that just as blatantly involve race in California and Ohio.[81]

Why has O'Connor privileged compactness, but applied it only to minority opportunity districts?[82] Why did the *Miller* majority introduce the concept of "race as a proxy," which so contradicted the "predominant intent" standard that it set out? Why did that majority not apply the intent criterion to California and the race-as-a-proxy rule to Ohio? In such cases as *U.S. v. Paradise* (1987), *City of Richmond v. Croson* (1989), and *Adarand Constructors, Inc. v. Pena* (1995), Kennedy, Scalia, Thomas, and, less certainly, O'Connor and Rehnquist, endorsed the radical policy that governments should never distinguish between citizens on the basis of race, even to prevent or remedy discrimination against specific groups. How could the same justices approve the Supreme Court's actions in *De Witt* and *Quilter II*?[83] In other words, why did they adopt "colorblind" standards that especially disadvantaged minorities, and why did they carve out exceptions?

As in many instances of legislative action, the evidence is presently largely circumstantial. The opposition of the *Shaw* justices to minorities' requests for governmental action or protection certainly explains the "colorblind" standard. Ever since William Rehnquist, while a law clerk to Justice Robert Jackson, wrote an infamous memorandum stating "I think *Plessy v. Ferguson* was right and should be re-affirmed," his views and behavior on racial matters have been those of what one of his fellow law clerks at the time called "a reactionary." A Republican activist in Phoenix in the 1960s, Rehnquist challenged black voters at the polls and fought against an antidiscrimination ordinance and a school desegregation program, asserting that Americans should be "no more dedicated to an 'integrated' society than we are to a 'segregated' society." As a Nixon administration lawyer, he drafted a constitutional amendment that would have allowed segregation of public schools and prohibited busing for school integration. Elevated to the Supreme Court after a controversy over his racial views, Rehnquist was long the Court's chief antagonist of school desegregation and affirmative action. It was a perfect background for an apostle of "colorblindness" (Kluger 1976, 606–9; Tushnet 1994, 110–12, 190, 351; Davis 1989, 12–15, 56–62; Simon 1995, 31–37). Except for Souter, the Reagan-Bush appointees shared Rehnquist's racial opinions. In their concurrences in *Vera* (1996), 1971, 1973, Justices Kennedy and Thomas agreed that any consciously created majority-minority districts should be subject to strict scrutiny; Thomas asserted in his concurrence in *Holder v. Hall* (1994), 2596, that minority groups may not be entitled to any seats at all in a majoritarian system; and Scalia joined in both of Thomas's opinions.

But why, then, should these four justices vote for any perpetuation of minority opportunity districts at all, especially without subjecting them to strict
scrutiny? Why did they not agree with Abigail Thernstrom's condemnation
of all majority-minority districts, rather than just "ugly" ones, and why did
they not respond favorably to Thernstrom's appeal for courts to "intervene"
to destroy such districts (Thernstrom 1995, 936)? Upon what principle or
even unconscious bias can one square their opinions in *Shaw II, Vera,* and
Holder with the same justices' silent acquiescences in the Court's actions in
De Witt and *Quilter II*? No explanation based on following principle or precedent can possibly account for the radicals' decisions in all of these cases,
because they were so patently inconsistent. Their uncompromising adherence to "colorblindness" collapsed when the interests of the Republican party
were at stake.

Four other potential explanations focus on the pivotal O'Connor, the first
Reagan-appointed justice, although some of them apply to other justices,
as well. The first is moderation through incoherence. According to Nancy
Maveety, an uncritical biographer, O'Connor is an "accommodationist" or
"pragmatic centrist" whose "fact-centered jurisprudence" has "deidologized
the Court's judicial standards." In this view, O'Connor moderates the extrem-
ists on each side by joining, not leading, opposing factions; by writing concurrences, not principal opinions; and by stretching her own and others' interpretations in order to stress what she, but few others, see as common ground
between them. In her positions on racial issues, Maveety argues, she "has
attempted an accommodation between two distinct philosophies of racial
identity and civil rights: colorblind individualism and group-conscious community empowerment." Thus, her opinions are often somewhat muddled,
because she does not have the clear ideological position of a Scalia on the
right or a Marshall on the left, and because she shifts sides strategically
(Maveety 1996, 1-5, 121). There are several difficulties in applying this thesis
to her opinions in racial cases, and especially to racial gerrymandering cases.
Here, O'Connor has been a leader, not a follower, writing the principal opinions in *Croson, Adarand, Shaw I, Hays,* and *Vera,* all of which, save *Hays,* take
quite radical ideological positions and contain strong, absolutist statements
of "colorblind individualism." More generally, in thirty-nine of the forty-
one civil rights cases decided by 5-4 or 6-3 margins from 1981 through 1997,
O'Connor has voted against the minority litigant (*LAT,* April 12, 1998, M:2).
Although her votes in redistricting cases where she did not write opinions
have wavered on some issues, there has been one consistent thread in all of
these positions of the only member of the Court during her tenure that had
previously served in major elective office: She favored outcomes and standards that helped Republicans, but opposed them if they helped Democrats.

The moderate muddle thesis therefore fails because O'Connor has not been centrist or reticent on racial issues, at least since *U.S. v. Paradise* (1987), and because it does not explain the major thread of consistency that connects her opinions.

The second hypothesis is unintended consequences. Perhaps O'Connor has a civics-textbook fondness for tidy-looking districts and an aversion to the sort of interest-group bargaining that produces racial preferences and sinuous boundary lines, and those tastes just happen to disadvantage blacks, Latinos, and Democrats. This theory founders on the facts that her position does nothing to prevent Republicans and white Democrats from overwhelmingly white areas from arranging to draw "bizarre" districts, and because it does not explain her biased employment of the notion of "race as a proxy." Moreover, considerable evidence in the briefs and opinions shows that O'Connor and her fellow *Shaw* Justices were aware of the partisan implications of the North Carolina, Texas, and Ohio cases. Awareness does not prove intention, but it makes it more difficult to believe in coincidence.

Third is the "expressive harms" thesis—that O'Connor dislikes noncompact minority opportunity districts because they broadcast an emphasis on race. But the briefs from true believers in "colorblindness" insisted that any minority opportunity district spotlighted race, and, as pointed out above, lots of governmental activities, including drawing majority-white districts, underline racial distinctions. This thesis also fails to explain why O'Connor would endorse the notion of "race as a proxy," a notion that undermines her "representational harms" conjecture. Moreover, using race as a proxy deemphasizes race in instances when Democrats add a leaven of minorities to a majority-white district in order to buttress the chances of an integrated Democratic party.

Only one explanation accounts simultaneously for O'Connor's abandonment of the "colorblind" standard that she fostered in *Croson* and *Adarand*, for her endorsement of compactness for minorities only, and for her use of "race as a proxy" against Democrats but not Republicans—partisanship. It is hardly anomalous that racial issues should be connected to partisan interests. It has been so through much of American history. In the 1850s, the Republican party organized to contain and destroy slavery, and Democrats who remained in their party staunchly defended black servitude. During and after Reconstruction, the purest dividing line between the two parties was over racial issues. Although not all Republicans were stalwart antiracists, especially after 1890, not one Democratic member of Congress or the Supreme Court ever voted for black civil rights in the nineteenth century. In nearly 100 school racial discrimination cases heard at various levels of courts in the nineteenth century, my unpublished research shows, about two-thirds of Democratic judges opposed black rights, while two-thirds of Republican judges supported them. For a time in the post–World War II era, region, not party, chiefly demarcated white racial attitudes and behavior, but since 1964, the Democrats have increasingly become a unified party of civil rights, while the Republicans have been even more united against the rights of African-Americans and Latinos. To invent constraints on redistricting that might cost Democrats tens of seats in Congress and hundreds in state legislatures is to forward not only "conservative" policies in general but "conservative" racial policies in particular and, potentially, to solidify Republican legislative margins for a generation. What greater triumph could the most ideological and racially illiberal Supreme Court majority since 1937 achieve?

In the 1980s, Benjamin Ginsberg, the redistricting chief for the Republican National Committee, pushed a strategy of alliances of convenience with African-Americans and Latinos, in which packed minority opportunity districts, largely in the central cities, would be swapped for safe Anglo Republican seats in the suburbs. He could not have predicted, however, that the Supreme Court would find a way to ban the drawing of such districts when their boundaries helped Democrats while approving them when the boundaries helped Republicans and at the same time allowing any amount of finagling with the peripheries in overwhelmingly white areas.[84] Only by keeping Section 2 from being declared unconstitutional, thus preserving the *Gingles* compactness requirement, could O'Connor deliver the ultimate Republican deal, Ben Ginsberg's deal, this time blessed by the oracles of the Constitution.

The 1997 Cases: Further Erosion of the VRA

The opinions on voting rights that the Supreme Court issued in 1997 attracted less attention than those of the previous three terms, but two of the cases subtly undermined the VRA without actually declaring it unconstitutional, and they starkly illustrated the continuing ambiguity and inconsistency of the Court's standards. While Justice O'Connor's principal opinion in *Vera* had seemed to exalt compactness at the expense of *Miller*'s predominant-motive criterion, Justice Kennedy's 1997 opinion in the second iteration of the Georgia congressional redistricting case reaffirmed the motive standard and multiplied what he referred to as traditional districting principles, thereby diluting the importance of compactness. He also weakened the VRA by refusing to overturn the district court's conclusion that the degree of racial polarization of voting in Georgia was insufficient to violate Section 2 (*Abrams v. Johnson*). In a case from "Bloody Bossier," a northern Louisiana parish that had been among the most prone to lynching in the South after the First Reconstruction (Tolnay and Beck 1995, 46 [map]), Justice O'Connor overturned the Justice

Department's denial of preclearance under Section 5 of the VRA to a redistricting change that considerable evidence showed to have been adopted with the purpose and effect of discriminating against African-Americans.

When the Supreme Court remanded *Miller* to the district court, the panel first gave the Georgia legislature a chance to redistrict, but the legislature deadlocked. In subsequent legal papers, the State, half-heartedly, and private parties, more forcefully, argued that the 1991 legislature had had a preference for two black-majority districts before being pressed by the Justice Department to draw a third one, that the court should follow the Supreme Court's 1982 decision in *Upham v. Seamon* and honor the legislature's preference, and that it was easy to draw a second majority-black district that was much more compact than the one that the Supreme Court had overturned in *Miller.* In response, the majority of the three-member court contended that the State had drawn more than one black-majority district in 1991 only under unseemly pressure from the Justice Department and that the judges were therefore fulfilling the State's true preference by reducing the number of black-majority seats to one. Two other seats in the new plan were between 30 and 35 percent African-American in voting-age population, which could hardly have been avoided, since the state's voting-age population was 25 percent black and the racial composition of the state was far from uniform. The panel also discovered traditional districting principles that, it asserted, could not be satisfied while drawing more than one majority-minority district. The judges did not take account of the preference of the black caucus in the Georgia legislature, which was for three minority opportunity districts, or the traditional Georgia districting principle of taking race into account—adversely to African-Americans—in redistricting (*Johnson v. Miller* [1995]).

The predictable five-person majority of the Supreme Court managed to sign on to a single opinion by Justice Kennedy, as it had in *Miller,* while the equally predictable four dissenters endorsed an opinion by Justice Breyer. Kennedy reiterated the principal findings and words of *Miller*—"legislative purpose," "predominant, overriding desire," "predominant factor"—as though no 1996 opinions had intervened. Again the justice, whose principal occupation before he ascended to the bench was that of lobbying the California legislature, strongly condemned the lobbying efforts of the ACLU and the more circumspect regulatory role of the Justice Department. Without reviewing the evidence, he accepted the district court's designation of Georgia's traditional districting principles as "maintaining district cores, four traditional 'corner districts' in the corners of the State, political subdivisions such as counties and cities, and an urban majority-black district in the Atlanta area," in addition to "protecting incumbents."

Although Georgia had drawn a black-majority Atlanta district in 1971 and

1981 only after its earlier plans had been refused preclearance by the Justice Department—the same sort of federal pressure that both the district and Supreme courts had so bitterly lambasted in *Miller*—Kennedy affirmed the district court's transparent rationalization that the black-majority Atlanta district "had become a state districting principle" (McDonald, Binford, and Johnson 1994, 87–89; *Abrams v. Johnson* [1997], 1931–37). This allowed the district court to take race into account in drawing the Atlanta district, keeping the black proportion at 62 percent, as it had been in 1991, without having to apply the same race-conscious principle to the other black-majority districts. It also avoided a dilemma at the Supreme Court level. The current Supreme Court majority has never squarely ruled that Section 5 of the VRA is constitutional when it allows race-conscious districting, and Justices Kennedy, Scalia, and Thomas almost surely believe it is not. Ruling that the Atlanta black district qualified as a traditional districting principle circumvented the problem of either resting its perpetuation on Section 5, thereby possibly splitting the Supreme Court majority if Rehnquist or O'Connor disagreed with the other three justices, or ruling unconstitutional both that relatively compact district and the core of the VRA, Section 5, if Rehnquist and O'Connor went along. If the Atlanta district could not survive the majority's scrutiny, it is hard to imagine that any minority opportunity district in the South could, and throwing them all out would have been a public relations embarrassment for the "colorblind" policy.

Kennedy did not note that the district court's plan actually abandoned the "four corners tradition," as the 1981 and 1991 redistrictings had. Nor did he explain why the desires of North Carolina or Texas to protect the cores of Democratic incumbents' districts provided no justification for those states' decisions to draw majority-minority districts, while the district court's willingness to protect Republican incumbents in Georgia (all the state's white congressmen in 1996 were Republican) gave the judges an adequate reason for refusing to draw majority-minority districts in the Peach State. Kennedy gave no guidance to lower courts in identifying "traditional districting principles" or in deciding how much weight to allot to each when they conflicted, which they often did. Nor did he provide any general rationale for assigning them so much importance, leaving the whole idea of such principles mired in ad hockery. To imagine that the equal protection clause or unspecified provisions of the U.S. Constitution mandated that redistricters count a defunct "four corners" habit that was not even mentioned in a state law as precluding any efforts to counteract past and present racial discrimination against African-Americans in the Deep South—discrimination that Kennedy pointedly ignored—showed the absurdities to which the radical majority on the Supreme Court was prepared to go.

Kennedy's discussion of racially polarized voting was also troubling for future vote dilution cases. The district court had found "a general willingness of white voters to vote for black candidates" in the former Eleventh Congressional District on the basis of the fact that black candidates in nonpartisan judicial contests, a Democratic primary for the minor office of state labor commissioner, and the first primary in the 65 percent black Eleventh in 1992, received 38–55 percent of the estimated votes of whites. The lower court panel even considered that the 23 percent of the white vote that African-American Cynthia McKinney got in the Eleventh District Democratic runoff in 1992 indicated widespread white cross-over voting. But the principal exhibit of white cross-over voting, available only after the district court had set the new boundaries, was the fact that the two black members of Congress whose districts had been redrawn to make them majority-white won reelection with virtually all of the African-American vote and 30–35 percent of that of white voters (*Abrams v. Johnson* [1997], 1936–37; Bositis 1997). Kennedy did not note that two-term incumbents Cynthia McKinney and Sanford Bishop faced virtually unknown Republican challengers, whom they outspent by nearly two to one, or that their redrawn districts were the second and third most heavily Democratic in the state, as measured by the percentage received by President Clinton in 1996, behind only John Lewis's 62 percent black district in Atlanta (Reeves 1997, 110; Barone and Ujifusa 1998, 397–436). Those Deep South whites who remain Democrats in the 1990s are no doubt more likely than other whites to vote for otherwise acceptable African-American candidates. Nor did Kennedy focus on the most relevant statistic, the average proportion of white cross-over votes, which was 14 percent in 51 elections during the 1980s and 26 percent in the most hotly contested statewide election involving a black candidate, the 1990 Democratic primary runoff for governor (McDonald, Binford, and Johnson 1994, 84–85). No African-American candidate has received more than 26 percent of the white vote in a statewide runoff election in Georgia (Allan Lichtman, personal communication, Sept. 24, 1997). And Kennedy failed to observe, as Justice Breyer underlined in dissent, that all but one of the forty-four African-Americans in the Georgia legislature in 1996 were elected from majority-black districts (*Abrams v. Johnson* [1997], 1945). If judges could pick and choose unrepresentative statistics and label a 14–30 percent cross-over a proof of the general will of whites, then it would be very difficult to prove minority vote dilution anywhere, and Section 2 would be significantly weakened.[85]

Kennedy's endorsement of the district court's denial of racial bloc voting in Georgia also contradicted a crucial part of the Court's opinion in *Quilter I*. According to O'Connor's opinion in that case, packing African-Americans into a small number of state legislative districts in Ohio did not amount to vote dilution because there was little racially polarized voting (*Voinovich v. Quilter* [1993], 1158). If a majority of whites was regularly willing to vote for African-American candidates, she implied, then Ohio blacks needed no special protection and were just another interest group that could be packed, stacked, or cracked in the usual rough-and-tumble of redistricting politics. But if the district court was right about white voters' lack of bias in Georgia, why did race-conscious districting in that state not survive a parallel challenge? Why should courts step in and overturn the results of a political process in which lobbyists from the ACLU and the Justice Department assisted the Georgia black caucus while it wheeled and dealed? The radical majority wanted to have it both ways: if voting was not racially polarized, blacks could neither be protected against dilution nor allowed to protect themselves like a typical interest group.

IN 1990, the twelve-member Bossier Parish School Board was elected from single-member districts by majority vote. When the School Board chose a redistricting plan containing no black-majority districts over a local NAACP plan with two such seats, the Justice Department refused to preclear the electoral change because it diluted the votes of the 20 percent of the population in the parish that was black. Under Departmental regulations adopted in 1986, no change in election laws that clearly violated Section 2 of the VRA could be precleared under Section 5. The Department based its rule on three grounds. First, to preclear a provision that would almost certainly be struck down by a court under Section 2 or the Constitution would seem to endorse patently illegal practices. Second, even if Justice Stewart's majority opinion in *Beer v. U.S.* (1976) had glossed the "effect" test of Section 5 as prohibiting only "retrogressive effects," it had also said that laws that violated the Constitution could not be precleared, and it had cited the redistricting statutes at issue in *White v. Regester* (1973) as examples. But in 1982, Congress explicitly wrote standards derived from *Regester* into its discussion of the amended Section 2. Therefore, *Beer*'s constitutional exception to the retrogressive effect standard, *White v. Regester*, had been incorporated into Section 2, and the proper way to follow the *Beer* precedent was for the Department to refuse to preclear a change that had a discriminatory purpose or either a retrogressive or a dilutive effect. Third, Congress explicitly endorsed this interpretation in the contemporaneous 1982 Senate report on the VRA and in a 1986 House report that resulted from oversight hearings in which even Reagan administration appointees testified in favor of the new understanding of Section 5 (*Reno v. Bossier Parish School Board* [1997], 1507–11 [Stevens dissent]; U.S. Senate 1982b, 12 n. 31; U.S. House of Representatives 1986, 5).

Justice O'Connor employed three mutually contradictory theories of interpretation to arrive at the conclusion that, contrary to its plain meaning, Section 5 does not overrule laws with the intent and effect of diluting minority votes. More specifically, according to O'Connor's opinion, the Department of Justice must preclear district lines, even if they may have a discriminatory purpose and effect, so long as they have no "retrogressive effect" and what O'Connor, in a striking innovation, termed "retrogressive intent." O'Connor's first interpretative theory was implied by her endorsement of the *Beer* case. Justice Stewart's majority opinion in *Beer* had ignored the plain meaning of Section 5—the law said "effect," not "retrogressive effect"—and had relied instead on reports by congressional committees, including two issued ten years after the language at issue in Section 5 had been adopted. Over harsh dissents by Justices White and Marshall, Stewart concluded that only retrogressive effects were banned by Section 5 (*Beer v. U.S.* [1976], 1359–64). In endorsing *Beer,* O'Connor was adopting her first mode of interpretation, a preference for extraneous materials rather than the text of the law. But in her second interpretative theory, only the text mattered. When she came to interpreting the 1982 revisions of the VRA, the justice denigrated a precisely relevant portion of the contemporary Senate Report as merely "dropping a footnote" and dismissed the House Committee's endorsement of the same conclusion issued four (not ten) years after the passage of the revisions as offering only "a hazardous basis for inferring the intent" of the 1982 changes because it appeared too late. Congress's amendments to Section 2 and their explication in hearings and reports were not enough, O'Connor declared. Only if Congress altered the language of Section 5 could the Justice Department's regulations be changed (*Reno v. Bossier Parish School Board* [1997], 1500).

O'Connor's third implicit hermeneutic theory exemplified what Professor William Eskridge termed the " 'free inquiry approach,' in which a court's role is to reach the best[86] result, formally unconstrained (though perhaps influenced or persuaded) by the statute's text and legislative history" (Eskridge 1988, 275). Disregarding the plain language of the "purpose" requirement of Section 5 and the fact that no congressional report had suggested that Congress meant only to ban laws or practices intended to make blacks demonstrably worse off than they currently were, she coined the phrase, at least in Supreme Court voting rights cases, "retrogressive intent" (*Reno v. Bossier Parish School Board* [1997], 1501). Although O'Connor made no effort to justify or define retrogressive intent or to provide guidance for distinguishing it from any other sort of discriminatory intent, the phrase seemed to have ominous implications. Suppose white southerners in 1965 had been able to predict that the Supreme Court would effectively amend Section 5 by inserting the word "retrogressive" before "purpose" and "effect." Then all those in covered jurisdictions, none of which then sent a single African-American to a state legislature or Congress, would have had to do was to keep changing laws with the intent and effect of preserving the white monopoly on offices, and they could have remained unaffected by Section 5. To be sure, they would have been subject to suits under the Constitution, but that had always been true, and in the ninety or so years since the first suffrage restriction laws had passed, such suits had not often endangered white supremacy. Section 5 is scheduled to expire in 2007. That is not, apparently, soon enough for the radical Supreme Court majority.

Inconsistencies and Unanswered Questions in the Racial Gerrymandering Cases

In their dissents in *Vera*, Justices Souter and Stevens had called for the Court to abandon the *Shaw* line of cases as mistaken and unmanageable intrusions into essentially legislative matters. At the end of her plurality opinion in that case, Justice O'Connor responded with a creative misreading, as though the dissenters had only said that *Shaw* threatened the judiciary by departing from precedent: "Our legitimacy requires, above all, that we adhere to *stare decisis*, especially in such sensitive political contexts as the present, where partisan controversy abounds" (*Vera* [1996], 1964, 1993, 2013).[87] Her response to criticism was as disingenuous as it was misleading. This was the same justice who in 1984 had denied standing to African-Americans because they were merely protesting "abstract stigmatic harms," who in 1986 had wanted to throw out the partisan gerrymandering claims of Indiana Democrats because they were not "a discrete and insular group vulnerable to exclusion from the political process by some dominant group," and who in 1995 had overturned a five-year-old affirmative action decision after misrepresenting it as a departure from precedent. Yet in *Hays* and other cases, O'Connor had granted standing to anyone who lived in a district to protest unproven representational harms. Indeed, O'Connor just a year before had remarked that "remaining true to an 'intrinsically sounder' doctrine established in prior cases better serves the values of *stare decisis* than would following a more recently decided case inconsistent with the decisions that came before it" (*Allen v. Wright* [1984]; *Davis v. Bandemer* [1986], 152; *U.S. v. Hays* [1995]; *Adarand Constructors, Inc. v. Pena* [1995], 2115, overruling *Metro Broadcasting, Inc. v. FCC* [1990], which followed *Fullilove v. Klutznick* [1980]).

More significantly, following precedent is difficult in this instance because *Shaw I* and its successors are inconsistent with each other. *Shaw I* (1993) stressed compactness, appeared to apply only to "segregated" African-American or Latino districts, required race to be the "sole" reason for the shape or composition of a district, postulated three harms to society that "racial gerrymandering" allegedly caused and distinguished, but did not overrule, *UJO* (1977). *Miller* (1995), however, largely ignored compactness, applied to any district in which a "significant" number of blacks or Latinos was "placed"; required that race be only the "predominant" reason for the decision to draw the district or include certain people in it; reduced the variety of posited harms to only one—stereotyping; and explicitly discarded *UJO*. *Hays* (1995) temporarily revived the issue of representational harm. The summary affirmance of *DeWitt* (1995), treated backhandedly in *Miller,* became an important precedent representing a clear principle, that any compact district is constitutional, in the plurality opinion in *Vera* (1996). In addition to restoring compactness to a predominant role, *Vera* underlined the importance of using race as a proxy for Democratic partisan interests, which it ruled unconstitutional unless the districts were as compact as a presumably nonpartisan judge would have drawn them. It also held that no district could be drawn in order to satisfy Section 5 unless it was the successor to a previous minority opportunity district, and that the new district could not have a higher proportion of minorities than the old one did just before the new redistricting. *Shaw II* (1996) dismissed evidence of specific historical discrimination as affecting only "some" legislators and hinted that race-conscious districts could not be drawn even to remedy perfectly documented discrimination against minority groups. The 1996 remand of the second lower-court *Quilter* decision, with the vaguest of instructions, seemed to undermine the *Miller* predominant-motive standard and appeared to treat Republican partisan interests much more favorably than *Vera* and *Shaw II* treated Democratic partisan interests. *Abrams* (1997) appeared to restore *Miller,* to downgrade compactness by multiplying the number of admissible traditional districting principles, and to contradict both *Vera* and *Shaw II* in allowing incumbency protection to justify the drawing of redistricting lines that had an effect on minority political power. Which principles does the splintered majority, its ad hoc answers differing in each case, wish to preserve?

Shaw I and its offspring also leave many questions unanswered and many others unasked, at least by the Court. Among the topics that subsequent cases may clarify are the following. First, can race-conscious districts be drawn, by courts or legislative bodies, as a remedy for past or present discrimination?[88] If they cannot, then a ban on "discrimination between" individuals on the basis of race will have eliminated governmental efforts to combat "discrimination against" minority groups, Section 2 will no longer apply to electoral structures, the Fifteenth Amendment will not prevent abridgements of minority electoral power, and, if analogous interpretations are extended to other areas of the legal system, the equal protection clause will henceforth merely bar governments from safeguarding any African-American or Latino. It would also seem inconsistent to require jurisdictions to observe Section 5, because any non-retrogression standard must be race-conscious. At least three justices—Kennedy, Scalia, and Thomas—seem to prefer this position. Chief Justice Rehnquist raised the issue and explicitly left it open in *Shaw II*, and the justices' academic defenders insist on it (Butler 1995, 610–17; 1996, 355; O'Rourke 1995, 756).

Second, is using race as a proxy for political interests unconstitutional when it helps Republicans by allowing them to pack their most predictable partisan opponents into the fewest districts or to spread them thinly across districts or otherwise to waste their votes in order to maximize Republican political power? Is using race as a proxy for Democratic interests unconstitutional in districts that do not border on minority opportunity districts? If the answers to these two questions are different, why? How large is a "significant" number of minorities, and how is one to know whether they have been "placed" in a district? Does the answer involve whether they are on the edges or near the geographical center of a jurisdiction, and if so, how can the Constitution be said to make such a distinction? If the differences in the treatment of Republicans and Democrats formally involve compactness, then how is that stance consistent for anyone except O'Connor?

Third, is it unconstitutional to use partisanship or socioeconomic variables as proxies for race, for instance, by dividing the most Democratic areas of central cities into separate districts? If African-Americans are as strongly Democratic elsewhere as they are in Dallas, what is the effective difference between using one or the other as a proxy? [89]

Fourth, are all compact districts always constitutional, must all minority opportunity districts and only minority opportunity districts be compact, and what is the definition or measure of compactness? Would a consciously drawn, compact minority opportunity district be subject to strict scrutiny, according to the "no race-conscious decisions" principle? And, if so, then would a preference for "traditional districting principles," untethered to any law or constitutional provision or to whatever shreds of Section 2 survived, validate the district by satisfying both the narrow tailoring and compelling state interest requirements? The silent assents of Kennedy, Scalia, and Thomas to the Court's affirmance of *De Witt* and its remand of the second *Quilter* case suggest that this might be their position, although they might simply favor the elimination of minority opportunity districts altogether, contending that no interest is sufficiently compelling to justify any race-conscious governmental action. To reconcile their stated position in *Vera* that only districts that were not consciously drawn as minority opportunity districts were constitutional, they might assume that the reason for creating a compact district was to adhere to "traditional districting principles" and that its demographic or political composition was, by definition, entirely coincidental. Some purely formal argument like this one, which has no connection with real motivations, would be necessary in order to soften the apparent contradiction between their stances in *Vera, De Witt,* and *Quilter II.* O'Connor and perhaps Rehnquist would presumably rule that any compact, contiguous district would be subject only to a "rational basis" test, which it would automatically pass.

Fifth, if O'Connor's preference for compactness continues to be pivotal in the Court's decisions, what is the status of the *Miller* predominant-motive test? In other areas of equal protection law, plaintiffs have to prove *both* intent and effect. Does O'Connor's concentration on appearance imply that in pro-minority districting cases, plaintiffs need prove *neither*? Does *Abrams*'s reaffirmation of *Miller*'s intent test mean that O'Connor has abandoned the "expressive harm" position that she took in *Vera*?

Sixth, where does compactness live, so to speak? If it is just part of Section 2, through *Gingles,* must districts drawn to comply with Section 5 or to remedy constitutional violations be compact, especially since the Court's 1997 disentangling of Sections 2 and 5 in *Reno v. Bossier Parish*? Why did the Court not interpret Congress's refusal to adopt a compactness requirement in the redistricting law proposed by the Bush administration as an implicit statement that compactness was not mandated by federal law? If compactness is a constitutional constraint, what part of the Constitution does it come from—perhaps Article I, Section 2's mention of elections "by the People," as suggested in a brief by the Pacific Legal Foundation (La Fetra 1995, 18, 25)? If it is truly a constitutionally derived concept, why has it lain dormant for two centuries and why does it apply only to minority opportunity districts? If compactness is merely a sound principle of public policy, as Butler and others seem to believe, one of many such principles that judges are free to discover or invent anytime they please, then what constrains those inventions?[90] What is to stop a majority of the Supreme Court from declaring any other of their prejudices or preferences to be law?[91]

Seventh, what is the legal and constitutional significance of the other "traditional districting principles," how does one determine what qualifies as a traditional districting principle, and how should redistricters and judges weigh each principle against the other and against any desire that legislators may have had to alleviate discrimination against minorities? In the pre-*Shaw* cases, the Court articulated two rationales for incorporating such principles in the evaluation of redistricting plans. In his concurrence in *Karcher v. Daggett* (1983), 754–60, Justice Stevens suggested that low scores on mathematical compactness indexes, deviations from established political boundaries, and biased processes of drawing districts might indicate questionable intentions. Justice Marshall, in his dissent in *Beer v. U.S.* (1976), 1374, employed them as possible compelling state interests to be considered after strict or other scrutiny had been imposed on a race-conscious decision. Although there were echoes of both these rationales in the theoretical chaos of *Shaw I* and its successors, traditional districting principles in these cases are perhaps better understood to have functioned more as judicially created benchmarks, naturalizing principles, or stopping points with which to distinguish the acceptable from the excessive use of race in redistricting or as indications of how districts would have been drawn had race not been taken into account at all (*Shaw I* [1993], 2826–27; *Miller* [1995], 2481, 2486, 2488; *Vera* [1996], 1952–55, 1960, 1970, 1973; *Shaw II* [1996], 1900–1901). After all, *Miller*'s holding that a decision to "place" minorities anywhere might be illegal demanded some means of distinguishing between situations in which they have been "placed" in a district from situations in which they just happen to reside in one.

But if a redistricting authority's actions would be legal if it adhered to its own principles when it drew minority opportunity districts or districts containing "significant" numbers of minorities, then why isn't the extent of its adherence to those principles in all districts relevant, and why is it particularly important that the principles be traditional? If white districts do not meet judges' aesthetic criteria, or if they cut city or county or precinct lines, or if they protect incumbents, then how have minority opportunity districts that do the same thing departed from a baseline? If the reply is that all white districts would have been sufficiently tidy if race had not been taken into account in drawing the minority opportunity districts, the answers are, first, that this just assumes the conclusion, which should be established by a much more systematic look at the evidence; and second, that even if this is so, why should drawing minority opportunity or influence districts be weighed so much less heavily than whatever goals justify other districting principles? Doesn't this amount to a ban on considering race at all and not merely on its excessive or predominant use? In reapportionment cases such as *Reynolds v. Sims* (1964) and *Lucas v. Colorado General Assembly* (1964), the Supreme Court overrode states' traditional districting principles because of what the Court said was a constitutional command for equally populated districts, which the Court declared outweighed the states' traditions. Whatever the intent of those traditions, the Court thought their disproportionate impacts on individuals who lived in urban and suburban areas more important than tradition. Why is the effect of the often artificial or inconsistently followed state traditional districting principles on minorities' political influence not equally significant? And what command about minority opportunity districts parallels that of "one person, one vote" in the reapportionment cases? Is the command that the Fourteenth Amendment prohibits the protection of minorities during redistricting, though it allows the protection of any other group or interest, unless the minority placement is incidental to more important goals, such as drawing districts in the four corners of a state or not splitting precincts that are continually redrawn for administrative convenience?

There is also a series of questions that the Court is not likely to address unless for some reason the radicals decide to respond to critics. First, why is it not contradictory to the alleged goal of a "colorblind" society to say that no other factors than race and perhaps political subdivision boundaries can be taken into account in drawing minority opportunity districts? In the world according to *Vera*, a district undergoes strict scrutiny when race matters too much but survives scrutiny if only race and a desire for regularity determine its shape. Is Justice O'Connor aiming to diminish or increase color-consciousness? Second, how can it be that for O'Connor, compactness is not mandated by the Constitution, and color-consciousness, incumbent protection, and partisan advantage are not prohibited, except when they affect minority opportunity or influence districts? If "neutral principles" become binding only when they decrease minority political power or suspect only when they increase it, then it is not adherence to the principles but a desire to inhibit the power that must motivate the justices who hold that view. Third, why are the hurdles of standing and strict scrutiny in voting rights cases so much higher for minorities than for whites? To achieve standing to sue, minorities have to prove that they are harmed; whites do not. To make out a Section 2 case, minorities must demonstrate racial bloc voting by both whites and themselves, that they live in a compact area, and that they are sufficiently numerous to make up a majority of a district in the jurisdiction. Then they must show a history of discrimination and that the discrimination against them continues in politics in the present. To invoke strict scrutiny or prove a purpose case under Sections 2 or 5, minorities must go to elaborate lengths, as described in Chapters 2 through 4, to show that race was the predominant motive for the choice of an electoral rule; and even then, a judge who wishes to believe, on the flimsiest of evidence, that the electoral rule might have been chosen if there had been no racial reasons for doing so can avoid imposing strict scrutiny (*Brooks v. Miller* [1996]). Whites, by contrast, need show only that someone said they wished to draw a minority opportunity district or that a district does not appear compact, and they are over the second hurdle. In voting rights, the principal achievement of the Rehnquist majority has been to construct an unequal protection clause.

Implications of the Racial Gerrymandering Cases for the Redistricting of 2001

Unless *Shaw* and its progeny are overturned, the process of redistricting in 2001 will be markedly less favorable to minorities than that of 1991 was. How is it likely to differ? First, the courts are sure to be even more involved than in previous years. Since the Supreme Court's standards are so unclear, redistricting plans in every area containing enough minority group members to form a majority or a near-majority of a district or even to influence the outcome of a district's election significantly will be subject to challenge by partisan, minority, or "colorblind" organizations, or simply by ambitious lawyers. Every hearing will be conducted, every speech delivered, every deal made, every boundary line drawn with a consciousness of how they will resonate in court. Confused legal standards promote judicial activism. Second, the deepened shadow of litigation will insure that the redistricting process is much less open. In 1991, computer redistricting software in many states calculated and displayed the African-American and Latino percentages of each district, as well as partisan proportions, every time the lines were shifted, and the partisan and racial consequences of each plan could therefore easily be understood by all. Advocates of "colorblindness" advise the removal of all racial statistics from redistricting computers (Blumstein 1996, 513), a proposal that would simply shift the information away from the public process into private, parallel operations, in which interest groups and partisans perform the calculations behind closed doors and conduct sham discussions in public. In the past, redistricting has often been a matter of hard private bargains decorated with public rhetorical flourishes; in 2001, it may not even be possible for knowledgeable observers to discover the effects of that intrigue until after elections are held. Third, the Justice Department will no longer be an ally of minorities who live in jurisdictions covered by Section 5, pressuring redistricters to treat minorities fairly, but will instead be an opponent, enforcing the Supreme Court's ban on increasing the number of minority opportunity districts or the percentage of minorities in each. The "purpose or effect" language of Section 5 notwithstanding, that provision has been reduced, in the case of redistricting, to a mechanical formula, with the result that the Justice Department's role, which so infuriated judges after 1991, will be shrunk to that of a mere tabulator. Fourth, the general understanding of 1991 that failure to draw possible minority opportunity districts was likely to be declared illegal under Section 2 will be replaced in 2001 by the fear that taking minorities' race into account at all in setting boundaries will be ruled unconstitutional. To the *Shaw* justices, white is the norm, the nonrace race.[92] The incentive to maximize the number of minority opportunity districts will be supplanted by an incentive to minimize.

There will also be marked partisan effects. Negotiations between black, Latino, and Anglo Democrats will be short and secret. Because any statements indicating an agreement between these parties to draw minority opportunity districts or influence districts will be considered evidence that race played a predominant role in the drawing of a district or that it was used as a proxy, no such statements will be made. Since the circumstantial evidence of ethnic percentages and district shape will also possibly prove racial gerrymandering, there will, in fact, be a strong incentive for minority and Anglo Democrats not to deal with each other at all. By contrast, Republicans will be in an excellent position to bargain openly with minorities. Whereas the compromises between Democratic congressmen Martin Frost and John Bryant and aspiring congresswoman Eddie Bernice Johnson in Dallas convinced judges that race had been used as a proxy in Texas, the endorsement by the Ohio NAACP of the Republican packing of African-Americans into house districts in that state helped to insulate the Republican plan from a Section 2 challenge, without seeming to count against the Republicans in a challenge to racial gerrymandering (*Voinovich v. Quilter* [1993]; [1996]). Under the O'Connor standard, packing minorities for Republican political advantage is legal, so long as the resulting districts appear compact to her, while distributing them in order to maximize a combination of Democratic support and minority seats is illegal. Moreover, those Republican redistricters who are not overly concerned with protecting Republican incumbents may deliberately place relatively small proportions of minority voters in strongly Republican districts in order to keep the overwhelmingly Democratic minority voters away from districts more favorable to Democratic politicians of all races. This is exactly what Judge Edith Jones did in her *Vera* remand plan—increasing the minority proportions in the districts of two of the safest, most conservative Republicans in Texas, congressmen Sam Johnson and Tom DeLay (*AAS*, Aug. 7, 1996, A:1). Such action may not be considered using race as a proxy, because the object of the population shifting will not be to affect the districts into which the minorities are moved but to change the results in districts from which they are taken or into which they could potentially be placed.

Thus, in the harshest of ironies, *Shaw* and its successors have transformed the Reconstruction Amendments and the VRA, which had gradually restored the political effectiveness of blacks and enlarged that of Latinos, into laws to diminish minority political power. The Fourteenth and Fifteenth Amendments had prohibited disfranchisement and vote dilution; now, they prohibit pro-minority redistricting. The amended Section 2 had allowed dilution suits on the basis of effect alone; now, it requires minority opportunity districts to meet a vague compactness standard. Section 5 had prevented suspect states and localities from making electoral changes that decreased minority political rights; now, it prevents them from making changes that enhance minority political rights. The Justice Department had been a valuable ally for minorities; now, it is required to be a foe. Minorities had been able to negotiate openly with Republicans and Democrats and to offer and accept the sorts of compromises that have long characterized the politics of redistricting; now, they can deal publicly with only one side, the side of their day-to-day enemies, and they can negotiate with their friends only at the risk of having a judge use their bargaining to overturn its result. In a word, institutions that benefited minorities have been hijacked by the radical Supreme Court majority and turned into engines of oppression.

Alternative Redistricting Standards If *Shaw* Is Reversed

Suppose that, realizing the deficiencies of the *Shaw* line of cases, a new majority of the Supreme Court were to decide to reverse it. What should take its place, and what would be the rationale for a revised judicial oversight of voting laws? The overall theme is easy to state: the equalization of the equal protection clause. Standing should be granted only to parties that can demonstrate that they are injured, that the laws or district lines at issue have a racially discriminatory effect, an effect evidenced by a disproportionately low percentage of potentially winnable seats for that group. This change, which merely puts *Shaw*-type plaintiffs on the same level as all other equal protection claimants, would by itself eliminate the vast majority of "racial gerrymandering" cases. Most redistricting should proceed with a minimum of judicial supervision and legalistic posturing. Within limits, judges ought to let politicians, including minority politicians, politick. Anyone who achieves standing should be required to pass the *Miller* predominant-motive test. Whenever a plaintiff could show, as in *Garza*, that a partisan or incumbent-protecting goal could be achieved only by discriminating against a historically disadvantaged group and that the intertwined motives predominated in the decision, then strict scrutiny should be imposed. As Chapter 7 showed, an intent criterion is workable, and a predominant or very significant motive test is preferable to "sole motive" or "contributing factor" standards, or to the inevitably artificial burden-shifting approach. But the examination of evidence ought to be more rigorous than merely looking at a few statements of major or minor actors or glancing at a map. It ought to involve the same sort of "totality of the circumstances" inquiry established for vote dilution cases by *White v. Regester* (1973), codified in the Senate Report on the 1982 amendments to the VRA (U.S. Senate 1982), and organized by a scheme such as that presented in Chapter 7. Rationales for all elements of this framework should be the same as for minority vote dilution cases, which were also laid out in Chapter 7.

If strict scrutiny is imposed, then the same sorts of compelling state interests as were mentioned in *Shaw II* and *Vera* ought to be available, but their interpretations ought not to be the same as they were represented to be in those cases. Each asserted compelling interest ought to be seriously examined, and if it appears to have motivated key actors or a large number of other decisionmakers in the particular instance, or if a combination of compelling interests did, then one should move on to the question of narrow tailoring. Historic discrimination should be shown to be specific to the type of electoral structure at issue, such as redistricting. If race-conscious districting discriminated against members of a distinct group in the past and if a desire to remedy that discrimination importantly moved the redistricters, who proposed an effective remedy that did not unduly burden innocent third parties, then the law should be declared constitutional. Prudent legislators will issue reports detailing the previous discrimination and showing how the current redistricting remedies it. Satisfying the requirements of Section 2 should also serve as a compelling state interest if redistricters have a reasonable basis for believing that voting in the jurisdiction is racially polarized and that the totality of the circumstances proves that certain groups do not enjoy an equal chance to participate in politics and to elect candidates of their choice. Legislators should not be required to prove a Section 2 violation in court or even through a formal presentation of evidence before drawing minority opportunity districts, as Thernstrom (1995, 930) has proposed, because that would relegate minorities to an unequal position in bargaining over redistricting and severely reduce the incentive for Anglo legislators to agree to such districts.

Districts should not necessarily have to be "compact" because, as shown throughout this chapter, compactness is a vague, unworkable concept that is biased against one political party and that tends to encourage packing of minorities, which discriminates against them by reducing their influence in the political system. Not grounded in the Constitution, compactness has been specifically and repeatedly rejected by Congress. A pattern of geographical and demographic patterns may help, as in *Gomillion* or *Garza*, to reveal a discriminatory purpose, but it is patently unfair to make minority opportunity districts meet a compactness standard that disproportionately Anglo districts do not have to satisfy. Finally, Section 5 should serve as a compelling state interest, but instead of being interpreted as a grandfather clause preventing white power from retrogressing, as in the current formulation, it should be restored to its original intent, stressing the plain meaning of its text. Any electoral change with the "purpose or effect" of discriminating against minorities should not be precleared, and covered jurisdictions should be able to take affirmative action in order to comply voluntarily with the provision. In all of these activities, states and localities should be given more leeway to protect historically disadvantaged minorities than to insulate members of the majority race from adversity. The reasons for this differentiation can be found only in a study of the history of race relations.

CHAPTER NINE

History and Equality

*H*istory defines the Fourteenth Amendment. Its provisions do not mention race, ethnicity, gender, or religion, or single out any particular social group or governmental policy for special emphasis. A visitor from another country who knew nothing of American history could not discern from its words that the equal protection clause was particularly concerned with *racial* discrimination. If told that that clause banned the deliberate placing of significant numbers of some particular group into an electoral district, the visitor would have no less reason to believe, from the plain meaning of the text or from any abstract philosophical notion of equality, that the prohibited classification was of blue-collar workers or city dwellers or farmers or suburbanites or Democrats than that it was of African-Americans or Latinos. Only the history and continuing reality of racial discrimination and the connection of that discrimination with the adoption and development of the equal protection clause make racial differentiations especially relevant to it. Therefore, any gloss on that clause contains an implicit or explicit interpretation of the history of race relations in the country, and, conversely, every substantial difference in the interpretation of the history of race relations has implications for the understanding of the clause. Philosophy offers no guide to the Fourteenth Amendment or, rather, too many. For the equal protection clause, history, and only history, matters. Unless we get the history right, we cannot get the equal protection clause right.

The sketches of the history of voting rights offered by the *Shaw* justices and their defenders are either false or incomplete, and the lessons they draw from those sketches are at best misleading and at worst non sequiturs. Justice William Brennan was right when he wrote that "to read the Fourteenth Amendment to state an abstract principle of color-blindness is itself to be blind to history" (quoted in Hoffer 1992, 271). In 1993, in *Shaw I*, Justice O'Connor noted that literacy tests were used to "deprive black voters" of their rights, gerrymanders to "exclude black voters" from equal political power, at-large systems to "reduce or nullify minority voters' ability" to elect candidates of their choice. She did not consider connections between disfranchising and diluting devices or the Court's own role in facilitating antiblack political rules by adopting a rigid formalism in its voting rights decisions from 1876 until 1944, a formalism that returned in *Shaw I*. Under the Fourteenth Amendment, O'Connor continued, proof of a discriminatory purpose and effect was necessary to convince courts to overturn electoral rules or structures that diluted "a minority group's voting strength," while under the 1982 amendments to the VRA, proof of a discriminatory effect alone sufficed. In this sketch of the American past, the justice made no distinction between individual and group rights, and she considered only clearly disadvantageous distinctions to be illegal. When she turned to the claims of the *Shaw* plaintiffs under the "new cause of action," however, O'Connor glossed the equal protection clause as prohibiting "purposefully discriminating *between* individuals on the basis of race," and she divorced the clause from the concept of individual or group harm (*Shaw I* [1993], 2822–24, italics added). It was as if history had ended and the only examples of unequal rights that she had given, discrimination against minorities, were no longer relevant to the Reconstruction Amendments. O'Connor made no attempt to explain why the Fourteenth Amendment had suddenly shifted, why the Court should cease being concerned with protecting minority rights, with deprivations of real political power, and instead should care only about assumed societal harms and symbolic distinctions.

In *Miller, Vera*, and *Shaw II*, the *Shaw* justices made no further historical reflections, but in their short concurrences in the closely associated *Adarand* affirmative action case, Justices Scalia and Thomas did offer fragmentary historical revisions that took extreme anti-institutional positions. Government, Scalia contended, should never adopt policies designed "to 'make up' for past discrimination" against minorities, because to do so would be "to reinforce and preserve for future mischief the way of thinking that produced race slavery, race privilege and race hatred" (*Adarand Constructors, Inc. v. Pena* [1995], 2118–19). It was not the interaction of laws and private discrimination against African-Americans by whites that caused slavery, segregation, and disfranchisement, he implied, but merely a "way of thinking." In Scalia's cultural determinist view, racial discrimination against African-Americans was entirely a matter of ideological hegemony; all else was superstructure.[1] The thought patterns that produced these evils were not white supremacist but merely reflected, Scalia implied in another case, a "tendency . . . to classify and judge men and women on the basis of their country of origin or the color of their skin" (*City of Richmond v. Croson* [1989], 520). To Scalia, apparently, it was purely coincidental which group was enslaved and which privileged, and the facts of enslavement and privilege had no long-term social or political consequences. It was a vignette of some other society, of some other country's history.

Justice Thomas went even further down the radical, anti-institutional path, announcing that "government cannot make us equal," disdaining affirmative action as merely "some current notion of equality," and equating policies motivated by "benign" impulses with those flowing from "malicious" purposes (*Adarand Constructors, Inc. v. Pena* [1995], 2119). Since a government incapable of promoting equality is presumably innocent of previously fostering inequality, it is difficult to imagine how, on Thomas's view, slavery, segregation, and disfranchisement were established, maintained, or destroyed. Thomas's sentiments also eerily echo two statements in racial discrimination cases of the turn of the twentieth century. Justice Henry Billings Brown had remarked in *Plessy v. Ferguson* (1896, 1143) that "if one race be inferior to the other socially, the constitution of the United States cannot put them upon the same plane." And Justice Oliver Wendell Holmes had announced in *Giles v. Harris* (1903, 642), the Alabama disfranchisement case, that the only relief that the Supreme Court could provide for what the black plaintiffs thought was a "great political wrong" was just "an empty form." In interstate commerce law, Justice Thomas has called for a return to the doctrines that the laissez-faire Court proclaimed in the 1890s, disregarding the experience of the Court and the development of the economy since then (*U.S. v. Lopez* [1995], 1642–51). Thomas obviously believes even more strongly in a return to the same laissez-faire policies in race relations that the federal government adopted or enunciated a century ago, and he is impatient to dismantle the web of protective laws and institutions so carefully and gradually spun out during the last half of the twentieth century.

After the First Reconstruction, a restrictive and unsympathetic Supreme Court and a Congress split between a fervent, doctrinaire, southern-dominated political party and a cautious, pragmatic, northern-based party paralyzed national action aimed at protecting the civil rights of African-Americans from private persons and from state and local governments that were determined to make sure that blacks were not equal. The parallels with the Rehnquist Supreme Court and the Gingrich Congress of today are not comforting.

The "conservative" justices have been joined by their academic followers in distorting history and contemporary reality. Prof. Katharine Butler, for example, has asserted that "until the Voting Rights Act of 1965 enfranchised blacks in the South, Southern legislators had little interest in the racial make up of election districts" and that "districts are seldom created 'for' white voters." These statements, for which she provides no evidence whatsoever, merely represent an effort to deny the long history of racial gerrymandering against minorities by disregarding the First Reconstruction and the discriminatory electoral rules and structure that destroyed it as well as much recent history, for example, in North Carolina and Texas. Likewise, she has portrayed gerrymandering for any reason as "non-standard" in the American experience, so rare as to make recent pro-minority gerrymanders almost unique, and therefore deeply suspect. This view cannot survive even the slightest glance at the history of American redistricting practices. Butler has also condemned efforts to create minority opportunity districts because " 'group representation' is antithetical to the nation's founding principle that we be 'one people,'" an expression that echoes Justice Scalia's comment in *Adarand* that "we are just one race here. It is American." Butler has joined Scalia, too, in deriding what she calls "the folly of attempting to fix past historical wrongs" (Butler 1995, 598, 618; 1996, 327, 333, n. 79, 360; *Adarand Constructors, Inc. v. Pena* [1995], 2119). In such statements, the law professor and the justice ignore altogether the history of discrimination against blacks, Latinos, Asians, and Native Americans; of ethnic conflict among groups now all homogeneously considered "white"; of ethnic political machines, ethnically balanced tickets, ethnic appointments to office, and ethnically based representative districts. Historians have long rejected the idea that the "melting pot" metaphor was accurate, as they have recognized that black and Latino individuals have faced discrimination not because of their individual characteristics but on account of their ethnic characteristics (Abramson 1980; Holt 1980). Group discrimination and group preferences may not have been the ideal, but they have been a great deal of the reality of American history. For Butler and Scalia, facts recede before slogans, and righting wrongs is either undesirable or fatuous.

Another *Shaw* defender, Prof. Abigail Thernstrom, has both drawn lessons from the history of American race relations and proclaimed the end of history. But her lessons are superficial and her proclamation premature. Like Justice Scalia, Thernstrom has declared that past discrimination against minorities can never justify race-conscious remedies in the present, for "it is precisely the history of racism that makes those race-conscious policies so dangerous." Although quick to condemn the "hyperbolic rhetoric" that she claims "is the language of discourse among civil rights spokesmen," Thernstrom has hardly tempered her own. The drawing of minority opportunity districts, she has charged, is "racist," an activity fostered by "the forces of segregation." These intellectual descendants of *Plessy v. Ferguson,* she alleges, oppose "commingling" and favor "Jim Crow districts" as apartheid " 'homelands' for black voters." Turning the point of her usual confederate, Justice Thomas, on its head, Thernstrom has announced not only that government cannot help but that it can only hurt—"on the question of race, the state is not to be trusted." Rather than powerless, the state is potentially too powerful, and always with baleful results. At the current juncture, however, both views lead to the same conclusion: Governments should do nothing to help minorities overcome discrimination against them and only refrain from "distinguish[ing] between [individuals] on the basis of race" (Thernstrom 1994, 36–37, 42–44, 53–54). To Thernstrom and Thomas, there has been only a negative equal protection clause, at least for minorities. All the clause said to governments was "Do no wrong, and since any action will necessarily be wrong, do nothing."

While it is true that in the past American governments have generally heightened or solidified societal discrimination against various minority groups, those actions have nearly always been directed by majority groups and the powerful against groups that were already disadvantaged, not vice versa. As Figure 1.1 in Chapter 1 displays most dramatically, and the rest of this book substantiates, governments have the power to help or hurt minorities, and in the matter of voting rights they have no alternative but to use the power one way or another. Either minorities will be allowed to vote or they will not. Either they will be placed into districts in order to give them an equal opportunity to influence policies, or they will be inserted into districts that will afford them less than equal opportunities. There are no "natural" baselines for district boundaries, and governments cannot refrain from defining political rights. Although the national state should not be trusted unreservedly, it must act or allow other levels of government a free hand. As the history of the disfranchisement and reenfranchisement of African-Americans shows, leaving local white majorities to define minority political rights without safeguards has generally sacrificed those rights, at least in areas that contained substantial percentages of minorities. The lessons of American history are not colorblind. When that history is analyzed more closely than it has been by Scalia, Thomas, and Thernstrom, it does not reinforce their predetermined conclusion that governments can or should act only to protect whites from distinctions that might help minorities.

In redistricting, Thernstrom has called on courts to throw out not just "bizarre" minority opportunity districts but all of them. "Majority-minority districts are here to stay," she has warned, "unless courts intervene." Any race-conscious governmental action during redistricting is wrong, she believes, because it forces courts implicitly to decide such empirical and normative questions as whether African-Americans and Latinos are distinctive groups, who best represents them, whether they are better off with a great deal of influence over a few representatives or a little influence over a larger number of representatives, and how to move toward a "colorblind society" (Thernstrom 1994, 43; 1995, 936). But there is no escape from these questions. Banning minority opportunity districts does not avoid them, leaving them to "the political process" to solve, as she contends. On the contrary, such a ban is an intervention in the political process by courts to overturn a modus vivendi that Congress, the Justice Department, and state redistricters have worked out fitfully over a generation.

It is also worth noting that history and current reality offer answers to Thernstrom's questions, answers that differ systematically from those that she gives when she abandons her skeptical pose. Thernstrom has contended that African-Americans (she largely ignores Latinos) are not distinctive because they are heterogeneous: "Black suburbanites, quite simply, are as different from black inner-city residents as white suburbanites are from white inner-city residents. . . . Middle-class blacks nationwide are often more middle class than black" (Thernstrom 1994, 46). This position ignores both history and current politics, and it vastly understates the *political* homogeneity of African-Americans and their distinctiveness from whites as a group on particularly salient political issues. While there are certainly growing economic and social distinctions among blacks—as well as among Latinos, even those of the same country of origin—those distinctions have led to few systematic differences in political attitudes and behavior for three reasons. First, memories of blatant, pervasive, and severe discrimination against them persist and provide a convenient framework for interpreting the meaning of new events. It was not difficult to convince black members of the O. J. Simpson criminal jury that the Los Angeles police had planted evidence, because so many black families have had bad experiences with those police. Second, white discrimination continues, and middle-class minorities, who interact more with whites than lower-class minorities do and whose aspirations bring them up against racial barriers and stereotypes more frequently, may perceive even more discrimination than their lower-class counterparts do because they may personally experience more. Third, white Republican politicians have increasingly stressed such issues as affirmative action and immigration, exploited racial stereotypes in attacks on crime and welfare, and endlessly denounced "government," which middle-class minorities widely recognize has provided employment and benefits on a less racially discriminatory basis than the private sector has. It should not be surprising, therefore, that on such issues as social welfare, military and domestic spending, and the redistribution of income, as well as in presidential voting patterns, the first book that Thernstrom cites as support for her position on the political relevance of black class differences concludes that there is "a relatively distinct Afro-

American mass culture that cuts across class lines . . . class plays a much more significant role in structuring mass opinion in the white community than it does in the black" (Smith and Seltzer 1992, 47–48, 66–67, 80, 81). Far from supporting her black class-conflict interpretation, the books and articles Thernstrom cites almost uniformly come to the opposite conclusion.[2]

Questions about who best represents minorities and whether they are better off with concentrated or dispersed influence are empirical, not, as Thernstrom implies, theoretical. And even her theoretical position is hopelessly self-contradictory (Thernstrom 1994, 54).[3] Besides the evidence presented in Chapters 5 and 6 above, the most methodologically sophisticated study of this issue (Cameron, Epstein, and O'Halloran 1996) concluded that the best way to maximize the substantive influence of black voters in the South is to create as many districts as possible in which the voting age population is approximately 47 percent African-American, while in the North, "the most important objective for minority representation . . . is to elect Democrats, either black or nonblack." It is noteworthy that all seventeen districts in the South with voting-age populations that were 46 percent or more black elected African-American representatives in 1992, and that because of racial differences in age distributions, the total population in such districts was 50 percent black or more.[4] That is to say, based on this evidence, the best way to maximize African-American influence in the South is to draw districts that have a bare majority of minority voters. (For parallel findings, see Lublin 1997, 87–97.) No less important, *Vera*'s preference for compact districts and its indictment of the use of race as a proxy for Democratic support will, if these authors are correct, diminish black influence overall, and not just the number of black faces in Congress, because it will make it more difficult to create majority- or near-majority-black districts in the South and Democratic districts everywhere. Under certain circumstances, as Cameron and his colleagues have noted, "a trade-off does exist between substantive and descriptive representation," that is, between electing more minorities and electing more members of Congress who are at least somewhat sympathetic to minorities (Cameron, Epstein, and O'Halloran 1996, 807–8, 810; Congressional Quarterly 1993c). What they and Thernstrom fail to point out is that *Miller* and *Vera* largely eliminated the dilemma by making *both* more difficult.[5]

To those who fear the consequences of outlawing minority opportunity districts and dismantling much of the VRA, Thernstrom offers the Panglossian view that they are no longer needed, because "the past is not the future." White racial attitudes, she contends, "have been changing fast, and the record of black electoral success in 1975 tells us little about the prospects for such success today."[6] In fact, she announced, after the 1996 elections produced the first three African-American winners from majority-white southern congressional districts since 1976—incumbents who considerably outspent their little-known white opponents and who received about a third of the white vote in heavily Democratic districts—"I think there is an enormous willingness [among whites] to vote for black candidates in this country." "Racist campaigns," she and Stephan Thernstrom assert, "have almost entirely disappeared." The notorious race-tinged television ads that Jesse Helms ran against Harvey Gantt in the 1990 North Carolina Senate election, they claim, without presenting any evidence, probably had little effect on the outcome. The Democratic response to the Willie Horton ads in the 1988 presidential campaign, they reassure us, "is one more sign of heartening racial change" (Thernstrom 1995, 933; *NYT*, Nov. 23, 1996, I:1; *WP*, Nov. 26, 1996, A:15; Thernstrom and Thernstrom 1997, 308–10). On such important matters, scattered, anecdotal evidence and superficial examinations of evidence are not sufficient. Do systematic examinations show a complete transformation of white attitudes, a withering away of prejudice, an elimination of policy differences between blacks and whites?

The most comprehensive recent studies of racial attitudes in America disagree on whether self-interest or less rational "racial resentments" account for white attitudes, but they agree that there is a continuing gulf in policy preferences between African-Americans and whites.[7] Whites may assent to the abstract proposition that blacks should be treated equally, but when asked whether governments should take any action to integrate schools or prevent discrimination against minorities in housing, employment, or the enforcement of criminal laws, they are much less supportive (Schuman, Steeh, and Bobo 1985). Carefully designed attitudinal experiments devised to test Abigail Thernstrom's assertion that whites do not respond to subtle racial appeals by voting against black candidates convincingly reject Thernstrom's contention (Reeves 1997, 76–90). Whites and blacks differ dramatically on the questions of how much racial discrimination against African-Americans persists; how hard blacks try to work, achieve, and overcome hardships; and how much blacks deserve assistance and need protection from bias against them (Kluegel and Smith 1986). White racial resentments against blacks' alleged character defects strongly affect white views, in the words of one study, "not just on affirmative action or school desegregation, but on welfare, capital punishment, urban unrest, family leave, sexual harassment, gay rights, immigration, spending on defense, and more. . . . the most arresting feature of public opinion on race remains how emphatically black and white Americans disagree with each other . . . Divisions by race are nothing new to American politics, but if anything, they are more prominent now than they were a generation ago" (Kinder and Sanders 1996, 272, 287–88). Whatever the causes of differences in attitudes on these matters of great political consequence, whites and blacks and, to a lesser degree, non-Cuban Latinos differ so much on so many issues that to destroy minority opportunity districts is to exclude a distinctive voice from policy debates, to leave most minorities unrepresented. Whites and blacks, whose neighborhoods are now more segregated from each other than they were in 1900, see the world differently because, unfortunately, they still largely inhabit different worlds. Affluent, well-educated African-Americans are just as segregated from whites as are those who are poorer and less educated (Farley and Allen 1987, 136–57; Massey and Denton 1993). And unobtrusive measures in survey-experiments demonstrate that the apparent liberalization of the visceral racial opinions of white male southerners really represents a tendency to give "socially desirable" responses. "When given a chance to express what they really feel," three survey researchers conclude, "sizable numbers of white people, many concentrated in the South, say unequivocally that they feel anger and hostility toward black people" (Kuklinski, Cobb, and Gilens 1997, 346). Whatever the right way is to move toward a "colorblind society," it cannot be the way that Thernstrom and the *Shaw* justices insist on, which is to act as if that society had already been achieved.

In a dissent from a decision that made it much harder for minorities to prove that employers had discriminated against them, Justice Harry Blackmun wondered "whether the majority still believes that race discrimination —or, more accurately, race discrimination against non-whites—is a problem in our society, or even that it ever was" (*Ward's Cove Packing Co., Inc. v. Atonio* [1989], 662). It is worse than that. The *Shaw/Adarand* majority has consciously used vague and misleading notions of previous discrimination to prevent legislative and administrative attempts to combat present discrimination against minorities. For Scalia and Thernstrom, O'Connor and Blumstein, Thomas and Butler, minorities are twice cursed. Not only did African-Americans have to undergo slavery, segregation, disfranchisement, and discrimination against them in every area of life. That very fact makes it impossible to grant them any relief from present discrimination and the continuing effects of past discrimination. For suffering injustice, they are condemned to continue to suffer.

But this conclusion does not follow from the history of discrimination against minorities in the U.S., if that history is properly understood. There is nothing in our history to support Butler's speculation that Americans will "increase the chances that [race] will matter less if we steadfastly reject measures that affect individuals, positively or negatively, based on their membership in an immutable group" (1995, 599). For such a "principled" position merely facilitates private and sophisticated public discrimination against currently disadvantaged groups and reduces the representation of those groups in public office and other prominent positions, thus making it even less likely that effective action against discrimination will be taken. As the history of school segregation and especially of the Fourteenth and Fifteenth Amendments and the VRA makes clear, discrimination against individuals on account of their membership in a group cannot be remedied by ignoring the nature of the discrimination. Instead, group discrimination demands a group remedy. Nor do recent changes in white racial attitudes or the growing class differences within minority communities support the contention that political opportunities for African-Americans and Latinos are now and will remain equivalent to those of Anglos, so that protective rules can safely be overturned, for the changes in white opinions have not yet been sufficiently large, and blacks and Latinos are each still politically united and quite distinct from Anglos. History is not over yet. Americans still need the Reconstruction Amendments to do what they were designed to do—to guarantee those minorities who would otherwise lose out in the political struggle protection from private and public discrimination against them.

Shaw I and its progeny are wrong—as wrong as *Plessy,* as wrong as *Dred Scott. Dred* attempted to end political controversies over slavery and thereby tighten the shackles around African-Americans by outlawing the positions that Republicans and most northern Democrats had taken on slavery. *Plessy* sought to muffle racial strife by blessing what everyone knew to be the subordination of blacks to whites. *Shaw* aims to reverse the growing power and influence of minority voters, just as, in other decisions, the Rehnquist Court has striven to hamper school integration and governmental enforcement of nondiscrimination in private industry and to torpedo efforts to foster minority businesses (*Freeman v. Pitts* [1992]; *Missouri v. Jenkins* [1995]; *Martin v. Wilks* [1989]; *Patterson v. McLean Credit Union* [1989]; *Ward's Cove Packing Co. v. Atonio* [1989]; *City of Richmond v. Croson* [1989]; *Adarand Constructors, Inc. v. Pena* [1995]). Thus, *Dred, Plessy,* and *Shaw* all buttressed a seemingly uncertain white supremacy.

Many of the flaws in the minority racial gerrymandering cases parallel those in *Dred* and *Plessy.* First, the slavery, segregation, and racial gerrymandering decisions all foundered on the question of whether the parties of concern were individuals, groups, or the nation as a whole. In *Dred,* Chief Justice Roger Brooke Taney treated individual African-Americans as having no rights, whether they were slave or free, northern or southern. He yearned to decide the slavery question for the nation forever by guaranteeing slaveholders' rights against any legal attacks by the national government. To secure the "liberty" of individual southern slaveholders, Taney had to assume that blacks were an undifferentiated mass without any liberties; to "save" the nation, he had to imagine its interests as unitary by denying the political platform of its northern half. In *Plessy,* Justice Henry Billings Brown considered blacks faceless members of a separate group, not individuals who deserved the same right as white individuals to sit in comfortable railroad cars, if they could afford to. It was individuals, not races, who bought tickets on trains or boats, individuals who ate at restaurants or attended public performances, individual students who learned or failed to learn, but Brown ignored the nature of the behavior that the State of Louisiana was regulating. Justices O'Connor, Kennedy, and Thomas conceived of voting as a purely individual right, when it is in fact exercised in a way that is fundamentally different from the social processes that underlie judicial decisions in school segregation or employment discrimination. Voting and redistricting are inherently group-oriented processes because success depends not only on your own vote but on the votes of people like you, not only on what district you are in but on who else is in your district. In Justice Lewis Powell's words, "groups of voters elect representatives, individual voters do not." In an electorate where opinions and behavior are sharply divided on the basis of race, to fail to take race into account in districting is to deny any particular member of a minority group the opportunity to have her views represented. In other words, to deny group representation is to deny individual representation (*Davis v. Bandemer* [1986], 167; Karlan and Levinson 1996). Whether minorities are considered as individuals or members of groups, O'Connor, according to the most generous interpretation of her actions, was willing in *Shaw I* and its successors to refuse blacks and Latinos an equal voice in political decisions in order merely to save society from being symbolically confronted with the continuing reality of racial divisions.

Second, like the earlier decisions, *Shaw I* and its successors were abstract, formalistic, and factually incorrect. Free people of color were recognized as citizens in many states at and after the time of the adoption of the Constitution, contrary to Taney's assertion, so Dred Scott deserved standing to sue on that ground alone. Not even Deep South states stripped slaves, much less freed people and their descendants, of all rights, as the slaveholder Taney asserted. And Taney's extraordinary reading of the territorial clause of the Constitution and his radical extension of the Fifth Amendment due process clause to protect slaveholders' rights in U.S. territories and to repeal the Missouri Compromise ignored seventy years of the nation's history (Fehrenbacher 1978, 335–88; Nieman 1991, 3–48). Likewise, Brown's assertion that segregation laws were neither caused by a desire to discriminate against blacks nor had the consequence of injuring them was completely contrary to facts that Brown and everyone else knew well. His pretense that separate was or was ever meant to be equal fooled only those who desired to blind their eyes to the reality of discrimination against African-Americans. O'Connor's parallel contentions in *Shaw I*—that the societal harms that she condemned had something to do with irregularly bounded minority opportunity districts or even with the most compact of such districts or that decreasing minority representation would move the society toward, rather than away from, "colorblindness"—were as fanciful as anything Brown or Taney imagined. All three decisions exalted shallow slogans over careful examinations of the facts about rights and equality. Blacks in America, Taney asserted, had never enjoyed any "rights which the white man was bound to respect." Laws, Brown declared, were "powerless to eradicate racial instincts," and the Fourteenth Amendment, "in the nature of things . . . could not have been intended to abolish distinctions based upon color." Minority opportunity districts whose shapes she did not like, O'Connor insisted, did not follow "traditional districting principles." Even though they contained only slight majorities of African-Americans, such districts resembled "political apartheid" and threatened to "balkanize" Americans—who, she implied, had previously ignored race in their political decisions—into "competing racial factions" (*Dred Scott v. Sandford* [1857], 407; *Plessy v. Ferguson* [1896], 1140, 1143; *Shaw v. Reno* [1993], 2827, 2832).

Easy slogans—prejudices disguised as principles—do not make good law or policy. The founding fathers of the Fourteenth Amendment were steeped in the history of the struggle to abolish slavery and establish equal rights for all men because they had participated in that struggle. The founding men and women of the Second Reconstruction were equally aware of its narrative for the same reasons, and they appreciated the history of the institutions they were reforming. Martin Luther King Jr., for example, once termed C. Vann Woodward's *Strange Career of Jim Crow*, originally published in 1955, "the historical Bible of the civil rights movement" (Woodward 1986, 92). The Civil War and the two Reconstructions, more than any other events, have defined America as a nation and built the institutions that undergird our modern law. When radicals purposely distort the history of those times and the repressive intervening years in an effort to wipe out the legacies of those epic struggles, when they employ "colorblind" rhetoric in what is actually an attempt to redeem white supremacy once more, by deconstructing the Second Reconstruction, it becomes the duty of a historian to set the story straight.

Notes

INTRODUCTION

1. A word about editorial conventions and terminology must intrude at the outset. Endnotes are reserved for comments that would distract unnecessarily from the chief argument in the text. Sources are noted parenthetically, in social scientific style. Full source information appears in the references list, which is divided into four sections: newspapers, court cases, depositions, and all other documents.

Although the names used to refer to ethnic groups will never satisfy everyone, I have tried to be sensitive to current usage as I understand it. I use "black" and "African-American" interchangeably, the latter hyphenated on the grounds that Africans brought to the Americas as slaves had not African but only tribal or ethnic identities at the time. America homogenized and transformed the disparate cultures of African slaves, added European elements, and created a man and woman much newer than Crevecoeur's famous "new man, this American" (Kolchin 1993, 41–42). Because they became African and American simultaneously, I employ a hyphen. I avoid "Negro" or "colored" (except in quotations) as no longer acceptable.

The names for persons of Latin American origin are less settled. "Mexican-American" is too limited, because even where people of Cuban or Puerto Rican forebears are scarce, as in California and Texas, there are too many Central Americans intermingled with Mexican-Americans to overlook. "Chicano," another name for Mexican-Americans, is a 1960s coinage often associated with radical, ethnically nationalistic politics. Terms such as "Tejano," "Nuevo Mexicano," and "Hispano" are very regional, used chiefly in Texas and New Mexico. "Hispanic," the word chosen by the Census Bureau for the 1980 census to replace "Spanish-surnamed," has taken on a middle-class, rather conservative cast. Its use dwindles the farther west one goes in the United States, but it is still widely employed in Texas. Since Californians tend to prefer "Latino," I have used "Hispanic" in the chapter on Texas and "Latino," except in referring to demographic statistics, in the chapter on Los Angeles.

I refer to "whites" where the meaning is unambiguous and to "Anglos" or the "majority group" where I wish to contrast them with both blacks and Latinos. "Asian-American" is seemingly less troubling in this generation, though diversity within the group and a high rate of exogamous marriage will make the classification much less meaningful soon. When I want to refer to blacks and Latinos together, I call them "minorities" or "members of a minority group." "People of color" sounds too stilted and too reminiscent of "colored people," and it may imply that I mean to include Asian-Americans at times when I do not.

2. See Kleppner 1995 for a masterfully done parallel analysis of the Chicago City Council.

3. For examples of such distortions, see Blumstein 1995, 523; Butler 1995, 603.

CHAPTER ONE

1. Besides the attacks on minority officeholders and the Supreme Court's decisions in school segregation and job discrimination cases, a brief catalog would include the racialization of the crime and welfare issues, the political assaults on legal and illegal immigrants, the California and congressional pushes for totally dismantling affirmative action, and the middle-brow tracts of Hernstein and Murray (1994), D'Souza (1995), and Roberts and Stratton (1995). For a devastating critique of Hernstein and Murray, see Devlin et al. 1995.

2. Opposing the Nixon Administration's proposal to repeal Section 5 of the VRA, Clarence Mitchell, the longtime lobbyist for the NAACP, told the Senate Judiciary Committee in 1970 that he had to recount in detail the inadequacies of the civil rights laws since 1957 and their successive replacement by more effective protections of electoral rights because "I have been reading much of the history of our country, and particularly I have been reading about the Reconstruction Period of our history, and I think we are making some of the same mistakes now that we made in the Reconstruction Period" (U.S. Senate 1970, 273).

3. Astute readers may note the resonance of these observations with those of Key 1949. Key is still, at least for me, the brooding omnipresence in studies of southern and even American politics.

4. And as some scholars carelessly charge. See Gillette 1965, 161-62.

5. Section 2 of the Fourteenth Amendment requires reduction of the congressional representation of any state in which the suffrage "is denied to any of the male inhabitants of such state, being twenty-one years of age, and citizens of the United States, or *in any way abridged,* except for participation in rebellion, or other crime" (italics supplied). According to one of the leaders of this 39th Congress (Blaine 1886, 2:418-19), this language barred states from passing even facially neutral property, literacy, or religious tests. During the first quarter of the twentieth century, repeated attempts to enforce this section failed in Congress.

6. That they had a particular instance in mind, of course, does not mean that they would have opposed application of the amendment to other examples of abridgement. They were, after all, enacting a broad constitutional principle, rather than a minor statute that aimed to correct a transient situation.

7. Compare Belknap 1987, 10: "It was only with great reluctance that the Republican majority in Congress moved beyond the sort of negative intervention represented by statutory and constitutional prohibitions limiting what states could do to the enactment of legislation authorizing the federal government itself to prosecute wrongdoers who otherwise would have evaded punishment." Whatever reluctance congressmen felt did not slow them down appreciably.

8. African-Americans also composed a quarter of the delegates to the 10 state

conventions that reshaped the southern constitutional order between 1867 and 1869 (Hume 1982, 133).

9. In these instances, there was probably not quite so much fraudulent counting as in the presidential race. Several of the Democratic candidates openly appealed for black votes, while some of the independents had such bad civil rights records that many black voters deserted their tickets.

10. Belknap (1987, 29) notes only six civil rights–connected murders in the four years beginning in 1955 in the eleven states of the former Confederacy.

11. Of course, I do not mean to belittle the violence of the 1950s and 60s, nor the suffering it caused. My point is that the violence in the First Reconstruction claimed perhaps a hundred times as many victims.

12. The list comes from Trelease 1971, xliv, 129; and Tunnell 1984, 173–209.

13. In six of the nine counties in which meaningful comparisons can be made, the Republican percentage of the two-party vote in the post-violence election was lower than in the pre-violence election, though in two of these six the decline was less than 10 percent. Violence, especially if accompanied by fraud, could certainly have an important effect. My point is that that effect was not unlimited.

14. All statistics about congressional districts in North Carolina, South Carolina, and Mississippi are from Parsons, Beech, and Dubin 1986 and Parsons, Dubin, and Parsons 1990.

15. For examples of such tactics in South Carolina, see Tindall 1952, 72; in Mississippi, see the contested congressional election cases of *Buchanan v. Manning* and *Chalmers v. Morgan*, in Rowell 1901, 373–75, 457–57; in Virginia, see *Stovell v. Cabell*, *Waddill v. Wise*, and *Langston v. Venable*, in Rowell 1901, 393, 452–54, 457–60.

16. That this delegate, John Fielding Burns of Dallas County, was undoubtedly grossly exaggerating only strengthens the case for the racist motivation behind the provision. As evidence of Burns's racial purposes, one might take the preamble to a resolution that he offered during the convention to disfranchise illegitimate sons of "mixed blood," which he claimed would eliminate 48,000 voters: "Whereas, mixed bloods seldom inherit even the impaired virtues of their progenitors, and in every section of our country are always found among the most vicious and vindictive class of citizens; and whereas, this Convention was called with the understanding and for the purpose that white boys of Alabama should not be forced to compete with any others, whose only qualification for suffrage lies in their ability to memorize . . ." (Alabama Constitutional Convention 1901, 4429–30, 4786–87, 4790).

17. This position was taken by Prof. Wayne Flynt in his testimony in the remand cases of *Bolden v. City of Mobile* (1982) and *Brown v. Board of School Commissioners of Mobile County* (1982).

18. In 1890, the radical Harrison Kelley (R-Kans.) did introduce a bill, drafted by former North Carolina carpetbagger Albion Tourgee, that required congressional districts to be equal in population, and gave Congress the right to draw district boundaries. It also made the secret ballot mandatory in congressional elections and required states to allow all adult males except felons to vote. Tourgee appeared before a congressional committee to testify for his bill, and Speaker Thomas B. Reed endorsed

some parts of it, but the bill was too radical for the Republican caucus (Crofts 1968, 252–61).

19. See, e.g., *NYT*, July 13, 1882, 5; July 27, 1882, 5. In his first annual message in 1889, President Benjamin Harrison asked: "When and under what conditions is the black man to have a free ballot? When is he in fact to have those full civil rights which have so long been his in law? When is that equality of influence which our form of government was intended to secure to the electors to be restored?" In his second annual message in 1890, he remarked, "Equality of representation and the parity of the electors must be maintained or everything that is valuable in our system of government is lost" (Richardson 1900, 9:56, 127–29).

20. Thus, Roswell P. Flower (D-N.Y.) condemned the 1890 supervisory bill as an attempt to "revolutionize the Government and set up on the ruins of our free institutions a government by fear, force, and fraud." Richard Vaux (D-Pa.) thought the authors of the bill were aiming at the "overturning of the Constitution of the United States and destroying our form of government." William McAdoo (D-N.J.) denounced the effort as "drastic and revolutionary." William J. Stone (D-Mo.) referred to proponents of the bill as "damned, odious traitors." *Cong. Rec.*, 51st Cong., 1st sess., 6601, 6603, 6674, 6848. Democratic bills to repeal the Reconstruction supervisory act passed both houses of Congress, on strict party-line votes, in 1878 and 1894. In the former, President Hayes vetoed the bill, even though it was a rider to an Army appropriations act. In the latter, President Cleveland signed the bill. DeSantis 1959, 85; Hirshson 1962, 56–57; Richardson 1940, 461–64.

21. This fact has either gone unnoticed or been treated as unproblematic or unimportant. For instance, Huckfeldt and Kohfeld (1989, 179) comment: "To the extent that both major parties depend upon black votes, they would both be forced to become parties of civil rights." As they show, blacks are overwhelmingly Democratic, yet on voting rights issues the two parties were both parties of civil rights from 1957 through 1982. Even as late as 1991, a civil rights law reversing five conservative Supreme Court decisions of 1988–89 passed the House 381–38 and the Senate 93–5 and was signed by President George Bush; only 5 Democrats and 38 Republicans opposed the bill on final passage. Congressional Quarterly 1991, 257–60.

22. The most important liberal in the House in the 1960s and 70s, Phillip Burton, was well aware of the fact that the safety of his seat allowed him to devote his considerable talents to policymaking (Jacobs 1995, 198–99).

23. Few historians have yet studied the nature and degree of competition for congressional seats over a long period of time in the nineteenth century, and we know almost nothing about the reapportionment process of the time—a much more crucial element in explaining political outcomes than are the biographies that historians used to write or the studies of political culture, ideology, or informal politics that mesmerize them now. Political scientists' series, which concentrate on the incumbency advantage alone and often leave out crucial elections, such as those immediately after decadal reapportionments, are also inappropriate for my purposes (see, e.g., Garand and Gross 1984; Alford and Brady 1989). To make the data entry task manageable, I focused on three states that were key to both eras.

24. At-large contests have been excluded from these tallies, as have been votes for minor parties. No minor party candidate won a seat from these states in either period. The Greenback Party in 1878 apparently drew votes from minority parties in a large number of districts, increasing the margin of the two-party vote for the winners.

25. The standard deviation is the most common statistical measure of the dispersion of the values of any variable around its average.

26. Another possible explanation for the contrast—that Congress was not considered a career in the nineteenth century and that incumbents therefore were much less likely to run for reelection then than in the twentieth century—can be ruled out, at least for the period before 1890. Before the secret ballot was adopted, parties prepared their own ballots, which most often just listed all the party nominees and no one else. Although there was some split-ticket voting at the local level even in the pre-Australian ballot era, there appears to have been little of that in the voting for federal offices. In an era of straight-ticket voting, candidate quality did not matter so much.

27. For a trenchant analysis of the act, see the dissent of Justice Ward Hunt, *U.S. v. Cruikshank* 1876, 572.

28. Unlike the Fifteenth Amendment, which bans discrimination in voting "on account of race, color, or previous condition of servitude," the Fourteenth Amendment does not mention race;in fact, in the period before 1937 it was used extensively to guarantee the rights of corporations, which have no race. Zuckert 1986 demonstrates conclusively that in the debate over the Ku Klux Act, Congress relied on the Fourteenth Amendment and that it adopted the "state failure" rather than the "state action" interpretation of that amendment. In other words, if Congress anticipated that a state would fail to protect its citizens against other individuals, Congress could directly provide that protection.

29. To consider merely one fact, extensive reports from the South emphasizing persecution not only of blacks but of southern ex-Unionists were crucial in building support for Radical Reconstruction from 1865 on. See, e.g., Foner 1988, 225–26. That the Fourteenth Amendment was meant to protect the rights of all citizens is argued most forcefully in Curtis 1986.

30. The Republican majority in the Senate did pass a bill restoring the provisions of the Enforcement Act that the Court had voided in *Reese*, this time unmistakably limiting their scope to denials based on race, but the Democratic-controlled House, naturally, did not act on the bill (Magrath 1963, 131).

31. As a Copperhead state legislator in Illinois during the Civil War, Melville Westin Fuller had—after the Emancipation Proclamation—introduced a bill to endorse a constitutional amendment guaranteeing slavery against legislative or executive action by the national government (King 1950, 116).

32. *Giles v. Harris*, 1903. In *Guinn and Beal v. U.S.*, 1915, the Oklahoma grandfather clause case, Chief Justice White entirely ignored *Williams v. Mississippi* and *Giles*. Invalidating the grandfather clause enfranchised no blacks, because that patently unconstitutional device merely allowed illiterate whites to register legally. Throwing out *Giles*, however, would have allowed blacks to vote, since *Giles* was a challenge to the administration of the Alabama Constitution. A former member of the "conservative" faction

of the Democratic Party in Louisiana, which had opposed the grandfather clause in that state's constitutional convention in 1898, White wished to rule that escape clause unconstitutional, but he did not want to endanger white Democratic supremacy in the South. Consequently, he paid no attention whatsoever to the most obvious precedents. For a more extensive discussion of these and other federal court cases, see Chapter 7, below.

33. Chief Justice Fred Vinson's fortuitous death just before the reargument in *Brown v. Board of Education* in 1953 has often been noted. Justice Felix Frankfurter remarked of that timely demise that "This is the first indication I have ever had that there is a God" (quoted in Kluger 1975, 656).

34. Abraham 1974, 121, 129. On Edmunds, see Adler 1934; *CDG*, Dec. 15, 1879, 1; Mar. 8, 1882, 1, 4. Conkling called Justice John Marshall Harlan's racially liberal dissent in *The Civil Rights Cases* the "noblest opinion in history" (quoted in Maddocks 1959, 57).

35. Brewer and Brown did dissent in *Giles*.

36. What of the explanations offered by other scholars, sketched at the beginning of this paper, of the failure of the First Reconstruction? Violence was less effective than has often been supposed. Land reform is of fairly small relevance to politics, for the same violence that kept blacks from the ballot box could have deprived them of their property, and the petty property-holding of "forty acres and a mule" did not guarantee political power in the scattered coastal areas where it was tried, anyway. Northern resolve did not weaken uniformly or decisively until late in the nineteenth century. Republican factionalism and inability to appeal to whites could have been overcome if Republican voters could have been adequately protected and their votes counted, as the Independent and Populist movements in the South after 1877 showed. But it was not that the federal government was *unable* to protect the right to vote so much as that Democrats and some Republican Supreme Court justices were *unwilling* to do so. Like Valelly (1995), I would stress political self-interest and the actions of politicians (including judges) who controlled major political institutions as primary factors in the failure of the First Reconstruction. In that regard, the depressions of the 1870s and 1890s were critical, because they removed from office Republican elites who were committed, in varying degrees, to black rights. But after the passage of constitutional disfranchisement laws and the Supreme Court's demonstration that it was unwilling to overturn them, there was little that presidents or members of Congress could do to reenfranchise African-Americans in the South, whatever their electoral incentives. Although courts by themselves may not be able to protect minority rights, those rights can surely never be protected in America unless the Supreme Court says so.

37. Although the Court had ruled white primaries unconstitutional under the Fourteenth Amendment, without considering the Fifteenth, in *Nixon v. Herndon* (1927), it in effect reversed that decision in *Grovey v. Townsend* (1935). The opinion in *Allwright* does not explain why the Court chose to base its decision on the Fifteenth Amendment. This is especially peculiar because *U.S. v. Classic* (1941),the decision that intervened between *Grovey* and *Allwright* and was said to have reopened the question of whether the primary was so integral a part of the election system that its regulations constituted state action, was a Fourteenth Amendment case. The brief for the NAACP in *Allwright* challenged the white primary on the grounds of both amendments.

38. For more detailed discussions of *Gomillion* and other voting rights cases, see Chapter 7 below.

39. In *Lassiter v. Northampton Election Board* (1959), the Supreme Court had refused to rule literacy tests unconstitutional under the Fifteenth Amendment, departing from the generally liberal Warren Court trend on voting rights and necessitating congressional action in the 1964 Civil Rights Act and the VRA.

40. In a multimember district, when several places on a board or legislative body are voted on at the same time, minorities often try to elect one candidate of their choice by voting only for their favorite candidate. This is referred to as "single-shot" or "bullet" voting.

41. Seven justices joined in the substance of Chief Justice Warren's opinion, and Justice Hugo Black agreed with its interpretation of the VRA, although the Alabamian, referring to an outdated interpretation of the First Reconstruction, thought Section 5 unconstitutional.

42. In her concluding chapter, Thernstrom denies this implication of her earlier argument, saying that she would keep Section 5 to guard against intentional discrimination (which she proposes no standards for proving) and backsliding from the previous proportion of minority seats enjoyed (which, in using an implicit proportional representation standard, contradicts arguments she makes throughout the book). Because of the inconsistency between this isolated paragraph on page 236 and the burden of Thernstrom's rationale, I have emphasized what seems to me the main line of her case.

43. Thomas's citations to Justice Frankfurter's dissent in *Baker v. Carr* 1962 (*Holder v. Hall* 1994, 2593–94) imply, as does some of his language, that he would like the Court to abandon apportionment litigation completely, allowing the extremely wide population disparities that existed before 1964, when the Court ruled in *Reynolds v. Sims* that the right to vote "includes the right to have the vote counted at full value without dilution or discount" (*Reynolds v. Sims* 1964, 555 n. 29).

44. Katzenbach went on to note the following:

"Section 5 has had its broadest impact, however, in the areas of redistricting and reapportionment. A substantial majority of the objections have been directed at this type of change. A redistricting plan or election system can be arranged so that a black candidate will have little chance of winning even with the full support of the black community. A gerrymandered election plan which splinters a black community into several districts, a change from a ward to an at-large system, the imposition of a numbered post system, or a majority requirement are all changes that almost routinely receive objections from the Department of Justice. Objections to this type of change, more than any other, have allowed blacks to achieve a greater measure of political self-determination." (U.S. Senate 1975a, 124).

45. Of course, no one doubts that that was their *chief* concern. Thernstrom's claim goes much further.

46. Although Thernstrom surely does not disagree with *Gomillion*, she barely mentions it (15, 176–77) and misrepresents its findings when she does. The connection

between disfranchisement and dilution, so obvious in *Gomillion,* would no doubt interfere with the argument that she wants to make. For a thorough critique of Thernstrom's book, see Karlan and McCrary 1988.

47. According to *Los Angeles Times* Supreme Court reporter David Savage, "Most justices employ their clerks to do research or write preliminary drafts, but their final opinions tend to reflect their own personal styles. Not so with Thomas" (*LAT Magazine,* Oct. 9, 1994, 18).

48. Thomas did not even mention that U.S. Senate 1982b, 39–43, did declare it to be the intent of Congress to circumvent exactly that point in *Bolden* by stating that the enforcement sections of the Fourteenth and Fifteenth Amendments give Congress the power to go beyond what is constitutionally required. In other words, if Congress determines that the purposes of the Reconstruction Amendments are best served by prohibiting structural discrimination, then, the Senate report contended, the amendments allow it to do so.

49. In his concurring opinion in *Holder v. Hall* (1994), Justice John Paul Stevens three times refers to Justice Thomas's opinion as "radical" (*Holder v. Hall* 1994, 2628–29).

50. Long before the so-called "Dole Compromise" of 1982 amended Section 2 to make clear that it did not guarantee ethnic proportional representation, the following colloquy took place between Congressman Don Edwards of California and voting rights lawyer Armand Derfner.

> MR. EDWARDS: There is no constitutional right to get any particular proportion of any group of people elected.
>
> MR. DERFNER: Certainly not. This is a red herring that has been thrown at us, I don't know how many times. . . . That is why we are not talking about the quota system, but a system in which there is a fair chance to start with. The only reason we bring up disparities between the number of blacks or Spanish-Americans elected and their proportion of the population is as a benchmark. If the degree of strength minority group voters can exert in the county differs markedly from what the numbers would suggest they ought to be able to do, then the burden shifts symbolically and legally under the Voting Rights Act, to explain why that is the result. The disparity may the result of a perfectly fair apportionment system, or election system; but it is worth close scrutiny." (U.S. House of Representatives 1975a, 634)

CHAPTER TWO

1. Many of the facts in this chapter, such as this one, are drawn from unpublished, loose-leaf copies of parts of the case record in *Garza v. Los Angeles County* (1990). Since the relevant documents are cited in great detail in Kousser 1991b, I refer interested readers to that article for more specific references. Here I cite, besides published works, only newspapers, the transcripts of depositions of witnesses in legal cases, and reports that, while not printed, circulated fairly widely in photocopy form.

2. In August, Chace died in an auto accident, and Gov. Ronald Reagan appointed Hayes to the seat, making him the incumbent by November.

3. Increasingly identified with the pro-developer Republican wing of the Board, Debs ran behind then–Los Angeles city councilman Edelman, 36–31, in a poll taken before Debs decided not to run. Only 13 percent of those polled in his district recognized Debs as their supervisor. Some retirements are not entirely voluntary. *LAT,* Oct. 18, 1973, I:3, 30; Nov. 13, 1973, II:1.

4. Contemporary newspapers, as well as many depositions, reflect understanding of the fact and the significance of the four-vote requirement. See, e.g., *LAT,* Sept. 19, 1981, II:1; *PSN,* Sept. 23, 1981, A:14. The chief Republican reapportionment expert, San Franciscan Joseph Shumate, did not know of the four-vote requirement when he began to draw up reapportionment plans. "When I realized that, I thought it would be very difficult," he said during his deposition (266–67). His proposed concentration of Hispanics in the Third District would threaten Mr. Edelman eventually with a "viable Hispanic [opponent]. . . . Politicians in general don't like that kind of thing," he continued.

5. Naturally, other small changes could have reduced the population deviations further. The point of the hypothetical is to show that obvious changes that preserved city boundaries and the demographic character of the previous districts could have been made, but they would have increased the Hispanic percentage in the Third District.

6. Edelman's aide Alma Fitch, who was to be Edelman's first appointee to the Boundary Commission in 1981, compiled the population figures for Edelman in this reapportionment, and she negotiated with aides of other councilmen to determine what changes were acceptable to their bosses.

7. Santillan 1983, 128–29, notes the participation of the Beverly Hills Bar Association in CFR. In 1970, Braude had voted against expanding the Los Angeles City Council, a move that was explicitly designed to make it possible to elect a Hispanic (*LAT,* July 28, 1970, II:1; July 31, 1970, II:1). By 1972, the chief issue between him and Hayes was expanding the board of supervisors to make it easier to elect members of racial and ethnic minorities; by then, Braude favored expansion of the council (*LAT,* Sept. 16, 1972, II:1, 10).

8. The splitting of Districts 13 and 14 to create a new Fourteenth District with a two-thirds Hispanic majority in the population—an increase in what was already the most Hispanic district from 40 percent to 68 percent—contrasts sharply with the repeated decreases of the proportion of the Third County Supervisorial District in each succeeding reapportionment.

9. Reuben Jacinto, who ran against Snyder for the city council in 1967, described Snyder as "a masterful politician" who developed "a strong following in the Hispanic community" (Jacinto dep., 29–30). Snyder was "extremely responsive" to Hispanics in his district, according to the deposition of Los Angeles vice-mayor Grace Montanez-Davis (46–48). On Snyder's fundraising, see *LAT,* Mar. 16, 1974, I:18; Jan. 3, 1985, I:1, 3.

10. The *Garza* trial's opening date was put off during December 1989 to allow negotiations between attorneys of the county and the plaintiffs. The county offered to settle the lawsuit on the basis of a plan drawn up by Joseph Shumate, which targeted the strident Pete Schabarum, raising the percentage of the Hispanic population and

Hispanic registered voters in his district to 63 percent and 36.5 percent, respectively. Bitterly denouncing Deane Dana, who had teamed with Democrats Edmund Edelman and Kenneth Hahn to approve the proposal, Schabarum contacted Republican leaders throughout the state to crack the party whip over Dana. Under Shumate's plan, Dana shed heavily black Compton and anti-developer Malibu from his district, and Mike Antonovich picked up ten wealthy Republican suburbs to pad his majorities. Talks collapsed when the county refused to negotiate after the plaintiffs made a counter-proposal that would have raised the Hispanic population percentage in Schabarum's district to 70 and the Hispanic registered voter percentage to 47. See *LAT*, Dec. 6, 1989, B:1, 6, 8; Dec. 7, 1989, B:1, 4; Dec. 13, 1989, A:1, 35–36; Dec. 15, 1989, B:3, 6; Dec. 16, 1989, B:3, 4; Dec. 19, 1989, B:1, 3; Dec. 20, 1989, A:1, 26; Dec. 22, 1989, B:2; Jan. 3, 1990, B:1, 8; *PSN*, Dec. 13, 1989, A:1, 11.

11. Although he had huffily refused to appear at a television debate hosted by CBS newsman Bill Stout because Stout had editorialized against his billboards as "close to racism," Dana later blithely denied that he had "ever" heard anyone suggest that "by raising the issue of forced busing, there would be a concern that you were appealing to racial sentiments" (*LAT*, Sept. 13, 1980, III:14; Dana dep., 407). Privately, the campaign was even less subtle, one Dana fundraiser reportedly pitching for funds to a group of white businessmen with the line "We have to get that black bitch out" (Burke dep., 41–43, quote on 42–43).

12. Compare the following statement of the 1988 Republican national campaign chairman, South Carolina native Lee Atwater: "I, to this day, will not acknowledge that the Willie Horton matter had anything at all to do with race" (*LAT*, Oct. 26, 1989, A:34).

13. In 1991, Shumate became California governor Pete Wilson's major adviser on reapportionment. In 1996, he was one of a secret team of American campaign consultants who advised Russian president Boris Yeltsin's spectacular comeback victory (Kousser 1995b; Kramer 1996).

14. People involved in the redistricting process in 1981 sometimes reflected on what philosophers would term a "counterfactual" in exactly this way. For example, Bob Bush, Hahn's longtime chief deputy and his appointee to the 1981 boundary commission, noted: "If the redistricting would have taken place a year before, the structure of the supervisors would probably be different today than it is . . . we had a minority supervisor. We probably could have readjusted the district somewhat to make sure she [Burke] got reelected" (Bush dep., 38).

15. Skerry (1993, 335) has contended that it was not possible in 1981 to draw a supervisorial district in Los Angeles County with a majority of Latino registered voters. In fact, the demographic evidence on this and other points was complex and much disputed during the *Garza* trial. Whether or not it is true, that is merely a legal standard, not a political one; that is, several judges had interpreted part of the *Gingles* test, mentioned above in Chapter 1, to hold that one could not prove a violation of the VRA unless it could be shown that a compact district with a majority of voting age citizens from a minority group could be drawn in the challenged jurisdiction. But if some Anglos or African-Americans cross over to vote for a well-qualified Latino candidate, as both Skerry and I believe they would in contemporary California, then the 50 per-

cent voting age population or registered voter criterion is arbitrary and nonsensical. Latinos in many situations can be elected from districts with smaller Latino populations. See Kousser 1993.

16. Note that the Third District stopped moving north just where the concentration of the Hispanic population becomes dense.

17. Suppose that ethnic data had been entirely unavailable. Could partisanship have been used as a proxy for it, with the same results? The answer is that while Republicans might have been able to exclude nearly all African-Americans and Latinos from their districts on the basis of purely partisan statistics, Democrats would have been unable to separate blacks from Latinos or from many heavily Jewish, reliably Democratic areas. The boundaries between the Second and Third Districts might have been considerably different. On the other hand, politicians are generally very well aware of the ethnicity of areas where they seek votes, even if they do not have firm statistical evidence available. Those more informal understandings might well have been combined with partisan data to produce lines resembling those actually adopted.

18. Although Skerry treats Flores's showing in this primary as evidence that the *Garza* suit was unnecessary, because it showed that Latino candidates could win under the 1981 boundaries, the inarticulate and little-known candidate would have had much more difficulty in a runoff, with the hopes of torpedoing the lawsuit thwarted. Skerry does not inform his readers of Flores's subsequent unsuccessful campaign in the redrawn First District, when she had to face other Latino candidates who were much more experienced and representative of the Latino community (Skerry 1993, 333).

19. Without presenting any evidence at all, Skerry (1993, 332) has charged that the *Garza* case represented a partisan Republican effort "to ingratiate themselves with Hispanics." Having been involved with the case long before it was filed, I never saw or heard of any facts to support such an allegation of misconduct. Moreover, the Justice Department's rejection of the Republicans' post-trial plans in favor of boundaries that everyone knew would result in the replacement of a Republican by a Democratic majority on the board weighs heavily against the partisan accusation.

20. Some of the information in this and succeeding paragraphs comes from telephone interviews with Gary Blasi. General relief recipients who were deemed qualified to work were required to perform menial labor for the county in addition to looking for private-sector jobs (*LAT*, Apr. 2, 1991, B:14).

21. It was informative during the *Garza* case to compare the plush law offices of the private attorneys for the county, in a shiny skyscraper in spotless Century City, with the rented quarters of the team from the Department of Justice, located in a rather dilapidated downtown Los Angeles building whose side entrances and sidewalks were almost invariably occupied by homeless people.

22. Robert Rensch eventually managed to qualify for Supplemental Security Income, a federal program for the disabled.

CHAPTER THREE

1. The fact that the *MPS* continued to use the term "negro" (uncapitalized) long after other big-city southern newspapers had adopted "Negro" (capitalized) is a sign

of its continued and self-conscious racial conservatism. To preserve the racial insensitivity of the usage, I reproduce the word just as the *MPS* published it.

2. The upper-class government also repudiated the debts owed to out-of-state bondholders, as it was meant to do. See *MDAV*, Jan. 1, 1879, 1; Jan. 14, 1879, 1; Jan. 30, 1879, 4; Bejach 1950; H. C. Davis 1964.

3. Other members apparently abstained or were absent from the 8–7 vote.

4. Although statewide estimates of black voting in Tennessee are very small from 1896 through at least 1910, locally various factions of Memphis politicians, including E. H. Crump, appear to have allowed blacks whose votes they could control to register to vote in the early twentieth century (Kousser 1974, 120; Miller 1964, 56, 74, 102–3). The most detailed work on race relations in the city during this period is Roitman 1964.

5. For two divergent judgments of Crump, see Miller 1957 and 1964; Tucker 1980. Tucker's antagonistic picture is much better substantiated.

6. James C. Dickerson to Edwin Meeman, Oct. 30, 1940, in Meeman papers, folder 16. The "Pittsburgh" phrase is apparently a reference to the *Pittsburgh Courier*, a militant black newspaper that circulated nationally.

7. Dillard was a former Crump ally, but he would not have been elected without black support. The *Memphis World* (Nov. 18, 1955, 1) estimated that Orgill received about 15,000 of about 22,000 black votes cast in the contest. Since Orgill's margin over Overton was 19,116, blacks were unnecessary to his victory. On the split in the black leadership, see *MTSD*, Nov. 5, 1955, 1.

8. To insure that whites did not vote for Wilbun by mistake, the *Press-Scimitar* wrote "(negro, independent candidate)" beside Wilbun's name on its sample ballot. The paper printed nothing beside the names of any of the other ten candidates. Wilbun finished tenth of eleven candidates, with the top eight—there were eight seats to fill—running safely ahead of the last three in the Democratic primary (*MPS*, Aug. 6, 1958; Aug. 11, 1958, Y:18).

9. A fifth-generation Memphian, Ayres ran for mayor in 1959 after Orgill dropped out. Prominent features of Ayres's 1959 campaign were his endorsement of a runoff and his criticism of Partee Fleming, another mayoral candidate, because Fleming had been backed by the black *Tri-State Defender*, which Ayres referred to as "the voice of integration." For himself, Fleming declared that "the white people of Memphis are unanimous in their heartfelt conviction that present segregation customs are necessary" (*MPS*, July 13, 1959, 9; July 16, 1959, 31; July 20, 1959, 1; Aug. 12, 1959, 8, 21).

10. In a post-election hearing on what it should do during the 1959 session, the newly elected Shelby legislative delegation heard retired businessman and Chamber of Commerce leader June Rudisill call for reinstatement of the poll tax, a return to a nonpermanent voting registration law, and a "full-slate" law requiring voters to cast as many votes as there were offices to be filled in multimember contests (*MPS*, Nov. 14, 1958, 1).

11. In 1962, Briggs was the candidate of Lt. George W. Lee's "Old Guard" faction for the Republican nomination for Congress, unsuccessfully opposing the much more racially conservative "New Guard" candidate, Robert James (*MCA*, Aug. 3, 1962, 19).

12. A story in the *Commercial Appeal* was nearly as explicit: "Attention has been

focused recently on the runoff requirement by the entry of a Negro candidate, Russell Sugarmon Jr., in the seven-man race for public works commissioner. He stands the chance of being elected by a solid Negro vote, while the other candidates are splitting the white vote" (*MCA*, June 10, 1959, 15).

13. As old-line leader Lt. George W. Lee put it, "Nowhere was the hand of fellow-ship extended to the negro population of Memphis, inviting them to participate in our municipal election. Everywhere there was shock at the idea of a negro candidate. The negroes themselves had no desire to offer a list of negro candidates. They would have much preferred a ticket composed of whites and negroes. Under those circum-stances they would have not asked for over much. Their leadership understands that time is the important factor and several years must elapse before the negro will be invited to share equally with the whites in the responsibility of the community life" (*MPS*, Aug. 22, 1959, 2).

14. When Hooks first announced for office, *Press-Scimitar* reporter Clark Porteous announced, "The situation [in the municipal judgeship contest] is similar to the Pub-lic Works Commission race, which has six white entries and one negro entry. Negro voters could elect a negro, if the white votes split evenly enough." Slowly, whites dropped out. When Robert V. Bickers withdrew, he advised another white candidate to follow the same course "in order that we might have a white judge the next four years" (*MPS*, July 17, 1959, 19; July 25, 1959, 1).

15. *MPS*, June 9, 1959, 1. The report went on to relate the barely veiled code words to the political crisis then facing white Memphis:

> "The last Legislature, in an attempt to prevent the possibility of a candidate being elected by single-shotting (i.e., voting for only one candidate, ignoring all the others), passed a local bill for Memphis and Shelby County providing that candidates must run for specific offices, as for a certain position on the City Commission, and not just for City Commissioner.
>
> "This law, coupled with the fact that only a plurality of votes is needed (meaning an edge over the next highest candidate's vote), has disturbed some by its possible results in the race for Commissioner of Public Works, where six white candidates are opposed by one negro candidate. If the six white can-didates split the vote in anything approximating equality, the negro candidate might win."

16. Ellington may also have opposed runoffs in general because plurality elections favored the Clement-Ellington administration forces that held the governorship from 1952 through 1970. In 1958, the first plank in the platform of former governor Jim McCord, who received 32.4 percent of the vote as an independent against Democratic nominee Ellington, was the adoption of a statewide runoff law. "With the vote so split and without a run-off provision," McCord contended, "the incumbent state ad-ministration will almost always be able to name its successor, leading to a political totalitarianism and a political tyranny in Tennessee" (*MPS*, Oct. 11, 1958, 11; Nov. 20, 1958, Y:7). To foster a local runoff while opposing a statewide runoff would have been embarrassing for Ellington.

17. When he dropped out of the contest for public works commissioner in order

to prevent the election of "the negro candidate" by a "minority bloc of votes," A. W. "Ott" Anderson decried the lack of a runoff law. "If Memphis had such a law—and I earnestly hope we will have next election—this decision would not have been forced upon me" (*MPS*, July 23, 1959, 1).

18. At the outset of the campaign, Public Works Commission candidate Ott Anderson's invitation to "the other five white candidates for public works to [attend] a meeting this week to decide who will run against the one negro candidate August 20" finally fell flat after much discussion. Anderson himself was a staunch segregationist. "As I announced in my platform, 90% of the negroes of Memphis do not care to mix with whites, and if they are given certain facilities such as playgrounds, swimming pools and schools they will be satisfied" (*MPS*, June 22, 1959, 1; June 23, 1959, 1, 13; July 18, 1959, 3).

19. One letter writer appealed to the then conventional racist version of southern Reconstruction history:

"It is obvious to even a casual observer [that] if they [the white candidates for public works commissioner] refuse to abide by a fair process of elimination, they will do irreparable harm to Memphis and the South. The sacrifice they are called upon to make is small in comparison with those made by our forefathers when Carpetbaggers and Northern radicals disfranchised the white voters of the South and placed unqualified negroes in public office." (*MPS*, Aug. 5, 1959, 6)

20. Like nearly every other prominent white candidate, Farris had pledged support to the DCC platform plank in favor of segregation. Most used the same formula as Farris, who endorsed "the maintenance of segregation of the races by all legal means." Their positions reinforce the picture of a solid racist consensus among the white political elite in Memphis at the time, which reflects on the motives of those who framed election laws during the period. For the pledges, see *MPS*, July 14, 1959, 7, 12; July 15, 1959, 4; July 16, 1959, 4, 31; July 18, 1959, 3; July 20, 1959, 7; July 21, 1959, 15; July 22, 1959, 32; July 24, 1959, 7.

21. The fact that Sugarmon staunchly opposed runoffs as a member of the Program of Progress committee in 1966 shows that he did not really believe that that electoral provision would increase black political influence. For other predictions that the legislature would be pushed to adopt a runoff, see *JCL*, Aug. 20, 1959; Wright 1962, 31–32.

22. The paper implicitly assumed that all Shelby County state legislators would favor a runoff and that blacks would be unable to barter their support for one or more whites in the Shelby delegation in return for a pledge to veto a runoff bill.

23. The other proposal would have eliminated the numbering of candidate names on the often long and complex Memphis ballot, a move that obviously would have made it difficult for the less literate black population to vote for every office as they wished.

24. Black representation was also a major issue in Nashville in 1962. To assure black support for the 1962 metro charter, the Nashville Metro Charter Commission very carefully drew six safe black districts. Davidson County's population in 1960 was 19 percent black. Assuming that blacks could not carry any at-large seats, the six district positions gave them 15 percent of the council (Doyle 1985, 207–10).

25. In the context of Memphis Republican politics at the time, "Old Guard" white Republicans were those who were unwilling to expel African-Americans—most prominently, Lt. Lee—from all leadership roles in the party. Hanover appeared prominently at a testimonial dinner for Lt. Lee in June 1962 (*MPS*, June 4, 1962, A:10).

26. Tucker 1971 is a veritable catalogue of such humiliations. Even Miller's rosy picture of Crump's planter benevolence toward favored and compliant African-Americans recognizes that those who won Crump's favor were—the phrase is Miller's—"Uncle Toms." See Miller 1964, 206. In 1940, for instance, Hunt, principal of Booker T. Washington High School and a minister, lauded Crump as "a human idol" to Memphis blacks (quoted in Melton 1982, 192).

27. Lt. George Lee, who had held a seat on the Republican State Executive Committee for twenty years, lost that position in August 1962. The highly publicized refusal of the Goldwater-dominated Republican National Convention of 1964 to seat Lee was the most potent symbol of the southern "New Guard's" break with the party's devotion to southern black rights. See Tucker 1971, 179–99.

28. In actuality, it was 1974 before an African-American was elected from the Ninth District, and the winner was Harold Ford, not a member of the SCDC faction.

29. Because the electorate had authorized runoffs at the August election, Ingram could not have been referring to someone getting elected with a minority of the votes. He must have been pointing out that blacks would be elected. In fact, four of the seven districts were at least 39 percent black.

30. Only 43.5 percent of the registered voters cast ballots on the POP question, even though on the same ballot 58 percent of the registrants voted in the Frank Clement–Howard Baker contest for the U.S. Senate. The municipal change was not wildly popular.

31. Why did this moderate patrician push for the runoff? Three reasons may be suggested, although there is little direct evidence on the point. First, he probably shared the view that the election of a black as mayor would be bad for Memphis, because more white homeowners and businessmen would flee what would be perceived as a black-controlled city. (Although Lane and others may not themselves have been hostile to blacks because of their race, by acting on the view that many whites *were* racists, they entangled or infected their motives with racism.) Second, as a moderate, Lane could expect to win the black vote in a runoff against Loeb or, alternatively, much of Loeb's following in a runoff against Ingram (see *MPS*, Oct. 2, 1967, 1, 8). As a relative unknown himself, however, he could not reasonably hope to win a plurality against such well-established candidates. Third, because of his comparative obscurity, he needed a newspaper endorsement to get voters to take him seriously. The *Press-Scimitar* and, to a lesser extent, the *Commercial Appeal* were tireless advocates of the runoff and might look more favorably on a candidate who labored for it (see *MPS*, Sept. 26, 1967, 6).

32. With African-American population and voter registration rising in District 1, the City Council in 1971 shifted over 3,000 white registered voters from overwhelmingly black District 7 to District 1 and over 8,500 black registered voters from District 1 to District 7 (Ripy 1973, 85). More important than the further segregation of the districts was the fact that the interchange of population "stacked" the black population

at a percentage below which African-Americans had little hope of electing a representative of their choice.

33. For further discussion of notions of intent and causation, see Chapter 7 below.

34. After much less intensive discussions of some of the events dealt with here, Pohlmann and Kirby (1996, 68–69) conclude that "there was no clear pattern of intent to discriminate on the part of the whites involved" in the POP, but they immediately qualify that conclusion by stating that "the process was not exonerated from discrimination, either." They do not consider the crucial passage of the runoff at this point nor do they explicitly connect the evidence on intent to their conclusions. They also do not treat contrary interpretations of the POP contained in other works, including an earlier version of this chapter, which they were sent before the publication of their book.

35. The trial was initially set for April 1992, but after the election in October the case never went forward. *MCA*, Oct. 2, 1991, A:5.

36. In 1995, the majority-white city council abolished at-large elections for itself, dividing the six former at-large seats into two large, three-seat districts: a majority-white, eastern district and a majority-black, western district. African-American candidates won seven of thirteen seats in 1995, taking a majority, but a bare one, of the city council for the first time in history. Had all of the seats remained at-large, argue Pohlmann and Kirby (1996, 207), blacks would have won all six, instead of only those in the western district.

CHAPTER FOUR

1. Discriminatory purging is implied by the flattening out of the percentage of blacks registered from 1956 through 1964, apparent from Figure 4.1, together with the December 1962 registration figures by county (U.S. Commission on Civil Rights 1968, 234–39), which show forty-three counties with more than 100 percent of the eligible whites registered compared to only two counties in which comparable percentages of blacks were registered.

2. Bloch was defense attorney and Donald Hollowell, the leading African-American lawyer in the state, was civil prosecutor in a $170,000 lawsuit against police officers in Americus brought by the widow of a black man beaten to death by the police while in custody. The all-white jury ruled the police innocent (*MT*, Feb. 5, 1963, 1). Bloch was also a leading defender of the county unit system in court (Bernd 1972, 300–301).

3. In his majority opinion in *Rogers v. Lodge*, Justice White detailed the history in Burke County of racial bloc voting, exclusion of blacks from the suffrage and from equal participation in the affairs of the Democratic Party, discrimination in the selection of appointed officials and employees of the county, school segregation, the unresponsiveness of officials, and the depressed socioeconomic status of blacks. Six members of the Court ruled that at-large voting, a designated post system, and a majority-vote provision were being maintained in Burke County for a racially discriminatory purpose. Ironically, the lawyer for the challengers to discrimination in Burke County, David Walbert, later represented the state in its defense of the majority-vote requirement as nondiscriminatory.

4. In an op-ed piece (*AC,* May 27, 1990, G:7), two political scientists who assisted the state in the majority-vote litigation, Charles S. Bullock III and Loch K. Johnson, claimed that the 1907 majority-vote law could not have had a racially discriminatory purpose because blacks were already disfranchised. In fact, 28 percent of the state's blacks had been registered to vote in 1904 (Kousser 1974, 218–23), and black voters were thought to be so great a threat that the state had to pass the disfranchising constitutional amendment in 1908. In addition, it seems unlikely than an election law with obvious racial implications could have passed a legislature elected in the wake of the furiously racist Hoke Smith–Clark Howell gubernatorial campaign in 1906 and the infamous Atlanta race riot of the same year and in which the chief election-related issue was the disfranchisement of blacks, without some appreciation of its racial consequences.

5. Groover's account seems trustworthy because it is basically consistent with newspaper reports in February 1963. See, e.g., *MT,* Feb. 21, 1963, 1; *AC,* Feb. 21, 1963, 6. Groover's boast is perfectly consistent with the thesis that the rural legislators responded to the racial appeal of Groover's remarks, putting aside whatever small interest they may have had in keeping the ability to decide on plurality or majority rule in their counties as it fit their immediate political needs, for the larger value of preserving as much as possible of the racial status quo.

6. Presumably to avoid a repetition of this performance, the attorney for the state in the majority-vote case cued Groover twice with the phrase "labor bloc vote" when introducing the subject during Groover's 1994 deposition (Groover dep. 1994, 154).

7. See also similar remarks by Milton Carlton in *Brooks v. Harris* trial transcript, 5: 25–27.

8. Formally, anyone who could read and write a section of the state constitution did not have to take the 30-question test, but in practice local registrars could choose a difficult passage and apply subjective standards to grade the prospective registrant or, more simply, just require him or her to take the 30-question test anyway. The Terrell County case, described above in the text, makes it clear that such practices were followed, and the tiny proportion of blacks registered in many counties implies that the practices were widespread.

9. A lawyer is guilty of barratry if she solicits clients. Attorneys in class action suits, of which integration suits were the pertinent example at the time, often try to convince people to become prospective plaintiffs.

10. In 1962 there were 103,801 white but only 46,380 black registered voters in Fulton County (U.S. Commission on Civil Rights 1968, 234–39).

11. From the judge's point of view, of course, to call *Constitution* editor Ralph McGill by the derogatory "Jim Crow" name "Rastus" was an even greater insult than calling him an integrationist; it was to refer to a white man as black.

12. On ordered probit analysis, see, e.g., Maddala 1983, 46–49.

13. The results do not change substantially if counties with very few blacks are omitted, if the difference between the percentage of whites and blacks registered is substituted for the percentage of blacks registered, or if the relationships are estimated by running two separate logit or probit equations comparing proponents first to abstainers, and then to opponents.

14. In 1962, only 10.9 percent of the blacks but 96.2 percent of the whites in Macon County, where Montezuma is located, were registered to vote (U.S. Commission on Civil Rights 1968, 234–39).

15. Even in 1990, Sanders still believed that illiterates should be barred from voting (*Brooks v. Harris* trial transcript, 4:224).

16. Judge Freeman's conclusion is called into question at the outset, since he went so far out of his way to make it. Having ruled that plaintiffs had to prove both a discriminatory intent and effect and that they had not demonstrated the requisite effect, Freeman went on to rule, in a textbook example of a *dictum*, that even if the majority-vote requirement did have a discriminatory effect, plaintiffs had failed to demonstrate a discriminatory intent. His discussion also illuminates the frailties of the so-called *Arlington Heights* standard, discussed in Chapter 7 below.

17. Here are a series of statements by Patterson in the 1991 interview and the 1996 trial:

On the 1962–63 legislature:

1991: [T]he legislature was in the hands still of the country segregationists. . . . The racially motivated segregationist resisters to elections of blacks . . . made up the majority of votes in that legislature. . . . Sanders had far from a rubber stamp legislature. And Groover was the leader of, was one of the leaders of the segregationist wing. (Lawson 1991, 4, 13–14, 27)

1996: The governor had practically dictatorial powers over the legislature, certainly over the House. [Segregationists in the legislature were] under the thumb of the Governor [Sanders] who was a moderate. (*Brooks v. Miller* trial transcript, May 15, 1996, 447, 455)

On whether the legislature passed the majority vote law for racial reasons:

1991: I'm sure that's why the legislature passed the law. As I said in the beginning, racial motivations were everything in the politics of that period. And so the country segregationists probably saw this as some means to diminish the influence of blacks. (Lawson 1991, 25)

1996: Governor Sanders had appointed an Election Study commission to bring him a bill, a reform bill to make sense out of the Georgia election laws. They were a hodgepodge at the time. . . . The Election Law Study Commission did bring in a report, and it recommended, among other things, that a majority vote requirement for victory in a primary or an election become a statewide requirement of Georgia law, so that you could get some uniformity in the practice of democracy in this state. (*Brooks v. Miller* trial transcript, May 15, 1996, 440)

Although Prof. Lawson informed Patterson before the interview that he had been employed by the U.S. Department of Justice to study the motives behind the adoption of the majority-vote requirement in connection with the pending *Brooks* case, and although Lawson was accompanied to the interview by an attorney from the Department of Justice, Patterson attempted to account for the stark inconsistencies of his opinions expressed in 1991 and 1996 by claiming that Lawson earlier "was blind-siding me" and "trying to creep up on me to endorse his conclusion" (Lawson 1991, 44, 51; *Brooks v. Miller* trial transcript, May 15, 1996, 446, 468). Coming from a lifelong newspaper reporter, editor, and publisher, this complaint seems rather disingenuous.

CHAPTER FIVE

1. In 1976, a black former World Bank official, Elbert G. Rudasill, joined two other challengers to Fountain and received only 9 percent of the vote in a minor campaign. Fountain's chief opponent, six-term state legislator J. Russell Kirby, nearly managed to force the incumbent into a runoff (*RNO*, July 22, 1976, 10).

2. The JRC files contain a copy of a 1981 congressional bill that sought to mandate that districts be "compact in form." It is instructive to note that paragraph (h) of the bill, which did not pass and on which the North Carolina legislature took no recorded action, states that "nothing in this section shall be construed to supersede any provision of the Voting Rights Act of 1965."

3. Frye presented a map that put Durham County into the Second District, but deleted Orange from it. Frye appears to have been more concerned with making the Sixth District, where he lived, winnable by a liberal Democrat than with the exact composition of the Second District. Senate Congressional Redistricting Committee Minutes, June 1, 1981, in JRC files; *RNO*, May 31, 1981, 1.

4. Under *Beer v. U.S.* (1976), a change in an electoral system was said not to have a discriminatory effect and therefore might be precleared by the Justice Department if it did not lead to a "retrogression" in minority political influence. The Court in *Beer* did not consider whether the law was adopted with a racially discriminatory purpose, which was a separate ground for refusing to preclear a change under Section 5 of the VRA.

5. A week earlier, the Justice Department had ruled that the 1968 amendment to the state constitution requiring that whole counties be used in state legislative districts was illegal under the VRA (*RNO*, Dec. 8, 1981, 7).

6. Referring unmistakably to Rep. Daniel T. Blue's election to the House in 1980, the *RT* remarked that "Wake and other big multi-seat counties have elected black legislators partly via swapped-support agreements among white and black candidates" (Dec. 14, 1981, A:4).

7. Although it keeps some records of registration cross-classified by both race and party, the state of North Carolina does not make them available for all counties. My estimates are based on the figures for fifty-three North Carolina counties in 1993, supplied as part of the supplementation to Thomas Hofeller's deposition in *Shaw v. Hunt*. In these counties, the proportion of black registrants who were Democrats was 94 percent. Other, scattered mentions of the party affiliation of blacks in the newspapers are very similar. To arrive at the partisan percentages given in the text, I simply multiplied the total black registration in each district by 0.94 and divided the result by the number of Democrats.

8. In a much less heated contest for the Democratic nomination in the Fourth

Congressional District, incumbent Ike Andrews held off Howard Lee and John Winters, a minor black candidate, in the first primary. Lee raised only $8,195, compared to Andrews's $24,042, Spaulding's $72,585, and Valentine's $188,781 (*RNO,* Apr. 21, 1984, C:5). Engstrom estimated that Lee received 24.3 percent of the white vote in the nearly invisible contest. My discussion reflects the focus of the media and the voters, as indicated by their increased registration and turnout, on the Spaulding-Valentine race.

9. During the *Shaw v. Hunt* trial before the three-judge federal panel, none of the plaintiffs offered either evidence or arguments to counter the historical testimony, including that about the 1981 redistricting, that was presented by the various defendant parties, assuming, correctly, that the judges would largely ignore such matters. Potential competing explanations, such as that legislators were unaware of the racial consequences of drawing the "Black Second" in the nineteenth century or the fishhook in 1981, are so implausible that it would be a useless exercise to examine them at length.

10. In his dissent in *Shaw v. Hunt,* 1994, 488, Judge Richard Vorhees asserted that Judges J. Dickson Phillips Jr. and W. Earl Britt found that "the State has failed to demonstrate any basis in evidence for a conclusion that such remedial action was necessary." What they in fact found was that the number of North Carolina legislators who acted purely from a motive of remedying past discrimination did not constitute a majority of both houses (473). The three-judge panel majority's rather casually drawn conclusion would perhaps have been more difficult for Judge Vorhees to misstate if their opinion had discussed the evidence for that conclusion in more detail. This chapter supplies that missing discussion. Moreover, since in any legislative body most issues are decided by coalitions of legislators, the intentions of any large or important subgroups are hardly irrelevant to the final outcome of a bill. Thus, the motives of African-American and liberal white legislators, many of whom no doubt sincerely wished to redress past discrimination in redistricting, are quite pertinent to determining whether such redress constituted a "compelling state interest."

11. The Republican National Committee joined Robinson Everett in challenging the plan that the legislature finally adopted in 1992.

12. In the best-known blatant appeal to racism of that political season, Helms, whose Democratic opponent was African-American Harvey Gantt, ran an advertisement that pictured the hands of a white male tearing up a letter rejecting him for a job for which he allegedly was qualified but which he purportedly lost because the job had to be given to an anonymous and dehumanized "minority."

13. The well-educated Michaux's syntax in this instance was no doubt deliberate, presumably reflecting the way in which he assumed North Carolina Republicans viewed all African-Americans.

14. The politically active and overwhelmingly Democratic Lumbee tribe of native Americans comprised only 1.2 percent of North Carolina's population in 1990 and 0.8 percent of its registered voters in 1994, but their concentration in Robeson County gives them some power in the politics of southeastern North Carolina. They made up from 7 to 10 percent of the registered voters in whatever congressional district contained Robeson County in all of the plans proposed in 1991–92.

15. Although the LWV claimed that 40 percent would be sufficient, because the ma-

jority vote requirement had been relaxed to allow a winner to be declared if a candidate received 40 percent or more of the vote, the organization ignored the fact that 50 percent was still required in a two-person contest like the Valentine-Spaulding race.

16. In his deposition, Gerry Cohen reported that during committee meetings on redistricting, he heard three reasons given for drawing majority-minority districts in North Carolina in 1991-92: "One was that the VRA required it; second, that it was the right thing to do. The third was that districts had been deliberately drawn in the 1980 plan so as to reduce the ability of minorities to be elected—and had been so since the turn of the century—and that the legislature in response to a past pattern of discrimination had some duty to remedy this wrong" (254-55).

17. Economists use the term "stylized facts" to mean the characteristic features or fundamental facets of reality, at least as some group of people, such as neoclassical economists, see them. As one economist noted about the "facts" asserted by the originator of the term, "it is possible to question whether they are facts" (Boland 1987, 535).

18. In *Batson v. Kentucky* 1986, 104, Justice Marshall explains carefully that the equal protection clause "prohibits a State from taking any action based on crude, *inaccurate racial stereotypes*" (italics supplied)—not actions based on accurate generalizations.

19. Every elected official, but perhaps particularly members of Congress, provide "casework" or "constituency services" for virtually anyone in their districts and sometimes for people outside their areas, whether or not those people supported the member in the last election (Cain, Ferejohn, and Fiorina, 1987). In this sense, most officials may be responsive to almost anyone, and the shape of the district or the particular party, ideology, or race of the representative may not matter systematically to voters. A survey of constituent contacts during 1993, for instance, showed that whites were approximately twice as likely to contact newly elected North Carolina members of Congress Mel Watt and Eva Clayton, who are black, as were African-Americans (Lichtman 1994, table 43). If constituency service is what Justice O'Connor had in mind, then the evidence from North Carolina seems to refute her speculation.

20. Much of Swain's book is based on interviews with members of Congress, in which they apparently told her what she seemed to want to hear, and she believed them. For instance, when more quantifiable or systematic data disagrees with her interview impressions, as in the section on North Carolina congressman Tim Valentine, 159-68, Swain trusts her impressions.

21. Two advantages of the CQ index over those generated by special interest groups are, first, that it contains more roll calls and that it is based on a larger range of issues. A few deviant votes have little effect on a legislator's CQ index. In any event, scores on the CQ index are fairly closely related to those of the most prominent interest groups (see Kousser 1995c, 662, n. 161). Second, its advantage over one that is invented especially for a particular piece of research is that the inventor might consciously or unconsciously bias the invented index to fit the needs of the moment or make some error in calculating it. Anyone can recheck the CQ scores.

22. In particular, Tim Valentine's Conservative Coalition score from his first election in 1982 was very similar to that of his predecessor, L. H. Fountain.

23. The 1993-95 scores of Watt and Clayton were almost identical to the average of

the Conservative Coalition scores of all other African-Americans elected to Congress from the eleven ex-Confederate states for every session since 1972. This implies that if districts in which African-Americans had an opportunity to elect candidates of their choice had been drawn earlier in North Carolina, the people elected would have voted very differently from other representatives from the state.

24. In her concurring opinion in *Davis v. Bandemer* (1986), 151–52, Justice O'Connor suggested that individual members of traditionally protected minority groups could be protected as group members against political discrimination—not just as individuals—if "the racial minority group can prove that it has 'essentially been shut out of the political process.'" Figure 5.1 would seem to constitute such proof.

CHAPTER SIX

1. The phrase "political thicket," referring to redistricting, is attributed to Justice Felix Frankfurter in *Colegrove v. Green* (1946).

2. The Justice Department was involved because in 1975 Texas became a "covered jurisdiction" under the VRA. As a consequence, under Section 5, every change in district lines had to be precleared by the department, a development that provided all sides in 1980 with a further strategic tool.

3. A libertarian, Paul voted with the *Congressional Quarterly* "Conservative Coalition" only 62 percent of the time in 1981, far below the 94 percent average of the other four Texas Republicans in that session (*Congressional Quarterly Almanac* 1981, 39-C).

4. In 1970, there were only 220,412 African-Americans in Dallas County, or 47.2 percent of the population needed for a congressional district, even if all could somehow have been included. The campaign for an African-American congressional district was no doubt influenced by the fact that Dallas blacks were then in the midst of what was eventually a two-decades-long effort, resulting in seven federal district court decisions, to obtain adequate representation on the Dallas City Council (*Williams v. City of Dallas* [1990], 1331).

5. In 1981, Mattox and Frost were the two most liberal Anglo congressmen in Texas. On the *Congressional Quarterly* Conservative Coalition index, Mattox scored 25 out of 100 on the roll calls on which he was present, second in the delegation only to black congressman Mickey Leland's 9 percent. Henry Gonzales of San Antonio was third, with 32 percent, and Frost fourth, with 56 percent. The average for the five Texas Republican congressmen in the same session was 88 percent (*Congressional Quarterly Almanac* 1981, 39-C). In the rankings of the Leadership Conference for Civil Rights for the 1980 session, Frost and Mattox both scored 71, ranking behind only Gonzales, Leland, Jim Wright of Fort Worth, and Bob Eckhardt of Houston (Black and Hispanic Members of the Texas Legislature 1981b, 6–7). Eckhardt lost the 1980 election.

6. Patterson had won her position on the city council in 1973 when she managed to be included on the slate of the embodiment of Dallas's white business establishment, the Citizens' Charter Association (*Williams v. City of Dallas* [1990], 1321).

7. The contrast between this view and that held by blacks in North Carolina, who insisted that nonminority representatives were not responsive to minority views, is

presumably due to the more urban nature of Texas. Urban, Anglo Democratic voters appear to be less generally conservative than those from rural areas. In North Carolina, the districts of the least conservative white Democratic members of Congress were usually centered in the state's more urban areas, either in Greensboro/High Point or the Research Triangle area of Raleigh, Durham, and Chapel Hill.

8. Although the 287,541 blacks constituted 18.5 percent of the total population in Dallas County in 1980, the 180,640 over the age of 18 represented only 16.3 percent of the total voting-age population in the county. If the same ratio of voting-age to total population held in the S.B. 1 "black district," then blacks would have constituted only 41–42 percent of the voting-age population. If they registered and turned out at levels comparable to the whole state, they might have constituted only about 35–38 percent of the total electorate in the district, even if almost no Hispanics voted. Since the district was packed with Democrats and there was no requirement that one be a long-time member of a particular political party to vote in its primary, blacks could probably not hope to constitute much more than 40 percent of the Democratic primary electorate in the district.

9. The Southwest Voter Research Institute reported that in 1980, 68.4 percent of the Anglos, 60 percent of the blacks, and 57 percent of the Hispanic citizens of voting age were registered. In the Democratic primary in 1980, 68.4 percent of the registered Anglos, 17.69 percent of the registered blacks, and 17.3 percent of the registered Hispanics took part. In the general election, 60.9 percent of the Anglos, 50.5 percent of the blacks, and 52 percent of the Hispanics turned out (Black and Hispanic Members of the Texas State Legislature 1981a, 17). Although a spirited black campaign might have spurred African-American voters to turn out at much higher levels in a primary, it seems very doubtful that they could have closed the 50-percentage-point gap between black and white participation rates.

10. While no state or federal law requires members of Congress to live within the districts they represent, most do so, at least formally, for fear of being labeled "carpet-baggers" otherwise.

11. I am not arguing here that voting for the Democratic Party was in a normative sense in the best interests of African-Americans or Latinos, but only that the actions of minorities indicate that they believed that it was. It is certainly true, however, that public opinion polling data shows that on the vast majority of issues, blacks are substantially more liberal than whites, as are the records of such African-American members of Congress as Barbara Jordan, Mickey Leland, and Craig Washington. See Table 5.2 above and references in the accompanying text to the relevant literature. Evidence on Latino opinion is sparser. The point is that Republicans win *despite* the votes of the vast majority of blacks and Hispanics, and that therefore, Republican members of Congress are essentially outside of their influence.

12. Since she had been chief counsel for the Republican State Committee of Texas during the political and legal struggle over reapportionment from 1981 to 1983, Judge Edith H. Jones must have been fully cognizant of the connection between partisanship and race during Texas redistrictings prior to 1991 and of charges of "racial gerrymandering" during the 1981 reapportionment. Under the circumstances, some judges

would have recused themselves from deciding *Vera v. Richards*. Certainly, one would have expected Judge Jones not to ignore evidence of past discrimination in redistricting as a possible compelling state interest when it was presented to her and when she knew of a great deal of it from personal experience. In the event, Judge Jones's opinion, which was too extreme in several respects even for the Supreme Court majority, ignored all evidence of historical discrimination.

13. It was disingenuous for opponents of the 1991–92 reapportionments to compare the number of divisions in counties and precincts with those of the 1980s plans, because the "zero tolerance" that many redistricters thought the *Karcher* decision required forced many more cuts. For examples of such disingenuity, see Judge Richard Vorhees's dissent in *Shaw v. Barr* (1994), 477, and Judge Edith Jones's opinion in *Vera v. Richards* (1994), 1334.

14. If only 55–60 percent of the district's voters could be expected to participate in a Democratic primary and 43 percent of the population was black and all the blacks were Democrats, blacks could compose $^{43}/_{60}$ or more than two-thirds of the expected voters in a Democratic primary. If they united behind the black candidate, their choice would likely prevail even allowing for a good deal of slippage for a younger age structure and a lower turnout among blacks and even if a black candidate did not get a single Hispanic or Anglo vote.

15. The district Johnson proposed was actually less safe for an African-American in the Democratic primary than that in the Frost proposal. Since only 33 percent of the district's vote went for President Bush in 1988, perhaps 67 percent might be expected to vote in the Democratic primary; in the Johnson plan this would yield a black Democratic proportion of $^{45}/_{67} = .672$, while in the Frost plan it would be $^{43}/_{60} = .712$.

16. This example demonstrates how unrealistic is Prof. Samuel Issacharoff's notion that whites included in majority opportunity districts are merely "filler people" (Aleinikoff and Issacharoff 1993, 631). Politics is too uncertain and potential candidates and winning coalitions too numerous for one to ignore facets of a district's composition other than the percentage of one political or ethnic group, unless that percentage is overwhelming. The concept is also demeaning and cynical.

17. The parallel with State Sen. Barbara Jordan's actions in 1971 and her subsequent victory over the more vociferous Curtis Graves for Congress, described earlier, is almost exact. Johnson faced no substantial opposition at all when she ran for the seat she had so carefully designed for herself.

18. Evidence of Johnson's moderation as a member of Congress comes from the *Congressional Quarterly*'s Conservative Coalition scores. In her first three years in Congress, from 1993 through 1995, Johnson voted with the conservative coalition 33 percent of the time, which was quite comparable to the 37 percent score attained by Dallas liberal John Bryant of the Fifth District and not wildly different from the 47 percent average of Houston's "Hispanic district" congressman Gene Green. It was considerably more conservative than the 15 percent obtained by Craig Washington and his successor Sheila Jackson Lee in the state's only other African-American district, in Houston. Martin Frost, who had scored 39 percent and 43 percent in 1989 and 1990 soared to 56 percent in 1991, 71 percent in 1992, and 77 percent from 1993 through 1995,

apparently "voting his district" each time but shifting his behavior as the ideological complexion of the voters that he would have to face changed. Frost's shifts as he first anticipated (1991-92) and then received (1993-95) a more conservative constituency constitute strong testimony on the responsiveness of members of Congress to the voters.

19. Defending Justice O'Connor's use of the concept of "traditional districting principles," Butler (1996, 345) has contended that "states do not generally attempt to create a district for the rich by joining together the wealthy suburbs of several cities via a corridor no wider than an interstate highway."

20. The two exceptions were District 4, where Democrat Ralph Hall was particularly popular, and District 23, where Democrat Albert Bustamante was plagued by scandal.

21. All of the results in this paragraph were calculated by the author from data provided by the Texas Legislative Council and made available during the *Vera v. Richards* (1994) litigation. Election data in this form for years before 1992 was available to legislators when they drew and assessed plans during 1991.

22. The Democratic major plans reviewed were those given the following numbers in the legislature's computer system: 500, 505, 525, 551, 552, 574, and 657; the chief Republican plans reviewed were those designated 503, 521, 557, and 615.

23. By analyzing returns from only a small number of unrepresentative elections and by comparing the electoral results to only the combined percentages of black and Hispanic voters and not to each individual group's percentages, Flores rendered his results meaningless (trial testimony of Allan Lichtman, *Terrazas v. Slagle*, Dec. 12, 1991, 251-60).

24. Those debating redistricting in Texas in 1991 appear to have assumed that retrogression in District 18 would be said to occur if African-Americans could in fact no longer control the choice, not just if the black percentage were reduced, as is implied by Justice O'Connor's prevailing opinion in *Bush v. Vera* (1996), 1959. This instance shows the impracticality of O'Connor's formalistic definition, because if Hispanics, a large portion of whom were noncitizens or under 18 years old, were extracted from District 18 to build up the Hispanic percentage in District 29, the Anglo percentage in District 18 would increase. In such a case, with racially polarized voting, African-Americans could easily lose control of the district even if their percentage stayed the same or even rose slightly, because the black percentage of actual voters in District 18 would plummet as voting Anglos were substituted for nonvoting Latinos.

25. These figures were calculated from data supplied by the Texas Legislative Council at the congressional district level for districts situated partly or wholly in Harris County.

26. See Chapters 8 and 9 for a more detailed discussion of this and other recent cases.

27. At points in her contradictory and loose-ended opinion, Judge Edith Jones seemed implicitly to accept the plaintiffs' theory, but in the end she rejected it because the districts did not appear excessively ugly to her eye and because the racial percentages in the irregularly drawn parts of the districts did not constitute large enough

proportions of the district totals to matter to her (*Vera v. Richards* [1994], 1326–28, 1339, 1344–45). It is difficult to uncover the principle at work here.

28. There is a fascinating study to be done of the influences on reapportionment of such Texas judges as Nowlin, Edith Jones, and, before them, William Wayne Justice, who wrote the district court decision in what became known in the Supreme Court as *White v. Regester* (1973). Unfortunately, I must leave that task to others.

29. A state senate plan approved in a compromise settlement by a state court, which was adverse to the conservative Lucio, was eventually overturned by a three-judge federal court, which substituted the "Nowlin plan," one much less favorable to Lucio's liberal Hispanic opponents (*HC*, Oct. 8, 1991, A:13; *CCCT*, Oct. 22, 1991, 1; *HVMS*, Feb. 28, 1992, A:1).

CHAPTER SEVEN

1. I am not claiming that this is a complete explanation, which would have to account for the lack of previous African-American winners as well as for Jordan's victory in a minority-black, though majority black and Latino, district. Note also that a narrative account of Texas politics, the growth of black influence, or Jordan's career might well include the same explanation fragment given in the text, even if it did not overtly mention causes or explanations. It might remark, for example: "In 1972, state senator Barbara Jordan, who as a member of the Senate Redistricting Committee was allowed to draw the boundaries of a black-plurality Houston congressional district, became the first African-American ever elected to Congress from Texas."

2. Pildes (1997, 2537–47) has criticized motive-based approaches to redistricting as posing unintelligible questions and as irrelevant to his version of Justice O'Connor's views. But it is not clear that O'Connor, much less any other justice, is willing to cut redistricting litigation entirely off from the rest of equal protection jurisprudence, especially because, as Chapter 8 shows, intent has been an integral part of O'Connor's redistricting opinions from *Shaw v. Reno* (1993) on. I do not think the question of whether race was the predominant motive in a redistricting is any less intelligible than the question of what the shape of a district must be for it to cause "expressive harm."

3. Judges and law professors sometimes differentiate between these latter three terms, using "intent" to denote what the legislators wanted the terms of a law to mean, "purpose" to refer to their larger goals in the legislation, and "motive" to indicate what values or feelings or interests caused them to act (Eisenberg 1977, 106 n. 321; Weinzweig 1983, 308; Kousser 1995c, 642 n. 68). However, the concepts are so closely related and conventional usage is so imprecise that it seems hopeless to attempt to hew to a strict linguistic differentiation. I therefore use the terms interchangeably.

4. I assume that, as their practice in cases detailed in this chapter indicates, judges mean delineations of intent to be factual inquiries, not roundabout ways of weighing competing interests.

5. In other areas of the law, the Court had much earlier refused to examine legislators' motives, for instance, in the Georgia land speculation case of *Fletcher v. Peck* (1810) (Eisenberg 1977, 107 n. 322).

6. By "direct evidence," I mean statements about someone's motives for doing something.

7. It is also the traditional standard of intent in tort law (Parker 1983, 743 n. 136).

8. Mississippi allowed illiterates to register if they could prove to a registrar's satisfaction that they understood a section of the state constitution when it was read to them. The requirement was often applied to literate African-Americans and offered obvious room for discrimination.

9. At the same time that the Supreme Court was considering Jackson Giles's challenge to disfranchisement in Alabama, the U.S. House of Representatives was deciding a challenge to disfranchisement in South Carolina brought by Alexander P. Dantzler, who contested the seating of the elected representative from a congressional district that blacks had long controlled. The House decided that Dantzler's case belonged in court, not before a political body, a "judicial question" doctrine that cruelly mirrored Holmes's "political question" doctrine. But it was not inconceivable at the time that if Holmes had ruled the Alabama constitution unconstitutional or ordered registrars to apply its standards fairly to blacks, Congress might have taken some supportive action, such as unseating contested representatives, which could not have been blocked by a filibuster and would have been in the interest of the nationally dominant Republican Party. President Theodore Roosevelt, who as governor of New York had actively supported a law mandating integrated schools and whose chief patronage referee in Alabama was Booker T. Washington, who had secretly raised most of the funds for the *Giles* challenge, might well have endorsed limited federal court action to ensure some measure of fairness in the registration of voters. The power of the courts was less limited than Holmes pretended.

10. Despite repeated efforts to organize a public high school for white boys, the estimate of only twenty prospective students in 1895 was too low to convince the Board to spend the money (*AuC*, June 19, 1895, 2). The Academy of Richmond County, a school that had existed, sometimes with public subsidies, since before the Civil War, satisfied most of the small demand for high school education for white boys in the area. If the 1895 estimate of twenty white boys desiring public education in the county is correct, then the public schools were satisfying approximately 88 percent of the white demand before and after the closing of Ware. Kull's one-sided version of colorblindness ignores the percentages of blacks who could attend public school, or the changes in those percentages, as long as the white percentages were less than 100.

11. Similar views were developed in the Heritage Foundation and other neoconservative organizations in the 1970s, brought to power in the Reagan administration in 1981, and rejected by overwhelming majorities of both parties in Congress in 1981–82, at least with respect to voting rights (Crenshaw 1988, 1337). For a forceful statement of the Reagan orthodoxy, see Reynolds 1984, answered devastatingly by Marshall 1984. In the discussion that follows, I spotlight Blumstein and Butler only because they apply the "colorblind" interpretation of *Brown* to voting rights more directly than anyone else.

12. For a strikingly parallel argument by Malcolm X, see Peller 1997, 201. Justice Thomas is only the most recent manifestation of an alliance between black nation-

alists and "conservatives." For 150-year-old precedents, see Kousser 1988b, 982–83, 993–99.

13. Likewise, Blumstein (1995, 551 n. 199) could not accept that *Brown* rested on "potentially disprovable" facts, rather than on a priori principles.

14. A notoriously "result-oriented" judge, Douglas strongly dissented when a 7–2 majority of the Supreme Court approved an 86.3 percent nonwhite congressional district in Harlem against a contention that it was unconstitutionally racially gerrymandered (see Chapter 8 below). In school questions, Douglas came to believe that race had to be taken into account, even if no governmental action by school authorities had produced the problem. In cases on redistricting and admission to law schools, he sometimes applied a per se rule against taking race into account (*Wright v. Rockefeller* [1964]; *DeFunis v. Odegaard* [1974]). But note that Douglas sustained far-reaching and racially conscious powers under the VRA and the Court's principal decision on vote dilution (*Allen v. Board of Elections* [1969]; *White v. Regester* [1973]). Douglas simply did not follow abstract doctrines slavishly.

15. Although Frankfurter attempted to rest the decision wholly on Fifteenth Amendment grounds and would later deny that it had any implications for the Fourteenth Amendment, other justices disagreed, and *Gomillion* was prominently cited to support the Court's move into the reapportionment thicket in *Baker v. Carr* (1962), 229–31, 267, 300.

16. In speaking of "proportional representation" here, I refer not to proportional representation of voter *preferences,* but to proportional representation of geographically based *interests,* such as urban or suburban interests, which were massively underrepresented in many legislatures of the 1950s and early 60s (Altman 1998, chap. 3). By denying them fair representation, rural interests prevented nonrural people from adequately expressing both the preferences they *shared* (because they had fewer representatives than their numbers warranted) and also those they *differed* on (because their districts were too large and undifferentiated). *Reynolds* therefore allowed a much fuller articulation of the diverse interests, including racial interests, in metropolitan areas, thereby providing a closer approximation to proportional representation of preferences.

17. It is especially curious that the "one person, one vote" opinions should have been phrased in such essentially individualistic terms, since the cases were brought by urban and suburban interests. The arguments in such cases as *Baker v. Carr* explicitly and repeatedly focused on the urban/rural nature of the discrimination, and California during Chief Justice Warren's very active political career had repeatedly held referenda on the state senate's horrendous malapportionment, which had been mandated by a 1926 initiative sponsored by the Farm Bureau Federation (see Kousser 1995b). Perhaps, as Lowenstein (1995, 23) suggests, Warren resorted to individualistic phraseology because he was defensive about the charge that the basis for the reapportionment cases was really the guarantee-of-republican-government clause, which is widely believed to be discredited as a basis for judicial action because it is so undefined and open-ended. The reference to racial dilution shows that *Reynolds* was not based wholly on an individualistic conception of voting.

It is also strange to characterize vote dilution as an individual right because, as

Gardner (1997, 920 n. 135) points out, in large electoral districts, no individual has an appreciable effect on an election by herself except in extremely unusual instances. If a constituency contains 100,000 voters, then each person's vote may be valued at $1/100,000$ or 0.00001. Suppose her constituency were reduced, through a more equitable apportionment, tenfold. Then the value would be $1/10,000$ or 0.0001—still very small and hardly noticeably different from before. But the power of the group of urban, or Republican, or African-American, or whatever voters might grow by many legislators after a more equitable apportionment. For instance, the Los Angeles County delegation in the forty-member California state senate grew from 1 in 1964 to 16 in 1965, representing quite a noticeable rise in the group's power.

18. To argue, as Bierstein (1995, 1490–91) does, that *Whitcomb v. Chavis* rested on an individual rather than a group view of voting rights requires one to overlook Justice White's treatment of political parties as groups, to dismiss the "participate . . . and to elect" language as "incoherent" (Bierstein 1995, 1495 n. 124), and to ignore the fact that Justice White two years before joined in the obviously group-oriented *Allen* decision and two years later wrote the majority opinion in the group-oriented *White v. Regester* case.

19. A "slating group" is a nonparty organization that endorses candidates in elections. The principal Dallas slating group in the 1960s and early 70s was controlled by major businesspersons.

20. Only 2 percent of the state's veterans were women, and only 2 percent of the state jobs that went to women were filled by veterans. The Court's printed opinion does not give complete statistics on the labor force in and out of state government in Massachusetts.

21. This was consistent with *Whitcomb v. Chavis* and, less clearly, with *White v. Regester*. But the *White* and *Zimmer* cases were usually interpreted by courts and civil rights lawyers to have turned solely on effect. See, e.g., *City of Mobile v. Bolden*, 71–73; McDonald 1989, 1261–63.

22. As this instance suggests, inquiries into the meaning or interpretation of a case or, more broadly, of an action are often not unrelated to inquiries into the motives of the framers or actors. The principal difference is that some rules of thumb, such as the "plain meaning rule," constrain the search for meanings, whereas the search for motives is much less structured by well-recognized apothegms.

23. In his misleading treatment of *Bolden*, Blumstein (1995, 539–41) contradictorily denies that Stewart thought that impact provided evidence of intent at all but insists that Stewart believed historical discrimination was irrelevant unless it could be shown to have an "ongoing impact." More generally, Blumstein appears to believe that *Bolden* was concerned only with distinctions between people on the basis of race, not with discrimination against them, which is ridiculous, because at-large elections do not discriminate *between* voters. If Blumstein's insistence that the Fourteenth Amendment bans only discriminations *between* voters were true, then all at-large election cases ought to have been dismissed at the outset.

24. For a similar criticism of Justice O'Connor's opinion in the capstone affirmative action case, see Marshall's dissent in City of *Richmond v. Croson* (1989), 746–47.

25. Congress assumed that it could go beyond what the *Bolden* plurality had said

were the limits of the Fifteenth Amendment by amending Section 2 of the VRA. Although the Supreme Court has not ruled directly on this issue since 1982, it and other courts have acted as if Congress had that power. As Chapter 8 below points out, in her concurring opinion in *Bush v. Vera* (1996), Justice O'Connor indicated that a majority of the Court believes that the amended Section 2 is constitutional.

26. Plaintiffs showed that the Alabama crimes provision also continued to have a racially disproportionate impact on African-Americans. My point is that the Court put greater emphasis on intent than impact in this case, while in the statutory rape case, it gave the legislature's purposes no weight.

27. For an argument that the plurality's standard was not unmanageable and a description of a simple method to make it work, see Kousser 1995a.

28. I assume that, in order to gain standing to sue, plaintiffs must in any event prove that they were adversely affected by the law or regulation or practice in question. What I mean to exclude is the necessity of showing that those who passed the law were openly bigoted against the plaintiffs' group.

29. The Court described the standard in *Arlington Heights* as a "but for" cause, concluding that but for racial considerations, the change would not have taken place. The more usual terminology for what appears to me to be the same concept outside the law is "necessary."

30. Although it is obvious that judges who draw districts may bias plans in favor of one party or another or one group or another, as the examples of Judge Nowlin in Texas and a series of judges in California show (see Kousser 1995b), courts are generally presumed to be nonpartisan and without racial bias (*Seamon v. Upham* [1982], 944; *Turner v. Arkansas* [1991], 580; *Burton v. Sheheen* [1992], 1345; *Emison v. Growe* [1992], 446). Because this presumption makes it unlikely that judges and their employees will be treated like other officials and be forced to testify and turn over documents in redistricting cases, any assessment of their intentions will necessarily have to rely almost completely on studies of impact. For example, when after the remand case of *Bush v. Vera*, Judge Edith Jones, the former chief counsel for the Texas Republican State Committee, denied that the judges considered the partisan consequences of their redrawing of nearly half of the state's congressional seats as a result of a successful challenge to three of them, her statement was unlikely to be assessed by deposing her and her staff; however, such tactics were applied to similar statements by the Texas politicians and operatives who worked on the original redistricting plans, statements that played important roles in Judge Jones's original opinion in *Vera*. As a consequence, more weight than usual should be placed on the fact that the Jones Plan significantly reduced the election chances of two moderate to liberal white Democrats, causing an official of the Republican Congressional Campaign Committee to predict major GOP gains (*AAS*, Aug. 7, 1996, A:1; *DMN*, Aug. 7, 1996, A:1; *HC*, Aug. 7, 1996, A:1). In the election, Democrats lost a Dallas-area seat that they had carried since 1981, but the popular incumbent in the Houston area seat survived, though he was forced into a runoff (Barone and Ujifusa 1998, 1351–52, 1396–98).

31. The most extensive discussions of such factors that I have found in a federal voting rights case are Judge William Wayne Justice's separate opinion in *Seamon v. Upham*

(1982), which in turn cites precedent cases in several fields of law, and Judge John Minor Wisdom's opinion of the court in *U.S. v. Marengo County Commission* (1984). Among Supreme Court opinions, *Arlington Heights, Rogers v. Lodge,* and a series of separate opinions by Justice Stevens list factors that overlap with my discussion here but do not usually develop their rationales in much detail. It is very odd that "conservative" judges, who have been more insistent than liberals on requiring proof of intent, have not discussed more fully just what is required in order to demonstrate it.

32. Voting rights lawyers who argue cases before such judges say they expect to lose because the judges' policy views prevent them from considering either laws or evidence dispassionately. Judge Eisele's view of the evidence about these electoral devices, for example, is captured in his statement that the policy of runoffs is "strong, laudable, reasonable and fair to all" (*Whitfield v. Democratic Party of Arkansas* [1988], 1386), as well as in his declaration in a later case that no amount of evidence of racially discriminatory intent or effect could possibly invalidate a majority vote provision, because majority rule is part of the notion of a "republican form of government" guaranteed by Article IV, Section 4 of the U.S. Constitution (*Jeffers v. Clinton* [1990], 610 [Eisele, dissenting]).

33. For examples of the many interests the Supreme Court has found "compelling," see Strauss 1986, 29 n. 78.

34. This is the opposite of the point made by Judge Frank Easterbrook (1983, 547–48), who suggests that because someone with control over the agenda may be able to manipulate a legislature into doing something, institutional intent is meaningless. On the contrary, the legislative intent then reduces to that of the person who controlled the agenda.

35. This pivotal group, or pivot, might also be conceived of as an especially powerful legislator who by dint of formal position or force of personality could set or substantially influence the setting of the legislature's agenda.

36. For a more detailed discussion, see Kousser 1991b, 716–19.

37. This example differs from the previous one in one subtle respect: In the *Arlington Heights* paradox, the legislature was nearly equally divided. The opinions of nearly all the members counted, and if one had not been decisive, another might have been. In the example about predominant motives, a singularly dominant individual determined the outcome, and the other members' opinions on the issue might be considered altogether irrelevant. If ninety-eight of ninety-nine members favored a bill out of racial concerns, but one all-powerful legislator had no racial concerns whatsoever, and the bill passed, then it is unclear whether a "predominant" criterion would judge that the bill had a racial purpose.

CHAPTER EIGHT

1. There is no basis in the printed opinion for Professor Katharine Butler's assertion (1996, 328) that the "clear implication" of the majority opinion "is that the Court would have found drawing districts along racial lines to be unconstitutional" if the evidence had been more extensive. If the seven majority justices had been of this view,

they could easily have remanded the case to the lower court for more hearings, joined the dissenters, or at least included a statement that they might have ruled otherwise if other facts had been before them.

2. Comparisons like Justice Douglas's and Professor Butler's (1996, 338–39) of minority opportunity districts with racial lists drawn independently of geography and strictly segregated by ethnicity are misleading because racial lists are not geographically based, minority opportunity districts are not strictly segregated, and there is no guarantee in minority opportunity districts that the candidate favored by most minority group members will be elected. Furthermore, under geographical districting, most minority group members will live in majority-Anglo districts and have a chance to influence the election of other candidates, probably Anglos.

3. In contrast to the Los Angeles County redistricting case, partisan and racial motives were not inextricably intertwined in *Wright*, because Republicans could have drawn the districts in ways that preserved the silk-stocking district without packing blacks into one district. For instance, they could have cut the northern Manhattan districts on north/south, rather than east/west lines or extended one or more of them into the Bronx. Powell's personal desire for reelection was tied to racial lines, but his actions deprived no racial group of representation roughly proportional to its population percentage, so under the pre–*Shaw v. Reno* standards, it had no discriminatory effect and was therefore legal.

4. The Rehnquist Court has so regularly overturned precedents that it has become conventional for "conservative" judges on every court level to cite dissents as precedents. See, e.g., *Croson*, 731, and *Adarand*, 2113, quoting Stevens dissent in *Fullilove v. Klutznick*; *Adarand*, 2111, 2116, quoting Stewart dissent in *Fullilove v. Klutznick*; *Adarand*, 2114, quoting O'Connor dissent in *Metro Broadcasting*; *Holder v. Hall*, 2593, 2598, quoting Frankfurter dissent in *Baker v. Carr* and Douglas dissent in *Wright v. Rockefeller*.

Rick Pildes's (1997, 2526–28) attempt to use the Douglas and Goldberg dissents in *Wright* and the Brennan concurrence in *UJO* to deflect criticism of *Shaw v. Reno* (1993) is unconvincing, because he does not note the subtleties of the earlier opinions or sufficiently emphasize the factual differences between *Wright* and *Shaw* (for instance, an 86 percent nonwhite district in the former versus a 57 percent black district in the latter).

5. Four Brooklyn districts, two of which divided largely African-American areas, were the focus of the district court decision in *Wells* (*NYT*, May 11, 1967, 42).

6. Justice Marshall, who would surely have agreed with the majority in general, took no part in the case.

7. Butler (1996, 329) not only fails to mention Rehnquist's participation in the prevailing opinion in her textual discussion but misrepresents White's opinion by directly denying that this section of it existed: "The Court specifically did not address whether, in the absence of Section 5 of Voting Rights Act, a state could employ race-based districts to enhance minority voting strength."

8. Apparently because the lower court decisions preceded the Supreme Court's announcement of a "non-retrogression" standard in *Beer*, the record was devoid of facts about the nonwhite percentages in particular districts in the previous reapportionment, which had taken place in 1966. But instead of ordering a new trial to determine

whether the state had gone beyond non-retrogression, as Chief Justice Burger called for in dissent, White merely announced that the plaintiffs had presented no evidence of this fact. White's maneuver may have reflected, as Burger surmised, an uneasiness on the part of some justices with *Beer*'s non-retrogression standard, which seemed at odds with the words of Section 5. *Beer* was, after all, a 4–3 decision, with Stevens not participating and White, Marshall, and Brennan in dissent. Further facts might have forced the Court to revisit *Beer* and have further fractured the majority.

9. Even the staid *Congressional Quarterly* described the Republican tactics as "Machiavellian" (Congressional Quarterly 1993a, 201).

10. As Prof. Cass Sunstein has explained, this is essentially the same as saying that the plaintiffs have no standing to sue, even though a 1970 case created a legalistic distinction between these two grounds for dismissal (Sunstein 1993, 52).

11. Likewise, in a later brief to the U.S. Supreme Court, the chief counsel of the Republican National Committee attacked the districts because of "the diversity of interests and communities" in each (Hess 1994, 8).

12. Voting rights cases heard by special three-judge federal courts are appealed directly to the U.S. Supreme Court without passing through the intermediate circuit courts of appeal.

13. In his brief to the Supreme Court in *Shaw v. Hunt* (1996), Everett shamelessly castigated the North Carolina legislature for not attempting to establish districts with smaller percentages of African-Americans than it had and claimed to believe that racial bloc voting and racial appeals were things of the past in North Carolina. As proof of the decline of racial bloc voting in North Carolina, he cited the election of one black Republican legislator in a majority-white district in North Carolina and two black Republican congressmen from Connecticut and Oklahoma (Everett 1995b, 30, 41–42).

14. As evidence of the injury suffered by white constituents, Everett later referred to Twelfth District congressman Mel Watt's statement that the *Shaw* litigation was based on "racist assumptions" such as that black members of Congress could not properly represent white constituents. According to Everett, Watt also injured whites by refusing to form "interracial coalitions" (Everett 1995b, 44 n. 42). Everett did not call for dissolving the districts of all white candidates who did not work to form interracial coalitions. In fact, Watt did seek white support, and won that of the only two plaintiffs in the case who lived in his district.

15. Along with his son, Robinson Everett was one of the five plaintiffs in the case.

16. By the time of *Shaw v. Hunt* (1996), Everett had apparently changed his mind, contending that Congress must have meant to mandate compactness for all districts (Everett 1995b, 38). He did not mention the fact that Congress dropped a compactness requirement from its reapportionment law after 1911 and has repeatedly rejected attempts to reinstitute it since (Martis 1982, 7, 11; Congressional Quarterly 1989, 50).

17. Although there has never been a good empirical study on the subject, Republican and Democratic redistricting experts agree that because the most loyal Democrats (blacks, Hispanics, Jews, and lower-income voters in general) seem to be more geographically segregated than Republican voters are, compact districts would tend to minimize the number of seats Democrats win (Lowenstein and Steinberg 1985).

18. On Helms's 1990 campaign and the racial impact of his "wringing hands" television ad, see Prysby 1996 and Kern and Just 1995.

19. Butler (1996, 334, 357) has said that because the racial impact of the provisions in such cases was "clear," judges' statements about the need to prove effect are dicta, a strange standard under which good evidence invalidates explicit law. In an earlier article (1995, 602), she had remarked that what was unconstitutional in these cases was the "impact on minorities."

20. The question put to the parties was this: "Whether a state legislature's intent to comply with the Voting Rights Act and the Attorney General's interpretation thereof precludes a finding that the legislature's congressional redistricting plan was adopted with invidious discriminatory intent where the legislature did not accede to the plan suggested by the Attorney General but instead developed its own" (*Shaw v. Barr*, U.S. 1992, 653–54). This was an uninformed question, because under the VRA, the attorney general does not "suggest" plans. But if the question had ended after the second use of the word "intent," it could have been restated accurately as: "Should *UJO* be overruled?"

21. In three leading cases that are prominently cited in *Shaw I* and its successors, the Court majority derided the goal of correcting "societal discrimination" as a justification for affirmative action programs (*Wygant v. Jackson Bd. Of Educ.* [1986], 274; *City of Richmond v. Croson* [1989], 499; *Adarand Constructors, Inc. v. Pena* [1995], 2118–19). By contrast, in *Shaw* the majority justified striking down the recognition of racial communities in the same way as all other interests in redistricting on the grounds of speculations that such recognition would lead to vague societal evils. Why general charges of past discrimination should fail to support legislative action when equally general projections of future bad outcomes should vindicate judicial action, the Court did not explain.

22. The most heavily African-American congressional district in the South in 1992, the Alabama Seventh, had a 67.5 percent black population (Congressional Quarterly 1993c, xviii). In her haste to defend every aspect of *Shaw I*, Butler (1996, 356 n. 150) terms 25 percent black districts more "integrated" than 35 percent white districts, at least in a state in which the population is 25 percent African-American.

23. " 'When *I* use a word', Humpty Dumpty said, in rather a scornful tone, 'it means just what I choose it to mean—neither more nor less.'

" 'The question is', said Alice, 'whether you *can* make words mean so many different things.'

" 'The question is', said Humpty Dumpty, 'which is to be master—that's all.' " (Carroll 1939, 196)

24. O'Connor also contradictorily announced that Adam Clayton Powell's district from *Wright v. Rockefeller* (1964), which Justice Douglas had castigated as having very irregular boundaries, was not too bizarre, while she also approvingly quoted Douglas's rhetorical denunciations of racial gerrymandering (*Shaw v. Reno* [1993], 2826–28).

25. See Altman 1998, chap. 3, for a survey of districting throughout the country's history, showing that contiguity, compactness, and equal population are *not* traditional districting principles.

26. Butler (1995, 602) has suggested that noncompact districts can have no legitimate purpose, that the only purpose of noncompact minority opportunity districts must be to have a racial impact and that, therefore, plaintiffs in such cases need not prove a discriminatory impact, as they would have to do under the standards of *Washington v. Davis* (1976) and its progeny. The challenged actions in *Washington v. Davis* and other cases, such as administering standardized tests, no doubt had legitimate purposes. The troubles with this argument are that it assumes the conclusion—that there cannot be "legitimate" purposes for ugly districts—and that it ignores the history of gerrymandering in the country. Why should a practice long used by whites and which continues to be used by whites with the approval of the Court be illegal when it is employed in behalf of minorities?

27. More recently, Pildes (1997, 2534–35) has defended O'Connor's emphasis on compactness by suggesting that critics would not accept noncontiguous districts or racial registers that identified, for instance, all African-Americans in a state and let them vote in set-aside districts. In fact, as Altman 1998, chap. 3, shows, there have been many examples of noncontiguous congressional districts in American history, so contiguity is not an unambiguous "traditional districting principle." The "racial register" example is a traditional law school "imaginary horrible" that no one who favors geographical districting, as I do, needs to confront.

28. To Butler (1995, 601) and probably to the *Shaw* majority, it does not matter whether the "stereotype" that African-Americans, non-Cuban Latinos, and whites are politically largely distinct is true. Thus, Butler (1995, 604) contrasts the stability of racial divisions with what political scientists still consider the strong differentiations between identifiers in the two major political parties. To the radicals, the Constitution implicitly prohibits legislatures from acting on empirically well-established facts that even the majority justices and their supporters often implicitly recognize.

29. Of course, the charge proves too much, for since every voter must be "placed" in some district and someone will be a minority, in some sense, nearly everywhere, then nearly every district might be ruled unconstitutional, unless Butler does not mean to apply the criterion to white-majority districts. As roll call votes in Congress show, blacks and Latinos in Republican or conservative Democratic districts are ignored to a much larger extent than are Anglos in minority opportunity districts.

30. At least one radical opponent of affirmative action, Jim Sleeper, has called for the abolition of racial or ethnic categories in the census on this basis (*LAT*, Aug. 31, 1997, M:2).

31. It is possible—and *Bush v. Vera* (1996), discussed below, implies that it is true—that Justice O'Connor initially favored interpreting *Shaw*-type claims as Pildes believes. It has also been suggested that Pildes rationalized O'Connor's incompletely formed position in *Shaw v. Reno* and that she later endorsed his formula. But as later cases show, Justices Kennedy, Thomas, Scalia, and probably Rehnquist favored other interpretations of *Shaw*. At the very least, O'Connor was ambiguous in *Shaw* in order to forge a majority for her opinion.

Even if O'Connor by 1996 believed that the "racial gerrymandering" cases turn on district appearance rather than intent (even Richard Pildes, who most strongly argues this view, notes anomalies in her position) and even if she were the swing vote on the issue (she has always swung toward the same side since 1993), it seems odd to allow this minority of one, in a series of very ambiguous opinions, to define the true meaning of *Shaw* and its successors (Pildes 1997). As I have argued elsewhere (Kousser 1988a), the ideal point of the median voter should not be assumed to reflect the intent of a deliberative body. But even if the racial gerrymandering cases privilege compactness, they do not necessarily do so for the reasons O'Connor sets out, as I argue below.

Increasingly committed to a very strict reading of the Court's messy "racial gerrymandering" opinions, Pildes is forced to pick and choose, chide, and sometimes sidestep statements that do not fit his interpretation, as in his remark that "*Shaw* does not recognize an individual right against excessive racial classification, its own language notwithstanding" (1997, 2544).

32. All passages quoted are from Justice O'Connor's opinion in *Shaw v. Reno*, with page numbers in brackets after the passage quoted; italics have been added. Internal citations to *Village of Arlington Heights v. Metro. Hous. Dev. Corp.* (1977), 266; *Gomillion v. Lightfoot* (1960), 341; and *Wright v. Rockefeller* (1964), 59, have been omitted.

33. It is extremely ironic that in equal protection law the triad of strict scrutiny, compelling state interest, and narrow tailoring should be said to derive originally from the Japanese exclusion cases of 1943–44, not only because the Court in those cases allowed that massive deprivation of rights to proceed but also because the U.S. government almost certainly could have proven, on the basis of information that it made public then, that it had a compelling interest and that its actions were narrowly tailored (Irons 1983). The compelling interest was preventing a potential Japanese invasion from being assisted by people the government would have claimed to be suspicious, and the action was tempered by being aimed only at Japanese-Americans on the West Coast, where such an invasion would have been most likely. In other words, the test by itself would not even have outlawed the paradigm case it is aimed at, unless the Court had been willing to contest the government's presentation of facts. Thus, the classic formulation of modern equal protection theory rests not on a formal theoretical structure, but on the judiciary's willingness to get at the underlying facts. In equal protection law, it is facts, not theories, that really matter.

34. "Intermediate scrutiny," applied in equal protection law to gender discrimination, requires less weighty justification, while under a "rational basis" test almost any plausible reason that a state may give for a policy will suffice. In another irony, affirmative action for women, including explicit quotas and avowed intentions to provide separate but equal programs, has been held to be legal, on the grounds that gender discrimination was never so bad as to make gender always a suspect category (*Brown University v. Cohen [1996]*). In other words, because women have suffered *less* than blacks, programs to guarantee gender equality can use tools that the "conservative" majority of the Supreme Court would never allow to be used in efforts to promote racial or ethnic equity.

35. The extensive evidence of racial bloc voting and minority cohesion produced for the *Gingles* litigation was not formally before the Court at the time of the Court's

deliberations. This might well have satisfied O'Connor, as she implied in *Shaw v. Reno*, 2831.

36. As Parker 1995, 48–51, points out, *Beer* itself allowed a denial of preclearance not only for retrogressive changes but for those that violated the Constitution; and the Report of the Senate Committee on the Judiciary insisted that the Department of Justice should not preclear any changes that would violate Section 2 (U.S. Senate 1982b, 12 n. 31). Department of Justice regulations 28 C.F.R. Sec. 51.52 and Sec. 51.55(a)(2) prohibited preclearance under these circumstances until the Supreme Court's 1997 decision in *Reno v. Bossier Parish School Board*. For a discussion of the reasoning behind them, see Days 1992, 57. Thus, O'Connor again distorted both the *Beer* precedent and congressional intent.

O'Connor did not consider that choosing not to draw a minority opportunity district or choosing not to draw one unless it met standards of compactness or other principles that white districts did not have to meet might reflect discriminatory purposes and thus be denied preclearance under the purpose prong of Section 5. To her in this case, Section 5 was practically reduced to retrogressive effects.

37. This phrase drawn from *UJO*, the only time O'Connor relied on that earlier decision, after ignoring its contrary thrust throughout the rest of her opinion, was rebuffed by the author of the prevailing opinion in *UJO*, Justice White, who declared that "district irregularities . . . have no bearing on whether the plan ultimately is found to violate the Constitution" (*Shaw v. Reno* (1993), 2834, 2841).

38. In *U.S. v. Paradise* (1987), 196–201, Justice O'Connor, joined by Chief Justice Rehnquist and Justice Scalia, demonstrated exquisite concern for a tiny number of white Alabama state troopers who might be passed over for promotions in an attempt to remedy decades of perhaps the most intransigent discrimination by any state agency in the country against African-Americans. Black exclusion from office does not seem to elicit the same response from her.

39. White's opinions for the court included *Swann v. Adams* (1967), *Whitcomb v. Chavis* (1971), *White v. Regester* (1973), *Gaffney v. Cummings* (1973), *White v. Weiser* (1973), *UJO* (1977), and *Rogers v. Lodge* (1982), as well as notable dissents in *Wells v. Rockefeller* (1969), *City of Mobile v. Bolden* (1980), and *Karcher v. Daggett* (1983).

40. I do not think it is possible to suppress consideration of the largest cleavage in American society for the last 375 years, especially since race is so closely connected to the political fortunes of the people doing the redistricting or to their bosses. Across the country, the 1991 reapportionment processes were probably the most open in our history and the rules for drawing districts the most explicit and fair in avoiding discrimination against any person or group. In the wake of *Shaw* and its successors, the fear that openly race-conscious redistricting will legally endanger a plan may inhibit redistricters from using and publicizing racial statistics and from openly considering the racial consequences of different apportionment schemes, but defenders of minority rights are unlikely to surrender altogether. Instead, they will have to resort to clumsy and inefficient subterfuges. Is this progress? Is a charade that employs proxies of race such as Democratic registration and poverty to set up black and Latino dis-

tricts or to pack minorities into districts really preferable to honest public discussions not conducted in coded language?

41. On the deep difficulties with indeterminant benchmarks in post–New Deal constitutional law, see Seidman and Tushnet 1996, 72–90, 112–16.

42. I ignore, as Souter did, the particular geographic distribution of the population, the size of the legislature, and the size of the relevant groups.

43. It was conceivably significant that in the Carrollton case the circuit court found discriminatory intent in the adoption of the single-commissioner form of government, while in Bleckley County there was a contention of discriminatory motive only in the maintenance of the system. Both cases turned primarily on discriminatory effect.

44. The stark contrast between the 1994 and 1995 decisions suggests that the Supreme Court may still be "follow[ing] the 'illection' returns," in the famous phrase of nineteenth-century humorist Finley Peter Dunne. Perhaps the Republican tide in the 1994 congressional elections emboldened the Court's revolutionaries too. Suggestive of the climate of opinion at the time is the fact that the day the Court heard oral arguments in *Miller* and *Hays*, newspapers reported that President Clinton had just held his first press conference in eight months, a press conference at which he announced plaintively that despite the 1994 elections, the president's place in the constitutional order "gives me relevance." In what was interpreted as a deliberate slight to a badly wounded president, only one of the three major commercial television networks even bothered to broadcast the press conference, the same coverage that the triumphant House speaker, Newt Gingrich, had attracted, almost unprecedentedly, in his press conference the week before (*NYT*, Apr. 19, 1995, A:1).

45. Harold Ford was elected in 1974 from a Memphis district that may well have been majority black by that time but which had not been according to the 1970 census figures. No ethnic group held a majority in Barbara Jordan's Houston district in 1972, but fewer people were white than black. In 1996, three African-American incumbents previously elected from heavily black districts successfully sought reelection in majority-white districts that were redrawn by federal district courts after *Miller*: Corrine Brown of Florida and Cynthia McKinney and Sanford Bishop of Georgia. The redrawn black minority opportunity districts in Texas, which were 37.1 and 31.9 percent white, also reelected black incumbents. African-Americans constituted the plurality group in each of these Texas districts.

46. As explained later in this chapter, Justice O'Connor's interpretation of nonretrogression in *Bush v. Vera* would have made it illegal to raise the black percentage in the Fifth District at all, much less by Wilson's comparatively liberal 7 percent, unless the shape of the district met O'Connor's undefined aesthetic criteria.

47. Under *Bush v. Vera* (1996), both *Busbee* and the State of Georgia's action that led to it would presumably be illegal, because it is now unconstitutional to raise the minority percentage in an existing minority opportunity district and claim Section 5 as a justification. On the other hand, if the resulting district appeared compact to Justice O'Connor, it might be ruled constitutional whatever its ethnic proportions.

48. The Supreme Court had ruled, e.g., in *Perkins v. Mathews* (1971), 385, and *McCain*

v. Lybrand (1984), 246–47, that only the district court of the District of Columbia could overrule a Section 5 objection.

49. Kennedy's casual discussion of whether African-Americans in the Eleventh District formed a community of interest—expert witnesses on both sides had presented reports on the issue to the district court—seemed to imply that he believed that a racial minority might form a community of interest that could constitutionally be recognized by redistricters. Believing the plaintiffs' expert, Kennedy concluded that African-Americans in Atlanta and Savannah were "worlds apart in culture." This has given some observers hope that legislators in 2001 might build a community-of-interest case for drawing minority opportunity districts (Malone 1997). But in contradiction to this view, Kennedy in succeeding pages referred to the view that blacks might form a community of interest as a priori "offensive and demeaning," and he contrasted "actual shared interests" to "racial considerations," implying that empirical proof that such a community existed was irrelevant, because recognizing such a community would be unconstitutional (*Miller v. Johnson*, 2484, 2486, 2488). Although the contradiction between these two views may provide hope for lawyers, forced to rely on scraps of language when logic fails, they do not offer either side a very firm foundation.

50. Defenders of the *Shaw* line of decisions unaccountably also confuse "sole" with "predominant." Thus, in consecutive sentences, Butler (1996, 337) equates "the primary purpose" with "no purpose other than."

51. Whether compactness and respect for political subdivisions are in fact racially neutral is an empirical question that depends on the spatial distribution of various populations, the relationship between that distribution and municipal and other boundary lines, and the number of districts. An extremely clustered population that could be packed into a few districts might be hurt badly by a compactness standard, as might a population with smaller, widely separated clusters (Altman 1998, chap. 3). The point is that formally race-neutral criteria may have racially biased effects, and whether they do or not is an empirical, not a formal, legal question. Justice O'Connor noted in *Shaw v. Reno* (1993), 2826, that district lines are formally neutral ("A reapportionment statute typically does not classify persons at all; it classifies tracts of land, or addresses"), but the "conservative" majority has not stopped there. Instead, it has investigated the reality beneath the formalism. That it has not applied the same skepticism toward compactness and the preservation of political subdivisions is yet another example of the "conservatives'" double standards.

52. The reasoning is much more straightforward than is suggested by Butler's caricature of it as circular (Butler 1996, 350).

53. Blumstein (1995, 568–72), who was harshly critical of the 1982 amendments to Section 2 as an "affirmative race-based entitlement" during congressional testimony in that year, later claimed, in effect, that he had prevailed and that Section 2 did not accomplish what he had warned that it would. His is not a unique stance. In 1866, Democrats in and out of Congress shouted that the Fourteenth Amendment would require integrated schools, churches, graveyards, and marriage beds. After the amendment passed, they denied that it had any effect whatsoever.

54. The Thernstroms' lack of a citation to Canon's readily available study is just one of a very large number of examples of their failure to confront opposing facts or interpretations. Repeatedly, they cite articles or parts of articles that lend support to a point they are making but not others in the same article, book, journal issue, or hearing that tend to undermine their position. For examples, see chapter 16 on voting rights in Thernstrom and Thernstrom 1997, notes 20, 50, 52, 53, 54, 56, 69, 71, 82, 88, 90, 92, 97, 105, 116, 117, 119.

55. That such a standing doctrine, even if not extended to other areas of the law, would greatly expand opportunities for lawyers and for judicial intrusion into redistricting is more certain than that it would lead in the direction of a "colorblind" society.

56. As Justice Stevens pointed out in his dissent in *Vera* (1996), 1984 n. 22, the fact that eliminating the "tentacles" that lowered the district's compactness score would have *raised* its black percentage signaled that O'Connor's emphasis on compactness undercut the *Miller* "predominant motive" standard.

57. Pildes (1997, 2547) has said he believes that *De Witt* might represent "the best indication of how the Court will apply *Shaw* in the coming years," even though three-fifths of the *Shaw* majority denounced the compactness-as-safe-haven interpretation of *Shaw*. Pildes ignores the widely discussed partisan context of the California redistricting (Kousser 1995c) and the facts that the special masters did not even claim that the districts were geographically compact and that no evidence of their shape was on the record. He also misrepresents the sequence of events, saying that the special masters "interpreted *Shaw*" as requiring them to comply with traditional districting principles. In fact, they did their redistricting before *Shaw* was decided, and the first principle of redistricting that they discussed in their report clearly implied the maximization of the number of "functionally compact" minority opportunity districts in order to stave off any possible challenges under Section 2 of the VRA (*Wilson v. Eu* [1992], 748–49).

58. Preserving incumbents' positions had been ruled a sufficient reason for deviating from strict population equality and for irregularities in district boundaries in *Burns v. Richardson* (1966), 89 n. 16; *White v. Weiser* (1973), 791, a Texas case; and *Karcher v. Daggett* (1983), 740. Butler (1996, 345–48) ignores these cases and most of American redistricting history when she contends that incumbent and partisan protection cannot serve as reasons that would defeat a *Miller* predominant motive inquiry because otherwise "future redistrictings will be driven entirely by the self interests of legislators."

59. The districts that Judge Jones approved after *Vera* was remanded to her illustrate the point well. She reduced the black and Latino percentage, and thus those groups' influence, in two marginally Democratic districts, the Fifth and the Twenty-fifth, in the Dallas and Houston areas, respectively. Although the popular, moderate incumbent Democrat in the Twenty-fifth survived when the Republican Party splintered in the primary, Republicans captured the Fifth, Democratic since 1981, replacing the most liberal Anglo Democrat in the Texas delegation with a conservative Republican and reducing the influence of blacks, of whom 97 percent in Dallas were

Democrats, to zero (*AAS*, Aug. 7, 1996, A:8; Barone and Ujifusa 1997, 1351–52, 1396–98). Republican crusades against legal and illegal immigrants, in which racism often poked through a surface of stern law-and-order slogans, has solidified the allegiance of Latinos in the Southwest to the Democratic Party.

60. It seems especially odd that Chief Justice Rehnquist would join in this assertion of O'Connor's, in view of his statement in *Batson v. Kentucky* (1986), 1744–45, that "the use of group affiliations, such as age, race, or occupation, as a 'proxy' for potential juror partiality, based on the assumption or belief that members of one group are more likely to favor defendants who belong to the same group, has long been accepted as a legitimate basis for the State's exercise of peremptory challenges."

61. If race were used as a proxy to leach Democrats from marginally Democratic districts into safely Republican districts, racial bloc voting in a state would probably increase. That the current Supreme Court majority believes such a move is constitutional is indicated by its refusal to review the districts that Judge Jones drew in the *Vera* remand.

62. In his dissent in *Vera* (1996), 1980 n. 12, Justice Stevens playfully noted the contradiction between the "race as a proxy" argument and the "apartheid" rhetoric used in *Shaw I*.

63. The brevity of O'Connor's treatment of Houston made her failure to mention the election of an Anglo in a "Latino district" less obvious than it would have been otherwise. Justice Stevens, who discussed the evidence in more detail, certainly noted it (*Vera* [1996], 1976 n. 6).

64. Although they continued to believe that the boundaries of all thirty Texas congressional districts were "drawn exclusively to achieve the desired racial composition," the plaintiffs in *Vera* did not appeal Judge Jones's decision that the other twenty-seven districts they had contested had insufficiently irregular boundaries to be unconstitutional, although they "respectfully disagree[d]" with it. Apparently, the fact that the same attorney handled both the Louisiana and Texas cases strained the plaintiffs' legal resources (Hurd 1994a, 11 n. 16; Hurd 1995, 13, 21 n. 22). The question of whether using race as a proxy was unconstitutional per se was thus not properly before the Supreme Court in *Vera*.

65. O'Connor's discussion of compactness was further confused because it mixed two notions of compactness, one that emphasizes the length of the perimeter of the district and another based on the length and width of the district, regardless of its boundary squiggles. By the second definition, it would be especially egregious to invalidate only the three districts in question, since they were all in densely populated urban areas and had much shorter axes than more rural districts, majority Latino ones as well as majority Anglo (*Vera* [1996], 1954–55).

66. Rationality review asks only if the law is rationally related to a legitimate governmental goal (Tribe 1978, 994–96).

67. No justice responded to the plaintiffs' contention that Section 2 was "irrelevant" unless the State had shown that minorities were "essentially shut out of the political process" by first redistricting without paying attention to vRA considerations and then losing in court. Only when it was crafting a remedy for a judicially deter-

mined violation, the argument went, could the State legally consider complying with the VRA (Hurd 1995, 46–47).

68. Under a North Carolina law in effect in 1992, a candidate who received 40 percent of the votes in a primary election became the party nominee. In the first primary in the First Congressional District in 1992, a white candidate finished ahead with 39 percent of the vote, eventually losing to African-American Eva Clayton in a runoff (Hodgkiss 1994, 18). Abigail Thernstrom (1995, 917–18) misrepresents the facts when she says of the post-1991 minority opportunity districts that they in effect "have a sign posted on them: 'No white candidates need apply.'"

69. I owe this point to Dan Lowenstein. It further undercuts Pildes's (1997, 2543–44) attempt to constrain O'Connor's position to one of "expressive harm" connected only to "extremely bizarre" minority opportunity districts.

70. Souter did not even contemplate the technical problems involved in compactness measures. Which one should be adopted and why? How high does the correlation with race have to be before a particular compactness threshold counts as unconstitutional? Nor did he explore the difficulties in a "computerized process of color-blind randomness." Which process? What nonrandom "traditional districting principles"—such as contiguity, equal population, respect for jurisdictional boundaries, partisan considerations, and incumbent protection—would be built into it? What defines whether a tolerably small deviation from any or all of these principles has been reached? Technical fixes in this area are much more complicated than many people imagine (Altman 1998, chap. 5). Similarly, when Pildes (1997) chooses Souter's third alternative, a quantitative compactness standard, he ignores the problems of settling on one measure of it.

71. Citing *Hays*, the chief justice granted standing to challenge the Twelfth District to the two plaintiffs who lived in it. It was especially ironic to give Ruth Shaw and Melvin Shimm standing based indirectly, through *Hays*, on "representational harm," since both of them voted for African-American Mel Watt for Congress in the Twelfth District (Everett 1995c, 6 n. 14; Speas 1995, 31). Because none of the five plaintiffs lived in the rural First District, the opinion did not concern itself with that district.

72. Rehnquist assumed without actually deciding the question that an intention to comply with the VRA, properly interpreted, would constitute a compelling state interest. As in *Miller*, the chief justice said, "we do not reach that question" (*Shaw v. Hunt* [1983], 1903).

73. Even Justice Scalia at least used to disagree with this position, though he seems to have hardened his position more recently (*City of Richmond v. Croson* [1989], 524; *Adarand Constructors, Inc. v. Pena* [1995], 2118–19).

74. This position, which echoed that in the North Carolina Republicans' brief (Farr 1995a, 41–43), was said to follow from *Gingles*, but it did not. *Gingles* challenged an electoral structure, at-large elections in urban counties with significant proportions of blacks, and asked for single-member districts as a remedy. It would have been absurd to remedy an at-large system in Raleigh, for instance, by drawing a minority opportunity district in an eastern North Carolina rural county. Furthermore, if such a rural district had initially been drawn, it would not have been relevant to whether

the at-large system elsewhere had a discriminatory effect. By contrast, in a prospective challenge to the district lines in a system composed entirely of single-member districts, the statewide percentage of minority opportunity districts is clearly relevant to an assessment of discriminatory intent as well as effect. Because there would be no distinctive electoral structure to focus on, in a Section 2 case about single-member districts it would matter much less just where a minority opportunity district were drawn. The North Carolina Republicans and the chief justice applied *Gingles* to single-member districts much too mechanically.

75. In light of the strongly partisan actions of Republican federal judges such as James Nowlin and Edith Jones of Texas in redistricting cases, the districts that a judge might draw as a remedy for a Section 2 or constitutional violation should not be viewed as likely to be dispassionate creations.

76. When *Shaw II* was remanded to the district court, after North Carolina had held primary elections and little more than four months before the 1996 general election, the judges refused a request from a "colorblind" Republican office seeker to throw out three majority-black state legislative districts as well as a request from Robinson Everett to redraw or force the state legislature to redraw all the state's congressional districts. With the state House controlled by Republicans and the state Senate by Democrats, the legislature had enough trouble trying to agree on a budget. By the same 2-1 split as in previous *Shaw* cases, the judges put off the redistricting in order to "avoid undue disruption of state electoral processes." In March 1997, the legislators passed a plan that protected all incumbents and was predicted to preserve the 6-6 partisan split in the congressional delegation that the Democrats had gained in the 1996 elections. Among the incumbents seemingly protected were African-Americans Eva Clayton, whose district was reduced from 57 percent to 50 percent black, and Mel Watt, whose district went from 57 percent to 47 percent; in both cases, the new percentages were probably enough to elect well-financed, well-known incumbents if growing numbers of whites voted in the Republican primary and a quarter to a third of white Democrats stayed loyal to the party nominee in the general election. The First and Twelfth Districts retained their cores but lost some of their perimeter-extending tentacles. Black politicians whose chances to replace Watt or Clayton had been diminished joined "colorblind" whites critical of all minority opportunity districts and of treating black incumbents like white incumbents in opposition to the bipartisan compromise. Republican judge Richard Vorhees approved the plan along with the two Democratic judges, J. Dickson Phillips and W. Earl Britt. Since none of the *Shaw* plaintiffs lived in the redrawn Twelfth District, they lacked standing, under the ruling in *Hays v. Louisiana*, to challenge the legislatively redrawn districts (*RNO*, July 4, 31, Dec. 29, 1996; March 26, 28, May 22, June 10, Sept. 16, 1997).

But after the dismissal by Phillips, Britt, and Vorhees, Robinson Everett signed on with new plaintiffs and renewed his suit, challenging six of the state's twelve congressional districts as racial gerrymanders, before a much more sympathetic three-judge panel consisting of Vorhees, former Jesse Helms staff member Terrence Boyle, and Democrat Sam Ervin III. Thus, *Hays*'s illogical standing rule facilitated forum shopping by opponents of minority opportunity districts. In a brief order issued little more than a month before the scheduled primary date of May 5, 1998, the new court ruled that the truncated Twelfth District was still illegal, because it was constructed with race predominantly in mind, and it gave the legislature only five days to redraw the state's districts. The two Republicans, Vorhees and Boyle, concurred in the opinion, written by Boyle, while Ervin dissented. The decision threw the state's election plans into what election officials, who had already finished preparations for the May primaries, described as "chaos." While some Republican members of Congress worried that a court-ordered redistricting would collapse the Twelfth District and increase the number of black Democrats in their districts, the state Republican Party looked forward to gaining new seats in such a plan. The Supreme Court rejected the state's attempt to block the Boyle panel's decision from going into effect (*RNO*, Dec. 5, 1997; Jan. 10, Feb. 5, Mar. 17, 18, Apr. 4–7, 1998).

77. After *Miller*, the Republicans claimed that Tilling's notes were irrelevant to the question of intent because there were changes between his original plan and the one finally adopted and that the Board majority's report was irrelevant because it was a rationalization in response to the lower court's first ruling (Goodman 1996a, 3–6, 14–15). But the changes were relatively slight, and courts have considered similar documents from other states probative of intentions.

78. I have argued elsewhere (Kousser 1993) that racially polarized voting is a relative, not an absolute, concept; that courts should recognize that it is possible to discriminate against minorities by refusing to form "influence districts"; and that there is no logical "bright line" between influence districts and "control districts," because the line shifts with the degree of racial bloc voting. A Supreme Court more interested than its current majority is in protecting the rights of ethnic minorities and in creating the conditions for integrating political life would develop these fairly obvious observations, instead of cutting them off with mechanical formulas.

79. There were actually three post-*Shaw I* opinions in *Quilter II*, and their progression partially confirms Republican charges of partisan Democratic motives. When the second Democrat on the original three-judge panel, John W. Peck, died, he was replaced by Anthony Celebreeze, another Democrat and a former cabinet member in the Kennedy and Johnson administrations. After the panel's first opinion in *Quilter II*, issued on April 28, 1995, Celebreeze retired, but Sixth Circuit chief judge Gilbert Merritt, also a Democrat, allowed Celebreeze to continue on the *Quilter* case. The April 28 opinion, issued before the Supreme Court announced the "predominant motive" standard in *Miller*, merely called race "a substantial and motivating factor" in the drawing of the Ohio legislative districts. A slightly altered opinion on May 26, 1995, concluded that the State had ignored the Ohio constitution's provision in Article XI, Section 7(D) requiring the Redistricting Board to preserve existing districts insofar as possible, an arguable violation of a "traditional districting principle" that strengthened the opinion's connection with *Shaw I*. After *Miller* was issued on June 29, 1995, Judges Jones and Celebreeze on August 11, 1995 issued a third, more substantially revised version of *Quilter II* to bring it into congruence with the new standard announced in *Miller*. Celebreeze was eventually replaced on the panel by Judge Karen Nelson Moore, a Clinton appointee dubbed a "quota judge" by right-wing Republican activist Clint Bolick (Goodman 1996b, 6–9, 17–18; Bolick 1996).

80. Judge Douglas D. Dowd Jr., the Republican dissenter on the lower court, subjected Ohio's action to strict scrutiny but, without any detailed discussion or the application of any objective criteria, concluded that the districts were not "bizarre" and that an intent to draw compact districts constituted a compelling state interest (Goodman 1996b, 52a–56a). In *Voinovich v. Ferguson* (1992), the Ohio Supreme Court ruled that the Apportionment Board had followed some of the redistricting principles mandated by the Ohio state constitution and that when those principles conflicted, the Board was the sole judge of which ones to abide by. In other words, traditional districting principles were anything the Board did.

81. On the partisan nature of the "Special Master's" plan in California, see Kousser 1995b.

82. Pildes (1997, 2550–51) has proposed a standard that expresses the inequality of *Shaw* perfectly: that minority opportunity districts, but not white districts, be subject to a specific quantitative compactness standard. He does not specify one or explain how such patent racial inequity could be squared with the equal protection clause. In fact, his reductio ad absurdum (2554) might well be read as a subtle effort to abandon *Shaw* and impose compactness requirements on all districts or at least to create what he calls a new "redistricting culture" in which all districts would become compact.

83. Moderate Republicans Souter and Stevens seem to take their positions in spite of partisan considerations, not because of them.

84. It is only by gliding over the surface of the Supreme Court's opinions and completely ignoring their partisan implications as well as by disregarding the voting records of conservative southern Democrats that the Thernstroms (1997, 483) could possibly make their mischievous suggestion that *Shaw I* and its successors "may well have been a political gift to black voters."

85. The judges' academic allies follow a similar distorting course. Thus, after citing a series of elections in which 25 to 43 percent of whites are estimated to have crossed over to vote for black candidates, Thernstrom and Thernstrom (1997, 296) admit that "of course race determines how *some* whites vote *some* of the time" (italics added). But even their own evidence, which is based on a set of elections carefully culled to provide examples that seem to sustain their point, would be more accurately summed up by saying that "race determines how *most* whites vote *most* of the time."

86. "Best," of course, is in each individual judge's eyes.

87. Unintentionally undermining her own argument, O'Connor went on to quote from several quite recent cases, including *Batson v. Kentucky* (1986), 104, in which Justice Marshall had denounced not the use of racial stereotypes per se but the employment of "crude, inaccurate" ones, a phrase O'Connor quoted. As she had noted in *Vera*, 97 percent of African-Americans in Dallas voted in the Democratic primary. To stereotype Dallas blacks as Democrats was about as precise as one could possibly be.

88. Even since *Shaw I*, two circuit courts have ruled that race can be taken into account in such circumstances (*Clark v. Calhoun County* [1996]; *Sanchez v. State of Colorado* [1996]).

89. Although she recognizes that African-Americans are "overwhelmingly Democrats," Butler (1996, 348) states that it is unconstitutional to use blacks as a proxy for Democrats but that it is not a racial gerrymander if Democratic precincts are gathered

514 Notes to Pages 448–62

together. Since precinct lines are wholly artificial, this is a distinction without a difference, a matter, as in Texas, of which color-coded category appears on the computer screen.

90. Butler (1996, 346, 350) contends that a jurisdiction should not have to comply with Section 5 if it is required to draw a "bizarre" district to do so but holds that "bizarre" majority-white districts are only "arguably" unconstitutional. For Butler, then, compactness cannot be required by the Constitution.

91. Finding that compactness was a constitutionally derived concept would clear the way for the Court to overturn the VRA, as it applies to vote dilution, entirely. As I argued above, O'Connor's concurrence in *Vera* implies that there are already four votes to overturn Section 2. If *Gingles* were no longer necessary to provide a precedent for requiring compactness, then O'Connor would have no reason to continue to uphold Section 2, and she could take a position against race-consciousness in election laws under any circumstances, which would be more in line with her *Croson* and *Adarand* positions. While Section 5 is useful for O'Connor because it provides an administratively simple way to insure that no more minority opportunity districts are drawn in covered jurisdictions, a constitutionally based rule that no minority opportunity districts could be drawn unless they were as compact as a hypothetical judge might make them would also suffice. Since three of the radical justices have already signaled that they believe Section 5 may be unconstitutional if it requires race-conscious districting, all that would be left would be to secure Chief Justice Rehnquist's vote and the VRA would no longer protect against minority vote dilution in redistricting.

92. To the academic defenders of *Shaw*, minority opportunity districts amount to a "racial spoils system," "natural" districts are overwhelmingly majority white, and eliminating minority opportunity districts is "cleansing the political process of racialism" (Blumstein 1995, 555, 581; Butler 1995, 608 n. 41, 618). This is reminiscent of the excuse offered by Los Angeles police chief Darryl Gates for the deaths of African-Americans at the hands of police officers who used choke-holds: "We may be finding that in some blacks when [a carotid restraint] is applied, the veins or arteries do not open up as fast as they do on normal people" (*LAT*, May 11, 1982, I:1).

CHAPTER NINE

1. Similarly, Prof. Katharine Butler (1995, 622–23) has asserted that America's "lasting protection for all individuals, including minorities" is a product only of "our philosophical base," which she reduces to a disavowal of "group rights."

2. The only other book Thernstrom cites concludes with the following statement: "However, let us not overstate this contrast, for in most of these perceptions and opinions, better-off blacks have much more in common with lower-status blacks than they do with lower-status or better-off whites. Although some socioeconomic differences are obvious in blacks' racial perceptions, attributions, and opinions, these tend to be fairly limited and inconsistent" (Sigelman and Welch 1991, 167). Although one of the two studies she cites in support of her judgment did find class differences within

the African-American community on the issues of government guarantees of jobs and racial self-help, it also indicated that middle-class blacks were actually more race-conscious and more supportive of antidiscrimination policies than were lower-class blacks (Parent and Stekler 1985). The other study she cites concludes by offering the following "basic finding": "upper status blacks are somewhat more conservative than their lower status race peers (although still quite liberal) but markedly more liberal than their white higher status peers" (Gilliam and Whitby 1989, 97). For similar and related findings, see Dawson 1994 and Hochschild 1995.

3. Although Thernstrom has claimed that "basic democratic premises" require that voters be treated only as individuals rather than as members of groups, that "ours is still a nation of individual citizens, not a confederation of racial and ethnic groups," she herself treats them as indistinguishable group members when she considers whether they might be better off with more substantive and less descriptive representation: "In two districts that are each 35% black, African-American voters will often be the decisive swing vote. Concentrate that electorate in one 70% black district, however, and they will have lost the chance to have two representatives beholden to their support." It is also worthy of note that she believes that members of Congress would be "beholden" to African-American voters if they constituted only 35 percent of the voters but that "majority-minority districts are not 'integrated.'" In such districts, she says, "the white voters they contain are merely 'filler people,' . . . these are districts in which only black ballots are meant to count" (Thernstrom 1994, 54–55; 1995, 917–18, 941). Why whites must be assumed to have no influence on their members of Congress when they constitute 46 percent of the voters, as in the First and Twelfth Districts in North Carolina, but blacks could be imagined to exercise considerable power over representatives when they comprised 35 percent of the electorate, Thernstrom does not explain.

Karlan (1997, 300) points to other contradictions in Thernstrom's arguments. Unless blacks and whites have distinctive preferences, neither minority opportunity nor influence districts would have any significance. But unless a substantial number of whites is willing to defect from the white-preferred candidate and coalesce with blacks, blacks can never influence the winner in districts where the black percentage is only moderate. Thus, Thernstrom assumes racial bloc voting or racially homogeneous preferences when it fits one of her arguments, and factionalism within each racial group or racially heterogeneous preferences when it fits other arguments.

Moreover, Thernstrom ignores the possibility that any interest group may be able to maximize its influence by electing a few representatives and then playing a balance of power or logrolling strategy in the legislature or seeking to occupy key positions, such as committee chairs (Karlan 1997, 300–302). Or a group may do best by following a mixed strategy, shifting between influence in the legislature and influence in the electorate as conditions vary. Again, which strategy is best is an empirical question.

4. In 1992 there were no southern congressional districts that were between 40 and 45.7 percent African-American in voting-age population and only three that were between 45 and 50 percent. It is not possible in this instance to tell whether the race of the member of Congress made a difference, because in that year there were no

white congressional representatives from the South serving any of the districts with a voting-age population that was more than 40 percent black . It is perfectly possible that the effects that Cameron, Epstein, and O'Halloran (1996) attribute to the predominantly black constituency are partly the product of the interaction between the constituency and the representative of the same ethnic group, of black faces *and* black interests, rather than just of black interests alone.

5. Cameron, Epstein, and O'Halloran (1996) finessed the difficult problem of including Latinos in their analysis by lumping them together with Anglos. This is unfortunate for two reasons. First, it makes it impossible to determine systematically what the relationship is between the percentage of Latino voters and the degree of representation of Latino interests and subsequently, how to design districts in order to maximize the representation of substantive Latino interests. Second, since many African-Americans live close to or interspersed with Latinos, at least in the Southwest, minority opportunity districts represented by blacks will often contain large percentages, even majorities, of Latinos. Since a larger proportion of Latinos than of Anglos are noncitizens or under age 18, the black proportion that is necessary to elect a black or even a very sympathetic Anglo member of Congress may be much lower in those districts than in districts with few Latinos. This may have caused the authors to underestimate the black proportion needed to maximize black substantive representation and/or to misunderstand the relationships between the black proportion and patterns of voting in Congress, compared to what they would have found if their key independent variable had been the percentage of non-Hispanic whites. It is as dangerous for political scientists as for practical redistricters to treat all but the target population as "filler people." It may make a great deal of difference who *else* is in a district.

6. Butler, another Panglossian, has declared that "America is the most successfully integrated nation in the world," implicitly asserting that blacks share in all of the benefits of integration (Butler 1995, 622).

7. There are fewer studies of Latino opinion. The Latino National Political Survey of 1989–90 (de la Garza et al. 1992) generally found differences between people of Cuban, Puerto Rican, and Mexican origin, with Cubans generally closer to Anglos in political opinions and Puerto Ricans and Mexicans closer to African-Americans. But the patterns of opinion and participation are too complicated to discuss here in the detail that they deserve.

Bibliography

NEWSPAPERS

Newspapers are referred to by the abbreviations shown below.

AAS	Austin (Tex.) American Statesman	LAN	Los Angeles Newsletter
ABH	Athens (Ga.) Banner-Herald	LAT	Los Angeles Times
AC	Atlanta Constitution	MA	Montgomery (Ala.) Advertiser
ADW	Atlanta Daily World	MCA	Memphis Commercial Appeal
AH	Albany (Ga.) Herald	MDA	Memphis Daily Appeal
AI	Atlanta Inquirer	MDAV	Memphis Daily Avalanche
AJ	Atlanta Journal	MN	Macon (Ga.) News
AJC	Atlanta Journal-Constitution	MO	Moultrie (Ga.) Observer
AN	Amarillo (Tex.) News	MPS	Memphis Press-Scimitar
ASNG	Amarillo (Tex.) Sunday News-Globe	MT	Macon (Ga.) Telegraph
AT	Atlanta Times	MTN	Macon (Ga.) Telegraph and News
ATR	Americus (Ga.) Times-Recorder	MTSD	Memphis Tri-State Defender
AuC	Augusta (Ga.) Chronicle	MV	Meriwether (Ga.) Vindicator
AuCH	Augusta (Ga.) Chronicle-Herald	MW	Memphis World
AuH	Augusta (Ga.) Herald	NT	Nashville Tennessean
BN	Brunswick (Ga.) News	NYT	New York Times
BPS	Bainbridge (Ga.) Post-Searchlight	PIA	Petersburg (Va.) Index and Appeal
CCCT	Corpus Christi (Tex.) Caller-Times	PSC	Plano (Tex.) Star Courier
CD	Cordele (Ga.) Dispatch	PSN	Pasadena (Calif.) Star-News
CDG	Cincinnati Daily Gazette	RNO	Raleigh (N.C.) News and Observer
CE	Columbus (Ga.) Enquirer	RoN	Rome (Ga.) News
DDT	Delta Democrat-Times	RoNT	Rome (Ga.) News-Tribune
DKNE	DeKalb (Ga.) New Era	RT	Raleigh (N.C.) Times
DMN	Dallas Morning News	SAE	San Antonio Express
DRC	Denton (Tex.) Record Chronicle	SAL	San Antonio Light
DTH	Dallas Times-Herald	SDI	Sumter (S.C.) Daily Item
FWST	Fort Worth (Tex.) Star-Telegram	SEP	Savannah (Ga.) Evening Press
GDN	Griffin (Ga.) Daily News	SGVT	San Gabriel Valley (Calif.) Tribune
GNR	Greensboro (N.C.) News and Record	SMN	Savannah (Ga.) Morning News
HC	Houston Chronicle	SSA	Selma (Ala.) Southern Argus
HP	Houston Post	TCT	Tyler (Tex.) Courier-Times
HS	Hapeville (Ga.) Statesman	TDB	Torrence (Calif.) Daily Breeze
HVMS	Harlingen (Tex.) Valley Morning Star	VT	Valdosta (Ga.) Times
		WJH	Waycross (Ga.) Journal-Herald
JCL	Jackson (Miss.) Clarion-Ledger	WP (NWE)	Washington Post (National Weekly Edition)
LADJ	Los Angeles Daily Journal		
LADN	Los Angeles Daily News	WSJ	Wall Street Journal

518   *Bibliography*

COURT CASES

The shorter names of frequently cited cases are shown in brackets.

Abrams v. Johnson, 117 S. Ct. 1925 (1997)
Adarand Constructors, Inc. v. Pena, 115 S. Ct. 2097 (1995)
[*Allen*] *Allen v. Board of Elections,* 393 U.S. 544 (1969)
Allen v. Wright, 104 S. Ct. 3315 (1984)
[*Allwright*] See *Smith v. Allwright.*
Anthony v. Commonwealth, 415 F. Supp. 496 (D.Mass. 1976)
[*Arlington Heights*] See *Village of Arlington Heights.*
Baker v. Carr, 369 U.S. 16 (1962)
Batson v. Kentucky, 476 U.S. 79 (1986)
Barbier v. Connolly, 113 U.S. 27 (1884)
[*Beer*] *Beer v. U.S.,* 425 U.S. 130 (1976)
[*Bolden*] See *City of Mobile.*
Bolden v. City of Mobile, 542 F. Supp. 1050 (S.D. Ala. 1982)
Bolling v. Sharpe, 347 U.S. 497 (1954)
Briggs v. Elliott, 132 F. Supp. 776 (1955)
Brooks v. Harris (N.D. Ga., Civil Action No. 1: 90-CV-1001-RCF, July, 1990)
Brooks v. Miller (N.D. Ga., Civil Action No. 1: 90-CV-1001-RCF, Sept., 1996)
Brown v. Board of Commissioners of Chattanooga, Tennessee, 772 F. Supp. 380 (E.D. Tenn. 1989)
Brown v. Board of School Commissioners of Mobile County, 542 F. Supp. 1078 (S.D. Ala. 1982), *aff'd* 706 F.2d 1103 (11th Cir. 1983), *aff'd* 465 U.S. 1005 (1983)
[*Brown*] *Brown v. Board of Education of Topeka, Kansas,* 347 U.S. 483 (1954)
Brown University v. Cohen, 100 F.3d 155 (1996), *cert. denied* 117 S. Ct. 1469 (1997)
Burns v. Richardson, 384 U.S. 73 (1966)
Burton v. Sheheen, 793 F. Supp. 1329 (D.S.C. 1992)
Bush v. Vera, 116 S. Ct. 1941 (1996)
Busbee v. Smith, 549 F. Supp. 494 (D.D.C. 1982), *aff'd,* 459 U.S. 1166 (1983)
Buskey v. Oliver, 565 F. Supp. 1473 (1983)
Calderon v. City of Los Angeles, 93 Cal. 361 (1971)
Carrollton Branch of NAACP *v. Stallings,* 829 F.2d 1547 (11th Cir. 1987), *cert. denied, sub nom. Duncan v. Carrollton Branch of* NAACP, 485 U.S. 936 (1988)
Castorena v. City of Los Angeles, 34 Cal. App. 3d 901 (1973)
Chisom v. Roemer, 111 S. Ct. 2354 (1991)
City of Mobile v. Bolden, 446 U.S. 55 (1980). [*Bolden*]
City of Port Arthur, Texas v. U.S., 517 F. Supp. 987 (D.D.C. 1981)
City of Richmond v. Croson, 488 U.S. 469 (1989)
Clark v. Calhoun County, 88 F.3d 1393 (5th Cir. 1996)
Colegrove v. Green, 328 U.S. 549 (1946)
County Council of Sumter County, S.C. v. U.S., 444 F. Supp. 694 (D.D.C. 1983)
[*Croson*] See *City of Richmond v. Croson.*
[*Cumming*] *Cumming v. Richmond County Board of Education,* 175 U.S. 528 (1899)

Davis v. Bandemer, 478 U.S. 109 (1986)

DeFunis v. Odegaard, 416 U.S. 312 (1974)

[*DeGrandy*] See *Johnson v. DeGrandy.*

[*DeWitt*] *DeWitt v. Wilson,* 856 F. Supp. 1409 (E.D. Cal. 1994), *aff'd* 115 S. Ct. 2637 (1995)

Dillard v. Crenshaw Co., Ala., 640 F. Supp. 1347 (M.D. Ala. 1986); 649 F. Supp. 289 (M.D. Ala. 1986)

[*Dred Scott*] *Dred Scott v. Sandford,* 60 U.S. 393 (1857)

Dunston v. Scott, 336 F. Supp. 206 (E.D. N.C. 1972)

Elmore v. Rice, 72 F. Supp. 516 (E.D. S.C. 1947)

Emison v. Growe, 782 F. Supp. 427 (D.Minn. 1992)

Ex parte Clarke, 100 U.S. 339 (1880)

Ex parte Siebold, 100 U.S. 371 (1880)

Ex parte Yarbrough, 110 U.S. 651 (1884)

[*Feeney*] See *Personnel Administrator of Mass. v. Feeney.*

Fortson v. Dorsey, 379 U.S. 433 (1965)

Freeman v. Pitts, 503 U.S. 467 (1992)

Fullilove v. Klutznick, 448 U.S. 448 (1980)

Gaffney v. Cummings, 412 U.S. 735 (1973)

[*Garza*] *Garza v. Los Angeles County Board of Supervisors,* 756 F. Supp. 1298 (C.D. Cal., 1990), *aff'd,* 918 F.2d 763 (9th Cir. 1990), *cert. denied,* 111 S. Ct. 681 (1991)

Gayle v. Browder, 352 U.S. 903 (1956)

Georgia v. Reno, 881 F. Supp. 7 (D.D.C. 1995)

Giles v. Harris, 189 U.S. 475 (1903)

[*Gingles*] See *Thornburg v. Gingles.*

Gingles v. Edmisten, 590 F. Supp. 345 (E.D. N.C. 1984)

[*Gomillion*] *Gomillion v. Lightfoot,* 364 U.S. 339 (1960)

Graves v. Barnes, 343 F. Supp. 704 (W.D. Tex. 1972); *aff'd sub nom. White v. Register,* 412 U.S. 755 (1973); *Graves v. Barnes,* 378 F. Supp. 640 (W.D. Tex. 1974)

Gray v. Sanders, 203 F. Supp. 158 (N.D. Ga. 1962), 372 U.S. 368 (1963)

Green v. County Board of Education, 391 U.S. 430 (1968)

Grovey v. Townsend, 295 U.S. 45 (1935)

Growe v. Emison, 113 S. Ct. 1075 (1993)

[*Guinn*] *Guinn and Beal v. U.S.,* 238 U.S. 347 (1915)

Hainsworth v. Martin, 386 S.W.2d 202 (Tex. Civ. App.—Austin, writ ref'd n.r.e.), *vacated as moot,* 382 U.S. 109 (1965)

[*Hays*] See *U.S. v. Hays.*

Hays v. Louisiana, 839 F. Supp. 1118 (W.D. La. 1993), 862 F. Supp. 119 (W.D. La. 1994)

Hendrix v. McKinney, 460 F. Supp. 626 (M.D. Ala. 1978)

[*Holder*] *Holder v. Hall,* 114 S. Ct. 2581 (1994)

Holland v. Illinois, 110 S. Ct. 803 (1990)

Holmes v. City of Atlanta, 350 U.S. 879 (1955)

Hunter v. Underwood, 471 U.S. 222 (1985)

Irby v. Fitz-Hugh, 692 F. Supp. 610 (E.D. Va. 1988); 693 F. Supp. 424 (E.D. Va. 1988); 889 F.2d 1352 (1989)

Jeffers v. Clinton, 740 F. Supp. 585 (E.D. Ark. 1990)

Johnson v. De Grandy, 114 S. Ct. 2647 (1994)

Johnson v. Miller, 864 F. Supp. 1354 (S.D. Ga. 1994)

Jones v. Montague, 194 U.S. 147 (1904)

Jordan v. Winter, 541 F. Supp. 1135 (1982)

Karcher v. Daggett, 462 U.S. 725 (1983)

Keyes v. School District No. 1, Denver, Colo., 413 U.S. 189 (1973)

King v. Chapman, 62 F. Supp. 639 (1945), *aff'd* 154 F.2d 460 (1946), *cert. denied* 327 U.S. 800 (1946)

Kirkpatrick v. Preisler, 89 S. Ct. 1225 (1969)

Lassiter v. Northampton Election Board, 360 U.S. 45 (1959)

Lawyer v. Department of Justice, 117 S. Ct. 2186 (1997)

Lemon v. Kurtzman, 403 U.S. 602 (1971)

Lodge v. Buxton, 639 F.2d 1358 (5th Cir. 1981). See also *Rogers v. Lodge*.

Loving v. Virginia, 388 U.S. 1 (1967)

Lucas v. Colorado General Assembly, 377 U.S. 713 (1964)

Lujan v. Defenders of Wildlife, 112 S. Ct. 2130 (1992)

LULAC v. Clements, 999 F.2d 831 (5th Cir. 1993), *cert. denied*, 114 S. Ct. 878 (1994)

McCain v. Lybrand, 465 U.S. 236 (1984)

McLaughlin v. Florida, 379 U.S. 184 (1964)

McMillan v. Escambia County, Fla., 638 F.2d 1239 (1981)

Major v. Treen, 574 F. Supp. 325 (E.D. La. 1983)

Martin v. Wilks, 490 U.S. 755 (1989)

Mayor of Baltimore v. Dawson, 350 U.S. 877 (1955)

Metro Broadcasting, Inc. v. FCC, 497 U.S. 547 (1991)

Michael M. v. Superior Court of Sonoma County, 450 U.S. 464 (1981)

Miller v. Board of Supervisors of Santa Clara Co., 46 Cal. Rptr. 617 (1965)

[*Miller*] *Miller v. Johnson*, 115 S. Ct. 2475 (1995)

Milliken v. Bradley, 418 U.S. 717 (1974)

Missouri v. Jenkins, 115 S. Ct. 2038 (1995)

Muir v. Louisville Park Theatrical Assn., 347 U.S. 971 (1954)

Myers v. Anderson, 238 U.S. 368 (1915)

NAACP v. Gadsden County School Board, 691 F.2d 978 (1982)

Nevett v. Sides, 533 F.2d 1361 (5th Cir. 1976)

New Orleans Park Improvement Assn. v. Detige, 358 U.S. 54 (1958)

Nixon v. Herndon, 273 U.S. 536 (1927)

Northcross v. Board of Education of Memphis, Tenn., 302 F.2d 818 (1962)

[*Palmer*] *Palmer v. Thompson*, 403 U.S. 217 (1971)

Patterson v. McLean Credit Union, 491 U.S. 164 (1989)

Perkins v. Mathews, 400 U.S. 379 (1971)

Personnel Administrator of Mass. v. Feeney, 442 U.S. 256 (1979)

[*Plessy*] *Plessy v. Ferguson*, 16 S. Ct. 1138 (1896)

Pope v. Blue, 809 F. Supp. 392 (W.D. N.C. 1992), *aff'd* 113 S. Ct. 30 (Oct. 5, 1992)

[*Quilter I*] See *Voinovich v. Quilter*.

[*Quilter II*] *Quilter v. Voinovich*, 794 F. Supp. 695 (N.D. Ohio 1992), 794 F. Supp. 756 (N.D. Ohio 1992), 857 F. Supp. 579 (N.D. Ohio 1994), 912 F. Supp. 1006 (N.D. Ohio 1995)

Ratliff v. Beale, 20 So. 20 (1896)

Reno v. Bossier Parish School Board, 117 S. Ct. 1491 (1997)

Regents of University of California v. Bakke, 438 U.S. 265 (1978)

[*Reynolds*] *Reynolds v. Sims*, 377 U.S. 533 (1964)

Robinson v. Commissioners Court, 505 F.2d 674 (1st Cir. 1974)

Rogers v. Lodge, 458 U.S. 613 (1982)

Rybicki v. Board of Elections, 574 F. Supp. 1082 (1982)

Sanchez v. State of Colorado, 97 F.3d 1303 (10th Cir. 1996)

Seamon v. Upham, 536 F. Supp. 931 (E.D. Tex. 1982); *Upham v. Seamon*, 456 U.S. 37 (1982); *Seamon v. Upham*, 536 F. Supp. 1030 (E.D. Tex. 1982); *Seamon v. Upham* (Civil Action No. P-81-49-CA, E.D. Tex., slip opinion, Jan. 30, 1984)

Selden v. Montague, 194 U.S. 154 (1904)

[*Shaw I*, also *Shaw v. Reno*] *Shaw v. Barr*, 808 F. Supp. 461 (E.D. N.C. 1992), *cert. granted*, 113 S. Ct. 653–54 (1992), *rev'd sub nom. Shaw v. Reno*, 113 S. Ct. 2816 (1993)

[*Shaw II*] *Shaw v. Hunt*, 861 F. Supp. 408 (E.D. N.C. 1994), 116 S. Ct. 1894 (1996)

Smith v. Allwright, 321 U.S. 649 (1944)

Smith v. Paris, 257 F. Supp. 901 (M.D. Ala. 1966)

Solomon v. Liberty County, 865 F.2d 1566 (11th Cir. 1988)

Soon Hing v. Crowley, 113 U.S. 703 (1885)

South v. Peters, 339 U.S. 276 (1950)

Strauder v. West Virginia, 100 U.S. 303 (1880)

Swann v. Adams, 385 U.S. 440 (1967)

Swann v. Charlotte-Mecklenburg Board of Education, 402 U.S. 1 (1971)

Sweatt v. Painter, 339 U.S. 629 (1950)

Taylor v. Haywood County, Tenn. Commission, 544 F. Supp. 1122 (W.D. Tenn. 1982)

Terrazas v. Slagle, 789 F. Supp. 828 (W.D. Tex. 1991)

The Civil Rights Cases, 3 S. Ct. 18 (1883)

Thornburg v. Gingles, 478 U.S. 30, 106 S. Ct. 2752 (1986). [*Gingles*]

Toombs v. Fortson, 205 F. Supp. 248 (N.D. Ga. 1962)

Turner v. Arkansas, 784 F. Supp. 553 (E.D. Ark. 1991)

[*UJO*] *United Jewish Organizations of Williamsburgh v. Wilson*, 510 F.2d 512 (1974), *aff'd sub nom. United Jewish Organizations of Williamsburgh v. Carey*, 430 U.S. 144 (1977)

U.S. v. Armstrong, 116 S. Ct. 1480 (1996)

U.S. v. Bibb County Democratic Executive Committee, 222 F. Supp. 493 (1962)

U.S. v. Carolene Products Co., 304 U.S. 144 (1938)

U.S. v. City of Memphis, (W.D. Tenn., Civil Action No. 91-2139)

U.S. v. Classic, 313 U.S. 299 (1941)

U.S. v. Cruikshank, 92 U.S. 542 (1876)

U.S. v. Dallas County, Ala., Commission, 548 F. Supp. 875 (S.D. Ala. 1981)

U.S. v. Hays, 115 S. Ct. 2431 (1995)

U.S. v. Lopez, 115 S. Ct. 1624 (1995)

U.S. v. Lowndes Co., Ga. (Civil Action No. 83-108-VAL)

U.S. v. Marengo County Commission, 731 F.2d 1546 (11th Cir. 1984)

U.S. v. O'Brien, 391 U.S. 367 (1968)

U.S. v. Paradise, 480 U.S. 149 (1987)

U.S. v. Raines, 172 F. Supp. 552 (M.D. Ga. 1959), *rev'd* 362 U.S. 17 (1960)

U.S. v. Reading Co., 226 U.S. 324 (1913)

U.S. v. Reese, 92 U.S. 214 (1876)

U.S. v. Wayte, 470 U.S. 598 (1985)

[*Vera*] See *Bush v. Vera.*

Vera v. Richards, 861 F. Supp. 1304 (S.D. Tex. 1994)

Village of Arlington Heights v. Metro. Hous. Dev. Corp., 429 U.S. 252 (1977). [Arlington Heights]

Voinovich v. Ferguson, 586 N.E.2d 1020 (Ohio 1992)

Voinovich v. Quilter, 113 S. Ct. 1149 (1993). [Quilter I]

Ward's Cove Packing Co., Inc. v. Atonio, 490 U.S. 642 (1989)

Washington v. Davis, 426 U.S. 229 (1976)

Washington v. Finlay, 664 F.2d 913 (4th Cir. 1981)

Watson v. City of Memphis, 373 U.S. 526 (1963)

Wells v. Rockefeller, 394 U.S. 542 (1969)

Whitcomb v. Chavis, 403 U.S. 124 (1971)

White v. Regester, 412 U.S. 755 (1973)

White v. Weiser, 412 U.S. 783 (1973)

Whitfield v. Democratic Party of Arkansas, 686 F. Supp. 1365 (E.D. Ark. 1988), 890 F.2d 1423 (8th Cir. 1989)

Wilson v. Eu, 1 Cal. 4th 707; 4 Cal. Rptr. 379; 823 P.2d 545 (1992)

Williams v. City of Dallas, 734 F. Supp. 1317 (N.D. Tex. 1990)

Williams v. Mississippi, 170 U.S. 213 (1898)

Wood v. Georgia, 370 U.S. 375 (1962)

Wright v. Rockefeller, 211 F. Supp. 460 (1962), 376 U.S. 52 (1964)

Wygant v. Jackson Bd. of Educ., 106 S. Ct. 1842 (1986)

Yick Wo v. Hopkins, 118 U.S. 356 (1886)

Zimmer v. McKeithen, 485 F.2d 1297 (5th Cir. 1973)

DEPOSITIONS

Unless otherwise noted, the deposition transcripts and memoranda listed here were collected for the trial of *Garza v. County of Los Angeles.* All depositions are in the possession of the author.

Alatorre, Richard. July 6, 1989.

Antonovich, Michael. Aug. 31, 1989.

Bannister, Wayne. Apr. 24, 1989.

Bush, Robert. June 2, 15, 1989.

Burke, Yvonne. Aug. 29, 1989.

Cohen, Gerry F. Nov. 12, 1993, in *Shaw v. Hunt.*

Crow, Kathleen. June 30, Sept. 5, 1989.

Dana, Deane. July 12, 31, Sept. 13, 1989.

Duron, Armando. May 12, 1989.

Edelman, Edmund. Aug. 2, Sept. 1, 1989.

Fitch, Alma. May 16, 30, 1989.

Fonda-Bonardi, Peter. Apr. 24, 1989.

Fukai, Mas. June 2, 1989.

Garcia, Miguel. May 26, 1989.

Gilbert, Donald. Apr. 26, 1989.

Groover, Denmark. Apr. 23, 1984, in *U.S. v. Lowndes Co.*

———. Sept. 8, 1994, in *Georgia v. Reno.*

Hayes, James. Aug. 28, 1989.

Heslop, David Alan. July 25, Sept. 14, 1989.

Hofeller, Thomas. Dec. 13, 1983, in *Jordan v. Winter.*

Hoffenblum, Allan. June 30, July 7, Aug. 15, 1989.

Huerta, John. May 25, 1989.

Jacinto, Reuben Alexandro. May 24, 1989.

Johnson, Eddie Bernice. June 13, 1994, in *Vera v. Richards.*

Lear, Davis. Apr. 27, 1989.

Lewis, Michael William. July 27-28, Sept. 14, 1989.

Marlow, Harry. June 27, 1989.

Marr, George. May 19, June 2, 1989.

Marshall, William Thomas. Sept. 12, 1989.

Martinez, Roman. June 16, 21, 1991, in *Vera v. Richards.*

Melendez, Jesus. Apr. 28, 1989.

Merritt, John. Dec. 22, 1993, in *Shaw v. Hunt.*

Molina, Gloria. Aug. 10, 1989.

Montanez-Davis, Grace. May 26, 1989.

Murdoch, Norman. Apr. 25, 1989.

Neri, Lauro. May 15, 1989.

Perkins, Robert Hillary. May 16, 1989.

Pozorski, Edward G. June 13, 1989.

Quezada, Leticia. Aug. 16, 25, 1989.

Quevedo, Frederic. Apr. 27, May 17, 1989.

Sanborn, Blake. June 1, 1989.

Santillan, Richard A. June 7, 1989.

Schabarum, Peter. Aug. 9, 28, 1989.

Schoeni, Richard. July 12-13, Sept. 12, 1989.

Schwellenbach, Baxter Ward. Aug. 17, 1989.

Seymour, Jeff. July 14, 21, Aug. 14, 1989.

Sharman, Christopher Martin. June 18, 1994, in *Vera v. Richards.*

Shumate, Joseph. July 29, Aug. 22, 1989.

Smith, Ron. Aug. 23-24, 1989.

Turner, Deborah A. May 17, June 12, Aug. 16, 1989.

Uranga, Steven Daniel. June 8, 1989.
Walters, Robert. May 16, 1989.
Washington, Craig. Nov. 24, 1981, in *Seamon v. Upham.*

OTHER SOURCES

Abel, Douglas D., and Bruce I. Oppenheimer. 1994. "Candidate Emergence in a Majority Hispanic District: The 29th District in Texas." In Kazee 1994, 45–66.
Abraham, Henry J. 1974. *Justices and Presidents: A Political History of Appointments to the Supreme Court.* New York: Oxford University Press.
Abramson, Harold J. 1980. "Assimilation and Pluralism." In Thernstrom, ed., 1980, 150–60.
Adkins, Walter P. 1935. "Beale Street Goes to the Polls." Unpublished master's thesis, Ohio State University.
Adler, Selig. 1934. "The Senatorial Career of George Franklin Edmunds, 1866–1891." Unpublished Ph.D. dissertation, University of Illinois.
Akin, Edward N. 1974. "When a Minority Becomes the Majority: Blacks in Jacksonville Politics, 1887–1907." *Florida Historical Quarterly* 53: 123–45.
Alabama Constitutional Convention. 1901. *Official Proceedings.* Wetumpka, Ala.: Wetumpka Printing Co.
Alabama, State of. Serial. *Acts.* Montgomery: various publishers.
Aleinikoff, T. Alexander, and Samuel Issacharoff. 1993. "Race and Redistricting: Drawing Constitutional Lines After *Shaw v. Reno.*" *Michigan Law Review* 92: 588–651.
Alford, John R., and David W. Brady. 1989. "Personal and Partisan Advantage in U.S. Congressional Elections, 1846–1986." In *Congress Reconsidered,* edited by Lawrence C. Dodd and Bruce I. Oppenheimer. 4th ed. Washington, D.C.: Congressional Quarterly Press.
Alston, Chuck. 1991. "Incumbents Share the Wealth, With Redistricting in Mind." *Congressional Quarterly Weekly Report* 49 (May 31, 1991): 1343–50.
Altman, Micah. 1998. "District Shape and Democratic Representation." Unpublished Ph.D. dissertation, California Institute of Technology.
Amir, Yehuda. 1976. "The Role of Intergroup Contact in Change of Prejudice and Ethnic Relations." In *Towards the Elimination of Racism,* edited by Phyllis A. Katz, 245–308. New York: Pergamon.
Anderson, Eric. 1981. *The Black Second: Race and Politics in North Carolina, 1872–1900.* Baton Rouge: Louisiana State University Press.
"Another Negro Suffrage Case" [editorial]. 1903. *The Outlook* 74: 634–35 (July 11, 1903).
Appleby, Joyce, Lynn Hunt, and Margaret Jacob. 1994. *Telling the Truth About History.* New York: W. W. Norton.
Arden, Wayne R., and Jeffrey M. Wice. 1993. "Brief *Amici Curiae* on behalf of the Democratic National Committee, Democratic Legislative Leaders Association, Democratic Congressional Campaign Committee, and Democratic Governors' Association in Support of the Appellees" (brief in U.S. Supreme Court, *Shaw v. Reno*). Mimeo.

Argersinger, Peter H. 1984. "Electoral Processes." In *Encyclopedia of American Political History,* edited by Jack P. Greene, 3:489–512. New York: Charles Scribner's Sons.

———. 1989. "The Value of the Vote: Political Representation in the Gilded Age." *Journal of American History* 76: 59–90.

———. 1992. *Structure, Process, and Party: Essays in American Political History.* Armonk, N.Y.: M. E. Sharpe.

Attlesey, Sam. 1981. "A Stunning Victory for Conservatives." *Texas Business,* October, 105–11.

Axelrod, Robert. 1984. *The Evolution of Cooperation.* New York: Basic.

Bacote, Clarence A. 1955. "The Negro in Georgia, 1880–1908." Unpublished Ph.D. dissertation, University of Chicago.

Baker, Gordon. 1984. "Representation and Apportionment." In *Encyclopedia of American Political History,* edited by Jack P. Greene, 3:1118–30. New York: Charles Scribner's Sons.

Ball, Howard, Dale Krane, and Thomas P. Lauth. 1982. *Compromised Compliance: Implementation of the 1965 Voting Rights Act.* Westport, Conn.: Greenwood.

Banfield, Edward C., and James Q. Wilson. 1963. *City Politics.* New York: Vintage.

Barone, Michael, and Grant Ujifusa. 1998. *The Almanac of American Politics.* Washington, D.C.: National Journal.

Barr, Alwyn W. 1971. *Reconstruction to Reform: Texas Politics, 1876–1906.* Austin: University of Texas Press.

———. 1986. "Black Legislators of Reconstruction Texas." *Civil War History* 32: 340–52.

Bartley, Numan V. 1969. *The Rise of Massive Resistance: Race and Politics in the South During the 1950s.* Baton Rouge: Louisiana State University Press.

———. 1983. *The Creation of Modern Georgia.* Athens: University of Georgia Press.

Bass, Jack, and Walter DeVries. 1976. *The Transformation of Southern Politics.* New York: Basic.

Beifuss, Joan Turner. 1989. *At the River I Stand: Memphis, The 1968 Strike, and Martin Luther King.* Brooklyn, N.Y.: Carlson.

Bejach, L. D. 1950. "The Taxing District of Shelby County." *West Tennessee Historical Society Papers*: 5–27.

Belknap, Michal R. 1987. *Federal Law and Southern Order: Racial Violence and Constitutional Conflict in the Post-Brown South.* Athens: University of Georgia Press.

Benedict, Michael Les. 1974. "Preserving the Constitution: The Conservative Basis of Radical Reconstruction." *Journal of American History* 61: 65–90.

———. 1978. "Reconstruction and the Waite Court." *Supreme Court Review* 39–79.

Bensel, Richard Franklin. 1990. *Yankee Leviathan: The Origins of Central State Authority in America, 1859–1877.* Cambridge: Cambridge University Press.

Bernd, Joseph. 1972. "Georgia: Static and Dynamic." In *The Changing Politics of the South,* edited by William C. Havard, 294–365. Baton Rouge: Louisiana State University Press.

Beth, Loren P. 1992. *John Marshall Harlan: The Last Whig Justice.* Lexington: University Press of Kentucky.

Bickel, Alexander, and Benno C. Schmidt. 1984. *The Judiciary and Responsible Government, 1910–21.* New York: Macmillan.

Bickerstaff, Steve. 1991. "State Legislative and Congressional Reapportionment in Texas: A Historical Perspective." *Public Affairs Comment* 37, no. 2 (Winter). University of Texas, Austin: LBJ School.

Bierstein, Andrea. 1995. "Millennium Approaches: The Future of the Voting Rights Act After *Shaw, De Grandy,* and *Holder.*" *Hastings Law Journal* 46: 1457–1531.

Biles, Roger. 1983. "Robert R. Church, Jr. of Memphis: Black Republican Leader in the Age of Democratic Ascendancy, 1928–1940." *Tennessee Historical Quarterly* 42: 362–82.

Binion, Gayle. 1983. " 'Intent' and Equal Protection: A Reconsideration." *Supreme Court Review*: 397–457.

Black and Hispanic Members of the Texas State Legislature. 1981a. "Comment on the Texas Congressional Redistricting Submission by Black and Hispanic Members of the State Legislature." In Texas 1981.

———. 1981b. "Retrogressive Effect of Texas Congressional Redistricting Plan: Reduced Ability of Minority Groups to Elect Their Choices to Office." In Texas 1981.

Black, Earl. 1976. *Southern Governors and Civil Rights: Racial Segregation as a Campaign Issue in the Second Reconstruction.* Cambridge: Harvard University Press.

Blacksher, James U. 1996. "Dred Scott's Unwon Freedom: The Redistricting Cases as Badges of Slavery." *Howard Law Journal* 39: 633–91.

Blacksher, James U., and Larry T. Menefee. 1982. "From *Reynolds v. Sims* to *City of Mobile v. Bolden*: Have the White Suburbs Commandeered the Fifteenth Amendment?" *Hastings Law Journal* 34: 1–64.

Blaine, James G. 1886. *Twenty Years of Congress.* 2 vols. Norwich, Conn.: Henry Bill.

Blake, Nelson M. 1935. *William Mahone of Virginia, Soldier and Political Insurgent.* Richmond, Va.: Garrett and Massie.

Blasi, Gary L. 1987–88. "Litigation Strategies for Addressing Bureaucratic Disentitlement." *New York University Review of Law and Social Change* 16: 591–603.

Blue, Frederick J. 1987. *Salmon P. Chase: A Life in Politics.* Kent, Ohio: Kent State University Press.

Blumstein, James F. 1995. "Racial Gerrymandering and Vote Dilution: *Shaw v. Reno* in Doctrinal Context." *Rutgers Law Journal* 26: 517–93.

———. 1996. "*Shaw v. Reno* and *Miller v. Johnson*: Where We Are and Where We Are Headed." *Cumberland Law Review* 26: 503–13.

Boland, Lawrence A. 1987. "Stylized Facts." In *The New Palgrave,* edited by John Eatwell, Murray Milgate, and Peter Newman, 4:535. New York: Stockton Press.

Bolick, Clint. 1996. "Clinton's Judges: A Preliminary Analysis," Goldwater Institute Issue Analysis Series, no. 5 (April). Phoenix: Goldwater Institute.

Bonner, James C. 1963. "Legislative Apportionment and County Unit Voting in Georgia Since 1877." *Georgia Historical Quarterly* 47: 351–74.

Bositis, David A. 1997. "The Persistence of Racially Polarized Voting in the 1996 Elections." *Voting Rights Review,* Summer, 5–9.

Boyd, Thomas J., and Stephen J. Markman. 1983. "The 1982 Amendment to the Voting Rights Act: A Legislative History." *Washington and Lee Law Review* 40: 1347-1428.

Braeman, John. 1988. *Before the Civil Rights Revolution: The Old Court and Individual Rights.* Westport, Conn.: Greenwood.

Brest, Paul. 1971. "*Palmer v. Thompson*: An Approach to the Problem of Unconstitutional Legislative Motive." *Supreme Court Review,* 95-144.

Brewer, J. Mason. 1935. *Negro Legislators of Texas.* Dallas, Tex.: Mathis Publishing.

Briffault, Richard. 1995. "Race and Representation After *Miller v. Johnson.*" *University of Chicago Legal Forum* 1995: 23-82.

Brischetto, Robert, David R. Richards, Chandler Davidson, and Bernard Grofman. 1994. "Texas." In Davidson and Grofman 1994, 233-70.

Brown, Gloria. 1982. "Blacks in Memphis, Tennessee, 1920-1955: A Historical Study." Unpublished Ph.D. dissertation, Washington State University.

Brown, Canter, Jr. 1995. Letter to author, Dec. 16.

Bryson, William C., et al. 1993. "Brief for the Federal Appellees" (brief in U.S. Supreme Court, *Shaw v. Reno*). Mimeo.

Bunche, Ralph J. [1935] 1973. *The Political Status of the Negro in the Age of FDR.* Chicago: University of Chicago Press.

Buni, Andrew. 1967. *The Negro in Virginia Politics, 1902-1965.* Charlottesville: University Press of Virginia.

Burka, Paul. 1992. "Battle Lines." *Texas Monthly,* March, 50-56.

Burnham, Walter Dean. 1955. *Presidential Ballots, 1836-1892.* Baltimore, Md.: Johns Hopkins University Press.

Burns, Haywood. 1987. "The Activism Is Not Affirmative." In H. Schwartz, 1987, 95-108.

Butler, Katharine Inglis. 1995. "Affirmative Racial Gerrymandering: Fair Representation for Minorities or a Dangerous Recognition of Group Rights?" *Rutgers Law Journal* 26: 595-624.

———. 1996. "Affirmative Racial Gerrymandering: Rhetoric and Reality." *Cumberland Law Review* 26: 313-63.

Cain, Bruce E. 1983. "Latinos in the Law: Meeting the Challenge—Reapportionment." *Chicano Law Review* 6: 39-41, 55-57.

———. 1984. *The Reapportionment Puzzle.* Berkeley: University of California Press.

Cain, Bruce E., and D. Roderick Kiewiet. "Ethnicity and Electoral Choice." *Social Science Quarterly* 65: 315-27.

Cain, Bruce E., John Ferejohn, and Morris Fiorina. 1987. *The Personal Vote: Constituency Service and Electoral Independence.* Cambridge: Harvard University Press.

Caldwell, Elizabeth. 1990. "Few Black Legislators Served This Century." *Arkansas Democrat,* March 26, B1.

California State Advisory Committee to the U.S. Commission on Civil Rights. 1971. "Political Participation of Mexican Americans in California." Mimeo.

———. 1982. "Access to Political Representation: Legislative Reapportionment in California." Mimeo.

Calvert, Robert A., and Arnoldo De Leon. 1990. *The History of Texas.* Arlington Heights, Ill.: Harlan Davidson.

Cameron, Charles, David Epstein, and Sharyn O'Halloran. 1996. "Do Majority-Minority Districts Maximize Substantive Black Representation in Congress?" *American Political Science Review* 90: 794-812.

Canon, David T. 1995. "Redistricting and the Congressional Black Caucus." *American Politics Quarterly* 23: 159-89.

Canon, David T., Matthew M. Schousen, and Patrick J. Sellers. 1994. "A Formula for Uncertainty: Creating a Black Majority District in North Carolina." In Kazee 1994, 23-44.

Capers, Gerald M. 1947. "Memphis: Satrapy of a Benevolent Despot." In *Our Fair City,* edited by Robert S. Allen, 211-34. New York: Vanguard.

Carmines, Edward G., and James A. Stimson. 1989. *Issue Evolution: Race and the Transformation of American Politics.* Princeton, N.J.: Princeton University Press.

Carroll, Lewis. 1939. "Through the Looking Glass." In *The Complete Works of Lewis Carroll.* London: Nonesuch.

Cartwright, Joseph H. 1976. *The Triumph of Jim Crow: Tennessee Race Relations in the 1880s.* Knoxville: University of Tennessee Press.

Catledge, Turner. 1971. *My Life and The Times.* New York: Harper and Row.

Clark, J. Morris. 1978. "Legislative Motivation and Fundamental Rights in Constitutional Law." *San Diego Law Review* 15: 953-1039.

Claunch, Ronald G., Wesley S. Chumlea, and James G. Dickson Jr. 1981. "Texas." In *Reapportionment Politics: The History of Redistricting in the 50 States,* edited by Leroy Hardy, Alan Heslop, and Stuart Anderson, 311-16. Beverly Hills, Calif.: Sage.

Comacho, Jose, et al. 1982. "Brief of Intervenors Matt Garcia, et al." (in *Seamon v. Upham*). Mimeo.

Congressional Quarterly. 1957-1993. *Congressional Quarterly Almanac.* Washington, D.C.: Congressional Quarterly.

Congressional Quarterly. 1961. "Redistricting Report." *Congressional Quarterly Weekly Report* (Nov. 17): 1868-74.

———. 1975. *Guide to U.S. Elections.* Washington, D.C.: Congressional Quarterly.

———. 1981. *Congress and the Nation.* Vol. 5, *1977-1980.* Washington, D.C.: Congressional Quarterly.

———. 1991. *Jigsaw Politics: Shaping the House after the 1990 Census.* Washington, D.C.: Congressional Quarterly.

———. 1993a. *Congressional Districts in the 1990s.* Washington, D.C.: Congressional Quarterly.

———. 1993b. *CQ's Guide to 1990 Congressional Redistricting, Part 1.* Washington, D.C.: Congressional Quarterly.

———. 1993c. *CQ's Guide to 1990 Congressional Redistricting, Part 2.* Washington, D.C.: Congressional Quarterly.

Connolly, Harold X. 1977. *A Ghetto Grows in Brooklyn.* New York: New York University Press.

Conway, Alan. 1966. *The Reconstruction of Georgia.* Minneapolis: University of Minnesota Press.

Cook, James F. 1988. "Carl Sanders and the Politics of the Future." In Henderson and Roberts 1988, 169–84.

Cooley, Thomas McIntyre. 1868. *A Treatise on the Constitutional Limitations which Rest upon the Legislative Power of the States of the American Union.* Boston: Little, Brown.

Crenshaw, Kimberle Williams. 1988. "Race, Reform, and Retrenchment: Transformation and Legitimation in Antidiscrimination Law." *Harvard Law Review* 101: 1331–87.

Cresswell, Stephen. 1995. *Multiparty Politics in Mississippi, 1877-1902.* Jackson: University Press of Mississippi.

Crofts, Daniel W. 1968. "The Blair Bill and the Elections Bill: The Congressional Aftermath to Reconstruction." Unpublished Ph.D. dissertation, Yale University.

Curtis, Michael Kent. 1986. *No State Shall Abridge: The Fourteenth Amendment and the Bill of Rights.* Durham, N.C.: Duke University Press.

D'Souza, Dinesh. 1995. *The End of Racism: Principles for a Multi-Racial Society.* New York: Free Press.

Daniel, John Thompson. N.d. "Memphis 1975: The Campaign Strategy of a Black Political Candidate." Unpublished master's thesis, Southwestern University.

Daniels, Roger. 1988. *Asian Americans: Chinese and Japanese in the United States Since 1850.* Seattle: University of Washington Press.

Davidson, Chandler. 1990. *Race and Class in Texas Politics.* Princeton, N.J.: Princeton University Press.

———. 1992. "The Voting Rights Act: A Brief History." In Grofman and Davidson 1992, 7–51.

———, ed. 1984. *Minority Vote Dilution.* Washington, D.C.: Howard University Press.

Davidson, Chandler, and George Korbel. 1981. "At-Large Elections and Minority Group Representation: A Re-examination of Historical and Contemporary Evidence." *Journal of Politics* 43: 982–1005.

Davidson, Chandler, and Bernard Grofman, eds. 1994. *Quiet Revolution in the South: The Impact of the Voting Rights Act, 1965-1990.* Princeton, N.J.: Princeton University Press.

Davidson, Donald. 1980. *Essays on Actions and Events.* Oxford, Eng.: Clarendon.

Davis, Henry Clifton. 1964. "Some Aspects of the Formation, Operation and Termination of the Taxing District of Shelby County, Tennessee." Unpublished Master's thesis, Memphis State University.

Davis, Peggy Cooper. 1997. "Performing Interpretation: A Legacy of Civil Rights Lawyering in *Brown v. Board of Education.*" In Sarat 1997, 23–48.

Davis, Sue. 1989. *Justice Rehnquist and the Constitution.* Princeton, N.J.: Princeton University Press.

Dawson, Michael C. 1994. *Behind the Mule: Race and Class in African-American Politics.* Princeton, N.J.: Princeton University Press.

Days, Drew S., III. 1992. "Section 5 Enforcement and the Department of Justice." In Grofman and Davidson 1992, 52–65.

————. 1995. "Reply Brief for the United States" (brief in U.S. Supreme Court, *Bush v. Vera*). Mimeo.

Days, Drew S., III, et al. 1994. "Brief for the United States" (brief in U.S. Supreme Court, *U.S. v. Hays*). Mimeo.

————. 1995a. "Brief for the United States" (brief in U.S. Supreme Court, *Bush v. Vera*). Mimeo.

————. 1995b. "Brief for the United States as Amicus Curiae Supporting Appellees" (brief in U.S. Supreme Court, *Shaw v. Hunt*). Mimeo.

de la Garza, Rodolfo O., Louis DeSipio, F. Chris Garcia, John Garcia, and Angelo Falcon. 1992. *Latino Voices: Mexican, Puerto Rican, and Cuban Perspectives on American Politics*. Boulder, Colo.: Westview.

Derfner, Armand. 1982. "Nondiscrimination in Districting." In *Representation and Redistricting Issues*, edited by Bernard Grofman, Arend Lijphart, Robert B. McKay, and Howard A. Scarrow, 65-76. Lexington, Mass.: Lexington Books.

DeSantis, Vincent P. 1959. *Republicans Face the Southern Question: The New Departure Years, 1877-1897*. Baltimore, Md.: Johns Hopkins University Press.

Devine, Patricia G. 1989. "Stereotypes and Prejudice: Their Automatic and Controlled Components." *Journal of Personality and Social Psychology* 56: 5-18.

Devlin, Bernie, Stephen E. Fienberg, Daniel P. Resnick, and Kathryn Roeder. 1995. "Galton Redux: Eugenics, Intelligence, Race, and Society: A Review of *The Bell Curve: Intelligence and Class Structure in American Life*." *Journal of the American Statistical Association* 90: 1483-88.

Doyle, Don H. 1985. *Nashville Since the 1920s*. Knoxville: University of Tennessee Press.

Drago, Edmund L. 1982. *Black Politicians and Reconstruction in Georgia: A Splendid Failure*. Baton Rouge: Louisiana State University Press.

Dubay, Robert W. 1988. "Marvin Griffin and the Politics of the Stump." In Henderson and Roberts 1988, 101-12.

Dyer, Thomas G. 1985. *The University of Georgia: A Bicentennial History, 1785-1985*. Athens: University of Georgia Press.

Easterbrook, Frank. 1983. "Statutes' Domains." *University of Chicago Law Review* 50: 533-52.

Edmonds, Helen G. 1951. *The Negro and Fusion Politics in North Carolina, 1894-1901*. Chapel Hill: University of North Carolina Press.

Edsall, Thomas Byrne, and Mary D. Edsall. 1991. *Chain Reaction: The Impact of Race, Rights, and Taxes on American Politics*. New York: Norton.

Ehrenhalt, Alan. 1983. "Pulling Away from the Racial Gerrymander." *Perspectives* (Winter-Spring): 33-37.

Eisenberg, Theodore. 1977. "Disproportionate Impact and Illicit Motive: Theories of Constitutional Adjudication." *New York University Law Review* 52: 26-171.

Eisenberg, Theodore, and Sheri Lynn Johnson. 1991. "The Effects of Intent: Do We Know How Legal Standards Work?" *Cornell Law Review* 76: 1151-97.

Election Law Study Committee (ELSC). 1968. *Report*. Mimeo in Georgia State Public Library, Trinity and Pryor St. Branch, Atlanta.

————. Files. Georgia Department of Archives and History, Atlanta.

Ely, John Hart. 1970. "Legislative and Administrative Motivation in Constitutional Law." *Yale Law Journal* 79: 1025-1341.

———. 1980. *Democracy and Distrust: A Theory of Judicial Review*. Cambridge: Harvard University Press.

Enelow, James M., and Melvin J. Hinich. 1984. *The Spatial Theory of Voting*. New York: Cambridge University Press.

Engstrom, Richard L., and Michael D. McDonald. 1981. "The Election of Blacks to City Councils: Clarifying the Impact of Electoral Arrangements on the Seats/Population Relationship." *American Political Science Review* 75: 344-54.

———. 1987. "The Election of Blacks to Southern City Councils: The Dominant Impact of Electoral Arrangements." In *Blacks in Southern Politics*, edited by Lawrence W. Moreland, Robert P. Steed, and Tod A. Baker, 245-58. New York: Praeger.

Epstein, Lee, Jeffrey A. Segal, Harold J. Spaeth, and Thomas G. Walker. 1994. *The Supreme Court Compendium*. Washington, D.C.: Congressional Quarterly.

Eskridge, William N., Jr. 1988. "Politics Without Romance: Implications of Public Choice Theory for Statutory Interpretation." *Virginia Law Review* 74: 275-338.

Estrada, Leobardo. 1983. "Demographic Characteristics of Latinos." *Chicano Law Review* 6: 9-16.

Everett, Robinson O. 1993. "Appellants' Brief on the Merits" (brief in U.S. Supreme Court, *Shaw v. Reno*). Mimeo.

———. 1995a. "Appellants' Brief in Opposition to Appellees' Motions to Dismiss or Affirm" (brief in U.S. Supreme Court, *Shaw v. Hunt*). Mimeo.

———. 1995b. "Brief of Appellants Shaw, et al., on the Merits" (brief in U.S. Supreme Court, *Shaw v. Hunt*). Mimeo.

———. 1995c. "Reply Brief of Appellants Shaw, et al." (brief in U.S. Supreme Court, *Shaw v. Hunt*). Mimeo.

Farley, Reynolds, and Walter R. Allen. 1987. *The Color Line and the Quality of Life in America*. New York: Russell Sage Foundation.

Farr, Thomas A. 1995a. "Brief of Appellants Pope, et al. on the Merits" (brief in U.S. Supreme Court, *Shaw v. Hunt*). Mimeo.

———. 1995b. "Reply Brief of Appellants Pope, et al." (brief in U.S. Supreme Court, *Shaw v. Hunt*). Mimeo.

Fehrenbacher, Don E. 1978. *The Dred Scott Case*. New York: Oxford University Press.

Field, Phyllis F. 1982. *The Politics of Race in New York: The Struggle for Black Suffrage in the Civil War Era*. Ithaca, N.Y.: Cornell University Press.

Findlay, Stephen M. 1975. "The Role of Bi-Racial Organizations in the Integration of Public Facilities in Memphis, Tennessee, 1954-1964." Unpublished paper, Memphis Room, Memphis Public Library.

Fischer, Roger A. 1974. *The Segregation Struggle in Louisiana, 1862-1877*. Urbana: University of Illinois Press.

Fiss, Owen M. 1993. *Troubled Beginnings of the Modern State, 1888-1910*. New York: Macmillan.

Fletcher, Anthony Q. 1994. "Recent Development, White Lines, Black Districts—The

Dilution of the Anti-Dilution Principle." *Harvard Civil Rights-Civil Liberties Law Review* 29: 231-55.

Foner, Eric. 1988. *Reconstruction: America's Unfinished Revolution, 1863-1877.* New York: Harper and Row.

———. 1993. *Freedom's Lawmakers: A Directory of Black Officeholders during Reconstruction.* New York: Oxford University Press.

Fontenay, Charles L. 1980. *Estes Kefauver, A Biography.* Knoxville: University of Tennessee Press.

Fortson, Ben. Papers. In Georgia Department of Archives and History, Atlanta.

Fraser, Walter J., Jr. 1975. "Black Reconstructionists in Tennessee." *Tennessee Historical Quarterly* 34: 362-82.

Friedman, Leon. 1969. "Salmon P. Chase." In Friedman and Israel 1969, 2:1113-28.

Friedman, Leon, and Fred I. Israel, eds. 1969. *The Justices of the United States Supreme Court, 1789-1969.* New York: Chelsea House.

Garand, James C., and Donald A. Gross. 1984. "Changes in the Vote Margins for Congressional Candidates: A Specification of Historical Trends." *American Political Science Review* 78: 17-30.

Garcia, F. Chris, Rodolpho O. De La Garza, and Donald J. Torres. 1985. "Politics: Introduction." In *The Mexican American Experience,* edited by Rodolfo O. de la Garza et al., 185-200. Austin: University of Texas Press.

Gardner, James A. 1997. "Liberty, Community and the Constitutional Structure of Political Influence: A Reconsideration of the Right to Vote." *University of Pennsylvania Law Review* 145: 893-985.

Gatewood, Willard B., Jr. 1970. *Theodore Roosevelt and the Art of Controversy.* Baton Rouge: Louisiana State University Press.

———. 1972. "Negro Legislators in Arkansas, 1891: A Document." *Arkansas Historical Quarterly* 31: 220-33.

Georgia, State of. Serial. *Laws.* Atlanta: various publishers.

Georgia Democratic State Executive Committee. 1962. "Rules and Regulations of the State Democratic Executive Committee of Georgia Governing Democratic Primary Elections" (April 18, 1962). In *Brooks v. Miller,* Defendant's Exhibit No. 1.

Georgia Government Documentation Project. 1989. "Interview with William P. Randall and William C. Randall, conducted by Cliff Kuhn and Duane Stewart" (Feb. 4, 1989). Transcript in author's possession.

Georgia House of Representatives. Serial. *Journal of the House of Representatives.*

Georgia Senate. Serial. *Journal of the Senate.*

Gillette, William. 1965. *The Right to Vote: Politics and the Passage of the Fifteenth Amendment.* Baltimore, Md.: Johns Hopkins University Press.

———. 1979. *Retreat from Reconstruction, 1869-1879.* Baton Rouge: Louisiana State University Press.

Gilliam, Armistead W., Jr. 1992. "Motion to Dismiss Appeal and to Affirm Ruling of Trial Court" (brief in U.S. Supreme Court, *Voinovich v. Quilter*). Mimeo.

———. 1996a. "Motion to Dismiss Appeal and to Affirm Ruling of Trial Court" (first brief in U.S. Supreme Court, *Quilter II*).

———. 1996b. "Motion to Dismiss Appeal and to Affirm Ruling of Trial Court" (later brief in U.S. Supreme Court, *Quilter II*).

Gilliam, Franklin D., Jr. and Kenny J. Whitby. 1989. "Race, Class, and Attitudes toward Social Welfare Spending: An Ethclass Interpretation." *Social Science Quarterly* 70: 88–100.

Glasser, Susan B. 1991. "For Texas Redistricting, It's Make or Break Time." *Roll Call,* May 20, 1, 27.

Griswold del Castillo, Richard. 1979. *The Los Angeles Barrio, 1850–1890: A Social History.* Berkeley: University of California Press.

Going, Allen J. 1951. *Bourbon Democracy in Alabama, 1874–1890.* University: University of Alabama Press.

Goldfarb, Joel. 1969. "Henry Billings Brown." In Friedman and Israel 1969, 2:1553–63.

Goldstein, Thomas C. 1994. "Unpacking and Applying *Shaw v. Reno.*" *American University Law Review* 43: 1135–96.

Gonzalez, Alberta L., and Adaljiza S. Riddell. 1981. "Representation or Illusion? District Elections, with an Overview of San Francisco." In Santillan 1981, 156–83.

Goodman, N. Victor. 1992a. "Brief in Opposition to Motion to Dismiss Appeal and to Affirm Ruling of Trial Court" (brief in U.S. Supreme Court, *Voinovich v. Quilter*). Mimeo.

———. 1992b. "Jurisdictional Statement" (brief in U.S. Supreme Court, *Voinovich v. Quilter*). Mimeo.

———. 1996a. "Defendants' Brief on Second Remand" (brief in District court remand of *Quilter II*). Mimeo.

———. 1996b. "Jurisdictional Statement" (brief in U.S. Supreme Court, *Quilter II*). Mimeo.

Gottlieb, Stephen E. 1993. "Introduction: Overriding Public Values." In *Public Values in Constitutional Law,* 1–30. Ann Arbor: University of Michigan Press.

Graglia, Lino A. 1976. *Disaster by Decree: The Supreme Court Decisions on Race and the Schools.* Ithaca, N.Y.: Cornell University Press.

Graham, Hugh Davis. 1967. *Crisis in Print: Desegregation and the Press in Tennessee.* Nashville, Tenn.: Vanderbilt University Press.

———. 1990. *The Civil Rights Era: Origins and Development of National Policy, 1960–1972.* New York: Oxford University Press.

Graves, John W. 1967. "Negro Disfranchisement in Arkansas." *Arkansas Historical Quarterly* 36: 199–225.

Gray, Richard E., III, and Roger Moore. 1995a. "State Appellants' Brief on the Merits" (brief in U.S. Supreme Court, *Bush v. Vera*). Mimeo.

———. 1995b. "State Appellants' Reply Brief on the Merits" (brief in U.S. Supreme Court, *Bush v. Vera*). Mimeo.

Greene, Lee S., David H. Grubbs, and Victor C. Hobday. 1975. *Government in Tennessee.* 3d ed. Knoxville: University of Tennessee Press.

Grofman, Bernard. 1982. "Should Representatives Be Typical of Their Constituents?" In *Representation and Redistricting Issues,* edited by Bernard Grofman, Arend Lijphart, Robert B. McKay, and Howard A. Scarrow, 97–99. Lexington, Mass.: Lexington Books.

Grofman, Bernard, and Chandler Davidson, eds. 1992. *Controversies in Minority Voting: The Voting Rights Act in Perspective.* Washington, D.C.: Brookings Institution.

Grofman, Bernard, Lisa Handley, and Richard G. Niemi. 1992. *Minority Representation and the Quest for Voting Equality.* New York: Cambridge University Press.

Gross, Jimmie Franklin. 1969. "Alabama Politics and the Negro, 1874–1901." Unpublished Ph.D. dissertation, University of Georgia.

Grossman, Lawrence. 1976. *The Democratic Party and the Negro: Northern and National Politics, 1868–92.* Urbana: University of Illinois Press.

Guinier, Lani. 1993. "Analysis: Lessons of 'History.'" *Voting Rights Review,* Fall, 3, 12, 14, 19.

Guinn, James Miller. 1902. *Historical and Biographical Record of Southern California.* Chicago, Ill.: Chapman Publishing Co.

Gunther, Gerald. 1972. "The Supreme Court, 1971 Term—Forward: In Search of Evolving Doctrine on a Changing Court: A Model for a Newer Equal Protection." *Harvard Law Review* 86: 1–48.

Gutierrez, David G. 1995. *Walls and Mirrors: Mexican-Americans, Mexican Immigrants, and the Politics of Ethnicity.* Berkeley: University of California Press.

Hair, Penda D. 1994. "Jurisdictional Statement" (brief in U.S. Supreme Court, *Bush v. Vera*). Mimeo.

Hair, William J. 1969. *Bourbonism and Agrarian Protest: Louisiana Politics, 1877–1900.* Baton Rouge: Louisiana State University Press.

Hamilton, Charles V. 1991. *Adam Clayton Powell, Jr.: The Political Biography of an American Dilemma.* New York: Atheneum.

Handler, Joel. 1987–88. "The Transformation of Aid to Families with Dependent Children: The Family Support Act in an Historical Perspective." *New York University Review of Law and Social Change* 16: 457–533.

Harmel, Robert, and Keith E. Hamm. 1986. "Development of a Party Role in a No-Party Legislature." *Western Political Quarterly* 39: 79–92.

Harris, Carl V. 1977. *Political Power in Birmingham, 1871–1921.* Knoxville: University of Tennessee Press.

Harris, William C. 1979. *The Day of the Carpetbagger: Republican Reconstruction in Mississippi.* Baton Rouge: Louisiana State University Press.

Hays, Samuel P. 1980. "The Politics of Reform in Municipal Government in the Progressive Era." In *American Political History as Social Analysis,* 205–32. Knoxville: University of Tennessee Press.

Henderson, Harold Paulk. 1991. *The Politics of Change in Georgia: A Political Biography of Ellis Arnall.* Athens: University of Georgia Press.

Henderson, Harold Paulk, and Gary L. Roberts, eds. 1988. *Georgia Governors in an Age of Change.* Athens: University of Georgia Press.

Hentoff, Nat. 1969. *A Political Life: The Education of John V. Lindsay.* New York: Alfred A. Knopf.

Herbert, Hilary A. 1890. *Why the Solid South? Or Reconstruction and Its Results.* Baltimore, Md.: R. H. Woodward and Co.

Hernstein, Richard J., and Charles Murray. 1994. *The Bell Curve: The Reshaping of American Life by Differences in Intelligence.* New York: Free Press.

Hess, Michael A. 1993. "Brief *Amicus Curiae* of the Republican National Committee in Support of Appellants" (brief in U.S. Supreme Court, *Shaw v. Reno*). Mimeo.

———. 1994. "Jurisdictional Statement" (brief in U.S. Supreme Court, *Shaw v. Hunt*). Mimeo.

Hicks, Renea, and Penda D. Hair. 1994. "Joint Brief in Opposition to Motion to Affirm" (brief in U.S. Supreme Court, *Bush v. Vera*). Mimeo.

Higginbotham, A. Leon, Gregory A. Clarick, and Marcella David. 1994. "*Shaw v. Reno*: A Mirage of Good Intentions with Devastating Racial Consequences." *Fordham Law Review* 62: 1593–1659.

Hinds, M. A. Papers. Mississippi Valley Collection, Old Brister Library, University of Memphis.

Hirshson, Stanley P. 1962. *Farewell to the Bloody Shirt: Northern Republicans and the Southern Negro, 1877–1893.* Bloomington: University of Indiana Press.

Hoar, George F. 1891. "The Fate of the Election Bill." *The Forum* 11: 127–28.

Hochschild, Jennifer L. 1995. *Facing Up to the American Dream: Race, Class, and the Soul of the Nation.* Princeton, N.J.: Princeton University Press.

Hodgkiss, Anita S. 1994. "Motion to Dismiss or Affirm of Appellees Ralph Gingles, *et al.*" (brief in U.S. Supreme Court, *Shaw v. Hunt*). Mimeo.

———. 1995. "Brief of Appellees Gingles *et al.*" (brief in U.S. Supreme Court, *Shaw v. Hunt*). Mimeo.

Hoffer, Peter Charles. 1992. " 'Blind to History' The Use of History in Affirmative Action Suits: Another Look at *City of Richmond v. J. A. Croson Co.*" *Rutgers Law Journal* 23: 271–96.

Holloway, Harry. 1969. *The Politics of the Southern Negro: From Exclusion to Big City Organization.* New York: Random House.

Holt, Thomas C. 1977. *Black Over White: Negro Political Leadership in South Carolina During Reconstruction.* Urbana: University of Illinois Press.

———. 1980. "Afro-Americans." In *Harvard Encyclopedia of American Ethnic Relations*, edited by Stephan Thernstrom, 5–23. Cambridge: Harvard University Press.

Honey, Michael. 1991. "Industrial Unionism and Racial Justice in Memphis." In *Organized Labor in the Twentieth-Century South*, edited by Robert H. Zieger, 135–157. Knoxville: University of Tennessee Press.

Hornsby, Alton, Jr. 1977. "The Negro in Atlanta Politics, 1961–1973." *Atlanta Historical Bulletin* 21: 7–33.

Huber, Peter William. 1993. "Sandra Day O'Connor." In *The Supreme Court Justices: Illustrated Biographies, 1789–1993*, edited by Claire Cushman, 506–10. Washington, D.C.: Congressional Quarterly.

Huckfeldt, Robert, and Carol Weitzel Kohfeld. 1989. *Race and the Decline of Class in American Politics.* Urbana: University of Illinois Press.

Hume, Richard L. 1982. "Negro Delegates to the State Constitutional Conventions of 1867–69." In *Southern Black Leaders of the Reconstruction Era,* edited by Howard N. Rabinowitz, 129–54. Urbana: University of Illinois Press.

Hurd, Paul Loy. 1994a. "Motion to Affirm" (brief in U.S. Supreme Court, *Bush v. Vera*). Mimeo.

———. 1994b. "Plaintiffs' Proposed Findings of Fact" (brief in District court case, *Vera v. Richards*). Mimeo.

———. 1994c. "Post Trial Brief" (brief in District court case, *Vera v. Richards*). Mimeo.

———. 1995. "Brief for Appellees" (brief in U.S. Supreme Court, *Bush v. Vera*). Mimeo.

Irons, Peter H. 1983. *Justice at War.* New York: Oxford University Press.

Issacharoff, Samuel. 1995. "The Constitutional Contours of Race and Politics." *Supreme Court Review* 1995: 45–70.

Issel, William, and Robert W. Cherny. 1986. *San Francisco, 1865–1932: Politics, Power, and Urban Development.* Berkeley: University of California Press.

Jackson, Luther Porter. 1945. *Negro Officeholders in Virginia, 1865–1895.* Norfolk, Va.: Guide Quality Press.

Jacobs, John. 1995. *A Rage for Justice: The Passion and Politics of Phillip Burton.* Berkeley: University of California Press.

Jacobson, Gary C. 1990. *The Electoral Origins of Divided Government: Competition in U.S. House Elections, 1946–1988.* Boulder, Colo.: Westview.

Jalenak, James B. 1961. "Beale Street Politics: A Study of Negro Political Activity in Memphis, Tennessee." Unpublished senior honors thesis, Yale University.

Johnson, Ross. 1983. "Latinos in the Law: Meeting the Challenge—Reapportionment." *Chicano Law Review* 6: 38–39, 59–60.

Jones, Elaine R. 1993. "Brief *Amici Curiae* in Support of Appellees of the NAACP Legal Defense and Education Fund, Inc." (brief in U.S. Supreme Court, *Shaw v. Reno*). Mimeo.

Kaczorowski, Robert J. 1972–73. "Searching for the Intent of the Framers of the Fourteenth Amendment." *Connecticut Law Review* 5: 368–98.

———. 1985. *The Politics of Judicial Interpretation: The Federal Courts, The Department of Justice and Civil Rights, 1866–1876.* New York: Oceana.

Kantor, Shawn Everett, and J. Morgan Kousser. 1993. "A Rejoinder: Two Visions of History." *Journal of Southern History* 59: 259–66.

Karlan, Pamela S. 1983. "Discriminatory Purpose and Mens Rea: The Tortured Argument of Invidious Intent." *Yale Law Journal* 93: 111–34.

———. 1989. "Maps and Misreadings: The Role of Geographic Compactness in Racial Vote Dilution Litigation." *Harvard Civil Rights-Civil Liberties Law Review* 24: 175–248.

———. 1993a. "All Over the Map: The Supreme Court's Voting Rights Trilogy." *Supreme Court Review* 24: 264–70.

———. 1993b. "The Rights to Votes: Some Pessimism About Formalism." *Texas Law Review* 71: 1705–40.

———. 1994. "End of the Second Reconstruction?" *Nation,* May 23, 698–700.

————. 1995. "Our Separatism? Voting Rights as an American Nationalities Policy." *University of Chicago Legal Forum* 1995: 83–109.

————. 1996. "Still Hazy After All These Years: Voting Rights in the Post-*Shaw* Era." *Cumberland Law Review* 26: 287–311.

————. 1997. "Loss and Redemption: Voting Rights at the Turn of a Century." *Vanderbilt Law Review* 50: 291–326.

Karlan, Pamela S., and Daryl J. Levinson. 1996. "Why Voting Is Different." *California Law Review* 84: 1201–32.

Karlan, Pamela S., and Peyton McCrary. 1988. "Book Review: Without Fear and Without Research: Abigail Thernstrom on the Voting Rights Act." *Journal of Law and Politics* 4: 751–77.

Karst, Kenneth L. 1978. "The Costs of Motive-Centered Inquiry." *San Diego Law Review* 15: 1163–66.

————. 1993. *Law's Promise, Law's Expression: Visions of Power in the Politics of Race, Gender, and Religion.* New Haven: Yale University Press.

Katzenbach, Nicholas deB., et al. 1993. "Brief of *Amici Curiae* Lawyers' Committee for Civil Rights Under Law, the American Civil Liberties Union, the Mexican American Legal Defense and Educational Fund, and the National Association for the Advancement of Colored People in Support of Appellees" (brief in U.S. Supreme Court, *Shaw v. Reno*). Mimeo.

Kay, Richard S. 1980. "The Equal Protection Clause in the Supreme Court, 1873–1903." *Buffalo Law Review* 29: 667–725.

Kazee, Thomas A., ed. 1994. *Who Runs for Congress? Ambition, Context, and Candidate Emergence.* Washington, D.C.: Congressional Quarterly.

Kelly, Alfred H. 1956. "The Fourteenth Amendment Reconsidered: The Segregation Question." *Michigan Law Review* 54: 1049–86.

Kelly, Michael. 1995. "Segregation Anxiety." *New Yorker* 71, no. 37 (Nov. 20): 43–54.

Kern, Montague, and Marion Just. 1995. "The Focus Group Method, Political Advertising, Campaign News, and the Construction of Candidate Images." *Political Communication* 12: 127–45.

Key, V. O., Jr. 1949. *Southern Politics in State and Nation.* New York: Vintage.

Kinder, Donald R., and Lynn M. Sanders. 1996. *Divided By Color: Racial Politics and Democratic Ideals.* Chicago: University of Chicago Press.

King, Willard L. 1950. *Melville Weston Fuller, Chief Justice of the United States, 1888–1910.* New York: Macmillan.

Klarman, Michael. 1991. "An Interpretive History of Modern Equal Protection." *Michigan Law Review* 90: 213–318.

Kleppner, Paul. 1982. *Who Voted? The Dynamics of Electoral Turnout, 1870–1980.* New York: Praeger.

————. 1995. "*Todo Cambia, Pero Nada Cambia*: Ward Redistricting Chicago Style." Expert witness report, *Bonilla v. City of Chicago*, No. 92 C2666 (N.D. Ill. 1996).

Kluegel, James R., and Elliot R. Smith. 1986. *Beliefs about Inequality: Americans' Views of What Is and What Ought to Be.* Hawthorne, N.Y.: Aldine de Gruter.

Kluger, Richard. 1975. *Simple Justice: The History of Brown v. Board of Education and Black America's Struggle for Equality.* New York: Vintage.

Kolchin, Peter. 1993. *American Slavery, 1619-1877.* New York: Hill and Wang.

Kousser, J. Morgan. 1965. "Tennessee Politics and the Negro, 1948-1964." Unpublished senior thesis, Princeton University.

———. 1973. "Post-Reconstruction Suffrage Restrictions in Tennessee: A New Look at the V. O. Key Thesis." *Political Science Quarterly* 88: 655-83.

———. 1974. *The Shaping of Southern Politics: Suffrage Restriction and the Establishment of the One-Party South, 1880-1910.* New Haven: Yale University Press.

———. 1979. "Making Separate Equal: The Integration of Black and White School Funds in Kentucky." *Journal of Interdisciplinary History* 10: 399-428.

———. 1980a. "Progressivism—For Middle-Class Whites Only: North Carolina Education, 1880-1910." *Journal of Southern History* 46: 169-94.

———. 1980b. "Separate but Not Equal: The Supreme Court's First Decision on Racial Discrimination in Schools." *Journal of Southern History* 46: 17-44.

———. 1984a. "Are Expert Witnesses Whores? Reflections on Objectivity in Scholarship and Expert Witnessing." *Public Historian* 6: 7-12.

———. 1984b. "Origins of the Run-Off Primary." *Black Scholar* 15: 23-26.

———. 1984c. "Suffrage." In *Encyclopedia of American Political History,* edited by Jack P. Greene, 3:1236-58. New York: Charles Scribner's Sons.

———. 1984d. "The Undermining of the First Reconstruction: Lessons for the Second." In C. Davidson, 1984. 27-46.

———. 1986. *Dead End: The Development of Nineteenth-Century Litigation on Racial Discrimination in Schools.* Oxford, Eng.: Clarendon.

———. 1988a. "Expert Witnesses, Rational Choice and the Search for Intent." *Constitutional Commentary* 5: 352-53.

———. 1988b. "'The Supremacy of Equal Rights': The Struggle Against Racial Discrimination in Antebellum Massachusetts and the Foundations of the Fourteenth Amendment." *Northwestern University Law Review* 82: 941-1010.

———. 1991a. "Before *Plessy,* Before *Brown*: The Development of the Law of Racial Integration in Louisiana and Kansas." In *Toward a Usable Past: Liberty Under State Governments,* edited by Paul Finkelman and Stephen C. Gottlieb, 213-70. Athens: University of Georgia Press.

———. 1991b. "How to Determine Intent: Lessons from L.A." *Journal of Law and Politics* 7: 591-732.

———. 1992. "Was Memphis's Electoral Structure Adopted or Maintained for a Racially Discriminatory Purpose?" Caltech Social Science Working Paper No. 807. Pasadena: California Institute of Technology.

———. 1993. "Beyond *Gingles*: Influence Districts and the Pragmatic Tradition in Voting Rights Law." *University of San Francisco Law Review* 27: 551-92.

———. 1995a. "Estimating the Partisan Consequences of Redistricting Plans—Simply." Caltech Social Science Working Paper No. 929. Pasadena: California Institute of Technology.

———. 1995b. "Reapportionment Wars: Party, Race, and Redistricting in California,

1971-1992." Caltech Social Science Working Paper No. 930. Pasadena: California Institute of Technology.

———. 1995c. "*Shaw v. Reno* and the Real World of Redistricting and Representation." *Rutgers Law Journal* 26: 625–710.

Kramer, Michael. 1996. "Rescuing Boris." *Time Magazine*, July 15, 29–37.

Kuklinski, James H., Michael D. Cobb, and Martin Gilens. 1997. "Racial Attitudes and the 'New South.'" *Journal of Politics* 59: 232–49.

Kull, Andrew. 1992. *The Color-Blind Constitution.* Cambridge: Harvard University Press.

Kutler, Stanley I. 1969. "William Strong." In Friedman and Israel 1969, 2: 1151–61.

La Fetra, Deborah J. 1995. "Brief *Amicus Curiae* of Pacific Legal Foundation in Support of Appellees, Al Vera, *et al.*" (brief in U.S. Supreme Court, *Bush v. Vera*). Mimeo.

Lamon, Lester C. 1977. *Black Tennesseans, 1900-1930.* Knoxville: University of Tennessee Press.

Lawrence, Charles R. 1980. "'One More River to Cross'—Recognizing the Real Injury in *Brown*: A Prerequisite to Shaping New Remedies." In *Shades of Brown: New Perspectives on School Desegregation,* edited by Derrick Bell, 48–68. New York: Teachers College Press, Columbia University.

Lawson, Steven F. 1976. *Black Ballots: Voting Rights in the South, 1944-1969.* New York: Columbia University Press.

———. 1985. *In Pursuit of Power: Southern Blacks and Electoral Politics, 1965-1982.* New York: Columbia University Press.

Lewinson, Paul. [1932] 1963. *Race, Class, and Party: A History of Negro Suffrage and White Politics in the South.* New York: Russell and Russell.

Lichtman, Allan J. 1994. "Final Report" (report in District court case, *Vera v. Richards*). Mimeo.

Lipsky, Michael. 1984. "Bureaucratic Disentitlement in Social Welfare Programs." *Social Service Review* 58: 3–27.

Loe, Victoria. 1981. "The Deal That Didn't Work." *Texas Monthly,* August, 136–39, 212–22.

Lofgren, Charles A. 1987. *The Plessy Case: A Legal-Historical Interpretation.* New York: Oxford University Press.

Logan, Rayford W. 1965. *The Betrayal of the Negro: From Rutherford B. Hayes to Woodrow Wilson.* New York: Collier.

Los Angeles County Citizens' Economy and Efficiency Commission. 1970. "Report" (July 14). Mimeo.

———. 1974. "Report." Mimeo.

Lowenstein, Daniel Hays. 1995. *Teachers Manual for Election Law: Cases and Materials.* Durham, N.C.: Carolina Academic Press.

Lowenstein, Daniel Hays, and Jonathan Steinberg. 1985. "The Quest for Legislative Districting in the Public Interest: Elusive or Illusory?" *U.C.L.A. Law Review* 33: 1–75.

Lublin, David. 1997. *The Paradox of Representation: Racial Gerrymandering and Minority Interests in Congress.* Princeton, N.J.: Princeton University Press.

Maddala, G. S. 1983. *Limited-Dependent and Qualitative Variables in Econometrics.* Cambridge: Cambridge University Press.

Maddex, Jack P., Jr. 1970. *The Virginia Conservatives, 1867-1879.* Chapel Hill: University of North Carolina Press.

Maddocks, Lewis I. 1959. "Justice John Marshall Harlan: Defender of Individual Rights." Unpublished Ph.D. dissertation, Ohio State University.

Magrath, C. Peter. 1963. *Morrison R. Waite: The Triumph of Character.* New York: Macmillan.

Malone, Stephen J. 1997. "Recognizing Communities of Interest in a Legislative Apportionment Plan." *Virginia Law Review* 83: 461-92.

Maltz, Earl M. 1990. "The Prospects for a Revival of Conservative Activism in Constitutional Jurisprudence." *Georgia Law Review* 24: 629-68.

Mann, Kimberley V. 1993-94. "*Shaw v. Reno*: A Grim Foreboding for Minority Voting Rights." *Maryland Journal of Contemporary Legal Issues* 5: 147-71.

Marable, Manning. 1991. *Race, Reform, and Rebellion: The Second Reconstruction in Black America, 1945-1990.* 2d ed. Jackson: University Press of Mississippi.

Marshall, Burke. 1984. "A Comment on the Nondiscrimination Principle in a 'Nation of Minorities.'" *Yale Law Journal* 93: 1006-12.

Martis, Kenneth C. 1982. *The Historical Atlas of United States Congressional Districts, 1789-1983.* New York: Free Press.

Massey, Douglas S., and Nancy A. Denton. 1993. *American Apartheid: Segregation and the Making of the Underclass.* Cambridge: Harvard University Press.

Mathews, John Mabry. [1909] 1971. *Legislative and Judicial History of the Fifteenth Amendment.* Reprint, New York: Da Capo Press.

Maveety, Nancy. 1996. *Justice Sandra Day O'Connor: Strategist on the Supreme Court.* Lanham, Md.: Rowman and Littlefield.

Mayer, Jane, and Jill Abramson. 1994. *Strange Justice: The Selling of Clarence Thomas.* Boston: Houghton Mifflin.

McClain, Charles J. 1994. *In Search of Equality: The Chinese Struggle against Discrimination in Nineteenth-Century America.* Berkeley: University of California Press.

McCrary, Peyton. 1984. "History in the Courts: The Significance of *Bolden v. The City of Mobile.*" In C. Davidson 1984, 47-63.

———. 1985. "Discriminatory Intent: The Continuing Relevance of 'Purpose' Evidence in Vote-Dilution Lawsuits." *Howard Law Journal* 28: 463-93.

———. 1990. "Racially Polarized Voting in the South: Quantitative Evidence from the Courtroom." *Social Science History* 14: 507-31.

McCrary, Peyton, and J. Gerald Hebert. 1989. "Keeping the Courts Honest: The Role of Historians as Expert Witnesses in Southern Voting Rights Cases." *Southern University Law Review* 16: 101-28.

McDonald, Laughlin. 1989. "The Quiet Revolution in Minority Voting Rights." *Vanderbilt Law Review* 42: 1249-97.

———. 1993. "Voting Rights and the Court: Drawing the Lines." *Southern Changes* (Fall): 15.

———. 1995a. "The Counterrevolution in Minority Voting Rights." *Mississippi Law Journal* 65: 271-313.

———. 1995b. "*Holder v. Hall*: Blinking at Minority Voting Rights." *District of Columbia Law Review* 3: 61-100.

McDonald, Laughlin, et al. 1994. "Brief of Appellants, *Abrams v. Johnson*" (brief in U.S. Supreme Court, *Miller v. Johnson*). Mimeo.

———. 1995. "Brief *Amicus Curiae* of the American Civil Liberties Union and the Lawyers' Committee for Civil Rights Under Law in Support of Appellees" (brief in U.S. Supreme Court, *Shaw v. Hunt*). Mimeo.

McDonald, Laughlin, Michael B. Binford, and Ken Johnson. 1994. "Georgia." In Davidson and Grofman 1994, 67–102.

McFeely, William S. 1991. "Two Reconstructions, Two Nations." *Massachusetts Review* (Spring): 39–53.

McMillan, Malcolm Cook. 1955. *Constitutional Development in Alabama, 1798–1901: A Study in Politics, The Negro, and Sectionalism.* Chapel Hill: University of North Carolina Press.

McKnight, Gerald D. [1984] 1989. "The 1968 Memphis Sanitation Strike and the FBI: A Case Study in Urban Surveillance." In *Martin Luther King., Jr. and the Civil Rights Movement*, edited by David J. Garrow, 2:637–55. Reprint, Brooklyn, N.Y.: Carlson.

McPherson, Edward. 1872. *Handbook of Politics for 1872.* Washington, D.C.: Phillip and Solomons.

———. 1876. *Handbook of Politics for 1876.* Washington, D.C.: Solomons and Chapman.

———. [1871] 1972. *The Political History of the United States of America During the Period of Reconstruction, April 15, 1865–July 15, 1870.* Reprint, New York: Da Capo Press.

———. [1890] 1974. *Handbook of Politics for 1890.* Reprint, New York: Da Capo Press.

Meeman, Edwin. Papers. Mississippi Valley Collection, Old Brister Library, University of Memphis.

Mele, Alfred R. 1992. *Springs of Action: Understanding Intentional Behavior.* New York: Oxford University Press.

Melton, Gloria Brown. 1982. "Blacks in Memphis, Tennessee, 1920–1955: A Historical Study." Unpublished Ph.D. dissertation, Washington State University.

Meier, August. 1957. *Negro Thought in America, 1880–1915.* Ann Arbor: University of Michigan Press.

Meier, Matt S., and Feliciano Rivera. 1972. *The Chicanos: A History of Mexican Americans.* New York: Hill and Wang.

Memphis and Shelby County Charter Commission. 1962. "Charter of the Consolidated Government of Memphis and Shelby County." In Program of Progress Papers, Old Brister Library, University of Memphis, folder 123.

Memphis Board of Education. Minutes. Files in Memphis City Schools Building, 2597 Avery, Memphis, Tenn.)

Memphis Business. 1961–62, various issues. In Program of Progress Papers, Old Brister Library, University of Memphis, folder 58.

Miller, Andrew P., and Mark A. Packman. 1987. "Amended Section 2 of the Voting Rights Act: What is the Intent of the Results Test?" *Emory Law Journal* 36: 1–73.

Miller, Barry A. 1977. "Proof of Racially Discriminatory Purpose Under the Equal Protection Clause: *Washington v. Davis, Arlington Heights, Mt. Healthy,* and *Williamsburgh.*" *Harvard Civil Rights–Civil Liberties Law Review* 12: 725–70.

Miller, William D. 1957. *Memphis During the Progressive Era.* Memphis, Tenn.: Memphis State University Press.

————. 1964. *Mr. Crump of Memphis.* Baton Rouge: Louisiana State University Press.

Moores, Merrill. 1917. *A Historical and Legal Digest of All the Contested Election Cases in the House of Representatives of the United States, 1901-1917.* Washington, D.C.: GPO.

Morris, Jack H. N.d. "Chronology of a Charter." Unpublished manuscript, in Program of Progress Papers, Old Brister Library, University of Memphis, folder 112.

————. 1991. "Affidavit" (brief in District court case, *U.S. v. City of Memphis,* July 18). Mimeo.

Murphy, Walter F. 1962. *Congress and the Court.* Chicago: University of Chicago Press.

Navarro, Carlos. 1981. "A Report on California Redistricting and Representation for the Los Angeles Chicano Community." In Santillan 1981, 132–54.

Navarro, Carlos, and Richard Santillan. 1981. "The Latino Community and California Redistricting in the 1980s: Californios for Fair Representation." In Santillan 1981, 50–117.

Newby, I. A. 1969. *Challenge to the Court: Social Scientists and the Defense of Segregation, 1954-1966.* Rev. ed. Baton Rouge: Louisiana State University Press.

Nieman, Donald G. 1991. *Promises to Keep: African-Americans and the Constitutional Order, 1776 to the Present.* New York: Oxford University Press.

Niemi, Richard G., Bernard Grofman, Carl Carlucci, and Thomas Hofeller. 1990. "Measuring Compactness and the Role of a Compactness Standard in a Test for Partisan and Racial Gerrymandering." *Journal of Politics* 52: 1155–81.

Niven, John. 1995. *Salmon P. Chase, A Biography.* New York: Oxford University Press.

Norrell, Robert J. 1985. *Reaping the Whirlwind: The Civil Rights Movement in Tuskegee.* New York: Knopf.

Norris, Christopher. 1992. *Uncritical Theory: Postmodernism, Intellectuals, and the Gulf War.* Amherst: University of Massachusetts Press.

North Carolina Joint Redistricting Committee (JRC). 1981. Files. North Carolina Legislature, Raleigh.

Note. 1976. "Reading the Mind of the School Board: Segregative Intent and the De Facto/De Jure Distinction." *Yale Law Journal* 86: 317–55.

Note. 1982a. "The Constitutional Significance of the Discriminatory Effects of At-Large Elections.: *Yale Law Journal* 91: 974–99.

Note. 1982b. "Making the Violation Fit the Remedy: The Intent Standard and Equal Protection Law." *Yale Law Journal* 92: 328–51.

Note. 1993. "The Supreme Court—Leading Cases." *Harvard Law Review* 107: 144–371.

Orr, Douglas Milton, Jr. 1970. *Congressional Redistricting: The North Carolina Experience.* Chapel Hill: Dept. of Geography, University of North Carolina.

O'Rourke, Timothy G. 1995. "*Shaw v. Reno*: The Shape of Things to Come." *Rutgers Law Journal* 26: 723–73.

Ortiz, Daniel R. 1989. "The Myth of Intent in Equal Protection." *Stanford Law Review* 41: 1105–52.'

Padgett, James A. 1937. "From Slavery to Prominence in North Carolina." *Journal of Negro History* 22: 433–87.

Padilla, Fernando V. 1981. "Chicano Representation by Court Order: Impact of Reapportionment." In Santillan 1981, 83–101.

Pajari, Roger N. 1988. "Herman E. Talmadge and the Politics of Power." In Henderson and Roberts 1988, 75–92.

Palmer, Bryan D. 1990. *Descent into Discourse: The Reification of Language and the Writing of Social History.* Philadelphia: Temple University Press.

Parent, Wayne, and Paul Stekler. 1985. "The Political Implications of Economic Stratification in the Black Community." *Western Political Quarterly* 38: 521–38.

Parker, Frank R. 1983. "The 'Results' Test of Section 2 of the Voting Rights Act: Abandoning the Intent Standard." *Virginia Law Review* 69: 715–64.

———. 1990. *Black Votes Count: Political Empowerment in Mississippi after 1965.* Chapel Hill: University of North Carolina Press.

———. 1995. "The Constitutionality of Racial Redistricting: A Critique of *Shaw v. Reno.*" *District of Columbia Law Review* 3: 1–59.

Parsons, Stanley B., William B. Beech, and Michael J. Dubin. 1986. *United States Congressional Districts and Data, 1843–1883.* New York: Greenwood.

Parsons, Stanley B., Michael J. Dubin, and Karen Toombs Parsons. 1990. *United States Congressional Districts, 1883–1913.* New York: Greenwood.

Paul, Arnold. 1969. "David J. Brewer." In Friedman and Israel 1969, 2: 1515–34.

Pearson, Jessica, and Jeffrey Pearson. 1978. "Denver: *Keyes v. School District No. 1.*" In *Limits of Justice: The Court's Role in School Desegregation,* edited by Howard I. Kalodner and James J. Fishman, 167–222. Cambridge, Mass.: Ballinger.

Peller, Gary. 1997. "Cultural Imperialism, White Anxiety, and the Ideological Realignment of *Brown.*" In Sarat 1997, 190–220.

Perman, Michael. 1973. *Reunion Without Compromise: The South and Reconstruction, 1865–1868.* Cambridge: Cambridge University Press.

———. 1984. *The Road to Redemption: Southern Politics, 1869–1879.* Chapel Hill: University of North Carolina Press.

Perry, Huey L., ed. 1996. *Race, Politics, and Governance in the United States.* Gainesville: University Press of Florida.

Perry, Michael J. 1977. "The Disproportionate Racial Impact Theory of Racial Discrimination." *University of Pennsylvania Law Review* 125: 540–89.

Pettigrew, Thomas F., ed. 1975. *Racial Discrimination in the United States.* New York: Harper and Row.

———. 1979. "Racial Change and Social Policy." *Annals of the American Academy of Political and Social Science* 441: 114–31.

———. 1980. "Prejudice." In S. Thernstrom 1980, 820–29.

———. 1985. "New Black-White Patterns: How Best to Conceptualize Them?" *Annual Review of Sociology* 11: 329–46.

———. 1989. "The Nature of Modern Racism in the United States." *Revue Internationale de Psychologie Sociale* 1989: 293–303.

Pettigrew, Thomas F., and Denise A. Alston. 1988. *Tom Bradley's Campaigns for Governor: The Dilemma of Race and Political Strategies.* Washington, D.C.: Joint Center for Political Studies.

Phelps, Timothy M., and Helen Winternitz. 1992. *Capitol Games: Clarence Thomas, Anita Hill, and the Story of a Supreme Court Nomination.* New York: Hyperion.

Pike, James S. 1874. *The Prostrate State: South Carolina Under Negro Government.* New York: D. Appleton and Co.

Pildes, Richard H. 1995. "Book Review: The Politics of Race." *Harvard Law Review* 108: 1359–92.

———. 1997. "Principled Limitations on Racial and Partisan Redistricting." *Yale Law Journal* 106: 2505–61.

Pildes, Richard H., and Richard G. Niemi. 1993. "Expressive Harms, 'Bizarre Districts,' and Voting Rights: Evaluating Election-District Appearances After *Shaw v. Reno.*" *Michigan Law Review* 92: 101–205.

Pitt, Leonard. 1966. *The Decline of the Californios: A Social History of the Spanish-Speaking Californians, 1846–1890.* Berkeley: University of California Press.

Piven, Frances Fox, and Richard A. Cloward. 1996. "Northern Bourbons: A Preliminary Report on the National Voter Registration Act." *PS: Political Science and Politics* 29(1): 39–43.

Plano, Jack C., and Milton Greenberg. 1976. *The American Political Dictionary.* 4th ed. New York: Holt, Rinehart and Winston.

Pohlmann, Marcus D., and Michael P. Kirby. 1996. *Racial Politics at the Crossroads: Memphis Elects Dr. W. W. Herenton.* Knoxville: University of Tennessee Press.

Politz, Henry A., et al. 1992. "*In Re*: The Complaint of Lewis H. Earl against United States District Judge James R. Nowlin under the Judicial Conduct and Disability Act of 1980" (May 15). Mimeo.

Polsby, Daniel D., and Robert D. Popper. 1993. "Ugly: An Inquiry into the Problem of Racial Gerrymandering Under the Voting Rights Act." *Michigan Law Review* 92: 652–83.

Popeo, Daniel J., and Richard A. Samp. 1993. "Brief of Washington Legal Foundation, U.S. Senator Jesse Helms, and the Equal Opportunity Foundation as *Amici Curiae* in Support of Appellants" (brief in U.S. Supreme Court, *Shaw v. Reno*). Mimeo.

Powell, H. Jefferson. 1993. "State Appellees' Brief" (brief in U.S. Supreme Court, *Shaw v. Reno*). Mimeo.

Program of Progress Papers. Mississippi Valley Collection, Old Brister Library, University of Memphis.

Prysby, Charles L. 1996. "The 1990 U.S. Senate Election in North Carolina." In H. Perry 1996, 29–46.

Public Commission on Los Angeles County Government. 1976. "To Serve Seven Million" (Feb.) Mimeo.

Purdon, [John]. 1930. *Purdon's Pennsylvania Statutes Annotated.* St. Paul, Minn.: West Publishing.

Pyles, Charles. 1988. "S. Ernest Vandiver and the Politics of Change." In Henderson and Roberts 1988, 143–56.

Rabinowitz, Howard N. 1978. *Race Relations in the Urban South, 1865–1890.* New York: Oxford University Press.

———. 1994. *Race, Ethnicity, and Urbanization.* Columbia: University of Missouri Press.

Reeves, Keith. 1997. *Voting Hopes or Fears? White Voters, Black Candidates and Racial Politics in America.* New York: Oxford University Press.

Regalado, James A., and Gloria Martinez. 1991. "Reapportionment and Coalition Building: A Case Study of Informal Barriers to Latino Empowerment in Los Angeles County." In *Latinos and Political Coalitions: Political Empowerment for the 1990s,* edited by Roberto E. Villarreal and Norma G. Hernandez, 126-43. New York: Praeger.

Reynolds, William Bradford. 1984. "Individualism vs. Group Rights: The Legacy of *Brown.*" *Yale Law Journal* 93: 995-1005.

Rice, Bradley Robert. 1977. *Progressive Cities: The Commission Government Movement in America, 1901-1920.* Austin: University of Texas Press.

Rice, Lawrence D. 1971. *The Negro in Texas, 1874-1900.* Baton Rouge: Louisiana State University Press.

Richardson, James D. 1900. *The Compilation of the Messages and Papers of the Presidents, 1789-1897.* Washington, D.C.: GPO.

Richardson, Joe M. 1965. *The Negro in the Reconstruction of Florida, 1865-1877.* Tallahassee: Florida State University Press.

Richardson, Leon Burr. 1940. *William E. Chandler, Republican.* New York: Dodd, Mead.

Ripy, Thomas B., Jr. 1973. "Changes in the Formal Structure of Municipal Government and Their Effect on Selected Aspects of the Legislative Process: A Case Study of Memphis, Tennessee." Unpublished Ph.D. dissertation, University of Kentucky.

Roberts, Gary L. 1988. "Tradition and Consensus: An Introduction to Gubernatorial Leadership in Georgia, 1943-1983." In Henderson and Roberts 1988, 1-21.

Roberts, Paul Craig, and Lawrence M. Stratton, Jr. 1995. *Redrawing the Color Line: How the Civil Rights Movement Destroyed Liberalism.* New York: Regnery.

Roberts, Ronald Suresh. 1995. *Clarence Thomas and the Tough Love Crowd: Counterfeit Heroes and Unhappy Truths.* New York: New York University Press.

Roitman, Joel. 1964. "Race Relations in Memphis, Tennessee, 1880-1905" Unpublished master's thesis, Memphis State University.

Romo, Ricardo. 1983. *East Los Angeles: History of a Barrio.* Austin: University of Texas Press.

The Rose Institute. 1988a. "The Demographics of California's Latinos: Maps and Statistics." Mimeo. The Rose Institute, Claremont, Calif.

————. 1988b. "Facts and Figures on California's Latino Voters." Mimeo. The Rose Institute, Claremont, Calif.

Rosen, Jeffrey. 1996. "Sandramandered." *New Republic,* July 8, 6, 41.

Rosenau, Pauline Marie. 1992. *Post-Modernism and the Social Sciences.* Princeton, N.J.: Princeton University Press.

Rothbart, Myron, and Oliver P. John. 1993. "Intergroup Relations and Stereotype Change: A Social-Cognitive Analysis and Some Longitudinal Findings." In *Prejudice, Politics, and the American Dilemma,* edited by Paul M. Sniderman, Philip E. Tetlock, and Edward G. Carmines, 32-59. Stanford, Calif.: Stanford University Press.

Rowell, Chester H., comp. 1901. *Digest of Contested Election Cases, 1789-1901.* Washington, D.C.: GPO.

Rumbaut, Carmen, and Penda D. Hair. 1995a. "Brief of Appellants" (brief in U.S. Supreme Court, *Bush v. Vera*). Mimeo.

———. 1995b. "Reply Brief of Appellants" (brief in U.S. Supreme Court, *Bush v. Vera*). Mimeo.

Safire, William. 1978. *Safire's Political Dictionary*. New York: Random House.

Sanchez, George J. 1993. *Becoming Mexican American: Ethnicity, Culture, and Identity in Chicano Los Angeles, 1900-1945*. New York: Oxford University Press.

Santillan, Richard, ed. 1981. *The Hispanic Community and Redistricting*. Claremont, Calif.: Rose Institute.

———. 1983. "The Chicano Community and the Redistricting of the Los Angeles City Council, 1971-1973." *Chicano Law Review* 6: 122–43.

Sarat, Austin, ed. 1997. *Race, Law, and Culture: Reflections on Brown v. Board of Education*. New York: Oxford University Press.

Saxton, Alexander. 1971. *The Indispensable Enemy: Labor and the Anti-Chinese Movement in California*. Berkeley: University of California Press.

Scammon, Richard M., and Alice V. McGillivray. 1976-1991. *America Votes*. Biennial. Washington, D.C.: Congressional Quarterly.

Schiesl, Martin J. 1977. *The Politics of Efficiency: Municipal Administration and Reform in America, 1800-1920*. Berkeley: University of California Press.

Schrag, Peter. 1996. "The Populist Road to Hell: Term Limits in California." *American Prospect* (Winter) 24: 24–30.

Schuman, Howard, Charlotte Steeh, and Lawrence Bobo. 1985. *Racial Attitudes in America: Trends and Interpretations*. Cambridge: Harvard University Press.

Schwartz, Bernard, ed. 1970. *Statutory History of the United States: Civil Rights*. 2 vols. New York: Chelsea House.

———. 1990. *The New Right and the Constitution: Turning Back the Legal Clock*. Boston: Northeastern University Press.

Schwartz, Herman, ed. 1987. *The Burger Years: Rights and Wrongs in the Supreme Court, 1969-1986*. New York: Penguin.

Seidman, Louis Michael, and Mark V. Tushnet. 1996. *Remnants of Belief: Contemporary Constitutional Issues*. New York: Oxford University Press.

Sellers, Joseph M. 1980. "The Impact of Intent on Equal Protection Jurisprudence." *Dickinson Law Review* 84: 363–94.

Shadgett, Olive Hall. 1964. *The Republican Party in Georgia, From Reconstruction to 1900*. Athens: University of Georgia Press.

Sherstruk, Katerina. 1993. "How to Gerrymander: A Formal Analysis." Caltech Social Science Working Paper No. 855 (July). California Institute of Technology, Pasadena.

Sigelman, Lee, and Susan Welch. 1991. *Black Americans' Views of Racial Inequality: The Dream Deferred*. Cambridge: Cambridge University Press.

Simon, James F. 1995. *The Center Holds: The Power Struggle Inside the Rehnquist Court*. New York: Simon and Schuster.

Simon, Larry G. 1978. "Racially Prejudiced Governmental Actions: A Motivation Theory of the Constitutional Ban Against Racial Discrimination." *San Diego Law Review* 15: 1041-1130.

Simpson, Brooks D. 1992. " 'This Bloody and Monstrous Crime.' " *Constitution* 4 (Fall): 38–46.

Skerry, Peter. 1993. *Mexican Americans: The Ambivalent Minority.* New York: Free Press.

Smallwood, James. 1974. "Black Texans During Reconstruction." Unpublished Ph.D. dissertation, Texas Tech University.

Smith, Arlo Hale. 1994. "Jurisdictional Statement" (brief in U.S. Supreme Court, *DeWitt v. Wilson*). Mimeo.

Smith, Paul M. 1995. "Brief *Amici Curiae* of the Democratic National Committee and the Democratic Congressional Campaign Committee Supporting Appellants" (brief in U.S. Supreme Court, *Bush v. Vera*). Mimeo.

Smith, Robert C., and Richard Seltzer. 1992. *Race, Class, and Culture: A Study in Afro-American Mass Opinion.* Albany: State University of New York Press.

Smith, Samuel Denny. 1940. *The Negro in Congress, 1870-1901.* Chapel Hill: University of North Carolina Press.

Smith, W. H. 1905. "Is the Negro Disfranchised?" *The Outlook* 79: 1047-49.

Sniderman, Paul M., and Thomas Piazza. 1993. *The Scar of Race.* Cambridge: Harvard University Press.

Soifer, Aviam. 1981. "Complacency and Constitutional Law." *Ohio State Law Journal* 42: 383-409.

South Carolina Constitutional Convention. 1895. *Journal of the Proceedings.* Columbia, S.C.: Charles A. Calvo, Jr.

Southern Regional Council. 1968. *Black Elected Officials in the Southern States.* Atlanta: Voter Education Project of the Southern Regional Council.

Spears, Ellen. 1992. "The Republicans Go to Court." Atlanta: Southern Regional Council. Mimeo.

——. 1994. "Black-Majority Districts Upheld in North Carolina; Struck in Louisiana." *Voting Rights Review,* Summer, 1-35.

——. 1996. "High Court Rules—Dismantling of Minority Districts to Continue." *Voting Rights Review,* Summer, 1-14.

Speas, Edwin M., Jr. 1994. "Motion to Affirm by Appellees, the Governor and Other Officials of the State of North Carolina" (brief in U.S. Supreme Court, *Shaw v. Hunt*). Mimeo.

——. 1995. "State Appellees' Brief" (brief in U.S. Supreme Court, *Shaw v. Hunt*). Mimeo.

Sperber, Hans, and Travis Trillschuh. 1962. *American Political Terms: An Historical Dictionary.* Detroit: Wayne State University Press.

Sperling, Jonathan M. 1994. "Equal Protection and Race-Conscious Reapportionment: *Shaw v. Reno.*" *Harvard Journal of Law and Public Policy* 17: 283-92.

Starr, Kenneth W. 1992. "Brief for the United States as *Amicus Curiae* Supporting Appellants" (brief in U.S. Supreme Court *Voinovich v. Quilter*). Mimeo.

Stavis, Morton. 1987. "A Century of Struggle for Black Enfranchisement in Mississippi: From the Civil War to the Congressional Challenge of 1965 and Beyond." *Mississippi Law Journal* 57: 591-673.

Stern, Robert M. 1989. *Money and Politics in the Golden State: Financing California's Local Elections.* Los Angeles: Center for Responsive Government.

Strauss, David A. 1986. "The Myth of Colorblindness." *Supreme Court Review* 1986: 99-134.

———. 1989. "Discriminatory Intent and the Taming of *Brown.*" *University of Chicago Law Review* 56: 935–1015.

———. 1995. "Affirmative Action and the Public Interest." *Supreme Court Review* 1995: 1–43.

Strong, Daniel G. 1985. "Supreme Court Justice William Strong, 1808–1895: Jurisprudence, Christianity, and Reform." Unpublished Ph.D. dissertation, Kent State University.

Student Nonviolent Coordinating Committee. [Oct. 1962] 1992. "Terrible Terrell." In *Let Freedom Ring: A Documentary History of the Modern Civil Rights Movement,* edited by Peter B. Levy, 100–101. New York: Praeger.

Sugarmon, Russell. Papers. Mississippi Valley Collection, Old Brister Library, University of Memphis.

Sunstein, Cass. 1993. "Standing Injuries." *Supreme Court Review* 37–64.

Swain, Carol. 1993. *Black Faces, Black Interests: The Representation of African Americans in Congress.* Cambridge: Harvard University Press.

———. 1995. "The Future of Black Representation." *The American Prospect* 23 (Fall): 78–83.

———. 1996. "The Supreme Court's Rulings on Congressional Districts Could Benefit Minority Voters." *Chronicle of Higher Education,* Sept. 27, B:3–4.

"Symposium: Reapportionment." 1983. *Chicano Law Review* 6: 34–62.

Tajfel, Henri. 1969. "Cognitive Aspects of Prejudice." *Journal of Social Issues* 25: 79–97.

Taper, Bernard. 1962. *Gomillion versus Lightfoot: The Tuskegee Gerrymander Case.* New York: McGraw Hill.

Tate, Katherine. 1993. *From Protest to Politics: The New Black Voters in American Elections.* Cambridge: Harvard University Press.

Taylor, Joe Gray. 1974. *Louisiana Reconstructed, 1863–1877.* Baton Rouge: Louisiana State University Press.

Taylor, Joseph H. 1949. "Populism and Disfranchisement in Alabama." *Journal of Negro History* 34: 410–27.

tenBroek, Jacobus. 1965. *Equal Under Law.* New York: Collier.

Texas House Committee on Regions, Compacts, and Districts. 1981. Hearing (transcript), July 21. Copy in author's possession.

Texas House Study Group. 1981. "Redistricting, Part Four: The Voting Rights Act." Special Legislative Report No. 60, in Texas 1981.

Texas. 1981. Submission Under Section 5 of the Voting Rights Act. (Files in Voting Section, Civil Rights Division, U.S. Dept. of Justice, Washington, D.C.)

———. 1983. Submission Under Section 5 of the Voting Rights Act. (Files in Voting Section, Civil Rights Division, U.S. Dept. of Justice, Washington, D.C.)

———. 1991. Submission Under Section 5 of the Voting Rights Act. (Files in Voting Section, Civil Rights Division, U.S. Dept. of Justice, Washington, D.C.)

Thernstrom, Abigail M. 1987. *Whose Votes Count? Affirmative Action and Minority Voting Rights.* Cambridge: Harvard University Press.

———. 1994. "*Shaw v. Reno*: Notes from a Political Thicket." *Public Interest Law Review,* 35–56.

———. 1995. "More Notes from a Political Thicket." *Emory Law Journal* 44: 911–41.

Thernstrom, Abigail M., and Stephan T. Thernstrom. 1995. "The Promise of Racial Equality." In *The New Promise of American Life*, edited by Lamar Alexander and Chester E. Finn Jr., 88-103. Indianapolis, Ind.: Hudson Institute.

Thernstrom, Stephan, ed. 1980. *Harvard Encyclopedia of American Ethnic Relations*. Cambridge: Harvard University Press.

Thernstrom, Stephan T., and Abigail M. Thernstrom. 1997. *America in Black and White: One Nation Indivisible*. New York: Simon and Schuster.

Tindall, George B. 1952. *South Carolina Negroes, 1877-1900*. Columbia: University of South Carolina Press.

―――. 1967. *The Emergence of the New South, 1913-1945*. Baton Rouge: Louisiana State University Press.

Tolnay, Stewart E., and E. M. Beck. 1995. *A Festival of Violence: An Analysis of Southern Lynchings, 1882-1930*. Urbana: University of Illinois Press.

Toobin, Jeffrey. 1997. "Clinton's Left-Hand Man." *New Yorker*, July 21, 28-32.

Trelease, Allen W. 1971. *White Terror: The Ku Klux Klan Conspiracy and Southern Reconstruction*. New York: Harper and Row.

Tribe, Lawrence H. 1978. *American Constitutional Law*. Mineola, N.Y.: Foundation Press.

Tucker, David M. 1971. *Lieutenant Lee of Beale Street*. Nashville, Tenn.: Vanderbilt University Press.

―――. 1972. "Black Politics in Memphis." *West Tennessee Historical Society's Papers* 26: 13-19.

―――. 1980. *Memphis Since Crump: Bossism, Blacks, and Civic Reformers, 1948-1968*. Knoxville: University of Tennessee Press.

Tunnell, Ted. 1984. *Crucible of Reconstruction: War, Radicalism and Race in Louisiana, 1862-1877*. Baton Rouge: Louisiana State University Press.

Tushnet, Mark V. 1977. "The New Law of Standing: A Plea for Abandonment." *Cornell Law Review* 62: 663-700.

―――. 1980. "The Sociology of Article III: A Response to Professor Brilmayer." *Harvard Law Review* 93: 1698-1726.

―――. 1987. *The NAACP's Legal Strategy against Segregated Education, 1925-1950*. Chapel Hill: University of North Carolina Press.

―――. 1991. "What Really Happened in *Brown v. Board of Education*." *Columbia Law Review* 91: 1867-1930.

―――. 1994. *Making Civil Rights Law: Thurgood Marshall and the Supreme Court, 1936-1961*. New York: Oxford University Press.

U.S. Bureau of the Census. 1883. *Population*. Washington, D.C.: GPO.

―――. 1972. *1970 Census of Population and Housing: Census Tracts: Los Angeles-Long Beach, Calif. Standard Metropolitan Statistical Area*. Washington, D.C.: GPO.

―――. 1985. *Congressional Districts of the 99th Congress*. Washington, D.C.: GPO.

U.S. Commission on Civil Rights. 1959a. *Hearings before the United States Commission on Civil Rights. Hearings Held in Montgomery, Alabama*. Washington, D.C.: GPO.

―――. 1959b. *Report*. Washington, D.C.: GPO.

―――. 1961. *Hearings before the United States Commission on Civil Rights. Hearings Held in New Orleans, Louisiana*. Washington, D.C.: GPO.

————. 1963. *Hearings before the United States Commission on Civil Rights. Hearings Held in Memphis, Tennessee, June 25-26, 1962.* Washington, D.C.: GPO.

————. 1965a. *Hearings Held in Jackson, Mississippi.* Washington, D.C.: GPO.

————. 1965b. *Voting in Mississippi.* Washington, D.C.: GPO.

————. 1968. *Political Participation.* Washington, D.C.: GPO.

————. 1975. *The Voting Rights Act: Ten Years After.* Washington, D.C.: GPO.

U.S. Congress. 1989. *Biographical Directory of the United States Congress, 1774-1989.* Washington, D.C.: GPO.

U.S. Department of Commerce. 1988. *County and City Data Book.* Washington, D.C.: GPO.

————. 1994. *County and City Data Book.* Washington, D.C.: GPO.

————. Annual, various years. *Statistical Abstract of the United States.* Washington, D.C.: GPO.

U.S. House of Representatives. 1965a. *Contested Elections in the First, Second, Third, Fourth, and Fifth Districts of the State of Mississippi: Hearings Before the Subcommittee on Elections of the Comm. on House Adm.,* 89th Cong., 1st sess. Washington, D.C.: GPO.

————. 1965b. *Hearings Before Subcommittee No. 5 of the Committee on the Judiciary, House of Representatives, 89 Cong., 1 Sess., on H.R. 6400.* Washington, D.C.: GPO.

————. 1965c. *House Report 439, 89 Cong., 1 Sess., "Voting Rights Act of 1965."* Washington, D.C.: GPO.

————. 1969. *Hearings on H.R. 4249, H.R. 5538, and Similar Proposals (Voting Rights Act Extension) before Subcommittee No. 5 of the House Committee on the Judiciary, 91st Cong., 1st Sess.* Washington, D.C.: GPO.

————. 1975a. *Hearings on H.R. 939, H.R. 2148, H.R. 3247, and H.R. 3501 (Extension of the Voting Rights Act) before Subcommittee on Civil and Constitutional Rights of the Committee on the Judiciary, 94th Cong., 1st sess.* Washington, D.C.: GPO.

————. 1975b. *House Report No. 94-196.* Washington, D.C.: GPO.

————. 1981. *"Extension of the Voting Rights Act," Hearings before the Subcommittee on Civil and Constitutional Rights of the Committee on the Judiciary, 97 Cong., 1 Sess.* Washington, D.C.: GPO.

————. 1982. *Voting Rights Act: Hearings Before the Subcommittee on the Constitution of the Committee of the Judiciary, United States Senate, 97 Cong., 2d Sess.* Washington, D.C.: GPO.

————. 1986. Subcommittee on Civil and Constitutional Rights of the House Committee on the Judiciary. *Voting Rights Act: Proposed Section 5 Regulations, 99th Cong., 2d Sess.* Washington, D.C.: Committee Print.

U.S. Senate. 1877. *Senate Reports.* No. 704, 44th Cong., 2d sess. Washington, D.C.: GPO.

————. 1878. *Senate Reports.* No. 855, 45th Cong., 3d sess. Washington, D.C.: GPO.

————. 1965. *Hearings Before the Committee on the Judiciary, 89th Cong., 1 Sess., on S. 1564.* Washington, D.C.: GPO.

————. 1970. *Hearings on S. 818, S. 2456, S.2507, and Title IV of S. 2029 (Amendments to the Voting Rights Act of 1965) before the Subcommittee on Constitutional Rights of the Committee on the Judiciary, 91st Cong., 1st and 2d Sess.* Washington, D.C.: GPO.

————. 1975a. *Hearings on S.407, S.903, S.1297, S.1409, and S.1443 before the Subcommittee on Constitutional Rights of the Senate Committee on the Judiciary, 94th Cong., 1st Sess.* Washington, D.C.: GPO.

————. 1975b. *Senate Report No. 94-295.* Washington, D.C.: GPO.

————. 1982a. *Hearings Before the Subcommittee on the Constitution of the Committee on the Judiciary, United States Senate, Ninety-Seventh Congress Second Session on S. 53, S. 1761, S. 1975, S. 1992, and H.R. 3112, Bills to Amend the Voting Rights Act of 1965.* Washington, D.C.: GPO.

————. 1982b. *"Voting Rights Act Extension," Report of the Committee on the Judiciary, United States Senate, 97 Cong., 2 Sess., Report No. 97-417.* Washington, D.C.: GPO.

Uzee, Philip D. 1950. "Republican Politics in Louisiana, 1877–1900." Unpublished Ph.D. dissertation, Louisiana State University Press.

Valelly, Richard M. 1993a. "Making the Rules Count: American Exceptionalism and Black Voting Rights Struggle, 1867–1965." Mimeo.

————. 1993b. "Party, Coercion, and Inclusion: The Two Reconstructions of the South's Electoral Politics." *Politics and Society* 21: 37–67.

————. 1995. "National Parties and Racial Disenfranchisement." In *Classifying By Race,* edited by Paul E. Peterson, 188–216. Princeton, N.J.: Princeton University Press.

Valien, Preston. 1957. "Expansion of Negro Suffrage in Tennessee." *Journal of Negro Education* 26: 362–68.

Vandiver, Ernest. 1988. "Vandiver Takes the Middle Road." In Henderson and Roberts 1988, 157–66.

Vedlitz, Arnold, James A. Dyer, and David B. Hill. 1988. "The Changing Texas Voter." In *The South's New Politics: Realignment and Dealignment,* edited by Robert H. Swansborough and David M. Brodsky, 38–53. Columbia: University of South Carolina Press.

Verrilli, Donald B., Jr. 1993. "Brief *Amici Curiae* of Bolley Johnson, Speaker of the Florida House of Representatives, and Peter R. Wallace, Chairman of the Reapportionment Committee of the Florida House of Representatives, in Support of Appellees" (brief in U.S. Supreme Court, *Shaw v. Reno*). Mimeo.

Vincent, Charles. 1976. *Black Legislators in Louisiana During Reconstruction.* Baton Rouge: Louisiana State University Press.

Walker, Jack. 1963. "Negro Voting in Atlanta, 1953–1961." *Phylon* 24: 379–87.

Warren, Charles. 1922. *The Supreme Court in United States History.* 4 vols. Boston: Little, Brown.

Watts, Eugene J. 1974. "Black Political Progress in Atlanta, 1868–1895." *Journal of Negro History* 59: 268–86.

————. 1978. *The Social Bases of City Politics: Atlanta, 1865–1903.* Westport, Conn.: Greenwood.

Wax, Jonathan I. 1968. "Program of Progress, A Step into the Present; Change in the Form of Government of Memphis, Tennessee." Unpublished senior thesis, Princeton University.

————. 1969-70. "Program of Progress: The Recent Change in the Form of Government of Memphis." *West Tennessee Historical Society's Papers* 23: 81–109; 24: 74–96.

Weinstein, James. 1968. "The Small Businessman as Big Businessman: The City Commission and Manager Movements." In Weinstein, *The Corporate Ideal and The Liberal State, 1900-1918*, 92–117. Boston, Mass.: Beacon.

Weinzweig, Marjorie J. 1983. "Discriminatory Impact and Intent Under the Equal Protection Clause: The Supreme Court and the Mind-Body Problem." *Law and Inequality* 1: 277–339.

Wharton, Vernon Lane. 1947. *The Negro in Mississippi, 1865-1900*. Chapel Hill: University of North Carolina Press.

Whiteside, Ruth. 1981. "Justice Joseph Bradley and the Reconstruction Amendments." Unpublished Ph.D. dissertation, Rice University.

Whitman, Mark, ed. 1993. *Removing a Badge of Slavery: The Record of Brown v. Board of Education*. Princeton, N.J.: Markus Wiener Publishing.

Wiggins, Sarah Woolfolk. 1977. *The Scalawag in Alabama Politics, 1865-1881*. Huntsville: University of Alabama Press.

———. 1980. "Alabama: Democratic Bulldozing and Republican Folly." In *Reconstruction and Redemption in the South*, edited by Otto H. Olsen, 48–77. Baton Rouge: Louisiana State University Press.

Wilkinson, J. Harvie, III. 1979. *From Brown to Bakke*. New York: Oxford University Press.

Williams, Wendy S. 1987. "Sex Discrimination: Closing the Law's Gender Gap." In H. Schwartz 1987, 109–24.

Woodburn, James Albert. 1906. *American Politics: Political Parties and Party Problems in the United States*. New York: G. P. Putnam's Sons.

Woodward, C. Vann. 1951. *Origins of the New South, 1877-1913*. Baton Rouge: Louisiana State University Press.

———. 1960. *The Burden of Southern History*. Baton Rouge: Louisiana State University Press.

———. 1974. *The Strange Career of Jim Crow*. 3d rev. ed. New York: Oxford University Press.

———. 1986. *Thinking Back: The Perils of Writing History*. Baton Rouge: Louisiana State University Press.

———. 1989. *The Future of the Past*. New York: Oxford University Press.

Work, Monroe N. 1920. "Some Negro Members of Reconstruction Conventions and Legislatures and of Congress." *Journal of Negro History* 5: 63–119.

Wrenn, Lynette B. 1983. "The Taxing District of Shelby County, A Political and Administrative History of Memphis, Tennessee, 1879-1893." Unpublished Ph.D. dissertation, Memphis State University.

———. 1986. "School Board Reorganization in Memphis, 1883." *Tennessee Historical Quarterly* 45: 329–41.

———. 1988. "Commission Government in the Gilded Age: The Memphis Plan." *Tennessee Historical Quarterly* 47: 216–26.

Wright, Brenda. 1995. "*Johnson v. DeGrandy*: Mixed Messages on Equal Electoral Opportunity under Section 2 of the Voting Rights Act." *District of Columbia Law Review* 3: 101–37.

Wright, Sharon D. 1996. "The Deracialization Strategy and African American Mayoral Candidates in Memphis Mayoral Elections." In H. Perry 1996, 151–64.

Wright, William E. 1962. *Memphis Politics: A Study in Racial Bloc Voting.* New Brunswick, N.J.: Rutgers University Press.

Wynes, Charles E. 1961. *Race Relations in Virginia, 1870–1902.* Charlottesville: University Press of Virginia.

Yarbrough, Tinsley E. 1995. *Judicial Enigma: The First Justice Harlan.* New York: Oxford University Press.

Zuckert, Michael P. 1986. "Congressional Power under the Fourteenth Amendment— The Original Understanding of Section Five." *Constitutional Commentary* 3: 123–55.

Index

commissioner, Hahn appointee),
100–102, 111–12, 118, 123, 478 (n. 14)
Bush v. Vera. See *Vera*
Bustamante, Albert (Hispanic congressman, D-Tex.), 309, 493 (n. 20)
Butler, Katharine Inglis: on *Brown*, 329–
30, 495 (n. 11); on harm in *Shaw I*,
388–89; on "natural" districts, 413,
503 (n. 29), 507 (n. 52); on remedying
past discrimination, 427; on basis of
compactness, 448, 514 (n. 90); distortions of history by, 458–59, 464,
503 (n. 26), 508 (n. 58); on futility of
government action, 459; on traditional
districting principles, 493 (n. 19); on
Wright v. Rockefeller, 499–500 (nn. 1,
2); distortion of *UJO* by, 500 (n. 7);
inconsistencies of, 502 (nn. 19, 22),
507 (n. 50); and truth of stereotypes,
503 (n. 28); and race as a proxy, 513–
14 (n. 89); and group rights, 514 (n. 1);
Panglossian views of, 516 (n. 6)
Byrd, Garland (lt. gov. of Ga.): and 1962
Democratic primary, 206, 241

Cain, Bruce E. (Calif. redistricting ex-
pert), 75
Calderon, Charles (Latino candidate for
L.A. supervisor), 134
Calderon, Richard (Latino L.A. politi-
cian), 108
Calderon v. City of Los Angeles, 87–88
Caldwell, Johnnie (state house member,
D-Ga.), 239
Caldwell, Tod (gov. of N.C.), 26
California, redistricting in. See *DeWitt*;
Minority opportunity districts
California Business Roundtable, 98, 109
Californios, 70–71
Californios for Fair Representation,
91, 109–10; and 1981 L.A. County
redistricting, 106, 112–15, 121–22
Cameron, Charles, 462, 515–16 (nn. 4–5)
Campos, Mark (Hispanic activist, Hous-
ton), 303

Campos, Tony (Hispanic activist, Houston), 303
Canale, John Ford (candidate for Memphis City Commission), 159, 183
Carlton, Milton (state sen., D-Ga.): and
term "bloc vote," 228; and anti-slate
card proposal, 234
Carmack, Edward Ward (anti-Crump
candidate for U.S. Senate, Tenn.), 143
Carmichael, James V. (candidate for gov.
of Ga., 1946), 213
Carrollton Branch of NAACP v. Stallings, 398,
506 (n. 43)
Carter, Robert (NAACP-LDF lawyer):
and *Gomillion*, 54; and *Brown*, 330
Carter, Jimmy, 255
Cary, Reby (African-American state house
member, D-Tex.), 289
Catledge, Turner (Memphis political
reporter), 143
Causation: notions of, 190–91, 230, 270,
427; importance of, in history, 347; and
mixed motives, 363; and interpretation
of *Shaw I*, 503–4 (n. 31)
Census, U.S.: 1990 undercount in, 293;
level of detail in, 293, 352, 409–10, 417
CFR. *See* Californios for Fair Representation; Chicanos for Fair Representation
Chace, Burton (L.A. County supervisor),
72, 477 (n. 2); and 1959–63 redistricting,
79–82
Chacon, Peter (Latino state house member, D-Calif.), 105
Chamber of Commerce: L.A., 92; Memphis, 163, 165–66, 168–69, 174–75, 179,
182, 189, 480 (n. 10)
Chambers, Sam (candidate for Memphis
City Commission), 159, 183
Chandler, Wyeth (city councilman and
mayor of Memphis), 186–87, 190, 193,
195
Chandler, Walter (mayor of Memphis),
179
Chapel Hill, N.C.: liberalism of, 247
Chapman, Jim (congressman, D-Tex.), 308

Hardaway, Thomas C. (African-American state house member, D-N.C.), 264

Harlan, John Marshall (U.S. Supreme Court justice, 1877–1911): and discrimination against a group, 324; inconsistency of, 324; and *Cumming* case, 324–27, 359; and *Civil Rights Cases*, 474 (n. 34)

Harm: expressive, 5, 244, 378, 387–89, 421–22, 467; representational, 270, 274–76, 387–88, 407–8, 416; in *Brown*, 327–32, 389, 395; in *Shaw v. Reno*, 368, 377–78, 380–81, 387–89, 407; in affirmative action cases, 377; Justice White on, 394; racial double standard of, 408; and race as a proxy, 416; and constituency services, 489 (n. 19)

Harris, Rod (African-American candidate for state senate, R-Ga.), 225

Harris, Roy (head of Ga. Citizens' Council), 224

Harrison, Benjamin, 472 (n. 19)

Harsh, David (Memphis county commission chairman), 165

Hartsfield, William (mayor of Atlanta), 203

Hatch, Orrin, 62

Hawke, Jack, Jr. (chairman, Republican state committee, N.C.): and partisanship in 1991–92 redistricting, 264–65, 269

Hawkins, Reginald (African-American gubernatorial candidate, N.C.), 246

Hayden, Tom (L.A. liberal), 94

Hayes, James (L.A. County supervisor), 72, 88, 92–93, 95, 106, 117, 477 (n. 2, 7)

Hayes, Edgar (director, L.A. County data processing), 100–101

Hayes, Rutherford B.: southern policy of, 21–22, 472 (n. 20)

Haynes, Clyde (state house member, D-Tex.), 280

Hays, Lake (Memphis charter commission member), 164

Hays (*U.S. v. Hays*), 369, 399–402, 407–9,

412, 437; contradictions with *Miller* of, 408; and expressive harm, 408; and encouragement of forum shopping, 511–12 (n. 76)

Hefner, W. G. (congressman, D-N.C.): and 1981–82 redistricting, 249, 251; and 1991–92 redistricting, 264

Helms, Jesse: and racial issues, 262, 273; and *Shaw I*, 381–82; and grandfather clause reading of *Beer*, 382, 393; and Gantt, 382, 463, 488 (n. 12); and color-blindness, 382; and post-*Shaw II* redistricting, 511 (n. 76)

Henry, Harold A. (L.A. city councilman), 79

Herenton, Willie (African-American mayor of Memphis), 193–95

Hernandez, Lisa (Hispanic activist, Houston), 301

Heslop, Alan (Calif. Republican redistricting expert): on Latinos and redistricting, 78, 109; and Rose Institute, 98, 115

Higgs, Otis W., Jr. (African-American candidate for mayor of Memphis), 193–95

Hill, John (gubernatorial nominee, D-Tex.), 282

Hill, Fred (state house member, R-Tex.), 298

Hinds, M. A. (sheriff of Memphis), 150, 168–70

Hispanics. *See* Latinos

History: and public policy, 8, 467; radicals' distortions of, 66–67, 242–45, 265, 270, 277–78, 331, 377, 413, 456–60, 464–67; importance of, in defining injury, 344; revision of radicals' version of, 426; and the Fourteenth Amendment, 456; and group rights, 464–66

Hittner, David (U.S. district court judge, Tex.), 418

Hoadly, George (gov. of Ohio), 39

Hobby, Bill (lt. gov. of Tex.), 282–83, 285, 308